ADVANCES IN URBANISM, SMART CITIES, AND SUSTAINABILITY

ADVANCES IN URBANISM, SMART CITIES, AND SUSTAINABILITY

Edited by
Uday Chatterjee, Arindam Biswas, Jenia Mukherjee,
and Sushobhan Majumdar

CRC Press
Taylor & Francis Group
Boca Raton London New York

CRC Press is an imprint of the
Taylor & Francis Group, an **informa** business

First edition published 2022
by CRC Press
6000 Broken Sound Parkway NW, Suite 300, Boca Raton, FL 33487-2742

and by CRC Press
4 Park Square, Milton Park, Abingdon, Oxon, OX14 4RN

CRC Press is an imprint of Taylor & Francis Group, LLC

Library of Congress Cataloging-in-Publication Data
Names: Chatterjee, Uday, editor. | Biswas, Arindam, editor. | Mukherjee, Jenia, editor. | Majumdar, Sushobhan, editor.
Title: Advances in urbanism, smart cities, and sustainability / edited by Uday Chatterjee, Arindam Biswas, Jenia Mukherjee, and Sushobhan Majumdar.
Description: First edition. | Boca Raton : CRC Press, 2022. | Includes bibliographical references and index.
Identifiers: LCCN 2021053493 (print) | LCCN 2021053494 (ebook) | ISBN 9780367641764 (hardback) | ISBN 9780367647735 (paperback) | ISBN 9781003126195 (ebook)
Subjects: LCSH: City planning--Case studies. | Smart cities--Case studies. | Sustainable urban development--Case studies.
Classification: LCC HT166 .A335 2022 (print) | LCC HT166 (ebook) | DDC 307.1/216--dc23/eng/20220105
LC record available at https://lccn.loc.gov/2021053493
LC ebook record available at https://lccn.loc.gov/2021053494

ISBN: 978-0-367-64176-4 (hbk)
ISBN: 978-0-367-64773-5 (pbk)
ISBN: 978-1-003-12619-5 (ebk)

DOI: 10.1201/9781003126195

Typeset in Times
by MPS Limited, Dehradun

Dedication

Dedicated to
Young scholars in the field of urban studies, urban planning, city planners, and smart city policy makers

Contents

Preface

In the neoliberal era, the pattern of urbanization comes with lots of challenges. Climate change, inequality, poverty, pollution, and physical and social conflicts continuously challenge the urban growth and development. It is impeding the physical glory of urban systems and restraining the overall human development in cities. Each city, irrespective of its development standard, is stretched to overcome the complexities and attain prosperity for its citizens. Unlike in the past, cities have been utilizing science and technology to their advantage. The advancement in data science, communication technology, big data analytics, and artificial intelligence provide new opportunities to study, comprehend, analyze, assimilate, and resolve urban issues with greater accuracy. Experts from different backgrounds collaborated to create newer opportunities for improving the quality of life and sustainability in urban areas. It is an intelligent amalgamation of know-how and technology steering towards the future of smart and creative urban development. Many believe that smart city ideas are unique because they allow real-time accurate decision support systems and save resources for the future, while others argue that a smart city is a tech-savvy tool to profit multinational conglomerates and less to solve real urban issues. Yet, as academicians, it is our responsibility to portray all the facets of a smart city and its impact on sustainable urban development.

The boois magnifies intellects of smart city approaches by harmonizing urban physical environment and societies, multidimensional approach on urban ecology, ecosystem services, sustainable landscapes, and recent advances in geographical and geospatial tools and techniques. It provides a detailed account of problems arising from growing urbanism in the world. This book also addresses how to present the state of the art and practice to develop smart cities in the world with proper illustrations for sustainable and advanced urbanism and sustainable development. Each contributor has demonstrated great intellects and aptitude and contributed wonderful notes on the theme with mature academic responsibility. They explored ideas from urban planning, geography, urban studies, science and technology studies, and innovation studies to go beyond the rhetoric of technological innovation and reveal the political, social, and physical implications of digitalizing the built environment. It particularly focuses on policies and programs to address the issues and challenges posed by cities. This book consists of five sections: 1) Urban Conservation, Land Transformation, and Regeneration; 2) Urban Health, Space, Governance, and Policy Implications; 3) Urbanism and Smart Cities—An Advanced Analysis; 4) Urban Sprawl, Resource Consumption, Management, and Smart Cities; and 5) Urban Smart Building, Modern and Geospatial Technology, and Smart Cities. Determining different sections to portray *Advances in Urbanism, Smart Cities, and Sustainability* was never easy. However, we selected the sections to include wider spectrums of urbanism and touch upon different spatial scales of a smart city's strategic interventions. We hope that academic scholars and practitioners from different disciplines will immensely benefit by the book's wider coverage of themes and multidisciplinary contributions.

Uday Chatterjee,
Arindam Biswas,
Jenia Mukherjee,
Sushobhan Majumdar

Acknowledgments

This volume stands as testimony to the efforts made by our contributors and the urban planners, city planners, and smart city policy makers who have helped in the process rendering validation to the theme and relevance of the book. We sincerely acknowledge the efforts of these professionals towards the analysis and the compilation of the chapters provided in this book. We express our gratitude to the anonymous reviewers for their feedback that resulted in significant enhancement in the quality of this work. Being in the works for a long time, preparing the volume was a major commitment of time for the editors. This would not have been possible without the unwavering support of our family and friends and the constant inspiration of our students, teachers, colleagues, and collaborators. We thank them all for being a source of support during the difficult times of the COVID-19 pandemic. We particularly thank Professor Virendra Kumar Tewari, Director, Indian Institute of Technology, Kharagpur; Professor Ajit Okay Chaturvedi, Director, Indian Institute of Technology, Roorkee; and Dr. Pabitra Kumar Mishra, Principal, Bhatter College, Dantan for their academic support and guidance. In conclusion, we also thank our publisher CRC Press-Taylor & Francis Group and Irma Shagla Britton, Senior Editor, CRC Press-Taylor & Francis Group, Shannon Welch, Editorial Assistant Taylor & Francis/CRC Press for their unremitting support and guidance in the publication of this book.

About the Editors

Dr. Uday Chatterjee is an assistant professor at the Department of Geography, Bhatter College, Dantan, Paschim Medinipur, West Bengal, India, and applied geographer with a post-graduate in applied geography at Utkal University and doctoral degree in applied geography at Ravenshaw University, Cuttack, Odisha, India. He has contributed various research papers published in various reputed national and international journals and edited book volumes. He has authored a jointly edited book entitled *Harmony with nature: Illusions and elusions from Geographer's perspective in the 21st Century*. He has also conducted (Convener) one Faculty Development Programme on "modern methods of teaching and advanced research methods" sponsored by the Indian Council of Social Science Research (ICSSR), Govt. of India. His areas of research interest cover urban planning, social and human geography, applied geomorphology, hazards and disasters, environmental issues, land use, and rural development. His research work has been funded by the West Bengal Pollution Control Board (WBPCB) Govt. of West Bengal, India. He has served as a reviewer for many international journals. Currently, Dr. Uday Chatterjee is the lead editor of Special Issue (S.I.) of *Urbanism, Smart Cities and Modelling*, Geojournal, Springer.

Dr. Arindam Biswas is an associate professor at the Department of Architecture and Planning, Indian Institute of Technology (IIT) Roorkee, India. He has a doctorate in urban planning from the University of Tokyo. He is recipient of the institute research fellowship for outstanding young faculty, ASEM Duo-India Fellowship, DAAD Fellowship (Germany), and MEXT Scholarship (Japan). He has also undertaken a certificate program on international environmental leadership (Asian Program for Incubation of Environmental Leadership, APIEL) from the University of Tokyo. He is presently pursuing researches sponsored by different research foundations of the government of India like the Department of Science and Technology (DST), Ministry of Education, Indian Council of Social Science Research, Ministry of Environment Forest and Climate Change, and National Building Construction Company. He is also working on research sponsored by the Royal Academy of Engineering and GCRF-UKRI, United Kingdom. He has published two editorial books and contributed four book chapters. He is presently working on three books to be published next year. He has also extensively published articles in peer journals on urban infrastructure, inclusive growth, resilience, housing and informality, innovation, and regional development.

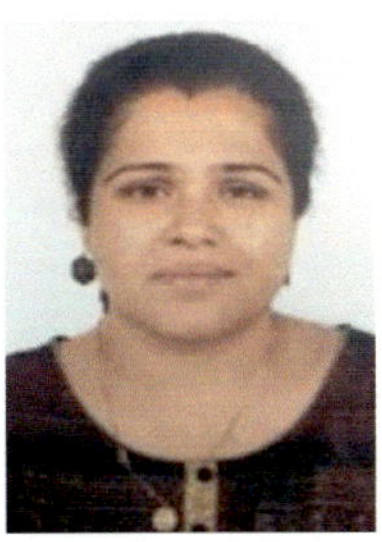

Dr. Jenia Mukherjee is an assistant professor at the Department of Humanities and Social Sciences, Indian Institute of Technology Kharagpur. Her research interest spans across urban studies and environmental history. She received the Australian Leadership Awards Fellowship in 2010 and 2015. She completed her book project: *Blue infrastructures: Natural Ecology, Political History and Urban Development in Kolkata* (Singapore: Springer Nature, 2020) and has widely published in peer-reviewed impact factor journals including *Environment and Planning E, International Journal of Urban Sustainable Development, Urban Research and Practice*, etc. and book chapters. She is a member of the editorial advisory board for the Routledge *Equity, Justice and the Sustainable City* series edited by Julian Agyeman.

Dr. Sushobhan Majumdar is an applied geographer with a post-graduate degree from Presidency University, Kolkata and doctoral degree from the Department of Geography, Faculty of Science, Jadavpur University, Kolkata. He is currently working on research on the geography of cities with its planning and development. His principal areas of research include urban geography, social geography, regional development and planning, remote sensing and GIS, and geography of transport. He is also engaged in the various developmental projects under the Socio-Economic Planning Unit of Kolkata Metropolitan Development Authority (KMDA) under the government of West Bengal. He has published various research papers in different journals, proceedings, and edited volumes of national and international repute. He has presented papers in more than 20 national and international seminars and conferences in India and abroad. He delivered special or invited lectures in various national and regional programmes. He is a life member of the Geographical Society of India, National Association of Geographers of India (NAGI), Institute of Indian Geographers (IIG), Regional Science Association of India (RSAI), etc. Recently he is deeply engaged in surface temperature mapping and modeling of metro cities in India and its impact on environment.

Foreword

It gives immense pleasure to write a foreword for the book entitled Advances in Urbanism, Smart Cities and Sustainability edited by Uday Chatterjee, Arindam Biswas, Jenia Mukherjee and Sushobhan Majumdar published by CRC Press/Taylor & Francis Group.

India is home to 11 per cent of the total global urban population where urban planning can provide the foundation for integrated development of cities, citizens, and the environment. By 2030, almost 70% of the national GDP will come from our cities as rapid urbanization facilitates efficiencies of agglomerations as per Ministry of Housing and Urban Affairs. The best-performing cities globally contribute five times more to national GDP than comparable Indian cities. Therefore, in becoming a five-trillion-dollar economy Indian cities need to generate a similar density of economic activity.

Transforming cities to make them smarter and more sustainable, is indeed a monumental task, but investments in the domain can help provide just the right financial and technical edge to help these potential tourism hubs to take advantage of their unique assets and turn into the most profitable ventures of the future. Smart cities are essentially a framework that make use of information and communication technologies to promote sustainable development. A city is known to be smart because of its innovative undertakings, and for any trade centric environment, the key is to generate business, through the power of tourism, which can be rapidly assisted through investments in the sector. This includes strides in e-governance, adequate water supply, sanitation and waste management, efficient public utility, and financial management. Systematic investments in the domain can help birth a well-rounded structure, for a future tourism powerhouse yielding great financial returns.

This volume of Advances in Urbanism, Smart Cities and Sustainability is compilation of five sections having 25 chapters. Section I - Urban Conservation, Land Transformation and Regeneration contains good discussion on placemaking, environmental impacts of city development, urban redevelopment and sustainable tourism. Section II – Urban Health, Space, Governance and Policy Implications, critically discusses the children friendly spaces, climate change and role of green spaces in fostering environmentally modified attitudes. Section III - Urbanism and Smart Cities- An advanced Analysisis about transport sustianbaility assessment, water quality index and urban spaces challenges in smart cities development. Section IV Urban Sprawl, Resource Consumption, Management and Smart Cities, contains discussions on urban blight, food security, and solid waste management in cities. The firnal and Section-V Urban Smart Building, Modern and Geospatial Technology and Smart Cities has very interesting discussion around resilience, geo-hazards and use of GIS technology in evaluation of urban spaces.

I would like to appreciate and congratulate the editors for their noble initiative in bringing out this precious volume of contemporary relevance. This book will be very useful for scholars in urban planning, and practitioners in smart cities development in India and abroad.

Dr. Anil Kashyap, PhD, MRICS, MRTPI, FHEA
Head of Department
Geography & Environmental Management
Faculty of Environment and Technology
University of the West of England (UWE Bristol)
Bristol BS16 1QY
England

Contributors

Dr. Mohammad Afsar Alam, assistant professor of geography in the Department of Social Science, College of Humanities and Education, Fiji National University, Fiji. His areas of research interest cover urban planning, social and human geography, hazards and disasters, tourism geography, climate change, and environmental Issues. He has contributed many research papers in various reputed national and international journals and edited book volumes. He has served as a reviewer for many International journals.

Dr. Mumtaz Alam, assistant professor in the Department of Social Science, College of Humanities and Education, Fiji National University, Fiji. His areas of research interest cover history of urbanization, medical history, environmental humanities, ecotourism, and ICT education with interdisciplinary approach. He has contributed various research papers in various reputed national and international journals. He is serving as an associate editor (Heliyon), editorial, advisory board, and reviewer for many International journals.

Mr. Mohammed Feroz Ali is the head of the Department Secondary and Sports Education at Fiji National University. His research is in physical education sports and rural development. He has published papers in reputable journals in psychological parameters in the fields of sports and physical education. Currently, he is a PhD research scholar at Mangalore university Karnataka, India.

Aireen Grace Andal is a PhD candidate under a double-PhD track at the Ural Federal University (Russian Federation) and Macquarie University (Australia). She is currently a research fellow at the Centre for Global Urbanism and Centre for Comparative Studies of Toleration and Recognition in Ural Federal University. The majority of her recent academic and research experiences involve children's geographies with a focus on urban spaces. Aireen is a scholar of and for children and their spaces.

Dr. Anzhelika Antipova is an associate professor in the Department of Earth Sciences, University of Memphis, Memphis, Tennessee, United States. Her areas of research interest cover urban planning, urban and economic geography, medical/health geography, and transportation studies. She has contributed various research papers published in various reputed national and international journals and edited journal special issues and book volumes. She has served as a reviewer for many International journals and books.

Aakriti Asim has completed her M.Sc. in environmental science from the Central University of South Bihar. Her research areas includes satellite monitoring of aerosols, urban aerosol dynamics, and aerosol climatology.

Reza Banai is a professor at the Department of City and Regional Planning, University of Memphis, Memphis. His areas of research interest cover urban planning, land use/land cover analysis, and transportation studies. He has contributed various research papers published in various reputed national and international journals.

Archisman Barat is currently pursuing his doctorate as UGC-SRF at the Central University of South Bihar. His core research areas include urban climate, aerosol-microclimate interactions, satellite meteorology, and high-resolution numerical modelling. He has educational degrees (B.Sc. (Hons.), M.Sc., and M.Phil.) in environmental science, and he has also qualified UGC-NET-JRF and ASRB-NET in environmental science.

Dr. Prabal Barua is a program manager of NGO named YPSA (Young Power in Social Action) with the focusing program on climate change adaptation issues. He achieved a PhD in environmental sciences from Jahangirnagar University, Bangladesh. His areas of research interest cover climate change, fisheries management, environmental issues, hazards and disasters, aquatic resource management, and rural development. He has contributed various research papers published in various reputed national and international journals and edited book volumes. He has served as a reviewer for many International journals.

Dr. Hamza Benacer is a lecturer architect and a researcher from the Institute of architecture and urban planning, University of Blida. His research interests lie in urban heritage giving focus to determine conflicts caused by the rapid growth and globalization phenomena at different levels. He has collaborated actively with researchers and laboratories in several other topics ranging from urban to architectural arriving to interior design scale.

Dr. Djihed Berkouk, born in 1990, is a lecturer in the Department of Architecture at Biskra University, Algeria. His research interests include studying the relationship between physical environment and space occupants, human comfort, thermal and luminous environment, soundscape, noise pollution, and urban morphology. Berkouk regularly participates at international conferences, and he has contributed to research articles published in reputable national and international journals.

Dr. Tallal Abdel Karim Bouzir is a lecturer and a researcher at the Institute of Architecture and Urbanism of the University of Blida, Algeria. His areas of research interest cover urban planning, noise pollution, soundscape studies, urban morphology and environmental issues, and architectural and urban atmospheres. He has a background in architecture and environmental sciences (master's and PhD).

Dr. Supernova Chakraborty is a full-time academician and teaching faculty at Lovely Professional University, Phagwara. She has done her MPhil from IBS, Hyderabad and PhD from JNU, Jaipur. She is an expert in research methodology, consumer behavior, and sales and marketing and has very good command over data analysis and visualization tool like SPSS, Tableau, AMOS, etc. She has contributed in many research works of both national and international repute. She is serving on the editorial board of various journals of repute.

Dr. Nilendu Chatterjee is an assistant professor in the Department of Economics, Bankim Sardar College, West Bengal, India. He has research interests in resource economics, general equilibrium, development economics, etc. He has published research papers in various national and internationally renowned journals, including the *International Journal of Sustainable Economies Management, Economic Affairs,* and *Foreign Trade Review.*

Soumen Chatterjee is an independent researcher from Durgapur, West Bengal, India. He has awarded a Ph.D from Visva Bharati University, India, in 2016 for completing doctoral thesis on land transformation over the Asansol Durgapur planning region. He mainly works on the field of urban and environmental issues for the past decade and published a number of research articles in several national and international journals.

Dr. Uday Chatterjee is an assistant professor at the Department of Geography, Bhatter College, Dantan, Paschim Medinipur, West Bengal, India, and applied geographer with a post-graduate in applied geography at Utkal University and doctoral degrees in applied geography at Ravenshaw University, Cuttack, Odisha, India. He has contributed various research papers published in various reputed national and international journals and edited book volumes. His areas of research interest cover urban planning, social and human geography, applied geomorphology, hazards and disasters, environmental issues, land use, and rural development. His research work has been funded by the West Bengal Pollution Control Board (WBPCB) Govt. of West Bengal, India. He has served as a reviewer for many international journals. Currently, Dr. Uday Chatterjee is the lead editor of Special Issue (S.I.) of *Urbanism, Smart Cities and Modelling*, Geojournal, Springer.

Zahra Chehragan obtained her master's degree in urban planning from the Iran University of Science and Technology. As a master student, she ranked first among her classmates in urban planning (2016–2019). Her research interests include solar urban planning, renewable urban planning, and sustainable urban planning.

Dr. Nirmalya Das, M.Sc., M. Phil., Ph. D., associate professor in geography of Panskura Banamali College (Autonomous), West Bengal. The interest of the research area is urban geography and marketing geography. He has published various research papers in reputed national and international journals as well as in edited book volumes.

Ms. Sanjali Das is currently pursuing her Ph.D in cultural geography from the Department of Geography, Adamas University. She is an alumnus of the University of Calcutta. Being specialised in tourism geography, her keen area of interest is understanding tourism dynamics and its interaction with the society, culture, and landscape of the neighborhood.

Mr. Subhrangsu Das received a M.Sc. degree in geography from Panskura Banamali College affiliated to Vidyasagar University, Medinipur, India. He also received a M.Phil. from Utkal University, Bhubaneswar, India in 2019. His research interests include urban and social geography.

Sujit Das has obtained a M.A. and Ph.D degree from Burdwan and Visva Bharati University, West Bengal, respectively. He has published a number of research articles in national and international journals and book chapters. Presently, he is serving as an assisstant teacher of geography in the West Bengal Govt. Aided School.

Apurva Deshmukh is a second-year student in the master of planning course with a specialization in housing. She has worked as an architect in a private firm on various housing projects, after graduating from D.Y. Patil College of Engineering & Technology, Kolhapur, India. With an experience of 1.5 years in the field of architecture, now she aims to gain the knowledge in the housing sector with respect to planning. Her fields of interest are disaster management, climate change, and materials and technology.

Prof. Megersa Olumana Dinka is an associate professor in the Civil Engineering Science Department of the University of Johannesburg, South Africa. His areas of research cover water management, hydraulics, and hydrology aspects. He has more than 15 years' experience as an academician and researcher and has supervised several postgraduate students. He has published and reviewed several articles in peer-reviewed journals.

Dr. Ganapathy Pattukandan Ganapathy is a professor at the Centre for Disaster Mitigation and Management, Vellore Institute of Technology (VIT), Vellore, Tamil Nadu, India. His areas of research cover geo-hazards mapping and monitoring and developing early warning systems. He has contributed various research papers in international and national journals, conferences, and edited book volumes. He is the editorial board member in international journals and also served as a reviewer for many international journals.

Dr. Mahshid Ghorbanian is an assistant professor in the Department of Landscape Architecture, School of Architecture and Environmental Design, Iran University of Science and Technology,

Tehran, Iran. As an urban designer and planner with more than 14 years of professional and academic experience, her research interests include urban modeling, urban spatial structure and health, morphological and visual analysis of city texture, and urban transportation in the complex city network. She has contributed various research papers published in widely reputed national and international journals and edited books as well as been the author of full books released by well-recognized publishers like the Taylor & Francis Group. Additionally, she has served as a reviewer for many international journals.

Sanat Kumar Guchhait has been a professor of geography at the University of Burdwan in West Bengal since 2001. His areas of research interest are environmental geography, social geography, and philosophy of geography. He has successfully completed one UGC Major Research Project on Soil Erosion, Conservation and Forest Ecology. He has supervised 11 doctoral students so far and published 83 research papers in different peer-reviewed national and international journals.

Mr. Santu Guchhait is working as a state aided college teacher (SACT-I) in the Department of Geography at Panskura Banamali College (Autonomous), West Bengal, India. He has received his M.Sc. and M.Phil. degree from Vidyasagar University (West Bengal, India) and Ravenshaw University (Odisha, India), respectively. His research areas are urban and regional geography, forest degradation, livelihood vulnerability, and application of RS and GIS.

Dr. Krishnendu Gupta is an assistant professor of the Department of Geography, Visva Bharati University, India, and formerly a senior project scientist and group head of the State Remote Sensing Centre, Department of Science & Technology, Government of West Bengal. He has vast academic and research excellence. His areas of interest are urban and regional planning, land degradation, applied geomorphology, and application of remote sensing. He has supervised and coordinated several research and technical projects in different times. More than 30 research articles have been published by him.

Dr. Md. Asif Iqubal is currently involved as a guest faculty in the Department of IDRS and GIS application as a GIS expert at Aligarh Muslim University, Aligarh. His research interests include urban planning; agriculture; livestock rearing; social, rural, and economic geography; climate change; and environmental issues. Dr. Iqubal was awarded the Young Geographer's award in an international conference held in the Department of Geography, Aligarh Muslim University, Aligarh, 2009.

Mr. Atham Lebbe Iyoob is a development officer in the Land Use policy Planning Department, District secretariat, Ampara, Sri Lanka. His areas of research interest cover remote sensing, social and human geography, hazards and disasters, environmental issues, land use, and rural development. He has contributed various research papers published in various reputed national and international journals. He has served as a reviewer for many international journals.

Divya Jain is a second-year student in the master of planning course with specialization in urban planning and completed her bachelors in planning from the Maulana Azad National Institute of Technology, Bhopal, India. She achieved the "Gold Medal" for securing first position in the university bachelor's degree. She is interested in urban planning, urban governance, disaster management, and policy making.

Cladia Anna Jose, is an engineer and urban planner by profession. The author holds a post-graduate from NIT Calicut in urban planning and B.Tech degree in civil engineering from Mahatma Gandhi University, Kerala. Her field of interest includes sustainable development, transport planning, spatial planning, etc.

Dr. Bappaditya Koley is presently the head of the Department in Geography, Bankim Sardar College, South 24 Parganas, West Bengal, India. He is involved in investigating in the field of applied geomorphology and landslide disaster mitigation studies. His areas of research interest cover landslide hazard, vulnerability and risk assessment; landslide early warning system; coastal risk assessment, coastal planning, and management; climate change; and environmental issues, etc. He has published research papers in various national and international reputed journals.

Sunny Kumar is a doctoral researcher at the Central University of South Bihar. His core research area includes meteorology with modelling and simulations aspects, aerosol-climate interactions, and hydrology. Having education (B.Sc. (Hons.), M.Sc. and M.Phil.) in the field of environmental science, he has qualified UGC-NET and ASRB-NET in his field.

Dr Sakul Kundra is an assistant professor of history in the Department of Social Science, School of Arts and Humanities at the Fiji National University. He has a Ph.D in history from Jawaharlal Nehru University (India) and is the recipient of a Gold Medal for PGD in education, USP. He has many high-ranked publications, research projects, conference presentations, and op-eds to his credit. His expertise includes urbanisation, historiography, Pacific history, tourism, and European travellers.

Dr. Sushobhan Majumdar is an applied geographer with a post-graduate degree from Presidency University, Kolkata and doctoral degree from the Department of Geography, Faculty of Science, Jadavpur University, Kolkata. He is currently working on research on the geography of cities with its planning and development. His principal areas of research include urban geography, social geography, regional development and planning, remote sensing and GIS, and geography of transport.

Nirmoha Mandal is a second-year student in the master of planning course with a specialization in urban planning. He is an architect who graduated from the National Institute of Technology, Raipur, India. He has experience working in the Public Works Department on a wide range of architectural projects. His fields of interest are urban planning, urban governance, climate change, and green building.

Dr. Richa Mitra is an experienced academician with a demonstrated history of working in the education management industry, skilled in soft skills, e-learning, student counselling, business development, and lecturing. A strong consulting professional with a doctor of philosophy (Ph.D.) focused in business administration and management, general from Aligarh Muslim University.

Dr. Firoz C. Mohammed is an architect and urban planner by profession. He holds a Ph.D. degree from IIT Kharagpur, post-graduate in urban and regional planning from CEPT University, and B.Arch. degree from NIT Calicut for which he was a university rank holder. He has been involved in teaching, researching, and consulting at NIT Calicut since July 2004. He was also engaged as a visiting teacher at the Architectural Association London (AA London) for the term May–June 2015. His fields of interest include rural urban interface studies, sustainable urban design and planning, regional development and planning, etc.

Ehsan Momeni is a Ph.D candidate in the Department of Earth Sciences, University of Memphis, Memphis, Tennessee, United States. His areas of research interest cover remote sensing, GIS, urban planning, land use/land cover analyses, and transportation studies. He has contributed various research papers published in various reputed national and international journals.

Dr. Navneet Munoth has been serving in his current position as an assistant professor in the Department of Architecture and Planning, MANIT Bhopal for the past 11 years. He is also as an honorary director of the Council of Architecture Training and Research Centre, Bhopal (COA-TRC) established at MANIT Bhopal for fostering the synergy for boosting the entrepreneurship culture as well as for facilitating skill development among the students, academicians, and professionals, which is in line with the vision of the government of India. He has been awarded the Prof. R. C. Singh Prize in December 2016 by The Institute of Engineers (India).

Anindita Nath has completed a M.Sc in geography and is presently working as a state aided college teacher in the Department of Geography, Bankim Sardar College, South 24 Parganas, West Bengal, India. She does research in coastal geomorphology and hazards studies. Her areas of research interest cover coastal hazard, vulnerability, and risk assessment; coastal planning and management; landside hazards studies; and environmental issues, etc. She has published research papers in various national and international reputable journals.

Unaisi Nobobo-Baba has had about 30+ years of working in the field of education (mostly higher education and development). Her work has been in teaching, researching publication, and other educational and development-related work in the Pacific Islands. She is a teacher, researcher, and a prolific author. Unaisi Baba is passionate about quality and relevance in education. Her research, publication, and consultancy interests include teacher education, education reform, and international aid in Pacific Education, Indigenous knowledge, research and development, higher education, education for sustainable development, women in leadership in the Pacific Islands, rural and remote education, among others.

Dr. Joan Nyika is an assistant lecturer in the Geoscience and the Environment Department of Technical University of Kenya, Nairobi. Her areas of research interest cover various environmental science topics including hydro-biogeochemistry, environmental chemistry, bioremediation, and biochemical techniques and instrumentation. She has published several articles in peer-reviewed journals and various book chapters in edited books. She is also involved in mentoring under- and post-graduate students.

Prof. Barbara Ocicka is at the SGH Warsaw School of Economics. Her research interests include strategies of global supply chains' reconfiguration, sourcing strategies, and best practices in logistics and supply chain management. She has authored and co-authored of over 50 publications. She is currently involved as a principal investigator in the SIMBIO Project entitled "New Frontiers in Social Innovation Research: Social Innovation for BIOPlastics" within the Trans-Atlantic Platform Social Innovation Programme.

Prof. Gopal Krishna Panda is presently working as a senior ICSSR fellow in the post-graduate Department of Geography at Utkal University, Bhubaneswar. He was awarded the prestigious emeritus fellowship of UGC in 2016. He has nearly 35 years of teaching and research in the areas of physical geography, coastal geomorphology, climate change, natural hazards and disaster management, and geospatial technology.

Dr. Ashis Chandra Pathy is an assistant professor in the P.G Department Geography, Utkal University, Bhubaneswar, Odisha, India. His areas of research interest cover remote sensing and GIS application in coastal geomorphology, urban planning, coastal geomorphology, applied climatology, and disaster management. He has contributed various research papers published in various reputable national and international journals and edited book volumes.

Mr. Tanmay Patra is a Ph.D. research scholar in the Department of Geography, Panskura Banamali College Research Centre (Autonomous), Vidyasagar University, Paschim Medinipur, West Bengal, India. His areas of research interest in urban geography and regional planning, contemporary social issues like women empowerment, gender inequality, and poverty.

Dr. Ravinesh Rohit Prasad is an assistant professor in the Department of Social Science, College of Humanities and Education, Fiji National University, Fiji. His research interests include urban and rural geography, biogeography, human geography, climate change, and education. He has contributed various research papers in various reputable national and international journals.

Dr. Dhanya Praveen is a scientist working with Tamil Nadu Agriculture University, Coimbatore, Government of Tamil Nadu India. Her areas of research interest cover climate change and agriculture, agro climatology, adaptation and risk assessment, coastal wetland conservation, sea level rise, urban geography, hazards and disasters management, environmental issues, social vulnerability and rural development, and forest carbon sequestration. She has handled various national and international projects for the government of Telangana. She has contributed research papers published in various reputed national and international journals and served as a reviewer for many international journals. She has written books on human geography in the regional language of Malayalam.

Dr. Anu Rai is an assistant professor in the Department of Geography, School of Basic and Applied Sciences, Adamas University, West Bengal, India. Being specialized in regional planning and development, she is much interested in exploring the anatomy of spatial events from the perspective of geography of decision-making. Her areas of research interest cover tourism geography, cultural studies, health geography, urban planning, landscape studies, and corporate geography. She has contributed various research papers published in various reputable national and international journals and authored a book on medical tourism.

Ms. D.K.D.A. Ranaweera is a lecturer in the Department of Geography, Faculty of Humanities and Social Sciences, University of Sri Jayewardenepura, Sri Lanka. Her areas of research interest cover urban geography, geographic information system, and remote sensing. She has contributed various research papers published in various reputed national and international journals.

Professor (Dr.) R.M.K. Ratnayake is a professor in geography in the Department of Geography, Faculty of Humanities and Social Sciences, University of Sri Jayewardenepura, Nugegoda Sri Lanka. His areas of research interest are urban planning, settlement geography, regional development, medical geography, and application of geo-spatial technology for many areas. He has published many books in geography, various research papers in reputed national and international journals, and contributed as an editor for government publications such as books, articles, and chapters. He has served as a reviewer for many national and international journals.

Hemadri Raut, an urban development professional, has done his post-graduate in urban and regional planning from the School of Planning and Architecture, Bhopal, Madhya Pradesh, India. He obtained his graduation in architechture from the School of Planning and Architecture, Vijayawada, Andhra Pradesh, India. He is currently working as a project associate for All India Institute of Local Self Government, Bhopal. As a scholar he has interned at the Deutsche Gesellschaft für Internationale Zusammenarbeit (GIZ) GmbH in their Sustainable Urban Development-Smart Cities (SUD-SC) project and Multidisciplinary Centre for Human Centric Research (CHCR), Design Innovation Centre, School of Planning and Architecture, Bhopal. His research areas includes urban development through real-time data processing and developing spatial data infrastructure (SDI) at an urban local level.

Dr. Bidhan Chandra Ray is a former professor in the Department of Chemistry at Jadavpur University, Kolkata. He is an expert in environmental management and also the president of the Professor Sukumar Maiti Polymer Award Foundation. He has contributed many research papers published in various reputable national and international journals.

Dr. Kakoli Saha completed her Ph.D. in applied remote sensing in 2010 from Kent State University, Kent, Ohio, USA. She joined the School of Planning and Architecture, Bhopal as an assistant professor in 2014. Since then, she has successfully completed many professional assignments. Dr. Saha was coordinator for the doctoral programme and was principal investigator for the DST project under the Young Scientist Scheme (2012- 2015). Currently, she is heading the Geoinformatics Centre, School of Planning and Architecture, Bhopal. Her research interest span covers application of GIS and remote sensing in physical planning and architecture. As the author of several scholarly articles, Dr. Saha is a recipient of the prestigious Erasmus Scholarship under the framework of Erasmus Plus Global Mobility Programme, 2016.

Prof. Dr. Subhajit Saraswati is a renowned professor in the Department of Construction Engineering at Jadavpur University, Kolkata. He is the former president of the Indian Concrete Institute and Executive Committee Member of Asian Concrete Federation. He is a member of the Institution of Engineers, Indian Roads Congress, and American Concrete Institute. He has contributed many research papers published in various reputable national and international journals.

Prof. Pradhan Parth Sarthi (M. Sc. (Tech); Ph.D. in geophysics (meteorology) from Banaras Hindu University, Post-Doctorate from CAS, IIT Delhi) is currently a professor in the Department of Environmental Science, CUSB, Gaya, India. He has guided a number of MPhil/Ph.D. students and published research papers in prestigious international journals. His research interests are Eurasian Snow, ISMR, climate modelling, and climate change. Presently, he is president of the India Meteorological Society, Patna Chapter, India, and steering committee member of Bihar State Action Plan on Climate Change.

Swatilekha Sen is presently working as a research fellow in the Department of Geography, the University of Burdwan, West Bengal. Her areas of research interest include environmental geography, urban studies, and human and social geography. She has contributed in various research papers in different peer-reviewed international journals and edited book volumes.

Dr. Amir Shakibamanesh is an urban designer with more than 12 years of professional experience. He currently works as an associate professor of urban design at the University of Art, Tehran, Iran. He is the author or co-author of more than 25 scholarly articles and monographs, and author of 9 books and book chapters. He is also the director of Virtual Reality And Emerging Technologies Lab (In Urban Design And Architecture). Dr. Shakibamanesh's research interests include smart cities, urban modeling and simulation, virtual and augmented reality, and urban scene analysis.

Dr. Madhuri Sharma is an associate professor in the Department of Geography, University of Tennessee, Knoxville, Tennessee, USA. Her research interests include racial/ethnic diversity/segregation, contemporary housing market, gender economy and social disparity, gentrification, new urbanism and placemaking, poverty and income inequality, and geographies of the developing world. She has published research papers in various international journals and edited book volumes, and she also serves as a reviewer for many international journals. She uses both quantitative and qualitative methods to answer research questions on human disparity.

Dr. Vishal Soodan is an assistant professor in the Centre of Management Studies, Jain (Deemed to be University) Bengaluru, India. He is UGC-NET qualified and has more than five years of teaching and research experience at the UG and PG level. His areas of specialization are technology adoption, consumer psychology, and business analytics. He has conducted workshops on business analytics and has several publications in both national and international journals. He is on the editorial board of various journals of repute and has actively participated in national and international conferences.

S.A. Sudusinghe is a member of the Sri Lankan administrative service, currently working as an assistant divisional secretary at divisional secretariat Siyambalanduwa, Sri Lanka. M.Sc. in GIS and RS, University of Sri Jayewardenepura and graduated from the Vavuniya campus of the University of Jaffna, Sri Lanka. Her areas of research interest cover urban planning, environmental management, disaster management, waste management, land use, and rural development.

Omid Veisi received his M.Sc. in urban design from the Art University in Tehran in 2020 and completed his bachelor's degree in architecture from the Razi University in Kermanshah in 2012. He defended his master thesis on the "Study Effect of Morphological Indices of Urban Block Design on Improvement of Passive Solar Energy Absorption Levels (Case Study: Farangian Phases 1 of Kermanshah)." Also, he has been working as a postgraduate researcher at the Department of Urban Planning and Design, School of Architecture and Urbanism, Art University in Tehran.

Dr. Grażyna Wieteska has a Ph.D in economic sciences in the field of management sciences. Her research interests include risk management, business continuity management, supply chain resilience, circular economy, and eco-product development. She has contributed in various research and educational projects performed in cooperation with European universities; author and co-author of over 50 publications; and is currently involved as the principal investigator in the SIMBIO Project entitled "New Frontiers in Social Innovation Research: Social Innovation for BIOPlastics" within the Trans-Atlantic Platform Social Innovation Programme.

Dr. Beata Wieteska-Rosiak has a Ph.D in economic sciences. Her research interests include adaptation to climate change, circular economy, sustainable cities, sustainable buildings, and public safety in the face of contemporary environmental, social, and economic threats. She is the author and co-author of many scientific publications and is a participant of many research projects. Presently, she is involved in the SIMBIO Project entitled "New Frontiers in Social Innovation Research: Social Innovation for BIO Plastics" within the Trans-Atlantic Platform Social Innovation Programme.

Section I

Urban Conservation, Land Transformation, and Regeneration

1 Crowdfunding and Place-Making Efforts in New Orleans

Madhuri Sharma
University of Tennessee, Knoxville, TN, United States

CONTENTS

1.1 INTRODUCTION

There has been marked increase in community engagement toward neighborhood development activities through crowdsourcing and crowdfunding efforts in several small-to-big towns of the USA and other parts of the world. These efforts have largely conceptualized due to increased prominence of neoliberal policies and continuously diminishing public funds to support community activities such as the arts, culture, community development, and the like. Crowdfunding is an online process of creating funds for projects through money donated from a "crowd" or bunch of people/backers who support the cause (Bouncken et al., 2015; Davies, 2014a, 2014b, 2014c; Elrod, 2014; Stiver et al., 2015). Thus, it is a new and unique way of funding compared to traditional borrowing that allows any one and everyone willing to fund — individuals, groups, communities, or economic actors and investors who want to support the activity. Thus, these project ideas and products become largely owned by the group of fundraisers (e.g., individuals/supporters/entrepreneurs), who seek for money to get their projects fulfilled. Thus, crowdfunding is an idea that acquires its financial resources through open calls for donations, grants, etc., and in exchange, it rewards the donors with a voice in the project's conceptions and ideas (Bouncken et al., 2015; Bugge, 2011; Davies, 2014a, 2014b, 2014c; Elrod, 2014; Hemer, 2011; McCracken, 2012). Over last few years, the widespread crowdfunding initiatives, especially in terms of its geographic outreach, money raised, and number of platforms globally, including various new types of crowdfunding initiatives have also occurred (Davies, 2014c; Doucette, 2015; Stiver et al., 2015). The issues and themes of focus may vary for these projects, and yet the context and the concept remain the same – funded by a crowd/public who

DOI: 10.1201/9781003126195-2

care enough to make the projects successful. More recently, these projects have largely focused on the arts, culture, music, urban farms, vegetable gardens, urban parks, community health, community mapping and needs assessment, reading groups, and any other social and economic cause that appeal to the public who care enough to support it (Davies, 2014a, 2014c; Miller, 2015; Soden and Palen, 2014; Sharma and Elrod, 2016).

Crowdfunding research so far has focused largely on assessing the network and motivation among people who commit to such causes online. On rare occasions, some scholars have examined the role of place and space (e., Brown, 2012, 2014 and Agrawal et al., 2015), wherein a project's spatiality/geographic attributes and the effectiveness in their implementation has been linked with the projects' success or failures (Agrawal et al., 2014, 2015; Copeland, 2015; Mollick, 2014; McCracken, 2012). In this regard, Brown's term "*Citizinvestor*" has really energized the community toward their innovative approaches to solving local community problems in developed and developing countries both (see Brown, 2012, 2014). This has opened avenues for initiating community-level projects to address numerous short-term problems (Davies, 2014a, 2014b, 2014c; Doucette, 2015; Miller, 2015; Soden and Palen 2014; Sharma and Elrod, 2016), and these efforts have been successful across many cities in the United States. Crowdfunding offers unique opportunities to individuals who lead these ideas on their unique individualities, identities and concepts (Copeland, 2015; Davies, 2014a, 2014b, 2014c; Mollick, 2014; McCracken, 2012). When a "common" need is identified by a community, which brings them together to generate funds by seeking donations from a crowd of people through a website/Internet sources, that in itself creates a unique opportunity of bringing "like-minded" people together (Beyers, 2002; Bugge, 2011; Tirdatov, 2014). However, crowdfunding initiatives have rarely been approached from quantitative angles (Bouncken et al., 2015), even though some recent work by Davies (2014c) and Brown (2014) have compiled and analyzed such projects by analyzing the dollar amounts generated from these, and the volumes/numbers of these projects functioning within the USA and Europe.

A kickstarter, on the other hand, provides a digital platform for projects' initiators to campaign online and seek funds by offering rewards to those who help them raise money from potential founders (Copeland, 2015; Howe, 2006a, 2006b; HTTP14; HTTP15; McCracken, 2012). The organizers of these sites look for projects with clear goal and adequate fitness into one of these categories: art, comics, dance, design, fashion, film, food, games, music, photography, publishing, or theater. Thus, the projects that do not require continued funding and maintenance after their completion are essential. Such projects have been operating since 2009 and work on an "all or nothing" approach (McCracken, 2012; Perry, 2014).

This research examines the grassroots level organic processes that initiate community-based crowdfunded projects that appeal to local communities and meets their emotional, physiological, and socio-economic needs in numerous ways (Doucette, 2015; Kerschberg, 2012; Sherman, 2011). As such, this research also explores how the kickstarters and crowdfunded projects contribute toward urban revitalization. By using New Orleans as a laboratory for this study, this chapter illustrates insights from select kickstarter projects that occurred in the city of New Orleans (NOLA hereafter) during 2009–2012, which helped them sustain the arts and the culture that would have otherwise diminished, given the economic and natural distress that NOLA frequently suffers from. While discussing the kickstarters in NOLA, readers are also informed about NOLA's communities' unique characteristics – resilience, commitment, and dedication – that are essential in sustaining and (re) creating personalized community spaces and safety nets (see Campo's [2014] discussion on Detroit and Buffalo; Fields et al.'s, (2015) and Ehrenfeucht's (2014) paper on New Orleans; Hyra's (2015) discussion on neighborhood redevelopment; and Barthel et al. (2015) and Beilin and Wilkinson (2015) on resilience and food security in urban context). This chapter links community-based initiatives with their local and global outreach and the enthusiasm that a "glocal" community shows by contributing toward the cause of these projects in New Orleans. By capturing the perceptions of initiators from select projects in New Orleans that were analyzed in another related work, and by comparing those findings from my own analysis of 13 projects analyzed in this work, this chapter contributes toward scholarly understanding of these questions from multi-layered and mixed methods approach.

The rest of this chapter has four sections. The literature review introduces readers with the concepts of crowdfunding, placemaking, and resilience in New Orleans. The research design discusses the study area, data collected, and the methods employed. Analysis and findings draw upon a broad overview of 13 projects in NOLA, their backers, and their local and global outreach. The conclusions discuss the process through which small, organic ideas come together to create a sense of placemaking. In doing so, these efforts reemphasize the presence of resilience and strong affinity toward maintaining arts and cultural heritage among NOLA communities.

1.2 BACKGROUND CONTEXT

1.2.1 CROWDFUNDING

Crowdfunding implies arranging for funds for an idea/concept by convincing a group of individuals or crowd of people to buy into their concept, instead of reaching out to professional parties or public/government funding institutions (Agrawal et al., 2014, 2015; Boudreau et al., 2015). This platform, thus, encourages initiators to directly appeal to like-minded people/community such that the seed capital generated out of such initiatives become self-sustainable entrepreneurial ventures without any dependency on conventional funding sources (e.g., banks, loans, etc.) or other capital (Elrod, 2014; Howe, 2006a; HTTP14; HTTP15; HTTP16; HTTP17). This very public nature of support makes such projects successful (Doucette, 2015; Davies, 2014a, 2014b). Often entrepreneurs in funding-deprived areas are more likely to engage in such community-based "crowdfunded" efforts (Agrawal et al., 2014). For example, spaces/places with limited services by banks/branches or in places/communities with depressed home prices, making home equity and traditional banking loans less valuable, and/or any other place/neighborhood less attractive to bank-sourced funding – are the spaces/places with more viable options for crowdfunded opportunities to initiate. In recent times, however, several news channels have also noted an increase in mismanagement of funds by fundraisers.

Davies's work had empirically analyzed crowdfunded projects and their outreach in terms of the revenue generated and the community impacts within the USA and other parts of the world (see Davies, 2014a, 2014b, 2014c; Doucette, 2015; Howe, 2006b; Miller, 2015). Other scholars have also explored the role of crowdsourced projects in solving everyday problems in the developing world (Kerschberg, 2012), and for crises management and community mapping tasks (Brown, 2014), especially in the lesser developed parts of the world (Soden and Palen, 2014), and for creative community arts/music (Sharma and Elrod, 2016), for public good and philanthropy work (Davies, 2014a, 2014b, 2014c; Doucette, 2015; HTTP14; HTTP17; HTTP18), and for community's revitalization and redevelopment work (Davies, 2014c; Sherman, 2011).

While many scholars have suggested that crowdfunding serves as a good alternative in an age of declining public funds to meet all community needs, Davies (2014a, 2014b, 2014c) also added a contradictory perspective to the mushrooming of such projects in that these projects serve various short-term needs of people, providing a model for "project-based" rather than "organizational-based" agenda, without offering any long term commitment or guarantees for the future, which make them more attractive to the contemporary demography. In addition, since the government agencies won't intervene, such projects get more focused attention of the crowd through crowdfunding (Davies, 2014a). Crowdfunding, thus, also helps develop a strong network among these investors who might later on share more ideas toward other similar passions and interests in the long run (Davies, 2014a, 2014b, 2014c).

The effectiveness of crowdfunding efforts, however, may also vary based on their geography. For example, Mollick's (2014) analysis of spatial discrepancies in fundraising outcomes were associated with geographic variations in the neighborhood's socio-economic attribute. In addition, varying levels of personal connections and friendships also determined the numbers and quality of projects that got funded (Davies, 2014c). Thus, while studies on crowdfunding have so far analyzed the funding networks as well as the community's motivations toward these projects, not many have examined the role of *place* and/or their association with the people and local communities which might be detrimental toward these motivations and initiatives.

1.2.2 Placemaking

Through her seminal book *The Death and Life of Great American Cities,* Jane Jacobs (1961) gained global fame due to her emphasis on the role of *place* in urban planning. This work paved pathways for various other studies, including *The Rise of the Creative Class* by Richard Florida (2012), which lays out a framework for the role of the *creative class.* In particular, Florida's attention to the "three Ts," – Talent, Tolerance and Technology – has gained momentum for their contributions toward making a place creative, that also serves as an attraction pole for diverse and yet like-minded people who make such places their home.

Concerning "place" and "emotional attachment to place," Yi Fu Tuan (1974) had long ago indicated that undifferentiated *space* becomes a *place* when one starts knowing a place better and endows it with values and meanings. Places acquire special meanings through the creation of sentiments and experiences (Tuan, 1974), which eventually also motivates residents to become more attached to their own communities. These experiences help accumulate higher levels of social cohesion and social capital, while gaining better control on their local environments, and have less fear of crime that eventually contribute toward significant and visible physical revitalization of neighborhoods (Manzo and Perkins, 2006). Rootedness adds a larger context to a person by linking its *being* as a manifestation of individual lived-in experiences as well as external social processes (Manzo and Perkins, 2006). Place attachments often get portrayed in different forms of arts, culture, music, etc. Thus, a creative place/city can be thought of as a hearth – an incubator for culture – where people, ideas, creativity, and organizations – all come together to nurture entrepreneurs and creativity that eventually create and produce next generation of *creative* workers (Fields et al., 2015; Finn, 2014; Sharma and Elrod, 2016).

In recent years, culture and the arts have gained significance due to their attractiveness and valuation among the creative class in cities and communities (Ehrenfeucht, 2014; Florida, 2012). Increasingly, a large number of people engaged in the arts and culture are now promoting artistic traditions from developing regions such as Africa, Asia, Latin America, and the Pacific Rim (Sidford, 2011). Not only are traditional art forms being appreciated highly as exotic commodities, but artists are also engaged in building communities that address various types of societal problems, injustices, and inequalities (Ehrenfeucht, 2014; Jabareen, 2014; Perry, 2014; Sidford, 2011). Further, many organizations focused on the culture and arts also continue to address issues of environmental/social (in)justice, and inequities in civil/human rights through various arts forms (Morgan, 2015). However, with the continued declines in public funds, these activities are the ones to be chopped off the list first, which, fortunately over the past few years, have found new lives through crowdfunding initiatives (Davies, 2014a, 2014b, 2014c; Miller, 2015; Sharma and Elrod, 2016).

1.2.3 The Role of Resilience in the Placemaking of New Orleans

Long before Hurricane Katrina hit New Orleans in 2005, the city had been a target of economic distress, with all types of jobs and population leaving the city for decades, with its school districts ranking at the lowest performing scales, and people and places plagued with high unemployment and poverty (Davidson, 2009; Rudowitz et al., 2006; Squires, 2008). Like Detroit where African Americans (the terms Black and African American have been used interchangeably in this chapter) and the poorest residents have generally been confined to the worst parts of the city (Grady and Darden, 2012), New Orleans too showed signs of distress that were most felt by the minorities, and in particular African Americans felt more challenged due to frequent encounters with natural disasters (Campo, 2014; Caputo et al., 2015; Davidson, 2009; Rudowitz et al., 2006; Sharma and Elrod, 2016; Turner, 2006). After Katrina, the scenes from the Superdome and the flooded streets of New Orleans had further exposed the poverty and vulnerability of the city's African Americans (Berube, 2007; Davidson, 2009; Turner, 2006).

However, despite Katrina, the low-income communities of NOLA have shown resilience and vitality to re-create the city (Beilin and Wilkinson, 2015; Berube, 2007; Campo, 2014; Davidson, 2009; Rudowitz et al., 2006; Turner, 2006). In this regard, McLeman and Hunter (2010) and Turner (2006) note that New Orleans's pre-Katrina population of 450,000 in 2005 had declined to 210,000 in 2006, and by 2008 it was still below 310,000, marking a net loss of almost 31% during 2005–2008. Despite population losses and high poverty, New Orleans retains unique characteristics that have sustained it through cycles of economic and natural distress. Many families have spent their entire lives and generations in these very neighborhoods, which has created strong social networks of families, friends, neighbours, and communities, which have eventually helped them weather hardships (Berube, 2007; Davidson, 2009; Turner, 2006). Likewise, many other U.S. metropolises have survived economic distress by taking refuge in local community initiatives for addressing redevelopment and economic revitalization (Campo, 2014; Caputo et al., 2015; Hyra, 2015). This chapter relies on secondary data analysis of projects initiated in New Orleans and the roles of such community-initiated projects in creating, sustaining, and preserving the local arts, culture, and heritage that also emphasize the New Orleans's resilient people and their dedication toward its *place-making* efforts through local and global contributions toward the cause.

1.3 RESEARCH DESIGN

1.3.1 Study Area

This chapter analyzes crowdfunding efforts in the neighborhoods of New Orleans that had a potential to help initiate projects that benefitted the community at large. In a preliminary analysis of crowdfunded projects across the USA, New Orleans was the only urban area, larger than 50,000 population, that ranked among the top 20 with regard to total numbers of kickstarter projects per 1,000 population (Elrod, 2014). Other qualifiers for selecting NOLA included repeat occurrences of natural disasters, its high levels of economic distress and poverty, and the city's extraordinary community resilience and rich cultural history (Beilin and Wilkinson, 2015). New Orleans, despite being a hub of culture, music, food, and fun, has always been one of the most divided mid-sized metro areas in the USA (Brown and Sharma, 2010; Darden and Kamel, 2000). All of these reasons collectively made NOLA an interesting study area for this analysis.

1.3.2 Data

Given the newness of the concept of crowdfunding, especially in terms of financing, with little to no research done on this concept from a spatial perspective, this study adopted a multi-step approach to complete this chapter. After collecting the data for all kickstarter projects from all over the United States (initiated during 2009–2012), each project was normalized by population (numbers of projects per 1,000 people) to gain insights into the per-capita community engagement efforts and its scalar and spatial variances across cities, towns, urban areas, and metropolises alike (see Elrod, 2014 for detailed analyses of U.S.-wide projects). These two columns of data were compared against Florida's (2012) ranking analyses of creative class cities wherein New Orleans, that had originally ranked among the top five in terms of total numbers of projects funded, had dropped to the 18th rank in the normalized-by-population rankings, and didn't show up among the top 50 in Florida's creative class cities. However, New Orleans was still chosen due to its specific attributes pertaining to economic distress, natural disasters, higher poverty, and health disadvantage, especially for its African American populations, along with the notoriety of its environmental injustice (Campo, 2014), while also being a unique and resilient cultural and arts hub (Caputo et al., 2015; Ehrenfeucht, 2014).

1.3.3 Methodology

After completing basic secondary data-based analysis of projects all over the USA, I focused on the projects in NOLA to identify the projects' initiators willing to fully participate in in-depth or semi-structured interviews. After sending out rounds of introductory emails, only 13 kickstarters were identified in New Orleans, and by the end of the interview completion period (June 25–August 26 of 2013[1]), only four of the eight willing participants had completed the online interviews on skype or through the online detailed questionnaires. Questions focused largely on examining the *what, why, where,* and *how* aspects of the kickstarters – i.e., the *processes* surrounding their conception and implementation, as well as the overall characteristics of their initiators, and how well these communities reacted toward the concepts of crowdfunding and crowdsourcing. These responses provided some insights into how they helped create sustainable urban communities, which also reflected the "resilient" nature of people of NOLA. The recorded interviews were later transcribed, analyzed, and compared with additional secondary data gathered from the websites of the 13 identified projects in NOLA. Based on the themes recurring in the interviews, all 13 identified projects were broadly analyzed for their overall focus along with backers' portfolio, and their domestic as well as international outreach in terms of their overall support – through funding and in terms of their support toward the projects' concepts. The analysis of the 13 projects is summarized along three dimensions: (i) tabular analysis of the projects and the global outreach of the backers, (ii) role of place and space, and (iii) grantfunding,

1.4 ANALYSIS

1.4.1 Tabular Overview of Projects and the Global Outreach of Backers

Table 1.1 briefly outlines the activities of the kickstarter projects in New Orleans. It also enumerates its overall "local-global" backers' geographical spread and their funding pledged – likening these with the conceptual outreach of these projects that bring together like-minded people. As noted, a majority of these 13 projects pertained to arts and culture, and none to food, even though NOLA is famous for its cuisine.

While the table suggests an interesting global outreach of these 13 projects, in a related field-based analysis conducted by Elrod (2014) that included some of these NOLA projects, Elrod actually mapped them and linked them with census tract-scale data on income, poverty, and racial/ethnic characteristics, and found some interesting patterns that largely corroborated what I found in the table (see Figures 10–15 on pages 46–51 in Elrod 2014). Elrod's (2014) analysis of the kickstarters' neighbourhoods suggested these projects seemingly initiated in areas with an older population (median age in 31–50 years) – suggestive of stronger kinship ties, especially in the inner-city locations where generations of families had lived. She also found that a majority of her mapped projects occurred in largely low-income ($20,000–$40,000) and mid-income ($40,000–$80,000) neighborhoods, even though the initiators were largely white, educated, and middle class.

Elrod's (2014) analysis overlapped with my own analysis of the tabulated projects (Table 1.1) wherein I illustrate a dedicated effort of backers – domestic and international, with some returning and some new, and a contribution of $49.68 per backer. These align quite well with an earlier analysis by Brown (2014) who had found similar patterns in his analysis of community-initiated projects in the cities of Providence and in Philadelphia. Across these three studies, however, the common thing was the desire to protect cultural and place-specific heritage – which were felt more strongly in the relatively poorer, low-income communities of NOLA. This is also evident from the table that shows many new supporters/backers who supported the project's objectives and donated

TABLE 1.1

Project Name and Type, Focus, and Backers' Profile (Interviewed Projects Are Shaded)

"Catapult" –Art

- Launched on October 14, 2010, this show concerns potentials for exploring art in New Orleans, had its first art opening at *T-Lot*, installed a new space in St. Claude to create a new studio (HTTP1).
- Its 19 backers pledged $720 to bring this project back to life.
- Backers belonged from NOLA (6), Chicago (2), Baltimore (1), Greensboro (1), Mandeville (1), Tuscaloosa (1), and Waltham (1), and other undisclosed locations.
- 15 of these 19 backers were new supporters.

"8th Annual Draw-a-Thon" –Art

- Press Street initiated *The Draw-a-Thon, which* was a 24-hour event free for all ages, open to the public of NOLA. This event encouraged creative work by letting interested participants draw on the temporary walls that were built and covered with papers suited for drawing and painting (HTTP2).
- Its 68 backers pledged $2,228
- 49 of its 67 U.S. backers were from NOLA, others from various cities
- 1 international backer (location unknown)
- 38 were new backers

"Golden Feather Mardi Gras Indian Gallery and Coffee House" –Art

- Initiated by Naimah and Shaka Zulu (HTTP3), this project showcased Mardi Gras Indian suits and provided space for buying supplies that were needed to build these astonishing yearly suits.
- Its 61 backers (by February 18, 2016) pledged $5,732.
- Backers belonged to NOLA (14) and other cities (Oakland, San Francisco, Brooklyn, Asheville, Chicago, Dayton, Lockport, etc.)
- Had international backers including from Brazil
- 47 out of 61 U.S. backers were new supporters and remaining 14 were returning

"The New Orleans Book Fair" –Publishing

- Created by Robin Watt, this project published community work (HTTP4)
- Its 49 backers pledged $1,639
- 45 out of 49 backers were from the USA and belonged to NOLA (26), Metairie (3), Austin (1), Baton Rouge (1), Burbank (1), Fort Collins (1), Gadsden (1), and other cities
- Its 4 global backers belonged to Ireland (1), United Kingdom (1), and 2 from unknown locations.
- 27 out of 49 U.S. backers were newcomers

"A Giant Ball Pit in an Abandoned House" –Art

- John Ente created this project to address the issue of abandoned homes in NOLA since the number of vacant homes had doubled since Katrina (HTTP5).
- Its 231 backers pledged a total of $3,304.
- Its 206 U.S. backers belong to NOLA (29), Brooklyn (25), New York (19), Chicago (13), Los Angeles (7), Cambridge (6), Berkeley (4), Boston (4), Atlanta (3), and Seattle (3).
- Had 231 backers from 10 countries
- 65 of 231 backers were newcomers, whereas the rest were returning

"Swoon Musical Architecture for New Orleans" –Art

- Musicians and kinetic sound artists were the main targets for this project that turned a house in NOLA into a sculpture that functioned like a musical instrument – called as *Dithyrambali.* This involved stamping interactive instruments into the walls and floorboards of this house that created trails and tests for singing walls, organ floorboards, and the percussion. It also provided support for the artists who created prototype instruments for this house (HTTP6).
- Its 357 backers pledged $23,977.
- 278 U.S. backers belonged from NOLA (27), New York (26), Brooklyn (26), Los Angeles (14), San Francisco (9), Austin (8), Oakland (8), and Boston (5)
- International backers from 9 countries included the UK (14), Canada (10), Australia (4), France (2), Germany (2), The Bahamas (1), Denmark (1), Dominican Republic (1), and Ireland 91).
- 252 of its 357 backers were returning supporters

"The Aquarium Gallery and Studios" –Art

- Jacob Martins convert gutted homes into studios and galleries for artists. This also served as an inexpensive and fun place for these artists to work together (HTTP7).
- Its 87 backers pledged $3,398.

(*Continued*)

TABLE 1.1 (Continued)

Project Name and Type, Focus, and Backers' Profile (Interviewed Projects Are Shaded)

- Its 64 U.S. backers belonged to NOLA (26), Kansas City (6), Chicago (3), Los Angeles (3), Colorado Springs (2), Brooklyn (2), Ames (1), and others.
- Global backers included the USA (64), Australia (1), United Kingdom (1), and others

"Spread the Creative Forces Program Model"– Theater

- Mat Schwarzman created this theater to change the lives of the "at-risk students in the high-school" by introducing curriculum for creative programs for students. It raised funds for curriculum development for high schools/universities, and other youth groups and/or youth serving projects (HTTP8).
- Its 33 backers pledged $3,013.
- Out of its 24 U.S. backers, 4 were from NOLA and the rest were from other cities.
- 9 of these 33 were international backers
- 29 of these 33 backers were new supporters, whereas 9 were returning backers

"The Alamo Underground" – Art

- Created by Casey, this project was a collective of local, underground food, music, art, and theater on Freret Street (HTTP9).
- Its 51 backers pledged $4,030.
- Out of its 27 U.S. backers, 11 were from NOLA.
- 40 of these 51 were new backers

"Block Party 2011" –Culture & Festival

- Created by Daniel Ray, this project raised money for DVDs and general logistics and helped host the 4th festival by the Community Records (HTTP10).
- Its 75 backers pledged $3,620.
- Its 47 U.S. backers belonged to NOLA (10) and others (Los Angeles, Albany, Austin, Arnold, Berkley, Big Rapids).
- 28 out of its 75 backers were international (Canada (2), UK (1), and others)
- 57 of its 75 backers were new supporters

"New Orleans Film Society: 'Movies to Geaux'"–Films

- Jolese Pinder, the creator, purchased a screening equipment for outdoors to bring back cinema to every pocket of the city. The idea of a neighborhood-based movie theater was drawn from the way music, galleries, and restaurants existed in every corner of New Orleans (HTTP11).
- Its 122 backers pledged $5,227.
- Its 120 U.S. backers belonged to NOLA (75), Metairie (5), and Los Angeles (4). Others include Brooklyn (3), Covington (2), Kenner (2), Nashville (2), Austin (1), and Baton Rouge (1).
- 2 international backers from London, UK
- 55 backers were new supporters, whereas 67 were returning

"Fair Housing Five" – Publishing

- Hannah Adams, the creator of this project, focused on an illustrated children's book that could help initiate/promote a conversation between parents, caregivers, teachers, and children about housing discrimination and systemic inequality. The idea was to teach ways to end these types of injustices by creating awareness among the community (HTTP12).
- Its 93 backers pledged $5,361.
- Its 63 U.S. backers belonged to NOLA (28), Boston (2), New York (2), Brooklyn (2), Atlanta (1), Austin (1), Beacon (1), Cherry Hill (1), Dermott (1), and Rast Hills (1).
- 65 of its 93 backers were new

"Parallel Play –2nd Annual Show at T-Lot" – Art & Theater

- This involved an exhibit of upcoming/emerging artists such that by raising funds, it could become a more permanent event. Its second annual exhibition was held on October 14, 2016 (HTTP13).
- Its 50 backers pledged $2,145.
- Its U.S. backers belonged to NOLA (21), Chicago (2), New York (2), Baltimore (1), Chattanooga (1), Knoxville (1), Los Angeles (1), Louisville (1), Mclean (1), and New Haven (1).
- 27 of these 50 backers were new, whereas 23 were returning members
- This project was not geocoded, and hence doesn't show up on the map.

Summary: Total funds raised: $64,394; total backers: 1,296; average funds raised per backer = $49.68.

funds just because these projects' ideas and concepts resonated with them. However, since my analysis here is based on only 13 tabulated projects, one must be aware of not generalizing the findings due to its small sample size.

Finally, based on the knowledge gathered from the interviewed initiators, and the idea that the majority of their promotional and geographic outreach was largely local – through Facebook, word-of-mouth, websites/fliers, and through the close-knit art community in the city – all highlighted the strong role of social capital and kinships. Given the small sample of 13 projects discussed in the table, one can broadly conclude that low-income neighborhoods could be good platforms for initiating such community-based projects as the short-term commitment and its democratic appeal served well in these neighborhoods (Davies, 2014c; Elrod, 2014).

1.4.2 Role of Place and Space

Since this chapter's aim was to provide insights into the processes of initiating these projects, the data gathered emphasized the *who, why, where,* and *how* aspects of the kickstarters and the ways in which their responses identified with the role of place/space, community needs, support from non-government funding, and the like (Elrod, 2014). A quick overview of the four initiators found that all the four respondents were white, females, had a bachelor's degree, and were artists of various types. These included a filmmaker, photographer/graphic designer, writer, and a visual artist.

Concerning the role of place, the only one to comment was the development director of *Press Street* who emphasized the uniqueness of spatiality, particularly in terms of class-based intermixed spaces. In her views, New Orleans's neighborhoods were interesting in that the poor and the wealthy blocks sat adjacent to each other. Also, even though many people came to New Orleans as visitors and for fun, they would live there for a few years before eventually departing for Austin, which was perceived as "as hip as NOLA," but with higher-paying jobs (Elrod, 2014). The project SWOON Musical Architecture for New Orleans brought together the artists after the event was over. This helped bring disparate communities together, despite their differences in terms of race, religion, and culture. The development director, thus, emphasized the significance of New Orleans in terms of it as a space and spatiality – that likened its people in terms of "kinship," "cordial attitude," "family bond," and "place-attachment" – all of which were so integral to New Orleans's *culture* and *place-making* attributes (Elrod, 2014).

The Fair Housing Five project reached out to new constituents while making them aware of housing discrimination through books, literacy, and awareness creation. Draw-A-Thon collaborated through the planning weeks/months by staying awake at nights for organizing these events, and later they also hung out together through the camaraderie thereafter – largely reflecting their solidarity. Parallel Play: 2nd Annual Show at T-LOT, on the other hand, arranged for and provided space for them to shop at the flea markets; it also arranged space for movie screenings for the entire community as well as for the young artists to experiment outdoor work. All of these networking and collaborative approaches highlight the social capital and desire of working together to help create an identity of New Orleans.

1.4.3 Grantfunding

Most of these projects in New Orleans were largely funded by local support from family and friends, with few exceptions. The Fair Housing Five received funding from friends/family as well as former supporters who liked their innovative ways of fundraising (Elrod, 2014). The funds for the Draw-A-Thon were raised from those who had attended an event earlier and/or from the networks of the organization. T-LOT raised funds largely from family/friends. In contrast, SWOON Musical Architecture for New Orleans was funded largely by strangers. Relationships with grantfunding was generally avoided due to the constraints presented by grants and were pursued only when it needed to be supplemented and/or to expand its grantfunding (Elrod, 2014). The Draw-A-Thon had its funding slashed by the Arts Council of Louisiana, which eventually made them ask for funds from the kickstarters. Swoon and Fair Housing both also acquired small grantfunding from others (Elrod, 2014). Tracy Davis (pseudo name) from SWOON Musical Architecture for New Orlean*s* emphasized on the decision-making power that kickstarters gave to people that helped them buy into a project idea and its audience (Elrod, 2014; Sharma and Elrod, 2016). As noted in her conversation:

> We want people to believe they can create magic in their own community. Post-Katrina, urban planning has become the domain of those in power. We think that projects like these empower collaborators and visitors to take a stand and have a voice in their own neighborhood.
>
> (Elrod, 2014:36)

As such, the most important element of such funding was the creative freedom it allowed for the project initiators. As quoted from the initiator of Draw-A-Thon's web-based illustration:

> We've potentially been able to go after corporate sponsors to fund these things if we wanted to, but we prefer the crowdfunding model to keep it totally organic and we won't be beholden to anyone or advertising anything or have to compromise any of what we're trying to create and achieve...[......]. Being able to maintain total control on creativity and ownership [.......] what we do is very refreshing.
>
> (Elrod, 2014:36)

When the initiator was asked about why the backers chose that site in particular, the responses included the aesthetics of the site, and their awareness about the kickstarter. These projects mostly made it to the site after rigorous vetting process. As such, these efforts were largely appreciated by the participants as it gave them a sense of belongingness and accountability. This idea has been also reiterated by Tuan (1974) who said that "undifferentiated *space* becomes a *place* when we start to know and understand a place better and endow them with meanings and values." Thus, places acquire special and far deeper meanings through our building of sentiments, emotions, and experiences with a place (Manzo and Perkins, 2006).

1.5 DISCUSSION AND CONCLUSIONS

This chapter examined the support from local as well as international backers toward attaining the goals set by the kickstarter projects that initiated in numerous communities of New Orleans. The fact that the ideas that had originated locally, and yet they had backers from across the globe, was quite interesting as it resonated with the goals and philosophies that brought people together regardless of their nationality, race, color, and the like. Further, the interviews discussed in the analysis provided broad insights into the organic ways in which such *community-driven* initiatives paved pathways for urban rejuvenation by preserving the arts, culture, and heritage in NOLA (Beyers, 2002, 2008; Elrod, 2014). In their analysis of cultural services, for example, Beyers (2002) indicates that with reduced contributions from the National Endowment for the Arts, even the support from the local and state government toward the arts had dwindled and been severely cut. As such, support from local citizens (i.e., *Citizinvestor* according to Brown, 2014) and communities are getting initiated across space, and often these efforts have benefited from personal networking and connections of the initiators (Agrawal et al., 2014, 2015; Brown, 2014). These 13 projects were able to raise an amount of $64,394 through their supporters (Table 1.1). This finding reemphasizes Davies's (2014a, 2014b, 2014c) theorization that the dwindling support from state/public system can indeed provide the needed push and momentum to local communities to get into action, which can facilitate crowd-sourced and crowdfunded projects. The city of New Orleans suggests a greater commitment toward preserving art and culture as a mainstay of the city's heritage. This indeed speaks volumes of the *place-making* aspects of New Orleans and its people who have, through their resilience and hard work, survived repeat encounters of economic and natural disasters.

Regarding geographic connectedness and outreach, a majority of the 13 projects in New Orleans had supporters not only from within NOLA and/or the United States, but also from Canada, United Kingdom, Ireland, Brazil, Australia, and other countries (Table 1.1). While these projects based in New Orleans have drawn maximum support from NOLA, the *cause* of these projects seemed to resonate well with communities from other parts of the USA and the world as well – hence creating a "glocal theme" and a "glocal community." The fact that almost 50% of the backers were returning supporters (Table 1.1) and almost the same numbers were new supporters is quite commendable in that the very cause that makes these projects initiate, sustain, and seek support from local and international backers reflects the significance of these issues, ideas, and causes that creates the urgency for the people to connect with others across the globe.

These projects in New Orleans were funded by family and friends, which also speaks of individual/community enthusiasm toward a cause they cared for. Most of these projects, so far, had been operational at a very small scale. Thus, analyzing the impacts of such small-scale initiatives proved too much of a nuisance and too early to be effective.

As Davies (2014a, 2014b, and 2014c) had suggested, the very essence of these projects' success is the non-commitment toward long-term funding needs. Given that these projects have survived based on community initiatives, it creates an impact on the larger community toward preserving their social, economic, and cultural heritage. Thus, such projects should be evaluated for their *value-preservation* perspectives, rather than their financial volumes. It is the essence, the motivation, the social-capital, and the ideas of belongingness, cultural collectiveness, and place-specific spirits among the people that played crucial roles in the *placemaking* of New Orleans.

This analysis also highlights the continuity and community-engagement perspectives inherent in New Orleans. Sometimes, letting the project continue and letting the people and community involve in their own community's development can keep their hopes alive. The Fair Housing Five project had provided some help. To further facilitate their venture, they had also discussed with the children and the community about creating healthy sustainable neighborhoods by educating the kids and creating awareness among others about housing discrimination. The Draw-a-Thon searched for funding after losing their grantfunding from the public funds/state. The SWOON Musical Architecture for New Orleans continued its previous efforts. T-Lot's was the second annual event, and the organizers were searching for innovative ways to make these events permanent.

This analysis also suggests that the networks and connections that are formed due to common goals, motives, and aspirations at finer scales of geographies through kickstarter initiatives may be critical toward rejuvenating the declining urban neighborhoods, and more specifically the inner-city poorer communities. Concerning the power of people and community-based initiatives, Jane Jacobs (1961) in her seminal book *The Death and Life of Great American Cities* had rightly noted,

> Cities have the capability of providing something for everybody, only because, and only when, they are created by everybody.

The previous quote speaks about the power of the people – the local communities – and how the elements of *belongingness* can *create* cities for everybody. This idea resonates with the perceptions illustrated above. This also speaks volumes on the *why* and *how* elements of community participation, and the intrinsic qualities of New Orleans's people that make the city resilient and powerful.

Finally, the above-mentioned quote links crowdfunding's role in neighborhood's revitalization – through organic ideas in art and creativity that can sustain and spread throughout the whole city while also empowering their citizenship and sense of belongingness – an idea reiterated by Tuan (1974).

While Jane Jacobs's observations and writings could elaborate on the attributes of neighborhoods that made cities great, this analysis of projects in New Orleans found that even though most projects were at their inception stages, the continued efforts of the communities (i.e., new supporters and returning backers) to sustain them into the future was still alive (see Beyers, 2002). Despite New Orleans's non-presence in Florida's "creative class" list of cities, it has continued to attract people who are loyal, passionate, and resilient, and who decline to leave it despite the repeat economic and natural vulnerabilities (Turner, 2006). The family and kinship values and the associated social capital in this city is what distinguishes it from others.

Crowdfunding's relationships with communities has been relatively new in academic discussion, given the relatively newer form of funding and the new economic geographies it has created. Cities are increasingly incorporating community-based initiatives and engagement that redefine new urban spaces (Beyers, 2002, 2008). The focus of crowdfunding initiatives has been gradually shifting. Now, more places/sites are mushrooming up with community-based place-specific ideas. These have now become a new way of financing businesses in contemporary times (Beyers, 2008; McCracken, 2012; Perry, 2014). The organic nature of these crowdfunded projects helps gauge the projects that have community support, which eventually helps revitalize neighborhoods.

Crowdfunding helps people add *value* to a place by strengthening a community's spirit, which helps build networks across people and places, and helps them find solutions to problems that might otherwise miss the attention of formal funding opportunities (Davies, 2014a, 2014b; Doucette, 2015; Miller, 2015; Sharma and Elrod, 2016; Sherman, 2011). This resonates with Tuan's (1974) ideas of *spaces* becoming *places* when endowed with values and meanings. This study examined New Orleans in light of these organic and community-supported funding that gave a new voice and a new identity to its people and spaces – *resilient* and *cultural heritage*. The appeal of New Orleans as a great place/city to live and raise a family exists. The project initiators are not limited by grants; instead, it is the supporters' monetary contributions that create a more democratic way to build and expand their communities without ruining its residents financially (Beyers, 2002). The people and cultures of New Orleans have created an *authenticity* with *special meanings* attached to this *city* and *place*.

ACKNOWLEDGEMENT

I thank Ms. Brenna Elrod for conducting the field work and preliminary analysis of some interview data that comprised part of her master's thesis work. This chapter has adopted some data collected during her thesis and they have been duly referenced. Additional secondary data were gathered from the websites of the kickstarter projects in New Orleans, and these have been tabulated and analyzed in writing this chapter. Earlier versions of this chapter were reviewed by anonymous reviewers and their suggestions have been taken to improve this chapter.

NOTE

1 Online interviewing in a research implies using the Internet as a medium of data collection and conversation rather that face-to-face in person interaction (Kee and Thompson-Hayes, 2012). There are various ways for web-based interviewing. These include Skype, instant messaging, and emails (Kee and Thompson-Hayes, 2012; James and Busher, 2006, 2009) and these days even the FaceTime, WhatsApp, and the like.

REFERENCES

Agrawal, A., C. Catalini, and A. Goldfarb. "Some simple economics of crowdfunding." *Innovation Policy and the Economy, University of Chicago Press* 14, no. 1 (2014): 63–97. http://www.jstor.org/stable/10.1086/674021

Agrawal, A., C. Catalini, and A. Goldfarb. "Crowdfunding: Geography, social networks, and the timing of investment decisions." *Journal of Economics and Management Strategy* 24, no. 2 (2015): 253–274.

Barthel, S., S. Parker, and H. Ernstson. "Food and green space in cities: A resilience lens on gardens and urban environmental movements." *Urban Studies* 52, no. 7 (2015): 1321–1338.

Beilin, R. and C. Wilkinson. "Introduction: Governing for urban resilience." *Urban Studies* 52, no. 7 (2015): 1205–1217.

Berube, A. "The geography of U.S. Poverty and its implications." *The Testimony before the Committee on Ways and Means, Metropolitan Policy Program* (2007): 1–10.

Beyers, W. B. "Culture, services and regional development." *The Service Industries Journal* 22, no. 1(2002): 4–34. 10.1080/714005056.

Beyers, W. B. "Cultural and recreational industries in the United States." *The Service Industries Journal* 28, no. 3 (2008): 375–391. 10.1080/02642060701856266

Boudreau, K. J., L. B. Jeppesen, T. Reichstein, and F. Rullani "Crowdfunding as 'Donations': Theory & evidence." Working Paper 16-038, Harward Business School (2015): 1–37.

Bouncken, R. B., M. Komorek, and S. Kraus "Crowdfunding: The current state of research." *International Business & Economics Research Journal* 14, no. 3 (2015): 407–415.

Brown, D. "Somerville mobile farmers market." *Citizinvestor* (2012). http://www.citizinvestor.com/project/somerville-mobile-farmersmarket (Accessed 09/28/2017).

Brown, D. "Do projects in rich neighborhoods perform better than those in poorer neighborhoods?" *Citizinvestor* (2014). http://blog.citizinvestor.com/post/76530391900/do-projects-in-rich-neighborhoods-performbetter-than (Accessed 09/28/2017).

Brown, L. A., and M. Sharma. "Metropolitan context and racial/ethnic intermixing in residential space: U.S. Metropolitan Statistical Areas, 1990–2000." *Urban Geography* 31, no. 1 (2010): 1–28.

Bugge, M. M. "Jacobian cluster mutation across advertising and internet-based market communication." *Tijdschrift voor Economische en Sociale Geografie* 102, no. 5 (2011): 515–531.

Campo, D. "Iconic eyesores: Exploring Do-It-Yourself preservation and civic improvement at abandoned train stations in Buffalo and Detroit." *International Research on Placemaking and Urban Sustainability* 7, no. 4 (2014): 351–389. 10.1080/17549175.2014.952322

Caputo S., M. Caserio, R. Coles, L. Jankovic, and M. R. Gaterell. "Urban resilience: Two diverging interpretations." *Journal of Urbanism: International Research on Placemaking and Urban Sustainability* 8, no. 3 (2015): 222–240.

Copeland, A. J. *Christian Century*, (May 27, 2015): 22–25.

Darden, J. T., and S. M. Kamel. "Black residential segregation in the city and suburbs of Detroit: Does socioeconomic status matter?" *Journal of Urban Affairs* 22 (2000): 1–13.

Davidson, N. M. "Reconciling people and place in housing and community development policy." *Georgetown Journal on Poverty Law & Policy* 17, no. 1 (2009): 1–11.

Davies, R. "Civic crowdfunding: Participatory communities, entrepreneurs and the political economy of place." Master Thesis submitted to Massachusetts Institute of Technology (June 2014) (2014a).

Davies, R. "Civic crowdfunding as a market place for participation in urban development." Series paper, Center for Work, Technology and Organization. Stanford University (Sep 1, 2014b).

Davies, R. "Civic crowdfunding: A new way of spending down?" (2014c). https://ssir.org/articles/entry/civic_crowdfunding_a_new_way_of_spending_down (Accessed 9/10/2017). DOI: 10.48558/a3de-ym60

Doucette, J. "Crowdfunding for public good and philanthrophy." (2015). https://medium.com/the-digital-civil-society-lab/crowdfunding-for-public (Accessed 09/28/2017).

Ehrenfeucht, R. "Art, public spaces, and private property along the streets of New Orleans." *Urban Geography* 35, no. 7 (2014): 965–979. 10.1080/02723638.2014.945260

Elrod, B. "Place and crowdfunding: An examination of two distressed cities." *Master's Thesis submitted to University of Tennessee* (2014). https://trace.tennessee.edu/utk_gradthes/2884

Fields, B., J. Wagner, and M. Frisch. "Placemaking and disaster recovery: Targeting place for recovery in post-Katrina New Orleans." *Journal of Urbanism: International Research on Placemaking and Urban Sustainability* 8, no. 1 (2015): 38–56.

Finn, D. "DIY Urbanism: Implications for cities." *Journal of Urbanism: International Research on Placemaking and Urban Sustainability* 7, no. 4 (2014): 381–398.

Florida, R. L. *The Rise of the Creative Class* – Revisited: 10th Anniversary Edition – Revised and Expanded. New York: Basic Books (2012).

Grady, S. and J. Darden. "Spatial methods to study local racial residential segregation and infant health in Detroit, Michigan." *Annals of the Association of American Geographers* 102, no. 5 (2012): 922–931.

Hemer, J. A snapshot on crowdfunding. Working papers: Firms and region. (2011). http://www.econstor.eu/handle/10419/52302 (Accessed 02/08/2015).

Howe, J. "The rise of crowdsourcing." *Wired Magazine* 14, no. 6 (2006a): 1–4.
Howe, J. "Crowdsourcing: A definition." January (2006b). *Crowdsourcing.com*. (Accessed 07/25/2012). https://scholar.google.com/citations?view_op=view_citation&hl=en&user=qJ -j3oAAAAAJ&alert_preview_top_rm=2&citation_for_view=qJ-j3oAAAAAJ:d1gkVwhDpl0C
HTTP1: https://www.kickstarter.com/projects/catapult/catapult-inaugural-opening-at-t-lot-new-studio-and
HTTP2: https://www.kickstarter.com/projects/press-street/6th-annual-24-hour-draw-a-thon-2011
HTTP3: https://www.kickstarter.com/projects/306003514/golden-feather-mardi-gras-indian-gallery-and-coffe
HTTP4: https://www.kickstarter.com/projects/1373450098/the-new-orleans-bookfair
HTTP5: https://www.kickstarter.com/projects/1394857195/a-giant-ball-pit-in-an-abandoned-house-naturally
HTTP6: https://www.kickstarter.com/projects/dithyrambalina/swoons-musical-architecture-for-new-orleans
HTTP7: https://www.kickstarter.com/projects/204316335/the-aquarium-gallery-and-studios-in-new orleans
HTTP8: https://www.kickstarter.com/projects/2122430087/spread-creative-forces-program-model
HTTP9: https://www.kickstarter.com/projects/20114987/the-alamo-underground
HTTP10: https://www.kickstarter.com/projects/communityrecords/block-party-2011-dvd-and-fundraising
HTTP11: https://www.kickstarter.com/projects/294366625/new-orleans-film-society-presents-movies-to-geaux
HTTP12: https://www.kickstarter.com/projects/202012700/the-fair-housing-five-a-childrens-book-about-fair?ref=discovery
HTTP13: https://www.kickstarter.com/projects/catapult/parallel-play-2nd-annual-show-at-t-lot?ref=discovery
HTTP14: Howe, Jeff. Video interview with Jeff Howe on 'What is Crowdsourced Placemaking', at http://www.sourcethestation.com/crowdsourcedplacemaking/ (Accessed 9/10/2017).
HTTP15: http://cspmgroup.com/ (Accessed 9/10/2017).
HTTP16: http://crowdsourceplaces.com/ (Accessed 9/10/2017).
HTTP17: http://cspmgroup.com/crowdsourcedplacemaking/ (Accessed 9/10/2017).
HTTP18: http://cspmgroup.com/about/ (Accessed 9/10/2017).
Hyra, D. "The back-to-the-city movement: Neighbourhood redevelopment and processes of political & cultural displacement." *Urban Studies 52*, no. 10 (2015): 1753–1773.
Jabareen, Y. ""Do it yourself" as an informal mode of space production: Conceptualizing informality." *Journal of Urbanism: International Research on Placemaking and Urban Sustainability* 7, no. 4 (2014): 414–428. 10.1080/17549175.2014.884975
Jacobs, J. *The Death and Life of Great American Cities*. Vintage Books, A Division of Random House, Inc. : New York (1961).
James, N., and H. Busher. "Credibility, authenticity and voice: Dilemmas in online interviewing." *Qualitative Research* 6, no. 3 (2006): 403–420.
James, N., and H. Busher. *Online Interviewing*. Sage Publications Limited; 1st edition (September 15, 2009), EnglishPaperback: 176 pages, ISBN-10: 1 412945321; ISBN-13: 978-1412945325, (2009).
Kee, K. F., and M. Thompson-Hayes. "Conducting effective interviews about virtual work: Gathering and analyzing data using a grounded theory approach." In *Virtual Work and Human Interaction Research*, Ed. Shawn Long (2012): 192–212. 10.4018/978-1-4666-0963-1.ch012 (Accessed 05/03/2013).
Kerschberg, B. "How crowdsourcing is tackling poverty in the developing world" (2012). https://www.forbes.com/sites/benkerschberg/2012/03/21/how-crowdsourcing-is-tackling-poverty-in-the-developing-world/print/ (Accessed 09/07/2017). Guest Post by Lauren Fisher.
Manzo, L. C., and D. D. Perkins. "Finding common ground: The importance of place attachment to community participation and planning." *Journal of Planning Literature* 20, no. 4 (2006): 335–350.
McCracken, H. "The kickstarter economy." *Time*. 180, no. 14 (2012): 1–7.
McLeman, R. A., and L. M. Hunter. "Migration in the context of vulnerability and adaptation to climate change: Insights from analogues." *WIRE's Climate Change* 1 (2010): 450–461.
Miller, A. B. "Civic crowdfunding and the public good." (January 27, 2015). https://www.shareable.net/blog/civic-crowdfunding-and-the-public-good (Accessed 9/10/2017).
Mollick, E. "The dynamics of crowdfunding: An exploratory study." *Journal of Business Venturing* 29, no. 1 (2014): 1–16.
Morgan, K. "Nourishing the city: The rise of the urban food question in the Global North." *Urban Studies* 52, no. 8 (2015): 1379–1394.
Perry, S. "Caution! The downsides of crowdfunding." *Chronicle of Philanthropy*, 26, no. 18 (2014): 1–5.
Rudowitz, R., D. Rowland, and A. Shartzer. "Health care in New Orleans before and after hurricane Katrina." *Health Affairs* 25, no. 5 (2006): 393–406.
Sharma, M., and B. Elrod "Crowdfunding and crowdsourcing initiatives in Detroit." *International Journal of Geospatial and Environmental Research*, 3, no. 1 (2016): 1–24. Article 1. http://dc.uwm.edu/ijger/vol3/iss1/1

Sherman, A. "How 3 cities are crowdsourcing for community revitalization" (2011). http://mashable.com/2011/07/20/crowdsourcing-city-tech/#H6x4lToETEqk (Accessed 09/07/2017).

Sidford, H. "Fusing arts, culture, and social change: High impact strategies for philanthropy." National Committee for Responsive Philanthropy, A Philanthropy at its Best Report, by the author, (October, 2011): 1–44.

Soden, R. and L. L. Palen. "From crowdsourced mapping to community mapping: The post-earthquake work of OpenStreetMap Haiti." *COOP 2014 – Proceedings of the 11th International Conference on the Design of Cooperative Systems* (27–30 May 2014, Nice, France) (2014): 311–326.

Squires, G. D. "Urban development and unequal access to housing finance services." *Heinonline* 53 (2008): 255–268.

Stiver, A., L. Barroca, P. M. Leonor, M. Richards, and D. Roberts "Civic crowdfunding: How do offline communities engage online?" In: *British HCI Conference*, 13–17 July 2015, Lincoln, ACM (2015): 37–45, 10.1145/2783446.2783585.

Tirdatov, I. "Web-based crowd funding: Rhetoric of success." *Technical Communication* 61, no. 1 (2014): 3–24.

Tuan, Y. F. *Topophilia*. Englewood Cliffs, NJ: Prentice-Hall (1974).

Turner, M. A. "After Katrina: Rebuilding opportunity and equity into the new New Orleans: A framework for policy and action." *The Urban Institute Series* (2006): 73–83. http://webarchive.urban.org/UploadedPDF/311406_after_katrina.pdf

2 Exploring the Spatial Pattern of Urban Heat Island Formation in Relation to Land Transformation: A Study on the Paschim Barddhaman District of West Bengal

Soumen Chatterjee, Sujit Das, and Krishnendu Gupta
Visva Bharati Santiniketan, West Bengal, India

CONTENTS

2.1 INTRODUCTION

The climate of the built-up areas and surrounding of the mining areas are altered due to several deliberate anthropogenic activities like modification in land use and land cover (LULC). Large-scale anthropogenic activities are gradually decreasing vegetation cover of the Earth's surface on the one hand and increasing

DOI: 10.1201/9781003126195-3

the opaque built-up areas on the other. Geospatial techniques such as satellite remote sensing (RS) and geographic information systems (GIS) are most effective techniques for evaluating, monitoring, and predicting the land use/land cover change (Mallick et al., 2008, Omran, 2012, Jalan and Sharma, 2014, Ali et al., 2017). The analysis of temporal remote-sensing imageries helps in comprehending the land cover changes and their impact on the environment (Baeza and Paruelo, 2020). The thermal and infrared bands of remote-sensing data of space-borne sensors help to retrieve land surface temperature (LST) (Ramachandra et al., 2012). The most imperative problem in urban and coal mining areas is the rising land surface temperature as a direct consequence of modification in the land use and land cover in the form of an increase in the bare land due to encroachment of urban land and increase in the built-up areas that is chiefly composed of impervious surfaces (Ahmed, 2011). The impervious surface absorbs most of the incoming solar radiation and their reflectivity is found to be very low. As a result, land surface temperatures (LSTs) of this area are higher than those of their surroundings (Mallick et al., 2012). Due to a rapid rate of urbanisation and peri-urban development, land cover gradually is converted into impervious cover such as pavement, roofs, asphalt, etc., which absorbs more heat than the natural land cover. As a result, these areas are commonly warmer than their rural and semi-rural counterpart, which actually helps to form an urban heat island (UHI) (Bharath et al., 2019).

Land surface temperature is commonly considered to be the temperature of the surrounding environment that can be measured when the land surface is in direct contact with the environment. Different techniques have been employed by several researchers to evaluate the LST for urban heat analysis, meteorology, and climatology. Common among them are brightness temperature (Joshi and Bindu, 2012), split window technique, and single channel technique (Juan-Carlos et al., 2014; Qinqin et al., 2010; Juan-Carlos and Sobrino, 2008; Rajeshwari and Mani, 2014; Xiaolei et al., 2004; Jeevalakshmi et al., 2017). The split-window algorithm is a very common and widely used technique for its inherent qualities and accuracy in results. Different scholars have mentioned that several factors are involved in the generation of LST as well as the UHI. In India, there are a number of studies that have been carried out by the different scholars, mainly over some metropolitan cities like Kolkata (Allaka et al., 2019), Mumbai (Grover and Singh, 2015), Chennai (Lilly Rose and Devadas, 2009), Jaipur (Jalan and Sharma, 2014), and Delhi (Mallick et al., 2008, ; Grover and Singh, 2015). But there has been less work in the small towns as well as emerging industrial regions (Pal and Ziaul, 2016). Few works have been carried out in small urban areas as well as mining and industrial areas, which started increasing the land surface temperature more than the surrounding regions. Dutta et al. (2020) have attempted a study over the industrial town of Durgapur to examine the intensity of the UHI formation. In this regard, the town has experienced massive and large-scale urban industrial growth for the last five decades. Choudhury et al. (2019) assessed the changes in the temperature pattern of several land use classes and found that the industrial and mining areas are composed of an impervious surface and are generally warmer than the surroundings in the Asansol Durgapur Development Region. Kamila and Pal (2015) have also considered that various anthropogenic activities profoundly influence the land surface temperature in the Asansol and Durgapur areas. Rahaman et al. (2020) found the loss of vegetation cover and agricultural land in the district of Barddhaman is alarming and that might have contributed to an increase in the LST pattern. Chatterjee and Gupta (2021) have identified that massive open pit mining and uncontrolled urban industrial growth have led to micro-climatic variation in the Jamuria area of the Paschim Barddhaman district. Keeping concern in mind, the present study has been conducted on Paschim Bardhhaman of West Bengal, a highly populated and emerging industrial region in Eastern India. In the Paschim Bardhhaman district, a few urban and industrial as well as mining conclaves are located in the Asansol, Durgapur-Faridpur, Raniganj, and Jamuria blocks. The Asansol Durgapur industrial zone is one of the largest industrial hubs in eastern India. Existance of open cast coal mining pit and newly developed industrial clusters transforming hectares of agricultural land. Hence, development of an industrial cluster, extension of open pit mining, and unplanned and rapid urbanization undoubtedly stimulated the rapid transformation of land use and land cover into barren lands, mining brown fields, and other built-up land by removing vegetation cover. So, the increase in the heat-absorbent concrete surface along with emission of aerosols and other greenhouse gases from

Industrial activities and mining sources are the major sources of anthropogenic heat generation and gradual increases of the surface temperature in the study area. Now it is a challenge to the researcher and urban planner to delineate the UHI that would ask facilities to take proper mitigation measures for sustainable urban design. An attempt has been made in this study to evaluate the relationship between the land use land cover change and land surface temperature in the Paschim Bardhhaman district. The study has been undertaken with two objectives: firstly, to categorize the patterns of land use land cover changes between 1995 and 2019, and secondly to investigate the impacts land use land cover change on the LST pattern during the stipulated time periods.

2.2 STUDY AREA

The Paschim Bardhhaman district of West Bengal lays on the western part of the Rarh plateau covers an area of 1603.17 sq. km. It lies between 23 °31′ 27.295″ N and 23 °50′ 2.38″ N latitudes and 86 °48′ 0.33″ E and 87 °28′ 32.094″ E longitude. Paschim Bardhhaman comprises two subdivisions i.e., Asansol Sadar subdivision and Durgapur subdivision, and eight (8) community development (CD) blocks (Figure 2.1). This district is known for coal mining (Raniganj: India's first coal mining) and industrial hub in the Rarh Bengal. Indian Iron and Steel Company (Burnpur), Chittaranjan Locomotive Works, Burn Standard (Asansol), Durgapur Steel Plant, and other industrial units function in the study area. The topography of the study area is undulating rocky pediments in the western parts, which is the extension of Chotanagpur plateau region, and alluvial plain (older and newer) in the eastern parts. The regional slope is from the northwestern parts to the southeastern parts.

As part of the monsoon weather system, the area experiences alternative wet and dry seasons. The winter months basically remain dry and cold with minimum temperature prevails of 7 to 10 °C, while the summer months remain hot and humid with maximum temperatures of 35 to 37 °C. The mean annual temperature range exceeds 13 °C and mean annual humidity remains below 65% in dry months. Almost 75% of the rainfall received is during the summer months of July to September.

2.3 DATABASE AND METHODOLOGY

2.3.1 Database

The present study employed sets of Landsat images during the summer and winter time (Table 2.1). The images have been downloaded from the official website of the United States Geological Survey (USGS). For the year 1995, L5-TM satellite data have been used, which have a pixel size of 30 meter with 7 bands, while for the year 2019, L7-ETM+ data with a spatial resolution of 30 m. have been used. Details of the images have been tabulated. Besides this, a Survey of India (SOI) topographical map and Google Earth images of different times have been used for land use classification (Table 2.1).

2.3.2 Image Processing and Classification

Atmospheric condition hardly remains same for the specified time span; hence, it is essential to make necessary atmospheric corrections for using thermal band in any scientific study. Actually, the re-radiated energy from Earth's surface is sometimes modified by the existing atmospheric situation, which must be corrected (Barsi et al., 2003). The free and open-source software "QGIS" has been used for the whole study and in this case the SCP or semi-automatic classification plug-in has been employed for the necessary atmospheric corrections.

Having a general knowledge on the (LULC) of the study area supervised image classification has been preferred with a maximum likelihood algorithm. The classification scheme followed in this study is based on the national remote-sensing agency with some minor modifications. Seven major land use land cover classes have been identified including built up, vegetation, agriculture, water body, sand bar, and barren land. Supervised classification provides a provision for the user to

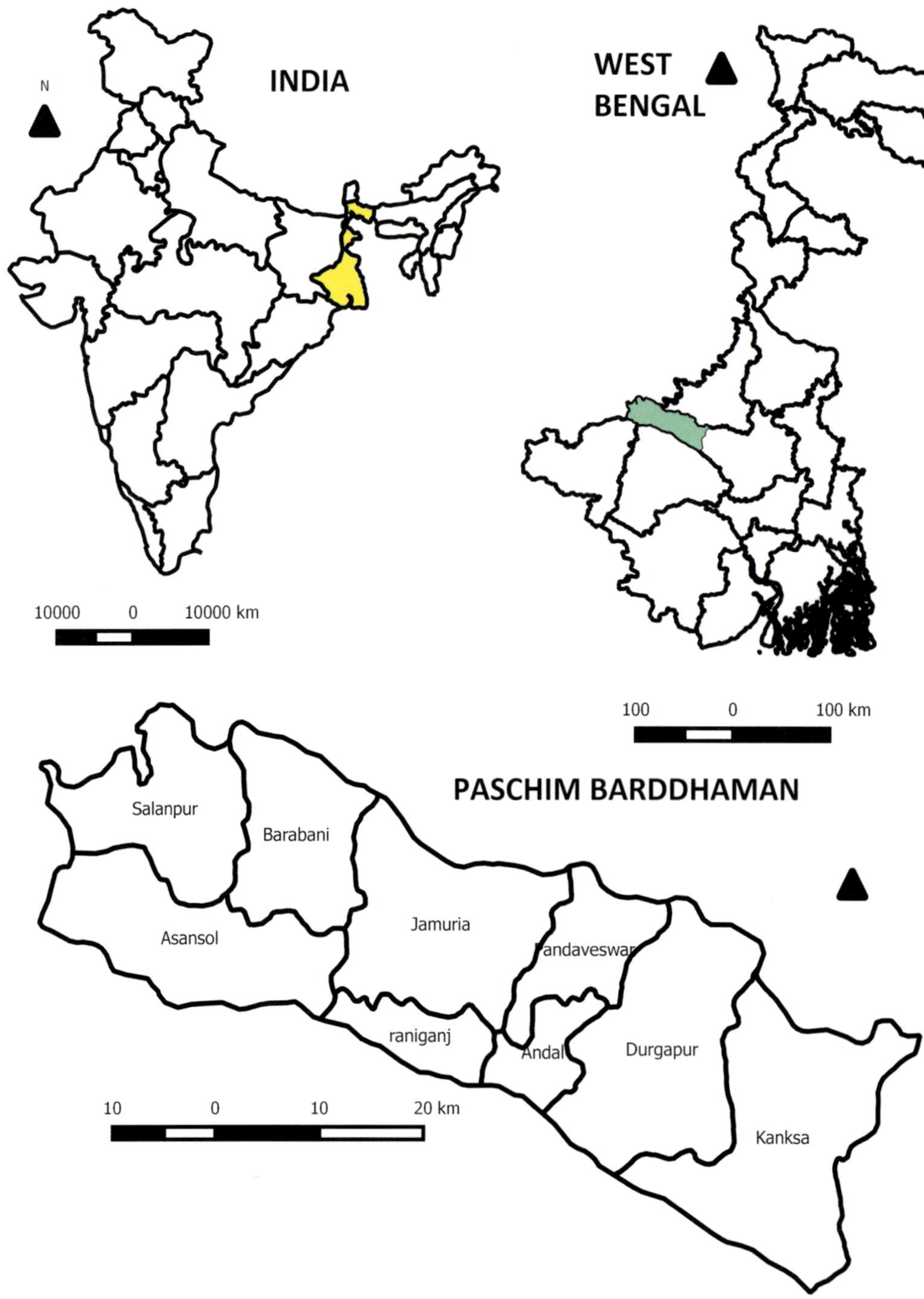

FIGURE 2.1 Location of the study area.

define the training site for each class. After the training site for each class has been defined, the whole image has been classified using the training pixels, which yield the final LULC map of the study area. The area of the respective class has been extracted from the classification report. The accuracy assessment of the final LULC image of the study area has been performed by comparing the classified raster with the Google Earth image, which has been used as a reference image. In the classified image, 365 random points have been created and each has been

TABLE 2.1
Satellite Images Used in the Study

Satellite	Sensor	Path/Row	Date of Acquisition
Landsat5	TM	139/044	1995-04-25
Landsat5	TM	139/044	1995-12-21
Landsat7	ETM+	139/044	2019-12-31
Landsat7	ETM+	139/044	2019-05-05

cross-checked with the reference map. The overall accuracy has been 86.83% and 89.61% for the years 1995 and 2019, respectively. Eventually change detection between both years has also been calculated for understanding the extent of the LULC change.

2.3.3 Calculation of Land Surface Temperature (LST)

2.3.3.1 Step I Calculation of Radiation Luminance Form Digital Number

Each terrestrial object is considered to have its own thermal expression. The thermal sensor of Landsat has been so designed that it can sense the outgoing radiation from each terrestrial object and is actually recorded as a sensor radiance value. It is commonly known as a digital number and preserved into an 8-bit scale that can be converted into ToA (top of atmosphere) reflectance using the following formula (landsathandbook.gsfc.nasa.gov/ pdfslandsat7_handbook.pdf):

$$L\lambda = Lmn\lambda + \left[\left\{\frac{Lmx\lambda - Lmn\lambda}{Qmx - Qmn}\right\} * Qdn\right]\ldots \quad (2.1)$$

where $Qmn = 0$, $Qmx = 255$, Qdn = Digital number of each pixel, $Lmn\lambda$ and $Lmx\lambda$ represent spectral radiances for B6 at the DN0 and DN255 levels, respectively.

2.3.3.2 Step II Estimation of At-Satellite Brightness Temperature (T_B) from Luminance of Radiance ($L\lambda$)

The spectral radiance value obtained from the previous equation needs to be converted into an effective satellite temperature, which is commonly expressed in Kelvin by using the following formula:

$$T_B = K_2 / In\left(\frac{k_1}{L_\lambda} + 1\right)\ldots \quad (2.2)$$

where T_B = at-satellite brightness temperature (K)

$L\lambda$ = spectral radiance in $W.\ m^{-2}.\ \mu m^{-1}$

K_1 *and* K_2 are the two pre-launched calibration contrasts

The resultant raster provides the LST in the Kelvin scale, which has been deducted with 273.15 to convert the result to the Celsius scale.

2.3.4 Derivation of Spectral Indices

Each terrestrial object is found to absorb and radiate different segments of the electromagnetic radiation; hence, it is easier for detect them on a specific band, which is a greatest benefit to using multispectral satellite images. Three indices have been applied in the present study to assess their relationship with LST. NDVI (normalized difference vegetation index) is a useful index for assessing the nature and extent of green vegetation cover in the study area. To analyze the extent and growth of the built-up area, NDBI (normalized differential built up index) has been applied. Finally, to identify the extent of barren land, NDBaI (normalized difference bareness index) has been used. They have been calculated by using following way:

$$NDVI = \frac{(B_4 - B_3)}{(B_4 + B_3)} \ldots \quad (2.3)$$

$$NDBI = \frac{(B_5 - B_4)}{(B_5 + B_4)} \ldots \quad (2.4)$$

$$NDBaI = \frac{(B_5 - B_6)}{(B_5 + B_6)} \ldots \quad (2.5)$$

where B_3, B_4, B_5 *and* B_6 represent the DN values of the corresponding red, near infrared, middle infrared, and thermal infrared bands, respectively.

2.3.5 Profile and Correlation Analysis

Finally, to establish a logical relation between the LULC pattern and the LST, two processes have been followed. Firstly, three profiles have been drawn on several directions that may cover all types of land use in the study region for both years using QGIS software to show the cross-sectional variation of the LST in respect to change of the LULC. Secondly, the correlation coefficient (r) has been calculated to find the relationship between the LST and the indices i.e., NDVI, NDBI, and NDBaI. A total of 591 samples have been collected randomly from the LST and other indices raster using a sample tool in the QGIS software. Correlations have been calculated using Microsoft Excel.

2.4 RESULTS AND DISCUSSION

2.4.1 Extent of Land Transformation

After classification of the satellite images for both years the land use land cover statistics have been represented in Tables 2.2, 2.3, and 2.4. To get a better view, land use land cover data has been extracted from the sub-district also. The blockwise change of LULC has been represented in Figure 2.2. Two distinguishable changes from those tables are that forest cover, cropland, and water bodies have decreased gradually and the built-up area and barren land rapidly increased.

There are nine CD blocks in the district of Paschim Barddhaman and here we have decided to elaborately discuss the pattern of the LULC for the block level so that a detailed scenario about the ongoing land transformation process can be presented. During 1990, only Kanska block have more than 1/4th of its total area under vegetation cover while the rest of the blocks found to have less than 15% of their total area under vegetation cover. Precisely vegetation cover in the other block ranges from just 2.77% to 11.51% (Table 2). In terms of agricultural land, only Barabani consists more than 3/4th of its total land under this use and, among the others, five blocks had half of their total land under agricultural use, whereas three blocks fell under less than 50% value of use. Five out of the nine blocks had built up land more than 25%, among them Asansol, Jamuria, and Raniganj occupy the first three positions according to their use of land under built-up growth with 44.54%, 42.45%, and 40.48%, respectively. The other two land use did not have much occupancy in the blocks, areas fell under barren land, and water bodies ranged from 0.21% to 3.49% and 0.87% to 12.33% in some respects.

TABLE 2.2
Pattern of LULC in Paschim Barddhaman (1995–2019)

LULC Classes	1995		2019	
	Hectares	Percentage	Hectares	Percentage
Vegetation	11,419.90	10.92	13,968.40	13.36
Agricultural land	58,629.00	56.06	52,759.30	50.45
Built-up land	27,736.70	26.52	31,602.80	30.22
Barren land	1,614.10	1.54	2,402.30	2.30
Water body	5,186.70	4.96	3,853.60	3.68

During the second phase of the study, there had been a noticeable change in the LULC pattern. As per the table: three shown below, in 2019, vegetation cover in all of the nine blocks was in between 4.30% and 29.13%, when five blocks had not even crossed the 10% level as per their use of land under vegetation cover. While measuring the area under agricultural use, it was found that not a single block passed the 75% level and four blocks claimed their position under the 50% level. Out of the nine blocks, five had more than 30% of their total land under a built-up area and the rest fell below the 30% level; among them, Raniganj, Asansol, and Jamuria account for 48.76%, 46.73%, and 44.76%, respectively. Again, in 2019, as like 1995, two LULC classes have slender coverage of land in the blocks and barren land rangeed from 0.95% to 6.82%, while water body ranged from just 0.83% to 7.77%.

Some clearly distinguishable changes have been evident from the discussion: i) vegetation, agricultural land, and water bodies decreased gradually and ii) built-up areas and barren land rapidly increased. Hence, to get a clear view about the changes between the 1995 and 2019 raster change detection analysis has been performed in GIS environment (Table 2.5).

During the past two decades, a manifold rise in built-up land and diminished forest cover and agricultural land were reported in this area. Consolidation of the existing urban area and their peripheral growth has been found all over the study area. The LULC pattern of 1995 and 2019 is shown in Figure 2.2.

2.4.2 Changing Pattern of the LST in Winter and Summer

The spatial distribution of the surface temperature pattern during April and December has been has been depicted in the following map (Figure 2.3 a, b, c and d). More or less three distinguishable patches of high-temperature zones were found to exist in 1995, where surface temperature has been recorded almost 35 degree celsius in summer and 23 degree celsius during winter. Mostly the built-up areas of the Asansol and Durgapur regions and barren land and the mining tract of tract of the Pandaveswar and Jamuria regions located in the central and western part of study region, respectively, fall under this zone. Cropland mostly occupied the Jamuria and Kanksa blocks of the study and were found to have low temperatures, below 19 degree celsius and 29 degree celsius during the winter and summer months, respectively. Besides, the forest land of Kanksa and Salanpur were found to be comparative colder than the surrounding regions. From the following, Figure 2.3 b and d, it can be stated that open pit mining and several small to medium industries in the different parts of the study area attributed to the formation of several patches where the LST is found to be greater than the surrounding region.

In the first instance, open pit mining areas at various places in Jamuria (Churulia) and Pandaveswar (Sonepurbazari) might have played an important role in increasing the LST in those areas. The rising temperature over those patches can be discernable from the cross profile (Figure 2.5) drawn for 1995 and 2019 over the study area. The LST of urban regions and open pit

TABLE 2.3
Spatial Distribution of LULC in 1995

Block	LULC Types	Vegetation	Agricultural Land	Built-up Land	Barren Land	Water Body	Total Area
Salanpur	hectare	863.80	7728.50	2010.00	223.40	789.00	11614.60
	%	7.44	66.54	17.31	1.92	6.79	100.00
Asansol	hectare	670.00	6145.80	6400.00	246.10	907.40	14369.80
	%	4.66	42.77	44.54	1.71	6.31	100.00
Barabani	hectare	837.80	8142.10	1128.00	199.00	220.50	10528.30
	%	7.96	77.34	10.71	1.89	2.09	100.00
Jamuria	hectare	810.30	6382.80	6785.00	34.10	1971.20	15982.40
	%	5.07	39.94	42.45	0.21	12.33	100.00
Raniganj	hectare	123.30	2186.80	1802.70	49.20	291.30	4453.10
	%	2.77	49.11	40.48	1.10	6.54	100.00
Pandebeswar	hectare	275.30	4577.80	1432.90	115.00	36.00	6437.40
	%	4.28	71.11	22.26	1.79	0.56	100.00
Andal	hectare	165.30	2401.00	1053.20	132.10	33.00	3783.60
	%	4.37	63.46	27.84	3.49	0.87	100.00
Durgapur-faridpur	hectare	1992.50	9643.30	4724.30	381.00	574.50	17316.50
	%	11.51	55.69	27.28	2.20	3.32	100.00
Kanksa	hectare	5681.60	11420.90	2400.60	234.20	363.80	20100.70
	%	28.27	56.82	11.94	1.17	1.81	100.00

TABLE 2.4
Spatial Distribution of LULC in 2019

Block	LULC Types	Vegetation	Agricultural Land	Built-up Land	Barren Land	Water Body	Total Area
Salanpur	hectare	954.30	7141.00	2608.00	110.20	801.20	11614.60
	%	8.22	61.48	22.45	0.95	6.90	100.00
Asansol	hectare	617.60	5838.60	6714.30	405.50	794.00	14369.80
	%	4.30	40.63	46.73	2.82	5.53	100.00
Barabani	hectare	1652.40	6522.70	2143.40	100.60	109.10	10528.30
	%	15.69	61.95	20.36	0.96	1.04	100.00
Jamuria	hectare	942.20	6592.70	7153.20	480.20	814.10	15982.40
	%	5.90	41.25	44.76	3.00	5.09	100.00
Raniganj	hectare	439.00	1397.30	2171.40	99.20	346.20	4453.10
	%	9.86	31.38	48.76	2.23	7.77	100.00
Pandebeswar	hectare	416.00	3692.00	2044.90	231.10	53.20	6437.40
	%	6.46	57.35	31.77	3.59	0.83	100.00
Andal	hectare	479.30	1571.30	1434.70	258.20	40.30	3783.60
	%	12.67	41.53	37.92	6.82	1.07	100.00
Durgapur-faridpur	hectare	2612.10	8662.60	5146.90	268.70	626.20	17316.50
	%	15.08	50.03	29.72	1.55	3.62	100.00
Kanksa	hectare	5855.50	11341.10	2186.00	448.60	269.30	20100.70
	%	29.13	56.42	10.88	2.23	1.34	100.00

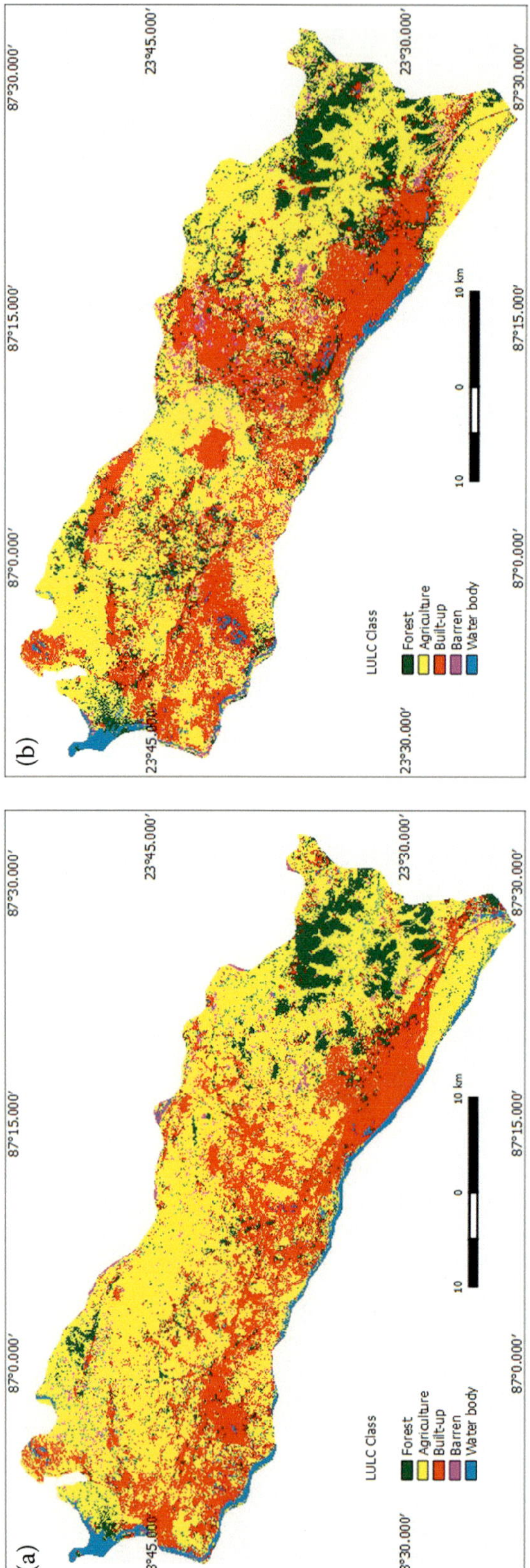

FIGURE 2.2 Land use/land cover of 1995 (a) and 2019 (b).

TABLE 2.5
LULC Change Matrix (in Hectare)

LULC Type	Vegetation	Agricultural Land	Built-up Land	Barren Land	Water Body
Vegetation	9847.7	3813.2	2898.7	73.6	280.2
Agricultural land	8387	68932.9	3703.2	2964.1	755.3
Built-up land	4437	10255.5	39010.1	332.1	1771.7
Barren land	346.3	3371.3	344.5	270.2	32.5
Water body	48.8	1943.3	1016.4	474.4	2488.6

regions was also found to rise by 3 degree Celsius to 5 degree Celsius. In the second instance, establishing an industrial cluster at Mangalpur of Raniganj and Banskopa of the Kanksa and Maithon regions of Salanpur is considered to play a pivotal role in the general increase in the surface temperature. There is a general consensus among the scholars that the urban areas are comparatively warmer compared to their rural counterparts (Ahmed et al., 2013) since the composition of the building materials of built-up areas are commonly opaque to solar radiation, which can store more heat than the land surface. As a matter of fact, an increase in the built-up areas and shrinking of the forest areas in the past decades must have altered the LST pattern of the study area.

To understand the seasonal variation in the surface temperature distribution, a comparison has been made between the summer and winter condition. The built-up area, barren land, and sand bar are the areas that comprise the high temperature zone. Here, both the summer temperature and winter temperature remains high. Apart from the sand bar region, the mining and industrial clusters remain the warmest places. Comparatively, low temperatures prevail over the forest land and crop land. It is now necessary to examine the highest temperature pattern of the study area during the summer and winter. It reveals that the summer months experienced 35 °C and 38 °C during 1995 and 2019, respectively. Contrary to this, the winter temperature during 1995 and 2019 was found to be 23 °C and 24.5 °C, respectively. Therefore, there has been a general increase of 2 to 3 °C in surface temperature over the past.

2.4.3 Regional Pattern

To have a manageable view over the regional pattern of surface temperature distribution, the range of temperatures in summer and winter have been calculated by deducting the maximum and minimum value from a set of raster. An almost 8 °C and 10 °C departure has been found during 1995 and 2019, respectively, which has been divided into five equal classes (Figure 2.4 and Table 2.6). The results showed that almost 60% of the study area has 29 to 32 °C temperatures in the month of May 1995. On the other, only 12% and 17% of the region have surface temperatures below 32 – 34 °C and above 27 – 29 °C, respectively, during the stipulated time frame. The figure also indicates that temperature patterns in most of the areas show a upward trend; for instance, Figure 2.6 indicates that during 2019 more than 80% of the study area experienced 29– 34 °C temperatures. On the other, almost 8% of the area has a surface temperature above 34 °C during 2019. The same area was found to be only 1.5% during 1995. Hence, there has a significant increase in the pockets of high-temperature patches in the form of an urban heat island. Surface temperatures during the winter, to some extent, reveal the same pattern. During 1995, almost 40% of the area has a surface temperature below 19 °C, whereas in 2019, only 12% of the area experienced temperatures below 19 degree celsius. On the other hand, only 5% of the area has a surface temperature above 21 degree Celsius; surprisingly that figure rose to 31% during 2019. It is also interesting to note that almost 8% of the area has a surface temperature above 23 °C but in 1995 the figure is only 1%. So there has been a significant alteration in the regional pattern of

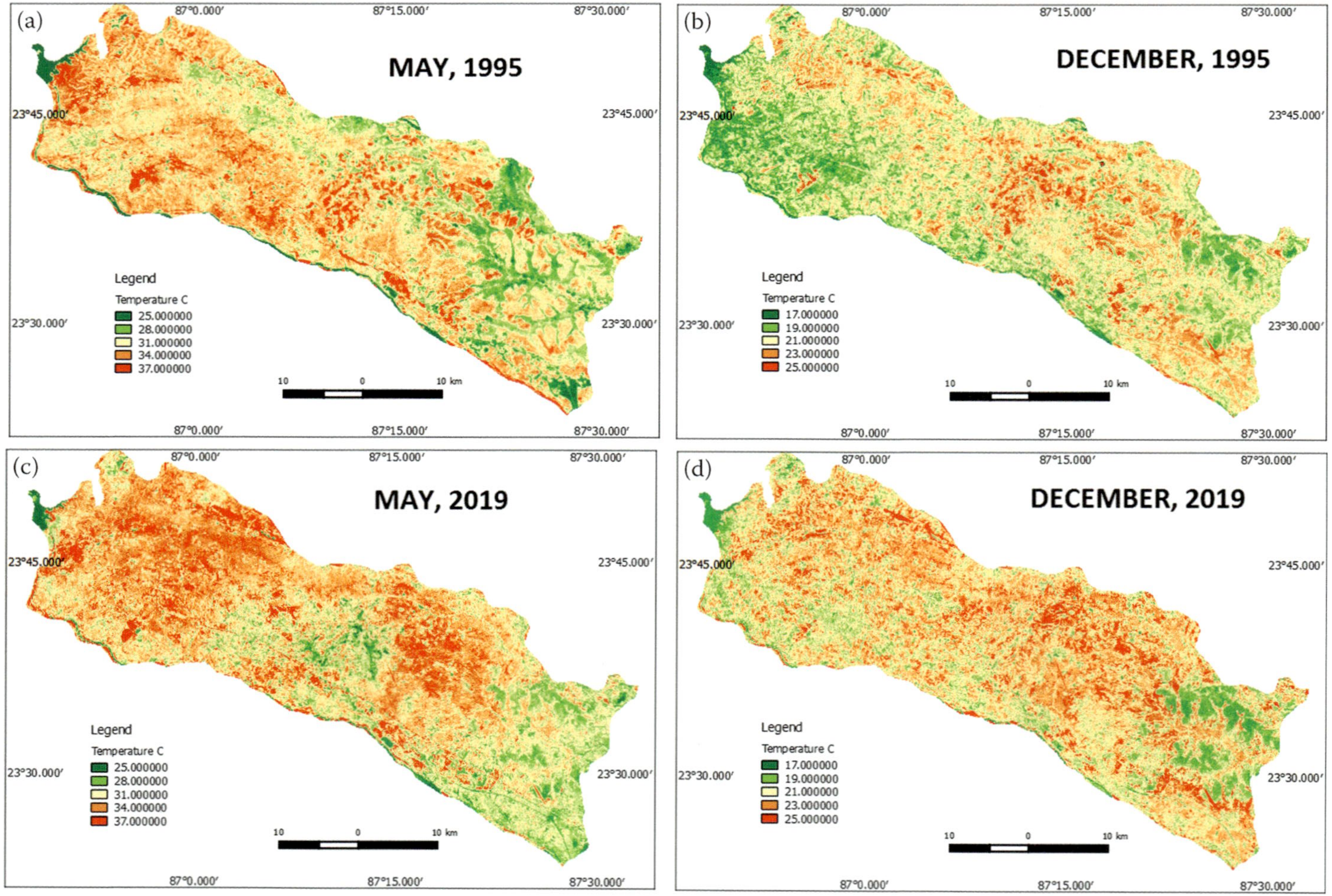

FIGURE 2.3 Land surface temperature during the month of May 1995 (a) and 2019 (b) and December 1995 (c) and 2019 (d).

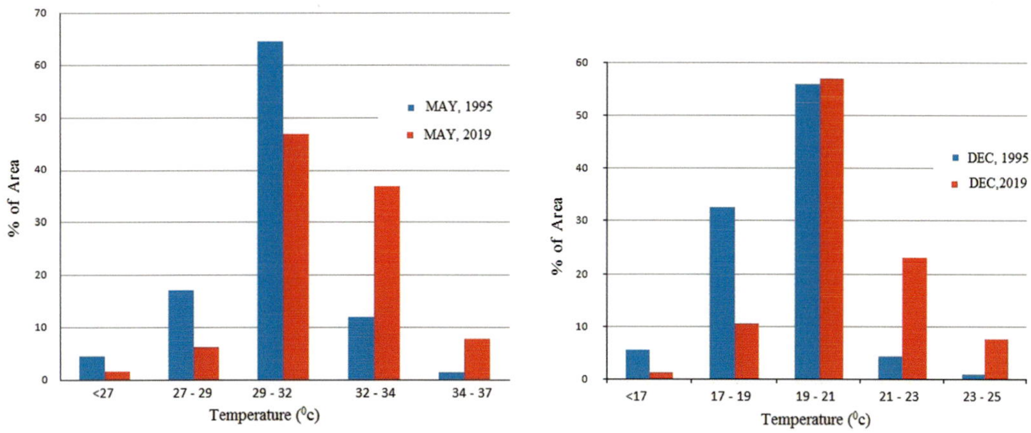

FIGURE 2.4 Spatial pattern of LST.

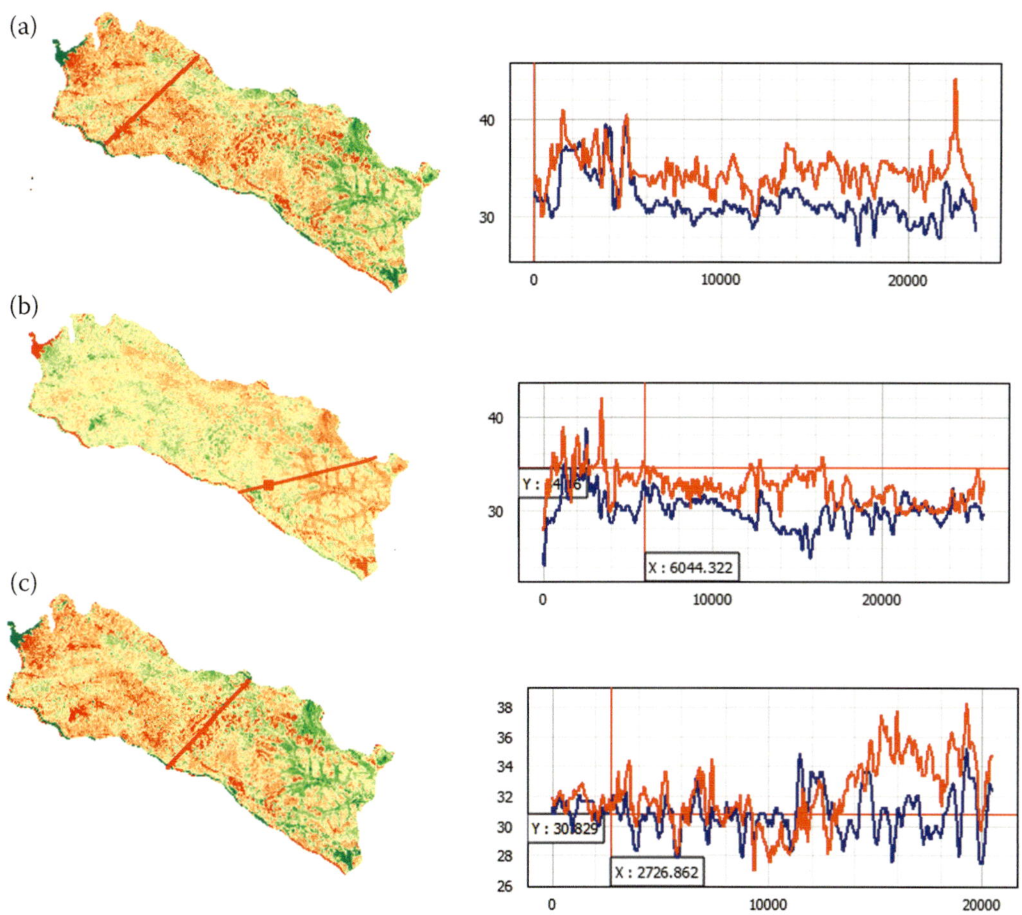

FIGURE 2.5 Cross-profile of temperature over various LULC types (blue line for 1995 and red line for 2019).

TABLE 2.6
Spatial Pattern of LST

	% of Area			% of Area	
Temperature (°C)	**May 1995**	**May 2019**	**Temperature (°C)**	**Dec. 1995**	**Dec. 2019**
< 27	4.62	1.76	< 17	5.73	1.35
27 - 29	17.27	6.35	17 – 19	32.75	10.69
29 - 32	64.58	47.08	19 – 21	56.11	57.08
32 - 34	12.04	36.94	21 – 23	4.39	23.13
34 - 37	1.49	7.87	23 – 25	1.02	7.75

surface temperature in the study area during the last two decades. This increase in the temperature pattern is mostly considered to be attributed to the large-scale land transformation in the form of urban industrial growth that largely contributed to the formation of urban heat island (Table 2.6).

2.4.4 Relations between LULC Change and LST Pattern

To establish a logical relation between the changing LULC and rising LST has been one of the major objectives of the present study. To fulfil this, a twofold approach has been undertaken. First of all, a series of cross-profiles have been constructed over various LULC units in different directions. Secondly, there are various indices like NDVI, NDBI, etc. that represent particular LULC categories. Hence, an analysis of their patterns over time may focus some light on the relation between LULC and LST. Eventually, calculating a linear relationship by using the coefficient of correlation (r) may help to understand the association between the LST and the LULC.

As mentioned earlier, three cross sections over the study area have been constructed in such a way that it could cover major land use types. The x-axis in the profile represents the LULC and the y-axis represents the LST for both years, presented by two different colours (Figure 2.5). Hence, one is able to detect the changes in the LST where there have been any changes in the LULC. The LULC change matrix shows most of the land in the study area changed from crop land to both built-up and barren land; hence, simultaneously the land surface temperature change rapidly in those areas of land use change. Here, we have drawn three cross-sectional profile to highlight the nature of LST change with respect to change in LULC. Profile "A," drawn in the northern portion of the region, shows a high surface temperature in and around 30–40 °C due to the conversion of agricultural land into built-up and barren land (mining activity). Profile "B," drawn over the southern section of the study area, reveals that the temperature remains mostly around 30 °C due to the prevalence of a non-built-up area. In profile "C," drawn through the middle of the region, shows an increasing trend of temperature from east to west because the western portion of the profile has an ascendancy of vegetation and agricultural land while in the north it is dominated by barren and built-up classes of land use.

Most of the change occurred in the blocks of Asansol, Salanpur, Barabani, Ondal, Jamuria, Ranigunj, and Pandabeswar where agricultural land transformed into built-up and barren land; more so in Asansol, Jamuria, and Ranigunj, built-up areas have grown the most during the last two decades, whereas in Ondal, Pandabeswar, and Barabani, barren land increased due to the rapid increase of mining activity.

2.4.5 Index: NDVI, NDBI, and NDBaI

In the second instance, different land use indices have been calculated to evaluate the relation between the LULC and LST patterns. Considering the major land use categories, three indices have been employed in the present study; these are NDVI, NDBI, and NDBaI. In this connection, NDVI is an effective indicator for measuring the status of vegetation cover. Several studies acknowledge the importance of vegetation cover to regulate the LST pattern. Negative relation is found to exist between the NDVI and LST patterns. A gradual decrease of the NDVI value in the study area indicates a gradual waning of vegetal cover. The NDVI values of the study area are between –0.15 to 0.35. The highest values of NDVI (0.35) indicate that the dense vegetation is prominent in the eastern and northwestern parts of the study area. The lowest values (–0.15) indicated that built-up areas were followed by water bodies (Figure 2.6). Over the 20 years (1995 to 2019), vegetation cover has decreased over time and increased non-vegetated cover gradually. Therefore, it can be said that NDVI values have been decreasing in the Paschim Bardhhaman district.

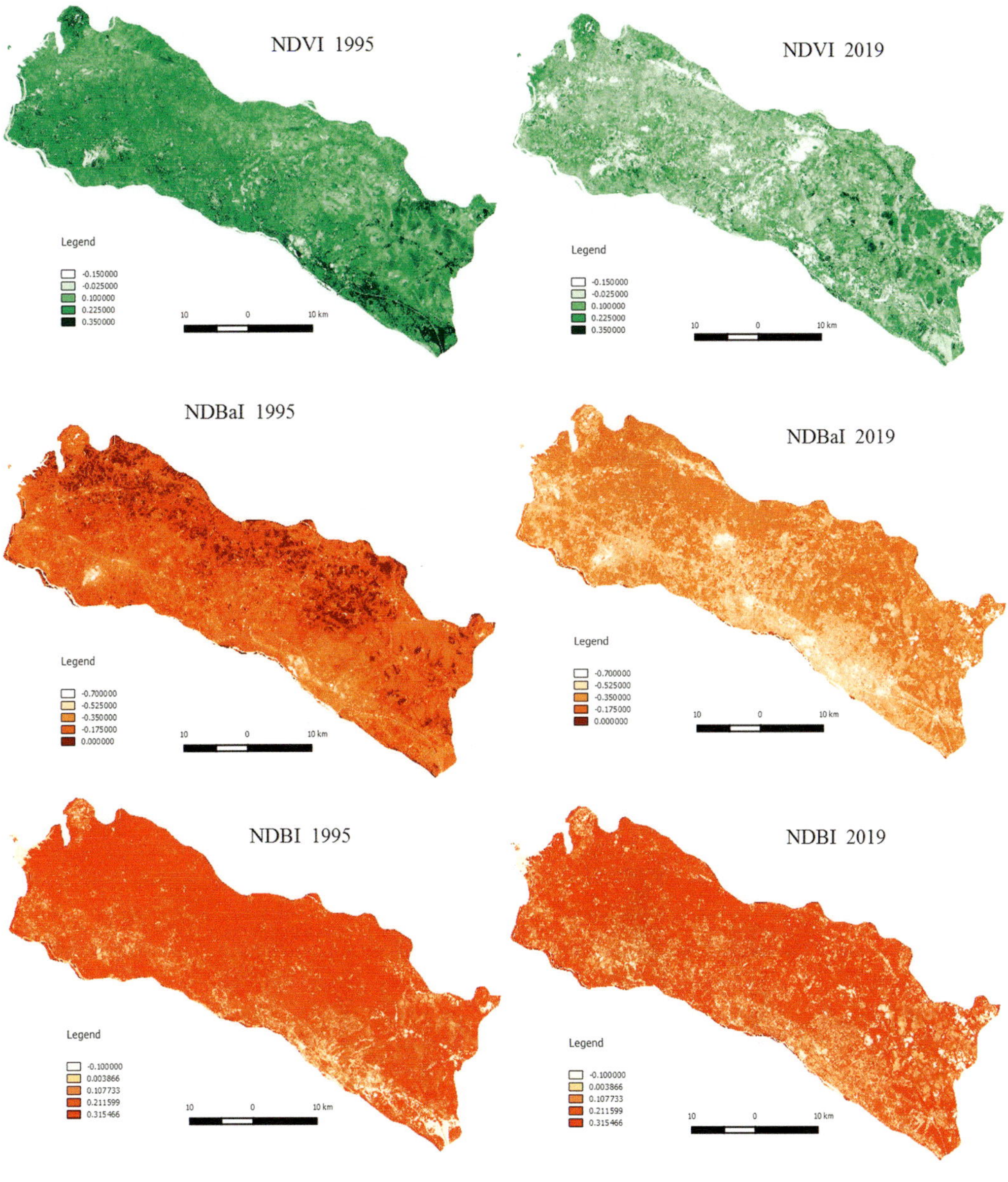

FIGURE 2.6 NDVI, NDBaI, and NDBI of 1995 and 2019.

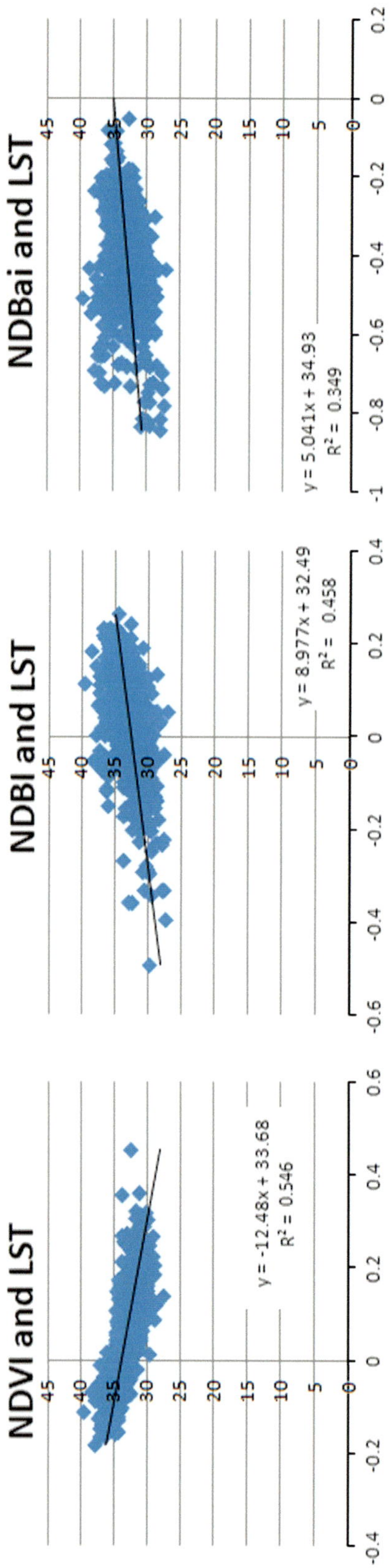

FIGURE 2.7 Relationship between LST and spectral indices.

Similarly, different research has established that normalized difference vegetation index (NDVI), normalized difference built-up index (NDBI), and normalized difference bareness index (NDBaI) also correlate strongly with the LST (Chen et al., 2006; Liu and Zhang, 2011; Essa et al., 2012, Rasul and Ibrahim, 2017; Sannigrahi et al., 2018). Built-up areas mostly composed of heat-absorbent materials like concrete make them warmer; hence, a positive relation exists between the LST and NDBI that represents the amount of built-up areas. So, an increase in the built-up area in the form of urban industrial growth and open pit mining must be responsible for the increase in the surface temperature. Urban expansion and proliferation of open pit mining also increase the amount of barren land. An increase in the NDBaI value in the present context indicates the increase of the barren land. It also positively correlated with the LST pattern.

2.4.6 Correlation

To measure the impact over the LST, we have prepared three land use land cover indices: NDVI, NDBI, and NDBaI. It is proved by previous research that the LST has a negative relation with NDVI, which means the LST increased with decreasing vegetation cover; here, this study also redirects the same status of relation (Figure 2.7). Built-up areas, high density of human activity, and industrial growth all have a close association with the LST, while Weng and Yang in 2004 argued that in the UHI effect, the lower vegetation coverage plays a role of a decision maker. Here also, NDBI (r^2 = 0.46) and NDBaI (r^2 = 0.35) indices reflect their positive relation with the LST, because impervious built-up cover and bare soil both have high reflectance capacity.

2.5 CONCLUSION

In conclusion, we must say that the study area is gradually converting into a cluster of heat islands; more particularly, Asansol, Raniganj, Jamuria, Pandabeswar, Ondal, and Durgapur, all six towns, irrespective of their size, influenced the whole study area to be a high-temperate region. Loss of crop land and forest cover are the two main factors to raise the temperature in the region, and those losses are amplified by the increase of built-up use and barren land all over the region and built-up growth caused by the continuous urbanization process, Loss of vegetation cover coupled with large scale and rapid increase in the open cast mining abruptly raise the barren land. So it seems the region is in need of a plan at either a regional level or local level; otherwise, the whole region will transform to large-scale heat island in the near future. Further, this study redirects the fact that although the whole region will not turn into an urban area in near the future, the transformation of land from barren to vegetation cover is needed, and the cities' planning should focus on the rise of urban greeneries. On the other hand, continuous monitoring of the changing pattern in the LULC in the urban region is needed to implement suitable and sustainable LULC policies.

REFERENCES

Ahmed, B. "Urban land cover change detection analysis and modeling spatio-temporal growth dynamics using remote sensing and GIS techniques: A case study of Dhaka, Bangladesh." Master's Thesis, Erasmus Mundus Program, Universidade Nova de Lisboa (UNL), InstitutoSuperior de Estatística e Gestão de Informação (ISEGI). Lisbon, Portugal (2011).

Ahmed, B., Kamruzzaman, M. D., Zhu, X., Rahman, S., and Choi, K. "Simulating land cover changes and their impacts on land surface temperature in Dhaka, Bangladesh." *Remote Sensing* 5 (2013): 5969–5998.

Ali, S. B., Patnaik, S, and Madguni, O. "Microclimate land surface temperatures across urban land use/land cover forms." *Global Journal of Environmental Science and Management* 3(3) (2017): 231–242.

Allaka, L., Gupta, N., and Aithal, B. "Land use pattern analysis and land surface temperature extraction: A case study of Kolkata." *IEEE 16th India Council International Conference (INDICON).* DOI: 10.1109/INDICON47234.2019.9028992 (2019).

Baeza, S., and Paruelo, J. M. "Land use/land cover change (2000–2014) in the Rio de la Plata Grasslands: An analysis based on MODIS NDVI time series." *Remote Sensing*, 12(381) (2020): 1–22. 10.3390/rs12030381.

Barsi. J. A., Barker. J. L., and Schott J. R. "An atmospheric correction parameter calculator for a single thermal band earth-sensing instrument." Retrieved from https://atmcorr.gsfc.nasa.gov/Barsi_IGARSS03.PDF (2003).

Bharath, H. A., Chandan, M. C., and Nimish, G. "Assessing land surface temperature and land use change through spatio-temporal analysis: A case study of select major cities of India." *Arabian Journal of Geosciences* 367 (2019). 10.1007/s12517-019-4547-1.

Chatterjee, S., and Gupta, K. "Exploring the spatial pattern of urban heat island formation in relation to land transformation: A study on a mining industrial region of West Bengal, India." *Remote Sensing Applications: Society and Environment* 23 (2021). doi.org/10.1016/j.rsase.2021.100581.

Chen, X.-L., Zhao, H.-M., Li, P.-X., and Yin, Z.-Y. "Remote sensing image-based analysis of the relationship between urban heat island and land use/cover changes." *Remote Sensing of Environment* 104 (2006): 133–146.

Choudhury, D., Das, K., and Das, A. "Assessment of land use land cover changes and its impact on variations of land surface temperature in Asansol-Durgapur Development Region." *The Egyptian Journal of Remote Sensing and Space Sciences* 22(2) (2019): 203–218. 10.1016/j.ejrs.2018.05.004.

Dutta, D., Gupta, S., and Kishtawal, C. M. "Linking LULC change with urban heat islands over 25 years: A case study of the urban-industrial city Durgapur, Eastern India." *Journal of Spatial Science* 65(3) (2020): 501–518.

Essa, W., Verbeiren, B., van der Kwast, J., van de Voorde, T., and Batelaan, O. "Evaluation of the DisTrad thermal sharpening methodology for urban areas." *International Journal of Applied Earth Observation and Geoinformation* 19(1) (2012): 163–172.

Grover, A., and Singh, R.B. "Analysis of urban heat island (UHI) in relation to normalized difference vegetation index (NDVI): A comparative study of Delhi and Mumbai." *Environments* 2(2) (2015): 125–138.

Jalan, S., and Sharma, K. "Spatio-temporal assessment of land use/land cover dynamics and urban heat island of Jaipur city using satellite data." *Remote Sensing and Spatial Information Sciences* 9(4) (2014): 767–772.

Jeevalakshmi, D., Reddy, S. N., and Manikiam, B. "Land surface temperature retrieval from LANDSAT data using emissivity estimation." *International Journal of Applied Engineering Research* 12(20) (2017): 9679–9687.

Joshi, J. P. and Bindu, B. "Estimating temporal land surface temperature using remote sensing: A study of Vadodara Urban Area, Gujarat." *International Journal of Geology, Earth and Environmental Sciences*, 2(1) (2012): 123–130.

Juan-Carlos, J. -M., and Sobrino, J. A. "Split-window coefficients for land surface temperature retrieval from low-resolution thermal infrared sensors." *IEEE Geoscience and Remote Sensing Letters* 5(4) (2008): 806–809.

Juan-Carlos, J. -M., Sobrino, J. A., Skoković, D., Mattar, C., and Cristóbal, J. "Land surface temperature retrieval methods from Landsat-8 thermal infrared sensor data." *IEEE Geoscience and Remote Sensing Letters* 11(10) (2014): 1840–1843.

Kamila, A., and Pal, S. C. 2015. Monitoring of land surface temperature and analyzing of environmental prediction on Asansol Durgapur Subdivision, Burdwan District West Bengal using Landsat Imagery. *International journal of remote sensing and geosciences*, *5*(10), 33–36.

Lilly Rose, A., and Devadas, M. D. "Analysis of land surface temperature and land use/land cover types using remote sensing imagery - A case in Chennai city, India." *The seventh International Conference on Urban Clim., held on 29 June–3 July 2009*, Yokohama, Japan (2009).

Liu, L., and Zhang, Y. "Urban heat island analysis using the Landsat TM data and ASTER data: A Case study in Hong Kong." *Remote Sensing* 3 (2011): 1535–1552.

Mallick, J., Kant, Y., and Bharath, B. D. "Estimation of land surface temperature over Delhi using Landsat-7 ETM+." *Journal of Indian Geophysical Union* 12(3) (2008): 131–140.

Mallick, J., Singh, C. K., Shashtri, S., Rahman, A., Mukherjee, S. "Land surface emissivity retrieval based on moisture index from Landsat TM satellite data over heterogeneous surfaces of Delhi city." *International Journal of Applied Earth Observation and Geoinformation* 19 (2012): 348–358.

Omran, E. E. "Detection of land-use and surface temperature change at different resolutions." *Journal of Geographic Information System* 4(3) (2012): 189–203.

Pal, S., and Ziaul, S. "Detection of land use and land cover change and land surface temperature in English Bazar urban centre." *The Egyptian Journal of Remote Sensing and Space Sciences*20(1) 2016): 125–145.10.1016/j.ejrs.2016.11.003.

Qinqin, S., Jianjun, T., and Yonghang, X. "An ERDAS image processing method for retrieving LSTand describing urban heat evolution: a case study in the Pearl River Delta Region in South China." *Environmental Earth Sciences* 59 (2010): 1047–1055. 10.1007/s12665-009-0096-3

Rahaman, S., Kumar, P., Chen, R., Meadows, M. E., Singh, R. B. "Remote sensing assessment of the impact of land use and land cover change on the environment of Barddhaman district, West Bengal, India." *Frontiers in Environmental Science* 8 (2020): 127. 10.3389/fenvs.2020.00127.

Rajeshwari, A., and Mani, N. D. "Estimation of land surface temperature of Dindigul district using Landsat 8 data." *International Journal of Research in Engineering and Technology* 3(5) (2014): 122–126.

Ramachandra, T. V., Aithal, B. H., and Sanna, D. "Land surface temperature analysis in an urbanising landscape through multi-resolution data." *Journal of Space Science & Technology* 1(1) (2012): 1–10.

Rasul, G., and Ibrahim, F. "Urban land use land cover changes and their effect on land surface temperature: Case study using Dohuk City in the Kurdistan Region of Iraq." *Climate* 5(1) (2017). 10.3390/cli5010013

Sannigrahi, S., Bhatt, S., Rahmat, S., Uniyal, B., Banerjee, S., Chakrborti, S., Jha, S., Lahiri, S., Santra, K., and Bhatt, A. "Analyzing the role of biophysical compositions in minimizing urban land surface temperature and urban heating." *Urban Climate 24* (2018): 803–819.

Xiaolei, Y., Xulin, G., and Zhaocong, W. "Land surface temperature retrieval from Landsat 8 TIRS-comparison between radiative transfer equation-based method, split window algorithm and single channel method." *Remote Sensing* 6 (2004): 9829–9852.

3 Mechanisms for Brownfield Redevelopment: A Case of Indore City

Hemadri Raut
All India Institute of Local Self Government, Bhopal, Madhya Pradesh, India

Kakoli Saha
School of Planning and Architecture, Bhopal, India

CONTENTS

3.1 INTRODUCTION

Most scientific literatures cite the definition of brownfield development provided by the Brownfields Economic Redevelopment Initiative under the U.S. Environmental Protection Agency (USEPA, 2006). According to the U.S. EPA, brownfields are abandoned, idle, or underused industrial and commercial facilities where expansion or redevelopment is complicated by real or perceived environmental contamination. In India, brownfields are defined as the vacant land parcels that may be built on previously, needing redevelopment (Bhattacharya and Rathi, 2015). Historically, brownfields are industrial or commercially used space located in urban boundaries

DOI: 10.1201/9781003126195-4

(Majumdar and Sen, 2018). There are several types of brownfields, such as 1) brownfields from old industrial areas – as outcomes of tremendous decline in industrial and respective mining sector employment in the late 20th century; 2) urban brownfields – as outcomes of the peripheral shift due to expanding urbanization; and 3) rural brownfields – as outcomes of abandoned land parcels due to a shift from primary sector activities. The common characteristics of brownfield sites are: 1. defunct and underutilized sites, 2. known/ suspected contamination issues, 3. primarily located in urban areas, and 4. require action plans to realize redevelopment potential (USEPA, 2006). These defunct spaces are eluded to as being hard to manage inside the setting of urban improvement inferable from the real or perceived pollution issues (Dulić and Krklješ, 2015). Brownfields are empty lands that have been used already but presently need redevelopment. Physical infrastructure is available in these lands because of its previous use. After the process of remediation, the land tends to seek regeneration (USEPA, 2006). Dixon (2006) proposed "marrying" brownfield and sustainability concepts to underpin the vision of "sustainable brownfield regeneration." He emphasized the need for better metrics and benchmarks to be developed to measure sustainable brownfield regeneration (Dixon, 2006). Beames et al. (2018) proposed amenity proximity analysis through GIS for sustainable brownfield redevelopment planning.

So far, no standard definition or rule for brownfield redevelopment is accessible in India. Brownfield redevelopment is gaining importance in the most recent government systems for several economic, environmental, and social benefits compiled from various literature (Doick et al., 2006; Turvani and Tonin, 2008; ICMA guidebook for Brownfield redevelopment) and outlined in Table 3.1.

Looking into the present government programs with the redevelopment as a procedure to provide urban development prerequisites, there is an absence of a city improvement model trying to address auxiliary disparity and deficiency (Patnayaka, 2018). Various development approaches from recent times indicate an unexpected jump from a socialist viewpoint to capitalist methodology and bring about the loss of inherent socio-economic urban environment. Such government activities often lack the basis for the choice of a space inside the city, the order in which various spaces will be chosen and the timeline by which the entire city would be secured (Patnayaka, 2018). This research for the first time provides a mechanism for brownfield redevelopment in an Indian context. The proposed method is comprised of two parts. The first part envisages the identification process of existing brownfield sites, and the second part consists of assessment of their redevelopment potential considering the economic feasibility, community benefits, and local context. For the study, the city of Indore of Madhya Pradesh, India, was chosen (shown in Figure 3.1). To select potential sites for brownfield redevelopment within Indore, a reconnaissance survey was performed. During the survey, lacking any comprehensive data attributes about all the brownfield land parcels in Indore was experienced. The majority of environmental data sets, including soil conditions and ground water quality, were not available. There was an absence of city-level environmental reports for the city of Indore to explore the respective conditions in detail.

TABLE 3.1
Benefits of Brownfield Redevelopment

Economic Benefits	Environmental Benefits	Social Benefits
• Increase in investment • Produce more employment • Additional property tax base • Better use of existing facilities and services	• Limit urban sprawl • Eradicate real or perceived contamination in the locality • Opportunity for open/green spaces, reduced congestion and pollution	• Improve public health • Improve public safety • Encourage neighborhood revitalization

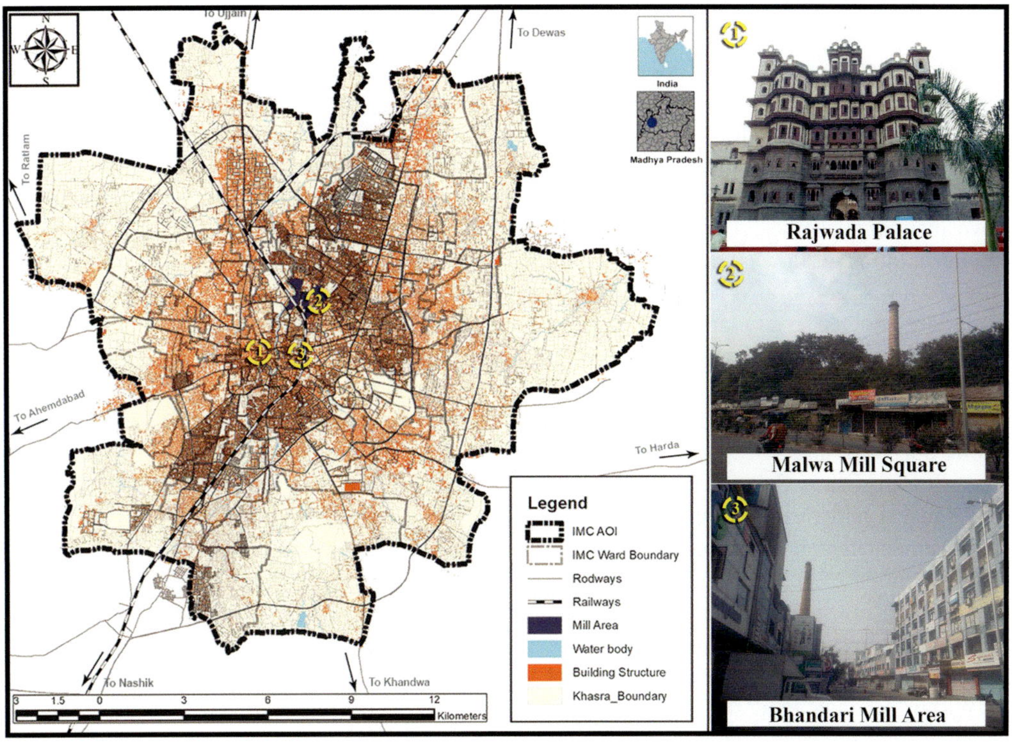

FIGURE 3.1 Maps showing the coverage of Indore Municipal Corporation and relevant landmarks.

3.2 BACKGROUND STUDY

3.2.1 Brownfield Redevelopment in India

India, being a nation with rich resources, has seen setting up of its secondary sector growth during the 19th century. With the establishment of railways by the East India Company as freight carrier prompted the advancement of the industrial sector (Majumdar and Sen, 2018). Demographic immigration into these industrial towns over some stretch of time has brought about high-density and inadequate infrastructure concerns to such towns (Patnayaka, 2018). It led to the process of developing tremendous opportunities of potential brownfield land parcels in India. In 2005, the first concrete step was taken for urban restoration in India through the Jawaharlal Nehru National Urban Renewal Mission with the aphorism of incorporating improvement; it dealt with goals like the supply of urban basic services to the urban poor, additionally to guarantee affordable tenure security, sanitation, and other physical infrastructure needs (Parlewar and Fukukawa, 2006). This was followed up by the Smart City Mission (launched in 2015) with the idea of Area Based Development and Pan City Initiatives. Although all the redevelopment techniques involved multi-scalar projects in India were detailed and executed under the reformed structure of urban planning standards, the primary spotlight was on land use, improvement of social and physical services, facilities, and utilities. Less light was thrown on logical methodology in managing brownfield destinations (Patnayaka, 2018).

Urban redevelopment practices in India are more of urban spatial strategies for distinguished underutilized land parcels managed under the dominating administrative structure (Majumdar and Sen, 2018). Certain methodologies, for example, pre-recognizable proof of plausible brownfield lands, site explicit specialized investigation, and logical remediation methodology, were proposed. An efficient and logical methodology in managing brownfields would accord the maintainable redevelopment.

3.2.2 Land Redevelopment Process in Madhya Pradesh

Since the research is based on Indore, located in Madhya Pradesh, the land development process of the state is studied in detail. The Madhya Pradesh Town and Country Planning Act (1973) refers to the practices and limitations of use of land resources within the administrative boundaries of Madhya Pradesh (Madhya Pradesh Real Estate Policy, 2019). It is an act to make better provisions for the preparation of development plan and zoning plans with a view for effective execution of town planning schemes. The Town and Country Planning Authority was constituted for proper implementation of town and country development plans and the Special Area Development Authority was constituted for the development and administration of special areas. The basic procedure adopted in any land development exercise in Madhya Pradesh can be summarized into the following steps: 1) pooling of land, 2) reconstitution of plot boundaries to acquire land for establishing adequate physical and social infrastructure, 3) the original owners will get their re-distributed plots along with development incentives, 4) automatic acquisition of land parcels for public purposes, and 5) expanse of development is regained through the resale of plots (Madhya Pradesh Real Estate Policy, 2019). The selection of the site is done within the physical and jurisdictional boundaries of the state to ensure the application of relevant policies and schemes on the site. Authorities call for objections or recommendations for any redevelopment proposal after the verification of public or private ownership. State government levy betterment charges for the enhanced infrastructural properties. It also increases the value of land ultimately keeping landowners in profit. The calculation of costs and compensations are based upon present as well as increased land value (Madhya Pradesh Real Estate Policy, 2019).

Within Madhya Pradesh, urban local bodies (ULBs) adopt different land development mechanisms. For example, Indore has now opted for a mutual land agreement method for any sort of land development. These development activities are called Indore development authority (IDA) schemes (Indore Development Plan, 2021). IDA starts with identifying the areas showcasing the opportunity for urban growth. Then they publish the preliminary initiative for the land development scheme after preparing the base map of accumulated land parcels and ask for suggestions or contradictions. The IDA also invites the landowners for investment based on public-private partnership models. This agreement provides the landowners with 25% of their original land parcels as developed and serviced plots in return against their willful submission of their underutilized or defunct plots to the authority. Additionally, they are also exempted from paying any stamp duties, additional development charges, or betterment levies to the IDA. The IDA follows a rule of thumb for such development schemes. The IDA returns 25% of the plots from the 50% of residential use category to landowners and 15% is kept secured for Low Income Group (LIG) and Economically Weaker Sections (EWS) in the ratio of 1:2. However, the IDA expenses 30% of the land for roads compared to the Ahmedabad model, which restricts it to 15% of the total land area only. This exposes the variation arising between the Development Plan and IDA schemes in Indore. When the IDA acquires possession, they go for necessary infrastructure development and disposal of plots. To secure greater profits, usually the IDA keeps the land parcels for longer time periods to seek the increase in market land value. Since the land acquisition process is lengthy, it keeps the reconstituted plots away from the reach of people who direly need them and the plots become unaffordable for middle-income and lower-income groups. The mechanism of potential assessment and prioritization proposed in this research can contribute to the speeding of redevelopment projects by ensuring the profit.

3.3 METHODOLOGY FOR REDEVELOPING BROWNFIELD SITES

According to the U.S. EPA (2006), the process of brownfield redevelopment involves seven steps: 1) identification of potential brownfield sites, 2) initial assessment of the identified sites, 3) economic assessment, 4) detailed site assessment, 5) project development and financing, 6) site cleanup and remediation, and 7) site redevelopment. Identification of potential brownfield sites starts through relating potential plots with the defined characteristics of brownfield sites (Ganser and Williams, 2007). Coffin and Meyer (2002) proposed the utilization of existing public databases for the respective identification of brownfields. According to them, there are four layers that can be considered for selection of target geographical areas, such as old industrial sites, areas with higher population densities, city centers (old business centers/downtown areas), and eco-sensitive areas. The ULBs can accurately identify the potential sites that have very little contamination in the form of local pollution control board records and property tax records. Such identification can be completed at the urban local level through linking industrial classification to local property tax records (Coffin and Meyer, 2002). Identification of potential brownfield sites is followed by initial assessment of the identified sites involving review of the land tenure details, on-site physical assessment, and other already documented data. While economic assessment (third step) involves assessment of various spatial and non-spatial site characteristics to ensure the viability of redevelopment, detailed site assessment (fourth step) is done through environmental impact assessment of the site and related site contamination assessments. At the stage of project development and financing (fifth step), financial feasibility assessment is performed. The feasibility assessment would entrust a profitable market investment with the redeveloped property resale greater than the cumulative cost of site remediation, construction, etc. Table 3.2 explains the identified criteria for feasibility analysis.

Besides financial feasibility, community benefits are to be explored to encourage the potential stakeholders. The listing of criteria as per Table 3.3 for community benefit analysis is done from secondary sources (Kurtović et al., 2014).

TABLE 3.2
Criteria for Redevelopment Feasibility Analysis

Criteria		Explanation
Condition of the site	Physical condition	The size of land parcel, quality of existing built infrastructure, etc. would influence the cost and redevelopment feasibility.
	Environmental condition	Type and extent of real or perceived contamination would impact the cost and time of site cleanup process.
Infrastructure and utilities	Utilities	Water supply and solid and liquid waste management network would affect the required capital for any redevelopment.
	Transport infrastructure	The proximity with transport network and transit infrastructure is essential in determining the future land use for the site.
	Communication facilities	Communication infrastructure is important for a majority of the future proposals in context to the city's importance.
Market factors	Customer proximity	This determines the accessibility to customers.
	Competitors	This forms the very basis of the shared market activities and any investment is highly influenced.
	Land pricing	The initial determinant of the project cost and associated profit or loss.
	Will of the owner	Owner's resistance would increase the project cost and initiation time.
Financing aspect	Policy incentives	Investments from strong developers can be attracted through property tax incentives.
	Financial support	Availability of a local financial base can overcome financial obstacles at the municipal level.

Source: Kurtović et al. (2014).

TABLE 3.3
Criteria for Community Benefit Analysis

Criteria		Explanation
Economic benefits	Development practices	Abundance of development activities in the city can drive the city towards new economic development and so the community benefits.
	Employment opportunities	Redevelopment can develop new job opportunities.
Environmental benefits	Regional environmental quality	Cleanup and remediation of brownfield sites can always improve the regional environmental quality.
Social benefits	Local interests	Redevelopment near sites of public interest or with special local values is always crucial for a community.
	Urban image	Redevelopment results in improved urban aesthetics and hence enhances the overall neighborhood quality.

3.3.1 Case Study References

To refine the methodology, two Indian cases of brownfield redevelopment practices were referred to. Both cases involve mill land redevelopment relevant to the case study city.

3.3.1.1 Reference Case 1: Girangaon Mill Land Redevelopment, Mumbai

Mumbai, a port city on the western coast of India, is an established industrial center in British India. As time passed, the industrial setup started to reach its threshold capacity to provide for such immigrating population and necessary infrastructure. Also, with the introduction to power looms, the cotton textile industry started suffering and proposals of shifting the mill out of central Mumbai and putting it to alternate uses had risen (D'monte, 2006).

In 1991, after the economic liberalization, the Maharashtra government amended its Development Control Regulations (DCR), particularly for the mill land redevelopment. There was a one-third formula for mill land readjustment as one-third of the total area each is to be shared among the mill owners: Maharashtra Housing and Area Development Authority (MHADA) and Bombay Municipal Corporation (BMC). While MHADA is responsible for affordable housing development, BMC would use their share to provide open spaces and public services. On the other hand, under rule 58(2), the mill owner would reimburse its ex-workers or modernize the mill and can sell 15% of the total land in incremental terms without following the one-third formula (Nallathiga, 2014). As a result, some mill lands were converted into shopping malls and recreational spaces to exploit the commercial value of land in central Mumbai. In 1996, a group led by Charles Chorea surveyed the 24 National Textile Corporation (NTC) mills as per the orders of the Maharashtra government and recommended a comprehensive approach of redevelopment against the one-third formula to ensure holistic planning of the city (Adarkar and Phatak, 2005). It also suggested the floor surface index (FSI) incentives for mill owners, but the report was not made public by the government. In 2001, the state government amended the DCR to allow the mill owners to surrender only the vacant land, not the land available after demolition of existing built structures. They clarified it by stating that built-up areas were exempted from the one-third formula, resulting in even fewer public spaces (D'monte, 2006).

This project shows the owner's will is the most important determinant of a brownfield redevelopment project. This was purely a market-driven redevelopment process. The commercial exploitation of this piecemeal approach of redevelopment under the umbrella of biased legislative DCR reforms has been considered a loss to the public. Out of the extensive 600 acres of land, 400 acres could have been utilized to create open spaces and affordable housing for a city suffering from the lowest levels in per-capita open space in the world. This project is an example of narrowminded and short-sighted development policies and strategies at an urban local level.

3.3.1.2 Reference Case 2: Bhendi Bazaar Redevelopment, Mumbai

In 1889, Bhendi Bazaar framed a piece of the downtown territories that housed workers working in the harbor of Mumbai. At first, it was intended to house lone rangers who had moved to the city for employment, but soon the chawls were full of their whole families. More than 70% of the occupants were living as inhabitants in a territory of under 350 sq. feet (Master and Dravid, 2015). As indicated by MHADA, more than 80 of the 250 structures are exhausted and have been announced weather beaten and unfit for living. A private body called the Saifee Burhani Upliftment Trust (SBUT) has taken up the redevelopment project of this area. It has purchased 87% of the structures and is procuring the rest. So far, the trust has wrecked more than 70 structures. The SBUT has made groups that helped inhabitants with the affirmation, including getting old records and in any event, having their homes estimated, and are utilizing old service charges as records. As per the administration rules, occupants of a redevelopment zone must get the proportionate space in the new undertaking that they had in their old structures and the new units must be at least 300 sq. ft, regardless of whether they recently lived in littler houses (Master and Dravid, 2015).

This project has emerged as a successful model for large-scale development with the help of detailed social impact assessment and environmental analysis. The project was supported by a unique cluster redevelopment policy developed by the state government of Maharashtra and adequately furnished transit accommodations by the SBUT. It recommends the creation of awareness for redevelopment and a methodological approach in convincing the tenants as an urban planning instrument to reduce sprawl. Both case references were further evaluated through criteria for brownfield redevelopment identified from a literature review, as shown in Table 3.4.

TABLE 3.4
Examining Suitability of Each Criterion for Comprehensive Assessment

Type of Assessment	Classified Aspects	Identified Criteria	Evaluation Score in Case 1	Evaluation Score in Case 2
Feasibility analysis	Site condition	Physical condition	Good	Poor
		Environmental condition	Medium	Poor
	Infrastructure	Utility infrastructure	Medium	Medium
		Transport infrastructure	Good	Good
	Market	Customer proximity	Good	Good
		Competition	Medium	Poor
		Land Price	Poor	Medium
		Owner's will	Poor	Good
	Financing	Policy incentives	Medium	Good
		Financial backup	Medium	Good
Community benefits analysis	Economic benefits	Development activities	Medium	Good
		Employment	Poor	Good
	Environmental benefits	Regional environmental quality	Poor	Good
	Social benefits	Public interests	Poor	Good
		Urban aesthetics	Poor	Good

Source: Author.

According to Table 3.4, the trust-led redevelopment in the second reference case was successful because of the negligible competition as the site's physical condition and infrastructure facilities were outdated and required high remediation costs. The traditional mill area with insufficient focus on labor housing and contamination issues in reference case 1 is seen as poor performance of environmentally beneficial criteria. The importance of up-to-date infrastructure is justified. Although it is necessary to put the regional environmental quality in assessment process but its performance is not a result of redevelopment process in any case. From this analysis, it can be concluded that incorporation of local criteria such as public interest, urban aesthetics, and policy incentives (Table 3.4) are necessary for successful implementation of brownfield redevelopment projects. The identified criteria are included in this research in the form of land re-use preferences, urban image, and local policy incentives.

3.4 SELECTION OF BROWNFIELD SITES FOR REDEVELOPMENT

At the start of the 21st century, the city of Indore was developed as a business and industrial capital of the state of Madhya Pradesh with an urban population of around 20 lakhs (Indore Development Plan, 2021). Modern spinning, weaving, and fabric processing units have contributed to increase garment manufacturing enterprises in the city. This city has also seen a paradigm shift from manufacturing to a service sector and in the process earning the tag of textile market center in central India. Newer capital-intensive industries have overtaken the old traditional mills and led to limited job opportunities (Indore Development Plan, 2021).

Unexpectedly, the old textile mills, which shaped the core of mechanical advancement in and around Indore, have been totally removed from the new vision of Indore urban planning approaches. The old textile mills had attracted the major share of business deployment due to the accompanying Swadeshi Movement and export possibilities arose out of the First World War (1914–1918). The new businesses were unmistakably more capital serious than the old plants. At that point, the laborers of the old material plants were viewed as unfit for the accessible employments (Patnayaka, 2018).

The identification of potential brownfield sites within Indore was done in a GIS platform following the Coffin and Meyer (2002) model (see section 3.3). The old industrial sites of Indore were overlapped (Figure 3.2a) with the areas of higher population density (Figure 3.2b). Based upon the census of 2011, the population density was calculated at the ward level within IMC. It was classified into five categories with the help of an equal method. The abandoned textile mills were situated in areas with a population density higher than 400 pph. As per the "Indore Development Plan (2021)," there were three proposed city centers in the city. The city core, Rajwada, was the first city center and was also selected for ABD through the Smart City Mission. The second one was Vijaynagar, with a proposed mixed-use commercial development. The third one was the Silicon city area proposed, as an IT hub. The proximities with these city centers can influence the surrounding areas. As there is no environmental plan in Indore for the urban local level, blue and green areas in the city have been used to generate eco-sensitive zones in the city of Indore (Figure 3.2c). The next step was overlaying these eco-sensitive areas upon the above-described densely populated and old industrial sites. Unlike the Coffin and Meyer (2002) model, pollution levies and tax delinquency data (refer section 3.3) could not be used due to unavailability. Through the overlay analysis in GIS, target geographical areas (Figure 3.2d) were identified.

The target geographical areas within Indore consist of an old mill area, old barracks, abandoned printing press, some government defunct buildings, and areas near the existing blue-green areas. Some of the potential sites lie in the historic cotton textile mill area from the Holkar administrative periods. There is also a ground verification to further finalize the potential brownfield sites in the case area. The old textile mills were declared sick in 1974 under the "Sick textile undertaking (Nationalisation) Act." A reconnaissance survey was conducted, which included several personal interviews and focused group discussions with the urban planners and city officials. There were

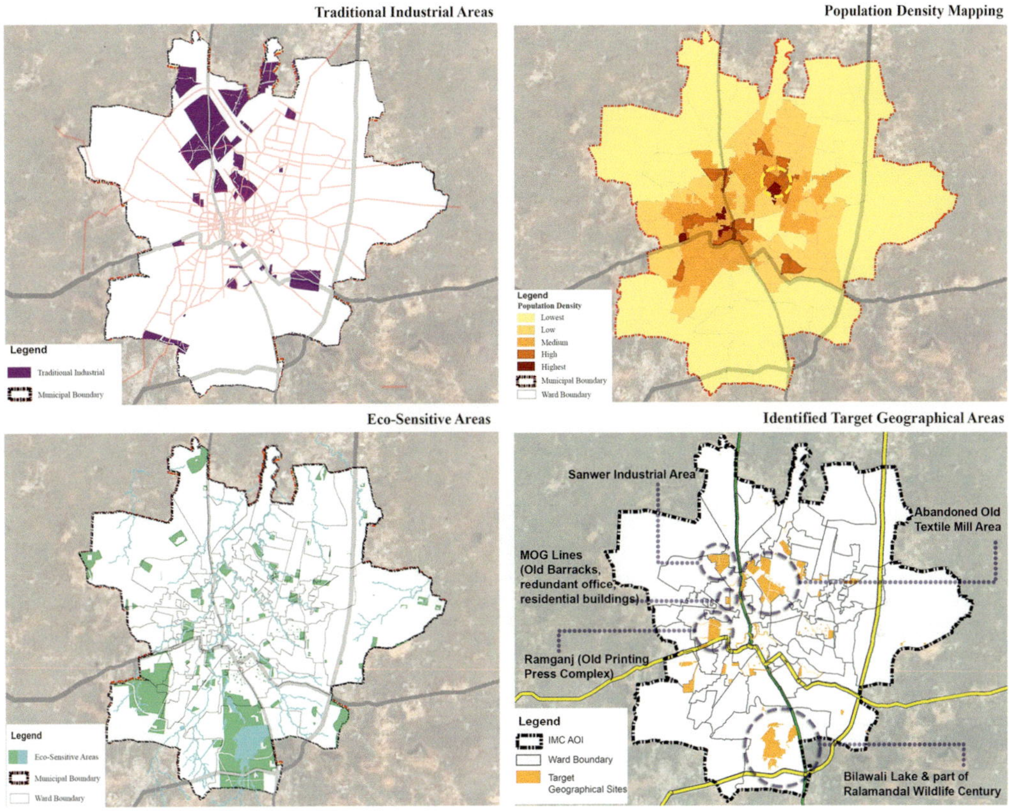

FIGURE 3.2 Maps showing the target geographical areas in Indore, including old industrial sites, highly populated areas, and eco-sensitive areas.

also some site visits to verify the existing conditions in the city. Based upon fieldwork and data limitations, finally six old and defunct industrial sites were selected: Kalyanmal United Mills, Swadeshi Mill, Bhandari Mill, Indore Malwa United Mill, Hukumchand Mill, and Rajkumar Mill (Figure 3.3). Both Kalyanmal United Mills and Swadeshi Mill were set up in 1919, taken over by the National Textile Corporations (NTC) after declared sick, and finally closed in 2002. Total vacant land under the public ownership available is 33.85 and 15.32 acres, respectively. Bhandari Mill was set up in 1922, bought by HOPE textile in 1973, and closed in 1973. The vacant land of 15.57 acres is under private ownership. Indore Malwa United Mill was set up in 1909, declared sick in 1974, and finally closed in 2003. This mill has 59.29 acres of vacant land available under public ownership. Hukumchand Mill was set up in 1916 and closed in 1991. This mill has 41.02 acres of land available under private ownership. Rajkumar Mill was set up in 1924, Madhya Pradesh Government bought 57% share in 1986, and final closure happened in 1999. Total vacant land available is 5.90 acres under public ownership.

3.5 DATA COLLECTION

After selection of the brownfield sites for redevelopment, the next step was to collect data to apply the identified methodology. Both primary and secondary data collection techniques were adopted. Data was collected from different agencies like Indore Municipal Corporation (IMC), Indore Development Authority (IDA), and Indore Smart City Limited (ISCL) during the dedicated fieldwork time (February, 2020). The IDA, an urban local body responsible for bringing out

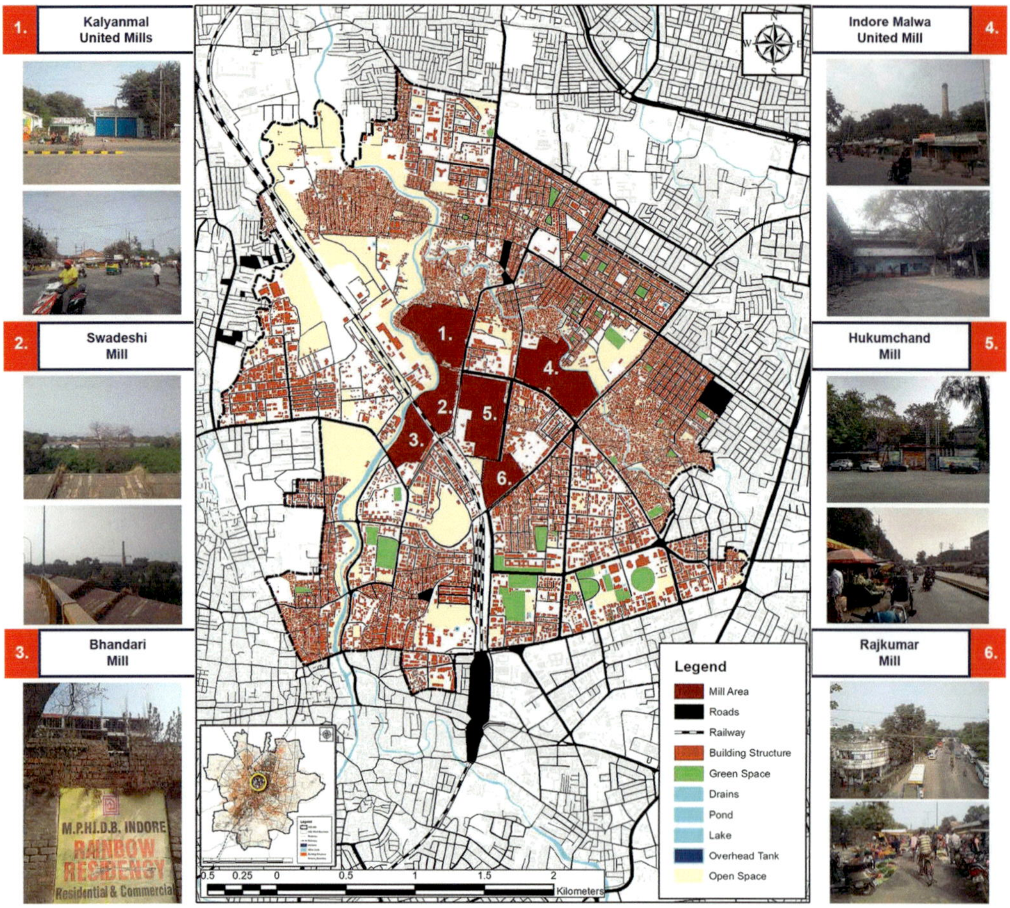

FIGURE 3.3 Identified brownfield sites in Indore.

various urban planning practices in the form of town planning schemes, provided some city-level development approaches. The primary data collection had a broad objective of learning about the local context of urban redevelopment. It included field visits undertaken to explore in detail the impact of local factors of brownfield redevelopment practices. For example, from site visits along with the responses from the interviews with city managers, it was observed that the ULB is focused on attaining the SDGs along with the optimized land use distribution, better employment opportunities, urban image of the city, and local policy incentives.

3.6 ASSESSING REDEVELOPMENT POTENTIAL OF IDENTIFIED BROWNFIELD SITES IN INDORE

Based on literature surveys and field visits, the assessment of redevelopment potential of identified sites is done based upon financial feasibility, community benefit, and local context. This assessment incorporates the multi-criteria evaluation (MCE) approach including spatial and non-spatial variables (Figure 3.4).

The required maps for spatial analysis are generated in ArcGIS (V. 10.6) to demonstrate the spatial criteria. The non-spatial attributes are computed in an effect table. The assessment has been carried upon six of the identified sites.

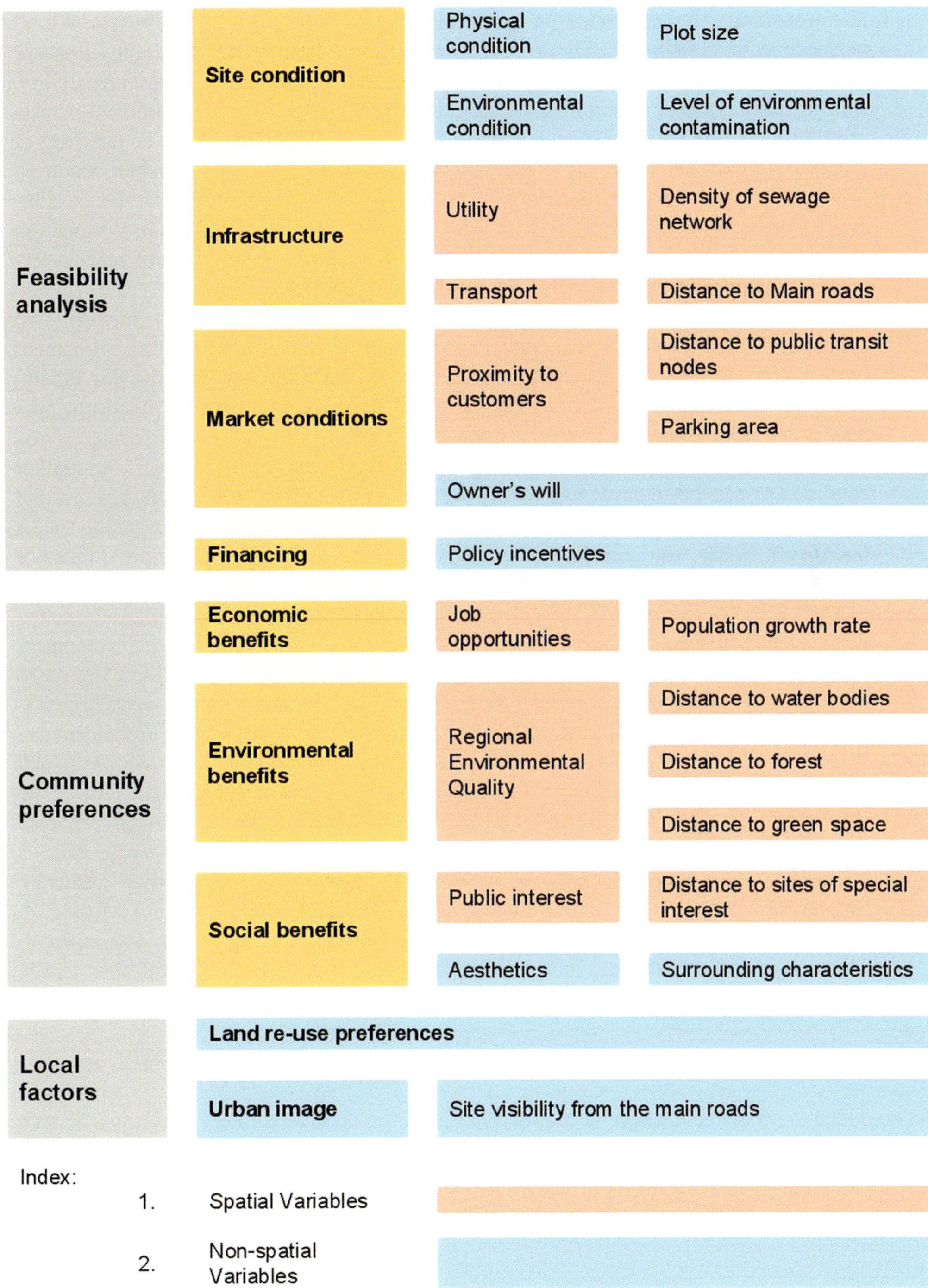

FIGURE 3.4 Criteria to assess the potential of identified brownfield sites.

3.6.1 Financial Feasibility Analysis

As discussed in the methodology section (section 3.3), there are four criteria for the feasibility analysis: site condition, infrastructure, market factors, and financing aspect.

i. Site Condition: The site condition was analyzed in a both physical and environmental perspective, as classified in Figure 3.4. To understand the physical condition, plot size was compared as it will majorly influence the cost for redevelopment and its feasibility. As per Indore Smart City Limited [ISCL], the minimum area for redevelopment parcels should be 0.2 Ha (Redevelopment, Smart City Indore, 2020). Hence, the comparison of plot size for each identified site is mentioned in Table 3.6. The environmental condition includes the level of environmental degradation as the extent and degree of contamination is always associated with time and cost of site remediation. As per the qualitative data gathered during the site visit, a qualitative classification of real or perceived contamination can be provided, as shown in Table 3.6.
ii. Infrastructure: This criterion was analyzed through utility and transport infrastructure mappings as their availability accounts for the required investment for the redevelopment process. The utility was understood through sewage infrastructure density. For Indore, the density of sewage service structure was found along the road network. Transport was understood through proximity to the major roads.
iii. Market Conditions: As discussed in the methodology section (section 3.3), the market condition was analyzed through customer proximities for a given area, its land pricing, and owner's will. While Figures 3.5a and b show the proximity of customers to public transit nodes such as bus stops and proposed metro stops, Figure 3.5c shows the proximities of sites with existing parking plots in the city. Existing residential and commercial values in Indore are shown in Figures 3.5j and k, respectively. Regarding owner's will, it was found that if a land parcel is owned by public authority, there is ease in acquiring the development rights. If the ownership does not belong to the public authority and land use rights are distributed to individuals or societies, the transfer process for development rights becomes complicated (Dair and Williams, 2006). Any resistance from one of the stakeholders can delay or cancel the proposed development on any site (Adams et al., 2001). Since the will of the landowner directly impacts both monetary and non-monetary costs of the project, the land owner can either raise the percentage or pricing in the agreement or simply refuse to cooperate (Haninger et al., 2012). This non-spatial variable is classified in Table 3.6.
iv. Financing: The financial aspect can be assessed through policy incentives attracting investment. For the city of Indore, there are options of TDR and additional FAR of 0.25 for the owners if they cooperate in the pooling of their land for any kind of development. This non-spatial variable (Figure 3.4) helped in evaluating the identified sites and is classified in Table 3.6.

3.6.2 Community Benefit Analysis

As discussed in section 3.3, community benefit analysis can be done through three aspects, such as economic, environmental, and social. The economic development can be triggered with the establishment of newer business in a vicinity. Hence, employment opportunities depend upon demographic growth rate (refer to ward-wise population density shown in Figure 3.2 and spatial development density shown in Figure 3.5i). Environmental benefit is illustrated with the distance of sites from environmentally sensitive areas/spaces to get an idea of regional environmental quality. The distance from lakes, rivers, green areas, and forest has been depicted in Figures 3.5e–h. Social benefits have been evaluated using the criteria of community imperative local public interests and urban aesthetics in a neighborhood. The map with proximity to major landmarks is shown in Figure 3.5d.

3.6.3 Local Context

As identified during data collection (discussed in section 3.5) the following local factors were considered for assessing the potential of case study sites.

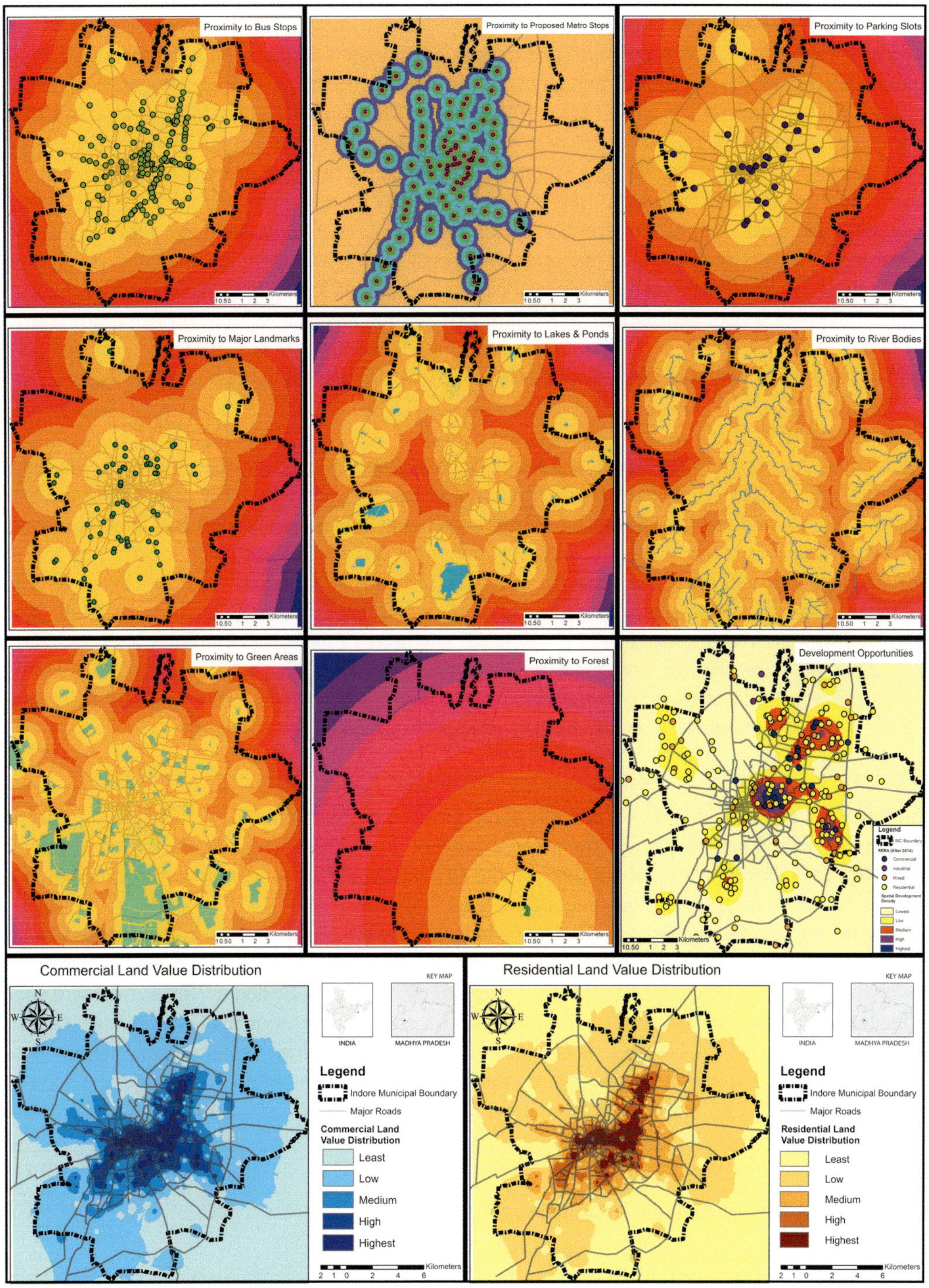

FIGURE 3.5 GIS-based proximity and isopleth analysis for spatial criteria assessment.

3.6.3.1 Land Reuse Preferences

Based upon the key interviewees (stake holders) and document analysis, a conclusion can be drawn about the prioritization of land reuse preferences of the brownfield redevelopment in Indore as recreational (mainly green and open spaces), mixed use, and residential (Indore Development Plan, 2021).

3.6.3.2 Employment in Inner-City Areas

The ever-expanding urban population, due to immigration and floating population, newly developed industrial zones of the city and IT hub have created pressure on the municipal services, facilities, and utilities (Indore Smart City ABD Master Plan, 2018). The core city areas, due to the tourism opportunities, house numerous informal sector activities. But the linear spatial growth has biased the land utilization by attracting investments at selected urban areas. These areas are enjoying the accessibility benefits of a single route BRTS system. This has resulted in higher values of land in inner-city areas and areas with better accessibility. Consequently, small manufacturing sites cannot afford the rising land costs and indefinite market requirements. This forces them to shift to areas with lower land values. However, the inner-city areas always attract population and business activities due to the higher quality of service distribution. This creates congestion issues, a serious problem in the core city of Indore. Thus, the city is in dire need to provide more job options in the inner-city areas and on the same track reduce transport complications (Indore Metro System Preliminary Project Report, 2016).

3.6.3.3 Urban Image

Urban image is indeed a key determinant for driving the brownfield redevelopment practices in Indore. The city government has invested good capital in this aspect through the ABD approach of the Smart City Mission. Additionally, Indore is frequently winning the title of the cleanest Indian city for the last four years under the Swachh Bharat Mission (launched in 2014). This can result in attracting a highly skilled population and even many enterprises to start investments in Indore. Good urban image is also an indicator of an improved standard of living in the city (Doick et.al., 2006; Dulić and Krklješ, 2015). The area targeted in this research is not only in the proximity of the main city center but it also has an incredible industrial heritage from the early 20th century. The sites are adjacent to existing and proposed rail, road, and metro transit networks. It has high visibility from prominent city squares and avenues and is surrounded by an established market from the southeast direction.

3.6.3.4 Local Policy Incentives

Interviewees at ULBs suggested that the local government does intend to redevelop underused/underutilized land parcels in city core areas to balance the rising land use demands and to limit the urban sprawl induced by greenfield redevelopment. This would also result in better economic drive with associated social and environmental benefits.

As per the Smart City Mission initiative in Indore, there are regulations for redevelopment of land parcels. It states the minimum area of the plot for redevelopment is 0.2 hectares and its ownership can be private (individual or group) or pooled from several owners or public bodies (Redevelopment, Smart City Indore, 2020). The smallest of the identified six sites covers an area of 6.19 hectares and the largest covers almost 24 hectares. It is always easier to acquire land rights if ownership is public (MoHUA, 2018). But private owners can also enjoy TDR rights or additional FAR rights, as shown in Table 3.5. There is allowance of reconstruction if the built structures are structurally weak or unsafe.

TABLE 3.5
Permissible FAR for Redevelopment Parcels

Permissible FAR for Redevelopment Parcels				
S. N.	Right of Way (RoW)	Base F.A.R.	Additional F.A.R. (50% TDR and 50% IMC)	Total permissible F.A.R.
1	30 m	1.5	1.5	3
2	24 m and 18 m	1.5	1	2.5

Source: Indore Smart City Limited (ISCL).

TABLE 3.6
Effect Table for Non-spatial Variables

Criteria	Site 1 (Indore Malwa Mill)		Site 2 (Swadeshi Mill)		Site 3 (Kalyanmal Mill)		Site 4 (Hukumchand Mill)		Site 5 (Bhandari Mill)		Site 6 (Rajkumar Mill)	
	Score	Std. Score	Score	Std. Score	Score	Std. Score	Score	Std. Score	Score	Std. Score	Score	Std. Score
Plot size (ha)	24.00	1.00	6.20	0.25	13.70	0.57	16.60	0.69	6.30	0.26	10.48	0.43
Environmental degradation	2	0.67	2	0.67	3	1.00	3	1.00	3	1.00	1	0.33
Owner's will	3	1.00	3	1.00	2	0.67	2	0.67	3	1.00	3	1.00
Policy incentive	3	1.00	2	0.67	3	1.00	3	1.00	3	1.00	3	1.00
Aesthetics	3	1.00	1	0.33	2	0.67	3	1.00	2	0.67	3	1.00
Land reuse preferences	3	1.00	3	1.00	2	0.67	3	1.00	3	1.00	3	1.00
Site visibility	3	1.00	2	0.67	2	0.67	3	1.00	3	1.00	3	1.00

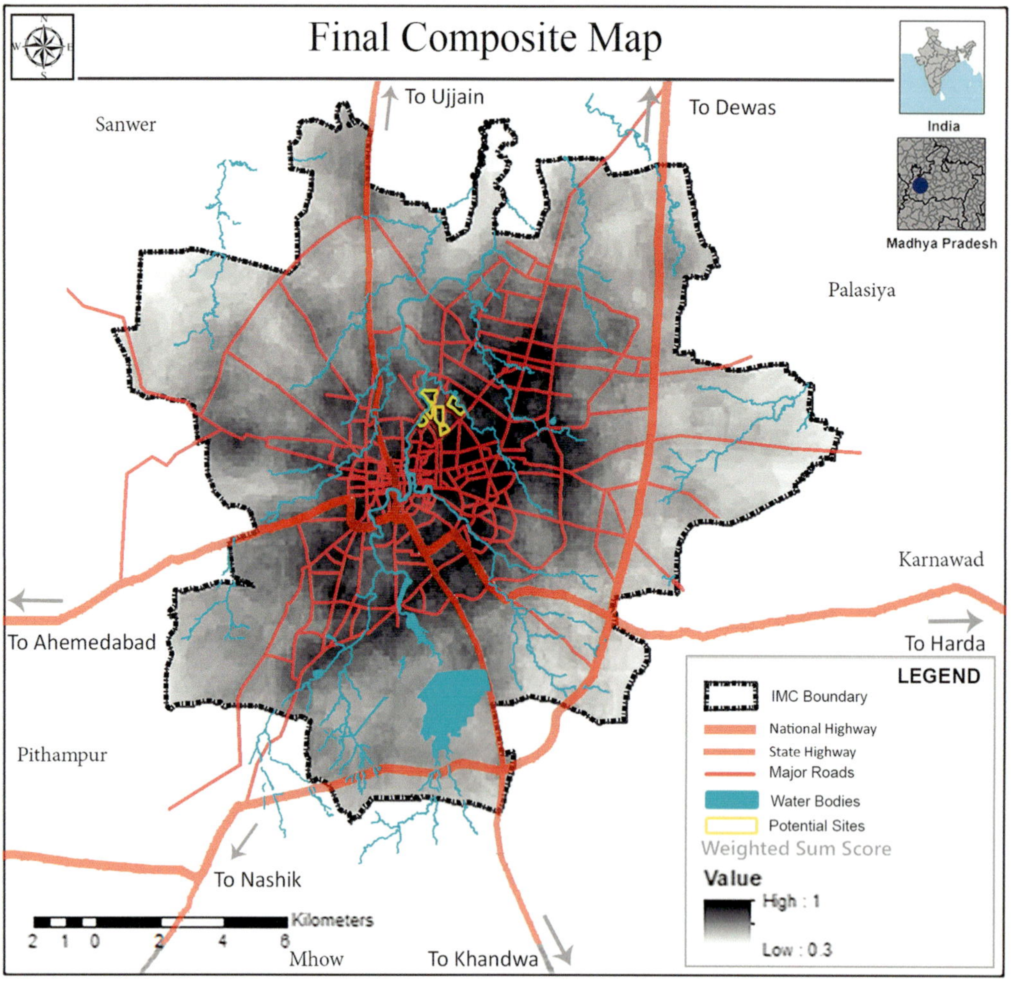

FIGURE 3.6 Map showing result of spatial analysis using weighted sum function.

3.6.4 Analyzing Spatial Variables

Analysis of spatial variables was performed in ArcGIS (V. 10.6) software. Using the function weighted sum, a result map (Figure 3.6) is generated where each spatial criterion was given equal weight, assuming each criterial has equal importance. Figure 3.6 is further used to extract individual weight for each site, as summarized in Table 3.7.

3.6.5 Analyzing Non-spatial Variables

As discussed in Figure 3.4, seven non-spatial variables were distributed among three criteria for potential assessment are considered for the potential assessment study. Table 3.6 is prepared in which each criterion had been made comparable by using the maximum scores from a 0 to 1 range bracket. Then, there is an assignment of weight by direct way assuming all the criteria have equal importance.

Finally, each of the sum values for each identified site is computed using the zoning function. To complete the overall assessment, the final value is obtained from the cumulative spatial criteria evaluation and the cumulative non-spatial criteria the through weighted sum tool, as outlined in Table 3.7.

TABLE 3.7
The Value-Based Evaluation Based on Weightage and Scoring

Weighted Sum Value	Site 1 (Indore Malwa Mill)	Site 2 (Swadeshi Mill)	Site 3 (Kalyanmal Mill)	Site 4 (Hukumchand Mill)	Site 5 (Bhandari Mill)	Site 6 (Rajkumar Mill)
Spatial analysis	0.92	0.74	0.59	0.51	0.79	0.83
Non-spatial analysis	0.95	0.65	0.75	0.91	0.85	0.82
Total	**1.87**	**1.39**	**1.34**	**1.42**	**1.64**	**1.65**

TABLE 3.8
Ranking of Identified Brownfields in Terms of Redevelopment Potential

Ranking According to Potential	Name of the Site
1	Indore Malwa Mill
2	Rajkumar Mill
3.	Bhandari Mill
4.	Hukumchand Mill
5.	Swadeshi Mill
6.	Kalyanmal Mill

According to Table 3.7, "Site 1" (Indore Malwa Mill) has the highest redevelopment potential, whereas "Site 3" (Kalyanmal Mill) has the least. "Site 1" (Indore Malwa Mill) reflects the greater plot size rationale along with the local government's preferences and policies' influence. Most of them performed relatively well in spatial aspects due to the locational advantages with the concentration of sound infrastructural services and population. "Site 4" (Hukumchand Mill) performed well in non-spatial aspects, but due to its remoteness from major roads and centric location amidst the concerned mill area, it got the least score in spatial aspects. The final ranking of the identified potential brownfield sites is mentioned in Table 3.8.

3.7 CONCLUSION

This research aims to develop a mechanism to identify and assess the potential of brownfield sites for improved redevelopment practices. To achieve the goal, a two-step mechanism is proposed using Indore of Madhya Pradesh, India, as a case study city. While the first step deals with the identification of existing brownfield sites, the second step involves assessment of their redevelopment potential. The multi-criteria evaluation (MCE) approach was adopted to perform both steps.

An exhaustive literature review and case study analysis was performed to identify criteria for analysis. Identification of brownfield sites within Indore was done by overlapping old industrial sites of Indore with the areas of high population density, established business opportunities, and good environmental quality. The major limitation observed in this stage was the unreliability and inaccessibility of required data. The most relevant database concerning the environmental conditions at an urban local level is limited to visual pollution and contamination. The integrated data center is missing as one tries to relate the underground water pollution, soil conditions, etc., at the municipal level. They are also not transformed into relevant real-time location databases such as property tax records and pollution levies. Six old and defunct textile manufacturing sites, popularly known as "mills," Kalyanmal United Mills, Swadeshi Mill, Bhandari Mill, Indore Malwa United Mill, Hukumchand Mill, and Rajkumar Mill, were identified for redevelopment potential assessment. After identification of brownfield sites, the next step was to assess redevelopment potential and prioritize. The criteria selected for assessment were financial feasibility, community benefits, and local context. Under the broad umbrella of these criteria, several spatial and non-spatial factors were considered. The spatial factors were analyzed using a weighted overlay technique in GIS and non-spatial factors were analyzed through observational survey followed by scoring. Total weight for each site was calculated by summing the value for both spatial and non-spatial factors and a rank list was prepared. "Site 1" (Indore Malwa Mill) ranked number one with the highest redevelopment potential, whereas "Site 3" (Kalyanmal Mill) ranked last with the least potential. The outcome indicates greater plot size rational along with the local government's preferences and policies influence the redevelopment potential of brownfield sites. The ranking will help the ULBs to prioritize and develop local-level strategies for brownfield redevelopment practices.

The mechanism applied in this research can certainly provide relevant information for the identification and assessment of brownfield sites for redevelopment practices. The outcome of this research suggests that there are three requirements for successful implementation of brownfield redevelopment practices: 1. a comprehensive brownfield redevelopment policy at the national level, 2. a brownfield redevelopment code at the state level, and 3. a mechanism for brownfield redevelopment at the urban local level with prioritization of redevelopment practices at such land parcels in Development Plans (DPs), Zonal Plans, and Local Area plans (LAPs). Establishment of a land bank at municipal levels is required and it can be marketed with attractive financial incentives such as TDR, additional FAR, etc.

The research can be further taken forward with application of the proposed method on other types of land parcels in other Indian cities. As each criterion can influence various stakeholders differently, a comprehensive stakeholder analysis can be conducted with the vision of a participatory planning approach.

REFERENCES

Adams, D., Disberry, A., Hutchison, N., and Munjoma, T. 2001. Ownership constraints to Brownfield redevelopment. *Environment and Planning A*, 33 (3), 453–477. 10.1068/a33200.

Adarkar, N., and Phatak, V. K. 2005. Recycling mill land: Tumultuous experience of Mumbai. Economic and Political Weekly, *40*, 5365–5368.

Beames, A., Broekx, S., Schneidewind, U., Landuyt, D., van der Meulen, M., Heijungs, R., and Seuntjens, P. 2018. Amenity proximity analysis for sustainable Brownfield redevelopment planning. *Landscape and Urban Planning*, *171*, 68–79.

Bhattacharya, S., and Rathi. S. 2015. Reconceptualising smart cities: A reference framework for India. Center for Study of Science, Technology and Policy, September, 80. www.cstep.in (last accessed on 20th April, 2021).

Coffin, S. L., and Meyer, P. B. 2002. Closing the Brownfield information gap: Practical methods for identifying Brownfields Practice Guide #3 Southeast Regional Environmental Finance Center EPA Region 4 University of Louisville. http://louisville.edu/cepm (last accessed on 20th April, 2021).

Dair, C. M. and Williams, K. 2006. Sustainable land reuse: The influence of different stakeholders in achieving sustainable Brownfield developments in England, July 2006. *Environment and Planning A*, 38(7), 1345–1366. 10.1068/a37370.

Dixon, T. (2006). Integrating sustainability into Brownfield regeneration: Rhetoric or reality? – An analysis of the UK development industry. *Journal of Property Research*, 23(3), 237–267.

D'monte, D. 2006. *Mills for Sale: The Way Ahead*. Mumbai: Marg Publications.

Doick, K. J., Sellers, G., Hutchings, T. R., and Moffat, A. J. 2006. Brownfield sites turned green: Realising sustainability in urban revival. *WIT Transactions on Ecology and the Environment*, 94, 131–140. 10.2495/BF060131. WITPress.

Dulić, O. and Krklješ, M. 2015. Brownfield Redevelopment as a Strategy for Preventing Urban Sprawl. Optimization of Architectural and Urban Planning and Design in Function of Sustainable Development in Serbia View Project Transdisciplinary Approach to Design of a Total Healing Environment, Chapter: Innovative Healthcare Systems for the 21st Century View Project. https://www.researchgate.net/publication/281651820.

Ganser, R., and Williams, K. 2007. Brownfield development: Are we using the right targets? Evidence from England and Germany. *European Planning Studies*, 15(5), 603–622.

Haninger, K. Ma, L. and Timmins, C. 2012. Estimating the impacts of brownfield remediation on housing property values. *Duke Environmental and Energy Economics Working Paper Series,* Working Paper EE 12-08.

ICMA Brownfield Redevelopment – A guidebook for local governments and communities – Second Edition, a publication of the superfund/ brownfield research institute. https://community-wealth.org/sites/clone.community-wealth.org/files/downloads/tool-ICMA-brownfields.pdf (last accessed on 15th July 2015).

Indore Development Plan. 2021. https://indore.nic.in/en/document (last accessed in 20th April 2021).

Indore Metro System Preliminary Project Report, 2016. http://www.mpmetrorail.com/files/PPR%20%20INDORE.pdf (last accessed on 20th April 2021).

Indore Smart City ABD Master Plan. 2018. Indore: Indore Smart City Development Limited. https://www.smartcityindore.org (last accessed on 20th April 2021).

Kurtović, S., Siljković, B. and Pavlović, N. 2014. Methods of identification and evaluation of brownfield sites. *International Journal of Research in Business and Social Science IJRBS, 3, p.105–120.* www.ssbfnet.com (last accessed on 20th April 2021).

Madhya Pradesh Real Estate Policy. 2019. http://mptownplan.gov.in/otherfiles/Real_Estate.Policy.pdf (last accessed on 20th April 2021).

Madhya Pradesh Town and Country Planning Act. 1973. https://mphed.nic.in/tcp-act1973.pdf.

Majumdar, M. and Sen, J. 2018. A spatio-temporal assessment of Brownfield transformation in a Metropolis: Case of Kolkata India. In Proceedings of the*Annual International Conference on Architecture and Civil Engineering*. Global Science and Technology Forum. 10.5176/2301-394X_ACE18.80.

Master, A. and Dravid, G. 2015. Ambitious mumbai project – Cluster development for large scale re-development of urban habitat. *CTBUH 2015 New York Conference*.

MoHUA, 2018. Pilot on Formulation of LocaL Area Plan (LAP) and Town PLanning Scheme (TPS) For Selected Cities. http://amrut.gov.in/upload/newsrelease/5d6f8bda8c3fd7amrutbook.pdf (last accessed on 20th April 2021).

Nallathiga, R. 2010. Redevelopment of industrial land in urban areas: opportunities and constraints. A case study of textile mill land redevelopment in Mumbai. *Theoretical and Empirical Researches in Urban Management*, 5(5 (14), 35–46.

Parlewar, P., and Fukukawa, Y. (2006). Urban regeneration of historic towns: Regeneration strategies for Pauni, India. *The Sustainability City IV: Urban Regeneration and Sustainability*, *93*, 209–228.

Patnayaka, R. 2018. Brownfield development scenario in India and prospective challenges. *International Journal of Innovation and Scientific Research*, 37. p.1-12, http://www.ijisr.issr-journals.org/. http://www.ijisr.issr-journals.org/abstract.php?article=IJISR-18-154-02121 (last accessed on 20th April 2021).

Redevelopment, Smart City Indore. 2020. *Indore Smart City Development Limited.* https://www.smartcityindore.org/redevelopment/ (last accessed on 28th May 2020).

Turvani, M., and Tonin, S. (2008). Brownfields remediation and reuse: An opportunity for urban sustainable development. In *Sustainable Development and Environmental Management* (pp. 397–411). Dordrecht: Springer.

USEPA. 2006. Revitalizing America's mills: A report on Brownfields mill projects. Washington D.C. https://www.epa.gov/sites/production/files/2015-09/documents/mill_report_110306.pdf (last accessed on 20th April 2021).

4 Religious Tourism in the Age of Commodification and Reconstruction of Heritagescapes: A Neighborhood-Based Study along the Stretch of River Hooghly, North 24 Parganas, West Bengal, India

Anu Rai and Sanjali Das
Adamas University, Jagannathpore-Barberia, Kolkata, West Bengal, India

CONTENTS

4.1 RELIGIOUS LANDSCAPE

Religious beliefs and practices transform mere space into a religious landscape that is defined as a semiotic complex system of the consecrated interaction among nature and religion (Singh, 2011). In the sphere of religion, religious landscapes incorporate myriad interactions between ritual, culture, myth, tradition, and beliefs that intervene with space and the individual (Keisteri, 2013;King, 2005). The intense interaction among space, convictions, body, and practices of varied locations often represent a visual image of the cosmic faith that easily fits into the emblematic

DOI: 10.1201/9781003126195-5

portrayal of the mythology, for instance, in the Indian context, the religious landscape is often defined as a sacredscape practicing sacrality since time immemorial (Singh, 2011). These sacredscapes are not the imaginary product of the mind; it is the visual representation of the landscapes of faith and belief—where space is reconstructed and transformed into a place of sacred power by the process of sacralization and ritualization (Singh, 2011). It is strongly believed that structurally, each religious landscape follows a unique spatial patterning and cosmic ordering (Singh, 2009). As a medium of contact between human belief and divine spirit (Mother Nature), religious landscapes are present in various forms at different places. It represents the visual image of the spatial manifestation that is widely accepted, respected, and recognized among folk tradition where the increasing sense of making social identity high, has encouraged the human quest to preserve their belief in forms of symbolic expressions (Singh and Rana, 2002).

Each of these landscapes, representing spatial ordering of faith, is valuable and meaningful for its visitors. The individual landscape has its imprints that carry a unique locational, historical, cultural, architectural, and economic value. For neighborhood communities, it offers a tool to develop social experiences, community relations, and cultural exchanges. With time, it becomes a cultural heritage for its followers that connects them with the feeling of similar history and culture. These cultural landscapes are often considered a social process rather than a physical object (Mydland and Grahn, 2011) that evolved with interaction among community participation and cultural knowledge (Maitseo and Kanduza, 2008). This intensive interaction of space, body, and practices constitutes the spatial arena where religions compete for members and resources (Alberto, 2010) and dynamically attempt to change the morphology of the places. Tandon and Sehgal (2017) explained how the faithscapes of the city Mathura (city in Uttar Pradesh, India) have changed the morphology and economy of the city. The city of Banaras (Uttar Pradesh, India) and its spatial geometry following cosmic ordering make it one of the holiest sacredscapes of the world (Singh, 2002). Similarly, the city of Allahabad (city in Uttar Pradesh, India) rapidly changed due to intensive religious activity (Chadha and Onkar, 2016). The dominance of religious activity also intervened in the urban planning of the city (Chadha and Onkar, 2016). Istanbul in Turkey (Egresi and Kara, 2016), Israel (Collins-Kreiner and Kliot, 2000), Mecca (Saudi Arabia), Lhasa (Tibet), Jerusalem (Israel), and many others represent the spatial arrangements of the city following the symbolic expression in divine context.

4.2 RELIGIOUS TOURISM AND ECONOMY

Spatial association and arrangements of cosmic forces in the form of the archetypal connotations creating sacred places are of long interest in the tourism economy (Stark, 2004). It is associated with the craving for peace, joy, and salvation, which are at the very core nature of human beings, as these are not sold in the materialistic market, have forced individuals to find solutions in supernatural forces (Stark, 2004). The result is that on a global scale, religious tourism constitutes a significant proportion of the global tourism economy as the UN World Tourism Organization (UNWTO) estimates that approximately 300 to 330 million tourists travel across the religious sites of the world every year (UNWTO, 2014). Tourism and religion together form the spatial market of faith where religions encourage social competition and attempt to include more members and resources (Singh, 2009; Alberto, 2010). This social competition is driven by the forces of the tourism economy, which further enhances the socio-cultural aspects of neighborhood community (Stark, 2004). On a neighborhood scale, such religious places are not only reconstructing the morphology of the landscape but creating tourism interest of national and international significance (Tandon and Sehgal, 2017; Chadha and Onkar, 2016).

Religious tourism and cultural value have long tied to history, where religious sites host more tourists who have a keen interest in the cultural values of such sites (Petrillo, 2003; Collins-Kreiner and Kliot, 2000). Tourism helps in the protection of the religious structures and offers a wide horizon of employment and job opportunities to neighborhood communities either in the type of organizations like lodgings, eateries, or gift shops, etc (Olsen, 2003; Shackley, 2006; Vukonic, 1998). Regular visitation of the sacred sites also develops the infrastructure of the region (Jackowski and Smith, 1992) and continually modified and altered by the market forces of demand and supply. Religious spaces are perceived as a market of exchange of a wide range of goods and services in terms of explanations of life and supernatural rewards (Stark, 2004). The rising number of visitors to religious sites is often associated with the commoditization of the faith (Egresi and Kara, 2016; Wall and Mathieson, 2006) controlled by market forces of promotion, marketization, and commercialization. The evolutions of the religious-tourism sites (Hughes, Bond, and Ballantyne, 2013) are the result of the interactions among economic, political, social, and cultural forces. Commercialization often encourages the inclusion of value-added tourism essence to the particular site among similar or near similar sites of current or past religious significance. Despite having common culture, heritage, history, and architecture, not all religious sites evolve as religious tourism attractions. Various political, cultural, economic, and social forces interact differently with various religious spaces that produce different levels of tourism interests while reshaping the spatial landscape and reconstructing spatial behavior more in favor of the tourism economy.

This chapter attempts to explore the evolution of religious tourism centering on the Dakshineswar Temple, one of the largest Hindu temples widely acknowledged as the center of international interest and national significance for India. The study will attempt to highlight the evolution of the Dakshineswar Temple as the center of international interest more ahead than its contemporary temples sharing similar or near similar heritage, history, and culture. It is found that in the age of commoditization, forces of globalization reshape religious marketplaces and alter the value of heritagescapes. The significance of religious tourism in reshaping the spatial landscape and reconstructing spatial behavior is also remarkable.

4.3 RESEARCH DESIGN AND METHODOLOGY

4.3.1 Framework

Any religious landscape is the product of religious practices and constitutes an intricate part of the daily social livelihood (Zhang and Wei, 2017). Over the years, with the increasing influence of religious economy and religious tourism (Bhuiyan et al., 2011), religious buildings and their surroundings often undergo conversion to multifunctional spaces, offering a multitude of services to the neighborhood community and its visitors. However, it is difficult to draw clear-cut boundaries delineating religious landscapes among fast-growing population clusters. especially in developing countries; one can easily understand how religious tourism actively modifies the landscape of the sacred sites of interest. The major research objective of this chapter is to draw attention to the significance of religious tourism and the promotion of faith in reshaping the spatial landscape and spatial behavior surrounding a religious building, showcasing sharp differences from its contemporary counterparts sharing similar or near similar heritage, history, and culture. The study adopts a case study approach and selects one among the largest Hindu temple of Dakhineshwar at Kolkata, situated at the eastern bank of River Hooghly.

4.3.2 Site Selection and Data Collection

To attain the objective of the study, we have adopted multi-purposive random sampling techniques to select equivalent sites for the detailed comparative assessment. In the first stage of the study, ancient maps of River Hooghly, prepared by the deputy surveyor general of India in 1856 and G.M. Das & D. N. Mazumdar in 1925,[1] were obtained from the National Library, Kolkata, India, and used to demarcate the religious buildings with similar or near similar historical significance. In total, 133 religious sites have been identified and the spatial composition of each site recorded, as shown in Table 4.1. We have also conducted several pilot-field studies from December 2017 to June 2018 for spatial data collection. In the second phase, detailed field observation and multiple interactions with the neighborhood community helped us to identify the major religious buildings with emotional value among the local community. Accordingly, all sites were visited and common sites with historical significance on the temporal scale were demarcated following experts' opinions. In terms of the elements sharing common spatial composition, detailed field observation, Google imagery analysis, and intensive interviews are included in the study. Adopting a deductive approach, and after multiple field visits, a detailed review of existing literature and the in-depth interviews of the experts from the religious community, temple management trusts, academia, and tourism board, in total 10 (ten) religious buildings (among 133 sites), Dakshineswar Kaali temple, Shyamnagar Mulajore Temple, Annapurna Temple, 26 Shiva Temple Ghats, 12 Temples, Bazarpara Ghats, Giribala Temple, Char Mandir, Joymitra Kalibari, and Alambazar Ghats, as shown in Figure. 4.1, were found suitable for the present study. These religious buildings share common locational, historical, and architectural similarities and are found most suitable for the comparative study. The detailed characteristics are further discussed in this chapter.

A semi-structured face-to-face questionnaire survey of tourists and visitors has been conducted from August 2018 to January 2019. The aim is to identify crucial factors adding tourism essence to the particular site among similar or near similar sites of current or past religious significance. From ten selected sites, in total 298 tourists have been surveyed, with 252 usable responses (84.57% usable response rate). There was no demographic control on the sample selection of the tourists and the tourists were surveyed on a random basis. Acknowledging the significance and impact on Dakhineswar Temple noted during the pilot study, a neighborhood-based case study was adopted to map the impact of religious tourism on the spatial economy. It is imperative to note here that Dakhineswar Kaali Temple is not among the great 51 Shakti Peethas, great mythological attractions of India (Singh, 2009); however, over time it has successfully been able to draw global attention and emerged as the center of the international repute among the religious tourism community visiting Kolkata and India. At the neighborhood scale, a detailed survey of the local community comprising households, lodgings, eateries, gift shops, etc. surrounding the selected site has been conducted. Site selection for household, market, and hotel survey is based on an areal stratified random sampling technique centering the selected site within the distance of 1,000 meters. To understand the crucial factors affecting the development and growth of specific religious buildings than others, a focus group survey has been conducted and views of six experts including members from the academia, religious community, and tourism industry have been collected, following Saaty's approach of pair-wise comparison (Saaty, 1992; Saaty and Vargas, 2001).

4.3.3 Measurement

The detailed methodology implied in this study is shown in Figure 4.2. We have used a questionnaire survey and detailed field observation for this study. Once the survey is completed with the given time constraint, the basic demographic data including gender, age, education, and occupation have been extracted from the respondents' group. The respondent community consists of two groups: guest community of tourists or visitors who visit religious sites and host community, rather dependent community, whose livelihood is partially or completely dependent on the religious economy of the selected site(s). The host community includes the household, eateries, gift shops, or staff and members of the stakeholder group engaged with the religious site and its surroundings. Most motivating factors affecting tourism or visitors' demand to visit particular religious sites, sources of first-hand information, attractions, and site perceptions were commonly collected information from the guest community. From the host community, the responses were collected mainly on the attitude towards the cost and benefit of religious tourism associated with the site and their rate of dependency and involvement with the tourism economy of the particular

TABLE 4.1
Spatial Composition of Ghats along the River Hooghly, North 24 Parganas, India

Name of the Ghats	Function					Spatial Association					Architecture of Associated Religious Building						Connectivity			
	Religious	Funerary Sites	Tourism and Recreation	Commercial	Historical	Religious Building	Residential Zone	Recreational Park	Market	Historical Buildings	Nine Spire Temple	Temple Facing Ghat	Square Shaped	Ring Shaped	Shakti Temple	Shiva Temple	Religious Path	Major Urban Road	Residential Streets	Ferry Service
1. Rani Rasmoni Ghat	*		*			*		*	*			*							*	
2. Mukheree Para Ghat	*						*												*	
3. Bakultala Ghat	*						*												*	
4. Nigamananda Ghat	*		*			*						*	*					*		
5. Bisaran Ghat	*																	*		
6. Burning Ghat (Halisahar)	*	*																*		
7. Dunlop Ghat				*														*		*
8. Ramprasad Ghat	*		*					*	*								*	*		
9. Bandha Ghat	*																	*		
10. Baidyapara Ghat	*					*						*				*		*		
11. Sidhyeswari Ghat	*					*		*				*		*	*			*		
12. Shyamasundari Ghat	*					*						*	*		*			*		
13. Sadhu Ghat	*					*						*	*			*		*		
14. Kona Ghat	*					*						*	*			*		*		
15. Bichuli Ghat																		*		*
16. Chandni Ghat	*		*				*	*											*	
17. Ramghat	*	*				*						*	*			*			*	
18. Chai Ghat																				*
19. Goalapara Ghat	*		*				*	*											*	
20. Banerjee Para Ghat	*						*												*	
21. Laxmimaster Ghat	*						*												*	
22. Loha Ghat	*																		*	
23. Ferry Ghat																				*
24. Mokreshwar Ghat	*						*	*											*	
25. Bhulu Babu Ghat	*																		*	
26. Muktapur Ghat	*	*					*												*	
27. Khetramistri Ghat	*						*												*	
28. Balaram Sarkar Ghat	*					*	*						*		*				*	
29. Meye Ghat	*						*											*		
30. Buno Ghat	*						*											*		
31. Badha Ghat	*																	*		
32. Bakultala Ghat	*																		*	
33. Rupdas Babu Ghat	*						*												*	
34. Rajkrishna Ghat	*					*	*					*							*	

(Continued)

TABLE 4.1 (Continued)

Spatial Composition of Ghats along the River Hooghly, North 24 Parganas, India

Name of the Ghats	Function					Spatial Association					Architecture of Associated Religious Building						Connectivity			
	Religious	Funerary Sites	Tourism and Recreation	Commercial	Historical	Religious Building	Residential Zone	Recreational Park	Market	Historical Buildings	Nine Spire Temple	Temple Facing Ghat	Square Shaped	Ring Shaped	Shakti Temple	Shiva Temple	Religious Path	Major Urban Road	Residential Streets	Ferry Service
35. Clerk Ghat	*						*											*		
36. Jagaddal Ferry Ghat																			*	*
37. Panchanan Ghat	*					*	*						*			*			*	
38. Nana Baba Ghat	*						*												*	
39. Mulajore Ghat	*		*			*			*		*	*			*		*		*	
40. Ferry Ghat							*												*	*
41. School Ghat	*						*												*	
42. Ratneswar Ghat	*	*				*										*			*	
43. Kangali Ghat																			*	*
44. Babu Ghat																			*	*
45. Garulia Ghat	*																		*	
46. Debitala Ghat	*	*					*												*	
47. Khudiram Basu Ghat							*												*	*
48. Gazi Ghat	*	*				*						*	*						*	
49. Bazar Ghat	*						*	*											*	
50. Biswas Ghat	*					*	*					*	*						*	
51. Mondal Ghat	*						*			*									*	
52. Kali Ghat	*						*												*	
53. Nawabganj Ghat	*	*																	*	
54. Roybagan Ghat	*						*												*	
55. Shitalatala Ghat	*					*	*					*	*						*	
56. Dey Para Ghat	*						*												*	
57. Du Poisa Ghat																			*	*
58. Ghatakpara Ghat	*						*												*	
59. Daspara Ghat	*						*												*	
60. Burning Ghat (Barrackpore)	*	*																	*	
61. Char Poisa Ghat							*												*	*
62. Bali Ghat	*						*												*	
63. GolaGhat					*		*												*	
64. Dhobi Ghat							*												*	*
65. Kusum Ghat	*					*				*		*		*					*	
66. Flagstaff Ghat			*		*			*											*	
67. Gandhi Ghat			*		*			*											*	
68. Rani Rasmoni Ghat	*		*			*					*	*			*				*	
69. Baranasi Ghosh Ghat	*					*	*					*	*						*	
	*	*																	*	

70. Burning Ghat (Titagarh)															
71. Laxmi Ghat				*	*		*		*	*					*
72. Bir Ghat	*			*	*				*				*		*
73. Raskhola Ghat	*			*	*				*		*				*
74. Nathu pal Ghat	*	*													*
75. Shiromoni Ghat	*		*		*										*
76. Kumorpara Ghat	*				*										*
77. R. Ghosh Ghat	*		*		*										*
78. Laxminarayan Ghat	*			*	*				*	*					*
79. Panchanan Ghat	*				*			*							*
80. N. Dutta Ghat	*				*									*	
81. ManasaTala Ghat	*				*									*	
82. Biharilal Pain Ghat	*				*									*	
83. Kasharipara Ghat	*				*									*	
84. I. Chatterjee Ghat	*				*									*	
85. Kedar Nag Ghat	*				*									*	
86. Haridas Ghat	*				*									*	
87. T. Pramanik Ghat	*				*									*	
88. Thakurbari Ghat	*				*									*	
89. Iswar Suri Ghat	*				*									*	
90. Dutta Ghat	*			*	*				*				*	*	
91. Tranbabu Ghat	*			*	*				*			*	*	*	
92. Gobinda home Ghat	*							*						*	
93. Sadhuka Ghat	*				*									*	
94. Da Ghat	*			*	*				*				*	*	
95. Sen Ghat	*				*				*					*	
96. Sri Chaitanya Ghat	*				*				*					*	
97. Ramdas Ghat	*				*									*	
98. Ferry Ghat														*	*
99. Bazar para Ghat	*			*	*				*				*	*	
100. Burning Ghat (Panihati)	*	*												*	
1001. Madan Bose Ghat	*				*									*	
102. Mallik Ghat	*				*									*	
103. Giribala Ghat	*			*	*				*					*	
104. Fultala Ghat	*				*									*	
105. Dumurtala Ghat	*				*									*	
106. Piyari Ghat	*				*									*	
107. Malapara Ghat	*				*									*	
108. Pituri Ghat	*	*				*								*	
109. Ferry Ghat														*	*
110. Burning Ghat (Kamarhati)	*	*							*				*	*	
111. D.D. Mondal Ghat	*				*									*	
112. Ferry Ghat							*							*	*
113. Jogoda Math Ghat	*							*						*	

(*Continued*)

TABLE 4.1 (Continued)

Spatial Composition of Ghats along the River Hooghly, North 24 Parganas, India

Name of the Ghats	Function					Spatial Association					Architecture of Associated Religious Building						Connectivity			
	Religious	Funerary Sites	Tourism and Recreation	Commercial	Historical	Religious Building	Residential Zone	Recreational Park	Market	Historical Buildings	Nine Spire Temple	Temple Facing Ghat	Square Shaped	Ring Shaped	Shakti Temple	Shiva Temple	Religious Path	Major Urban Road	Residential Streets	Ferry Service
114. Dakshineswar Ghat	*		*			*					*	*			*	*	*	*		
115. Shibtala Ghat	*						*											*		
116. Bhatar Ghat	*						*											*		
117. Bakultala Ghat	*						*											*		
118. Kalikrishna Ghat	*				*		*			*								*		
119. Govt Quarter Ghat	*						*											*		
120. Shanti Napit Ghat	*						*											*		
121. R. Ghosh Ghat	*					*	*					*				*		*		
122. Kolvin Ghat	*						*											*		
123. Burning Ghat (Baranagar)		*					*											*		
124. Chaitanya Ghat	*				*													*		
125. Ekmandir Ghat	*					*	*					*				*		*		
126. Joymitra Kali Ghat	*					*	*				*	*			*			*		
127. Kuti Ghat	*						*											*	*	
128. Munsibabu Ghat	*						*											*		
129. G. Mukherjee Ghat	*				*		*											*		
130. Snan Ghat	*																	*		
131. Sukdev Ghat	*						*											*		
132. Shila Ghat	*						*											*		
133. Satidaha Ghat	*				*												*			

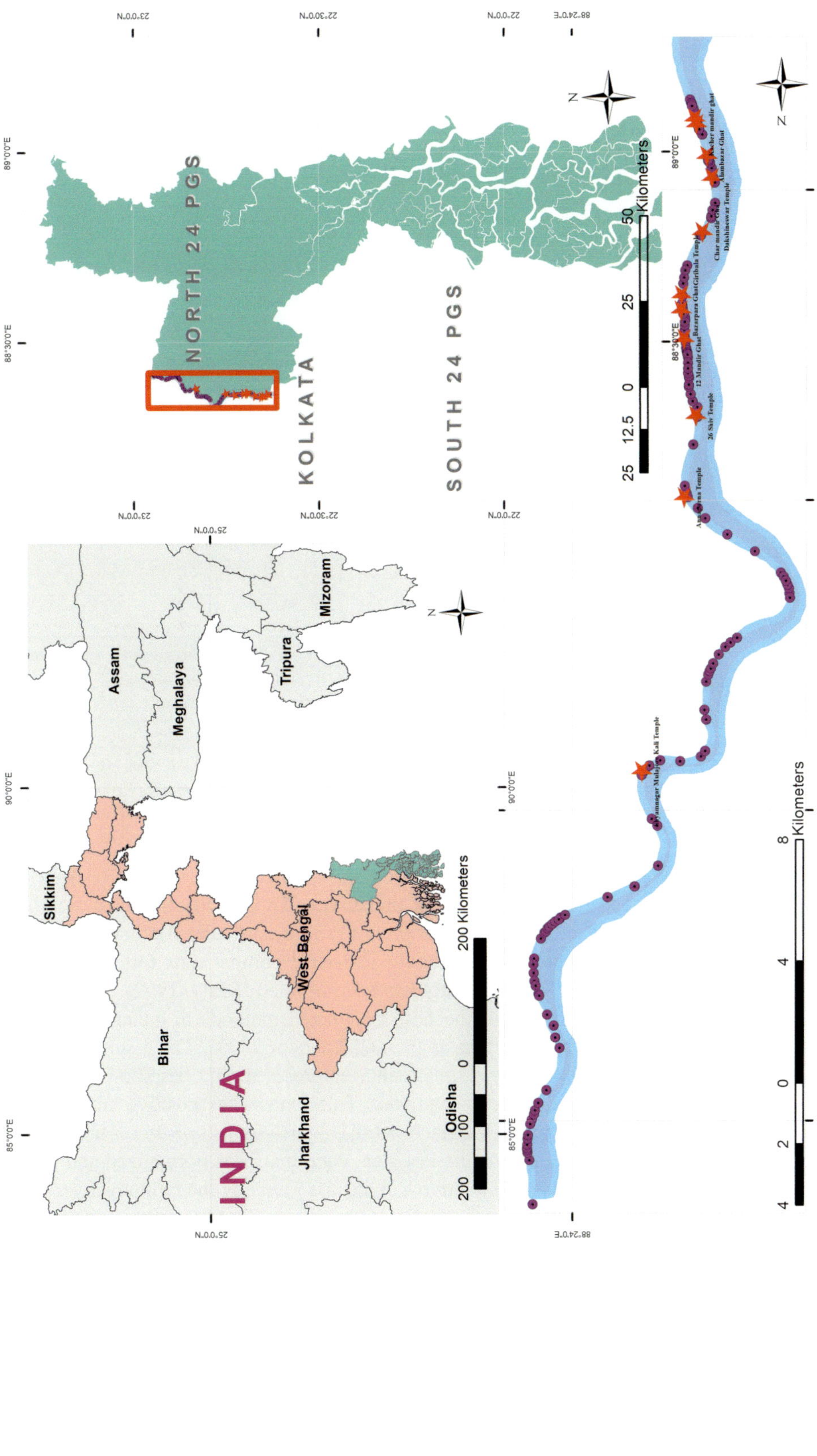

FIGURE 4.1 The sites of interest along the western boundary of North 24 Parganas.

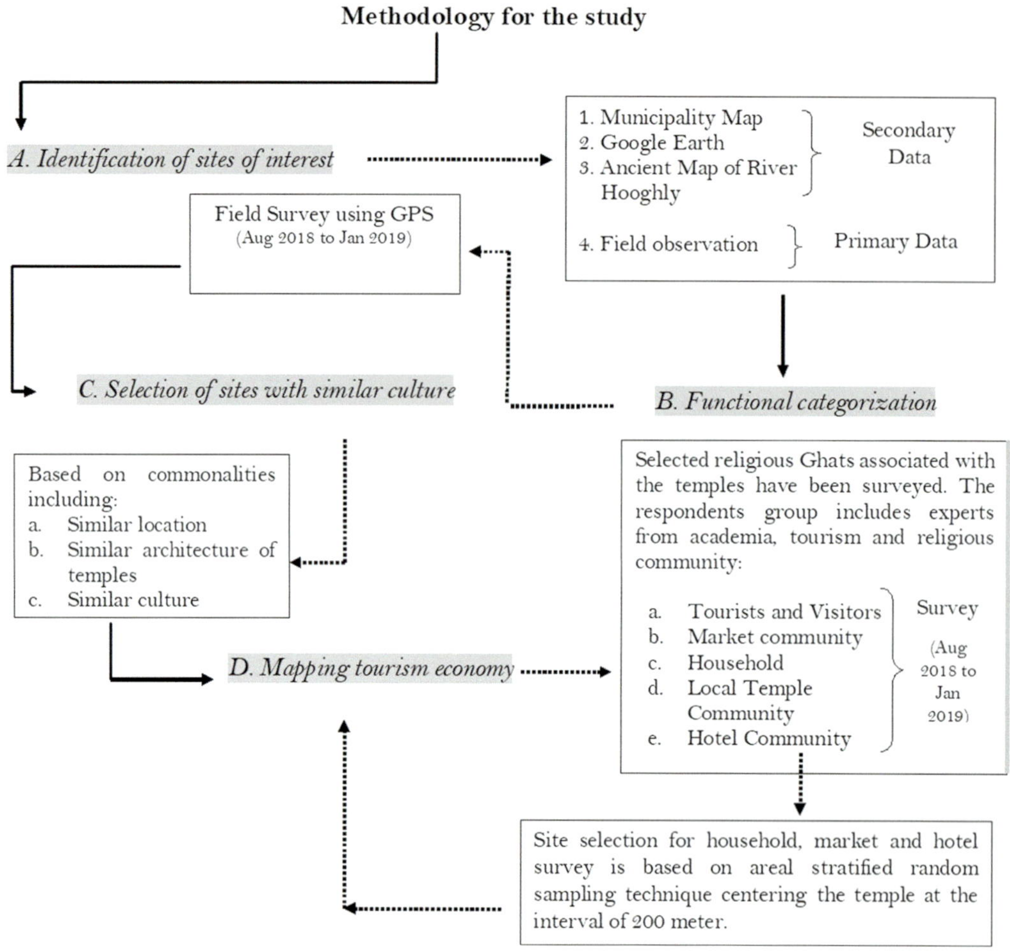

FIGURE 4.2 Schematic diagram showing methodology adopted to achieve the objectives of the study.

site of interest. The basic tools of geographical information science and statistical packages for social sciences are employed to draw the results of the survey. To quantify the most significant factors affecting the evolution of religious tourism economy at a particular destination, the analytical hierarchy process (AHP) approach of multiple pair-wise comparisons following relative scale of importance[2] as proposed by Thomas Saaty has been implied (Saaty, 1992). Imperative to note here, AHP weighting criteria is one of the best-recognized methods to quantify intangible judgments (Saaty and Kearns, 1985; Wickramasinghe and Takano, 2009). The result of the pair-wise comparison matrices can be shown by a square and reciprocal matrix based on the mean of experts' opinions for each pair of comparison matrices. This matrix has positive entries everywhere and satisfies the reciprocal property (Matrix A = (aij), aij = wi/wj, i, j = 1, … .n where w = relative weight of the criteria, aji = 1/aij). At the last step, each matrix is normalized and relative weights (priority scores) are calculated. The relative weights are given by the right eigenvector (w) corresponding to the largest eigenvalue (λmax as Aw = λmax. w). To test whether the pairwise comparisons or judgments are consistent (ajk = aik/aij, i,j,k = 1, … .n), the consistency analysis is performed. The final consistency ratio (CR) decides the consistency among the judgments of experts. It is calculated as the ratio of the consistency index (CI) and randon index for a given number of variables/factors (RIn) as conceptualized by Vargas (1982). The number 0.10 is the accepted limit for CR, if it is more the judgment matrix is inconsistent and needs reassessments.

Due to financial and time constraints, the search for sites for this study is limited to the western administrative boundary of the North 24 Parganas, forming an approximately 100-kilometer stretch along the River Hooghly. It flows along the western border of the district North 24 Parganas and creating imprints of its purity since time immemorial. From bath to transport, economy to worship, waste disposal to scenic beauty, the Hooghly River is the salvation for the local community.

4.4 RIVERFRONT GHATS PRACTICING HERITAGE

River Hooghly, a distributary of River Ganges in West Bengal, forming the western boundary of the district North 24 Parganas popularly known as "Ma Ganga" (The Mother Ganges) represents iconic significance on the land of 966 million Hindu. As the lifeline of the territory of India, River Ganges serves the need of millions and purifies the souls of billions. In search of the sites, we have visited about 133 holy sites or "ghats" along the 100-kilometer stretch of River Hooghly. Etymologically, it is believed that the word "ghat" has its origin in the Sanskrit word "Ghatta," meaning a series of stairways leading down to a river or water body. Being a profoundly refined and impressive example of South Asian architecture, ghats represent significant spiritual centers and places of human gatherings (Samant, 2004). Similar to other studies (Chadha and Onkar, 2016; Samant, 2004; Singh, 2002) the present study also observes the auspicious role of a ghat as a symbolic expression of strong Hindu values and beliefs. The ghats are an integral part of the lives of the neighborhood community and support a multitude of activities including religious, social, commercial, as well as domestic activities as listed in Table 4.1. In total, 113 ghats (85% of the total number, N = 133) exhibit their association with religious activities. Most of the ghats are used as an auspicious venue for the execution of religious and social ceremonies including weddings, fertility rites, and funeral ceremonies to name a few. During religious fairs and festivals, these ghats attract a large number of tourists and visitors. Some ghats are used for tourism and re-creational purpose throughout the year. Among 113 ghats associated with religious activities, 38 ghats are identified with their spatial association with the buildings of religious and historical significance. Most of the buildings are used for religious activities and are spatially built on the ghats following cosmic, geographical, and metaphysical orientations based on Hindu mythology and belief. For instance, most of the temples have domes, and the shikhara (a spire on a Hindu temple) of the temple rises to meet the sky, as captured in Figure 4.3.

The larger temples have big premises while smaller ones usually consist of a single cell structure. Temples are usually square and have ring-shaped geometry and generally face in the direction of a river that is well marked in Figure 4.4. A unique association of the ghats with the Hindu God and Goddess "Shiva" and "Shakti" is observed. In Hinduism, the Shiva symbolizes consciousness and masculine power while energy is symbolized as feminine power or Shakti. Four ghats, Mulajore Ghat, Rani Rasmoni Ghat, Dakshineswar Ghat, and Joymitra Kalibari Ghat, have similar architectural similarities in their association with the nine-spire temple. However, among all major religious ghats, Dakshineswar Ghat, on which the Dakshineswar Kali Temple is built, is popularly known as the favorite destination among religious tourists and pilgrims of India and abroad. Field investigations reveal that on average 35,000 devotees visit the temple per day while the number reaches up to 200,000 on auspicious occasions like New Year, Durga Puja, Diwali, etc., as captured in Figure 4.5. Such a huge inflow of tourists and visitors to the temple has actively altered the spatial morphology and economy of the neighborhood community surrounding the temple premises.

FIGURE 4.3 Temples with domes and shikharas – unique hindu architecture (Picture Courtesy: Sanjali Das, January, 2019).

FIGURE 4.4 Common geometrical orientation of the temples facing riverfront ghats (Google Earth, 2019).

4.5 HERITAGESCAPES – TALE OF COMMON HISTORY, PRACTICES, AND CULTURE

Along the western boundary of North 24 Parganas, following the holy stretch of River Hooghly or Ganges, our study has identified religious buildings of interest, sharing similar or near similar religious-cultural values comparable to the Dakshineswar Temple. With different stories of the current situation, historically, archeologically, and culturally they are contemporary to the Dakshineswar Temple. Namely, the Shyamnagar Mulajore Temple (CE 1820), Annapurna Temple (CE 1875), 26 Shiva Temple Ghats (CE 1920), 12 Temple (CE 1883), Bazarpara Ghats (CE 1950), Giribala Temple (CE 1852), Char Mandir (CE 1965), Joymitra Kalibari (CE 1835), and Alambazar Ghats (CE 1847), as shown in Figure 4.6, have been established during the same time scale as that of the Dakshineswar Temple (CE 1856). A few temples, Shyamnagar Kali Temples, Alambazar Temple, Joymitra Kalibari, and Giribala Temple, were older than Rani Rashmoni's Dakshineswar Kali Temple.

These temples are uniquely associated with the Hindu God and Goddess "Shiva" and "Shakti," symbolizing consciousness and energy share common beliefs and practices with the Dakshineswar Temple. The 26 Shiva temple, 12 Temple Ghat, Bazarpara Temple Ghat, Giribala Temple, Char Mandir Ghat, Alambazar Ghat were observed with its association with the Shiva while Shyamnagar

FIGURE 4.5 Visitors quest at Dakshineswar Temple.

(Picture Courtesy: Sanjali Das, Jan 01 2019 and Google Earth Pro 2019)

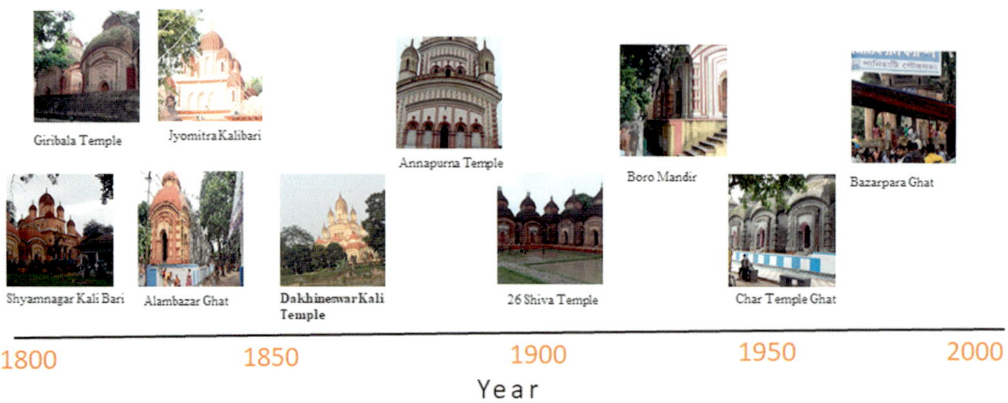

FIGURE 4.6 Estimated year of foundation of the temples along the stretch of River Hooghly.

Mulazore Kali Temple, Annapurna Temple, Joymitra Kali Bari, and Dakshineswar Kali Temple are associated with the worship of fierce and passionate derivation of energy, Goddess Kali. Along with the common historical and cultural similarities, these temples also exhibit common locational characteristics, a significant element of religious tourism. All of these temples are located along the stretch of River Hooghly, typically associated with the riverfront ghats shown in Figure 4.7.

Acknowledging the significance of ghats in Hinduism (Kutluturk, 2013), the common orientation of these buildings is inclined towards the westward riverfront. Analysis of the built environment exhibits the unique association of the temples along with Hindu mythology and belief. Domes and shikhara of the temples rising to meet the sky are common features. The belief is to represent the profound relationship of Hindu architecture with the abode of the supernatural

FIGURE 4.7 Locational similarities.

(Source: Google Earth, 2019).

power. The temples worshipping Goddess Kali uniquely follow the nine-spire Bengal architecture. The nine-spire architecture of temples represents the symbol of universal power and balance in Hinduism (Chaudhary, 2017). It is believed that Goddess Durga or Shakti is described in nine forms, parallel to eight directions and at the center she protects the cosmic territory (Amazzone, 2010). The number 9 (nine) is often compared with the number of planets in Hindu mythology, influencing the Earth and its mankind. The spatial-geometrical arrangements of the nine-spire temples are influenced by the nine derivations of Goddess Durga, exhibiting the three layers of spire crossing at the cardinal points, each of one representing the individual form of Shakti (Das, 2018). Annapurna Temple of Barrackpore is the identical twin of the famous Dakshineswar Temple (Das, 2018). It was established only 20 years after the one at Dakshineswar by the Rani Rasmoni's youngest daughter, Jagadamba, as illustrated in Figure 4.8. It was inaugurated on April 12, 1875, in the presence of the great Hindu religious leader Swami Ramkrishna Paramhansa. The Annapurna Temple is taller than the Dakshineswar Temple, where the idol of Goddess Kali is made of gold. The Annapurna Temple has only six Shiv temples compared to the 12 at Dakshineswar.

Similarly, another temple, Shyamnagar Mulajor Kalibari, was established around 200 years ago before the Dakshineswar Kali Temple. Relatives of Nobel Laureate Rabindranath Tagore set up the temple beside River Hooghly. Architecturally, Shyamnagar Mulajor Kalibari was also constructed following the nine-spire (Navaratna) architecture and associated with the eight-roofed (aatchala) Shiva temple. Joymitra Kalibari is located on the eastern bank of River Hooghly near Baranagar,

FIGURE 4.8 Architectural similarities.

(Source: Google Earth 2019; Picture Courtesy: Sanjali Das 2019).

established in 1848 by Jayram Mitra. It is also a nine-spired temple with 12 shrines dedicated to Shiva. The religious buildings associated with the worship of Shiva also exhibit the spatio-geometrical structure following the unique Bengal architecture. On the eastern bank of River Hooghly at Khardah, 26 Shiva temples were built with 100,000 Shivalinga. All of these temples are situated on the bank of the sacred River Hooghly, among them, five temples are riverfront facing, and the rest of the 21 arranged as a rectangle. Acknowledging the significance of its unique architecture representing the image of the Gaur period (medieval period of Bengal C.E.

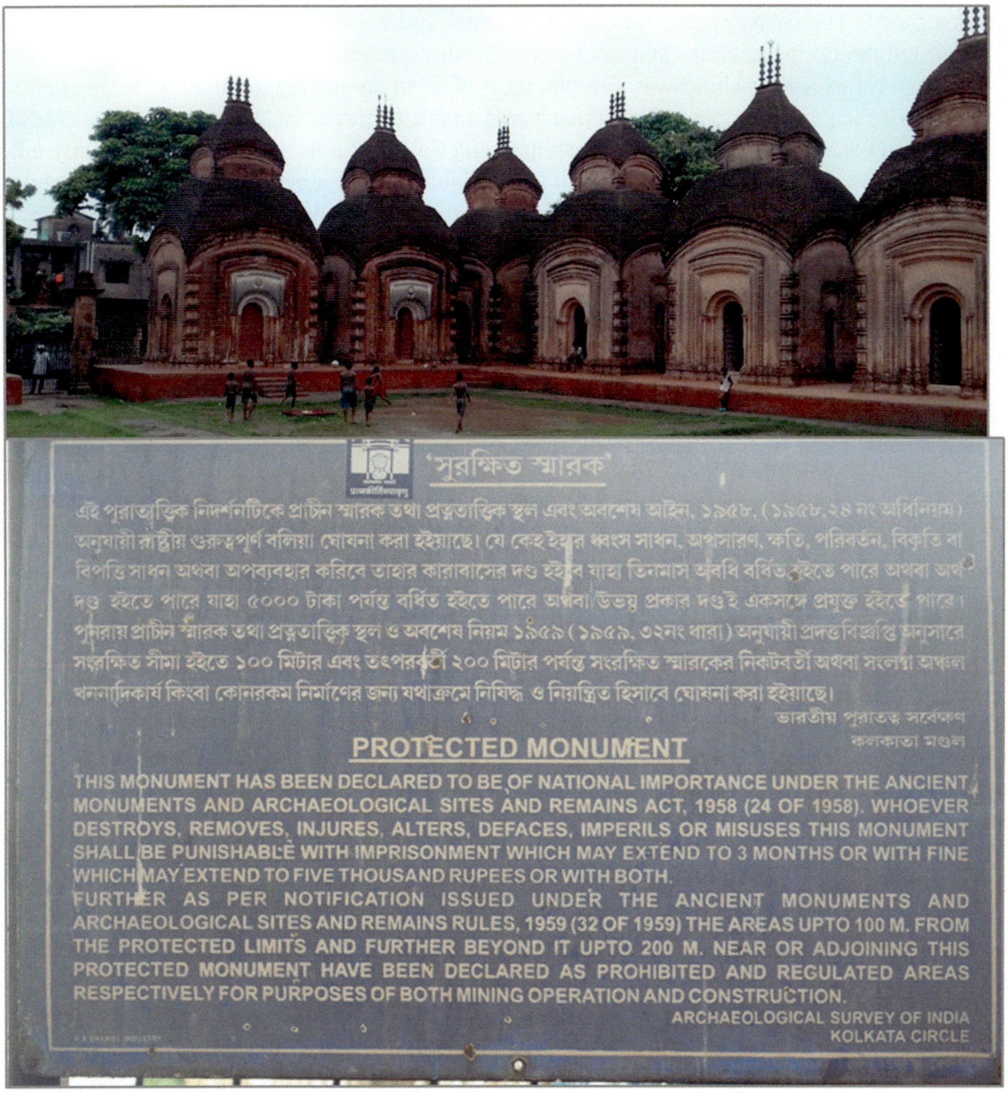

FIGURE 4.9 26 Shiva Temple, a protected monument by Anthropological Survey of India.

(Picture Courtesy: Sanjali Das 2019)

1450–1565), the Archaeological Survey of India (ASI) has declared the 26 Shiva temple to be of national importance under the Ancient Monument and Archaeological Sites and Remains Act, 1958 (24 of 1958). Under the act, this religious building of Shiva is a protected monument and it is committed that whoever destroys, removes, injures, alters, defaces, imperils, or misuses it shall be punishable. Further, any mining operation and construction activities are prohibited up to 200 meters near or adjoining this protected monument, as shown in Figure 4.9. Similarly, 12 Shiva temple ghat or popularly known as Baromandir Ghat (Panihati) and Bazarpara ghat with 4 Siva temples are a unique symbol of Bengal architecture and culture. Considering the spatial distribution perspective, an attempt has been made to analyze the spatio-economic characteristics of religious spaces surrounding these temples through detailed field visits and surveys. Results exhibit that surroundings of these temples practice religious, commercial, and tourism activities. However, the commercial activities and residential functions are common spatial characteristics of the neighborhood. These spaces are spatially connected and accessible through urban main roads. Though culturally, historically, and architecturally these religious buildings share many similarities, however except Dakhineswar Temple, most of them are unable to attract tourism attention. Even the identical twin temple of Dakshineswar is unable to attract much tourism attention despite its historical connection with the Rani Rashmoni and Swami Ramkrishna Paramhans. Only minor tourism-oriented commercial activities are noticeable surrounding the Shyamnagar Mulajor Kalibari Temple. In terms of the reception of infrastructure support and investments, sharp differences have been observed. The next section of the study will focus on the detailed investigation of religious tourism surrounding the Dakhineswar Temple to unwrap crucial factors that contributed to the sharp differences in tourism essence to the particular site among similar or near-similar sites of current or past religious significance.

4.6 DAKSHINESWAR TEMPLE IN QUEST FOR MARKETPLACE

The famous Hindu temple of Dakshineswar was founded by Rani Rashmoni in the small village of Dakshineswar along the eastern bank of the River Hooghly. The idols of the God and Goddess were installed with grand splendor on 31st May 1855 and the temple was opened to pilgrims of all strata of the society irrespective of their caste and religion (Dakshineswar Kali Temple, 2021). Shri Ramkrishna "Paramhans" (1836–1886), one of the leading Hindu spiritual leaders of 19th-century Bengal, had become the second chief priest of the temple and played a significant role in the socio-religious reforms of West Bengal and India. Among his disciples, the most famous was Swami Vivekananda (1863–1902), the family name Narendranath Dutta founder of the Ramkrishna Mission, who became the major contributor in the revival of Hinduism worldwide (Singh, 2018). Swami Vivekananda enlightened the world with his deep interest in Hinduism as an ideology of human development. He mesmerized the world's religious community with his speech during his visits to the United States, representing India at the 1893 Parliament of the World's Religions (Singh, 2018). Within its first century of establishment, Dakshineswar Temple has earned international recognition in light of its grand legendary association with Swami Vivekananda and Shri Ram Krishna "Paramhans" (Dakshineswar Kali Temple, 2021). The temple hosts approximately more than 35,000 visitors every day. The numbers reach up to 200,000 on special occasions including New Year, Durga Puja, Kali Puja, Diwali, etc. The scenic beauty of the temple and its legendary association with the great Hindu leaders attract tourists from not only the neighborhood of Kolkata or West Bengal but from a distinct corner of India and abroad. A Dakshineswar Temple visit has become one of the important parts and parcel of plans among tourists arriving at Kolkata. Increasing tourist flow to visit the Dakshineswar Temple has led to the commercialization of the faith in Goddess Kali, which is implanted by Rani Rashmoni, nurtured by the Shri Ram Krishna "Paramhans," and flowered by Swami Vivekananda. Perceived potentiality lies in the Dakshineswar tourism economy that has attracted the attention of the tourism stakeholders in the last decade. The resultant huge developmental projects and intervention of state and central government as shown in Table 4.2 has altered the spatial economy surrounding the religious building of Dakshineswar. In 2003, the Kolkata Metropolitan Development Authority has taken the major steps for the restoration of the Dakshineswar Temple that included the construction of a multi-complex plaza, the establishment of eateries, the construction of wider roads, and restoration and beautification of Kuthibari, Dudhpkur, and Hanspukur (The Telegraph, 2008). The further upgrade plans implemented during 2009 included the temple landscape construction, beautification, and preservation of water bodies, namely Dudhpukur and Hanspukur, construction of paved walkways and toilets, setting up of drinking water facilities, and development of parking spaces (The Telegraph, 2008). To fully cash in the potentiality of religious tourism, the state government has given more emphasis to the upgradate of the connectivity of the area. For the extension of the metro railway from Dumdum to Baranagar via Dakshineswar, the state government sanctioned INR2069.6 Cr. in 2011.

TABLE 4.2
Development Plan for Dakshineswar Temple

Year	Developmental Plans	Sources of Information
1847	On 6th September 1847 Rani Rasmoni purchased 54.4 bighas of land at the cost of Rs. 42,500 from James Hasty.	Dakshineswar Kali Temple, 2018
1855	On 31st May 1855 Rani Rasmoni placed luxminarayan Shila (founding stone) in the Navaratna Temple as per the wish of her late husband and also for the welfare of his soul.	Dakshineswar Kali Temple, 2018
1855	The temple was dedicated in the name of Rani's Guru, and Ramkumar who was the head priest. The idol of Kali in the new temple was installed in presence of Intellectuals of shastras (scriptures), Brahmin pundits, and celebrated scholars arrived from distant places like Kashi, Orissa, and Navadvip.	Dakshineswar Kali Temple, 2018
1986	Lokmata Rani Rasmoni Mission was established to maintain the temple and to pursue distinct social activities and reforms.	Lokemata Rani Rasmoni Mission (Field Visit)
2003	Restoration of the Dakshineswar Temple was finalized by KMDA. The plan includes construction of a multi-complex plaza and eateries for tourists, wider roads, relocation of kiosks along the roads, and restoration of Kuthibari, where Sri Ramakrishna dwelt from 1855 to 1871. Plans also include restoration of the two waterbodies, Dudhpukur and Hanspukur.	The Telegraph, 2003
2012	Jetty services for Dakshineswar Temple trough River Hooghly were sanctioned by the state government. The plan was implemented in August 2013.	The Telegraph, 2013
2015	Chief Minister of West-Bengal has announced to build a Skywalk through Dakshineswar Temple for the pilgrims. The skywalk is opened for visitors in 2018.	Times of India, 2013
2015	The prime minister of India visited Dakshineswar Temple assured the Temple authority to offer all possible help for the upgrade of the temple.	India Today, 2015
2017	The West Bengal Government has allotted Rs. 34 Crore for the development of Ghats of Dakshineswar Temple and Belur.	The Telegraph, 2017
2018	"Light and sound program" has been decided to start first in Dakshineswar Temple to aware the people about the history of the Dakshineswar Temple. The plan is under construction.	Anandabazar Patrika, 2018
2018	Upgrade of the official website of the Department of Tourism, Government of West Bengal and a detailed page dedicated to Dakshineswar.	Dakshineswar, 2018

Source: Collected from multiple sources and compiled by authors, 2018–19.

The plans for jetty services for the temple through River Hooghly was implemented in 2013. The Dakshineswar skywalk, 10.5 meters wide and 340 meters long elevated glass and steel pathway, connects the Dakshinewar Railway Station to the compound of the temple and has been inaugurated in November 2018. The walkway offers space for series of shops selling items of worship and food, as illustrated in Figure 4.10. The Ministry of Tourism is in the process of implementing a light and sound program incorporating the history and significance of the temple to spread more awareness among tourists and the locale. To attract more tourists, the Department of Tourism, Government of West Bengal showcases detailed information about the temple on its official website (Dakshineswar, 2018). Recently, the metro has also started to run from the core of the city.

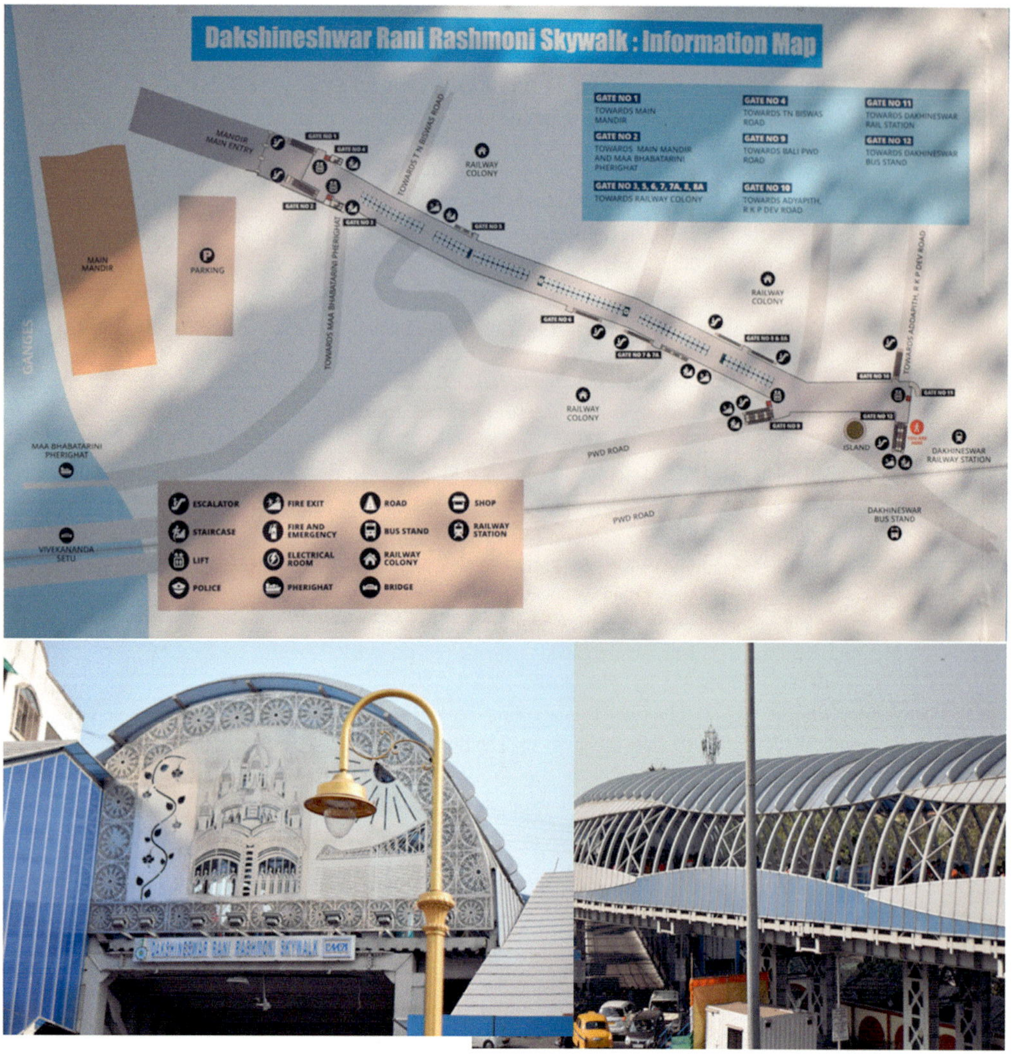

FIGURE 4.10 Views of skywalk connecting Dakshineswar Temple with Adyapith Temple.

(Picture Courtesy: Sanjali Das, 2018)

Over the years, the increasing impact of the Dakshineswar Temple economy, influenced by the age of commoditization, has witnessed the conversion of spatial morphology of this sacred space to commercialized space. A simple religious building and its surroundings have been converted to a multifunctional spatial arena offering a multitude of services to the neighborhood community and its visitors. An increase in communication channels; evolving diversification in the market economy; growing numbers of hotels, motels, guest houses, and eateries; and rising numbers of multi-complex plazas altered the spatial morphology surrounding the temple, as highlighted in Figure 4.11.

To understand how religious tourism and commoditization of religious value contributed to the reconstruction of spatial morphology of sacred space, a detailed survey on the neighborhood scale has been conducted. The survey found a positive perception among the local community. It is also observed that the surrounding neighborhood is full of hotels, restaurants, and shops that benefit from the tourism traffic visiting the temple. High inflows of investments have strengthened the basic need-based infrastructure and attract more involvement of the neighborhood community. A similar result is found in other studies (Tsai, Song, and Wong, 2009).

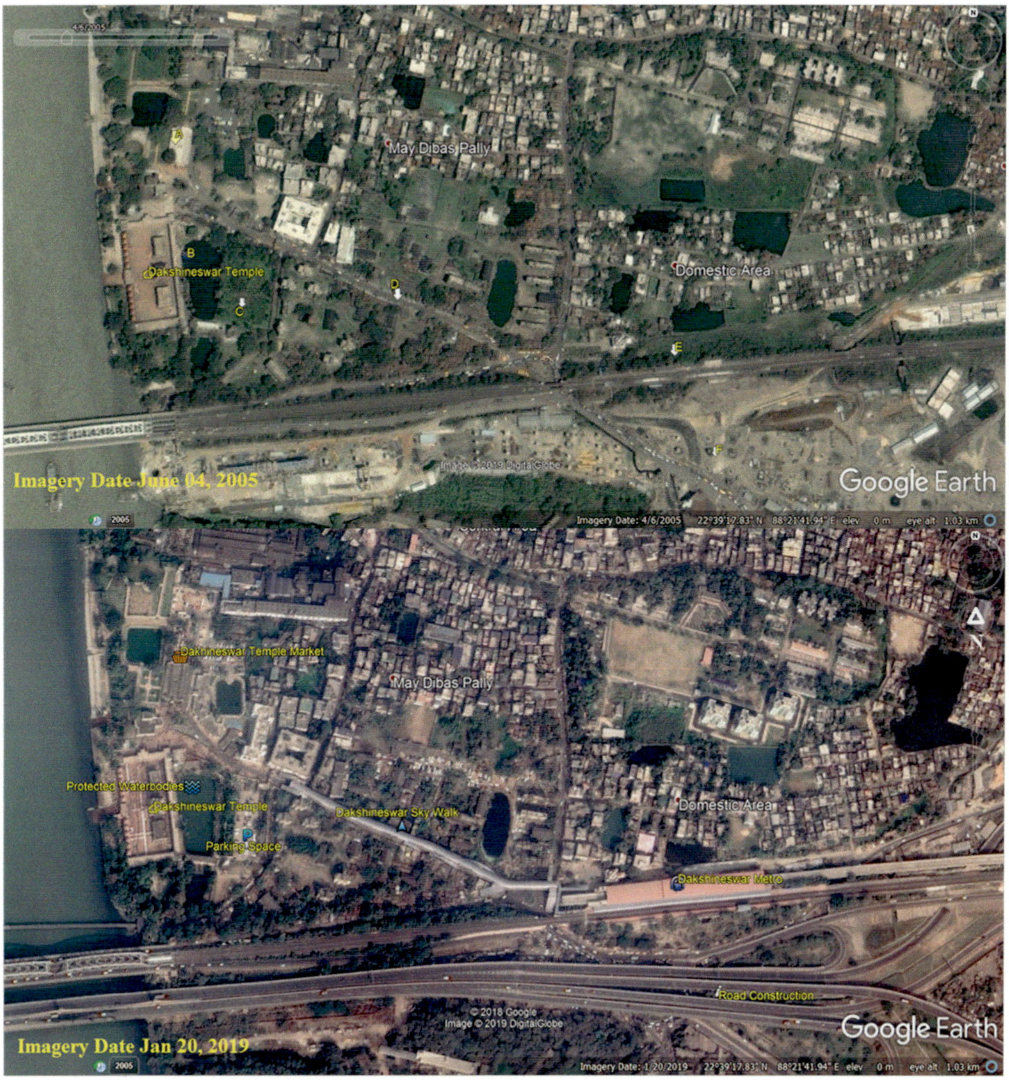

FIGURE 4.11 Infrastructural development in the neighborhood of Dakshineswar Temple.

(Source: Google Earth, 2005 and 2019).

4.7 SPATIAL MORPHOLOGY INFLUENCED BY SACRED ECONOMY

The religious value of the Dakshineswar Kali Temple and regular visitation of tourists in search of peace, joy, and salvation constitute a spatial arena, where driving forces of the tourism market enhance the socio-cultural aspect of the neighborhood community (Singh, 2009; Alberto, 2010). On a neighborhood scale, the rising influence of the tourism economy on religious belief and commoditization of services reconstruct the spatial morphology surrounding religious places (Olsen, 2003). Similar interest has changed the spatial morphology surrounding the Dakshineswar Temple of Kolkata. The present study observed a rapid change in the morphological and socio-economic characteristics of the Dakshineswar. Through a neighborhood survey of activity types and population features, it is found that within the premises of the Dakshineswar Temple the dominant activity is religious activities while the surrounding neighborhood exhibits the amalgamation of religious activities, tourism activities, and commercial activities. The tourism interest in the sacred value of temples has created commercial religious spaces (Zhang and Wei, 2017). Most of the businesses, including religious gift shops, lodgings, eateries, etc. were completely dependent on the devotees visiting the temple. More than 150 religious gift shops were present within the temple premises that are completely dependent on the religious and tourism crowd attracted by the temple every day. To accommodate a large number of tourists in the peripheries of the Dakshineswar Temple, many lodgings, eateries, and hotels have come up. Most of the residential households either fully or partially benefit from the tourist traffic attracted by the temple. Figure 4.12 displays the influence map showing responses of neighborhood communities on the share of their household benefits derived from the temple economy. It is observed that the socio-economic dependency of the neighborhood community is higher (more than 80%) near the periphery of the temple. The mixed religious-commercial dependency is observed with the increasing distance from the temple. As stated earlier, tourism interest in the Dakshineswar Temple and perceived economic benefits from the tourism economy have attracted huge investment opportunities surrounding the temple. An appreciation of tourism benefits by the neighborhood community is also remarkable.

4.8 RELIGIOUS TOURISTS AT THE DAKHINESWAR TEMPLE

The Dakshineswar Temple is today acknowledged as one among the major religious landscapes of Eastern India, compared to other contemporary temples sharing similar potentialities. We have employed a questionnaire analysis intending to understand the tourist's perception of this different spatial experience of similar or near-similar religious places of interest. The survey includes the visitors and tourists visiting these selected sites. Due to the huge popularity of the Dakshineswar Temple among the religious tourists and visitors of Kolkata, it was really difficult to have an equal distribution of samples from all places surveyed. As a result, nearly 81% (N = 203) of the total sample responses were collected from the Dakshineswar Temple and 19% (N = 49) from the other temples. The survey incorporates more or less equal share in terms of gender distribution (male = 50.40%; female = 49.60%). The mean age of respondents was 40.63 years, while the majority of the respondents (N = 171; 67.86%) were from the young age group (30–59 years). Most of the respondents were well educated, completed graduation, and above the level of education. Respondents were belonging to the diverse occupational sector; most of them belong to the service sector. Nearly, 51% of the respondents were coming from different parts of Kolkata, while 40% were coming from West Bengal but other districts of West Bengal. Nearly 6.35% of respondents were from other states of India while 2.38% of respondents surveyed were from other countries including Sweden, Russia, Bangladesh, and Myanmar. The detailed result of the demographic characteristics of the visitor community is illustrated in Table 4.3.

In our study, we found most of the respondents were same-day visitors to the site. A visitor is a traveler taking a trip to a destination outside his/her usual environment for any main purpose (business, leisure, or another personal purpose) other than to be employed at the place visited. This trip does not include an overnight stay. In our response group, 15.1% of responses were collected from tourists who are visitors but classified as a tourist if his/her trip includes an overnight stay. Most of them are regular visitors to the sites. Respondents were asked to identify major attractive motives of the visit to this unique religious site using a 5-point Likert scale. Unanimously, most of the respondents have acknowledged the role of their belief (strengthened mean = 3.87, SD = 1.687) by word-of-mouth recommendations made by their family, friend, relatives, and neighbors (mean = 4.32, SD = 1.303). Very interestingly, a newly opened skywalk of Dakhineswar at the time of the survey has obtained higher scores as well (mean = 3.92, SD = 1.565). The importance of the publicity measure (mean = 3.68, SD = 1.666) and scenic and natural landscape of the sites (mean = 3.24, SD = 1.672) are other attractants. However, family heritage and the role of architecture have little part to play here, where most of the pilgrims have given due emphasis to tourism and recreation as a unique reason for visit (N = 160, 63.7%), as shown in Table 4.4.

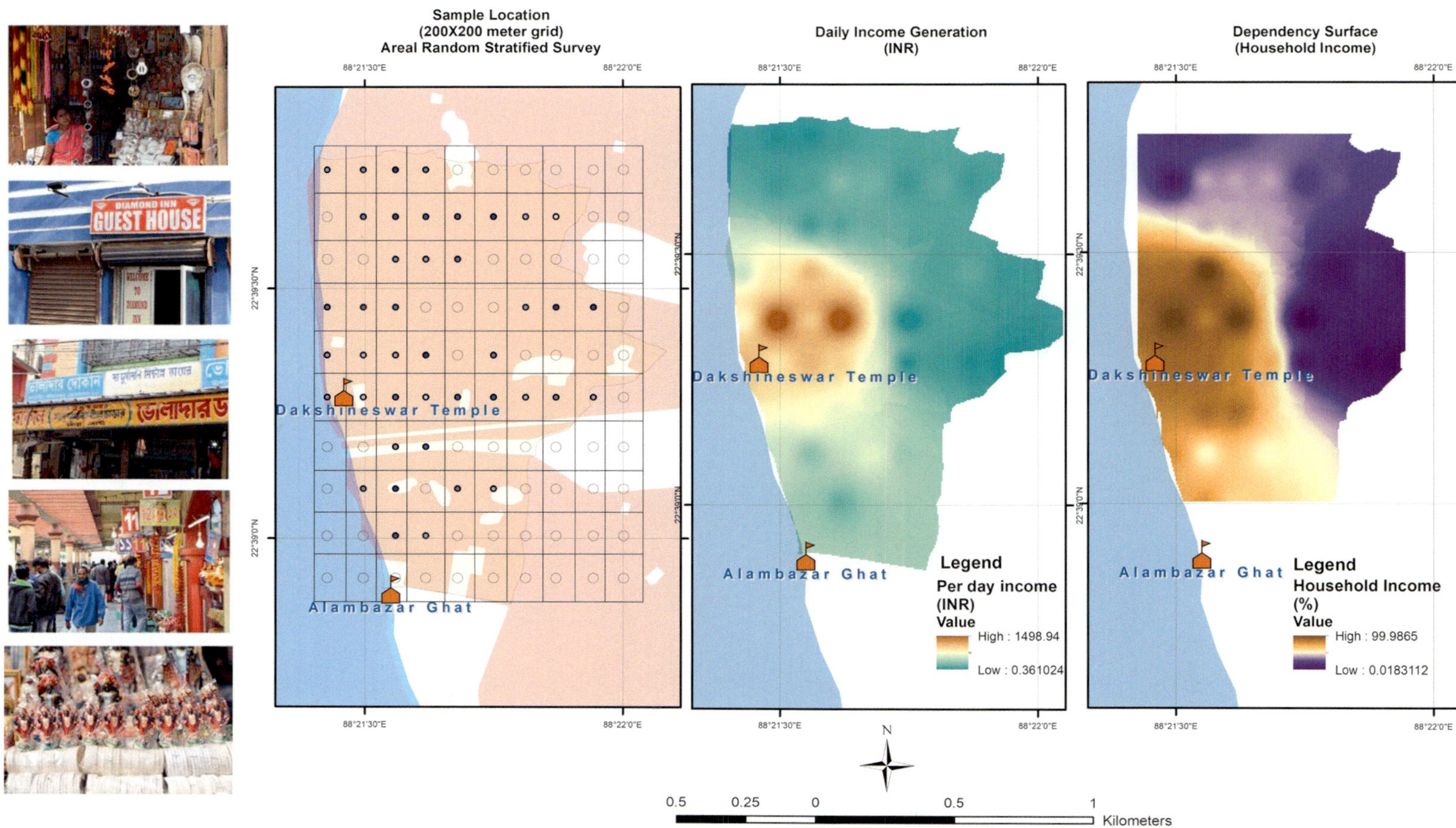

FIGURE 4.12 Zone of tourism influence surrounding Dakshineswar Temple.

(Source: Field Survey, 2019).

TABLE 4.3
Demographic Characteristics of the Respondents (N = 252)

Location of Survey (N = 252)		
Temple	**Frequency**	**Percentage**
Dakhineswar Temple	203	80.9
Shyamnagar Kalibari	30	12.0
Annapurna Temple	12	4.8
Joymitra Kalibari	6	2.4
Demographic Characteristics (N = 252)		
Gender	**Frequency**	**Percentage**
Male	125	49.60
Female	127	50.40
Age (Mean = 40.63; SD = 12.85 years)		
Age Group	**Frequency**	**Percentage**
Less than 30	55	21.83
30 –59	171	67.86
60 + and above	26	10.32
Education (N = 251)		
Level	**Frequency**	**Percentage**
Secondary	23	9.2
Higher secondary	57	22.7
Graduation	129	51.4
Post-graduation	42	16.7
Others	1	0.40
Places of Residents	**Frequency**	**Percentage**
Within district	129	51.19
Other districts of West Bengal	101	40.08
Outside West Bengal, other states of India	16	6.35
Outside India	6	2.38
Occupation (N = 251)	**Frequency**	**Percentage**
Agriculture	3	1.2
Artist	6	2.4
Business	36	14.3
Homemaker	61	24.3
Retired professional	13	5.2
Self-employed professional	17	6.8
Service sector	83	33.1
Student	32	12.7

In this contemporary age of commoditization, the Dakshineswar Temple has been successfully able to situate itself on the map of global tourism interests. To encash the religious tourism potentiality of the temple, a huge investment has been made in promoting the religious value of the place. The area surrounding the temple has received a high level of investments for its infrastructural development and upgrades to support the tourism economy. Such huge tourism interest and related investment plans have altered the spatial morphology surrounding the Dakshineswar Temple and creating a new space showcasing sharp differences from its contemporary counterparts sharing similar or near-similar historical, cultural, architectural, and religious interests. We found a similar perception among visitor community to the site, as shown in Table 4.5.

TABLE 4.4
Trip Characteristics and Major Motivational Constructs

Nature of visitation (N = 251)	**Frequency**	**Percent**
Tourist	38	15.1
Visitor	213	84.9
Frequency of visitation	**Frequency**	**Percent**
New visitor	4	1.6
Daily visitor	9	3.6
Once in 1 month	29	11.6
Once in 3 months	144	57.4
Once in 6 months	53	21.1
Once in 1 year	12	4.8
Motivational Constructs (N = 239; N of Items = 9)		
Scale of item: 5 = Strongly agree and 1 = Strongly disagree		
Reliability Statistics Cronbach's Alpha = 0.720	**Mean**	**Std. Deviation**
Attracted by believe in practice of a religion to render due worship and obedience to Goddess Kali	3.87	1.687
Attracted by family heritage and cultural practices	2.91	1.794
Attracted by scenic beauty and natural landscape	3.24	1.672
Attracted by architecture	2.93	1.595
Attracted by cleanliness and available infrastructure	3.23	1.656
Attracted to newly opened skywalk of Dakhineswar	3.92	1.565
Attracted by information and recommendations made by peers	4.32	1.303
Attracted by ease of access	3.97	1.459
Attracted by publicity measures	3.68	1.666
Unique reason to visit	**Frequency**	**Percent**
Pilgrimage and worship	91	36.3
Tourism and recreation	160	63.7

Most of the respondents strongly agreed and stated that the spatial landscape surrounding the Dakhineswar Temple has been changed rapidly. Among major changes, an increase in commercial activities and marketization of religious goods and services (mean = 4.46, SD = 0.871) with price hikes, overcrowding and congestion (mean = 4.46, SD = 0.852), and increased unwanted interferences of the temple trust's members are well-recognized by the respondents. Respondents also felt that religious sites of interest are now less respected among both guests and host community and cultural heritage is losing its glory amidst increasing means of recreation and entertainment. Most of the respondents were not aware of the presence of other religious buildings in the vicinity of the Dakshineswar Temple, as shown in Table 4.6. Nearly 50% of the tourists visiting the Dakshineswar Temple are aware of the presence of the Shyamnagar Kali Temple and 26 Shiva temples; however, very few of them have ever been visited.

4.9 FORCES OF MARKET ECONOMY CREATING DISSIMILARITIES AMONG SIMILARS

Acknowledging the perception of visitors and the neighborhood community, we have listed five major factors significantly affecting the emergence of the Dakhineswar Temple among the visitor

TABLE 4.5
Visitors' Perception on Changing Spatial Landscape Surrounding Dakhinewsar Temple (N = 203)

	N	Range	Minimum	Maximum	Mean	Std. Deviation	Variance	Skewness	Std. Error
Spatial landscape changed in last 5 years (Dakhineswar Temple)	203	2	3	5	4.46	0.852	0.725	−1.05	0.171
Congestion and overcrowding	203	4	1	5	4.2	1.183	1.4	−1.268	0.171
Increasing commercial activities and marketization of religious goods and services	203	2	3	5	4.46	0.871	0.727	−1.09	0.171
Price hikes in surroundings	203	4	1	5	3.73	1.129	1.275	−0.294	0.171
Increased interference of priest community (*pandas*)	203	4	1	5	4.08	1.293	1.671	−1.143	0.171
Unwanted interference and restrictions imposed by temple trust	203	5	1	5	4.24	1.26	1.587	−1.7	0.171
Decrease in respect to sites of religious interests	203	4	1	5	3.75	1.255	1.575	−0.364	0.171
Cultural heritage preserved at the site	203	4	1	5	2.55	1.473	2.169	0.273	0.171

Where, 5 = Strongly agree and 1 = Strongly disagree.

TABLE 4.6

Responses on Awareness on Similar Sites of Interests

Descriptive Statistics

	N	Range	Minimum	Maximum	Mean	Std. Deviation	Variance	Skewness	
	Statistic	Statistic	Statistic	Statistic	Statistic	Statistic	Statistic	Statistic	Std. Error
Adyapith	203	3	2	5	4.64	0.786	0.618	−2.421	0.171
Belur Math	203	3	2	5	4.89	0.505	0.256	−4.837	0.171
Annapurna Temple	203	4	1	5	2.17	1.602	2.566	0.723	0.171
Shyamnagar Kali Bari	203	4	1	5	2.82	1.695	2.873	−0.007	0.171
Joymitra Kalibari	203	3	1	4	1.69	1.258	1.581	1.298	0.171
Alambazar Ghat	203	4	1	5	1.84	1.454	2.114	1.303	0.171
Giribala Temple	203	4	1	5	1.87	1.474	2.172	1.255	0.171
12 Temple Ghat	203	4	1	5	1.94	1.503	2.258	1.127	0.171
26 Shiv Temple	202	4	1	5	2.77	1.798	3.234	0.115	0.171
Bazarpara Temple	203	4	1	5	2.12	1.656	2.742	0.905	0.171
Char Mandir Ghat	203	4	1	5	1.78	1.483	2.200	1.445	0.171

5-Point Likert Scale of awareness: 5 = Very much; 4 = Somewhat; 3 = Maybe; 2 = Not really; 1 = Not at all.

TABLE 4.7
Result of Opinion Survey on Factors Supporting Tourism Development Surrounding Dakshineswar Temple – Criteria Weight Is Derived from Pair-wise Comparison Based on Scale Proposed by Saaty and Vargas (2001)

Statement	S_1	S_2	S_3	S_4	S_5	Priority Score
Location, architecture and sanctity of the temple (**S_1**)	1.0	0.33	0.33	0.25	0.20	5.7%
Association of Swami Ramkrishna Paramhans and Swami Vivekanand (**S_2**)		1.0	2.0	2.0	0.25	20.0%
History and fame of Dakshineswar Temple (**S_3**)			1.0	2.0	0.33	15.9%
Infrastructure development surrounding the temple (**S_4**)				1.0	0.33	13.0%
Marketization and advertisement of Dakshineswar Temple (**S_5**)					1.0	45.4%

Maximum Eigenvalue =5.29297; C.I.=0.0732419.

community of Kolkata. The pair-wise comparison made following the methodology proposed by Saaty and Vargas (2001), which represents one among appropriate methodology in measuring intangible components including love, care, and emotions. We have collected the responses from the experts from temple management trusts, the tourism industry, and academia, on the evolution of the Dakshineswar Temple as a popular destination among the tourist and visitor community in comparison to its counterpart. The results of the analysis, as shown in Table 4.7, found a maximum weight to the marketization and advertisement of the Dakshineswar Temple (S5 = 45.4%) and its fame to both domestic and foreign markets followed by legendary association of Swami Vivekanand and Ramkrishna "Paramhans."

Huge disciple strength of the Swami Vivekanand and role of Ramkrishna Mission in promoting the image of the Dakshineswar Temple has introduced the world to the history and fame of the Dakshineswar Temple, leaving behind the cultural and architectural significance of the other temples far behind. In this age of commoditization, commercialization of the faithscape surrounding the Dakshineswar Temple has attracted huge investment and developmental plans. The active role of Rani Rashmoni Trust and the State Government of West Bengal in encashing the faith and belief associated with the Goddess Kali, Swami Ramkrishna, and Swami Vivekanand has successfully made Dakshineswar the center of international repute among the religious tourism community. The advertisement and marketization of the Dakshineswar Temple, promotion of the same on the official website of Ministry of Tourism, West Bengal, a huge investment for upgrade of infrastructure, beautification of the temple, improvement in connectivity, construction of the skywalk, and associated word-of-mouth recommendation followed by quality surrounding experience has added value to tourism essence surrounding Dakshineswar.

4.10 CONCLUSION

Creating tourism to preserve our history and culture is no doubt one among the best ideologies adopted by the UN World Tourism Organisation (UNWTO, 2014). Academicians, scholars, and stakeholders also acknowledged the role of tourism in preserving historical and cultural sites (Duncan, 2009; Logan, 2012; Lussetyowati, 2015; Mah et al., 2019). In consensus with the other studies (Duncan, 2009; Lungo, Sabia and Pacella, 2015; Mah et al., 2019; UNWTO, 2014), the present study also suggests adopting a proactive role in creating tourism surrounding aforementioned sites sharing similar or near-similar culture, architecture, and location. Experts' opinions unwrapped the demand and hope of priests and neighborhood communities surrounding these hidden places of tourism interest. Most of them hope that the state tourism department should include these sites in the Kolkata-Dakshineswar tourism circuits. Detailed contingent-valuation studies may help the state government in this regard to initiate the necessary policy. The present study successfully takes the primitive stage in this regard; however, detailed econometric analysis is required further. It is further noted that digitalization of the buildings of historical and religious importance and a virtual tour is a significant component of the 21st century's tourism economy (Mah et al., 2019). The creation of virtual tours of the aforementioned sites may raise awareness among the religious tourist community visiting Kolkata. We cannot ignore the role of revitalization to preserve and restore historic buildings which are getting more and more significant attention (Mukhopadhyay and Devi, 2017; Penićaa, Svetlana and Murgul, 2015), the state government may take necessary initiatives to restore and revitalize the selected religious buildings along the stretch of the Ganges to regenerate tourism essence. In line with the market economy of tourism, these religious buildings need to be assigned with the multi-purpose function, satisfying modern requirements. Acknowledging the role of market economy and commoditization of religious tourism (Azmi and Ismail, 2016; Hare, 1997; Hunt and Durham, 2012) proper advertising is necessary to direct tourists to equally attractive religious buildings. Proper initiative and awareness campaigning may encourage tourists to visit the neighborhood religious places around the Dakshineswar Temple to expand the zone of tourism benefits surrounding these shadow heritagescapes.

NOTES

1 Map archived from National Library Kolkata. *Bengal River Hooghly Panihati to Pulta to Gondalpara to Hooghly Bridge, Hooghly* published in 1925.
— *The City Environs of Calcutta including the government estate of Punchunnogram in 1852–1856* published in 1856.

Intensity of Relative	Definition
1	Equal importance
3	Moderate importance of one over another
5	Essential or strong importance
7	Very strong importance
9	Extreme importance
2, 4, 6, 8	Intermediate value between the two adjacent
Reciprocals	If factor *i* has one of the above numbers assigned to it when compared with factor *j*, then *j* has the reciprocal value when compared with *i*

Source: Saaty and Kearns, pp. 27, 1985.

2 Saaty's Scale of Relative Importance for quantification of intangible components

REFERENCES

Alberto, U. T. (2010). Tourist experience of heritage tourism in Macau SAR, China. *Journal of Heritage Tourism*, *5*(2), 157–168.

Amazzone, L. (2010). *Goddess Durga and Sacred Female Power*. United Kingdom: Hamilton Books.

Anandabazar Patrika. (2018). Retrived from https://www.anandabazar.com/state/light-and-sound-program-is-going-to-start-at-dakshineswar-1.774216

Azmi, E., & Ismail, Z. M. (2016). Cultural heritage tourism: Kapitan keling mosque as a focal point. *Procedia – Social and Behavioral Sciences*, *222*, 528–538.

Bhuiyan, M., Siwar, C., Ismail, S., & Islam, R. (2011). Potentials of islamic tourism: A case study of malaysia on east coast economic region. *Australian Journal of Basic and Applied Sciences*, *5*(6), 1333–1340.

Chadha, H., & Onkar, P. (2016). Changing cities in the perspective of religious tourism – A case of Allahabad. Proceedings of *International Conference on Emerging Trends in Engineering, Science and Technology (ICETEST – 2015), Proceedia Technology*, *24*, 1706–1713.

Chakravorty, S. (2000). From colonial city to global city? The far-from-complete spatial transformation of Calcutta. In Marcuse, P. and Kempen, R. (Eds.), *Globalizing Cities: A New Spatial Order?* (pp. 56–77). Oxford, UK: Blackwell Publishing.

Chaudhary, S. A. (2017). The role of five elements of nature in temple architecture. *International Journal of Scientific & Engineering Research*, *8* (7), 1149–1162.

Collins-Kreiner, V., & Kliot, N. (2000). Pilgrimage tourism in the holy land:The behavioural characteristics of christian pilgrims. *Geojournal*, *50* (1), 55–67.

Dakshineswar (2018). Dakshineswar [online]. Department of Tourism, Government of West Bengal. Retrieved from https://wbtourismgov.in/destination/place/dakshineswar

Dakshineswar Kali Temple (2018). Dakshineswar Kali Temple [online]. Retrieved from http://www.dakshineswarkalitemple.org/history.html

Dakshineswar Kali Temple (2021). Dakshineswar Kali Temple [online]. Retrieved from http://www.dakshineswarkalitemple.org/places_in_dakshineshwar.html

Das, S. (2018). Navadurga and the 9 Forms of the Hindu Goddess Durga [online]. Indian Art & Culture, Hinduism. Retrieved from https://www.learnreligions.com/nine-forms-of-goddess-durga-1770307

Duncan, E. (2009). Tourism and Cultural Heritage Preservation. 10.2139/ssrn.1399124

Egresi, I., & Kara, F. (2016). Residents' attitudes to tourists visiting their mosques: A case study from istanbul, Turkey. *Journal of Tourism and Cultural Change*, *16*(1), 1–21.

Google Earth Pro. (2019).Temples near Dakshineswar Kaali Mandir 22°39'34"N, 81°21'55"E, [Online] Available at: http://www.google.com/earth/index.html [Accessed 31 August 2019].

Hare, O. D. (1997). Interpreting the cultural landscape for tourism development. *Urban Design International*, *2*(1), 33–54.

Hughes, K., Bond, N., & Ballantyne, R. (2013). Designing and managing interpretive experiences at religious-tourism sites: Visitors' perceptions of canterbury cathedral. *Tourism Management*, (36), 210–220.

Hunt, A. C., & Durham, H. W. (2012). Shrouded in a fetishistic mist: Commoditisation of sustainability in tourism. *Tourism Anthropology*, *2*(4), 330–347.

India Today. (2015). PM Narendra Modi visits Dakshineswar temple [online]. Retrieved from https://www.indiatoday.in/india/story/narendra-modi-west-bengal-visit-dakshineswar-temple-252200-2015-05–10

Jackowski, A., & Smith, V. (1992). Polish pilgrim-tourists. *Annals of Tourism Research*, *19*, 92–106.

Keisteri, T. (2013). The study of changes in cultural landscapes. *Fennia – The International Journal of Geography*, *168*(1), 31–115.

King, W. (2005). Religion. In: Jones, L. (Eds.), *Encyclopedia of Religion: Vol. 11*. 2nd ed. (pp. 7692–7701). Detroite: Macmillan Reference US.

Kutluturk, C. (2013). Significance of Varanasi in terms of Indian religions. *IOSR Journal of Humanities and Social Science*, *10*(2), 36–40.

Logan, W. (2012). Cultural diversity, cultural heritage and human rights: Towards heritage management as human rights-based cultural practice. *International Journal of Heritage Studies*, *18*(3), 231–244.

Lungo, D. S., Sabia, A. C., & Pacella, C. (2015). Landscape and cultural heritage: Best practices for planning and local development: An example from southern Italy. *Procedia – Social and Behavioral Sciences*, *188*, 95–102.

Lussetyowati, T. (2015). Preservation and conservation through cultural heritage tourism. Case study: Musi riverside palembang. *Procedia – Social and Behavioural Sciences*, *184*, 401–406.

Mah, O. B. P., Yan, Y., Tan, J. S. Y. T., Tan, Y., Tay, G. Q. Y., Chiam, D. J., Wang, Y., & Feng, C. C. (2019). Generating a virtual tour for the preservation of the (In)tangible cultural heritage of tampines chinese temple in singapore. *Journal of Cultural Heritage*, 2(4), 202–211.10.1016/j.culher.2019.04.004.

Maitseo, M. & Kanduza, M. A. (2008). Critical factors of cultural tourism in Botswana. *Botswana Notes and Records*, *39*, 54–61.

Mukhopadhyay, C., & Devi, H. D. (2017). Landscape, heritage and technological innovation: Towards a framework of sustainability of cultural landscape in a desert town in India. *Landscape Research*, *43*(1), 1–14.

Mydland, L. & Grahn, W. (2011). Identifying heritage values in local communities. *International Journal of Heritage*, *18*(6), 564–587.

Olsen, H. D. (2003). Heritage tourism and the commodification of religion. *Tourism Recreation Research*, *28*(3), 94–104.

Penićaa, M., Svetlana, G., & Murgul, V. (2015). Revitalization of historic buildings as an approach to preserve cultural and historical heritage. *Procedia Engineering*, *117*, 883–890.

Petrillo, C. S. (2003). Management of churches and religious sites: Some case studies from Italy. In Fernandes, C., McGettigan, F. and Edwards, J. (eds.), *Religious Tourism and Pilgrimage* (pp. 71–86). Arnhem: ATLAS.

Saaty, T. L. (1992). How to make a decision: The analytic hierarchy process. *European Journal of Operational Research*, *48*, 9–26.

Saaty, T. L., & Kearns, K. P. (1985). *Analytical Planning: The Organization of Systems*. Oxford, New York:Pergamon Press.

Saaty, T. L., & Vargas, L. (2001). *Models, Methods, Concepts & Applications of the Analytic Hierarchy Process*. New York: Springer Science+Business Media, LLC.

Samant, S. (2004). Manifestation of the urban public realm at the water edges in India—A case study of the ghats in Ujjain. *Cities*, *21*(3), 233–253.

Shackley, M. (2006). Costs and benefits: The impact of cathedral tourism in England. *Journal of Heritage Tourism*, *1*(2), 133–141.

Singh, R. P. B. (2002). *Towards the Pilgrimage Archetype: The Panchakroshi Yatra of Benaras* (p. 3). Pilgrimage & Cosmology Series. Varanasi: Indica Books.

Singh, R. P. B. (2009). *Banaras: Making of India's Heritage City*. Germany: Cambridge Scholar Publishing.

Singh, R. P. B. (2009). Goddesses and spatial ordering. In Singh, R. P. (Eds.), *Cosmic Order and Cultural Astronomy: Sacred Cities of India* (pp. 186–208). Newcastle upon Tyne, U.K.: Cambridge Scholars Publishing.

Singh, R. P. B. (2011). Rolwaling: A sacred buddhist valley in Nepal. In Sechere, J. (Eds.), *Sacredscapes & Pilgrimage System* (pp. 153–174). Gurgaon: Shubhi Publication.

Singh, R. P. B. (2018). Swami Vivekananda (1863–1902). In David, S. (Eds.), *Key Thinkers on Development*. Routledge Key Guides Series (2nd Edition, pp. 515–518). London and New York: Routledge, Taylor and Francis Group.

Singh, R. P. B. & Rana, P. S. (2002). *Banaras Region: A Spiritual & Cultural Guide* (p. 1). Pilgrimage & Cosmology Series. Varanasi: Indica Books.

Stark, R. (2004). *Exploring the Religious Life*. Baltimore and London: The John Hopkins University Press.

Tandon, M., & Sehgal, V. (2017). Traditional indian religious streets: A spatial study of the streets of mathura. *Frontiers of Architectural Research*, 6(4), 469–479. https://doi.org/10.1016/j.foar.2017.10.001.

The Telegraph (2003). Dakshineswar temple restoration finalised [online]. Retrieved from https://www.telegraphindia.com/states/west-bengal/dakshineswar-temple-restoration-finalised/cid/1257648

The Telegraph (2008). Temple town upgrade [online]. Retrived from https://www.telegraphindia.com/states/west-bengal/temple-town-upgrade/cid/1259665

The Telegraph (2013). Jetty plan for Dakshineswar [online]. Retrieved from https://www.telegraphindia.com/states/west-bengal/jetty-plan-for-dakshineswar/cid/1287804

The Telegraph (2017). Govt gives Rs 34cr for Ghats' upgrade [online]. Retrieved from https://www.telegraphindia.com/states/west-bengal/govt-gives-rs-34cr-for-ghats-upgrade/cid/1396142

Times of India (2013). Dakshineswar temple to get a walkway [online]. Retrieved from https://timesofindia.indiatimes.com/city/kolkata/Dakshineswar-Temple-to-get-a-walkway/articleshow/21351069.cms

Tsai, H., Song, H. & Wong, F. K. (2009). Tourism and hotel competitiveness research. *Journal of Travel & Tourism Maeketing*, 26(5-6), 522–546.10.1080/10548400903163079

UNWTO. (2014, Feb 27). Tourism – a tool to preserve cultural heritage in Latin America and the Caribbean [online]. Communications – Press release. Retrieved from http://media.unwto.org/press-release/2014-02-27/tourism-tool-preserve-cultural-heritage-latin-america-and-caribbean

UNWTO. (2014, December 10). Tourism can protect and promote religious heritage [online]: UNWTO communications. Retrived from http://media.unwto.org/press-release/2014-12-10/tourism-can-protect-and-promote-religious-heritage

Vargas, L. G. (1982). Reciprocal Matrices With Random Coefficients. *Mathematical Modelling*, 3(1), 69–81. https://doi.org/10.1016/0270-0255(82)90013-6.

Vukonic, B. (1998). Religious tourism: Economic value or an empty box? *International Review of Economics and Business*, *1* (1), 83–94.

Wall, G., & Mathieson, A. (2006). *Tourism: Change, Impacts and Opportunities*. Harlow: Pearson.

Wickramasinghe, V., & Takano, S. (2009).Application of Combined SWOT and Analytic Hierarchy Process (AHP) for Tourism Revival Strategic Marketing Planning: A Case of Sri Lanka Tourism.*Journal of the Eastern Asia Society for Transportation Studies*, 8, 954–969.

Zhang, Y., & Wei, T. (2017). Typology of religious spaces in the urban historical area of lhasa, Tibet. *Frontiers of Architectural Research*, *6*(3), 384–400.

Section II

Urban Health, Space, Governance, and Policy Implications

5 Mapping of Urban Heat Islands and Mitigation Measures in the Durgapur-Asansol Industrial Region, India

Santu Guchhait, Tanmay Patra, and Nirmalya Das
Panskura Banamali College (Autonomous), West Bengal, India

Subhrangsu Das
Utkal University, Odisha, India

CONTENTS

DOI: 10.1201/9781003126195-7

5.1 INTRODUCTION

It is needless to say that the process of urbanization and industrialization has improved the level of comfortability and the quality of human's life effectively. But, at the same time, these two rampant developmental processes threaten the global environment and the existence of living organisms. Rapid urbanisation with high population growth and rural to urban migration accelerate the fast transformation of natural landscape into human-induced landscape (Golden, 2003; Weng, 2003; Luber and Mcgeehin, 2008) in the form of concrete pavements, lofty buildings, metalled roads, etc. These impervious surface materials with a high specific temperature absorb more heat (Sultana and Satyanarayana, 2019) and increase the surface and atmospheric temperature (Kolokotroni and Giridharan, 2008; Ghazanfari et al., 2009; Kolokotsa, Psomas, and Karapidakis, 2009; Roth, 2013; Shahmohamadi et al., 2011). In contrast, temperature is relatively lower in the rural areas with vegetated surface in comparison to the impervious surface of urban area (Xie and Zhou, 2015). This phenomenon of thermal inversion between urban centres and surrounding rural areas is known as an urban heat island (UHI) (Streutker, 2002; Odindi et al., 2015), which in turn affects the local and regional climate (Swain et al., 2017; Kotharkar and Surawar, 2016; Luck and Wu, 2002). Besides, it also affects the health of residents and the matter of grievance is that the morbidity due to urban ambient heat is increasing every year (Shahmohamadi et al., 2011).

In recent years, the Asansol-Durgapur industrial region which has the identity of a major industrial hub in eastern India, faced the problems of the UHI effect (Yadav, Santra, and Samanta, 2016; Kamila and Pal, 2015). Large industrial units like Indian Iron & Steel Company (IISCO), Durgapur Steel Plants, Durgapur Thermal Power Station, etc. and their allied urbanisation stimulated the rapid transformation of land use and land cover (LULC) into barren lands, factory outlet, pavements, and buildings with removal of surface vegetation (Wasige et al., 2013). Industrial activities along with pollutants and other greenhouse gases (GHGs) are the major source of anthropogenic heat generation and increase the surface temperature of the twin metropolitan city (Asansol-Durgapur) (Asimakopoulos et al., 2001). Another major activity is the open cast coal mining that refuelled the temperature and helped to form heat islands (Choudhury, Das, and Das, 2019; Fawzi and Jatmiko, 2015). So, it became a challenge to the researcher and urban planner and mapping of UHIs has a great relevance to take the mitigation measures for sustainable urban design. In the Asansol-Durgapur industrial region, a few studies have examined UHIs in the context of spatio-temporal variation (Gupta, Dey, and Mondal, 2019), relation with NDVI and NDBI (Das et al., 2020; Choudhury, Das, and Das, 2019) and land use/land cover (Dutta, Gupta, and Kishtawal, 2020). Studies have not identified the location of intensive UHIs and their specific causes nor propose any measure to mitigate the high surface temperature. Therefore, the present study aimed 1) to study the seasonal variation and mapping of surface temperature, 2) to identify intensive UHI spots and its forming causes, 3) to analyse the relationship of LST with NDVI and NDBI, 4) to analyse the spatial variation of LST with land use characteristics, and 5) to propose mitigation measures to reduce high heat influx.

5.2 MATERIALS AND METHODS

5.2.1 Study Area

The present study has been conducted in the Asansol-Durgapur industrial region located in the Paschim Barddhaman district (bifurcated from erstwhile Burdwan district on 7th April 2017) of West Bengal, India (Figure 5.1). It covers a geographical area of 1603.17 sq. km (Ministry of MSME 2019) and positioned in between 23°22′20" N to 23°53′59" N and 86°46′25" E to 87°29′03" E. At present, the district consists of eight CD blocks and two municipal corporations (Asansol and Durgapur) situated on the left bank of the Damodar River. The total population is about 2.88 million and experienced a high decadal growth rate of 12.90% from 2001 to 2011 (Census of India, 2011).

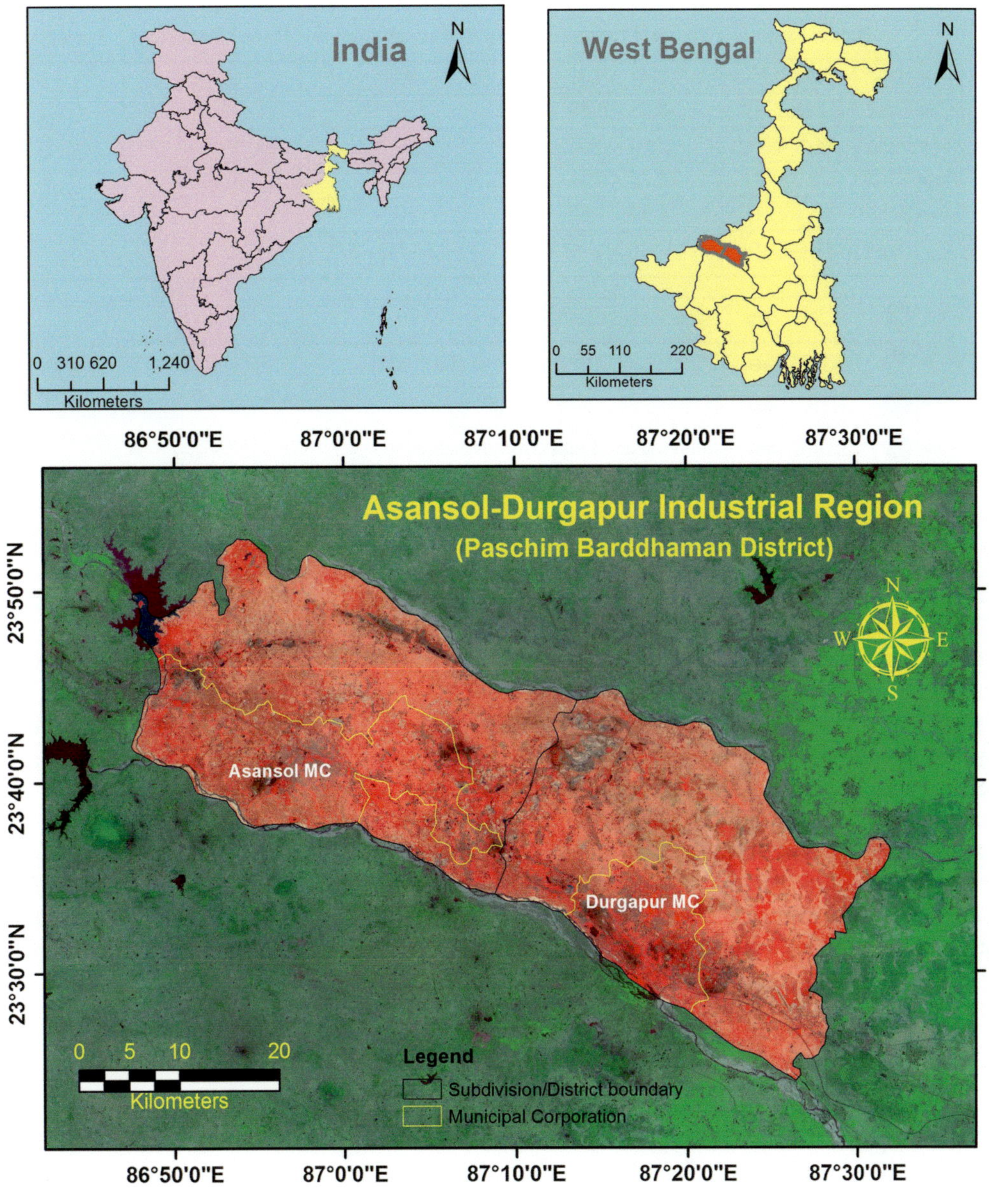

FIGURE 5.1 Location map.

The study area lies on the extension of Chhatonagpur plateau and rocky undulating topography with laterite soil found in the western part of the district, which extends up to the western part of the Durgapur subdivision. The climate of this region is characterized by tropical monsoons with hot-humid summer and cold-dry winter. The average summer temperature varies from 30° Celsius to 14° Celsius in winter with an annual average of 1,408 mm rainfall (Census of India, 2011). Earlier, the industrial base of the region was primarily coal, iron, and steel but recently experienced a rapid development and new industrial ventures comprising heavy engineering, fertilizers, and coal-based chemicals. This region is also renowned as the second-largest coalfield of India (Raniganj Coalfield) with more than 98 mines (Eastern Coalfields Limited, 2012). Major collieries under the Raniganj coalfield area are Kajora, Raniganj-Pandaveswar, Jhanjra, Kenda, Sonepur, Kunustoria, Satgram, Bankola Sripur, Sodepur, and Salanpur (partly) (Eastern Coalfields Limited, 2012).

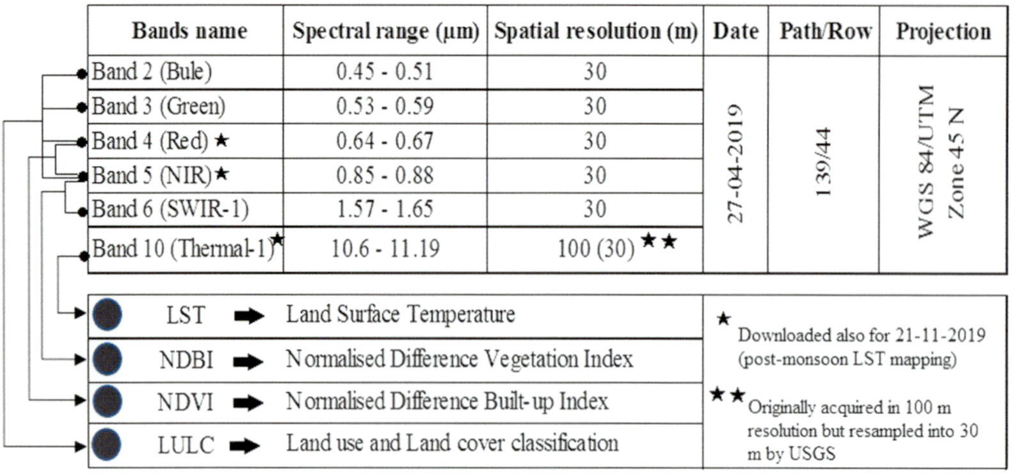

FIGURE 5.2 Band specification of Landsat-8 OLI/TIRS.

5.2.2 Data

For the purpose of the present study, the Landsat 8 Operational Land Imager (OLI) and thermal infrared sensor (TIRS) imagery were obtained from the U.S. Geological Survey (USGS) because of high spatial resolution and easy access (Yuan and Bauer, 2007; Nichol, 1994). Two scenes of daytime image of pre-monsoon and post-monsoon have been used for land surface temperature (LST) dated on 27th April and 21st November 2019, respectively. Both images are pre-georeferenced to UTM Zone 45 North projection using WGS-84 datum. Only the pre-monsoon image is used for land use and land cover (LULC) and other geospatial index analysis as the surface temperature was not pronounced in winter (post-monsoon). Band specifications of the analysis are listed in Figure 5.2. Areas of interest have been masked with the district boundary of the Paschim Barddhaman district collected from the District Census Handbook. All the image processing and mapping are carried out using ArcGIS 10.1, ENVI 5.1, and MS Excel 2016 tools.

5.2.3 Methods

At first, images are processed with radiometric calibration and atmospheric FLAASH (Fast Line-of-sight Atmospheric Analysis of Hypercubes) correction in ENVI 5.1 for better visual image interpretation and minimization of atmospheric noises. Most of the researchers (Ndossi and Avdan, 2016; Qin, Karnieli, and Berliner, 2001; Wan and Dozier, 1996; Waters et al., 2002) have taken land surface temperature (LST) to study a UHI as it is the radiative skin temperature of the Earth's surface, which exchanges energy and surface radiation with the immediate atmosphere (Voogt and Oke, 2003).

The method of the study adopted has two main parts, where first is the estimation of land surface temperature (LST), normalized difference built-up index (NDBI), normalized difference vegetation index (NDVI), and the preparation of land use land cover (LULC). The second part deals with the identification of urban heat islands (UHIs) as well as the analysis of LST and its relation with NDBI, NDVI, and LULC (Deng et al., 2018; Yue et al., 2007; Zhang, Odeh, and Han, 2009).

5.2.3.1 Estimation of LST

LST is considered the important parameter of surface urban heat island (SUHI) analysis. Every object of the Earth's surface have a temperature above absolute zero (−273.15 °C) and emit energy in the form of electromagnetic radiation (EMR). This emitted EMR is recorded by the thermal sensor and stored as a digital number (DN) value against each pixel of satellite image. We derived

LST from thermal band (Band 10: 10.6–11.19 μm) of the Landsat-8 OLI/TIRS sensor for both the pre-monsoon (April) and post-monsoon (November) month.

5.2.3.2 Conversion to TOA Radiance

The standard and the most robust method of LST retrieval from the raw Landsat-8 OLI/TIRS sensor requires the conversion of DN values into top of atmospheric (TOA) spectral radiance values using band-specific rescaling factors as follows (Equation 5.1) (Grigoraș and Urițescu, 2019; Malik, Shukla, and Mishra, 2019):

$$L_\lambda = ML \times QCAL + AL \tag{5.1}$$

where

L_λ = TOA spectral radiance value (W m^{-2} sr μm)
ML = Radiometric multiplicative rescaling factor of Band 10
QCAL = Quantized and calibrated pixel value (DN value)
AL = Radiometric additive rescaling factor of Band 10

5.2.3.3 Conversion to Spectral Radiance to At-Satellite Brightness Temperatures

The next step is to calculate at-satellite brightness temperature in degrees Celsius from the TOA spectral radiance using the approximation equation, as shown (Equation 5.2) (Choudhury, Das, and Das, 2019; Grigoraș and Urițescu, 2019; Malik, Shukla, and Mishra, 2019):

$$Tb = \frac{K2}{In\left(\frac{K1}{L\lambda}\right) + 1} - 273.15 \tag{5.2}$$

where

Tb = At-satellite brightness temperature (°C)
L_λ = TOA spectral radiance value (W m^{-2} sr μm)
K1 & K2 = Thermal conversion constant value of Band 10

5.2.3.4 Estimation of NDVI and Proportion of Vegetation (PV)

NDVI is an important indicator for land description (Julien and Sobrino, 2009) and is less sensitive to the change of atmospheric parameter. It is a simple ratio of infrared reflectivity and visible red reflectivity, shown in the Equation 5.3 (Carlson and Ripley, 1997; Sultana and Satyanarayana, 2019). This NDVI value is used to obtain proportion of vegetation (Pv) per each pixel of the data set. As the proportion of vegetation (Pv) is a dynamic variable of the land surface, it has been measured using Equation 5.4 (Choudhury, Das, and Das, 2019; Grigoraș and Urițescu, 2019) to separate dense vegetated surface from non-vegetated surface.

$$NDVI = \frac{(\rho NIR - \rho VISR)}{(\rho NIR + \rho VISR)} \tag{5.3}$$

$$Pv = \left[\frac{NDVI - NDVImin}{NDVImax + NDVImin}\right]^2 \tag{5.4}$$

where

NDVI = Normalised difference vegetation index
ρNIR = Reflectance in near infrared band (Band 5 for Landsat-8 OLI)

$\rho VISR$ = Reflectance in visible red band (Band 4 for Landsat-8 OLI)
Pv = Proportion of vegetation
NDVImin = Minimum value of NDVI
NDVImax = Maximum value of NDVI

5.2.3.5 Emissivity

Emissivity is the function of different properties of objects and it varies with different surfaces as well as different wavelengths of the EMR spectrum (Snyder et al., 1998). Therefore, measurement of surface emissivity (Ɛ) is quite important for incorrect estimation of LST from a satellite image. We have used the following Equation 5.5 for land surface emissivity estimation, adopting the result of Sobrinoa, Jiménez-Muñoz, Paolinib (2004).

$$\varepsilon = 0.004 \times Pv + 0.986 \tag{5.5}$$

5.2.3.6 Land Surface Temperature

In the final step, the at-satellite brightness temperature value has been converted into land surface temperature (LST) using Equation 5.6 (Choudhury, Das, and Das, 2019; Grigoraș and Urițescu, 2019, Sultana and Satyanarayana, 2019).

$$\text{LST} = \frac{Tb}{\left(1 + \lambda \frac{Tb}{\rho} \ln [\varepsilon]\right)} \tag{5.6}$$

$$\rho = h\frac{C}{\sigma}$$

where
LST = Land surface temperature (°C)
Tb = At-satellite brightness temperature (°C)
λ = Centre wavelength of emitted radiance (10.8 μm)
ε = Emissivity
h = Planck's constant (6.626×10^{-34} J s^{-1})
C = Velocity of light (2.998 × 108 m s^{-1})
σ = Boltzmann constant (1.38×10^{-23} J K^{-1})

5.2.3.7 Calculation of Normalize Difference Built-up Index (NDBI)

Calculation of NDBI is an important index for UHI analysis as it helps to extract the built-up areas of Earth's surface (Kaplan, Avdan, and Avdan, 2018; Guha et al., 2018). NDBI has been derived using the reflectance of short-wave infrared (SWIR) and near-infrared (NIR) band of Landsat-8 OLI/TIRS sensor (Equation 5.7) (Zha, Gao, and Ni, 2003). It is useful for mapping built-up areas because of higher reflectance in the short-wave infrared portion of EMR spectrum.

$$NDBI = \frac{(\rho SWIR - \rho NIR)}{(\rho SWIR + \rho NIR)} \tag{5.7}$$

where
NDBI = Normalised difference built-up index
$\rho SWIR$ = Reflectance in short-wave infrared band (Band 6 for Landsat-8 OLI)
ρNIR = Reflectance in near infrared band (Band 5 for Landsat-8 OLI)

5.2.3.8 Land Use and Land Cover (LULC) Classification

For the present study, the LULC classification has been carried out using the multispectral (blue, green, red, and infrared) bands of Landsat-8 OLI sensors. Different land covers/land uses of the Asansol-Durgapur subdivision are classified into eight main classes following USGS level I and level II LULC classification scheme: vegetation, agricultural land, water bodies, barren land, coal mine area, residential, industrial, and sand deposition. The maximum likelihood algorithm has been used for supervised classification (Ahmad and Quegan, 2012) of satellite images after taking distinct spectral signatures of different land classes (25 training sites are taken for each) compared with the high-resolution Google Earth images.

5.2.3.9 Relationship among Different Indices (LST, NDBI, and NDVI)

A total of 460 centre points of square grids (2 km × 2 km) are taken with equal intervals covering the entire study area. These points have been considered as sample points and extracted values of LST, NDBI, NDVI, and LULC class (OID value for specific land use type) against each point. A simple linear regression model and correlation methods have been applied to study the relationship among LST, NDBI, and NDVI. To study the relationship with the land use pattern, scatter plot and cross-section methods have been implied.

5.3 RESULTS AND DISCUSSION

5.3.1 Seasonal Variation of LST: Pre-monsoon and Post-monsoon

Land surface temperature is an important indication of lower-layer atmospheric conditions of any region. It is greatly affected by the nature of the Earth's surface and this surface temperature plays a great role in heat land formation by balancing the absorbed and radiative energy of Earth's surface. In this study, the LST of the pre-monsoon season has been used to depict the temperature range of the Paschim Bardhaman district. The LST distribution (summer) map shows that the maximum and minimum temperature of this region is that 43.97 degree Celsius and 25.48 degree Celsius (LST result has been cross-checked with the study of Yadav, Santra, and Samanta, (2016) and Gupta, Dey, and Mondal (2019), respectively (Figure 5.3a). The range of temperature is 18.49 degrees Celsius. The western part of this district, namely part of the Barabani and Salanpur block, as well as some part of the Asansol municipal corporation, shows a very high surface temperature because of its urban built-up impervious construction and mining areas. Some sporadic high-temperature zones are also identified around the Durgapur municipal corporation due its large number of heat intensive industries and urban residences (Dutta, Gupta, and Kishtawal, 2020). Some elevated barren land in the northern part of the Durgapur sub-division shows a high temperature. The minimum temperature is recorded in and around the water bodies.

Whereas during the post-monsoon period, LST ranges from 39.74 °C (maximum) to 22.38 °C (minimum) (Figure 5.3b). The high temperatures of a few places have been recorded in the mining areas and the sand deposition over the river bed. Except for these few clusters of high temperatures, the whole district shows a moderate level of temperature. The minimal temperature has been identified in the eastern and western part of the industrial region where the lands are covered by dense vegetation and a water body (Maithon Lake), respectively.

Throughout the literature, the distribution of LST (mapped in Figure 5.3a and 5.3b) also reveals that the urban heat effect is more pronounced during the pre-monsoon (summer) period. Therefore, the entire study has been analysed in the pre-monsoon period only.

5.3.2 Surface Temperature Zones and Heat Island Identification

As the urban heat island (UHI) is identified on the basis of the dictum that the temperature of the urban area is 2–3°C more than the surrounding rural area, the LST map (Figure 5.3a) is classified into six temperature zones with 2 °C intervals (Figure 5.4). Two temperature zones (32 to 34 °C and

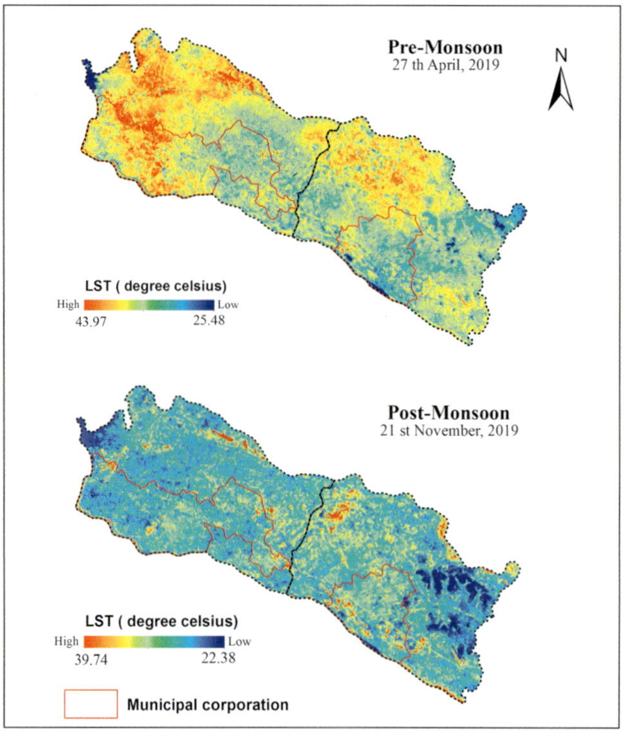

FIGURE 5.3 Land surface temperature (LST) a. Pre-monsoon, b. Post-monsoon.

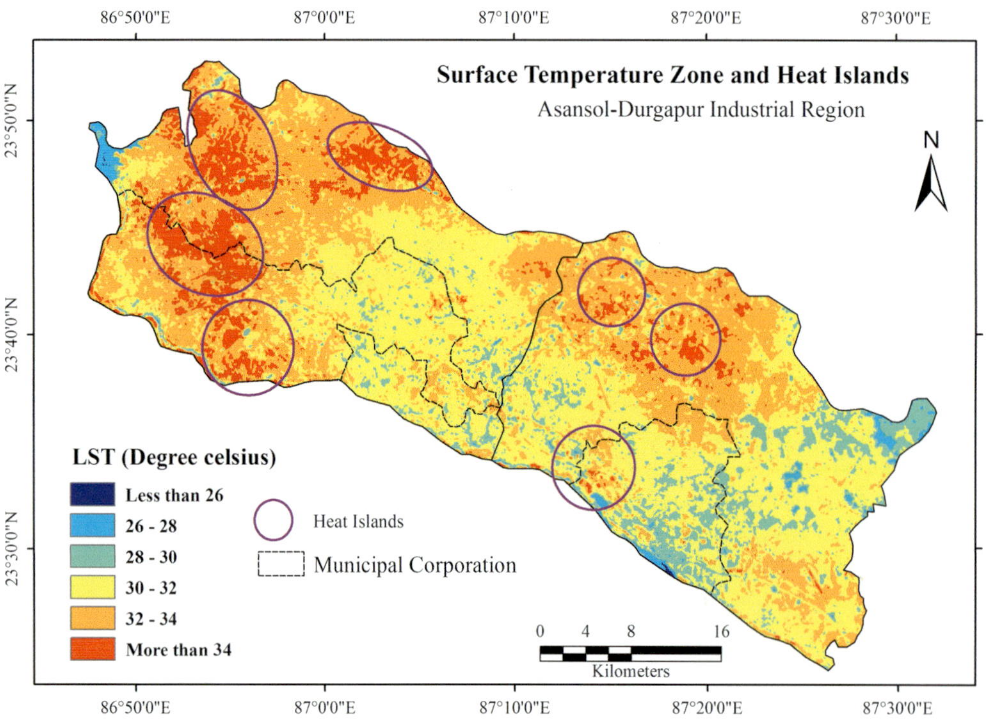

FIGURE 5.4 Surface temperature zones and heat islands.

TABLE 5.1
Location of Urban Heat Islands (UHIs) and Related Major Land Uses

Heat Islands	Location	Max/Min LST (°C)	Mean ± SD LST (°C)	Major Land Use
A	North of Barabani and Jamuria CD block	43.97 / 28.61	33.91 ± 1.36	Coal mine
B	Salanpur CD block, Chittaranjan Locomotive	37.39 / 28.03	33.86 ± 1.05	Coal mine, barren land, settlements
C	Kulti M, Barakar, Sitarampur	37.09 / 28.38	34.00 ± 1.11	Coal mine, settlements
D	Asansol MC, IISCO Steel Plant	38.65 / 28.08	33.05 ± 1.35	Settlements, industrial area
E	Durgapur MC, Steel plant	37.32 / 26.14	31.33 ± 1.41	Settlements, industrial area
F	Laudoha, Kalipur, Sirsa	35.76 / 29.40	33.19 ± 0.98	Barren land
G	Pandabeswar CD block, Kumardihi, Sonpur	36.28 / 27.67	33.03 ± 0.97	Coal mine

more than 34 °C) are distributed on the western part of the Asansol sub-division and northern part of the Durgapur sub-division with a small cluster on the eastern side. These two zones of high surface temperatures are found where the land is used either for mining and surrounding barren land or industrial cum urban residence. Zones (26 to 28 °C and less than 26 °C) with low surface temperatures are distributed only in a few places where water bodies are situated. The rest of the places has experienced temperature ranges from 28 °C to 32 °C covered with agriculture and vegetation.

The average temperature of the region remained close to 30 °C during the pre-monsoon (summer) season. We found that approximately 40% of the area of the industrial region portrayed more than 34 °C surface temperature (Figure 5.4) and Figure 5.3a has also revealed a maximum surface temperature of 43.97 °C concentrated in the centre of the coal mine area. Taking 34 °C as the threshold limit, we have determined seven heat islands (details are listed in Table 5.1) distributed over the region. Figure 5.5 has portrayed a surface temperature graph along the cross-sectional line of seven heat islands. All seven graphs have depicted that maximum and minimum temperature varies in between 35.76 °C to 43.97 °C and 26.14 °C to 29.40 °C, respectively. A heat island with the highest temperature (named as A) has been recorded north of the Asansol sub-division.

5.3.3 Relationship of LST with NDBI and NDVI

It is reaveled that the LST is an interpaly of various features of the Earth's surface. So far as the formation, intensity, and morphology of the heat island is concerned, the built-up area and the intensity of vegetation coverage of the land surface play an important role. In this respect, two important indices have been analysed such as normalized difference built-up index (NDBI) and normalized difference vegetation index (NDVI). The NDVI value has also been deployed here to know about the vegetation coverage and intensity. Mostly the Kanksa block of the Paschim Bardhaman district contains a high NDVI value (Figure 5.6a). Some built-up area, barren land, and some open cast mining areas exhibit very low NDVI values due to the absence of thick vegetation coverage. The NDBI is very useful for mapping the urban built-up areas and has been computed here (Guha et al., 2018; Morabito et al., 2016). The value of the NDBI ranges from −1 to +1. The positive value of the NDBI at its extreme end indicates highly built-up areas, whereas a negative value shows other land use (Figure 5.6b). In the study, two municipal corporation areas i.e.,

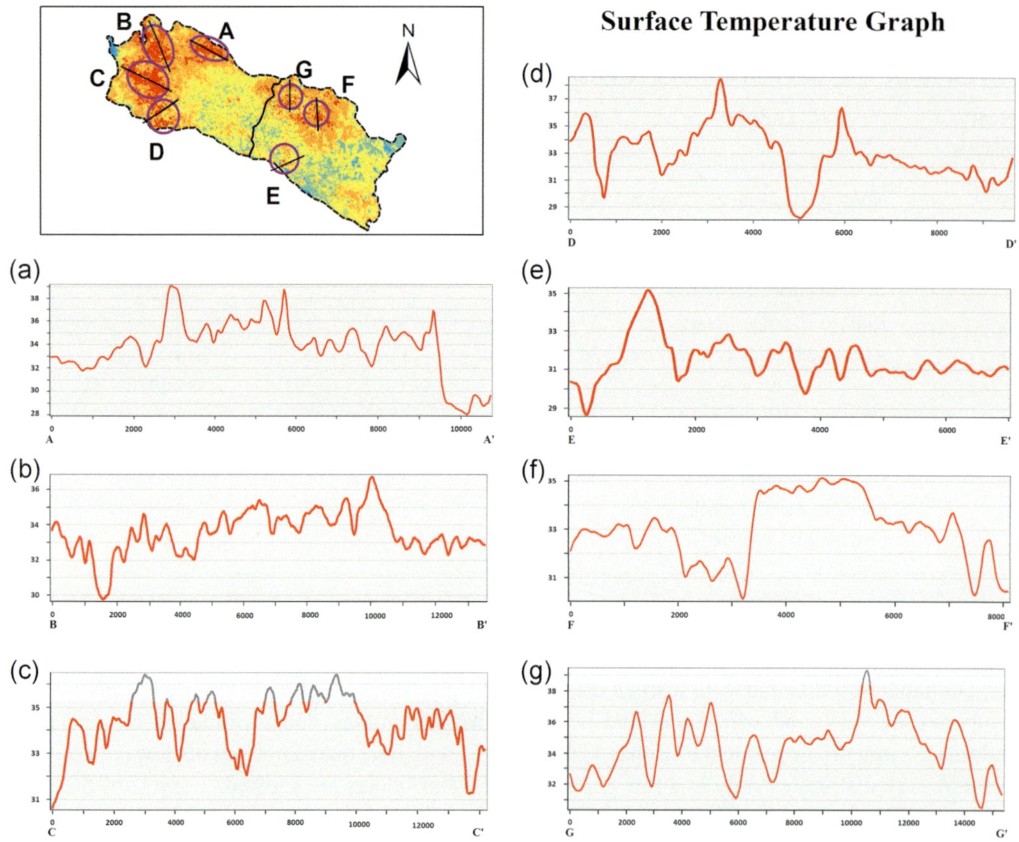

FIGURE 5.5 Surface temperature graph of seven heat islands.

Durgapur and Asansol, indicate a high NDBI value. Besides, the NDBI value is also high in the barren land due its reflection, same as the built-up area.

The relationship among the LST, NDVI, and NDBI has been analysed taking a sample of 460 points (Section 5.2.3.9) and respective values against each point data sets. The results reveal the strong positive correlation (r = 0.71, P = <0.001) with NDBI and negative correlation (r = –0.48, P = <0.001) with NDVI (Figure 5.7a and 5.7b). It means that the surface temperature increases with the increasing percentage of built-up area. Surface temperature is higher in the high-density built-up area and un-vegetated land. A high percentage of vegetation cover in and around the urban area has a significant influence on the thermal condition of cities. Vegetation can reduce the temperature of land surface through the process of evapotranspiration. It is statistically proved that a high percentage of dense vegetation experienced low surface temperature (Gomez-Martinez et al., 2021; Hamilton et al., 2018). But the correlation coefficient value (Figure 5.6a) is not high. The explanation can be cited here that the temperature is also influenced by the soil type and properties, elevation from sea level, slope of the land, aspect of the area, along with the vegetation cover. In spite of dense vegetation, some areas have depicted high temperatures due to lateritic soil and high elevation.

5.3.4 Land Use/Cover Pattern and Temperature Variation

The spatial pattern of a heat island is directly controlled by the nature of land use and land cover of Earth's surface. As LST is greatly influenced by the features of land use and land cover these three

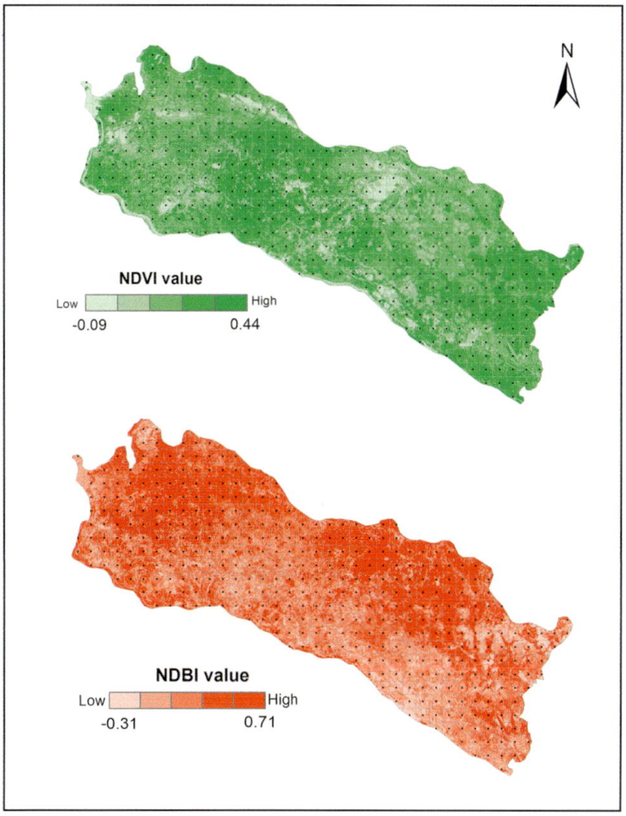

FIGURE 5.6 Distribution of a. NDVI and b. NDBI.

elements i.e., land use land cover, land surface temperature, and heat island formation, have a trio relationship among them. In the study, the LULC has been categorized into eight classes viz. vegetation, agricultural land, barren land, water bodies, coal mine, residential, industrial, and sand deposition (Figure 5.8). To find the relationship of the LST with land use/cover pattern, a chart has been prepared where the LST value is plotted against each land use/cover type (Figure 5.9).

This chart clearly indicates that the higher LST (36 °C) is recorded in a coal mine and residential area where a minimum LST (26 °C) is found in water bodies. A wide variation in LST is identified in agricultural land due to the variation of cultivation patterns, which change with the season. A transect chart has been prepared to prove how the temperature changes with changes in land use patterns (Figure 5.10). This chart has clearly showed the maximum temperature in the industrial area and minimum in water bodies.

5.3.5 Mitigation Measures

Elevated temperature due to the UHI, mainly during the pre-monsoon season, demands the high energy consumption for cooling purposes in urban areas. Moreover, it affects the local and regional environment and of course the health of inhabitants. This prime concerning issue has helped the policy maker and urban planner to develop the UHI mitigation measures through tree plantations, green roofs, and cool roofs, etc. It is found that the triggering causes for UHI are different and varies with land use patterns, as our study portrayed in Figure 5.10 and Table 5.1. The present study reveals the presence of large industries, high-density residence, barren land (unvegetated surface), and open

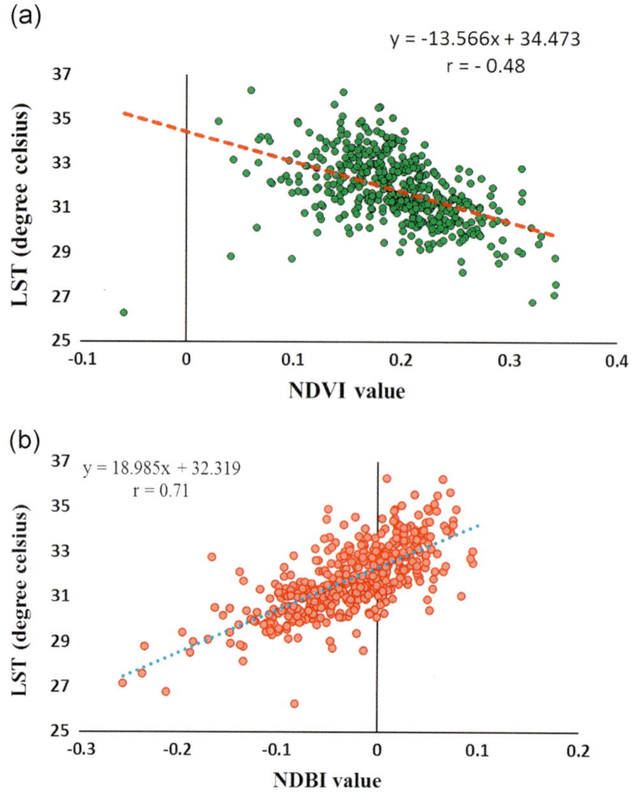

FIGURE 5.7 Correlation between a. LST and NDVI, b. LST and NDBI.

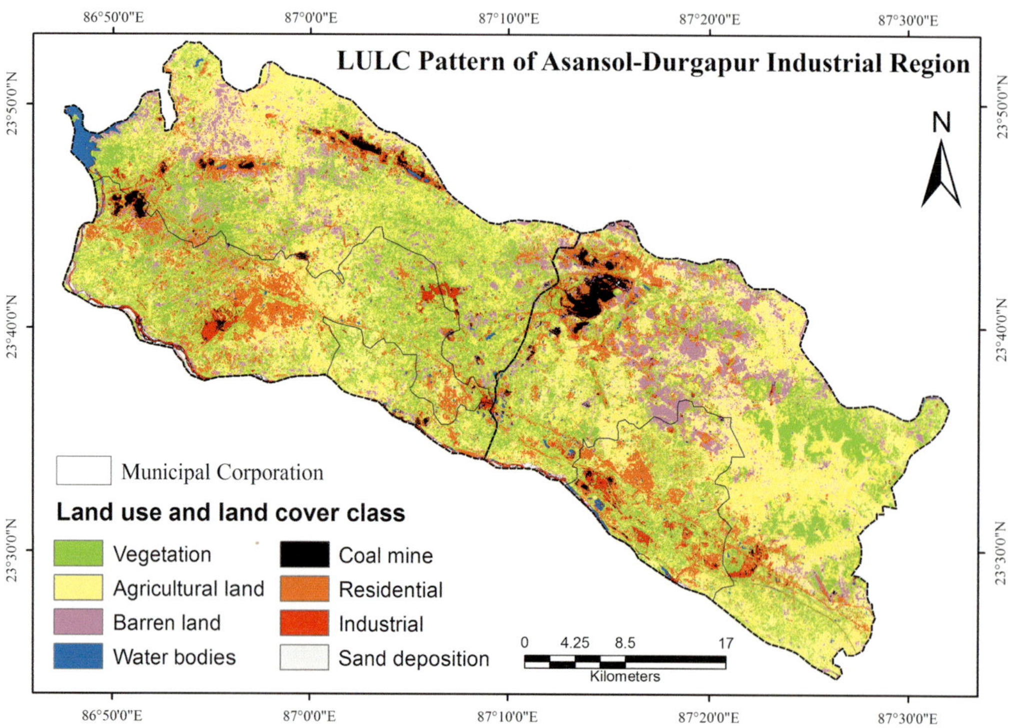

FIGURE 5.8 Land use and land cover (LULC) pattern.

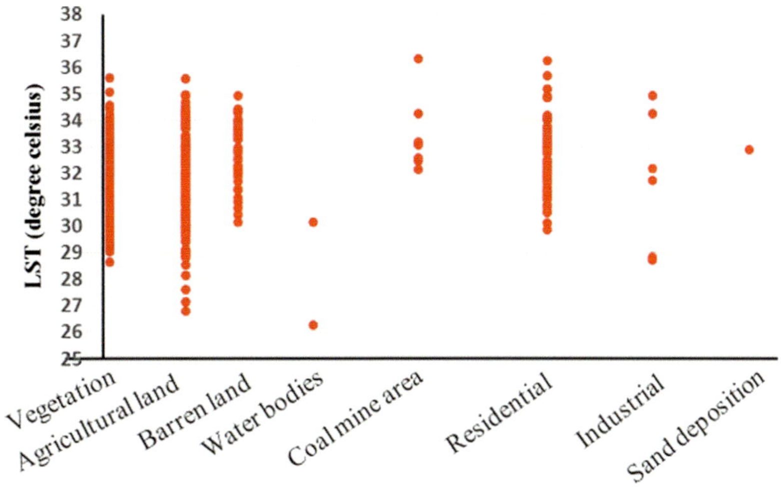

FIGURE 5.9 LST distribution against LULC class.

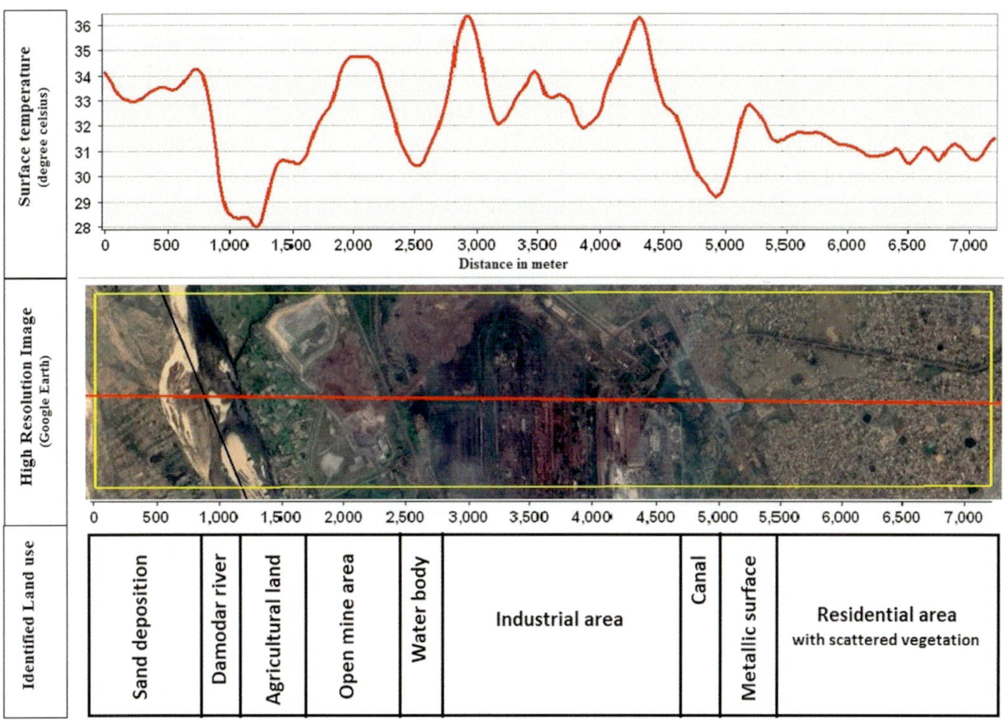

FIGURE 5.10 Surface temperature graph along a cross section.

cast coal mine are the major causes of UHI effects in the Asansol-Durgapur industrial region. A detailed insight on the distribution of a heat island depicted surface temperature is more intensive in and around the coal mine area. Therefore, mitigation measures should be location and sector specific, as portrayed in Figure 5.11, to reduce surface temperature of the study area.

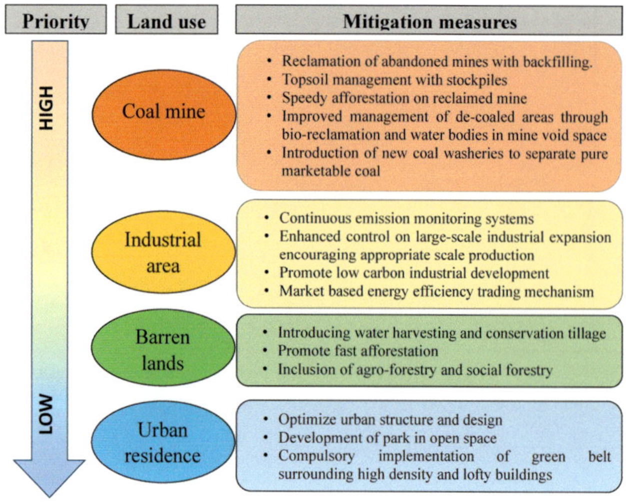

FIGURE 5.11 Mitigation measures.

5.4 CONCLUSIONS

The present study has been conducted to analyse and map the surface UHIs with an attempt to propose the mitigation measures in the Asansol-Durgapur industrial region. We have used the LST extracted from the thermal band of the Landsat-8 OLI/TIRS sensor and tried to correlate it with NDVI, NDBI, and land use patterns as well. The findings reveal the identification of seven heat islands distributed in both the Asansol and Durgapur sub-divisions. The intensity of the LST is high in the western and northern part of the region where most of the land is used for surface mining (open cast) and industrial development. It is found the presence of an open cast coal mine, industrial cum high-density residence, and barren land including unvegetated surface are responsible for intensive surface heating. A high positive correlation is determined between the LST and NDBI ($r = 0.71$), which support the increasing surface temperature with the built-up area. Other relations bring out negative correlations with NDVI ($r = -0.48$), which means the presence of vegetation lowers the temperature. Examining the overall analysis, sector-wise mitigation measures have been proposed to reduce the triggering causes of UHIs. Abandoned mine reclamation, bio-reclamation in de-coaled land, afforestation, green belt, and control of large-scale industrial expansion should be prioritized to minimise the surface temperature and thermal discomfort.

REFERENCES

Ahmad, Asmala, and Shaun Quegan. 2012. "Analysis of Maximum Likelihood Classification on Multispectral Data." *Applied Mathematical Sciences* 6 (129): 6425–36.

Asimakopoulos, D. N., V. D. Assimakopoulos, N. Chrisomallidou, N. Klitsikas, D. Mangold, P. Michel, M. Santamouris, and A. Tsangrassoulis. 2001. *Energy and Climate in the Urban Built Environment*, edited by M. Santamouris. New York, USA: Routledge, Taylor & Francis Group. https://doi.org/https://doi.org/10.4324/9781315073774

Carlson, T. N., and David A. Ripley. 1997. "On the Relation between NDVI, Fractional Vegetation Cover, and Leaf Area Index." *Remote Sensing of Environment* 62 (3): 241–52.

Census of India. 2011. "District Census Handbook Barddhaman". Village and Town Directory, Series-20, West Bengal, India.

Choudhury, Deblina, Kalikinkar Das, and Arijit Das. 2019. "Assessment of Land Use Land Cover Changes and Its Impact on Variations of Land Surface Temperature in Asansol-Durgapur Development Region." *The Egyptian Journal of Remote Sensing and Space Sciences* 22 (2): 203–18. https://doi.org/10.1016/j.ejrs.2018.05.004.

Das, Niladri, Prolay Mondal, Subhasish Sutradhar, and Ranajit Ghosh. 2020. "Sensing and Space Sciences Assessment of Variation of Land Use/Land Cover and Its Impact on Land Surface Temperature of Asansol Subdivision." *The Egyptian Journal of Remote Sensing and Space Sciences*, 24 (1): 131–49. https://doi.org/10.1016/j.ejrs.2020.05.001

Deng, Yuanhong, Shijie Wang, Xiaoyong Bai, Yichao Tian, and Luhua Wu. 2018. "Relationship among Land Surface Temperature and LUCC, NDVI in Typical Karst Area." *Scientific Reports* 8: 641. https://doi.org/10.1038/s41598-017-19088-x

Dutta, Debjani, Srimanta Gupta, and C. M. Kishtawal. 2020. "Linking LULC Change with Urban Heat Islands over 25 Years: A Case Study of the Urban-Industrial City Durgapur, Eastern India." *Journal of Spatial Science* 65 (3): 501–18. https://doi.org/10.1080/14498596.2018.1537198

Eastern Coalfields Limited. 2012. "Annual report & accounts 2012–13." Sanctoria, Dishergarh, Burdwan.

Fawzi, Nurul Ihsan, and Retnadi Heru Jatmiko. 2015. "Heat Island Detection in Coal Mining Areas Using Multitemporal Heat Island Detection in Coal Mining Areas Using." In Proceedings of the *36th Asian Conference on Remote Sensing*, 1–10. Metro Manila, Philippines.

Ghazanfari S., M. Naseri, F. Faridani, H. Aboutorabi, and A. Farid. 2009. "Evaluating the Effects of UHI on Climate Parameters (A Case Study for Mashhad, Khorrasan)." *WSEAS Transactions on Environment and Development* 5 (7): 508–17.

Golden, Jay S. 2003. "The Built Environment Induced Urban Heat Island Effect in Rapidly Urbanizing Arid Regions – A Sustainable Urban Engineering Complexity." *Environmental Sciences* 1 (4): 321–49. https://doi.org/10.1080/15693430412331291698

Gomez-Martinez, Filoteo, Kirsten M. De Beurs, Jennifer Koch, and Jeffrey Widener. 2021. "Multi-Temporal Land Surface Temperature and Vegetation Greenness in Urban Green Spaces of Puebla, Mexico". *Land* 10: 155.

Grigoraș, Georgiana, and Bogdan Urițescu. 2019. "Land Use/Land Cover Changes Dynamics and Their Effects on Surface Urban Heat Island in Bucharest, Romania." *International Journal of Applied Earth Observation and Geoinformation* 80: 115–26. https://doi.org/10.1016/j.jag.2019.03.009

Guha, Subhanil, Himanshu Govil, Anindita Dey, and Neetu Gill. 2018. "Analytical Study of Land Surface Temperature with NDVI and NDBI Using Landsat 8 OLI and TIRS Data in Florence and Naples City, Italy". *European Journal of Remote Sensing* 51 (1): 667–78. https://doi.org/10.1080/22797254.2018.1474494

Gupta, Koyel, Anindita Dey, and Biraj Kanti Mondal. 2019. "Geoinformatics Based Techniques for the Study of Spatialization of Urban Heat Island and Micro-Climatic Region in Asansol Durgapur Development Authority, West Bengal". In *Geo-Environmental Issues of the New Millennium*, 361–369. Kolkata, India:Dey's Publishing.

Hamilton, S. K., M. Z. Hussain, C. Lowrie, B. Basso, and G. P. Robertson. 2018. Evapotranspiration is resilient in the face of land cover and climate change in a humid temperate catchment. *Hydrological Processes* 32: 655–63. https://doi.org/10.1002/hyp.11447

Julien, Yves, and José A. Sobrino. 2009. "The Yearly Land Cover Dynamics (YLCD) Method : An Analysis of Global Vegetation from NDVI and LST Parameters". *Remote Sensing of Environment* 113 (2): 329–34. https://doi.org/10.1016/j.rse.2008.09.016

Kamila, Amrit, and Subodh Chandra Pal. 2015. "Monitoring of Land Surface Temperature and Analyzing of Environmental Prediction on Asansol and Durgapur Sub-Division, Burdwan District, West Bengal Using Landsat". *International Journal of Remote Sensing & Geoscience (IJRSG)* 4 (1): 33–6.

Kaplan, Gordana, Ugur Avdan, and Zehra Yigit Avdan. 2018. "Urban Heat Island Analysis Using the Landsat 8 Satellite Data: A Case Study in Skopje, Macedonia." *Proceedings* 2: 358. https://doi.org/10.3390/ecrs-2-05171

Kolokotroni, Maria, and Renganathan Giridharan. 2008. "Urban Heat Island Intensity in London : An Investigation of the Impact of Physical Characteristics on Changes in Outdoor Air Temperature during Summer". *Solar Energy* 82: 986–98. https://doi.org/10.1016/j.solener.2008.05.004

Kolokotsa, D., A. Psomas, and E. Karapidakis. 2009. "Urban Heat Island in Southern Europe : The Case Study of Hania, Crete". *Solar Energy* 83: 1871–83. https://doi.org/10.1016/j.solener.2009.06.018

Kotharkar, Rajashree, and Meenal Surawar. 2016. "Land Use, Land Cover, and Population Density Impact on the Formation of Canopy Urban Heat Islands through Traverse Survey in the Nagpur Urban Area, India". *Journal of Urban Planning and Development* 142 (1): 1–13. https://doi.org/10.1061/(ASCE)UP.1943-5444.0000277

Luber, George, and Michael Mcgeehin. 2008. "Climate Change and Extreme Heat Events." *American Journal of Preventive Medicine* 35 (5): 429–35. https://doi.org/10.1016/j.amepre.2008.08.021

Luck, Matthew, and Jianguo Wu. 2002. "A Gradient Analysis of Urban Landscape Pattern : A Case Study from the Phoenix Metropolitan Region, Arizona, USA." *Landscape Ecology* 17: 327–40.

Malik, Mohammad Subzar, Jai Prakash Shukla, and Satanand Mishra. 2019. "Relationship of LST, NDBI and NDVI Using Landsat-8 Data in Kandaihimmat Watershed, Hoshangabad, India". *Indian Journal of Geo-Marine Sciences* 48 (1): 25–31.

Ministry of MSME, Govt. of India. 2019. "District Industrial Profile PASCHIM BARDHAMAN 2018-19." Kolkata, Government of India.

Morabito, Marco, Alfonso Crisci, Alessandro Messeri, Simone Orlandini, Antonio Raschi, Giampiero Maracchi, and Michele Munafò. 2016. "The Impact of Built-up Surfaces on Land Surface Temperatures in Italian Urban Areas." *Science of the Total Environment* 551–552: 317–26. https://doi.org/10.1016/j.scitotenv.2016.02.029

Ndossi, Milton Isaya, and Ugur Avdan. 2016. "Application of Open Source Coding Technologies in the Production of Land Surface Temperature (LST) Maps from Landsat : A PyQGIS Plugin." *Remote Sensing* 8 (5): 413. https://doi.org/10.3390/rs8050413

Nichol, Janet E. 1994. "A GIS-Based Approach to Microclimate Monitoring in Singapore's High-RiseHousing Estates."*Photogrammetric Engineering & Remote Sensing* 60(10):1225–32.

Odindi, John, Onisimo Mutanga, Elfatih M. Abdel-Rahman, Elhadi Adam, and Victor Bangamwabo. 2015. "Determination of Urban Land-Cover Types and Their Implication on Thermal Characteristics in Three South African Coastal Metropolitans Using Remotely Sensed Data." *South African Geographical Journal* 90(1): 52–67. https://doi.org/10.1080/03736245.2015.1117015

Qin, Z., A. Karnieli, and P. Berliner. 2001. "A Mono-Window Algorithm for Retrieving Land Surface Temperature from Landsat TM Data and Its Application to the Israel-Egypt Border Region." *International Journal of Remote Sensing* 22 (18): 3719–46. https://doi.org/http://dx.doi.org/10.1080/01431160010006971

Roth, M. 2013. Urban heat islands. In *Handbook of Environmental Fluid Dynamics*, edited by H. J. Fernando, pp. 143–59. Boca Raton, Florida CRCPress/Taylor & Francis Group.

Shahmohamadi P., A. I. Che-Ani, K. N. A. Maulud, N. M. Tawil, and N. A. G. Abdullah. 2011. "The Impact of Anthropogenic Heat on Formation of Urban Heat Island and Energy Consumption Balance". *Urban Studies Research* 2011: 1–9. https://doi.org/10.1155/2011/497524

Snyder, W. C., Z. Wan, Y. Zhang, and Y. Feng 1998. "Classification-Based Emissivity for Land Surface Temperature Measurement from Space". *International Journal of Remote Sensing* 19 (14): 2753–74. https://doi.org/10.1080/014311698214497

Sobrinoa, Jose´ A., Juan C. Jiménez-Muñoz, and Leonardo Paolinib. 2004. "Land Surface Temperature Retrieval from LANDSAT TM 5". *Remote Sensing of Environment* 90: 434–40. https://doi.org/10.1016/j.rse.2004.02.003

Streutker, D. R. 2002. "A Remote Sensing Study of the Urban Heat Island of Houston, Texas". *International Journal of Remote Sensing* 23 (13): 2595–608. https://doi.org/10.1080/01431160110115023

Sultana, Sabiha, and A. N. V. Satyanarayana 2019. "Impact of Urbanisation on Urban Heat Island Intensity during Summer and Winter over Indian Metropolitan Cities." *Environmental Monitoring and Assessment* 191: 789. https://doi.org/https://doi.org/10.1007/s10661-019-7692-9

Swain, D., G. J. Roberts, J. Dash, K. Lekshmi, V. Vinoj, and S. Tripathy 2017. "Impact of Rapid Urbanization on the City of Bhubaneswar, India". *Proceedings of the National Academy of Sciences, India, Section A: Physical Sciences* 87: 845–53. https://doi.org/10.1007/s40010-017-0453-7

Voogt, J. A., and T. R. Oke 2003. "Thermal Remote Sensing of Urban Climates". *Remote Sensing of Environment* 86: 370–84. https://doi.org/10.1016/S0034-4257(03)00079-8

Wan, Zhengming, and Jeff Dozier 1996. "A Generalized Split- Window Algorithm for Retrieving Land-Surface Temperature from Space". *IEEE Transactions on Geoscience and Remote Sensing* 34 (4): 892–905.

Wasige, John E., Thomas A. Groen, Eric Smaling, and Victor Jetten. 2013. "Monitoring Basin-Scale Land Cover Changes in Kagera Basin of Lake Victoria Using Ancillary Data and Remote Sensing." *International Journal of Applied Earth Observations and Geoinformation* 21: 32–42. https://doi.org/10.1016/j.jag.2012.08.005

Waters, Ralf, Richard Allen, Masahiro Tasumi, Ricardo Trezza, and Wim Bastiaanssen. 2002. *(SEBAL) Surface Energy Balance Algorithms for Land.* Idaho Implementation. Advanced Training and Users Manual.

Weng, Qihao. 2003. "Fractal Analysis of Satellite-Detected Urban Heat Island Effect." *Photogrammetric Engineering & Remote Sensing* 69 (5): 555–66. https://doi.org/10.14358/PERS.69.5.555

Xie, Qijiao, and Zhixiang Zhou. 2015. "Impact of Urbanization on Urban Heat Island Effect Based on TM Imagery in Wuhan, China." *Environmental Engineering and Management Journal* 14 (3): 647–55. https://doi.org/10.30638/eemj.2015.072

Yadav, Naval Kishore, Abhisek Santra, and Amiya Kumar Samanta. 2016. "Identification of Urban Heat Islands from Multi Temporal MODIS Land Surface Temperature Data in the Southern Part of West Bengal, India." *International Journal of Engineering Sciences & Research Technology* 5 (5): 640–5.

Yuan, Fei, and Marvin E. Bauer. 2007. "Comparison of Impervious Surface Area and Normalized Difference Vegetation Index as Indicators of Surface Urban Heat Island Effects in Landsat Imagery." *Remote Sensing of Environment* 106: 375–86. https://doi.org/10.1016/j.rse.2006.09.003

Yue, W., J. Xu, W. Tan, and L. Xu. 2007. "The Relationship between Land Surface Temperature and NDVI with Remote Sensing: Application to Shanghai Landsat 7 ETM + Data". *International Journal of Remote Sensing* 28 (15): 3205–26. https://doi.org/10.1080/01431160500306906

Zha, Y., J. Gao, and S. Ni. 2003. "Use of Normalized Difference Built-up Index in Automatically Mapping Urban Areas from TM Imagery." *International Journal of Remote Sensing* 24 (3): 583–94. https://doi.org/https://doi.org/10.1080/01431160304987

Zhang, Youshui, Inakwu O. A. Odeh, and Chunfeng Han. 2009. "Bi-Temporal Characterization of Land Surface Temperature in Relation to Impervious Surface Area, NDVI and NDBI, Using a Sub-Pixel Image Analysis". *International Journal of Applied Earth Observation and Geoinformation* 11: 256–64. https://doi.org/10.1016/j.jag.2009.03.001

6 Approaches to Season-Responsive Urban Spaces for Children: Lessons and Challenges in Winter Cities

Aireen Grace Andal
Macquarie University, Sydney, Australia
Ural Federal University, Yekaterinburg, Russian Federation

CONTENTS

6.1 INTRODUCTION

This chapter seeks to contribute to the discussions on the ever-increasing role of weather in cities and urban governance discourses for their inclusiveness of urban residents more broadly, and that of children, in specific. It presents the relevance of children in understanding winter urban governance toward making child-friendly winter cities. The broader context in this study is grounded on two urban movements: winter cities and child-friendly cities. The winter season sets forth unique challenges for urban dwellers due to its "cold, snow- and ice-producing phenomenon of the water-land-atmosphere interface" (Hamelin, 2002: 43 cited in Chartier, 2007). Pressman (1985: 15) noted that "there is a unique beauty intrinsic to winter, but not all urban dwellers will be able to appreciate this beauty." Yet, as cold regions of the world urbanize, appreciation of winter has gained traction. For instance, the Winter Cities Movement emphasizes the unique context of urban settlements that experience winter (Erskine, 1968; Collymore, 1985). The Winter Cities Movement is a response to the urgency to adapt the urban context in view of the UN Sustainable Development Goals that specifically stipulate its Goal 11 on urban areas to prioritize resilience, sustainability, inclusivity, and safety. Recent visions of winter cities aim "to reduce winter's negative consequences and to emphasize its positive features and opportunities, to create more sustainable and livable settlements" (Davies, 2015: 278).

Alongside climate-responsive urbanization and sustainable development, the idea of child-friendly cities also received attention as response to the increasing population of children in cities

DOI: 10.1201/9781003126195-8

(Chawla and Van Vliet, 2016). In 1996, UNICEF (2004) launched the program called Child Friendly Cities Initiative (CFCI) with the premises of "nondiscrimination, the right to life and maximum development and respecting children's views" (Hörschelmann and van Blerk, 2012: 192). The challenge, however, is that most child-friendly city initiatives have limited models, thereby underrepresenting diverse urban climate conditions including winter cities. Moreover, although preceding urban scholars have provided wisdom on designing sustainable winter cities (see for example Blumenfeld, 1985; Gappert, 1987; Culjat and Erskine, 1988; Pressman, 1996), these accounts pay little attention to children's specific needs in winter. . Children are especially sensitive to weather changes as they are less able to adapt physiologically and metabolically compared to adults at adapting to coldness and other climate-related exposure. The lack of physical activities during the winter can be a major issue given that outdoor winter environments support both mental and physical health of children (Mendes et al., 2014). For example, a pertinent issue for children is having safe urban designs that are "walkable, runnable, [and] bikeable places that are also sledable, skiable [and] skateable places" for young people (Borys, 2017a). Moreover, while there have been efforts to provide a child-centered perspective on sustainable urban spaces, most available urban models for children remain applicable to ideal conditions (Costamagna et al., 2019). For instance, green spaces are applicable in cities under temperatures that accommodate plant survival, which is not applicable for cities that experience winter for half a year. Yet, designs of public space tend to focus on good weather and thus set aside the potential of challenges in children's circumstances in public space in the winter. Public playgrounds have some equipment not suitable for winter, such as the materials used under climbing equipment and swings, which lose their shock-absorbing quality in freezing weather.

To answer the question about how contemporary urban developments, city planning and policy-making encompass children's spaces during winter, this chapter reviews urban practices insightful for developing a child-responsive winter city agenda. This analysis builds on previous studies conducted on both child-friendly and winter cities, which have been instructive to urban policy and design. Through an examination of the literature on the best practices and challenges cities face in dealing with the winter, this work identifies a potential call-to-action for cities to be more season-responsive for children, such as making playgrounds with "more flexible design in which seasonal changes can be seen as useful and enjoyable" (Rooijmans, 2018: 205). Child-oriented protection and resilience systems remain important factors to combat urban vulnerability to temperature-related hazards. As such, the insights generated from this study are hoped to spark discussions on an alternative framework for winter cities to meet the child-friendly city ideals.

6.2 LITERATURE REVIEW: SHARED PRINCIPLES OF CHILD-FRIENDLY CITIES AND WINTER CITIES

There are four key areas that child-friendly cities and winter cities movements share: *First*, both question our assumptions about cities and suggest a paradigm shift on how to understand urbanity. Child-friendly cities challenge the adult-centric urbanity that oversees children's urban needs. Likewise, winter cities interrogate the idea that winter is "a negative force generating inconvenience and added costs – instead of a positive one" (Bergum and Beaubien, 2009). *Second*, mobility is a primary concern for both child-friendly and winter cities, especially that children have low physical activities during long periods of darkness in winter. Studies show that children spend less time moving and participating in play activities when the days are short, which implies unique challenges to winter cities in providing a healthier and vibrant public life (See Goodman et al., 2012; Horton, and Kraftl, 2018; Leung and O'Connor, 2019). *Third*, human–nature relationships are at the center of urban life. Child-friendly cities emphasize the importance of exposing children to nature such as urban gardens and sunlight (Hörschelmann and Van Blerk, 2012) and winter cities embrace snow, ice, and winter's coldness for residents to enjoy their experience with nature (Pressman, 1996). Even winter-safety health manuals for children promote spending time with nature (see for example, Canadian Paediatric Society, 2002). *Lastly*, both child-friendly and winter cities encourage community participation. Winter offers the opportunity for children and their communities to collectively appreciate the winter environment (Tourula et al., 2013). As such, a key urban objective of both child-friendly and winter cities is to create environments that promote children's community participation, allowing children to understand how the winter conditions influence their choices and opportunities.

6.3 METHODOLOGY

This chapter draws lessons from selected literature on the status of children in urban spaces during the winter season and offers direction for a reimagined way of integrating children further in the urban settings during winter. Specifically, this chapter gathers findings in the last 20 years from the (rather limited) literature relevant to the dialogue concerning children, urbanity, and seasons. This work adopts the definition of a winter city from the World Winter Cities Association for Mayors (World Winter Cities Association for Mayors, 2017): cities with an approximate average temperature below 0 °C at least one month per year and with at least 20 cm of snow per year. Note, however, that some studies have more specific definitions, such as settlements with "high degrees of seasonal climate variation, temperatures commonly below zero, precipitation that is mainly snow, and limited hours of sunshine and daylight. In such settlements, winter conditions and covers of snow and ice are a regular part of the built environment and can be in place for between 4 and 6 months of the year" (Chapman et al., 2019: 2; see also Pressman, 1989). While most of these cities are located almost exclusively in the Northern Hemisphere (Stout et al., 2018), countries from the Southern Hemisphere, such as Argentina, Australia, Chile, New Zealand, and South Africa, also experience winter.

The basic inclusion criteria for this study are materials published in the English language from 2000–2020 that contain reports on winter city practices related to children 5–12 years old. To clarify, this work does not incorporate any primary data that involve children participation. The examined materials are books, journal articles, conference papers, and other authoritative sources, including national and local governments (print and online sources), academic institutions, urban studies societies and leading non-government organizations. These materials were varied in focus on urban studies, of which children's experience can be only one aspect. Given the heterogeneous nature of the literature reviewed in this chapter, they could only represent certain geographies and consequently only present a partial picture of children's winter city experiences. There might be unidentified relevant materials, which ultimately restrict the scope of analysis of this study. These limitations, however, serve as key areas for future research. This chapter stands as a contribution in urban scholarship by drawing together literature of child-focused winter city practices and experiences.

6.4 FINDINGS: CHILD-FRIENDLY URBAN WINTER INITIATIVES

In what follows, this section presents successful visions and practices in winter cities that embody innovative opportunities for children to meaningfully experience the winter period. Of particular interest is how such city agendas serve as inclusive urban practices for children in winter cities, which transpire in at least five themes: paradigm shift, mobility, nature, participation, and protection and resilience.

6.4.1 Paradigm Shift

Winter cities initiatives have transformed the impression of winter from being an indoor season into an outdoor community experience, which "leverage[s] the characteristics that make it [winter] unique" (Neumann, 2013). For instance, winter cities creatively incorporate darkness into public art to reduce muted tones of winter (Coleman, 2010). Urban designers install strings of lights along business districts, thereby creating a delightful atmosphere for urban dwellers across all ages. In Edinburgh, for instance, dark streets turned into enjoyable sights with overhead lighting in mesh roofs for the streets. Likewise, Paris took advantage of darkness to re-create a "winter wonderland" dramatic ambiance through lighting trees with pale blue lights (Walljasper, 2015). Winter cities also acknowledge the affordances of cold weather such as having designated areas for spray-painting snow, building snow objects, and piling snow for climbing and sliding activities. This paradigm shift of embracing long periods of darkness and coldness has enabled winter cities to enjoy winter festivals with the principle that "snow is an asset and so it should be celebrated and promoted" (Neumann, 2013). Winter cities create specific design features to encourage families to occupy urban public space for civic affairs and community events. The City of Toronto, for example, partnered with Evergreen and La Pépinière to create Loose-Parts Play for children in which they can enjoy outdoor rinks in some of the city's parks through a place-making pilot called Rink Social (Evergreen, 2019). Moreover, Quebec is known for its winter carnival, where street vendors sell hot bread while Ottawa is famed for its Rideau Canal, where residents skate through a wintry landscape (Walljasper, 2009). Meanwhile, London's Hyde Park hosts a Winter Wonderland where one of the largest Christmas events occurs, featuring over 100 rides and attractions and attracting local and international visitors (Eldridge and Pappalepore, 2019). London also allots one-day events for children such as the "toy parade" in Regent Street (Gillett, 2016). Finally, following the examples of Winnipeg's winter hut competition and Washington's massive community snowball fights, Saint Paul, Minnesota, established its Winterhood Lab, a pilot project for neighborhood residents to visit public spaces during winter months (O'Connor, 2015).

6.4.2 Mobility

Perpetual challenges to winter cities include creating winter-adjusted environments and understanding how winter conditions influence residents' mobility choices (Katapally et al., 2016; Chapman et al., 2019). When scaled to the level of children, a key challenge is to have winter spaces that encourage movement, especially in terms of being "walkable, bikeable, and transit-friendly" for children (Borys, 2017b). Winter cities offer examples of play environments as democratizing spaces. Many cities in Sweden and Norway design their urban environment to encourage children's outdoor mobility such as having winter playgrounds with themes of mystery and adventure, role-playing, and interactive events (Steinsvik, 2004). In Moscow's parks, children use snow as "loose parts" to unleash their artistic talents (Gudova, 2016). Moreover, winter events such as the Vancouver Winter Olympics have increased the physical activity and sports participation among Canadian children in an otherwise mobility restrictive weather condition (Craig and Bauman, 2014). Likewise, in their first winter with pandemic distancing protocols, residents of Manitoba took the initiative to create winter outdoor projects such as winter arts and curling rinks where children within the vicinity can enjoy when they cannot go to parks (Bergen, 2021). Meanwhile, some cities encourage indoor mobility too. Edmonton's Green Shack program hosts supervised winter activities such as games, sport, crafts, music, drama, and special events for children aged 6–12 during after-school hours (City of Edmonton, 2018). Washington, D.C., also has a wealth of public libraries, museums, indoor playgrounds, and obstacles spaces for children during the winter months (Austermuhle, 2019). Arranging winter venues adjacent to each other is also functional, such as placing a skating rink and children's play area next to outdoor cafés, outdoor library reading rooms, or vacation markets to allow children and parents to go together whilst having different interests (Walljasper, 2009). Finally, to address issues on accessing indoor washrooms (such as in libraries, community centers, stores, or eateries) during the coronavirus pandemic, urban planners have been trying to increase the number of comfortable and clean park restrooms (880 Cities and AARP, 2020).

The mobility of children with disabilities is another issue during winter, including physical barriers, transportation struggles, and safety concerns (see Lindsay and Yantzi, 2014). The weather conditions make it more difficult for children with disabilities to participate in recreational activities during winter (Lindsay et al., 2015). In response, winter city initiatives offer adaptation strategies to enhance the outdoor participation of children with disabilities such as innovations on adapting mobility devices to enhance the safety of youth during winter (Buettgen et al., 2018). Moreover, neighborhoods are crucial to maintaining inclusive protocols for children with disabilities. For instance, in Edmonton, neighborhoods have universally accessible designs that ensure safety and security for children with disabilities in moving in snow and ice (City of Edmonton, 2016). Indeed, winter cities are gradually working on making high-quality urban design of neighborhoods so children with disabilities can independently safely move within their community.

6.4.3 Nature

Natural winterscapes also offer a unique aesthetic of nature in which children can witness how "winter brings a different and more analytical lens to the way we see landscape" (Chassé, 2005: 38). Snow and winter plants are the primary natural affordances of winter to children. Children can especially use snow as an available and renewable natural endowment from which they can make snowmen, snowballs, snow castles, and footprints (Gudova, 2016). They can imaginatively combine snow with other elements of nature such as fallen branches, stones, and wood or join adults in making snow artworks such as snow statues and snow/ice lanterns (Enai et al., 2004). Winter cities also encourage using nature-based and climate-sensitive designs in neighborhoods or city centers (Davies, 2015). The aesthetics brought by winter plants produce a "translucent facade of the winter garden [that] blurs the presence of the immediate surroundings, to distance them from the house" (Ruby and Ruby, 2001: 15). Moreover, plants are especially beneficial for winter hazard protection such as having dense coniferous vegetation on the parks to help block the wind and maximize heat from solar radiation (Foss, 2017). While the idea of Winter Gardens started in the 20th century (See Howard, 1946), advancement in botanical studies encouraged winter shrubs to be displayed in winter gardens to "enjoy the variety of winter colors, textures, and forms" of winter plants (Pelczar, 2009: 73). For example, the Ulster Museum located in the Botanic Gardens in Belfast includes exhibitions for all types of visitors, including schoolchildren (Daniels, 2005).

Winter cities also address natural winter hazards to create more comfortable microclimates for children such as snow removal and storage, creating barriers against the wind or vehicle traffic, and forming snow hills where children can play (Foss, 2017). In Denmark, landscape architects make efforts to appropriately design city parks based on wind and sunshine patterns, such as installing moveable benches, thereby making outdoor areas comfortable for adults and children alike. Meanwhile, the downtown sidewalks in Oslo installed heating coils for warmth and even melting of snow (Walljasper, 2015). The Environment Agency of London in cooperation with the local city government creates sustainable approaches to winter flood as a response to the expected freshwater flood flows from tributaries that drain into some urban spaces due to higher winter rainfall (Environment Agency UK, 2021).

6.4.4 Participation

Participatory approaches and place-making activities in winter cities have led to new practices in urban planning, highlighting local culture and vibrant physical environment. Winter cities conduct pilot programs and gather information from residents to guide winter city designs, establish solid winter communities, and create a better sense of place for children. At the forefront of placemaking is Edmonton for its participatory consultation called Winter City Strategy initiative, which paved the way for greater community engagement from all ages and walks of life to experience public life outdoors during winter (City of Edmonton, 2016). Participation also comes in forms of surveys on citizens' city-related concerns. St. Joseph, Michigan, opened two ice arenas in 2002 because of citizens' requests for ice rinks, which continue to increase in popularity today. Currently, the rinks are visited by casual skaters of all ages looking for a family-oriented activity. Children can also join figure skating classes or ice hockey leagues of all ages for both practice and tournaments (Kearny, 2010).

Showing recognition of young people's full citizenship, winter cities also place an emphasis on direct participation of children in urban planning such as having youth councils and youth consultants in urban planning (Driskell, 2002; Checkoway et al., 2005; Collins et al., 2016; Nir and Perry-Hazan, 2016). In Eindhoven, for instance, community city planning includes child-focused participatory activities such as gathering suggestions from children on play space improvements in winter during participant-led planning events (Krishnamurthy, 2019). Likewise, St. Petersburg holds planning workshops involving young people's suggestions such as "build[ing] glass cubes on the streets for socialising with Wi-Fi and climate control, that will be warm in winter and cool in summer" (Epeshina and Markova, 2018: 214). Meanwhile, in Eau Claire, the group 880 Cities held an after-hours children winter event to consult residents from 8 to 80 years old (Leung, 2019).

6.5 KEY AREAS FOR FURTHER RESEARCH

Making cities child-friendly and climate-responsive has been an emerging focus in urban studies (Mora and Deakin, 2019; van der Graaf, 2020). Yet, while children in winter cities are gaining visibility in urban development efforts, much work remains to be done in terms of child-related matters in various types of winter cities. Not all children are equally well-placed to embrace winter due to increased risks of climate conditions in winter cities under extreme conditions (Davies, 2015). Winter hazards pose threats to urban life, public space use, health, and overall well-being of children in terms of four areas: 1) coastal winter cities, 2) non–Northern Atlantic region, and 3) winter cities with child refugees. These conditions, however, are venues of opportunities to adopt the practices of the Winter Cities Movement.

First, aside from having a nuanced perspective on the differences in coastal cities, a broader concern is how winter cities are connected to other parts of the world, which ultimately affect children's lives. For instance, climate change events such as the irreversible meltdown of Greenland's ice glaciers pose threats to many coastal cities (National Snow and Ice Data Center, 2019). Winter cities with coastlines are forecasted to be submerged under water such as Amsterdam, Stockholm, and cities in New Jersey to name a few (Woodward, 2019). In the winter months, storms strike the North Atlantic region, which generates swell waves and winter floods (Semedo et al., 2011). Extreme conditions such as winter floods cause damage to child-related infrastructures and buildings such as homes, play spaces, schools, and health clinics. The potential damage from winter storms to educational buildings and significant cultural sites can lead to disruption in schooling, which has implications on children's education in the long run (Oppenheimer et al., 2019). Disruption in energy also affects children with pre-existing health conditions, disabilities, or reliant on electrically powered medical equipment such as ventilators and oxygen (Bell et al., 2016). Moreover, children face risks in exposure to high wave energies and sea level rise in coastal cities along the seaboard of Scotland (Kay et al., 2011; Angus and Hansom, 2021); southern and eastern coasts of the North Sea (Dangendorf et al., 2014; Feser et al., 2015); Southwest, South and Welsh coasts (Palmer et al. 2014); and the Mediterranean basin (Amponsah et al., 2018). Such climate conditions will have a disproportionate impact on the lives of children due to flooding, storm surges, saltwater intrusion, and other coastal hazards.

Second, little research has investigated winter cities outside the Northern Atlantic region, especially in Eastern Europe and Central Asia. Local leaders such as the World Winter Cities Association for Mayors (WWCAM) observe the disproportionate attention in favor of OECD countries in discussing urban winter conditions, whereas cities of the "Global East" such as Belgrade, Bibra, Dushanbe, Khabarovsk, Pyeongchang, Sibiu, Tbilisi, and Wuhan are "too marginal to be northern" (Müller and Trubina, 2020a: 628), practices in such cities are instructive. For instance, aside from Moscow and St. Petersburg, many Russian cities have creative ways to assist children during the winter. Yekaterinburg's Yeltsin Center provides child entertainment, showing how public space can be designed as an alternative indoor space in the harsh winter (Müller and Trubina, 2020b). Cities in the Murmansk region also participate in the 2024 Urban Development Plan in which city-skating rinks and outdoor play spaces will be constructed (The Government of the Murmansk region, 2019). In Harbin, China, public spaces are devoted to the construction of spaces for sports in cold city parks to promote children's physical activity such as having assembled playgrounds suitable for 4–10-year-old children (Xu et al., 2019). Meanwhile, Georgian cities like Tbilisi make winter streets more hygienic by improving their solid waste collection and cleaning the city, especially gritting the streets during winter (Asian Development Bank, 2016). In Bishkek, winter ski resorts feature diverse winter activities and accommodation spaces, which have become a hub not only for local children but also for those in neighboring vicinities (Schröder, 2016).

Although the Global East has its share of champions in attending to children's well-being during the winter, there remains a challenge for "Central Asia's forgotten children" (de Boer, 2004). Winter cities in Central Asia face a mix of challenges during the winter, which affects children's lives. For instance, Central Asian cities have kept the system of district heating plants inherited from the Soviet era. However, children at home can suffer from this heating system due to its poor insulation and low-quality piping, causing the loss of heat and water when needed in the winter (Coulibaly et al., 2012). Likewise, Dushanbe and Tbilisi face annual shortages of electricity, which give children cold winter nights (Center for Economic Research, 2013; Asian Development Bank, 2016). In many Central Asian urban areas, water infrastructure has not been updated since the 1950s, leading to winter flooding and affecting children's mobility (International Crisis Group, 2014). Cities in Uzbekistan, Turkmenistan, and Kazakhstan experience problems of uncontrolled winter flooding if transboundary rivers are not released in summer (Pohl et al., 2017). Moreover, children suffer from the scarcity of winter equipment and appropriate clothing. In Karakol, Kyrgyz, children in poverty lack basic winter needs such as proper clothes or a decent pair of shoes (de Boer, 2004). In Georgia's cities, street children find it difficult to spend winter months if not for shelters and orphanages (Wargan and Dershem, 2009).

Finally, making winter cities accommodating and safe for children refugees has been more challenging in recent years. During the past decade, an unprecedented number of children from around the world migrated to other countries due to conflict, persecution, or natural disaster, with over half of 30 million refugees under 18 years old (UNHCR, 2017). These children reside in unheated refugee camps in winter cities along European borders (Borger and MacDowall, 2015). Children of Syrian refugees who crossed the Russian-Norwegian border are not prepared for the Arctic winter (Hohmann and Laruelle, 2016). While a portion of Norwegians showed empathy by gathering warm clothing and other basic necessities for the refugees, not everyone welcomed the idea of having refugees, thereby dividing citizens on how to manage the refugee crisis (Boe and Horsti, 2019). Meanwhile, refugees in Greece from Afghanistan, Iraq, Syria, and Turkey, of which 30% were children, stayed in cold refugee camps, causing children to pass out from hypothermia (Borger and MacDowall, 2015; Giannakopoulosa and Anagnostopoulosa, 2016; Devi, 2020). Some refugees in Belgrade slept in railway stations or cold abandoned buildings (Ghosh, 2018). Fortunately, some winter cities have addressed the needs of refugee children. For instance, in the Serbian cities of Adaševci, Belgrade, Bujanovac, Preševo, and Šid, local governments collaborate with NGOs and humanitarian partners to provide children winter clothing, winterized family tents, and supplies to protect them from weather conditions (UNHCR, 2017; UNICEF, 2017).

6.6 CONCLUSION: TOWARD CHILD-FRIENDLY WINTER CITIES

Through examining selected literature from the last 20 years, this chapter has created a unified account of the best practices of child-friendly winter cities. The literature has shown that practices in winter cities for the past two decades have stood by the drive to "increase in the enjoyment of winter's positive aspects, and protection from the negative ones" (Blumenfeld, 1985: 47). However, challenges remain in terms of the disproportionate vulnerability of children from marginal dispositions in winter cities. In view that winter is not only a season to endure but more importantly a season to celebrate and promote (Stout et al., 2018), the results indicate the need to advance children's integration in the urban setting during the winter. This work has offered an alternative way of rethinking about children's place in winter cities and thus contributes to the analysis of urban spaces focused on child-season dynamics, a relationship that is hitherto underexplored.

A few notable pointers are instructive from the literature. *First*, the key to innovations for winter cities is not only working with what winter provides but also aligning winter resources according to children's needs. The point of winter cities is not to banish the climate, but to acknowledge, adapt, and where possible, embrace it (Alcoforado and Matzarakis, 2010). Best practices in winter cities provide examples of how embracing winter can be customized so children can fully engage and participate in winter events, feel safe, and included in the city. *Second*, options sensitive to children's backgrounds are crucial because children's needs vary in different winter cities. Examples of vibrant public spaces in winter cities assume that all children are equally positioned to enjoy winter cities, potentially neglecting less fortunate children and marginalizing some voices in the ongoing discussions on public space access and tensions surrounding it. Much work is to be done on how children's experiences of a winter city are shaped by their background, such as race, gender, ethnicity, or mobility among others. *Finally*, winter cities, albeit diverse, can learn from each other by observing each other's best practices and selecting strategies applicable to local conditions. For instance, frontier winter cities can also learn from communities in the Arctic, which implement a comprehensive approach of adaptive co-management strategies coming from both traditional and scientific knowledge (Berkes, 2007; Kenny, 2017).

The observations in this chapter resonate with Robinson's (1910: 89) timeless note that "children are not hibernating animals," but instead have a complex relationship with the climate where they reside, permanently or temporarily. The discussions raised in this work imply a plea to pay attention to the season's powerful influence in terms of children's urban encounters. This work has also shown the complexities of winter cities and what it means to critically engage with the climate embodied in children's immediate spaces. Through policy making, cities can provide safe and child-responsive outdoor play for children during winter.

Winter holds a special role in directing the way urban residents think and practice what winter cities are and how they will and should live in the future. The practices of winter cities have shown that it is possible to have a more equitable application of urban technology and planning by creating places that children find themselves included in, which support and fulfill the city's task to transform places into accommodating and equal spaces to all humanity in both efficient and just ways. Finally, this chapter endorses the framework of child-friendly winter cities that pushes for urban policies that incentivize the combination of creating sustainable winter cities sensitive to children's needs. This work will serve as a contribution to advance a child-focused approach to urbanization in winter areas. Ultimately, the point is to translate urban advancements into children's spaces to equip the next generation of urban dwellers who will confidently take a leading role in the future debate and action on winter cities. It is hoped that this work sparks conversations that examine in detail the relationship of children and the winter as part of their urban experience.

REFERENCES

Alcoforado, M. J., and A. Matzarakis. "Planning with urban climate in different climatic zones." *Geographicalia* 57 (2010): 5–39.

Amponsah, W., P.-A. Ayral, B. Boudevillain, C. Bouvier, I. Braud, P. Brunet, G. Delrieu, et al. "Integrated high-resolution dataset of high-intensity European and Mediterranean flash floods." *Earth System Science Data* 10 (2018): 1783–1794.

Angus, S., and J. Hansom. "Enhancing the resilience of high-vulnerability, low-elevation coastal zones". *Ocean & Coastal Management* 200 (2021): 105414.

Asian Development Bank. *Realizing the urban potential in Georgia: National Urban Assessment.* Mandaluyong, Metro Manila:Asian Development Bank (2016).

Austermuhle, M.. "With the building museum closed this winter, what the hell do we do with our kids?" *DCist* (2019). https://dcist.com/story/19/12/04/with-the-building-museum-closed-this-winter-what-the-hell-do-we-do-with-our-kids

Bell, J.E., S. C. Herring, L. Jantarasami, C. Adrianopoli, K. Benedict, K. Conlon, V. Escobar, et al. "Chapter 4: Impacts of extreme events on human health." In *The Impacts of Climate Change on Human Health in the United States: A Scientific Assessment*, pp. 99–128. Washington D.C:U.S. Global Change Research Program (2016).

Bell, V. A., A. L. Kay, S. J. Cole, R. Jones, R. J. Moore, and N. S. Reynard. "How might climate change affect river flows across the Thames Basin? An area-wide analysis using the UKCP09 Regional Climate Model ensemble." *Journal of Hydrology* 442–443, no. 6, 89–104 (2012).

Bergen, R. "Manitobans kick COVID-19 frustration with creative wintery outdoor projects." *CBC Canada.* Available at: https://www.cbc.ca/news/canada/manitoba/snow-maze-zamboni-curling-rink-ice-tower-manitoba-1.5859298 (2021, January).

Bergum, C., and L. A. Beaubien. "Smart growth and winter city design." *Smart Growth St. Albert Bulletin*, 14 (2009). Available at: http://wintercities.com/Resources/articles/Smart%20Growth%20and%20winter%20city%20design.pdf (2009, October)

Berkes, F. "Understanding uncertainty and reducing vulnerability: lessons from resilience thinking." *Natural Hazards* 41 (2007): 283–295.

Blumenfeld, H. "Problems of winter in the city." In *Reshaping Winter*, pp. 47–50. University of Waterloo Press (1985).

Boe C. S., and K. Horsti. "Anti-racism from the margins: Welcoming refugees at Schengen's Northernmost border." In *Racialization, Racism, and Anti-Racism in the Nordic Countries*, pp. 183–201. Palgrave Macmillan (2019).

Borger, J. and A. MacDowall. "Winter is coming: the new crisis for refugees in Europe". *The Guardian.* Available at: (https://www.theguardian.com/world/2015/nov/02/winter-is-coming-the-new-crisis-for-refugees-in-europe) (2015, November).

Borys, H. "2017 International winter cities shake-up conference." *City of Edmonton* (2017a). Available at: https://m.youtube.com/watch?v=Y7eDpGuX5m0

Borys, H. "Goodbye winter: Until next time, a few reminders on lovable winter cities". *Placemakers.* Available at: http://www.placemakers.com/2017/03/28/goodbye-winter-until-next-time-a-few-reminders-on-lovable-winter-cities/ (2017b, March).

Buettgen, A., A. Goodbrand, and S. Hardie. *Planning Transition Services for Youth with Disabilities: A Literature Review and Environmental Scan.* Canadian Centre on Disability Studies (2018).

Canadian Paediatric Society. Winter safety tips for parents and children. *Paediatrics & Child Health* 7 (2002), 33–34.

Center for Economic Research. *Urbanization in Central Asia: Challenges, Issues and Prospects.* The United Nations Economic and Social Commission for Asia and the Pacific (2013).

Chapman, D., K. L. Nilsson, A. Rizzo, and A. Larsson. "Winter city urbanism: Enabling all year connectivity for soft mobility." *International Journal of Environmental Research and Public Health* 16, no. 10 (2019): 1820.

Chartier, D. . "Towards a grammar of the idea of North: Nordicity, winterity." *Nordlit* 22 (2007): 35–47.

Chassé, P. "Lessons in design." *Landscape Architecture* 95 (2005): 38–45.

Chawla, L., and W. Van Vliet. "Children's rights to child friendly cities." In *Handbook of Children's Rights: Global and Multidisciplinary Perspectives*, pp. 533–549. Taylor and Francis (2016).

Checkoway, B., T. Allison, and C. Montoya . "Youth participation in public policy at the municipal level." *Children and Youth Services Review* 27 (2005): 1149–51162.

City of Edmonton. *Winter Design Guidelines Transforming Edmonton into a Great Winter City* (2016).

City of Edmonton. *Keep the Snowball Rolling: WinterCity Strategy Evaluation & Report* (2018).

Coleman, P. *The Livable Winter Community.* Michigan Municipal League (2010).

Collins, M. E., A. Augsberger, and W. Gecker. "Youth councils in municipal government: Examination of activities, impact and barriers." *Children and Youth Services Review* 65 (2016): 140–147.

Collymore, P. *The Architecture of Ralph Erskine.* London: Architext (1985).

Costamagna, F., R. Lind, and O. Stjernström. "Livability of urban public spaces in Northern Swedish Cities: The case of Umeå." *Planning Practice & Research* 34 (2019): 131–148.

Coulibaly, S., U. Deichmann, W. Dillinger, M. Heroiu, I. Kessides, C. Kunaka, D. Saslavsky. *Eurasian Cities: New Realities along the Silk Road*. World Bank. Available at https://openknowledge.worldbank.org/handle/10986/11877 (2012, September).

Craig, C. L. and A. E. Bauman. "The impact of the Vancouver Winter Olympics on population level physical activity and sport participation among Canadian children and adolescents: population based study." *International Journal of Behavioral Nutrition and Physical Activity* 11 (2014): 107.

Culjat, B., and R. Erskine. "Architecture and urban design in Sweden: Climate and energy considerations." In *Cities Designed for Winter*, pp. 347–364. Helsinki: Building Book Ltd (1988).

Dangendorf, S., S. Müller-Navarra, J. Jensen, F. Schenk, T. Wahl, and R. Weisse. "North Sea storminess from a novel storm surge record since AD 1843." *Journal of Climate*, 27, no. 10 (2014): 3582–3595.

Daniels, S. 2005. "Cultural geographies in practice: The garden in winter." *Cultural Geographies* 12, 366–370. 10.1191%2F1474474005eu336xx.

Davies, W. K. "Winter cities." In *Theme Cities: Solutions for Urban Problems*, pp. 277–310. Netherlands: Springer (2015).

de Boer, E. "Helping Central Asia's forgotten children." *The International Federation of Red Cross and Red Crescent Societies*. Available at: (https://www.ifrc.org/en/news-and-media/news-stories/europe-central-asia/uzbekistan/helping-central-asias-forgotten-children/ (2004, June).

Devi, S. "Greece 'deliberately depriving' care to child refugees." *The Lancet* 395, no. 10221 (2020): 323.

Driskell, D. *Creating Better Cities with Children and Youth: A Manual for Participation*. London: Routledge (2002).

Eldridge, A. and I. Pappalepore. "Festive space and dream worlds: Christmas in London." In *Destination London: The Expansion of the Visitor Economy*, pp. 183–204. University of Westminster Press (2019).

Enai, M., N. Pressman, A. Lüttgen, M. Y. Zheng and J. Heikkinen. *Schoolchildren's Adaptation to Winter in Cold Climates*. Winter Cities Institute (2004).

Environment Agency UK. Thames Estuary TE2100 Plan. (2021). Available at: (https://www.gov.uk/government/publications/thames-estuary-2100-te2100/thames-estuary-2100-te2100).

Epeshina, A. and A. Markova. "Transforming, feeling and seeing urban landscapes." In *The City at Eye Level*, pp. 212–215. STIPO Publishing (2018).

Erskine, R. "Architecture and town planning in the north." *Polar Record*, 14 (1968), 165–171.

Evergreen. "The importance of placemaking, even in winter." *Evergreen Canada*. Available at: https://www.evergreen.ca/blog/entry/the-importance-of-placemaking-even-in-winter/ (2019, February).

Feser, F., M. Barcikowska, O. Krueger, F. Schenk, R. Weisse, and L. Xia. "Storminess over the North Atlantic and northwestern Europe—A review." *Quarterly Journal of the Royal Meteorological Society*, 141 (2015): 350–382.

Foss, A. *Urban Thaw: Encouraging Human Connection within a Winter City*. Masters diss., North Dakota State University (2017).

Gappert, G. *The Future of Winter Cities* (*Vol. 31*). Newbury Park, CA: Sage Publications (1987).

Ghosh, B. *Refugee and Mixed Migration Flows*. Cham: Palgrave Macmillan (2018).

Giannakopoulosa, G., and D. Anagnostopoulosa. "Child health, the refugees crisis, and economic recession in Greece." *The Lancet 387*, no. 10025 (2016): 1271

Gillett, F. "Thousands of excited children lined regent street to see their favourite characters come to life at the Hamleys Christmas Toy Parade." *Evening Standard*. Available at: (https://www.standard.co.uk/news/london/hamleys-christmas-toy-parade-thousands-gather-to-watchlargerthanlife-characters-ride-through-regent-a3400206.html (2016, November).

Goodman, A., J. Paskins and R. Mackett. "Day length and weather effects on children's physical activity and participation in play, sports, and active travel." *Journal of Physical Activity & Health* 9, no. 8 (2012): 1105–1116.

Gudova, E. "'Slow! Children at play': Localization of childhood in Moscow playgrounds in winter." *Higher School of Economics Research Paper No. WP BRP 06/URB/2016* (2016). http://dx.doi.org/10.2139/ssrn.2881279.

Hamelin, L.-E. *Discours du Nord*. GÉTIC Université Laval (2002).

Hohmann, S. and M. Laruelle. "From the Mediterranean to the far North: A refugees corridor at the Russian-Norwegian border." *The Arctic Institute*. Available at: (https://www.thearcticinstitute.org/refugees-corridor-russian-norwegian-border/?cn-reloaded=1 (2016, August).

Hörschelmann, K., and L. Van Blerk. *Children, Youth and the City*. Abingdon: Routledge (2012).

Horton, J., and P. Kraftl. "Three playgrounds: Researching the multiple geographies of children's outdoor play." *Environment and Planning A: Economy and Space* 50, no. 1 (2018): 214–235.

Howard, E. *Garden Cities of To-Morrow*. London: Faber and Faber (1946).

International Crisis Group. "Water pressures in Central Asia." *Europe and Central Asia Report No. 233*. Available at: https://www.refworld.org/pdfid/5412a6444.pdf (2014, September).

Katapally, T. R., D. Rainham, and N. Muhajarine. "The influence of weather variation, urban design and built environment on objectively measured sedentary behaviour in children." *AIMS Public Health 3*, no. 4 (2016): 663–681.

Kay, A. L., S. Crooks, H. Davies and N. Reynard. *An Assessment of the Vulnerability of Scotland's River Catchments and Coasts to the Impacts of Climate Change: Work Package 1 Report*. NERC/Centre for Ecology & Hydrology (2011).

Kearny, K. "Survey says: Citizens want an ice rink." *The Review: Official Magazine of The Michigan Municipal League*. Available at: (https://www.mml.org/resources/publications/mmr/pdf/jan-feb2010mag.pdf (2010, January/February).

Kenny, M. J. "Urban planning in the Arctic: Historic uses & the potential for a resilient urban future." *Arctic Yearbook* 6 (2017): 133–146.

Krishnamurthy, S. "Reclaiming spaces: child inclusive urban design." *Cities & Health* 3, no. 1–2 (2019): 86–98.

Leung, C. "Wintermission Eau Claire: Understanding the challenges." *880 Cities*. Available at: (https://www.880cities.org/wintermission-eau-claire-understanding-the-challenges/ (2019, March).

Leung, C., and R. O'Connor "Winter is a threat to public health: How can cities fight back?" *BRINK*. Available at: (https://www.brinknews.com/winter-is-a-threat-to-public-health-how-can-cities-fight-back/ (2019, March).

Lindsay, S. and N. Yantzi. "Weather, disability, vulnerability, and resilience: exploring how youth with physical disabilities experience winter." *Disability and Rehabilitation* 36, no. 26 (2014): 2195–2204.

Lindsay, S., E. Morales, N. Yantzi, C. Vincent, L. Howell and G. Edwards. "The experiences of participating in winter among youths with a physical disability compared with their typically developing peers." *Child: Care, Health and Development* 41, no. 6 (2015): 980–988.

Mendes, A., D. Aelenei, A. Papoila, P. Carreiro-Martins, L. Aguiar, and C. Pereira. "Environmental and ventilation assessment in child day care centers in Porto: the ENVIRH Project." *Journal of Toxicol Environmental Health A* 77 (2014): 931–943.

Mora, L., and M. Deakin. *Untangling Smart Cities: From Utopian Dreams to Innovation Systems for a Technology-Enabled Urban Sustainability*. Amsterdam: Elsevier (2019).

Müller, M., and E. Trubina. "The Global Easts in global urbanism: Views from beyond North and South." *Eurasian Geography and Economics* 61, no. 6 (2020a): 627–635.

Müller, M., and E. Trubina. "Improvising urban spaces, inhabiting the in-between." *Environment and Planning D: Society and Space* 38, no. 4 (2020b): 664–681.

National Snow and Ice Data Center. *State of the Cryosphere: Ice Sheets*. Available at: https://nsidc.org/cryosphere/sotc/ice_sheets.html (2019, June).

Neumann, B. "What is a winter city's placemaking strategy?" *Michigan State University Extension*. Available at: https://www.canr.msu.edu/news/what_is_a_winter_citys_placemaking_strategy (2013, December).

Nir, T., and L. Perry-Hazan. "The framed right to participate in municipal youth councils and its educational impact." *Children and Youth Services Review*, 69 (2016): 174–183.

O'Connor, R. "Creating cool winter neighbourhoods: The winterhood lab project in St. Paul, Minnesota." *880 Cities*. Available at: https://www.880cities.org/creating-cool-winter-neighbourhoods-winterhood-lab-project-st-paul-minnesota/ (2015, August).

Oppenheimer, M., B. Glavovic, J. Hinkel, R. Van De Wal, A. Magnan, A. Abd-Elgawad, R. Cai, et al. "Sea-level rise and implications for low lying islands, coasts and communities." In *IPCC Special Report on the Ocean and Cryosphere in a Changing Climate*, pp. 321–445. Cambridge University Press (2019).

Palmer, T., R. Nicholls, N. Wells, A. Saultera, and T. Masond. "Identification of 'energetic' swell waves in a tidal strait." *Continental Shelf Research*, 88 (2014): 203–215.

Pelczar, R. "Striking stems provide winter interest." *Landscape Architecture* 99 (2009): 66–73.

Pohl, B., A. Kramer, W. Hull, S. Blumstein, I. Abdullaev, J. Kazbekov, T. Reznikova, et al. *Rethinking Water in Central Asia: The Costs of Inaction and Benefits of Water Cooperation*. Adelphi and CAREC (2017).

Pressman, N. *Reshaping Winter Cities: Concepts, Strategies and Trends*. Waterloo: University of Waterloo Press (1985).

Pressman, N. "Un/ece research colloquium on human settlements in harsh living conditions." *Habitat International* 13 (1989): 23–29.

Pressman, N. "Sustainable winter cities: Future directions for planning, policy and design." *Atmospheric Environment* 30, no. 3 (1996): 521–529.

Robinson, C. "Winter playgrounds." *Art and Progress* 1 (1910): 89–90.

Rooijmans, R. M. "Seasonal adaptive public space for children." In *The City at Eye Level*, pp. 205–206. STIPO Publishing (2018).

Ruby, I., and A. Ruby. "Naïve architecture: Notes on the work of Lacaton & Vassal". *International Architecture Review 2G* 21 (2001): 4–19.

Schröder, P. "Urban spaces and lifestyles in Central Asia and beyond: An introduction." *Central Asian Survey* 35, no. 2 (2016): 145–156.

Semedo, A., K. Sušelj, A. Rutgersson, and A. Sterl. "A global view on the wind sea and swell climate and variability from ERA-40." *Journal of Climate* 24 (2011), 1461–1479.

Steinsvik, R. "Playgrounds in kindergartens, schools and residential areas." *Winter Cities.* Available at: http://www.wintercities.com/Resources/playgrounds.pdf (2004, October).

Stout, M., D. Collins, S. Stadler, R. Soans, E. Sanborn, and R. Summers. "Celebrated, not just endured": Rethinking Winter Cities." *Geography Compass* 12, no. 8 (2018): 1–12.

The Government of the Murmansk Region. *Urban Development in Extreme Weather Conditions.* Murmansk: United Nations Economic Commission for Europe (2019). Available at: https://unece.org/fileadmin/DAM/hlm/sessions/docs2019/Presentations_1/2a_11_Chibis_Murmansk_Russia

Tourula, M., T. Pölkki, and A. Isola. "The cultural meaning of children sleeping outdoors in Finnish winter: A qualitative study from the viewpoint of mothers." *Journal of Transcultural Nursing* 24, no. 2 (2013): 171–179.

UNICEF. *Building Child Friendly Cities: A Framework for Action.* UNICEF Innocenti Research Centre (2004).

UNICEF Serbia. "A warmer winter for refugee children in Serbia." *UNICEF.* Available at: https://www.unicef.org/stories/warmer-winter-refugee-children-serbia (2017, November).

United Nations High Commissioner for Refugees. *Inter-Agency Operational Update – Serbia.* United Nations Serbia (2017).

Van der Graaf, S. "The right to the city in the platform age: Child-friendly city and smart city premises in contention." *Information* 11, no. 6 (2020): 285.

Walljasper, J. "Winter cities Show cold weather can be cool." *The Public Space Project.* Available at: https://www.pps.org/article/winter-cities (2009, January).

Walljasper, J. "Cold weather can be cool: How to keep places lively throughout the winter." *On the Commons.* Available at: https://www.onthecommons.org/magazine/cold-weather-cities-can-be-cool (2015, February).

Wargan, K. and L. Dershem. *Don't Call Me a Street Child Estimation and Characteristics of Urban Street Children in Georgia.* Save the Children (2009).

Woodward, A. "Coastal cities watch out: Greenland is approaching an irreversible meltdown." *Business Insider South Africa* (2019). Available at: https://www.businessinsider.co.za/greenland-approaching-threshold-of-irreversible-melting-2019-1

World Winter Cities Association for Mayors. *WWCAM Pamphlet.* Available at: https://www.city.sapporo.jp/somu/kokusai/wwcam/documents/pamphllet-e.pdf (2017, May).

Xu, J., Q. Bian, and X. Zhao. "Observations of physical activity in winter urban parks using UAVs: A case study of four city parks, Harbin, China." In *Sustainability in Energy and Buildings 2018. KES-SEB 2018. Smart Innovation, Systems and Technologies, vol 131*, pp. 63–73. Springer (2019).

8 80 Cities and AARP Livable Communities. "Winter is coming: 6 ways local leaders can help people warmly and safely social distance outdoors during COVID-19." *8 80 Cities.* Available at: https://www.880cities.org/winter-is-coming-6-ways-local-leaders-can-help-people-warmly-and-safely-social-distance-outdoors-during-covid-19/ (2020, December).

7 Urbanization in the Fiji Islands during the 21st Century: A Tourism Perspective

Sakul Kundra, Ravinesh Rohit Prasad, Mohammad Afsar Alam, Mumtaz Alam, Unaisi Nabobo-Baba, and Mohammad Feroz Ali
Fiji National University, Fiji

Asif Iqubal
Aligarh Muslim University, Aligarh

CONTENTS

7.1 INTRODUCTION

Tourism has been an integral part of the economies of South Pacific Island nations such as the Fiji Islands, offering employment, salaries, and foreign exchange. In 2014, the global happiness survey by WIN/Gallup proclaimed Fiji to be the happiest nation in the world, that is used in tourism marketing brand, "Fiji…Where Happiness Finds You!" but it comes along with some repercussions, especially the sector of growth in urbanization at the tourism hub of Fiji i.e., Nadi. Fiji is considered the "paradise of the Pacific" consisting of 332 small islands, 110 of which are permanently populated, with a gross land region of approximately 18,273 square kilometres. The bulk of the population resides on Viti Levu and Vanua Levu, the two largest islands (Figure 7.1).

The majority of Fiji's major cities and towns are concentrated in coastal areas vulnerable to cyclones, storm surges, and possible sea-level rise related to climate change. This island is situated in the tropical cyclone belt; thus, it experiences one cyclone on average every year as it is exposed to hydro-meteorological hazards (floods, droughts, and tropical cyclones) and geophysical hazards (landslides, tsunamis, and earthquakes) (Bernard and Cook, 2015). Suva, the capital, and Nadi (and Denarau), the tourism gateway, are the most populated areas. In this tourism capital, the extensive growth of tourism has led to the development of the urban regions and the emergence of an international chain of hotels, holiday homes, various tourism activities, and residential expansion.

DOI: 10.1201/9781003126195-9

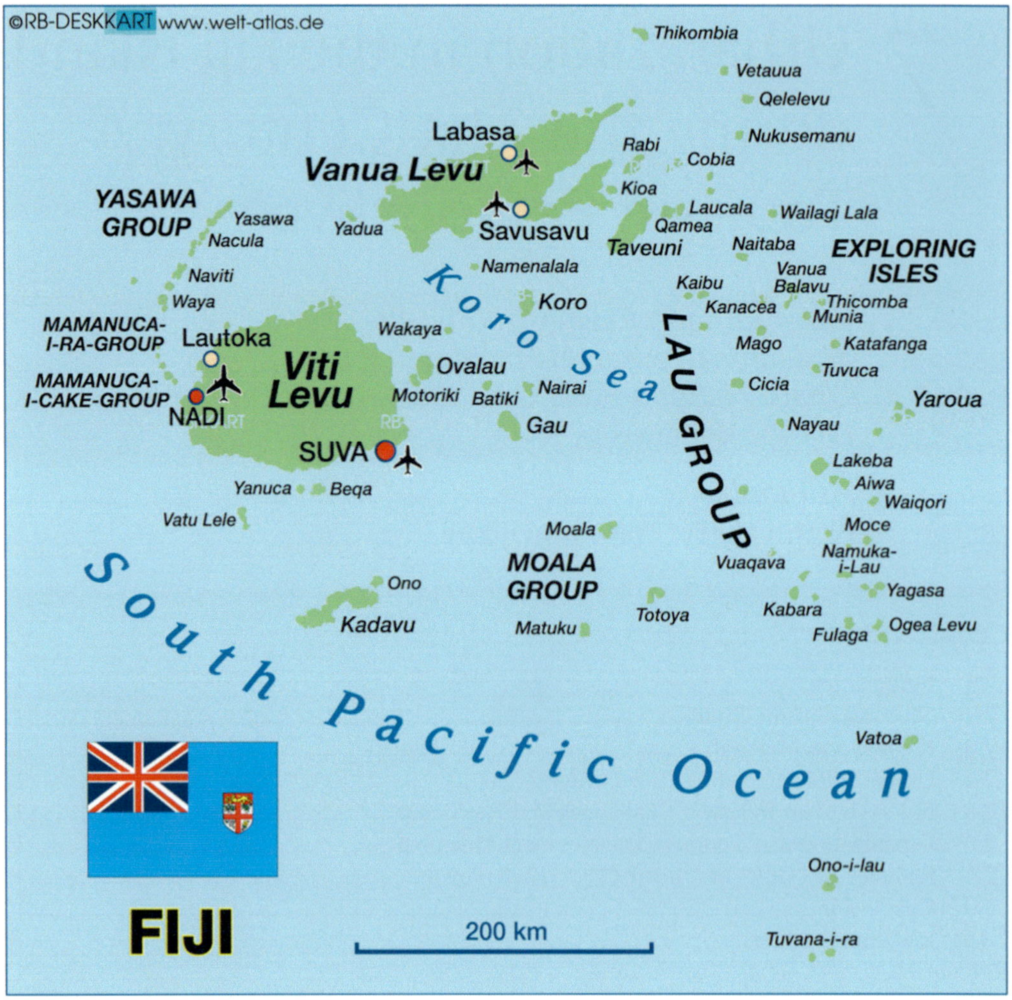

FIGURE 7.1 Location map.

Source: https://www.welt-atlas.de/map_of_fiji_3-354

Tourism-related undertakings led to an upsurge in the human settlement near urban coastal centers, put pressure on the living environment, public health, solid waste collection and water supplies, and exacerbate the risk of exposure to the local community in order to satisfy the increasing demand for urban cities. Therefore, the development of tourism is interrelated to the challenges of urbanization.

7.2 OBJECTIVES OF THE STUDY

- Examine the discourse of urbanization and its implications in Fiji.
- Outline the nature of existing linkages between Fiji's urbanization and tourism, and their vice versa impact.
- Examine the potentiality and hindrances to transform Nadi town into a city, and future smart city.
- Recommend methods and ways to move forward for sustainable tourism development in relation to planned urbanization growth.

7.3 METHOD AND MATERIAL

This study is descriptive in nature, primarily based on secondary sources of information related to urbanization and tourism. The information used in this study was gathered from various sources, i.e., research articles, the government published records, published books, and unpublished information and finally displayed in the form of tables and graphs.

7.4 URBANIZATION: IMPEDIMENT OR FORTUNE?

Urbanization is widespread in both the developing and developed worlds, as people migrate closer to towns and cities in search of "privileged" social and economic facilities and advantages. Better schooling, sanitation, health care, housing, transportation, and business opportunities are among these socio-economic benefits of this migration. Migration is primary considered an economic phenomenon (Todaro and Smith, 2011), "great promises" like full-time employment, social services, better housing, better wages, and infrastructure (Rakodi, 2008), while some migrate from the rural area to tourism poles in urban areas (Torres and Momsen, 2004). This has equal and opposite repercussions on rural and urban areas. Poverty, lack of and inadequacy of urban planning, migration, city economic development, shortage of established housing stock, political reasons, refugee influx, and other miscellaneous spatial-demographic reasons have all been described as factors in the creation and growth of squatter settlements (Asif and Wali, 2006, p. 48).

Indigenous Fijians (57%) and Indo-Fijians (*girmitiyas*) (38%) make up Fiji's population. Indo-Fijians are primarily descended from migrants compelled to work as indentured labour by British colonizers. Until the 1960s, colonial administrators across the Pacific strictly limited indigenous migration to urban areas (Chung and Hill, 2002), effectively confining *iTaukei* to the villages as a means of "preserving" indigenous culture and restricting urban growth. Both *iTaukei* and Indo-Fijian populations have experienced substantial rural-to-urban migration since these restrictions were lifted. This migration was accelerated by rising poverty in rural areas and increased possibilities in urban areas. A variety of socio-historical and politico-economic trends contribute to urban drift. Between 1997 and 2014, the expiration and non-renewal of thousands of sugarcane lease forced (and continues to push) many farming families and unemployed farmhands to urban areas, fuelling much of the current debate over Fijian land (Naidu, Matadradra, Sahib and Osborne, 2013). The percentage of Indo-Fijian farming families decreased by about 25% between 1997 and 2007 (Market Development Facility, 2013). The expiry of land leases and the sugar industry's decline, both of which are driving people to move from rural areas to cities in pursuit of better opportunities. In contemporary times, Fiji has over 57% of the population living in cities, and two out of every three Fijians are expected to live in cities by 2030. Tropical hurricanes like Winston in 2016 wreaked havoc on rural communities, and the resulting scarcity of construction supplies pushed even more people into cities. Official numbers on the number of informal settlements in Fiji are disputed; however, it is estimated that roughly 20% of Greater Suva inhabitants live in informal settlements, according to Father Kevin Barr, a poor advocate (Phillips and Narayan, 2017). The rate of urbanization in Fiji has increased dramatically. Fiji's urban population was 57.2% in 2020. Fiji's urban population rose from 35.1% in 1971 to 57.2% in 2020, increasing at a 1.62% annual rate. Fiji's total population versus urban population in per cent (Figure 7.2).

In selected municipalities in Fiji, Figure 7.3 indicates the urban-defined population and the additional urban population living in peri-urban areas. The results show that there are significant differences in how urban municipalities' boundaries are defined. In Nadi, for example, the peri-urban region (30,599 people) has more residents than the specified urban area (11,685 persons). The discrepancies between the urban and peri-urban populations have the effect of severely understating estimates of urbanization and urban growth rates in the Pacific, with actual urbanization and urban growth rates exceeding official estimates by 20–30%. Officially stated figures on national and regional economic development are skewed by such inequalities. In the same way,

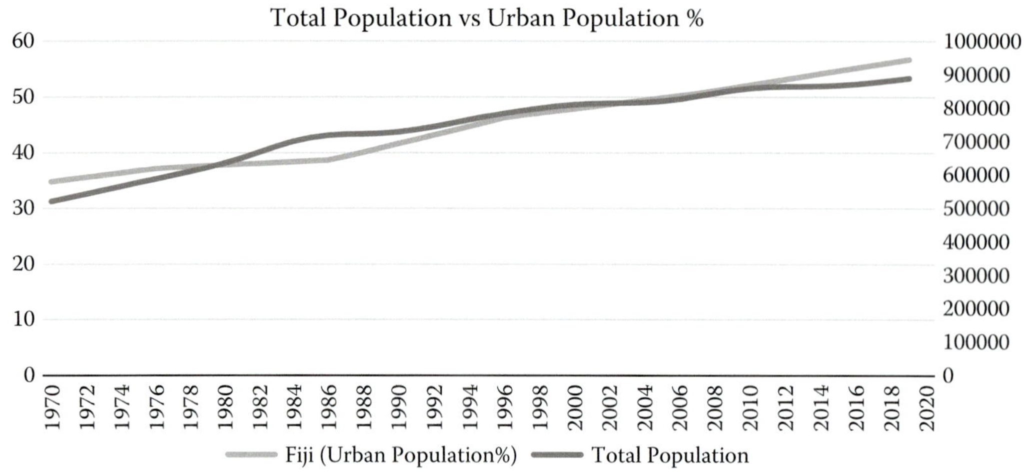

FIGURE 7.2 Growth of urban population and total population of Fiji.

Source: World Bank (License: CC BY-4.0)

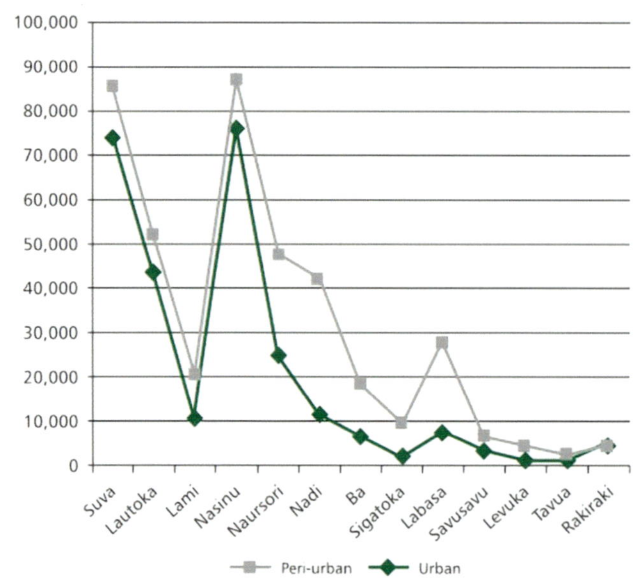

FIGURE 7.3 Fiji's urban and peri-urban population growth.

Source: Losana Rokotuibau, The Urban Government Agenda, 2011

estimates of urban poverty incidence are likely to be underestimated (while estimates of rural poverty incidence are likely to be exaggerated) in comparison to real levels (Figure 7.3).

7.5 FIJI'S TOURISM INDUSTRY: CHALLENGES AND RESILIENCE

The geographical central location of Fiji in the Pacific made it halt oversight stopover destination for refuelling aircraft and ships travelling from Australia and New Zealand to America during the 1970s. Gradually, visitors started to stay here for a longer duration as extended holidays. During the 1980s, the leading industry of Fiji sugarcane was surpassed by tourism to help earn the largest foreign exchange. The tourism sector has become the backbone of Fiji's economy, similar to many other small island developing nations. As per the Fiji Tourism Plan 2021s [FT 2021] vision is to develop into $2.2 billion industry by 2021, growing tourist arrivals to 930,000 and increasing visitor spending, thus spreading tourism benefits across the region, while developing a sector that is inclusive and sustainable in the future (Fiji Tourism 2021, 2018). Foreign direct investment (FDI) in hotels, resorts, and other infrastructure facilities has played a significant role in Fiji's tourism industry (Jayaraman and Choong, 2006). This growth was retarded temporarily due to Fiji witnessing four political coups (1987 May and September, 2000 and 2006) to see the fall in visitors and tourism earning (Kundra et al., 2021). Several post-coup recovery policies were adopted to regain the growth. In 2019, Fiji's travel and tourism sector has contributed 40% of Fiji's GDP, provides the principal earner of foreign exchange, and supports approximately one-third of Fiji's total labour force. According to FT 2021 (2018), tourists spend an average of 11.7 nights in Fiji, with repeated visitors staying longer than first-time visitors and Pacific Island visitors staying longer than those travelling from afar. Tourism initiatives attempted to increase visitor arrivals for vacations/holidays and increase their total duration of stay, resulting in more spending and attracting tourists through low seasons.

Fiji's tourist arrivals have noticed tremendous growth of 218% between 1999 and 2019, reaching 894,389 in 2019, a number is over the entire Fiji's population 889,953. Although, a decline in numbers was noticed in 2000 and 2006 coups, and floods in Nadi in 2009 and 2012 (Figure 7.4). In 2019, the majority of visitors coming to Fiji came from Australia (41%), New Zealand (23%), and USA (10.8%) (FBoS 2019). In the same year, the purpose of arrivals was holidays (73%), visiting friends or relatives (10.3%), business purposes (3.3%), and other reasons (13.0%) (FBoS 2019).

This tourism sector has several constraints that include overdependence on overseas capital, leakage of tourism profits, weak tourism policies, and environmental degradation, whereas negative impact of a rise in crime rate, health issues, poor quality of service delivery by the tourism business (Roberts et al., 2011). Tourism has been perceived as a "new form of colonialism," where Fijians only get "crumbs from the table" (Plange, 1996). The overdependence on foreign investors and international visitors, repatriation of profits, lack of local markets and human expertise, and lack of expertise in tourism planning always pressure further tourism development (Kundra et al., 2021). Due to tourism, Fijians are considered to be "live in a world of haves, half tradition and half modern" (Plange, 1996) that can be termed hybrid tourism culture. This had led to pressure on

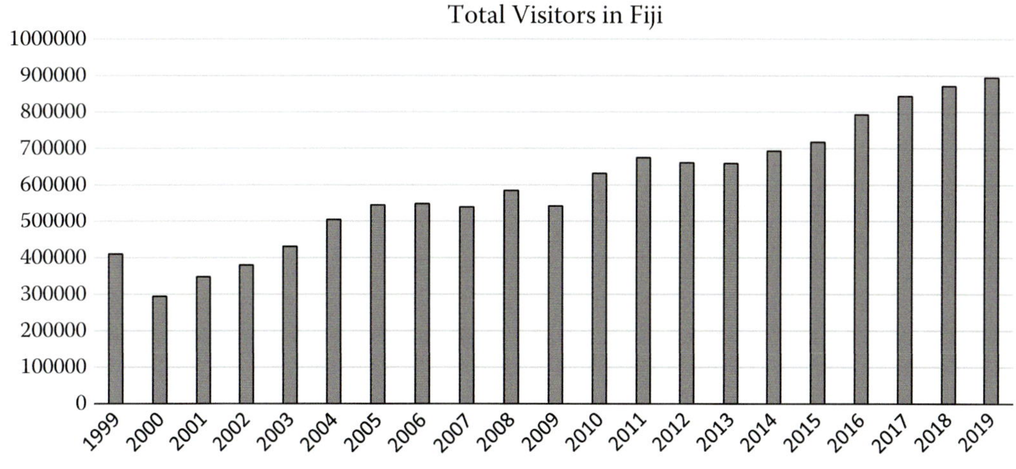

FIGURE 7.4 Variation of visitor's arrival in Fiji.

Source: Fiji Bureau of Statistics (FBoS)

urbanization and growth due to the development of tourism. Therefore, Fiji is forced to adopt sustainable tourism developments and conserve the needs of future generations. This increase in tourism is directly related to urbanization, but it is essential to determine if it is a hindrance or an aid.

7.6 URBANIZATION AND TOURISM: DEVELOPMENT DILEMMA

Varied studies support the impact of urbanization on tourism with both negative and positive impacts. Urbanization has shown some positive effects on tourism, as it increases production and consumption of goods and services in urban areas that have a positive impact on the tourism industry as the urban sector enhances their capacity to cater to the consumption demands of the tourists; further, urbanization boosts competition and innovations in these areas due to an upsurge in supply of workforce in the urban areas (Naidu, Chand, and Pandaram, 2017). Growth in tourism output signals an improvement in demand for Fiji dollars. As a result, if the price of anything in Fiji rises, the value of the Fijian dollar has increased (Naidu, Chand, and Pandaram, 2017). Tourism is already the cornerstone of Fiji's economy, and tourism would undoubtedly play a vital role in the urbanization phase in an economy where the tradable market and agriculture are underdeveloped (Naidu, Chand, and Pandaram, 2017). The increasing presence of visitors in urban centers in the economy would contribute to a rise in the salaries paid to the staff in Fiji. This will entice rural residents to relocate to urban areas (particularly tourism areas) in order to receive higher wages (Bernard and Cook, 2015). The urbanization also boosts competition and innovations in these areas due to an upsurge in the supply of human capital in the urban regions to support the tourism sector. This leads to a push towards innovative economic activities of the people living in urban areas. It also leads to providing more goods and services to tourists at competitive rates.

Fiji's tourism development requires land to flourish, but the problem of ownership is complicated, as 91.68% of customary land is managed by iTaukei Land Trust Board [TLTB] where the owner is known as *mataqali* (Karim, 2018). This land can only be leased through TLTB. The Department of Lands and Survey manages the rest of the land on behalf of the province and a portion of privately held land (7.94%) (UN-Habitat, 2012). The land right and development is a bone of contention between the Indigenous people and other races in Fiji, especially Indo-Fijians. Because of customary land ownership in Fiji, especially in rapidly increasing peri-urban areas, neoliberal ideologies face additional challenges in implementing them. The government does not have total influence over this territory, and many traditional owners disagree with neoliberal ideologies. This tenure structure with legal mechanisms will protect the rights of landlords and tenants when conflicts occur in order to improve urban equality and justice.

It has noticed a development discrepancy between Fiji's urban and rural areas. Rural areas lag in terms of tourism development as the government mainly invests in urban areas. Fiji's urban activities assist the rural activities by buying agricultural commodities of the rural areas used by the people of urban areas. Fresh vegetables and fruits are produced in rural areas and sold in urban areas. There are several "push and pull" factors for rural people to move towards urban areas. The push factors involve the scarcity of employment opportunities in rural areas, land availability, food insecurity, and congestion, whereas pull factors consist of bright city lights, the better prospect of medical, educational, and infrastructural facilities (Naidu, Chand, and Pandaram, 2017). Fiji's tourism activities are mainly concentrated around the urban areas. Therefore, the wage rate in urban areas is higher as people migrate to urban areas to get better employment opportunities.

The urbanization leads to a rise in informal squatter settlements in urban spaces where freshwater supplies are destroyed by rubbish spread by the poor and by a sewerage removal system used in the squatter settlements tarnishes the image of the nation in front of international visitors (Naidu, Chand, and Pandaram, 2017). Thus, contamination of freshwater supply and rising pollutants damage the tourism sector. Especially in the short run, urbanization does not affect the tourism output in Fiji as the problems of overpopulation of cities and towns is not severe compared to other countries (Naidu, Chand, and Pandaram, 2017). However, excessive urbanization due to tourism development is deterring foreign visitors from travelling to Fiji to avoid overcrowding and high pollution tourist destinations. It creates a negative image in front of tourists. This creates a hurdle to appreciate the urban scenery due to overcrowding and an unhealthy urban environment. Urban sprawl also creates pollution and poverty that give a negative impression on tourists. Since tourists are worried about their wellbeing, the tourist does not visit places with high emission levels. Currently, Fiji's metropolitan environment is safe enough to draw visitors. However, this might not be the case in the immediate term when human actions may have a detrimental effect on the urban climate.

Under the cultural tourism interactions of overseas tourists, making a visit in *iTaukei* village in a guided village tour also has a negative impact, of cultural gaze, spoiling the habits of locals (drinking and littering), sometimes disregarding village customs and is considered to be a threat to cultural beliefs. The excessive and unplanned tourism development is believed to be a significant threat to the mangrove forests in the vicinity of urban and peri-urban places. They have high negative environmental consequences; for example, Fiji's popular tourist destination, Denarau. Tourism is also seen as a recovery mechanism and an asset in dealing with the current environmental challenge in the Nadi region (Nolet, 2019).

Several studies have explored the negative effects of urbanization on housing, including flooding, inflation, hunger, homelessness, growth, violence, ecological destruction, and various others. This repercussion does not have a positive influence on the tourism sector, but both sectors are interdependent and have both good and bad effects on each other.

Fiji's tourism is the prime industry to contribute to the increase in per capita (Narayan, 2004). Narayan (2004) predicted the long-term effect of the boost in Fiji tourism and anticipated that if tourists raise their spending on Fiji by 10%, GDP would increase by 0.5%. According to Narayan (2004), as incomes from Fiji's source markets go up, the number of visitors coming to Fiji would rise. Results of another report, which looks at four Pacific Island nations (Fiji, Solomon Islands, Tonga, and Papua New Guinea), found that tourism-related exports had a substantial positive short-term and long-term effect on GDP in the area (Narayan et al., 2010). The tourism developments around the coastal areas are done at the cost of mangrove forests that disturb the ecosystem and have a negative effect on the environment.

The increase in the housing sector is a direct effect of the increase in tourism and transportation, as well as the fall of the sugar business in the Nadi region. The market is served by formal housing developments, which offer a variety of dwelling types. Because of the increased need for medium-density housing, detached houses are being transformed and renovated into multi-unit apartments and rental flats. This type of housing is very popular in high-growth locations near metropolitan sub-centers. Currently, these restrictions do not affect medium-density housing in Nadi, but if the trend toward denser housing continues, they are likely to hinder higher-density, high-rise apartment structures. The public and social housing estates are located outside of town. Within Nadi town, there are five *iTaukei* settlements. The Housing Authority has set out to develop around 400 serviced lots of various sizes at Matavolivoli in order to provide affordable housing. The number of housing developments in the city has increased dramatically, particularly on the outskirts. Housing estates now account for 20% of Nadi town's total housing supply. According to the DTCP's annual reports, 65% of the overall subdivision and rezoning plans received by the DTCP between 2009 and 2011 came from the Western Division, with 60% coming from the Nadi region. The Nadi region's proposals were mostly for residential and tourism development projects in proposed boundary extension regions. In terms of informal housing, the Nadi region includes *iTaukei* villages as well as informal communities on the outskirts of town. The Local Government Act exempts *iTaukei* settlements from council management. Due to poor or limited council oversight, informal settlements tend to be placed on the outskirts of town, where they can benefit from municipal services (UN-Habitat, 2012).

The Nadi International Airport and the Denarau Port are located in Nadi, Fiji's tourist capital. In Nadi, 85% of the total number of visitors to Fiji is concentrated. The town is growing at a rate of 2.5% each year, with a current population of roughly 42,000 people (including Nadi Town and the surrounding peri-urban areas). Nadi's economy is based mostly on three interconnected sectors: tourism, transportation, and real estate, where tourism growth has a direct impact on urbanization, which even raised the demand to convert Nadi town to city. Moreover, the dilemma exists to choose the appropriate policies as a way forward to achieve equal sustainable development of urbanization and tourism.

7.8 POTHOLES OF "CITY" OR "SMART CITY": NADI TOWN

Fiji is regarded as a vacation destination where visitors come to relax and rest, and this goal is primarily accomplished by visiting Fiji's tourism hubs of Nadi and Denarau. Nadi town is located in the western part of Viti Levu Island and is located in the Ba Province, western division. This town constitutes the third-largest population of Fiji, with a land area of almost 1,200 hectares. Nadi is the tourist capital due to its proximity to the Nadi International Airport, the Denarau Port, and a plethora of tourism-oriented events and facilities in and around the vicinity. This tourist town is the third-largest urban center after Lautoka and Suva (Figure 7.5).

Furthermore, while having the ability to be the most appealing tourist destination, debate arises that, would Nadi (and the nearby Denarau area) have the capacity to turn itself into a future tourism city and future smart city? Nadi is called the epicenter of Fiji's tourism as it constitutes about 85% of the total visitors to Fiji (Fiji Government, 2016). As per FT 2021 (2018) in 2017, 21% of all tourists remain in Nadi, 21% in Denarau, and 16% on the Coral Coast. As an overview, 58% of all tourists stay on the western side of Viti Levu, while 14% stay in Suva, the capital region; and the remaining 28% went to the Yasawa Islands (10%), the Mamanuca Islands (9%), or other parts of

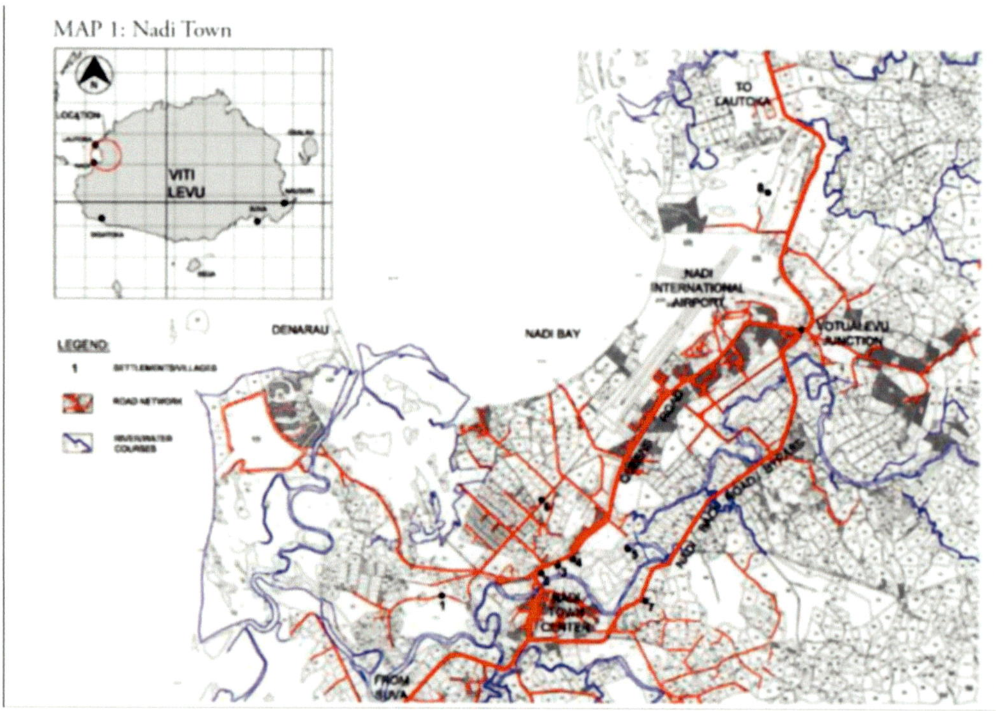

FIGURE 7.5 Nadi's map representing rising urbanization parameters and tourism.

Source: SCOPE cited by UN Habitat, 2012

Fiji (10%). Moreover, 42% of visitors from Nadi and Denarau generate 35% of Fiji's tourism earnings (FT 2021, 2018).

The majority of hotels are located outside the Nadi town boundary but the center in addition to sub-centers (Namaka and Martintar) provides all necessary services such as supermarkets, transport, retail, and eateries. This town has a small informal sector consisting of small businesses helping tourism and agriculture that are managed by NTC. A strong connection lies between tourism and transportation sectors with the real estate industry as they provide housing facilities to the workers serving in the tourism sector. The growth in the outskirts of town led to the enormous reduction of land dedicated to sugarcane cultivation. The expansion of the tourism industry has shifted the land-use trend of Nadi and the surrounding region from primarily residential to tourism-related growth, where the environmental review of tourism-related developments is under question, e.g., Denarau island developments (Karim, 2018).

Tourism development in Denarau that constitutes approximately 850 acres of area near the Nadi International Airport and Nadi town has become the major attraction. This area was earlier constituted of mangroves, swamps, small, low-lying islands, and mudflats (Bernard and Cook, 2015). There have been different developers who have contributed to this project during its extensive tourism development (mostly in 1988–1993) with the international gold course, marina, port, shopping malls, international premium resorts, and clubhouse. As massive incentives and concessions were given to a foreign investor who established an international hotel chain (such as tax-free status for 20 years, the low rental cost of the lease of land, permission to import construction materials, and exemption from sales tax) this was planned from the outset to target the high-end niche market of Fiji's tourism. These incentives were the part of the Short Life Investment Package (SLIP in 1996) with an investment of 40 million FJD and later in the Half Slip program with an investment of 7 million FJD. Providing high-end value-added tourism services and products to generate long-term profitability is an objective of Fiji's 2021 plan. In the development of the Denarau Port, a large amount of construction happened, demolishing an entire hill, bringing soil from other regions to occupy the ocean, large sections of mangroves removed, and even the course of the Nadi River was also changed (Bernard and Cook, 2015).

Since the majority of Fiji's land is customarily owned, the government implemented the first land tenure reorganization or "land swap" in 1996 in order to make room for Denarau development. This entailed exchanging 100 acres of customary land for a comparable region of government land in order to lure local and foreign investors (Bernard and Cook, 2015). In exchange for these improvements, the locals obtained some jobs; nevertheless, the main impediment was that the majority of the high-level management and executive positions were allocated to hotel owners or expatriates, whilst the locals received the majority of employees at the manager or below level.

The influx of businesses in this region became a pull factor for many people to come to Nadi and surrounding areas to provide products and services to Denarau visitors. The population density of the Nadi district has risen dramatically, but due to the past floodings of 2009 and 2012, these small business owners have suffered significant losses. The interest in further expansion of high-end tourism has negative repercussions on an area with respect to climatic hazards and urbanization. In order to support the tourism expansion and controlling floods, the Fiji government has adopted a mitigation programme of dredging the Nadi River, which has received mixed responses. The risk of floods in the Denarau region could be attributed to the impacts of climate change due to rapid growth. The central business area of the Nadi area has been majorly hit by frequent floods in comparison to fewer damages noticed by Denarau due to its exquisite planning and engineering.

Flood-prone Nadi has become a danger for tourist connectivity to the Nadi International Airport. The FT 2021 Plan (2018) attempted to focus on transit tourism by waiving the departure tax for visitors transiting through Fiji for less than 72 hours, providing an incentive to establish attractions in and around Nadi. This initiative will only be realized if proper accessibility is maintained between the Nadi International Airport and tourist attractions in the surrounding area.

Therefore, adequate planning for four-lane roads must be constructed from Nadi-Lautoka and the Nadi International Airport to Nadi town and Denarau.

Port Denarau is quickly displacing the Nadi town-Martintar-Namaka region as a preferred tourist shopping, entertainment, and evening leisure destination; moreover, it is better than the Nadi-Namaka strip connecting Denarau in the context of offered attractions, location, and amenities (Denarau Corporation Ltd., 2017). Locals have resented these developments but the construction carried on and suggested a need for an appropriate legal framework to require proper spatial planning suitable for the development of tourism, by ensuring sustainability is maintained in order to prevent the destruction of coastal resources (Bernard and Cook, 2015). Overall, assessment of these developments needs to be done through impartial analysis to assess the environmental and demographic impacts. The problem lies in the small island state like Fiji because attracting international investors and funds for tourism also brings a negative demographic problem that becomes an alarming issue.

The rapid growth of tourism in Nadi has placed a strain on residential developments; and similar commercial and industrial development has put immense pressure on agricultural land. The central government had stopped in intervals the development of state agricultural land to protect it against the expanding urban uses such as industrial, tourism, commercial, and residential sectors. Nadi's tourism activities are concentrated along the coastlines of the town. This has led to increased pressure to develop sensitive riparian mangrove zones in residential villa developments with associated marinas and commercial retail complexes. There is pressure on basic urban infrastructure and services facilities in the light of new development.

In the Nadi town, almost 60% of the townland is occupied by residential or housing purposes, whereas the left land is divided among industrial, commercial, and tourism purposes. Therefore, immense pressure is on peri-urban agricultural land due to the increased development of land within the municipal boundary. There is a need to establish an equilibrium in terms of development between urban and peri-urban areas as per the Urban Master plan. This has forced a solution of relocation to less vulnerable areas like Namaka, Martintar, or higher grounds like Votualevu, which has been rejected by many natives and businessmen. As a result, emergency risk prevention plans and interventions are being implemented in place of evacuation. Strong demand has been raised to include peri-urban areas on the periphery of the town to be included in the municipal boundaries.

The Nadi Town Council [NTC] takes care of the current municipal boundary area, whereas the Ministry of Provincial Development, via its Commissioner Western's office, takes care of the peri-urban and rural areas that surround the town (UN-Habitat, 2012). An integrated approach for local-level development is adopted by a partnership of two governing bodies that can address urbanization and proper management of urban resources. The Town Planning Scheme developed in 2000 and The Nadi Extension Town Planning Scheme of 2004 were created to manage growth and direct progress, but all of these schemes lack technological capability in terms of human resources at the part of the NTC (UN-Habitat, 2012). Their objective is to coordinate the growth of the town and incorporate the future development areas into the town boundary. Nadi Master Plan after formulation shall thrive to boundary expansion and increase the town's population base and also help in the transformation from town to much-desired city. Fiji is in dire need of a Urban Master Plan that should match national development goals. In order to become a city, it needs to construct a four-way road from Nadi town through the Nadi backroads. The demands of the city are facilities, standards, and environmental safeguards. There is massive reliability on a master plan to make a transition of Nadi from a status of a town to a city and in the future a smart city.

The biggest concern of Nadi town is the development of Nadi's urban area at the expense of the prime agricultural land that is placed on its periphery. NTC revenue collection is poor and it is also forced to widen the town's boundaries, as well as expanding municipal services. Urban problems of Nadi have become critical in terms of inadequate housing amenities, poor access to land, insufficient water supply and sanitation; insufficient urban infrastructures like road and sewerage systems; solid waste management issues; flood and poor drainage; extensive environmental degradation due to extensive private and tourism development increase the risk of climatic change and vulnerability (UN-Habitat, 2012). Rapid urbanization has created a problem of funds among the local government to manage, maintain, and sustain.

UN Habitat (2012) highlighted another hurdle towards transition as the sharing of responsibilities of infrastructure and basic services between central and local governments. The center provides power, water supply, arterial and rural roads, telecommunication, and sewage services, whereas the local government manages solid waste, drainage system, and maintenance to all secondary roads. Informal settlements and five *iTaukei* villages do not receive municipal urban services but they do take benefit of municipal waste management, services, and utilities. This creates a challenge for NTC in terms of regulating and maintaining hygiene, sanitation, and waste management. The Water Authority of Fiji's [WAF] connected sewerage system provides services to Nadi town and island tourism developments, including Denarau, but squatter settlements outside the town and five indigenous villages do not get these basic services. In regard to solid waste, NTC followed the Japan International Cooperation Agency (JICA) "3Rs" programme that believes in principles of reducing, reusing, and recycling to reduce solid waste (UN-Habitat, 2012). The NTC collects the waste of Nadi and dumps it at the Lautoka City Council's open waste dump by paying a fee. The squatter settlements and *iTaukei* villages also collect their waste to a nominated point by NTC. Illegal disposal has become an increasing problem as a result of insufficient council waste management facilities in peri-urban regions, informal settlements, and *iTaukei* villages.

Due to the rise in reliable water demand by Nadi's tourism sector, households, and businesses, the WAF had to face a water shortage in 2012 to find an additional source of water supply to Nadi town. The maintenance of the old pipes, water meters, and curbing illegal connections is necessary to provide constant supply without leakage of water. There are no formal pipeline easements, so the water pipelines have to obey unofficial access routes that are narrow. The problem also lies in inconsistent supply, slow repairs, and upgrades (FT 2021, 2018). FT 2021 intends to expand the potential of water supply, such as the Nadi-Lautoka water supply scheme, which would offer water to the people of Nadi and Lautoka, as well as the nearby rural areas (FT 2021, 2018). This is done to meet the needs of the rapidly growing tourist industry as well as subdivisions for industrial and residential use. Similarly, sewerage needs to be expanded and upgraded, and traffic congestion needs to be alleviated by the construction of new road and highway power (UN-Habitat, 2012). Inadequate seweage systems damage the ecosystem and restrict tourism growth by restricting tourism development plans (FT 2021, 2018).

Another concern is the housing development; although the housing authority tried to supply affordable housing that were located on the periphery, another big issue is informal housing at the periphery of the town that put pressure on municipal services (UN-Habitat, 2012). Growth in the tourism sector has led to an increase in demand in the housing sector, especially medium-density housing and housing estates have grown tremendously, especially in the outskirts of town. Inadequate road and drainage infrastructure, along with an ineffective waste disposal system, raises the town's susceptibility to natural hazards and environmental dangers.

Increasing energy demand in Nadi and Denarau by large, medium, and small tourism operators has become a source of concern. The latter two are hampered by a lack of financial capital and technological assistance in their efforts to transition to clean energy sources (FT 2021, 2018). Energy Fiji Limited [EFL], Fiji's largest power supplier, has built an optimized grid on Viti Levu to supply energy across the country. Energy consumption is strongest in metropolitan areas to meet the rising demand from the tourism sector. The capability of the cables running electricity to resorts is a challenge in certain places (FT 2021, 2018). These resorts in the Nadi and Denarau areas must partially or completely convert themselves to use green energy sources in order to reduce pressure on the surrounding areas. EFL intends to utilize sustainable sources of green energy in the future, such as solar, wind, biomass, and waste-to-energy, which can also be embraced by high-end tourism stakeholders as a sustainable energy solution.

This tourism town is highly vulnerable to climatic hazards such as flooding, storm surges, cyclones, and sea incursions. This coastal town is in danger due to the expected sea-level rise as a consequence of global climatic change power. Some studies claimed that Nadi shall be submerged by the sea in 2030 (UN-Habitat, 2012). Flooding is the primary threat to this town because of the town's topography and proximity to the river basin, continual mangrove removal along with the coast, poor agricultural practices in the upper area of the Nadi River, substantial reduction of mangrove trees as a result of land reclamation efforts, and catchment management activities (UN-Habitat, 2012). Recommendations have come up with land management and sustainable land use to avert the risk of regular floods in Nadi.

Although Nadi town does not experience widespread cyclone or hurricane activity during the cyclone season, heavy rain during the cyclone season, compounded by inadequate drainage, causes flooding. Heavy rain makes the Nadi drainage system insufficient and increases the risk of floods. Additionally, Nadi's tourism industry is affected by storm surges, as happened in 2010, which caused property destruction, beach erosion, significant sand depletion, and inundation.

Nadi town center faces traffic congestion, mainly along Queens Road (main highway) that faces long queues. The large number of vehicles entering the town, narrow roads, shops, and retail occupy both sides, lacking bus lanes and heavy cargo traffic creates congestion. This congestion becomes chronic when there are natural disaster events. In order to match up with tourism expansion in Nadi boundary areas, a new road has been constructed through state agricultural land connecting Denarau and Wailoaloa to the Queen's highway. Nadi has poor standards of roads due to poor sub-surface layers, inadequate roadside drainage, and shortage of capital to maintain regular and highway and poor drainage systems (UN-Habitat, 2012). The FRA has to maintain the quality of roads due to frequent emergence of potholes; many roads passing serviceability life plan and need entire rehabilitation; and substandard roads that leads to congestion during peak hours. Climatic change has increased the intensity of rainfall and flash floods that become grave due to poor drainage system that results in damage to roads. The lack of maintenance and wear and tear with a high cost to build a new road are major impediments.

Despite these constraints, Nadi town is the tourism hub that has sufficient potential to be transformed into a city in the near future and a smart city thereafter. With the purpose of achieving these goals, systematic planning and policy-making needs to be undertaken in order to contain these constraints.

7.9 CONCLUSION

The absence of economically competitive alternatives in SIDs like Fiji makes it overdepend on the tourism sector. Fiji's tourism growth is in a perplexed state, as it requires continuous investment in tourism-related infrastructure to accommodate the increasing demand, but that comes with its by-products, such as raising the vulnerability of urban areas. The way forward to eradicate the dilemma is to adopt sustainable and integration planning with adaptive and mitigation policies to curtail the negative ramifications of mass tourism on urbanization. The sustainability of tourism development can be achieved through formulating policies by engaging all tourism stakeholders and strategic planning of urbanization in order to support tourism hubs. These initiatives would help to turn Nadi from a town to a city, and then into a smart tourism city. This will render Fiji… Where Happiness (will inevitably) Find You!

7.10 RECOMMENDATIONS

This study finally concludes the work with the following recommendations that may help in the development of urbanization and the tourism sector symbiotically.

1. National and local governments should invest additional financial resources in the development of rural tourism activities, where alternative tourism forms can be of immense value.

2. Investing in agriculture will help to reduce the high rate of urbanization induced by tourism activities concentrated in Fiji's urban areas. Providing support to grow high-quality agricultural crops in rural areas so that locally grown products can be utilized by hotels and resorts, which shall eventually reduce the difference between urban-rural developments.
3. Proper urban planning should be formulated consisting of operational, developmental, and restorative planning and their proper implementation so that environmental damage and population expansion should be minimized. Operational planning should provide measures to develop local facilities, such as bridges, traffic, and transportation. A development strategy can place a premium on revitalizing recently annexed urban areas.
4. The issue of customary land ownership needs to be resolved by providing security to foreign investments and safeguarding customary Indigenous rights. Half of the responsibility also lies on tourism developers and decision makers to formulate adaptive tourism policies for sustainable tourism and urbanization development.
5. Hybrid policies of equal rural-urban development areas need to be adopted to curtail the urban-rural divide, and a concentration should be made to improve the current infrastructure of tourism hub, i.e., Nadi, and develop an Urban Master plan to support the transformation of Nadi town to a city or future "smart city."

REFERENCES

Asif, M., and Tariq Wali. "Asian Urbanization: Certain Public Health Consequences of Urban Social Stress." *The State of Indian Economy*. New Delhi: Serials Publications (2006).

Bernard, Karen, and Samantha Cook. "Luxury tourism investment and flood risk: Case study on unsustainable development in Denarau island resort in Fiji." *International Journal of Disaster Risk Reduction* 14(2015): 302–311.

David Hill. *Urban Informal Settlements in Vanuatu: Challenge for Equitable Development*. (2002).

Denarau Corporation Ltd. Destination Port Denarau. 2017. https://www.denarau.com/destination-denarau

Fiji Government. *Tourism Development Plan in Final Stages*, 18 January (2016). http://www.fiji.gov.fj/Media-Center/Press-Releases/tourism-development-plan-in-final-stages.aspx

Fiji Tourism 2021. Ministry of Industry, Trade and Tourism (2018).

Jayaraman, Tiruvalangadu K., and Chee-Keong Choong. "Foreign direct investment in the South Pacific Island Countries: a case study of Fiji." *World Review of Entrepreneurship, Management and Sustainable Development* 2, no. 4 (2006): 309–322.

Karim, Saiful. "Tourism and Residential Development in Suva and Nadi, Fiji," in *UN Habitat Report Strengthening Environmental Reviews in Urban Development*, Vol. 6 (2018): 94–107.

Kundra, Sakul, Mumtaz Alam, and Mohammad Afsar Alam. "How do political coups disrupt Fiji's tourism? Impact assessment on ecotourism at Koroyanitu National Heritage Park (KNHP), Abaca." *Heliyon* 7, no. 5 (2021): e07101.

Market Development Facility. *Study on Poverty, Gender and Ethnicity in Key Sectors of the Fijian Economy*. Report (2013).

Naidu, Vijay, Anawaite, Matadradra, Maria, Sahib, and Josaia, Osborne, "Fiji: The challenges and opportunities of diversity." (2013).

Naidu, Suwastika, Anand Chand, and Atishwar Pandaram. "Exploring the nexus between urbanisation, inflation and tourism output: empirical evidences from the Fiji Islands." *Asia Pacific Journal of Tourism Research* 22, no. 10 (2017): 1021–1037.

Narayan, Paresh Kumar, Seema Narayan, Arti Prasad, and Biman Chand, Prasad. "Tourism and economic growth: a panel data analysis for Pacific Island countries." *Tourism Economics* 16, no. 1 (2010): 169–183.

Narayan, Paresh Kumar. "Fiji's tourism demand: the ARDL approach to cointegration." *Tourism Economics* 10, no. 2 (2004): 193–206.

Nolet, Emilie. "5 A Tsunami from the Mountains: Interpreting the Nadi Flood." In *Pacific Climate Cultures*. De Gruyter Open Poland (2019): 60–72.

Phillips, Tarryn, and Akesh, Narayan. "Servicing the cities." *78 Development Bulletin* 78 (2017).

Plange, Nii-K. "Fiji." In C. M. Hall and S. J. Page (eds) *Tourism in the Pacific: Issues and Cases*. London: International Thomson Business (1996): 205–218.

Rakodi, Carole. "Prosperity or poverty?: Wealth, inequality and deprivation in urban areas." In *The Companion to Development Studies*. London: Hodder Education (2008).

Roberts, Graham, Wayne Irava, Timaina Tuiketei, Rigieta Nadakuitavuki, Sisa Otealagi, Sheetal Singh, and Odille Chang. "The Fiji islands health system review." *Vol. 1 No. 1. Manila: World Health Organization, Regional Office for the Western Pacific.* (2011).

Todaro, Michael P., and S. C. Smith. *Economic Development* (11th Edition). Essex: Pearson Educational Limited (2011).

Torres, Rebecca, and Janet Henshall Momsen. "Challenges and potential for linking tourism and agriculture to achieve pro-poor tourism objectives." *Progress in Development Studies* 4, no. 4 (2004): 294–318.

UN-Habitat. "Fiji: Nadi Town Urban Profile," United Nations Settlements Programme (2012).

8 The Maturity of Social Innovations for the Adaptation of Cities to Climate Change–The Case of Poland

Beata Wieteska-Rosiak and Grażyna Wieteska
University of Lodz, Lodz, Poland

Barbara Ocicka
SGH Warsaw School of Economics, Warsaw, Poland

CONTENTS

8.1 INTRODUCTION

Technical and technological progress as well as dynamic economic changes have always occurred whenever humans over-exploited the natural environment. The increase in the wealth of nations proceeded regardless of the consequences for the natural environment. The results of the IPCC research (Stocker et al., 2014) indicate that climate change is progressing to a large extent due to the high anthropogenic emission of greenhouse gases. Currently, climate change is recognized as the most important global threat to society, the economy, and the environment. Extreme climate-related events cause enormous loss of human life, health, damage to property, adversely affect economic activity, cultural heritage, and the natural environment. Climate change cannot be turned back, therefore adaptation becomes a challenge. The need for adaptation was recognized by the European Union, which back in 2013 developed the first EU Strategy on adaptation to climate change.

DOI: 10.1201/9781003126195-10

In Poland, in 2013, the national Strategic Adaptation Plan was adopted. The document indicated the need to develop urban adaptation plans for cities with more than 100,000 inhabitants (Ministry of Environment, 2013, p. 50). Urban areas are particularly vulnerable to the consequences of climate change due to the high concentration of population, infrastructure, buildings, economic activity, the high degree of surface sealing and the shortage of green areas. Cities are important centers of growth and concentration of socio-economic occurrences. Climate-related hazards such as heat and droughts, frost, heavy rainfall, floods, as well as rising sea levels can disrupt their sustainable development. The purpose of adaptation is to increase urban resilience and ensure further sustainable development, reduce material and non-material losses, improve the quality of life, and increase city attractiveness for investment.

Adaptation to climate change is a long-term process based on the systematic implementation of innovations. It consists in designing solutions that will respond to local needs and use the endogenous potential. Building urban adaptation requires a holistic approach and the involvement and participation of all stakeholders. It is important to develop cooperation between public authorities, society, NGOs, enterprises, public entities, and science and research centers. The involvement of various local actors is an opportunity to develop appropriate and sustainable urban projects. Social innovations (SI) support the creation of a cooperation network for the design and implementation of solutions for the sustainable development of the city. They support solving problems and eliminating barriers that block social development and reduce the quality of life and well-being of the inhabitants.

To investigate into social innovations in climate adaptation, there is a need to define them. Searches for an appropriate definition of SI have been a subject of spirited discussion among researchers. In short, SI is an innovation that has both social ends and means (Osburg, 2013, p. 18). In practical terms, SI is "a novel solution to a social problem that is more effective, efficient, sustainable, or just than existing solutions and for which the value created accrues primarily to society as a whole rather than private individuals" (Phills et al., 2008, p. 39). The SI development acts as an accelerator of a system transformation in view of the significant problems, including the climate change. The exploration of the SI potential for the solution of climate change problem has been widely studied in the book, *Global warming and social innovation: the challenge of a climate-neutral society,* whose authors put forward a thesis on the need for societal trend breaks to realize long-term substantive reductions in the emissions of greenhouse gases (Kok et al., 2002, p. 2). The research studies of other authors, as well as analyses of international institutions confirm that the broad and deep change triggered through the SI implementation and replication is needed to address the system-wide climate problems (Bergman et al., 2010; European Commission, 2014; Raja, 2020).

The development of SI for the adaptation of cities to climate change is a formative research area and a considerable process within sustainable cities. Researchers analyse the overall role of civil society participation and collaboration considering that their scope varies between cities depending on socio-political context (Mabon and Shih, 2021) and socio-economic barriers (Singh et al., 2021). The authors emphasize the importance of involving civil society in various initiatives for climate change adaptation, including promotion of green and blue infrastructure (Mumtaz, 2021), flood risk, stormwater management, and dealing with heat stress (Hegger et al., 2017). It is more and more often stressed in the literature that the involvement of civil society for solving urban problems leads to the generation of social innovations ecosystems (Andion et al., 2021). Today, social innovations are perceived as one of three main pillars (including also innovative technology and integration, governance innovation), that play a crucial role in decarbonizing European cities (Nerini et al., 2019). The authors agree that eco-innovations and nature-based solutions co-creation requires diversity and learning from social innovation (Frantzeskaki, 2019). On the one hand, the adaptation efforts are organized through policy efforts and public administration "to create, diversify and network social innovations in urban neighbourhoods" (Wolfram, 2018). On the other hand, they are inspired and generated through a "complex maze of different voluntary associations and networks including both public and private actors" (Winsvold et al., 2016). Simultaneously, there is a huge potential of synergy effects through multi actors' partnerships (Huang-Lachmann,

2019). Existing studies are often restricted in scope of the analysis presenting the overall role of civil society involvement or are focused on describing specific sources and types of social innovations based on selected case studies, but mostly in a static approach. There is a cognitive gap how to explore the development of SI for the adaptation of cities to climate change in a dynamic, comprehensive, objective and integrative way. There is limited understanding of the interdependency and interactions between nature of the climate change adaptation process and elements of the social innovation process that can contribute to meeting challenges of sustainable cities. To address the just-mentioned gap, we exploit a carefully selected consistent and process-oriented SI model adapted from Murray et al. (2010).

This chapter aims to identify social innovations for cities adaptation to climate change and to assess their maturity in Poland. Additionally, to achieve the chapter aims, three research questions were formulated:

1. What are the sources of creation and stimulation of social innovation and what are the types of social innovation in climate adaptation in Polish cities?
2. What is the maturity level of social innovations for adaptation to climate change in Polish cities?
3. How can cities achieve the highest degree of maturity of social innovation for urban climate change adaptation?

This chapter starts with the presentation of the materials and methods used in the study. The proper recognition of SI was possible thanks to the identification and screening of various documents, initiatives, and practices implemented in Poland. Subsequently, all the data collected was used as the input to the assessment of the maturity stage of social innovations for the adaptation of cities to climate change in researched country. The authors decided to focus on the largest cities, which are usually the leaders in the implementation of the policy of adaptation to climate change. Both the results of social innovations' screening and the assessment are presented in the results and discussion section. This section also indicates the ways of improving the maturity in the light of good practices of other European cities. In the last part of this chapter, general conclusions and limitations as well as implications are outlined.

8.2 MATERIALS AND METHODS

The effective implementation of the aim of considerations and the answers to the three research questions required a specific, applicable, and consistent methodological perspective. Therefore, the research regime employed two phases:

I. data collection phase and
II. collected data analysis phase.

Both phases were carried out between January and March 2021. The data collection phase began with the search for relevant materials that provide information on the social innovations for the adaptation of cities to climate change in Poland. Subsequently, the collected materials were subjected to a detailed screening to identify SI sources initiation and types, character, and number of SI for urban adaptation.

As there is no database of this type of materials in researched country, a decision was made to search for materials for the purpose of identifying the SI for the adaptation of cities to climate change, in two approaches:

- top-down approach, the starting point of which was the search for documents at the national and local level. This approach was a source of top-down social innovations and involved the analysis of urban adaptation plans of the largest cities in Poland, e.g.,

Warsaw, Cracow, Lodz, Wroclaw, and Poznan. The information and data available on the websites of city offices and public entities managing green areas were analysed.
- bottom-up approach, that was a source of bottom-up social innovations. It involved the analysis of information from social networking services, press publications, local portals, and non-governmental organizations operating in selected cities.

In the second phase of the study, based on the analysis of the collected data, the maturity stage of SI for cities' adaptation to climate change in Poland was assessed. For this purpose, the most suitable SI maturity model was employed.

Based on the literature review, the authors identified and analysed a plethora of frameworks for the SI development, among others, in the perspective of system thinking (Van der Bijl-Brouwer and Malcolm, 2020), designing innovation process (Oeij et al., 2019), building business models of enterprises (Gasparin et al., 2021), or changing social relations (Pel et al., 2020). The open character of social innovations was carefully considered, because of input from public and private actors, including civil society, and furthermore due to the creation of social relationships and new collaborative arrangements (European Commission, 2020). Moreover, the difference between social innovation and "normal" projects was analysed. The authors juxtaposed their characteristics and features and found out that SI is "multidisciplinary, aimed at integrated solution, focused on empowerment and working together, driven by demand, custom-made, approached in an open manner to allow the sharing of knowledge and intellectual property" (Social Innovation Academy, 2021).

The main criterion for selecting the appropriate SI model for the study was its consistency with the nature of cities' adaptation to climate change, which is perceived as a process of transformation. The authors chose the process-based framework designed by Murray et al. (2010), reflecting six stages of the SI process that form a coherent path from a problem to systemic change presented below in Table 8.1. In light of this model, spectacular power of the SI impact relies mainly on deep understanding of problems, high motivation to resolve them, and sufficient capabilities to replicate desirable solutions.

In the first stage of the SI process, the problem and its causes are diagnosed. Against this background, key questions are framed and the need for SI is inspired and prompted. The second phase is focused on generating proposals and ideas. It aims to use a number of methods to consider various options. In the third phase, ideas are tested in practice in different implementation settings. Prototyping and testing allow to improve potential solutions, as well as to enhance relationships between their stakeholders. The essence of the fourth phase is to sustain ideas in practice. It identifies resources (teams, budgets, infrastructure, etc.) and conditions (financial, legal, social, etc.) needed for the sustainable transformation. At the fifth stage, all strategies and efforts are concentrated on scaling and diffusion of solutions through powerful inspiration, education, or knowledge transfer and through more organic growth drivers, e.g., investments. The sixth stage – systemic change is the highest achievement of the SI process. It involves interdependencies and interactions of many elements, e.g., new ways of thinking and acting, business models, supply chain configurations, social activities and movements, laws and regulations, fiscal reforms, infrastructure, and technologies. As Murray et al. (2010, p. 107) note, "the most transformative innovations have been the ones that combine many elements in the new way." General systemic change implies changes in many subsystems, including the public sector, grant economy, market economy, and informal and household economy, aiming at synergies between them.

8.3 RESULTS AND DISCUSSION

8.3.1 Social Innovations for the Adaptation of Polish Cities to Climate Change

The analysis of the collected materials (first research phase) obtained an answer to the first research question: *What are the sources of creation and stimulation of social innovation and what are the types of social innovation in climate adaptation in Polish cities?*

TABLE 8.1

Stages of the Social Innovation Process

Stage 1 Prompts, Inspirations and Diagnoses	Stage 2 Proposals and Ideas	Stage 3 Prototyping and Pilots	Stage 4 Sustaining	Stage 5 Scaling and Diffusion	Stage 6 Systemic Change
Framing the question Triggers and inspirations Recognising problems From symptom to cause	Finding the right answer Imagining solutions Thinking differently Open innovation Participation Facilitating participation Institutions	Prototypes, pilots, and trials Finance for emerging solutions	Creating a business Ownership and organisational form Governance Organisation and management models OperationsRelational capital Venture finance Sustaining innovation through the public sector	Generative diffusion Inspiration Diffusing demand Scaling and diffusion in the public sector Commissioning and procurement Suppliers of innovation Transmitters Organisation and scale metrics	Ideas that energise systemic innovations Infrastructures and interstructures to support new system Formation of users and producers Strategic moves that accelerate systems change Regulatory and fiscal changes Information, accounting, and statistics Progressive coalitions and social movements Systemic finance

Source: Authors' own elaboration based on Murray et al., 2010.

The recognized social innovations are either top-down or bottom-up. The study shows that the development of **top-down social innovations** for the adaptation of cities to climate change is created by local policy, city authorities, and public entities managing green areas. Social innovation is stimulated by public investment projects and financial incentives. Researchers identified that city authorities use instruments of social participation to create and initiate the development of SI. The analysis of social participation instruments was used to identify in detail social innovations for adaptation to climate change e.g., public consultations, citizens' panels, local initiatives, and civic budgets. The **bottom-up social innovations** for the adaptation of cities to climate change come from the self-organized collective activities of society and are implemented directly by the inhabitants and non-governmental organizations. Further, it can be noted, that both types of social innovations are interconnected and stimulate each other. As a result, an increase in interdependence is observed between activities and initiatives in the network of relations linking city authorities and residents.

The research results are presented in a certain order. First, the results of the analysis of materials collected in the top-down approach are presented. At the end of this section, the results of the bottom-up material analysis are described.

The identification of top-down SI included an analysis of the city's policy. It was determined that the main document of the adaptation policy is urban adaptation plan. The plans of the largest cities in Poland were analysed. Based on their analysis, adaptation initiatives have been distinguished, which constitute the potential for SI development. These include the development of blue and green infrastructure in public and private space e.g., water curtains, fountains; development of green infrastructure in bicycle infrastructure; education that improves inhabitants' knowledge about ecology and climate change through education in schools and educational brochures; development of green buildings, revitalization and revalorization of degraded areas, development of river waterfronts and greenery; and development of green civic budgets (City of Lodz, 2018, pp. 42–46; City of Cracow, 2019, p. 84; City of Wroclaw, 2019c, pp. 107–137, City of Warsaw, 2021).

As part of the city's policy, public investment projects stimulating social innovation for the adaptation of cities to climate change are implemented. For example, the project titled "Green Streets" in Warsaw aimed at designing green streets in the city. Residents took part in developing the concept of creating green areas along several dozen streets. As a result, projects that are part of the city's green infrastructure are tailored to the needs of the residents. Moreover, green investment projects are implemented under the integrated revitalization program. The project "Green repair" has contributed to the creation of green squares and green areas. The activities are carried out in cooperation with the residents and in response to social needs (The City Greenery Board of the Capital City of Warsaw, 2018). In Wroclaw, the authorities implemented projects of green streets, parks, courtyards, public transport, city squares, and the revitalization of city areas. These projects also contain green solutions (City of Wroclaw, 2021a). The city implemented the project titled 100 streets for the 100th anniversary of independence under which residents could propose the locations for trees, shrubs, and flower meadows (City of Wroclaw, 2018). In addition, Wroclaw is taking part in the international "GrowGreen" project, which consists of testing solutions dedicated to the adaptation to climate change (nature-based solutions). As part of the project, pocket parks, green streets, and green courtyards are created. In all of these cases urban spaces are created with the participation of residents (City of Wroclaw, 2020a). Green projects that involve the local community are also implemented in Poznan; they focus on creating new squares, renovating parks, or constructing honey gardens (The City Greenery Board of Poznan, 2021). Within the Municipal Revitalization Program, since 2010, the "Change Your Backyard" campaign has been organized. Its aim is to stimulate the activity of the inhabitants as well as to strengthen integration within the local community. Residents work together to improve neighborhoods in which they live and the overall quality of life (Poznan City Hall, 2021a).

Apart from the local projects, financial incentives are also an important instrument supporting the development of top down innovation for adapting to climate change. Grants for adaptation solutions are offered from public funds. Residents can receive funds, e.g., collecting rainwater under the program "Catch the rain" (City of Wroclaw, 2020c). Another example is the tax exemption offered by the authorities for establishing green roofs and constructing living green walls of buildings in Wroclaw (Ekolokator, 2021). There is also the Civic Initiatives Fund at the state level. The program is aimed at non-governmental organizations. Its co-finances projects aimed at increasing the involvement of citizens and non-governmental organizations in public life (National Freedom Institute, 2021).

As established, the development of social innovation for the adaptation of cities to climate change is stimulated by the instruments of social participation used by the city authorities. The most important of them are:

- public consultations,
- citizens' panels,
- local initiatives,
- civic budgets.

The development of social innovations requires the creation and use of all instruments of social participation, but, above all, their promotion and dissemination among all the city's stakeholders.

The public consultations are an instrument for involving residents in the process of social innovation for the adaptation of cities to climate change. According to the report (Pistelok and Martela, 2020, pp. 14–27), few inhabitants engage in civic activity. There are barriers that restrict dialogue within public consultations (e.g., provisions that impose limits on such dialogue). The SI for adaptation to climate change require commitment, participation, and cooperation with residents. In accordance with the assumptions of the state policy, urban adaptation plans were developed in the largest Polish cities. Public consultations have been widely used in the development of the policy for city's adaptation to climate change. Residents, social organizations, entrepreneurs, scientists, and city authorities took part in developing the strategy. Social consultations provide an opportunity to jointly take a look at local problems and work out solutions that respond to the needs of local community.

Public consultations are organized by local authorities. They are an indispensable element of urban policy created and implemented at the municipal level. In the course of public consultations strategic and planning documents, as well as municipal investment projects are consulted with the society. Investment projects encourage and promote dialogue and cooperation with residents. City authorities also organize meetings with residents interested in specific social and environmental problems during which they together work out the solutions.

A citizens' panel is also an instrument aimed at deploying the community's potential to resolve climate change problems. Randomly selected residents are involved in discussions on issues important to the city. In this way, they can actively participate in decisions made by municipal authorities. The topics of the panels also concern climate change (Cracow City Hall, 2021). In Warsaw, the meeting was devoted to efficient use of energy in buildings and in the city (City of Warsaw, 2020a). There is a Cracow Climate Panel in Cracow, which is dedicated to climate change and the city's climate neutrality. The city's stakeholders are working together to develop solutions that reduce energy consumption and increase the use of renewable energy (Cracow City Hall, 2020). Citizens' panels are also organized in Lodz on themes, such as climate change and adaptation to it. The goal is to identify directions for the future development of green infrastructure and counteracting the effects of drought in the city. The question is how to create community gardens and how to increase residents' responsibility for green areas in the city (City of Lodz Office, 2021a). A citizens' panel on climate and transport was also organized in Wroclaw (City of Wroclaw, 2020b). Another panel entitled "How the Poznan authorities can act to counteract and adapt to climate change and the climate crisis" was organized in Poznan (Poznan City Hall, 2020a).

In Polish cities, it is possible to submit local initiatives that create social innovations for adaptation to climate change. The law obliges local governments to adopt resolutions on local initiatives. However, over 70% of local governments disregard it. Thanks to local initiatives, residents can submit projects directly or indirectly (through an NGO). The authorities of Warsaw have been using this participation instrument since 2014 (City of Warsaw, 2015). Thanks to local initiatives, innovative projects have been implemented that consider the problems of climate adaptation. Among them there are pocket parks and community gardens. The "Luxuriant Warsaw" program supports residents in establishing community gardens. In 2017, 13 gardens were implemented, and in 2019, 26 projects were created (Luxuriant Warsaw, 2021). There are also local initiatives in Cracow that tackle ecological aspects. In response to the need to manage rainwater, a rain garden was created. Another example is the planting of trees and shrubs in the city (Municipal Dialogue Center, 2019). In Lodz, local initiatives have been submitted since 2013. As part of the local initiative, new lawns and gardens, as well as parks and squares are created (City of Lodz Office, 2021b). In Wroclaw, city authorities use the Microgrants instrument to carry out social initiatives (City of Wroclaw, 2021b). Another solution is the Housing Estate Fund dedicated to housing estate projects. The projects concern adaptations to climate change, e.g., a rain garden and demolition of road plates (City of Wroclaw, 2019a). Moreover, Local Activity Centers were established in Wroclaw. Their goal is to create a strong community, solve common problems, satisfy the residents' needs, and create local cooperation networks also with enterprises. They represent a great potential for creating social innovations for the adaptation to climate change (City of Wroclaw, 2021c). There are Local Initiative Centers in Poznan to which residents can present various initiatives intended to solve problems and respond to the needs of the environment. The goal is to activate and integrate residents and build partnerships (Poznan City Hall, 2021b). Some applications that engage residents in green activities have been developed in Cracow and Warsaw. The Warsaw application, such as "Million trees," allows residents to report tree planting sites and greening the city (The City Greenery Board of the Capital City of Warsaw, 2019). Cracow has its "Collectively" application used for communication between residents and The City Greenery Board. Residents can submit proposals for the development of green areas, as well as problems identified in the city space (Cracow City Hall, 2017). An interesting pro-social and pro-ecological Lodz initiative is the "Forest of Young Lodz." The campaign encourages planting trees to commemorate the birth of a child (City of Lodz Office, 2017). Another solution activating the inhabitants is municipal competitions' "Green Poznan." Residents, enterprises, and institutions may propose green gardens, plots of land, and balconies to the competition. The aim of the program is to strengthen the "go green" attitudes among the inhabitants (Public Information Bulletin of Poznan, 2020).

Since 2013, diverse SI emerge under the so-called civic budget in Polish cities. A civic budget is "a separate part of the local government budget (most often the city budget), under which the predetermined amount of expenditure is allocated to investment initiatives and projects directly submitted by the local society (individually or by appropriate organizations) The Sejm of the Republic of Poland, 2021." The idea of the civic budget fits in with the concept of civic society and public governance. Its idea is to support bottom-up initiatives and enhance local development (Sobol, 2017). There are over several hundred civic budgets in Polish cities. It is an instrument whose importance and popularity is growing dynamically. Budgets allow residents to submit projects and vote for them. The winning urban projects are then implemented. Cities more and more often have green civic budgets directly dedicated to working out green and sustainable urban solutions and the adaptation to climate change.

In the capital city of Poland, nine different categories have been distinguished within the civic budget. Each submitted project can be assigned to several categories at the same time, including the category titled "environmental protection" and/or the category "municipal greenery." Eco-innovations proposed by society may cover a district or city-wide range. Their implementation is most often the responsibility of the Warsaw Green Spaces Authority. For example, the total amount allocated to the implementation of the civic budget for 2020 was over PLN 83 million.

Inhabitants submitted 486 projects for two eco-categories, of which about half were selected for implementation. The chosen projects related to various aspects, including measures supporting the adaptation of cities to climate change:

- planting anti-smog greenery (e.g., evergreen trees, shrubs) to reduce smog, improve oxygen conditions, protect fauna;
- planting flower meadows (home for insects and plants), honey plants, as well as creating boxes for insects in parks and squares to preserve the biodiversity (e.g., providing bees with a food base);
- creating rain gardens to limit the runoff of rainwater to the sewage system, and at the same time help to care for plants during drought;
- creating nesting towers for martin swallows and installing nesting boxes for bird swifts to fight mosquitoes, which multiply more easily in the conditions of global warming (City of Warsaw, 2020b).

Among the most common reasons for the decision to submit a project to the Warsaw civic budget is the desire to integrate the local community (34% of responses for the district level) and residents of various districts (24% of responses for the city-wide level) (Ośrodek Ewaluacji, 2019).

For several years, in some Polish cities, the authorities have been ring-fencing amounts from the civic budget for the so-called green civic budget which in their entirety are allocated for the implementation of green projects submitted by residents. Cracow, the second-largest city in Poland, has had a green civic budget for two years already. In 2020, more than half of all civic budget funds have been allocated to the green civic budget in the city. Cracow categorizes projects into a district or city relevance. Such efforts have an impact on the city's adaptation to climate change, but it can be noticed that the rationale and long-term effects presented in the descriptions of submitted eco-projects are focused on improving aesthetics and providing places for recreation rather than on environmental issues. Innovation proposals put forward by the public include, among others:

- construction and suspension of nest boxes in order to increase the number of birds, increase the biodiversity of the area, as well as naturally reduce the number of insects that are pests;
- creating a flower meadow to maintain biodiversity and educate the public;
- carrying out new plantings in order to clean the air off suspended dust and improve the quality of life of residents;
- creating pocket parks (The Management of the Cracow Municipal Greenspace Authority, 2021).

Lodz, the third-largest city in Poland, also has its civic budget but does not distinguish green categories within it. An analysis of 261 projects that were voted on by the city community in 2019 showed that eco-projects accounted for a minor fraction of the civic budget and their relevance to adaptation was relatively low. Only a few projects were identified for new plantings (e.g., green square, planting shrubs, and long-lived trees) or supporting bird species. At this point, the conclusion is that without distinguishing eco-categories or a green civic budget, a local community may fail to propose eco-innovations supporting adaptation to climate change (City of Lodz Office, 2021).

In Wroclaw, the civic budget has been implemented since 2013 (the first projects in 2014). The city is focused on green development, as evidenced by the efforts to apply for the European Green Capital Award, as well as the provisions in the Wroclaw 2030 Strategy, directly aimed at creating new green spaces for city dwellers. In the 2020 edition of the civic budget, the category "greenery/recreation" was included for the first time. Within this category, ten highly valuable projects were selected that mainly concerned creating new parks, flower meadows, and planting shrubs and trees. Wroclaw is struggling with smog. Therefore, the main goal of these urban eco-projects is to reduce air pollution. Nevertheless, alongside it, green projects support adaptation to climate change (City of Wroclaw, 2019b).

The analysis of over 230 projects delivered in 2020 in Poznan as part of the civic budget showed that they were relatively poorly focused on environmental issues. The greenest innovations submitted by society concerned creating new green areas or modernizing green areas in municipal housing estates as well as helping birds to access water in the summer (installation of drinkers). However, the first edition of green civic budget (projects will be implemented in 2022) has recently started in Poznan. The city authorities decided that within new green areas the percentage of biologically active area may not be less than 90%. Examples of green objects that may be submitted by the public include parks, squares, rain gardens, automatic irrigation systems, bioretention systems, meadows, avenues of trees, parks of one tree, and unconventional solutions that enrich the ecosystem (Poznan City Hall, 2019, 2020b).

Other cities in Poland are also showing interest in implementing urban eco-innovation as part of their civic budgets. In Lublin, a green civic budget has been announced since 2017 (first investments in 2018) (Lublin City Office, 2017). In Katowice, it includes the following tasks:

- greening public space;
- systemic revitalization of squares and parks;
- creating flower meadows, rain gardens, and small retention reservoirs;
- educating in the field of ecology and nature protection (Katowice City Hall, 2021).

As it has been established, adaptation to climate change can also be supported by **bottom-up social innovations** for the adaptation of cities to climate change. These include citizens' resolution initiatives that reveal their creativity and entrepreneurship, as well as use the potential of the local community. The flagship example of the bottom-up SI is the idea to create community gardens in many Polish cities. Gardens are taken care of and animated by local communities in areas owned by city authorities (e.g., urban green areas), individuals (e.g., allotments), informal groups (e.g., backyards in the neighbourhood), NGOs (e.g., roof squares), as well as other private or public entities and are open to all interested persons according to the rules laid down by the community (Agaciak, 2017; Grotowska and Ruman, 2019; Wolańska, 2019). The gardens are financed by their founders and users. They can also be financed from grants or city funds. The founders of the gardens often find neglected, serving as illegal waste dumps, spaces which are transformed into community gardens. The initiative is aimed at ecological cultivation of vegetables, fruits, herbs or ornamental plants, integration of local community, implementation of educational and cultural activities, improvement of the quality of public space, and care for biodiversity and the well-being of citizens. Gardens become meeting places and centers of social activity. The popular social initiative is the "Community Gardens of Cracovians." Residents organize themselves and jointly decide where a garden should be located, and they participate in the implementation of the project. After the garden is created, they take care of it themselves (The City Greenery Board of Cracow, 2020).

Furthermore, green areas are also created by citizens through social planting of trees campaigns for children in Cracow. In 2017, the residents planted trees themselves in Cracow. From the point of view of the hereto discussed problem, the above are other solutions that contribute to adaptation to climate change. The action was initiated by the inhabitants and is currently financed from public funds (The Management of the Cracow Municipal Greenspace Authority, 2017). As a result, the involvement of residents from many cities leads to the development of SI programs for the adaptation of cities to climate change supported by local governments.

The multitude of social initiatives and the number of people involved in them expand the scale of activities and thus strengthen their impact on solving the problem. Moreover, active information sharing about micro-initiatives through social media and blogs very effectively supports their dissemination in society. Additionally, many NGOs, e.g., the Sendzimir Foundation, Green Action Ecological Foundation, or the Institute for Sustainable Development, conduct promotional campaigns and deliver educational projects focused on environmental protection, mitigation of climate change, and sustainable development. Moreover, many social ideas are submitted to non-governmental organizations. Cooperation is based on shared resources and enables the acquisition of external funds to finance activities (Foundation Fenomen Miasto, 2020).

Summing up, the analysis of the collected materials shows that in Polish cities the source of social innovation in climate adaptation are the activities of the city authorities and entities managing urban greenery. They result from the city's development policy, implemented municipal investments, financial instruments, and the instruments of social participation used. Self-organizing inhabitants are the second source of social innovation. The analysis showed that the bottom-up and top-down SI interpenetrate strongly. Public authorities stimulate the emergence of social innovations through the offered instruments and the inhabitants use these instruments through their activity and entrepreneurship. Residents and NGOs are the source of the bottom-up SI. Often the ideas of the inhabitants are submitted to non-governmental organizations. These entities support residents in implementing their ideas as well as apply for financial support from the city. It is determined that social innovations are most often associated with the development of greenery, environmental education, and designing public spaces. The identification of SI has shown that they are rarely directly dedicated to adapting cities to climate change.

8.3.2 Assessment of the Maturity of the SI Process for Adaptation to Climate Change

The results of the in-depth analysis of sources and types of SI presented in 8.3.1 section and the application of the SI process model adapted from Murray et al. (2010), answer the second research question: *What is the maturity level of social innovations for adaptation to climate change in Polish cities?* In pursuit of an overall assessment, it is helpful to systemize and evaluate each stage in the model.

At the first stage, the main problems were framed in the national Strategic Adaptation Plan and, consequently, in many dedicated urban adaptation plans. Next, efforts at local levels are made to recognise the problem in depth, diagnose its relevance, and identify its causes in individual cities. An important change from symptoms to causes deeply rooted in society is taking place in many Polish cities, revealing at the same time the so far hidden potential of SI. As a result, the transformation process is inspired and initiated, aiming at the cities' climate adaptation through SI tailored to the needs of residents on a micro-scale. At the second stage of the SI process, the instruments of social participation, e.g., such as public consultations and citizens panels, are introduced by local public institutions to find the right answers to the question. These instruments integrate citizens thinking differently and play the role of facilitators of the open innovation co-creation. In addition, many NGOs (e.g., foundations, institutes, associations) conduct climate-related education, information campaigns or promotional activities, as well as ecological actions in the close cooperation with local government units. The especially important source of proposals and ideas are activities undertaken by residents who are aware and convinced of the need to counteract, prevent, and minimize climate change. Social initiatives, leading in the third stage of the SI process to prototyping, pilots, and trials, often have individual family and neighbourhood leaders who integrate communities. Many local initiatives are emerging solutions that later transform into programs or projects receiving financial and organizational support from local government institutions in cities. As a consequence of the SI evolution, initiatives building civic engagement are implemented and financed primarily from civic budgets in the medium and long-term perspective. The implementation of green civic budgets raises the maturity of the SI process for the Polish cities' climate adaptation to the fourth stage, characterized by sustaining innovations put in place through the public sector. However, this action is indicative of the beginning of this stage in Polish cities.

The first investments under the civic budgets have been recently successfully implemented in Poland (since 2014). Many Polish cities are just in the phase of announcing competitions for 2021 and at the same time many others still fail to distinguish civic budgets or green civic budgets. However, if city authorities decide to launch this instrument, it becomes a sustainable and consistently applied tool and competitions are announced in subsequent years. More and more cities are interested in introducing green criteria in civic budgets or even in distinguishing green civic budgets. Most likely, this is the effect of the implementation of strategies for the adaptation to climate change and the advancement of efforts to sustain environmental priorities. Civic budgets, especially green ones, are an effective instrument for supporting SI development by the public sector, especially as the society requires such organisation and management models. Most of the eco-projects are carried out under the responsibility and supervision of the City Greenery Boards, which as a rule outsource the drafting of documentation and physical works to external companies. Interestingly, residents are also invited to carry out some tasks (e.g., planting).

The authors of the chapter are aware of an urgent need to advance the SI process, as well as of some problems on the path towards increasing the maturity of this transformation. Key findings highlight the following main challenges:

- There is a need to increase the number of public investments directly named and dedicated to adapting cities to climate change. Their development and dissemination can create and stimulate the development of social innovations. Similarly, a shortage of public financial incentives dedicated to is identified.
- Investment projects implemented as a part of social participation exercise rarely directly tackle the adaptation to climate change. Most often they exhibit social and spatial dimensions. Most likely, the pro-environmental ideas are not seen as the most important in comparison to other residents' needs. Eco-design is very often integrated into projects aimed at creating the places for recreation and rest, improving the quality of life of society, and aesthetic value of public space. Although, the problem of the cities' adaptation to climate change is still rarely considered directly, it happens that the submitted ideas are motivated by the desire to improve the quality of air and reduce smog (especially in Cracow, because this city is one of the most affected by this problem in the world). However, these solutions are mainly mitigating climate change.
- Instruments, such as citizens panels or green civic budgets, supporting the SI process are relatively new tools implemented in Polish cities. It is difficult to clearly indicate the direction in which they will evolve and their future role in increasing the maturity of the SI process in the area of cities' adaptation to climate change. Generally, the social participation projects are highly diverse as to the subject and relate among others to transport or blue-green infrastructure, monitoring, security, and playgrounds. Some of the social projects are rejected due to the lack of funds.
- So far, civic budgets are the most popular instrument. Although this concept opens up the possibility of carrying out various types of activities, there is still a lack of projects aimed at creating rain gardens and small retention tanks. Most often, residents submit ideas for the creation of new or the protection of the existing green areas (new squares, street plantings) and the preservation of biodiversity (most often bird protection). This may be due to the fact that green civic budgets have been implemented recently, and new parks and plantings are seen as a priority by residents of Polish cities. An important barrier is also the shortage of financial resources for green civic budgets. However, it is observed that civic budgets and green civic budgets clearly dominate in terms of the degree of organization and formalization of initiatives, as well as the number and value of eco-investments carried out.
- The authorities of Polish cities have implemented instruments of social participation; however, there is a need to promote and disseminate them among residents. It is worth mentioning as an example, that within the Lodz citizens' panel entitled "Involving residents and creating community gardens," residents decided that "conducting information and

educational activities in the field of community gardens, including the preparation of a guide on creating community gardens" is the most important (City of Lodz Office, 2021c).
- Another aspect is the lack of knowledge about different potential eco-investments or the competence to describe them in the competition documentation that would fulfil formal requirements adopted for civic budgets organisation and management.

To sum up, the development of social innovations to adapt urban systems to the climate change is an emerging trend in Poland. Polish cities are on the path of increasing the maturity of the SI process for the adaptation to climate change. Their adaptation is evolutionary, characterized by reaching subsequent stages of the SI process gradually increasing the involvement and creating appropriate management instruments. Currently, the main groups of top-down and bottom-up innovations can be distinguished, covering instruments at different levels of the SI process maturity. Both public consultations and citizens' panels are mainly practised at the second stage, local initiatives are explored at the third one, and civic budgets are implemented at the fourth stage of the SI process. Each of the above-mentioned instruments can evolve to achieve higher stages of maturity. Certainly, the authorities of Polish cities should follow solutions adopted by more mature cities that exercise climate adaptation through social innovations at higher stages. Both exploitation and exploration of valuable experiences can provide inspiration and accelerate climate-related transformation of Polish cities.

8.3.3 Directions for Improving the Maturity of the SI Process for the Climate Adaptation of Polish Cities

The social innovation process is an appropriate model to solve the problems faced by modern cities. The main condition is cooperation and the use of resources originating from the public sector, households, and enterprises. The authors identified the development status of SI in the largest Polish cities at stage four. The urban adaptation plans for the largest cities were adopted even as late as in 2019, e.g., in Warsaw. This means that the policy of urban adaptation has been in place for a short time. Therefore, it can be concluded that the inclusion of adaptation policy in the integrated process of urban development is still taking place. The key question is, *how can cities achieve the highest degree of maturity of social innovation for urban climate change adaptation?*

Achieving the fifth (scaling and diffusion) and sixth (systemic change) stages of the SI process is conditioned by numerous factors (Table 8.1). Reaching a level of high maturity of social innovation is certainly a time-consuming process. The cornerstone of the development of mature social innovations is a high level of social capital and civil society (Kulik, 2013, p. 21) which, compared to Western European countries, is still rather low (SolAbility, 2020). Similarly, the involvement of enterprises in the development of SI may be conditioned by the degree of their social and environmental responsibility. Most companies in Poland still see "social problems in terms of philanthropy" (Kaczmarek and Tomkiewicz, 2013, p. 6). Therefore, it is important to support the development of enterprises whose business strategies are focused on sustainable development, which are open to new shareholders (crowdfunding), and cooperation-oriented in investing resources used to create common benefits (profit sharing).

Scaling and diffusion of social innovations requires increasing the spatial range of solutions. To achieve this phase, it seems particularly important that city authorities can identify initiatives that are key to climate change adaptation. Next, promote them among all stakeholders. This type of approach certainly facilitates the scaling and diffusion of social innovations, as well as enhances stakeholder network cooperation for their formalized and well-organized implementation following the continuous improvement philosophy. The development of SI can be activated by promoting the idea of adaptation together with city investment, education, lobbying, and promoting adaptation-related solutions with the use of recognizable brands of enterprises (Murray et al., 2010, pp. 85–87). The authors' research shows that adaptation to climate change is not always emphasized in the policy of Polish cities and urban investments. It is proposed to promote the term "adaptation to climate change" in public investment projects, revitalization, financial incentives, ecology education, and green budget. In this way, it is possible to spread SI to entire areas of the city and its surroundings. Stimulating the social innovations requires maintaining the involvement of innovation creators and supporting project financing (Komorowska and Wygnański, 2019, pp. 58–61). Therefore, the difficulty in diffusing social innovations may be caused by their costly nature, low involvement of creators and dependence on specific resources. Spreading SI and achieving high maturity requires embedding in the local community. In this case, the solutions become a constant inspiration for their duplication and implementation (Murray et al., 2010, pp. 82–105). In this way, they can also create a recognizable image of the city. Milan is an example of inspiration for Polish cities. Social innovation associated and recognizable in the city is urban gardening. The number of green areas (green roofs, parks) in the city has increased and they have become places where people meet and where relationships are built between residents (Gusti and Masperi, 2021). Another good example is Vienna. A network of fountains and fog showers has developed in the city (Eurocities, 2021).

The development of SI requires the integration of climate policy with other sectoral policies. This approach is needed in the policy of Polish cities. Adaptation measures must be considered in the strategic management of the city. In addition, it is essential to integrate climate change into spatial planning legislation. German cities can be a good example for Polish cities in terms of conducting politics (Naumann et al., 2020). Another model city is Copenhagen. For example, green construction is in force in new investments in downtown areas (Pardo, 2019). The analysis of Polish urban adaptation plans shows that adaptation solutions will also be disseminated through spatial planning or building standards. Changes are to be expected in the future.

Another instrument supporting scaling and diffusion is the development of green public procurement. The popularity of adaptive solutions in public procurement is an opportunity for the development of mature innovations in Polish cities. Additionally, it is possible to use the potential of Polish NGOs to implement the city's own tasks in the area of ecology and adaptation. It is essential to create platforms for the exchange of knowledge between stakeholders, to promote eco-events, and to involve the public and social media in promoting SI and adaptation to climate change.

Systemic change is the highest stage of the creation and absorption of social innovations. The stage is based on permanent cooperation in the network, diffusion of knowledge between offices, as well as capital, experience, and know-how. The mature SI becomes an instrument of adaptation and sustainable development of cities. Moreover, they become part of the life of the society and the functioning of enterprises in the city. Rotterdam is a good benchmark for Polish cities in terms of good practices in the field of climate change and water management. It can be considered as a city of mature social innovation. Dutch good practices are recognized all over the world (e.g., Water Square Benthemplein). The city of Rotterdam has always suffered from flooding due to its location in the delta. Therefore, its policy has always focused on strengthening resistance to the risk of flooding. It supports the spread of innovation through technologies. Besides, the city authorities are actively building eco-awareness of the society by promoting the slogan "many small activities make a big difference" (Urban green-blue girds, 2021). The city's struggle for survival forced out by its location has become the foundation for the development of a systemic approach to social innovation. The city of Rotterdam is a leader in innovative solutions; enterprises based there specialize in technology and offer attractive jobs. The transition to the phase of systemic change requires the inclusion of adaptive solutions in urban public and private space. Investing in disseminating adaptive solutions stems from the needs of households and is supported by the public sector and a wide range of products and services offered by enterprises. The highest phase of maturity of the SI process is based on the development of public and private blue-green infrastructure. It is important to stimulate and increase the involvement of private capital in the implementation of investments for climate adaptation.

To sum up, the maturity of social innovations for adaptation to climate change requires multi-sectoral actions and bold changes in the economy, society, and politics. Therefore, it is necessary to strengthen social capital, develop corporate social responsibility, promote adaptation actions in implemented investments, conduct an integrated development policy based on adaptation activities, development of green public procurement, develop technologies, strengthen the environmental awareness of residents, create and promote exchange platforms knowledge, and cooperation between stakeholders. The adaptation process requires transformations of the entire urban system. SI must permeate all stages of socio-economic life. We can conclude that the achievement of systemic changes in Polish cities will take place gradually. The occurrence of climatic phenomena and the increasing losses in property, economic activity, and cultural heritage are intensifying in cities. Therefore, effective adaptation and reduction of material and non-material losses require mature social innovations. Achieving mature SI for adaptation to climate change will improve the quality of life and investment attractiveness of Polish cities.

8.4 CONCLUSIONS

Climate change is progressing, and the occurrence of climate losses is increasing. Therefore, it is necessary to urgently focus on multi-directional adaptation measures in city policy, which will be implemented with the involvement of various city stakeholders.

The conducted research made it possible to achieve the assumed goal of the chapter and to answer the three research questions. There are two sources of creation of social innovations for the adaptation of cities to climate change. The first source is local policy, with city authorities and public entities managing green areas. The second source is residents and non-governmental organizations. It was specified bottom-up and top-down social innovation in climate adaptation. The review carried out showed that in Polish cities, SI for adaptation to climate change are stimulated by public investment projects, and financial incentives. They are also activated by all instruments of social participation. Adaptation to climate change requires both top-down and bottom-up social innovations. There is a strong connection between top-down and bottom-up SI in climate adaptation. Unfortunately, the social innovations are rarely directly dedicated to adapting cities to climate change. There is a need to increase the number of public investments, financial instruments, and participation instruments that will directly stimulate the development of SI in climate adaptation. The conducted maturity assessment led to the general conclusion that Poland reached the fourth stage of the SI process. In light of the assessment carried out, there is a need to enter the higher stages of maturity. It is necessary to involve the public and private sectors. The need for climate adaptation and SI must be embedded in all society. The development of mature social innovations can accelerate the adaptation of cities to climate change. However, it should be underlined that attaining the next stages of maturity should also be based on the simultaneous reinforcement of the previous ones. Improving SI maturity is certainly a long process while, in the country covered by the study, the policy of adaptation to climate change has been implemented quite recently. The full use of the potential of social innovation offers a chance for a holistic adaptation of cities to climate change. The cognitive gap indicated in the introduction has been filled using the consistent and process-oriented SI model adapted from Murray et al. (2010). The correct direction of adaptation activities was determined using the potential and dynamic approach to SI development.

The two-stage study that was conducted to achieve the purpose of the article has its limitations. Firstly, the analysis covers only the largest Polish cities. This decision was dictated by the assumption that in highly developed urban areas the issue of adaptation to climate change is strongly addressed in the urban policy. This approach enabled us to find out about the most up-to-date, developed, and diversified SI. Secondly, Internet sources account for a large share of literature sources on the subject which, however, could not be avoided considering the specifics of maturity assessment area.

This chapter provides several practical and theoretical implications. The maturity assessment based on the presented SI process is a practical approach for emerging economics wishing to learn at which stage they are and, consequently, to improve activities at the strategic and operational level aimed to deploy the inhabitants' potential to implement eco-initiatives. The presented approach is a unique one and can be treated as a pioneering one to the development of sustainable cities in the area of adaptation to climate change. The area of developing social innovations for adaptation to climate change is certainly an emerging one and requires many targeted actions. For future research directions, it is especially suggested to search for answers as to which system (including resources, stakeholders, communication channels, sources of financing, etc.) would be the most effective to achieve the highest stage of the SI process and how to measure its social, environmental, and economic outcomes.

REFERENCES

Agaciak, A. "Ogrody społeczne w każdej krakowskiej dzielnicy." *Dziennik Polski* 24 (2017). Available at: (https://dziennikpolski24.pl/ogrody-spoleczne-w-kazdej-krakowskiej-dzielnicy-zdjecia/ar/12271191), (2021, July).

Andion, C., G. Dias Alperstedt, J. Furlanetto Graeff, and L. Ronconi. "Social innovation ecosystems and sustainability in cities: a study in Florianopolis, Brazil." *Environment, Development and Sustainability* May (2021). https://doi.org/10.1007/s10668-021-01496-9

Bergman, N., N. Markusson, P. Connor, and L. Middlemiss. "Bottom-up social innovation for addressing climate change." (2010), Sussex Energy Group Conference. Available at: (https://www.researchgate.net/publication/271214929_Bottom-up_social_innovation_for_addressing_climate_change) (2021 February).

City of Cracow. "Plan Adaptacji Miasta Krakowa do zmian klimatu do roku 2030" (2019). Available at: (https://www.bip.krakow.pl/?dok_id=114317 (2021, March).

City of Lodz. "Plan adaptacji do zmian klimatu miasta Łodzi do roku 2030" (2018). Available at: (https://bip.uml.lodz.pl/files/bip/public/BIP_AB/WOSR_klimat_pro_181003.pdf) (2021, March).

City of Lodz Office. (2017). Available at: (https://uml.lodz.pl/czas-wolny/zielen-i-rekreacja/zarzad-zieleni-miejskiej/las-mlodej-lodzi/) (2021, February).

City of Lodz Office. (2021a). Available at: (https://uml.lodz.pl/panel-obywatelski/tematyka/ https://uml.lodz.pl/panel-obywatelski/tematyka/) (2021, March).

City of Lodz Office. (2021b). Available at: (https://uml.lodz.pl/decydujemy-o-lodzi/ngo/inicjatywy-lokalne/) (2021, March).

City of Lodz Office. (2021c). Available at: https://uml.lodz.pl/budzet-obywatelski (2021, February).

City of Warsaw. (2015). Available at: (http://inicjatywa.um.warszawa.pl/aktualnosci/wydarzenia/zrealizowane-inicjatywy) (2021, March).

City of Warsaw. (2020a). Available at: (https://zielona.um.warszawa.pl/temat-panelu) (2021, March).

City of Warsaw. (2020b). Available at: (https://twojbudzet.um.warszawa.pl/vi-edycja-budzetu-obywatelskiego) (2021, February).

City of Warsaw. (2021). Available at: (https://zielona.um.warszawa.pl/edukacja) (2021, March).

City of Wroclaw. (2018). Available at: (https://www.wroclaw.pl/rozmawia/100-ulic-na-100-lecie-niepodleglosci) (2021, March).

City of Wroclaw. (2019a). Available at: (https://www.wroclaw.pl/rozmawia/fundusz-osiedlowy) (2021, March).

City of Wroclaw. (2019b). Available at: (https://www.wroclaw.pl/rozmawia/wroclawski-budzet-obywatelski-edycja-2019) (2021, February).

City of Wroclaw. "Miejski Plan Adaptacji do zmian klimatu do roku 2030." (2019c). Available at: (https://bip.um.wroc.pl/artykuly/882/miejski-plan-adaptacji-do-zmian-klimatu-mpa) (2021, July).

City of Wroclaw. (2020a). Available at: (https://www.wroclaw.pl/growgreen) (2021, March).

City of Wroclaw. (2020b). Available at: (https://www.wroclaw.pl/rozmawia/panel-obywatelski) (2021, March).

City of Wroclaw. (2020c). Available at: (https://bip.um.wroc.pl/artykul/842/43956/zlap-deszcz-2020) (2021, March).

City of Wroclaw. (2021a). Available at: (https://www.wroclaw.pl/rozmawia/konsultacje) (2021, March).

City of Wroclaw. (2021b). Available at: (https://www.wroclaw.pl/mikrogranty/) (2021, March).

City of Wroclaw. (2021c). Available at: (https://www.wroclaw.pl/rozmawia/centra-aktywnosci-lokalnej) (2021, March).

Cracow City Hall. (2017). Available at: (https://www.krakow.pl/213716,artykul,collectively.html), (2021, March).
Cracow City Hall. (2020). Available at: (https://www.krakow.pl/klimat/247296,artykul,krakowski_panel_klimatyczny.html), (2021, March).
Cracow City Hall. (2021). Available at: (https://www.krakow.pl/klimat/247296,artykul,krakowski_panel_klimatyczny.html), (2021, March).
Ekolokator. (2021). Available at: (http://www.chronmyklimat.pl/projekty/eko-lokator/aktualnosci/dachy-i-sciany-zielone-we-wroclawiu-a-zwolnienia-od-podatku-uchwala-rady-miejskiej) (2021, February).
Eurocities. "Beating the heat in Vienna" (2021). Available at: (https://eurocities.eu/stories/beating-the-heat-in-vienna/) (2021, February).
European Commission. "Social Innovation. A Decade of Changes." (2014).
European Commission. "Social Innovation" (2020). Available at: https://ec.europa.eu/growth/industry/policy/innovation/social_en (2021, January).
Foundation Fenomen Miasto. (2020). Available at: (https://www.fundacjafenomen.pl/aktualnosci/437-fenomenalne-podworko-koscielna-4 (2021, July).
Frantzeskaki, N. "Seven lessons for planning nature-based solutions in cities." *Environmental Science and Policy* 93 (2019): 101–111.
Gasparin, M., W. Green, S. Lilley, M. Quinn, M. Saren, and C. H. Schinckus. "Business as usual: A business model for social innovation." *Journal of Business Research* 125 (2021): 698–709.
Grotowska, E., and H. Ruman. "Ogrody społeczne. Bank dobrych praktyk. Wrocławska Rewitalizacja Sp. z o.o." (2019). Available at: (https://www.funduszeeuropejskie.gov.pl/media/95443/9_wr_ogrodyspolecznee-book-1.pdf), (2021, July).
Gusti, R. A. T., and A. Masperi. Milan - NBS for urban regeneration (2021). Available at: (https://networknature.org.uk/casestudy/19446), (2021, February).
Hegger, D. L. T., H. L. P. Mees, P. P. J. Driessen, and H. A. C. Runhaar. "The rules of residents in climate adaptation: A systematic review in the case of the Netherlands." *Environmental Policy and Governance* 27 (2017): 336–350.
Huang-Lachmann, J. T. "Systematic review of smart cities and climate change adaptation." *Sustainability Accounting, Management and Policy Journal* 10 (2019): 745–772.
Kaczmarek, P., and Tomkiewicz, E. "Innowacje społeczne oczami uczestników Grupy Roboczej w projekcie Wizja 2050." In *Wizja 2050. Innowacje społeczne. Podsumowanie prac grupy roboczej w 2013 r* (2013).
Katowice City Hall. (2021). Available at: (https://www.katowice.eu/dla-mieszka%C5%84ca/zaanga%C5%BCuj-si%C4%99/konsultacje-spo%C5%82eczne/zielony-bud%C5%BCet), (2021, February).
Kok, M., W. Vermeulen, A. Faaj, and D. Jager. *Global Warming & Social Innovation. The Challenge of a Climate Neutral Society*. London: Earthscan Publications Ltd. (2002).
Komorowska Z., and J. J. Wygnański. *Pod rękę z Pomysłowym Dobromirem Podręcznik dla osób wspierających innowatorów społecznych, Pracownia Badań i Innowacji Społecznych "Stocznia" Warszawa* (2019).
Kulik, M. Bariery i szanse w rozwoju innowacyjności społecznej. In*Wizja 2050. Innowacje społeczne. Podsumowanie prac grupy roboczej w 2013 r,* MG, MŚ, and PwC FOB (2013).
Lublin City Office. (2017). Available at: (https://lublin.eu/mieszkancy/partycypacja/zielony-budzet-obywatelski/projekty-zbo-2017/), (2021, February).
Luxuriant Warsaw. (2021). Available at: (http://bujnawarszawa.pl/o-programie/), (2021, March).
Mabon, L., and W. Y. Shih. "Urban greenspace as a climate change adaptation strategy for subtropical Asian cities: A comparative study across cities in three countries." *Global Environmental Change* 68 (2021): 102248.
Ministry of Environment. Strategiczny plan adaptacji dla sektorów i obszarów wrażliwych na zmiany klimatu do roku 2020 z perspektywą do roku 2030 (2013).
Mumtaz, M. "Role of civil society organizations for promoting green and blue infrastructure to adapting climate change: Evidence from Islamabad city, Pakistan." *Journal of Cleaner Production* 309 (2021): 127296.
Municipal Dialogue Center. (2019). Available at: (https://dialogspoleczny.krakow.pl/inicjatywa-lokalna/inicjatywa-lokalna-fotorelacje-z-projektow/inicjatywa-lokalna-zrealizowane-projekty/), (2021, March).
Murray, R., J. Caulier-Grice, and G. Mulgan. *The open book of social innovation*. The Young Foundation. Nesta (2010).
National Freedom Institute. (2021). Available at: (https://niw.gov.pl/nasze-programy/fio/), (2021, June).
Naumann, S., M. Davis, E. Iwaszuk, M. Freundt, and L. Mederake. *Addressing climate change in cities –*

Policy instruments to promote urban nature-based solutions. Berlin, Krakow: Ecologic Institute, the Sendzimir Foundation (2020).

Nerini, F. F., A. Slob, R. Ericsdotter Engström, and E. Trutnevyte. "A research and innovation agenda for zero-emission European Cities." *Sustainability* 11 (2019): 1692.

Oeij, P. R. A., W. van der Torre, F. Vaas, and S. Dhondt. "Understanding social innovation as an innovation process: Applying the innovation journey model." *Journal of Business Research* 101 (2019): 243–254.

Osburg, T. "Social innovation to drive corporate sustainability." *Social Innovation*. Springer, Berlin, Heidelberg (2013): 13–22. https://doi.org/10.1007/978-3-642-36540-9_2

Ośrodek Ewaluacji. "Civic Budget 2020. Evaluation study of the 6th edition of the Civic Budget in Warsaw. Final report. Warsaw, November 2019. In turn, in Gdansk and Katowice, this year, residents can submit their ideas under the Green Civic Budget for 2021 for the first time" (2019).

Pardo, D. "Copenhagen's green future is built on the rooftops" (2019). Available at: (https://www.smartcitylab.com/blog/urban-environment/copenhagens-green-roofts/) (2021, January).

Pel, B., A. Haxeltine, F. Avelino, A. Dumitru, R. Kemp, T. Bauler, I. Kunze, J. Dorland, J. Wittmayer, and M. S. Jørgensen. "Towards a theory of transformative social innovation: A relational framework and 12 propositions." *Research Policy* 49 (2020): 104080.

Phills, J. A., K. Deiglmeier, and D. T. Miller. "Rediscovering Social Innovation." *Stanford Social Innovation Review* 6(4), Fall (2008): 33–43.

Pistelok, P., and B. Martela "Raport o stanie polskich miast. Partycypacja publiczna". Urban Policy Observatory (2020).

Poznan City Hall. (2019). Available at: (https://pbo2019.um.poznan.pl/i/pbo-2019/voting#projekt_02) (2021, February).

Poznan City Hall. (2020a). Available at: (https://www.poznan.pl/mim/info/news/poznanski-panel-obywatelski,153720.html) (2021, March).

Poznan City Hall. (2020b). Available at: (https://budzet.um.poznan.pl/pbo21/zielony-budzet/) (2021, February).

Poznan City Hall. (2021a). Available at: (https://www.poznan.pl/mim/rewitalizacja/-,p,38552,38582.html), (2021, March).

Poznan City Hall. (2021b). Available at: (https://www.poznan.pl/mim/main/centrum-inicjatyw-lokalnych,p,35745,37304.html), (2021, March).

Public information bulletin of Poznan. (2020). Available at: (https://bip.poznan.pl/bip/wydzial-dzialalnosci-gospodarczej-i-rolnictwa,15/news/konkurs-zielony-poznan,133015.html) (2021, March).

Raja, P. "This is how social innovators are leading the race to zero emissions" (2020). Available at: (https://www.weforum.org/agenda/2020/11/this-is-how-social-innovators-are-leading-the-race-to-zero-emissions/) (2021, January).

Singh, C. H., M. Madhavan, J. Arvind, and A. Bazaz. "Climate change adaptation in Indian cities: A review of existing actions and spaces for triple wins." *Urban Climate* 36 (2021): 100783.

Sobol, A. "Budżet obywatelski jako narzędzie rozwoju lokalnego." *Studia Ekonomiczne* 316 (2017): 172–182.

Social Innovation Academy. (2021). Available at: (https://www.socialinnovationacademy.eu/introduction-to-social-innovation/) (2021, February).

SolAbility. (2020). Available at: (https://solability.com/the-global-sustainable-competitiveness-index/the-index/social-capital) (2021, March 22).

Stocker, T., D. Qin, G.-K. Plattner, M. Tignor, S. K. Allen, J. Boschung, A. Nauels, Y. Xia, V. Bex, and P. M. Midgley (eds.) "Climate change 2013: the physical science basis: Working Group I contribution to the Fifth assessment report of the Intergovernmental Panel on Climate Change. Cambridge University Press" (2014).

The City Greenery Board of Cracow. (2020). "Sukces Krakowskich Ogrodów Społecznych." Available at: (https://zzm.krakow.pl/aktualnosci/718-sukces-krakowskich-ogrodow-spolecznych.html) (2021, March).

The City Greenery Board of Poznan. (2021). Available at: (http://zzmpoznan.pl/wiadomosci/1/wiadomosc/158369/czym_sie_zajmuje_zarzad_zieleni_miejskiej_w_poznaniu_i_plany_na_) (2021, March).

The City Greenery Board of the Capital City of Warsaw. (2018). Available at: (http://zzw.waw.pl/zieloneulice/) (2021, March).

The City Greenery Board of the Capital City of Warsaw. (2019). Available at: (http://zzw.waw.pl/2019/09/16/zapraszamy-do-wlaczenia-sie-w-akcje-warszawskie-swieto-drzewa-milion-drzew-dla-warszawy/) (2021, March).

The Management of the Cracow Municipal Greenspace Authority. (2017). Available at: (https://zzm.krakow.pl/dzialania-antysmogowe/395-akcja-park-krakowian.html) (2021, February).

The Management of the Cracow Municipal Greenspace Authority. (2021). Available at: (https://zzm.krakow.pl/aktualnosci/684-zielony-budzet-obywatelski-miasta-krakowa-2019-r-wyniki.html) (2021, February).

The Sejm of the Republic of Poland. "Budget lexicon" (2021). Available at: (http://sejm.gov.pl/Sejm7.nsf/BASLeksykon.xsp?id=667DCF4F24778F74C1257A710030C2E9&litera=B) (2021, February).

Urban green-blue girds. (2021). Available at: (https://www.urbangreenbluegrids.com/projects/water-sensitive-rotterdam/) (2021, February).

Van der Bijl-Brouwer, M., and Malcolm, B. "Systemic design principles in social innovation: A study of expert practices and design rationales." *The Journal of Design, Economics, and Innovation* 6(3) (2020): 386–407.

Winsvold, M., K. J. Hjeltnes, J. E. Klausen, and O. Langeland "Climate change adaptation through hierarchies and networks in the city of Bergen." *Climate Adaptation Governance in Cities and Regions: Theoretical Fundamentals and Practical Evidence* (2016): 285–304.

Wolańska, K. "Ogrody społeczne jako sposób na rewitalizację przestrzeni miejskiej i integrację sąsiedzką." (2019). Available at: (http://www.chronmyklimat.pl/projekty/eko-lokator/aktualnosci/ogrody-spoleczne-jako-sposob-na-rewitalizacje-przestrzeni-miejskiej-i-integracje-sasiedzka) (2021, July).

Wolfram, M. "Cities shaping grassroots niches for sustainability transitions: Conceptual reflections and an exploratory case study." *Journal of Cleaner Production* 173 (2018): 11–23.

9 Role of Urban Green Space Fostering Environmentally Modified Attitude and Behaviour: Reflection from a Highly Expanding Medium-Sized Town in India

Swatilekha Sen and Dr. Sanat Kumar Guchhait
The University of Burdwan, West Bengal, India

CONTENTS

9.1 INTRODUCTION

Is there any need for the development of urban green space in India for better liveability? Will it foster sustainable urban life-promoting environmental modified attitude and behaviour? To get a satisfactory answer, we have to look for the perspective of the man-nature integration: the emerging dimension of the post-structuralist city of the developed.

It is a necessity in the developing world as it ensures sustainable urban livelihood. The city life associated with green space is an antidote to post-modern restlessness urbanism that is gaining importance for the changing face of city infrastructures. The desired living for a natural environment to minimize the stress of hectic urban life (Maas et al., 2009) is gaining importance day

DOI: 10.1201/9781003126195-11

by day (Sen and Guchhait, 2021). So many city dwellers nowadays of the developing world favour green city space not as a fashion but for an urge for peaceful city life that ensures sound physical and mental health.

The social and spatial context of present-day urbanization can be explicable in multiple dimensions. Changing types of nature, forms, and perspectives of contemporary urbanization have interpreted the idea of city space, both hardware and software, city life, and the role of built-up green space in the post-modern city life of the western world, whether living in a gated community or slums or green surroundings. This enquiry seeks to unfold the role and need for green area development for rapidly escalating cities of India in a sequel to the importance of the interaction between individuals and the environment (Kruize et al., 2019) in an urban area.

Therefore, as crucial components of urban ecosystems, green spaces contribute to sustainable development, landscape, and environmental quality; quality of life; and citizen's health (Vargas-Hernández et al., 2017). For many urbanites, spending some quality time in green spaces is their only option to be surrounded by nature. Hence, the ascendancy of green space on the quality of urban life and the urban economy is now widely apprehended. Urban parks, as large outdoor open spaces, can provide residents with a green social environment in which to engage in outdoor activities (Xie et al., 2020). Better social and environmental factors are the crucial determinants of subjective wellbeing (Rajapaksa et al., 2018). Studies show that participants' attitudes towards, and affective connections with, the environment significantly predicted their intention to engage with nature (Anderson and Krettenauer, 2021).

A personal connection with nature plays an essential mediating role in relationships between environmental exposures and pro-environmentalism in individuals (Alcock et al., 2020; Martin and Czellar, 2017). Several pieces of research suggest that self-identity and biospheric values motivate people to engage in pro-environmental behaviour (Ruepert et al., 2016). It can be conceived of as a connectedness to nature (Mayer et al., 2009). Exposure to nature increases contact with and feelings of connectedness with the natural world, even among urban populations (Fuller and Gaston, 2009). The research findings suggest that those processes can enhance pro-social values and behaviour (Guéguen and Stefan, 2016; Zhang et al., 2014) and augment pro-environmentalism (Schwartz, 1994). Evans et al. (2018) show that pleasant experiences in nature lead to increased environmental responsibility.

With the growing disillusionment of hectic city life and poor liveability of the cities, restructuring of socio-spatial urban spaces is the need of the hour with the increasing demand for urban green space in the expanding towns of India in what has already been established for the planned cities of India like Chandigarh of Panjab and the Salt Lake City of West Bengal provinces, respectively. If the urbanites can access the desired environment through deep green cover and the chirping of birds and crawling of animals, it develops a rational mind for social integration and community development potentials (Miller et al., 2015; Van Hecke et al., 2017). Urban green space provides ecological benefits to the cities, such as regulating the urban heat island phenomena, reducing noise and air pollution, and various ecosystem services (Armson et al., 2012; Hamada and Ohta, 2010). It also extends multiple social, economic, and ecological roles, including therapeutic benefits, the desired surroundings for raising children, social integration, conservation easements, and community development potential (Miller et al., 2015; Hague and Siegel, 2002; Milton, 2002).

Hence, this chapter attempts to focus uniquely on human-nature connectedness (Biophilia-Wilson, 1984) through the study of humans on cities or nature in towns and the coupled relationship between them. Accordingly, the present research throws light to elucidate the environmental attitude and behaviour of urbanites through the framework of the SEM and validate the spatial differences of green space through MANOVA. In this regard, the impact variables of perceived green space attachment and environmental perception and attitudes on people's environmental behaviour have been assessed.

9.2 THE STUDY AREA

It is the urban century of India, urbanizing at an enhanced pace in recent decades (Ghosh and Kansal, 2014). Currently, India's urban population is about 34 per cent (World Bank, 2019). Indian cities are now subject to urbanize at rapid rates that create new challenges for infrastructure development, land use design and housing, and the urban ecology (Swerts et al., 2014; Nagendra et al., 2013; Vira and Vira, 2005). At present, all metropolitan areas are suffering from unplanned sprawl. Green and open spaces recede further and further. Large cities are reeling under the pressure of population and continuous built-up areas tending towards urban heat islands. If we are incapable of developing green space even in the 21st century, urban heat islands with massive populations will foster global warming. So, what will be the fate of urban sustainability and sustainable urban living?

Medium-sized cities are no exception to this; only the intensity is low. Henceforth, medium-sized towns are of vital importance as these are the places where the bulk of future urban development will happen in the upcoming decades. The study area comprises Bardhaman municipality (size: 26 sq. km, total population: 314,265, population density 11,949 persons/sq. km. Census of India, 2011); positioned at the centre of South Bengal, it is proliferating and shows rampant urbanization.

While considering the historical backdrop, the study area had deep green forest lands covered with various woody plants and different wildlife. Rivers like Damodar, Banka, and Khari have run through this area. Burdwan is well known due to its history. Burdwan Rajas ruled the city for over 350 years and contributed to its development as a built-up city. Since the beginning of the 21st century, this region has grown remarkably in land use and land cover changes, leading to environmental challenges. Due to the legacy of the Raj Dynasty, some places within the city space are protected and still bear the prominent signature as the preserved site for nature and biodiversity (Sen and Guchhait, 2021). On the other hand, other parts of the city are now congested and narrowed. The green and open spaces and wetlands have been grabbed by a developmental nexus in and around the cityscape.

9.2.1 Selection of Neighbourhood

For the present study, in general, BPA [Bardhaman Planning Area, as delineated by Bardhaman Development Authority (BDA), extends over 157.62 sq. km, accommodating about 4.07 lakh population, located in the south-central part of Bardhaman District, 107 km northwest to Kolkata metropolitan area (KMA) is selected as the setting for the study, considering the contrasting images of the city (Figure 9.1).

To fulfil our objective, whether the variability of green space connotes different pro-environmental behaviour, three neighbourhoods (ample points) are selected based on their locations within the city. The selected areas are (i) Study site-1: very close to built-up green space developed by Raj Dynasty that typically precludes the possibility of physical and psychological attachment towards nature while (ii) Study site-2: a busy built-up environment with the hustle and bustle of the city away from nature and (iii) Study site-3: embarks on intermediate or transitional zone comprising the physical characteristics of both the study sites located in the city's periphery. To assess the green cover, the spectral indices created by the NDVI (Normalized Difference Vegetation Index), MNDWI (Modified Normalized Difference Water Index), and NDBI (Normalized Difference Built-up Index) (using Arc-GIS 10.2.3) (Figure 9.2) help identify land cover types and, hence, these can identify the different neighbourhoods quickly. The availability of green spaces has been determined through GIS analyses and verified through field observations.

9.3 MATERIALS AND METHODS

9.3.1 Development of Indicators

A set of indicators and variables is constructed for assessing environmental attitude and pro-environmental behaviour. For this study, 15 items under four variables have been produced. Most

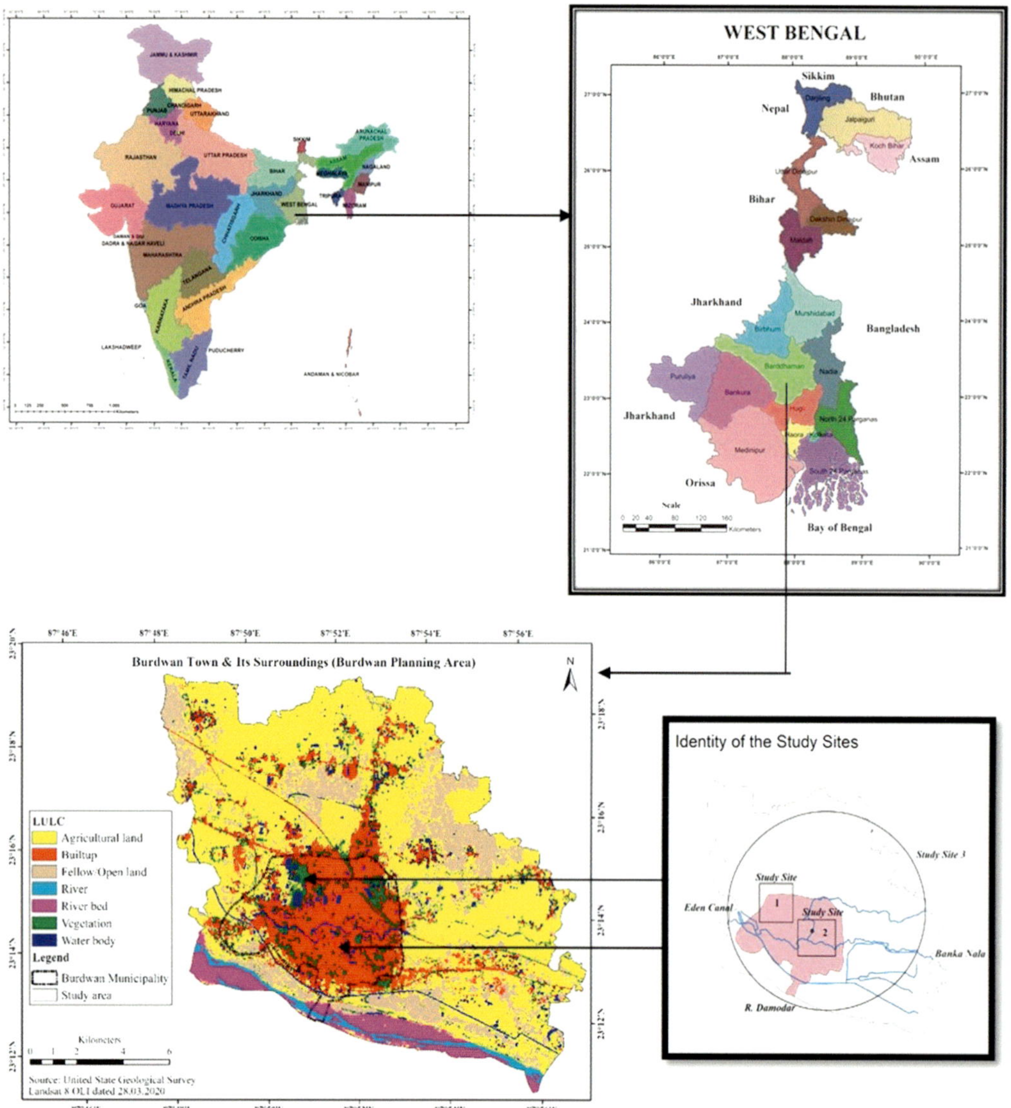

FIGURE 9.1 Location and identity of the study area.

of the dimensions are cited from notable literature: Alcock et al. (2020); Zhang et al. (2018); Arnberger and Eder (2012); Budruk et al. (2009) etc. The selected items of each dimension are also based on several relevant studies, e.g., environmental *attitude* following the ideas of Clayton (2012); Milfont and Duckitt (2010); Schultz et al.(2004), and environmental *behaviour* considered by Krajhanzl (2010).

9.3.2 The Present Research and Proposed Hypothesis

The study opts to address a positive relationship between nature connectedness in terms of proximity to green space, the number of visits, length of residence, and average time spent in the neighbourhood reflected in the environmental attitude and pro-environmental behaviour.

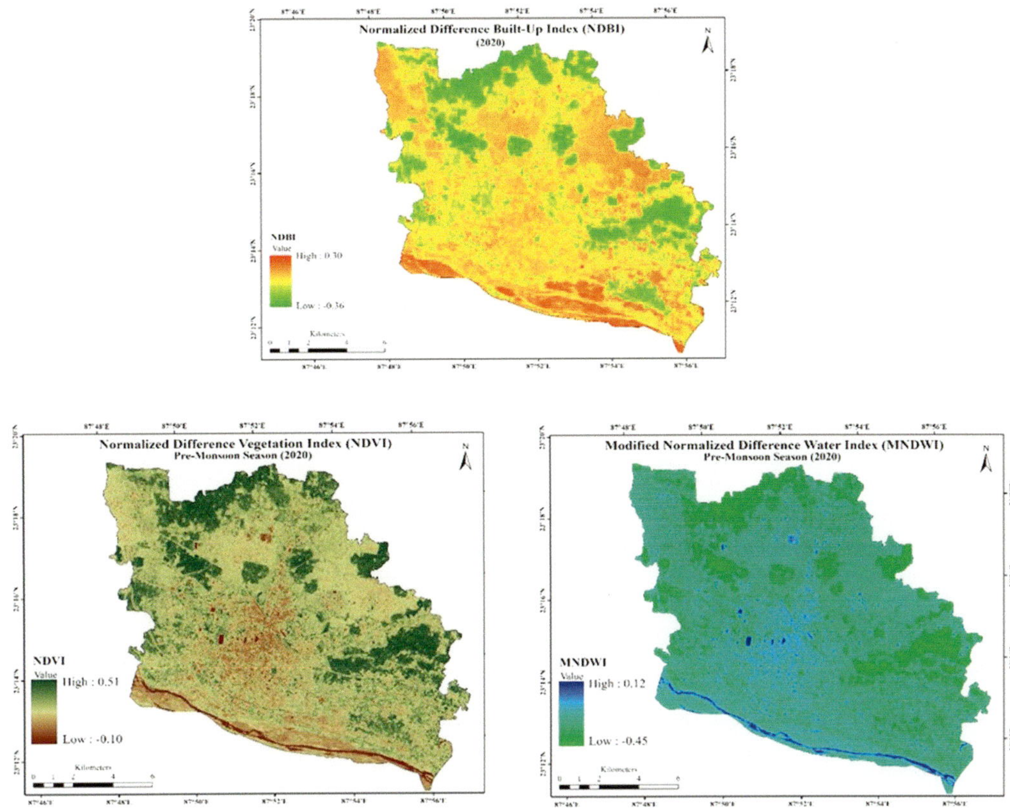

FIGURE 9.2 NDBI, NDVI, and MNDWI of the study area.

9.3.3 Hypothesized Model for Enquiry

The cognitive domain of environmental and psychological research commonly describes environmental attitude and behaviour as a mental judgment towards the value of environmental protection. Several studies (Li et al., 2019; Geiger et al., 2018; Capaldi et al., 2014; Klöckner, 2013) have been executed to explore the role of the variables in developing environmental attitude and behaviour. The structural framework of this study (Figure 9.3) explores how far connectedness to nature is crucial for judging environmental attitudes and behaviour.

9.3.4 Data Collection

In this paper, both qualitative and quantitative methods are employed together to obtain the complementary information. Since this analysis is mainly based on people's perception of surroundings, data used in the investigation have been collected by using constructed questionnaires for doing the primary field survey.

Firstly, primary questions were asked, and then some words were picked according to different persons. Sub-questions were added in addition to the initial questionnaire based on the responses made by various interviewees. Phase two involved developing the final questionnaire with a field survey where participants' responses were coded on the Likert Scale. The scale ranged from 1 to 5, where value-1 denotes "strongly disagree" and value-5 indicates "strongly agree." The questionnaire was designed into two sections to evaluate the four main areas of the study. The first part was intended to collect participants' socio-demographic identification (age, gender, level of education, occupation etc.), length of residence, rootedness, etc. Next, respondents were asked to reflect their opinion on different scale items.

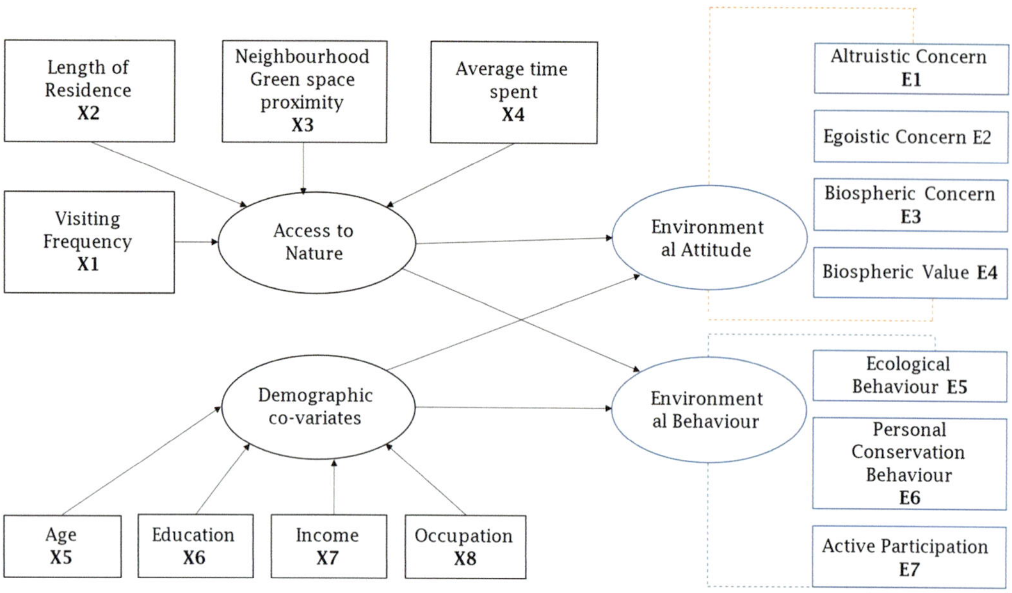

FIGURE 9.3 Hypothesized model of structural equation modelling.

9.3.5 Socio-demographic Overview of Respondents

The proportion of participants identifying with each province of residence and gender generally reflected the total population. Here, an attempt is made to use it to obtain a diverse as well as representative sample. There are more than 330 participants, of which 297 respondents' views are taken into consideration. These are split into three categories, based on whether they lived in core urban areas or periphery or intermediate zone of the study area (Table 9.1). The criteria for the respondents of the three sites are gender, age, education, income, and measures related to connectedness to nature. A slight gap is found for gender, age, education, and income among the three sites but others show some differences. The table is self-explanatory, and it will probably offer different dimensions between physical and social variables under specific measures.

9.4 RESULTS AND DISCUSSION

9.4.1 Structural Equation Model

After reviewing the backdrop, it is reasonably necessary to measure "how green space effects environmental attitude and pro-environmental behaviour among urbanites." To fulfil the present objectives, path analysis is instrumental in this case because of its ability to test simple processes of simultaneity based on a hypothesized model (Fassinger, 2000). Therefore, an SEM is applied to portray the relationship between nature connectedness, environmental attitude, and environmental behaviour. The structural model reports the relationships between exogenous variables and latent variables and among latent variables. When drawing a path diagram, the variables need to be placed in a structured way, such that the figure is easily interpretable (Boker et al., 2002). In the model, the adjusted Reingold–Tilford algorithm (1981) layout has been designed. However, variables of nature connectedness and demographic variables are represented by item X [accordingly, X1-X8], and environmental attitude and environmental behaviour are described by E (E1-E7) as observed indicators of these two latent variables. Each observed variable (item) has different effects on the development of these variables, as mentioned previously (Table 9.2).

TABLE 9.1
Overview of Socio-demographic Statistics of the Participants from the Three Neighbourhoods

Characteristics	Study Site 1 (Nearby Natural)	Study Site 2 (Busy Built Up)	Study Site 3 (Intermediate)
Respondents	87	95	115
Female in percentage	51.72	60	46.09
Average Age (in years)	48.61	49.66	49.56
Higher Education (in percentage)	75.86	55.79	57.39
Family Economic Status (%)			
Low/Lower-middle	10.34	22.10	27.82
Medium/High	89.65	77.89	72.17
Average Length of Residence (in years)	27.78	27.64	27.46
Frequency of Visits to Nearby Green Spaces (in percentage)			
Daily to Weekly	73.56	20	37.39
Monthly to Rare	16.09	80	62.60
Average Time Spent in Nearby Green Spaces (in percentage)			
Daily 1–1.5hrs	39.08	5.26	11.30
Monthly 15–20 hrs	33.33	9.47	26.96
Monthly <10–15 hrs	11.49	14.74	17.39
Rare/Never	5.74	70.52	44.34

TABLE 9.2
Criteria for Identification of Environmental Attitude and Environmental Behaviour with Their Mean Value and Standard Deviations

Criterion Environmental Attitude	Mean	SD	Cronbach's alpha .765
Egoistic Concern	3.10	1.58	
Altruistic Concern	2.75	1.45	
Biospheric Concern	3.21	1.17	
Biospheric Value	3.62	1.26	
Environmental Behaviour			**.830**
Ecological Behaviour	2.92	1.42	
Personal Conservation Behaviour	2.65	1.11	
Active Participation in Environmental Activities	2.69	1.25	

Visiting frequency (X1), length of residence (X2), average time spent on nearby green spaces (X3), and neighbourhood proximity (X4) are chosen as the determining factors of nature connectedness as those induce man-nature bond. A recent study has found that positive perceptions of green spaces are essential indicators of neighbourhood satisfaction (Douglas et al., 2019). In literature, age (X6), education (X7), and income (X8) show erratic patterns of associations with place attachment (Lewicka, 2011) and hence, consideration of socio-demographic status is important while judging the influence of green space on environmental attitude and environmental behaviour.

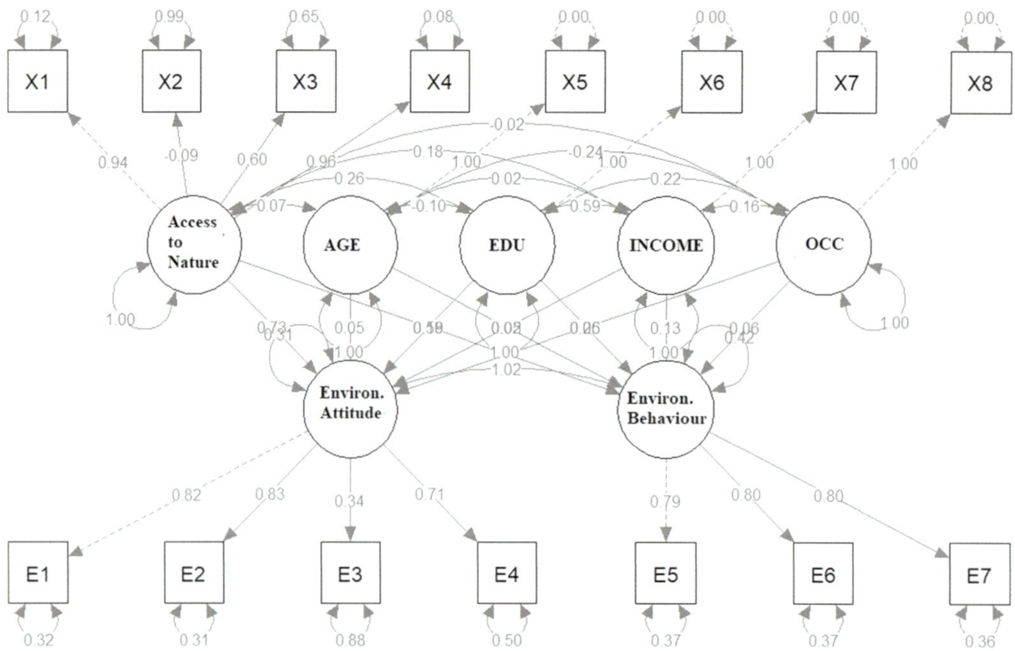

FIGURE 9.4 A standardized result of the structural equation modelling.

9.4.2 Descriptive Statistics of Input Variables

We tested the hypothesized model (Figure 9.3) under R Studio v1.4.1106. All standardized regression paths with a statistical significance of less than 0.05 have been included for the present analysis. Here, the consistency level is satisfactory. When a model is suggested to have an acceptable fit, then the focus must be on specific elements of fit: 1. the ratio of each parameter estimate to its standard error is distributed as a z-statistic and is significant at the 0.05 level if its value exceeds 1.96 2. Standardized parameter estimates are transformations of unstandardized estimates that remove scaling information (Suhr, 2006). It is generally determined that a positive co-efficient signifies that if the value of the independent variable increases; the mean of the dependent variable cater to increase also. So, when Figure 9.4 is examined, it is clearly observed that nature connectedness is a strong predictor of environmental attitude ($\beta = 0.73$, z-value = 13.509, P(>|z|) = 0.000) and environmental behaviour ($\beta = 0.59$, z-value = 9.843, P(>|z|) = 0.000). Among the socio-demographic variables, education plays the most crucial role. Significant parameter estimates for latent variables viz. nature connectedness includes X3, X4 (z-value = 11.994, 29.773), environmental attitude includes E2, E3, E4, (z-value = 16.956, 6.019, 13.635), and environmental behaviour includes E6 and E7 (z-value = 14.959, 15.061). Residuals or co-variances (association between the variables' error terms) are represented in the model as double-headed self-loops on endogenous and exogenous variables, as described by Boker et al. (2002).

In the resultant model (Figure 9.4), all indices confirm the goodness of model fit. Various standard indices are applied to assess the model fit in the present research. Chi-square ($\chi 2$) is utilized to test the relative fit of the hypothesized model employing Chi-square/df, adjusting for the degrees of freedom (Hesari et al., 2019). As recommended by Coovert and Craiger (2000), the other indices comprised the two most vital indices: the root mean square error of approximation (RMSEA) and the comparative fit index (CFI). The RMSEA (root-mean-square error approximation) value shows the consistency of structural equation modelling, with RMSEA = 0.10 (Chi square = 2483.708; df = 105; p = 0.000) indicates the acceptable character of the model.

[Note: Schermelleh-Engel et al. (2003) reported that when RMSEA≤0.05, the model was perfectly consistent and when 0.05≤RMSEA≤0.10, the model is acceptably consistent. The value of the standardized root mean square residual (SRMR) is 0.076 and comparative fit index (CFI) and Tucker-Lewis index (TLI) values are 0.889 and 0.861, respectively.]

9.4.3 Differentiating Nature Connectedness of Study Sites through MANOVA

SEM analysis indicates that there is a positive relationship between nature connectedness and environmental attitude and behaviour. It can be said that more orientation towards nature tends to modify environmental perspective positively as well as helps to increase environmentally responsible behaviour. But it is unable to assess the differences among the three sides. To test whether such difference significantly exists among the selected study site(s), multivariate analysis of variance is performed with effects on green space quality and nature connectedness. A MANOVA is conducted using SPSS v20 with the residence (study site) and as an independent variable and green space quality and nature connectedness as dependent variables. For green space quality, Study site-1 is significantly different from sites 2 and 3, respectively.

Similarly, Study site-2 is statistically different from sites 1 and 3. For connectedness to nature, site 1 is significantly different from study site 2 but not from site 3. On the other hand, Study site-2 is not substantially different from site 3. Therefore, it is interesting to note that a significant difference exists between sites 1 and 2 and vice versa, while there is no significant difference between Study sites-1 and -3 and Study sites-2 and -3. Hence, for the connectedness to nature criterion, Study site-3 has similar characteristics to Study sites-1 and -2 (Table 9.3).

To validate the model, **Wilks' Lambda** is used here. It shows that there is a statistically significant difference in green space quality and nature connectedness based on residents' situational environment [F (16, 140) = 6.093, $p < .0005$; Wilk's $\Lambda = 0.348$, partial $\eta 2 = .41$]. Follow up post-hoc test (Turkey HSD) is performed, and the result is presented below.

Connectedness to nature is considered as the intriguing factor for pro-environmental behaviour. To be associated with nature or to feel an urge to access nature is popularly known as biophilia (Wilson, 1984), a kind of eco-psychology (Bragg, 1996; Roszak, 1995), that develops through situatedness of green surroundings and connectedness to nature.

Average time spent in nearby green spaces (X4) and visiting frequency, i.e., the number of visits (X1) so far, play the most crucial role in determining nature connectedness. Closeness of the residence to the nearest available green urban space is of tremendous significance for how often individuals explore such places (Beheshti, 2010). In line with this, Coldwell and Evans (2017) found that people who spend more time in nature tend to have higher biodiversity knowledge, concern for nature, and pro-environmental behaviour. Echoing this, the present research analysis shows a good linkage between those two. Neighbourhood proximity (as an indicator of nature connectedness) also positively and significantly influences nature connectedness ($\beta = 0.60$). But, in contrast to the research hypothesis, length of residence does not satisfy the significance level criterion with its negative co-efficient ($\beta = -0.09$). However, as expected, selected socio-demographic co-variates, e.g., age, education, income, and occupation, show an erratic distribution pattern among the database. In this model, a lower association is observed between nature connectedness with age ($\beta = 0.26$) and education ($\beta = 0.18$), while it is not significantly related to income and occupation. As minor differences are found for socio-demographic variables over the three sites, it weakly regresses with the input variables.

9.4.4 Differences in Environmental Attitudes and Behaviour among Urbanites in Different Study Sites

Findings suggest that green space varies widely over the three sites, whereas socio-demographic variables have little differences. SEM analysis shows strong regressive behaviour with physical variables. So logically, three different sites for their functional characteristics and differences in

TABLE 9.3

Differentiation in Spatial Context through Multivariate Analysis of Variance (MANOVA)

Dependent Variable	(I) Neighbourhood	(J) Neighbourhood	Mean Difference (I-J)	Std. Error	Sig.	95% Confidence Interval	
						Lower Bound	Upper Bound
Green Space Quality	Study Site 1	Study Site 2	1.1168*	.14480	***.000***	.7707	1.4628
		Study Site 3	.4267*	.16201	.027	.0396	.8139
	Study Site 2	Study Site 1	−1.1168*	.14480	***.000***	−1.4628	−.7707
		Study Site 3	−.6900*	.15414	***.000***	−1.0584	−.3217
	Study Site 3	Study Site 1	−.4267*	.16201	.027	−.8139	−.0396
		Study Site 2	.6900*	.15414	***.000***	.3217	1.0584
Connectedness to Nature	Study Site 1	Study Site 2	.6394*	.15753	***.000***	.2629	1.0159
		Study Site 3	.3952	.17625	.070	−.0260	.8165
	Study Site 2	Study Site 1	−.6394*	.15753	***.000***	−1.0159	−.2629
		Study Site 3	−.2442	.16769	.318	−.6449	.1566
	Study Site 3	Study Site 1	−.3952	.17625	.070	−.8165	.0260
		Study Site 2	.2442	.16769	.318	−.1566	.6449

(Note: Based on observed means. The error term is mean square error = .228. *. The mean difference is significant at the .05 level.)

surroundings will show differences in terms of green space coverage and connectedness. But MANOVA results show that significant differences are there between Study sites-1 and -2 both for green space coverage and connectedness to nature (value 0.000) but Study sites-1 (built-up green space) and -3 (periphery) are not different at all except for the last combination (Table 9.3). Therefore, green space development is of utmost necessity for Study site-2.

Thus, the measures on environmental attitudes and environmental behaviour, used in the present study suggest that those who living nearby natural environment have the feelings, "*Living here we feel the man-nature bond, we feel urge for nature, and we must care for the environment.*"

9.5 LIMITATION AND FUTURE SCOPE OF THE STUDY

The present research outcomes provide an opportunity for reflection on the factors that profoundly affect environmental attitudes and pro-environmental behaviour and their implications on environmental awareness. It would be better if a comparison would be made for other towns. Besides, in future studies, the sample should be more categorical and improved. The selection should include more people who depend on the environment economically.

9.6 CONCLUSION

Urbanization has a universal appeal concerning the concentration of non-primary activity and related land use. However, urbanization has changed its paradigm from economical production space to gradual development of eco-space, from man-environment divide to man-environment integration. Therefore, living in or regularly accessing urban green spaces in the developed world has rendered love for and emotion towards nature due to the development of sensitive man-nature interaction with subsequent pro-environmental behaviour that has changed people's attitude and architecture of the city.

The present research confirms that environmental attitude and level of pro-environmental behaviour are a more well-developed sense of cognition with nature connectedness for those who live in close vicinity of nature. So, from the research perspective, the findings indicate that natural surroundings intensely condition human psychology, attitude, and urge. Therefore, the greening of the urban environment and urban eco-space development is the need of the hour for sustainable urban life. It also reveals the relevance of an individual's relation with the natural world by describing human-nature interactions. Hence, there is a hope that rootedness and nature connectedness can hold for a biophilic city through the cultural saga.

REFERENCES

Alcock, Ian, Mathew P. White, Sabine Pahl, Raquel Duarte-Davidson, and Lora E. Fleming. "Associations between pro-environmental behaviour and neighbourhood nature, nature visit frequency and nature appreciation: Evidence from a nationally representative survey in England." *Environment International* 136 (2020): 105441.

Anderson, Daniel J., and Tobias Krettenauer. "Connectedness to nature and pro-environmental behaviour from early adolescence to adulthood: A comparison of urban and rural Canada." *Sustainability* 13, no. 7 (2021): 3655.

Armson, D., P. Stringer, and A. R. Ennos. "The effect of tree shade and grass on surface and globe temperatures in an urban area." *Urban Forestry & Urban Greening* 11, no. 3 (2012): 245–255.

Arnberger, Arne, and Renate Eder. "The influence of green space on community attachment of urban and suburban residents." *Urban Forestry & Urban Greening* 11, no. 1 (2012): 41–49.

Beheshti, Shahid. "The role of urban green spaces in mood change." *Australian Journal of Basic and Applied Sciences* 4, no. 10 (2010): 5352–5361.

Boker, Steven M., J. J. McArdle, and Michael Neale. "An algorithm for the hierarchical organization of path diagrams and calculation of components of expected covariance." *Structural Equation Modeling* 9, no. 2 (2002): 174–194.

Bragg, Elizabeth A. "Towards ecological self: Deep ecology meets constructionist self-theory." *Journal of Environmental Psychology* 16, no. 2 (1996): 93–108.

Budruk, Megha, Heidi Thomas, and Timothy Tyrrell. "Urban green spaces: A study of place attachment and environmental attitudes in India." *Society and Natural Resources* 22, no. 9 (2009): 824–839.

Capaldi, Colin A., Raelyne L. Dopko, and John M. Zelenski. "The relationship between nature connectedness and happiness: A meta-analysis." *Frontiers in Psychology* 5 (2014): 976.

Clayton, Susan D. (2012). The Oxford handbook of environmental and conservation psychology.

Coldwell, Deborah F., and Karl L. Evans. "Contrasting effects of visiting urban green-space and the countryside on biodiversity knowledge and conservation support." *PloS one* 12, no. 3 (2017): e0174376.

Coovert, M., and P. Craiger. "An expert system for integrating multiple fit indices for structural equation models." *New Review of applied expert Systems and emerging technologies* 6 (2000): 39–56.

Douglas, Owen, Paula Russell, and Mark Scott. "Positive perceptions of green and open space as predictors of neighbourhood quality of life: implications for urban planning across the city region." *Journal of Environmental Planning and Management* 62, no. 4 (2019): 626–646.

Evans, Gary W., Siegmar Otto, and Florian G. Kaiser. "Childhood origins of young adult environmental behavior." *Psychological science* 29, no. 5 (2018): 679–687.

Fassinger, Ruth E. "Gender and sexuality in human development: Implications for prevention and advocacy in counseling psychology" (2000).

Fuller, Richard A., and Kevin J. Gaston. "The scaling of green space coverage in European cities." *Biology Letters* 5, no. 3 (2009): 352–355.

Geiger, S., C. Dombois, and J. Funke. "The role of environmental knowledge and attitude: Predictors for ecological behavior across cultures? An analysis of Argentinean and German students." *Umwelt psychologie* 22 (2018): 69–87.

Ghosh, Ruchira, and Arun Kansal. "Urban challenges in India and the mission for a sustainable habitat." *INTERdisciplpina* 2, no. 2 (2014): 281.

Guéguen, Nicolas, and Jordy Stefan. "Green altruism short immersion in natural green environments and helping behaviour." *Environment and Behaviour* 48, no. 2 (2016): 324–342.

Hague, Mary, and Nancy Siegel. "Municipal parks in New York City: Olmsted, Riis, and the transformation of the urban landscape, 1858–1897." *Transformations of urban and suburban landscapes: Perspectives from philosophy, geography, and architecture*. Lanham, MD: Lexington Books (2002): 153–191.

Hamada, Shuko, and Takeshi Ohta. "Seasonal variations in the cooling effect of urban green areas on surrounding urban areas." *Urban Forestry & Urban Greening* 9, no. 1 (2010): 15–24.

Hesari, Elham, Mina Peysokhan, Abbas Havashemi, Dariush Gheibi, Mitra Ghafourian, and Fatemeh Bayat. "Analyzing the dimensionality of place attachment and its relationship with residential satisfaction in new cities: The case of Sadra, Iran." *Social Indicators Research* 142, no. 3 (2019): 1031–1053.

Klöckner, C. A. "A comprehensive mod el of the psychology of environmental behaviour-A meta-analysis." *Global Environmental Change* 23 (2013) 1028–1038.

Krajhanzl, Jan. "Environmental and proenvironmental behavior." *School and Health* 21, no. 1 (2010): 251–274.

Kruize, Hanneke, Nina van der Vliet, Brigit Staatsen, Ruth Bell, Aline Chiabai, Gabriel Muiños, Sahran Higgins et al. "Urban Green Space: Creating a triple win for environmental sustainability, health, and health equity through behavior change." *International Journal of Environmental Research and Public Health* 16, no. 22 (2019): 4403.

Lewicka, Maria. "Place attachment: How far have we come in the last 40 years?" *Journal of Environmental Psychology* 31, no. 3 (2011): 207–230.

Li, Ding, Luman Zhao, Shuang Ma, Shuai Shao, and Lixiao Zhang. "What influences an individual's pro-environmental behavior? A literature review." *Resources, Conservation and Recycling* 146 (2019): 28–34.

Maas, Jolanda, Robert A. Verheij, Sjerp de Vries, Peter Spreeuwenberg, Francois G. Schellevis, and P. P. Groenewegen. "Morbidity is related to a green living environment." *Journal of Epidemiology & Community Health* 63, no. 12 (2009): 967–973.

Martin, Christian, and Sandor Czellar. "Where do biospheric values come from? A connectedness to nature perspective." *Journal of Environmental Psychology* 52 (2017): 56–68.

Mayer, F. Stephan, Cynthia McPherson Frantz, Emma Bruehlman-Senecal, and Kyffin Dolliver. "Why is nature beneficial? The role of connectedness to nature." *Environment and Behavior* 41, no. 5 (2009): 607–643.

Milfont, Taciano L., and John Duckitt. "The environmental attitudes inventory: A valid and reliable measure to assess the structure of environmental attitudes." *Journal of Environmental Psychology* 30, no. 1 (2010): 80–94.

Miller, Robert W., Richard J. Hauer, and Les P. Werner. *Urban forestry: planning and managing urban greenspaces*. Waveland Press (2015).

Milton, Kay. *Loving nature: Towards an ecology of emotion*. Psychology Press (2002).

Nagendra, Harini, Richard Lucas, João Pradinho Honrado, Rob H. G. Jongman, Cristina Tarantino, Maria Adamo, and Paola Mairota. "Remote sensing for conservation monitoring: Assessing protected areas, habitat extent, habitat condition, species diversity, and threats." *Ecological Indicators* 33 (2013): 45–59.

Rajapaksa, Darshana, Moinul Islam, and Shunsuke Managi. "Pro-environmental behavior: The role of public perception in infrastructure and the social factors for sustainable development." *Sustainability* 10, no. 4 (2018): 937.

Roszak, Betty "The spirit of the goddess." *Ecopsychology* (1995): 288–300.

Ruepert, Angela, Kees Keizer, Linda Steg, Fridanna Maricchiolo, Giuseppe Carrus, Adina Dumitru, Ricardo García Mira, Alexandra Stancu, and Daniela Moza. "Environmental considerations in the organizational context: A pathway to pro-environmental behaviour at work." *Energy Research & Social Science* 17 (2016): 59–70.

Schermelleh-Engel, Karin, Helfried Moosbrugger, and Hans Müller. "Evaluating the fit of structural equation models: Tests of significance and descriptive goodness-of-fit measures." *Methods of Psychological Research Online* 8, no. 2 (2003): 23–74.

Schultz, P. Wesley, Chris Shriver, Jennifer J. Tabanico, and Azar M. Khazian. "Implicit connections with nature." *Journal of Environmental Psychology* 24, no. 1 (2004): 31–42.

Schwartz, Shalom H. "Are there universal aspects in the structure and contents of human values?" *Journal of Social Issues* 50, no. 4 (1994): 19–45.

Sen, Swatilekha, and Sanat Kumar Guchhait. "Urban green space in India: Perception of cultural ecosystem services and psychology of situatedness and connectedness." *Ecological Indicators* 123 (2021): 107338.

Suhr, Diana "The basics of structural equation modeling." *Presented: Irvine, CA, SAS User Group of the Western Region of the United States (WUSS)* (2006).

Swerts, Elfie, Denise Pumain, and Eric Denis. "The future of India's urbanization." *Futures* 56 (2014): 43–52.

Van Hecke, Linde, Jelle Van Cauwenberg, Peter Clarys, Delfien Van Dyck, Jenny Veitch, and Benedicte Deforche. "Active use of parks in Flanders (Belgium): an exploratory observational study." *International Journal of Environmental Research and Public Health* 14, no. 1 (2017): 35.

Vargas-Hernández, José G., Karina Pallagst, and Justyna Zdunek-Wielgołaska. "Urban green spaces as a component of an ecosystem. Functions, services, users, community involvement, initiatives and actions." *Revista de Urbanismo* 37 (2017): 1–26.

Vira, Bhaskar, and Shiraz Vira. "Governing India's urban environment: Problems, policies and politics." *Urbanization and Governance in India* (2005): 29–60.

Wilson, Edward O. *Biophilia*. Harvard University Press (1984).

World Bank. (2019).https://data.worldbank.org/indicator/SP.URB.TOTL.IN.ZS

Xie, Jing, Shixian Luo, Katsunori Furuya, and Dajiang Sun. "Urban parks as green buffers during the COVID-19 pandemic." *Sustainability* 12, no. 17 (2020): 6751.

Zhang, Yachen, Brent D. Moyle, and Xin Jin. "Fostering visitors' pro-environmental behaviour in an urban park." *Asia Pacific Journal of Tourism Research* 23, no. 7 (2018): 691–702.

Zhang, Yuling, Hong-Lei Zhang, Jie Zhang, and Shaowen Cheng. "Predicting residents' pro-environmental behaviors at tourist sites: The role of awareness of disaster's consequences, values, and place attachment." *Journal of Environmental Psychology* 40 (2014): 131–146.

Section III

Urbanism and Smart Cities—An Advanced Analysis

10 Urban Spaces and Smart City Development: Issues and Future Challenges

Vishal Soodan
CMS Business School, Jain (Deemed To Be University), Bengaluru, India

Supernova Chakraborty and Richa Mitra
Jagan Institute of Management Studies, Jaipur, India

CONTENTS

DOI: 10.1201/9781003126195-13

10.1 INTRODUCTION

The agenda set by United Nations for the year 2030 unveiled a new setting which includes shifting the mainstream to sustainability in the global development strategy. The spotlight is on the metrics used in the urban context to measure the extent of reduction in carbon emissions during productive activities and other related actions concerning waste management, urban infrastructure, energy and water management, and urban and transportation mobility. A study by Phillis et al. (2017) stated that, as a result of going beyond the permissible boundaries, unexpected implications can be seen in the biosphere, "change in the climate, biodiversity loss and harmful effects on the nitrogen cycle are the three areas where humanity embarking on an experiment which has the capacity to threaten the foundations of sustainability."

The future vision shared by its citizens is known as a sustainable city. The vision involves providing a better quality of life and expanding the chances of prosperity and wellbeing of future generations. According to Mori and Yamashita (2015), a city can be termed sustainable when it has not only the potential to generate socio-economic benefits but also to maintain environmental and other parameters. Environmental protection concepts characterizing cities have led to initiatives such as green cities, smart cities, low carbon cities, etc (Trindade et al., 2017). As there are considerable number of concepts that can be related to sustainability, it has a great occurrence as well as similarity with other cities (De Jong et al., 2015). The concept of smart cities started gaining importance recently (Lara et al., 2016) as the people are moving towards the urbanization which is making the necessity to have smart cities to meet the need (Chatterjee et al., 2021).

Therefore, this chapter terms ideal cities of the 21st century "smart and sustainable" (Yigitcanlar and Kamruzzaman, 2018). The scientific literature available in the text has highlighted the gaps in developing a mutual understanding and has also emphasised the difficulty of presenting a universal definition for the concept of sustainable and smart city (Maiello et al., 2011). These disparities also indicate a need for development of smart city frameworks or enhancing the present-day understanding of smart city concept (Ahvenniemi et al., 2017). Hence, there is an urgent need of looking beyond the traditional measures for developing an all-inclusive approach that leads to the development of the city (Ding et al., 2015). In addition, a city should also define the environmental restrictions to become more eco-friendly (Mori and Yamashita, 2015). Due to these features, it becomes important and challenging to assess smart and sustainable cities (Yigitcanlar, 2009).

10.2 CONCEPT OF A SMART CITY

The concept of a smart city is an evolving one and a clear definition of this concept is not yet available among academics and learners. Simply, a smart city is a location where existing traditional and related networks can be transformed into more convenient, efficient, and informative, enhancing its operations for the holistic development of its residents using digital and telecommunication technologies (Gabrys, 2014). Another way to theorize a smart city is its recognition as an icon of a sustainable and liveable city (Chourabi et al., 2012). In other words, the features of the smart city include the transformation of digital technologies into improved services for citizens and to make better use of resources while minimizing the impact on the environment. Scholarly studies have effectively highlighted the frameworks and technologies that can be used to develop smart cities (Maeda, 2012; Lee et al., 2014).

There are many components of smart cities that together distinguishes them from other cities or urban centres as well, highlighted by previous research (Mardacany, 2014). A smart city adopts different points of these smart attributes based on the needs of the people living in the area. In addition to the above-mentioned attributes of smart cities, there are some other additional factors that determine the role of technology in the development of an urban centre. The additional factors include quality of life, happiness, and other psychological factors that contribute significantly towards the development of a smart city. It is pertinent to mention that there are factors like governance, energy, and climate change apart from social, economic, and health issues that determine the sustainability of a smart city. There are various additional facets of a smart city which include smart living and smart mobility that adds to the smartness of the city infrastructure.

The four core themes around which a smart city can be conceptualized includes society, economy, environment, and governance. The society plays a role in signifying the message that the city exists just because of its people. On the other hand, the economy reflects the continuous development of the city in terms of job growth and sustainability economically. The environment-related concept ensures that the city can sustain and learn some best practices from other cities of the world to ensure a better and brighter future for generations to come. The governance in a city is responsible for policy making and combining the practices are helpful in making lives better inside the city limits (Figure 10.1).

10.2.1 Smart Buildings

A city infrastructure includes all physical, electrical, and digital assets that are the mainstay of a city well equipped with technology. A smart city's infrastructure includes a rapid transportation system with an efficient network; a road network with effective traffic supervision and control; a waste management system with adequate recycling facilities; a high-speed railway network; a power supply system with a backup, fool-proof fire system; a health system with specialized doctors and staff; apartments with around-the-clock electricity supply; and tourist infrastructure with standardised hotels to name a few. The backbone of a smart infrastructure transforms the normal physical infrastructure into smart and efficient systems. The information communication technology (ICT) infrastructure plays a vital role and acts as a central nerve of any smart city. It helps in coordinating and connecting various networks and elements of existing infrastructure. There are various elements that act as an integrated system and help in different types of interactions between responsible elements. The ICT infrastructure in a city holds the key to the development and expansion of smart cities and depends on aspects related to its accessibility and

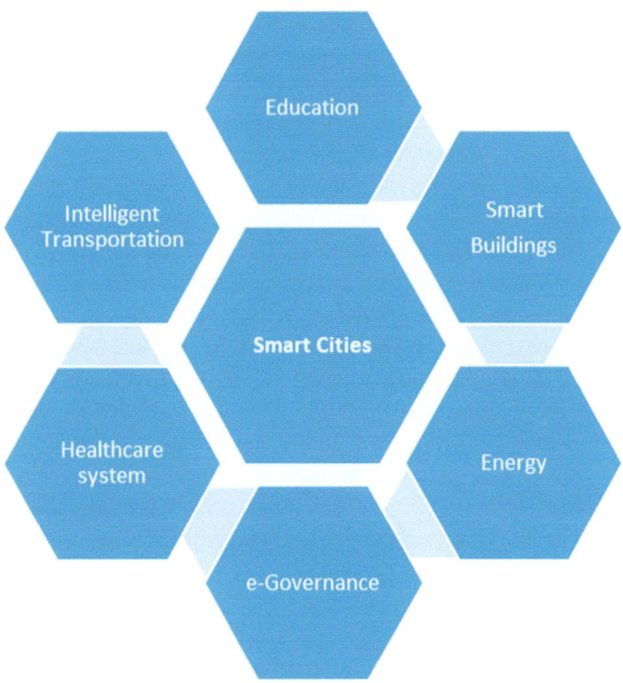

FIGURE 10.1 Components of a smart city.

Source: Self Drawn or Authors

implementation. The ICT infrastructure of a smart city includes a good communication infrastructure which is supported by technologies like optical fibre networks, a fast Wi-Fi network, and other information systems. Smart infrastructure in such cities is cost-effective, safe to use, and has an enhanced level of security as compared to typical city infrastructure. Smart infrastructure as a backbone of an ICT also includes sensors, software, and hardware as a combined force that plays a key role in determining a smart infrastructure.

Apart from different ICT support systems, middleware plays a key role in smart city infrastructure. Middleware is a specific type of software that is responsible for the rapid response of automation and smart infrastructure. This software works in the direction of data integration and uses it for further analysis and reporting. An inseparable part of the smart infrastructure of a city is an uninterrupted supply of electricity.

A smart grid includes effective mechanisms for continuous power supply to the city to meet their energy requirements. Smart infrastructure also includes smart buildings that make maximum use of technology to share information about the building and between systems to optimize the performance of the building. This information from the building is used to power various processes like heating and ventilation, which includes air conditioning and safety. A smart building has many distinctions that make it an additional asset of a smart city. A smart building can connect with ease to other buildings, its people, and with the outer world by using appropriate technology and at the same time can connect with the power grids and local (Figure 10.2).

10.2.2 Intelligent Transportation

A smart city cannot be called smart when there is no smart traffic. An intelligent transport system in a smart city helps to transform cities into digital communities and makes the lives of its citizens easier in every aspect. Awareness is an important concern in any city; it is the transportation system that is used by citizens to travel to and from school, college, and office or for any other purpose. An intelligent transportation system saves the time of the city dwellers and makes the city smarter.

An intelligent transportation system, or ITS, is a technology that helps a smart city to achieve results based on applications that monitor, operate, or enhance the quality of transportation within city limits. The intelligent transportation system relies heavily on data collection and analysis. Sensors play an important role in data collection. Because of intelligent transportation networks, smart cities have opened endless possibilities of converting the cities as the hub of transportation activities which are not limited to the domestic transportation hubs, but also serve as international transit points; for example, Singapore.

Singapore has initiated the projects with the help of a digital platform to assist the people of Singapore at a much lower cost. These service platforms have been designed to provide digital services at a fast rate with maximum effectiveness. The platform named CODEX involves various attributes that collect data and uses it for improving the standards related to the quality of life amongst its residents. The city has an extensive sensor platform that boosts city-level functions including municipal services, planning, and security at the national level. The city systematically uses data and has a well-developed infrastructure of sensors that leads to better urban planning, reliability, and responsive public transportation. Another additional feature of an intelligent transportation system includes effortless and automated ticketing technology, which is helpful for families having kids, and elderly people who have difficulty getting in and out of train stations. With autonomous shuttles operating in the city, this system provides better mobility and connectivity from one city to the other, especially to those with infirmities and senior citizens.

10.2.3 Energy

In these modern times, cities determine the future of technology and its use. It is estimated that by 2030, around 60% of people will live within city limits. Densely populated cities have huge sources of electricity demand, which makes up roughly around two-thirds of the world's energy

FIGURE 10.2 Smart building technology.

Source: www. Jhonsoncontrols.com

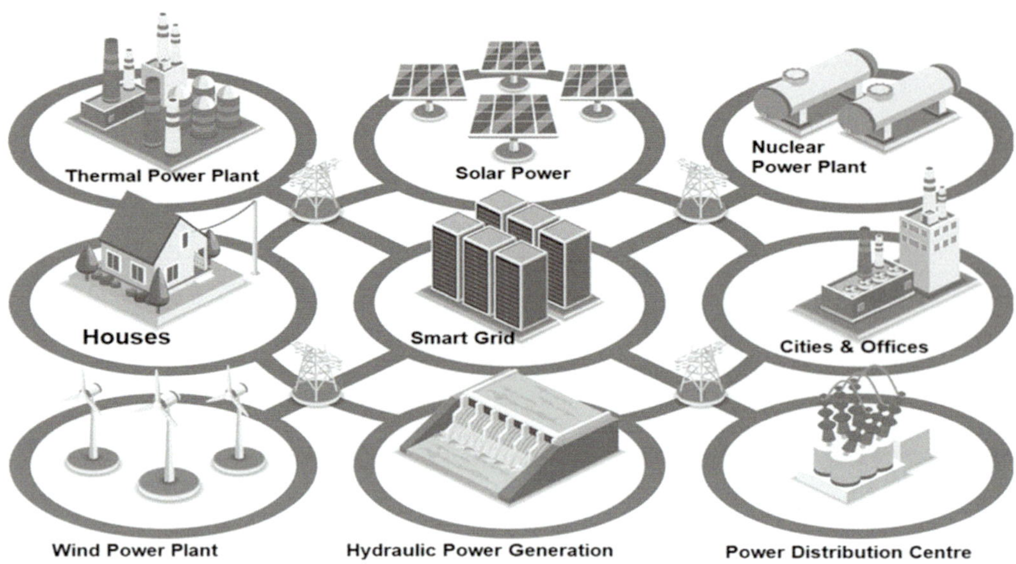

FIGURE 10.3 Smart grid solutions.

Source : Uday Chatterjee (2021)

and produce an equal proportion of global carbon emissions. It puts cities at the centre stage of the climate change debate.

Energy savings is one of the benefits that arise from the concept and lay down capabilities suggested by smart cities. In the wake of the existing scenario where almost every country is going through a financial crisis, it seems more important to save energy for a better future for its citizens. These savings depend on the innovation of the technology and the usage habits of the people, so it is necessary to provide them with the tools in a way that they can adapt. Smart cities have smart grids and their main objective is to provide a consistent and efficient power system with low losses and high quality, tailored to customer needs. Smart networks receive real-time information, which is another feature that a smart city usually can think to have. Smart networks that help to function more efficiently and adapt to the needs of the time helps a lot in saving time to have access to the data and not to wait so long for such insights (Figure 10.3).

10.2.4 Smart Health Care

The main objective of a smart city always revolves around the goal to improve living standards, economic access, and security for those living in cities and surrounding areas. Due to the growing digital ecosystem and the demands of government systems, municipal and state leaders around the world are reaching out for IT to modernize systems, while at the same time improving the quality of life of citizens. Smart health care comprises the most recent digital and mobile devices. They not only treat a disorder or a disease but also deal with it at the right time so that it remains always under control. There are various examples of the Internet of Things (IoT) in health care that operate through an extensive network of sensors and collect patient data remotely. An integration of biomedical and healthcare-related data, can help healthcare organizations to revolutionize the medical treatments and customized medication (Dash et al., 2019). Therefore, AI and big data can be used effectively by physicians, researchers, and healthcare professionals to evaluate this data for prompt solutions and for possible outcomes. Smart cities can utilize various technological advancements for the development of an efficient healthcare system. The best technology that can play a vital role in making health care more productive and safer, Artificial Intelligence can be used for the development of the system. AI now, with the help of sample identification, identifies patients who are at risk of developing a condition or whether it is exacerbated due to lifestyle, environmental, genetic, or other factors. With the emergence of pandemics like COVID-19, AI in the healthcare system could ensure a reduction in fatalities and further spread of this deadly virus.

There are various state-of-the-art artificial intelligence techniques that are used to develop ambient intelligence in the health sector (Acampora et al., 2013). Countries like Singapore and Malaysia have become smarter in how they provide care and services. Using technology, design thinking, and lean management, hospitals in these countries keep patients in a healthcare centre while at the same time reducing wait time and eliminating wasteful processes.

10.2.5 e-Governance

The use of technology by cities and governments to increase access to and distribution of public services is undoubtedly consistent with greater efficiency, accuracy, and consistency that benefits citizens, business partners, and employees. This can be regarded as a revolution as it ensures that all citizens should have access to the government and its services. Most essentially, the adoption of e-governance allows more government citizens, government business, and government employee transactions and is one of the primary drivers contributing to the development of e-governance programs.

E-governance or "digital government" has created the potential for the existing governments in building smart cities around the world. There are various countries that have already adopted e-governance. Asians country like South Korea have adopted e-governance and has been moving to full implementation of e-government since 2000. This has led to an increase in efficiency, transparency, and effectiveness of administrative work in South Korea. Additionally, e-governance has led to improved delivery of more relevant information and services to companies and the general public in the country (Figure 10.4).

10.2.6 Smart Education

There is an increased amount of attention being given to creative education imparted to the students in the smart cities. To achieve the objective, more progress has been made in building "smart schools" for students of smart cities. These schools are technologically sound and have advanced programs that will pave the way for the future of education; this in the future can become the backbone to education development in such cities. In this way, through the introduction of smart education programs, education and training is being imparted to smart citizens.

10.3 WHAT IS URBAN SPACE?

Urban space or urban public space is the area which is by and large open and accessible to every individual of the city. Streets including the footpaths, public squares, playgrounds, and seashores are regularly viewed as open spaces. Partly, government structures that are available to people in general, for example, public libraries, are public spaces, despite the fact that they will, in general, have confined regions and restricted accessibility. The term "public space" is mostly misinterpreted to mean different things, for example, "gathering place," which is a component of the broader idea

FIGURE 10.4 Components of e-governance.

Source: Self Drawn or Authors

of social space. For example, no fees or paid tickets are required for entry. Malls are the best example of private spaces that are also the entity of the public space (Kuzilenkova, 2016).

10.3.1 Need for an Urban Public Space?

A city provides something for every person living there and that, too, created using indigenous resources. Both physical and psychological wellbeing is greatly impacted by the urban space. It is assumed that citizens are aware of the behaviourism they need to showcase when they are alone versus in public (Jacobs, 2016).

10.3.2 Importance of Urban Public Spaces

To determine an urban public space there are some criteria. A public space is a spot that is attainable by the public at any point of time, including parks, beaches, roads, sidewalks, etc. All of these spaces are meant for different utilization. Still, with the mass gathering, they can be turned into dynamic, lovely spaces that help people to come together and enjoy a quality life (Yang, 2015). There are plenty of reasons why urban public space is important.

a. Benefits on human health

In a busy city life where the open space is a big concern, a citizen can enjoy a refreshing moment in a public space like a park. It helps us to reduce the carbon emission and enjoy a pollution-free atmosphere (Yang, 2015). Some of the well-known urban public parks in India are Jubliee Park Jameshedpur, Shivaji Park Mumbai and Maidan Kolkata.

b. Driving economic growth

In every Kumbh or Ardh Kumbh, lakhs of devotees gather on the banks of Ganges in India. This kind of event or gathering highlights the fact that open and shared space pulls traffic and is beneficial for the local business and strengthens the economy through business turnover by levying the taxes and increases the job scope.

c. Transforming wasted space

Today in India there are several places in different cities that have turned into beautiful gardens, where joggers enjoy their time and a clean environment. A beautiful example can be cited for this is a municipal dump yard on Marine Drive converted into a lush green park, ideal for hosting picnics. In conclusion, it can be said that if a proper place is created, people do visit the place (Yang, 2015).

d. City character and enhancing architectural diversity

Today, all the cities have become a jungle of concrete, where a mark of an open space, an art installation, makes a huge difference in the city life of the people. Consider the Cubbon Park of Bangalore, an urban recreation place in the centre of the city. Cubbon Park has space for both residents and tourists to hang out among planted flowers and tree-lined paths. Another example of using and lighting up public space is the help of art installations. Take the example of Descension, in Fort Kochi in India or the example of the fearless girl in New York City, Wall Street. The artworks or exhibitions not only complements the city's architecture but also motivates the common people to get themselves involved with the art pieces (Yang, 2015) (Figure 10.5).

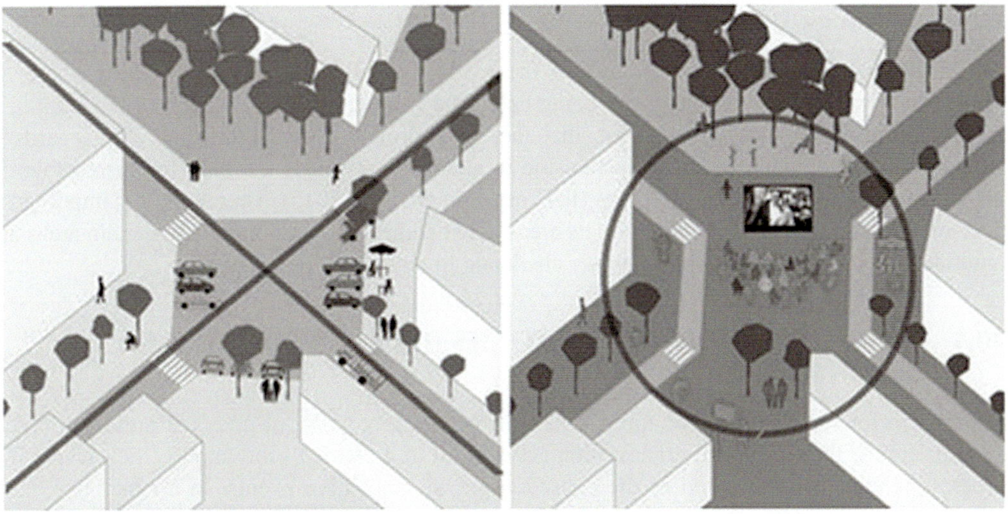

FIGURE 10.5 Sustainable planning of urban spaces.

Source: https://urbannext.net/charter-for-ecosystemic-planning/

10.4 SUSTAINABLE DEVELOPMENT AND URBAN SPACES

In the recent decades, these interconnected affairs and developments have begun to contribute afresh towards smart and sustainable cities. Urban spaces in a sustainable city can be developed by following the best available practices and keeping in mind the emerging issues related to development of such areas.

Hence, a "good urban governance" can be achieved by moving along a well-defined framework and resolving problems such as political and legal, leading to a concept of private partnerships and people participation. Presently, an urban local government is expected to achieve good urban governance in order to deliver both governance and management roles. Urban spaces can be developed in a sustainable city by keeping in mind the following issues.

10.4.1 Environmental Issues

Development of urban spaces in a sustainable city requires environmental consideration as an important aspect that cannot be ignored. It was the result of efforts made by The Brundtland Commission Report to put the idea of sustainable development on the existing plans and subsequent conferences highlighted the significance of provincial execution of the issues and activity to subside worldwide ecological and social concerns.

10.4.2 Population

Today, 3.6 billion people live in cities, a 52% increase over the past 100 years. According to a report published by the United Nations Department of Economic and Social Affairs, more than half of the world's population is now living in cities. It is expected that by 2050, the urban population will represent 67% of the world's population. In more developed areas, by 2050, 86% of the population will depend on urban dwellers. As UNESCO points out, much urbanisation takes place through the development of existing urban areas. Therefore, development of urban spaces should include this vulnerable aspect to contribute towards smart and sustainable city development.

10.4.3 Uniform Development

As urban areas contain more than half of the world's population, this is the place where the utilisation of most of the resources are being held. The continuous centralisation of population, in urban regions along these lines infers that these are progressively significant with regards to sustainable development. In short, sustainable urban development is the base for sustainable development (Editorial, Internet of Things (IoT) and Smart Cities, 2015). Therefore, it is important to develop urban spaces in a city all along its areas. Confinement of development to certain areas and ignoring other spaces may pose a serious challenge to smart city development.

10.5 COMMUNICATION TECHNOLOGIES (CLOUD AND SERVICE ARCHITECTURE)

Enthusiasm for sustainable development stems from the perception of coercive pressure on ecosystems around the world, and urbanization is the result of individuals moving to cities, where ICT progress is regularly perceived as the consequences of innovative events. In a smart city, communication technology plays a vital role as the progressions of ICT has impacted the way individuals proceed with their lives and on how work, entertainment, and society are made. In identifying and further developing urban spaces in a smart city, the ICT can be considered its backbone. The cloud and services architecture supports the development of communication technologies within urban limits. The integration of various components help to align all its facilities together (Figure 10.6).

10.6 SUSTAINABLE URBAN SPACES AND GOVERNANCE

The meaning of "sustainable development," by Brundtland (1987) gives details about the global context of this concept. The development of urban communities and towns should be liveable to guarantee a better-than-average personal satisfaction and impartial open door for all residents. Urban spaces and their development consider liveability as an inseparable part of smart city

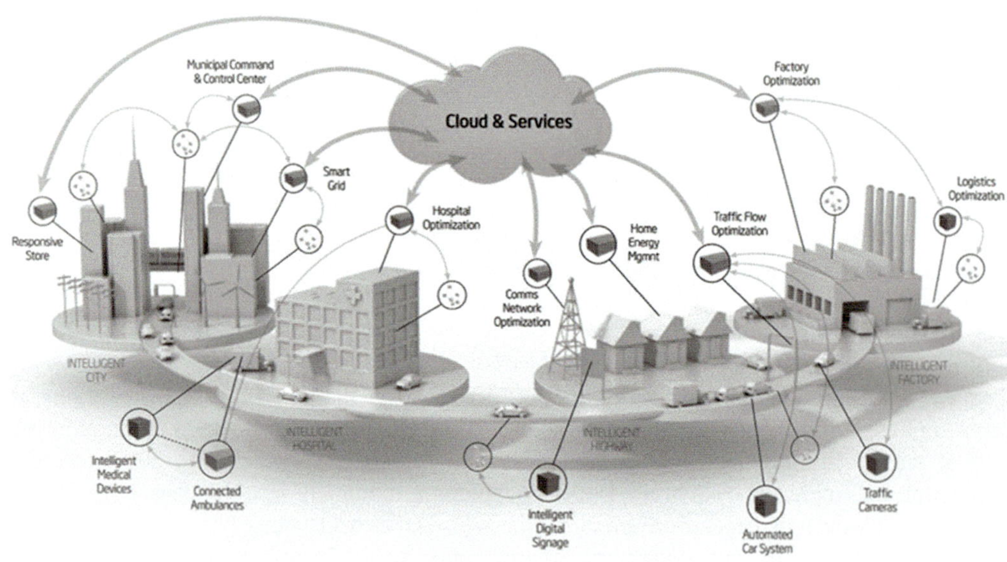

FIGURE 10.6 Intelligent services in a smart city.

Source: Uday Chatterjee (2021)

development. Therefore, a "sustainable urban space" is a liveable part of the city that fulfils the requirements of the current occupants without diminishing the limit of things for future inhabitants to fulfil their need.

The multidimensional urban approach recommends some shared objectives for all urban communities and provincial governments. Be that as it may, it would be executed diversely in better places with the pace, needs, and operational instruments relying upon the political duty and limits of the nearby and local governments and other primary stakeholders. There are additional expected clashes and trade-offs among the four objectives. A few cities may seek money-related and monetary increases to the detriment of value and essential personal satisfaction for all its residents. Others may receive approaches intended to improve government assistance that are monetarily unreasonable or that truly block business motivating forces to contribute. In any case, the urban strategic approach to be embraced by a city must consider each of the four components of maintainable urban areas after due considerations of various stakeholders. At the same time, the urban poor and underadvantaged should be considered first for its wellbeing.

10.6.1 Sustainable Urban Development

Sustainable urban development deals in the creation of areas to upgrade and create cities and towns that serve the overall objective of improving the health of humans and the natural environment on the earth. It is considered that sustainable urban development holds the key and also suggests the forward path to the cities to reduce the negative impact of environment deterioration. Sustainable urban development gives access for including local people and hence provides ample opportunities and resources with a proper mix of health and mobility.

10.6.2 Urban Spaces and Information Communication Technologies

There has been an extraordinary growth of ICT (information and communication technologies) over the last few years due to advancement and need for well-developed communication system. It has been reported that usage of ICT in cities for a wide range of activities has influenced urban operations. An urban space in a smart city can be considered the largest collection of labels compared to the labels used for other cities. The world population has grown significantly over the past decades and so have living standards. It is estimated that by 2050, 70% of the world's population will live in cities (United Nations, 2018). Cities currently consume one-third of the resources and energy, accounting for 80% of greenhouse gas emissions. Therefore, cities and their expansion will have an impact on the environment over the next few decades. This makes the concept of sustainable urban spaces mandatory and worth including in the agenda of urban development. The concept of creating sustainable urban space is a natural strategy that is instrumental in reducing the problems posed by city infrastructure and continuous growth of population. Cities with sustainable urban spaces consume less energy, water, and emit less carbon.

Urban centres around the world are very diverse in terms of their features, responsibilities, and mechanisms. It is well known that standards play a vital part in the growth and development of these urban centres; there are various standards available that provide globally recognized features that complement the growth of these urban pockets, but at the same time keep its focus on quality, efficiency, and safety (e.g., International Organization for Standardization; ISO). Standards help monitor the technical and functional performance of urban centres and are also effective in addressing climate change, safety, transportation issues, and water services.

10.7 SUSTAINABLE URBAN SPACES: THE FUTURE

In the current scenario, cities make up more than half of the world's 7 billion population. Clearly, metropolitan areas make up only 2% of the land area and are responsible for 80% of the land use of natural resources. With the growth of cities and the unequal use of physical and social resources, traditional systems depend on cities to provide resources. While urban growth and urbanization are contributing to global carbon emissions, local action is crucial to achieving a low-carbon future. In the absence of international climate action in line with the spirit of the Kyoto Protocol, as well as less effective leadership in many state governments, cities are now moving forward and developing strategies to mitigate the effects of climate change and address it through adaptation measures. In many ways, cities are the best hope for tackling climate change to address the issues of "global warming" and "food security."

In addition to the climate issues, urban spaces face more challenges and these areas need to address issues such as population growth, governance, and meeting the basic needs of city dwellers. Apart from these problems, sustainable urban spaces need to be simple in their approach and take tough measures against disasters and failures. Failure of the system can occur for a number of reasons, such as failure of information and communication technology or lack of performance of any critical factor. Any smart city consisting of these urban spaces needs to take these disasters and failures into account so that smart cities can recover quickly from such situations in a short period of time. These challenges affect the cost of designing and maintaining smart cities. The efficient use of smart components in urban spaces has enabled smart cities to process and store bulky data.

10.7.1 Big Data and Issues

Big data is a collection of complex data sets that are complicated to deal with using simple analysis tools or typical data processing applications. The Internet of Things (IoT) and big data are all tied up, as needed. Urban data is big data that is tagged in space and time and generated in smart cities. Urban spaces can create large amounts of data from sensors, databases, emails, websites, and social media. Big data processing requires new approaches to better decision making, insight innovation, and process optimization. Advanced data analysis techniques are needed to search and gather valuable samples and knowledge from the big data. Another challenge stems from the enormous amount of information that must be constantly collected, analyzed, and shared. The physical assets needed to store the information, and the energy it uses, requires a lot of power supply and space and in further action it produces a lot of carbon. Currently, smart frameworks are heavily dependent on visual data, which are too high to collect, strictly proportional, and not always reliable.

10.7.2 Governance and Funding

Political cycles and their elements affect the turn of events and development of urban spaces. Changes in the upper level of management or government point of view can delay ventures or other smart projects. Government and authorities can delay the advancement of sustainable urban spaces by not cooperating with each other, whereas to make the task complete, a joint effort needs to happen.

10.7.3 Street Fatalities

Despite measures to improve safety of urban transportation, street fatalities are expanding in numerous urban communities in India (Ministry of Road Transport and Highways, 2019). Urban population density combined with different class of vehicles pose a serious threat to the city residents, whether walking, cycling or riding a motorbike. The safe transportation has become one of the biggest challenges for society and as sustainable urban spaces need a growth engine, such fatalities need to be checked.

10.7.4 Overreliance on Technology

With the latest and biggest innovations and technical advancement, urban spaces including smart and connected components have increased the risk of digital threats. Cybercriminals take advantage of existing gaps in the description of cyber crime at the global level (Alghamdi, 2020). These criminals may barge into sensetive data, thereby affecting a city's control framework. This digital or cyber threat can cause dysfunction in the transport system and can lead to a big problem.

10.7.5 The Challenge of People/Skill Sets

The workers of different specialist co-ops from various urban spaces within a city likewise should be made familiar with the new vision, re-skilled on the utilization of innovation, and urged to adhere to the standard working methods.

10.8 CONCLUSION

This chapter discussed the sustainable urban spaces and has also focused on the challenges and future directions for development of these areas within cities. Due to a significant mobilisation of people from rural areas to the urban centres, there is excess pressure on cities. It is a need of the hour to convert the cities into smarter and more sustainable places of living where everything is governed by technology. In addition, it can be said that these sustainable urban spaces not only contribute to their individual people but also contribute towards the overall development of a smart city. A city can only be termed as worth living and problem solving if it is sustainable as well as smart. Hence, both sustainability and smartness of cities must go hand in hand and it can be achieved through sustainable urban spaces. Since there is no perfect city that is away from all lacunas, efforts can made to create these perfect cities with every available resource. Governing bodies across the world should take leads from available technology and should maintain their commitment towards environment. Additionally, smart cities should keep their focus intact on development of such urban pockets having high data privacy which is a very sensitive issue in this technology dominated world. Any data which is a part of a particular area must be utilized for the welfare and policy implications and should be protected to ensure privacy of citizens. Keeping a close watch on all such issues will not only ensure emergence of cities as a better place to live, but will ultimately help to conserve the vital resources of the world.

REFERENCES

Acampora, Giovanni, Diane J. Cook, Parisa Rashidi, and Athanasios V. Vasilakos. "A survey on ambient intelligence in healthcare." *Proceedings of the IEEE* 101, no. 12 (2013): 2470–2494.

Ahvenniemi, Hannele, Aapo Huovila, Isabel Pinto-Seppä, and Miimu Airaksinen. What are the differences between sustainable and smart cities? *Cities* 60 (2017): 234–245.

Alghamdi, Mohammed I . "A Descriptive Study on the Impact of Cybercrime and Possible Measures to Curtail its Spread Worldwide."*International Journal of Engineering Research & Technology* 9, no. 6 (2020).

Brundtland, G. H. *Report of the World Commission on environment and development: "our common future"*. UN (1987).

Chatterjee, U., G. A. Bhunia, D. Mahata and U. Singh. "Smart cities and their role in enhancing quality of life". *Quality of Life*, pp. 127–143. CRC Press, Taylor and Francis Group (2021).

Chourabi, H., T. Nam, S. Walker, J. R. Gil-Garcia, S. Mellouli, K. Nahon,... and H. J. Scholl. Understanding smart cities: An integrative framework. In 2012 45th Hawaii international conference on system sciences (pp. 2289–2297). IEEE (2012, January).

Dash, S., S. K. Shakyawar, M. Sharma, and S. Kaushik. "Big data in healthcare: management, analysis and future prospects." *Journal of Big Data* 6, no. 1 (2019): 1–25.

De Jong, M., S. Joss, D. Schraven, C. Zhan, and M. Weijnen. "Sustainable-smart-resilient-low carbon-eco-knowledge cities; making sense of a multitude of concepts promoting sustainable urbanization." *Journal of Cleaner Production* 109 (2015): 25–38.

Ding, Xiaohui, Weizhou Zhong, Richard G. Shearmur, Xiaoling Zhang, and Donald Huisingh. An inclusive model for assessing the sustainability of cities in developing countries – Trinity of cities' sustainability from spatial, logical and time dimensions (TCS-SLTD). *Journal of Cleaner Production* 109 (2015): 62–75.

Gabrys, Jennifer. Programming environments: Environmentality and citizen sensing in the smart city. *Environment and Planning D: Society and Space* 32, no. 1 (2014): 30–48.

International Telecommunications Union (ITU) 2015. Agreed definition of a smart sustainable city. Focus Group on Smart Sustainable Cities, SSC-0146 version Geneva. Accessed March 25, 2021. https://www.itu.int/en/ITU-T/focusgroups/ssc/Pages/default.aspx

Jacobs, Jane. *The Death and Life of Great American Cities*. New York: Vintage Books (2016).

Kuzilenkova, Nadezda (2016). "Social urban project. From the ghetto to a healthy neighborhood in 6 steps." Accessed August 12, 2021. https://www.politesi.polimi.it/handle/10589/121104

Lara, Alexander Prado, Eduardo Moreira Da Costa, Thiago Zilinscki Furlani, and Tan Yigitcanla. "Smartness that matters: towards a comprehensive and human-centred characterisation of smart cities." *Journal of Open Innovation: Technology, Market, and Complexity* 2, no. 2 (2016): 8.

Lee, Jung Hoon, Marguerite Gong Hancock, and Mei-Chih Hu. "Towards an effective framework for building smart cities: Lessons from Seoul and San Francisco." *Technological Forecasting and Social Change* 89 (2014): 80–99.

Maeda, Akira. "Technology innovations for smart cities." In *2012 Symposium on VLSI Circuits (VLSIC)*, pp. 6–9. IEEE (2012).

Maiello, Antonella, Massimo Battaglia, Tiberio Daddi, and Marco Frey. "Urban sustainability and knowledge: Theoretical heterogeneity and the need of a transdisciplinary framework. A tale of four towns." *Futures* 43, no. 10 (2011): 1164–1174.

Mardacany, Emile. "Smart cities characteristics: Importance of built environment components," IET Conference on Future Intelligent Cities (2014): 1–6.

Ministry of Road Transport and Highways. (2019). Crash data. Accessed January 21, 2021. https://morth.nic.in/state-wise-data

Mori, Koichiro, and Tsuguta Yamashita. "Methodological framework of sustainability assessment in City Sustainability Index (CSI): A concept of constraint and maximisation indicators." *Habitat International* 45 (2015): 10–14.

Neirotti, Paolo, Alberto De Marco, Anna Corinna Cagliano, Giulio Mangano, and Francesco Scorrano. "Current trends in Smart City initiatives: Some stylised facts." *Cities* 38 (2014): 25–36.

Phillis, Yannis A., Vassilis S. Kouikoglou, and Catalina Verdugo. "Urban sustainability assessment and ranking of cities." *Computers, Environment and Urban Systems* 64 (2017): 254–265.

Piro, Giuseppe, Ilaria Cianci, Luigi Alfredo Grieco, Gennaro Boggia, and Pietro Camarda. "Information centric services in smart cities." *Journal of Systems and Software* 88 (2014): 169–188.

Smart Building TechnologiesLeveraging Building Data, IoT, and AI to Make Buildings Smart. Accessed June 29, 2021, https://www.johnsoncontrols.com/digital-solutions/smart-buildings

Stocker, Thomas, ed. *Climate Change 2013: The Physical Science Basis*. Working Group I contribution to the Fifth assessment report of the Intergovernmental Panel on Climate Change. Cambridge University Press (2014).

Trindade, Evelin Priscila, Marcus Phoebe Farias Hinnig, Eduardo Moreira da Costa, Jamile Sabatini Marques, Rogério Cid Bastos, and Tan Yigitcanlar. "Sustainable development of smart cities: A systematic review of the literature." *Journal of Open Innovation: Technology, Market, and Complexity*, 3, no. 3 (2017): 11.

United Nations Department of Economic and Social Affairs, 68% of the world population projected to live in urban areas by 2050. Accessed June 9, 2021, https://www.un.org/development/desa/en/news/population/2018-revision-of-world-urbanization-prospects.html.

United Nations Department of Economic and Social Affairs, Population Division: World Urbanization Prospects, the 2011 Revision: Highlights. United Nations, New York (2012).

World Commission on Environment and Development: *Our Common Future*. Oxford: Oxford University Press (1987).

Yang, Lisa (2015). Why Public Space is Important. Accessed April 23, 2021. https://culturedays.ca/en/blog/why-public-spaces-matter.

Yigitcanlar, Tan. "Planning for smart urban ecosystems: information technology applications for capacity building in environmental decision making." *Theoretical and Empirical Researches in Urban Management* 4, no. 3(12) (2009): 5–21.
Yigitcanlar, Tan. "Position paper: benchmarking the performance of global and emerging knowledge cities." *Expert Systems with Applications* 41, no. 12 (2014): 5549–5559.
Yigitcanlar, Tan. "Smart cities: an effective urban development and management model?" *Australian Planner* 52, no. 1 (2015): 27–34.
Yigitcanlar, Tan, and Md Kamruzzaman. "Does smart city policy lead to sustainability of cities?" *Land Use Policy* 73 (2018): 49–58.

11 Urban Soundscape and Noise Pollution: An Introduction

Tallal Abdel Karim Bouzir and Hamza Benacer
Blida University, Blida, Algeria

Djihed Berkouk
Biskra University, Biskra, Algeria

Uday Chatterjee
Bhatter College, Dantan, Kharagpur, West Bengal, India

Sushobhan Majumdar
Jadavpur University, Kolkata, India

CONTENTS

11.1 INTRODUCTION

In recent years, the field of urban noise pollution, as well as soundscape, has more importance in scientific research and gradually in the politics of states and the international agency of sustainability, health, and environmental protection because of the significant link between the quality of life, the public health, and the fragile urban ecosystem and the quality sound

DOI: 10.1201/9781003126195-14

environment (Aziz et al. 2012; Bouzir, Zemmouri, and Berkouk 2017; K. Kryter 1994; K. D. Kryter 2013; Seidman and Standring 2010).

In developed countries, the axis of urban acoustics becomes omnipresent in research laboratories, which represents the sensitivity of society on the importance of this area of research and the political will of the states to improve the current situation. In developing countries, urban acoustics are still a gray area, especially in Africa; scientific production in this geographic area is still beginning despite the quality of the published works (Anomohanran and Osemeikhian 2005; Dahech and Rekik 2012; Bouzir and Zemmouri 2017, 2018; Berkouk et al. 2020). More interesting works are published in Asian and Latin American countries (Alam 2011; Alam, Aribam, and Singh 2018; Goswami 2009; Hunashal and Patil 2012; Ozer et al. 2009; Zannin, Diniz, and Barbosa 2002).

This chapter arises from the noticed lack of theoretical information concerning these concepts as well as their characteristics in a single document, which can be an introduction to this field of research which is not very usual for the town planner, architects, and the specialists who are working on the quality of life in cities (Bouzir 2018). These concepts are better detailed in other disciplines like ecology, for example, where there are many interesting reviews and papers published (Pijanowski, Villanueva-Rivera, et al. 2011; Pijanowski, Farina, et al. 2011; Farina 2013; Farina et al. 2014).

In the first part of this chapter, the soundscape concept was presented as it has been mentioned in the scientific literature, highlighting its types, components, and structure. On the other hand, the second part has been reserved for the noise pollution concept, by focusing on its definition, its sources, and its effects on the inhabitant's health and the immediate environment. The last part was devoted to identify and analyse the main recent research methods that are interested in the urban sound environment while addressing the advantages and disadvantages of each methodology.

11.2 URBANSCAPE

The landscape is defined as the overview of any place (city, forest, etc.). It is the terrestrial part seen by an observer, as it can also be defined as the results of an intersection between the human visual field and the characteristics of a natural or urban place (Euler, Perera, and Thompson 2000; Krönert, Steinhardt, and Volk 2001).

The urban landscape is perhaps captured by a photographer, the painting of an artist, or the view of an observer of a part of the city (Carrozza 1996; Roger 1995; Vincent Jost n.d.). We can note that the authors of these definitions summarized the urban landscape in the narrow definition of the visual landscape and ignored the olfactory and sound experience of human beings during the discovery and use of urban spaces, although these two parameters also affect the perception of the urban landscape.

In a study carried out in Canada to analyze the urban landscape of the city of Montreal, from a series of photos and soundtracks recorded in this city, it was concluded that sound analysis does not replace the visual analysis of the urban landscape, but it makes it possible to extract additional useful information that supplements the visual analysis of the landscape (Vincent Jost n.d.).

Based on this research, as well as several other studies (Dubois, Guastavino, and Raimbault, 2006; McLean 2017; Raimbault and Dubois 2005), we can define the urban landscape as the following set of components: smellscape, soundscape, and landscape, which is, generally, the most important, because it dominate over the other sub-landscapes most of the time.

A landscape is the set of visual information obtained from an urban composition by an observer, such as texture, color, geometric composition, vegetation, and human presence (Roger 1995; Donadieu and Mazas 2002).

Smellscape is a new concept invented in 1990 by Porteous (Dann 2002) to describe all the smells that characterize a space and make it different olfactory-wise compared to other places in the city.

The olfactory landscape, like the visual landscape, changes from one place to another. A big difference may be observed between the olfactory landscape of a boulevard where we can smell the diesel, a market, a garden, or a public square where natural smells are perceived (Malnar and Vodvarka 2004; Dufft 2009).

The soundscape is a concept invented by the Canadian Schaefer in 1976 in his book "*The Soundscape, our sonic environment and the tuning of the world,*" to describe all the sounds perceived by a human in their environment and without positive or negative judgment (Semidor 2004; 2006a; Radicchi 2019; Semidor 2006b).

11.3 SOUNDSCAPE

Following the definition of Schafer, which left a great echo in several disciplines, other researchers have developed other definitions in order to better describe this term as the definition of Botteldooren et al. (Botteldooren, Coensel, and Muer 2006), who defined the soundscape as an environment created by or with sound, or that of Farina et al. (Pijanowski et al., 2011; Farina 2013; Farina et al. 2014) who defined the soundscape as an acoustic composition resulting from a voluntary or spontaneous combination of natural sounds and/or urban. The same author has defined the soundscape as the set of sounds in a given area as perceived by organisms, however, Pijanowski defined the soundscape based on its components as the complex arrangement of sounds from multiple sources, including biophony, geophony, and anthrophony (Pijanowski, Villanueva-Rivera, et al. 2011; Pijanowski, Farina, et al. 2011).

The urban soundscape can be defined based on the previous definitions as the set of sounds and noises resulting from human activities in the public space, such as talk, trade, works, leisure, and transport, which generally dominate by their noise over the other components of the soundscape in addition to other natural and animal sounds as swaying trees in the wind, water, wind, and animal sounds such as birds, dogs, etc. (Botteldooren, Coensel, and Muer 2006; Figure 11.1).

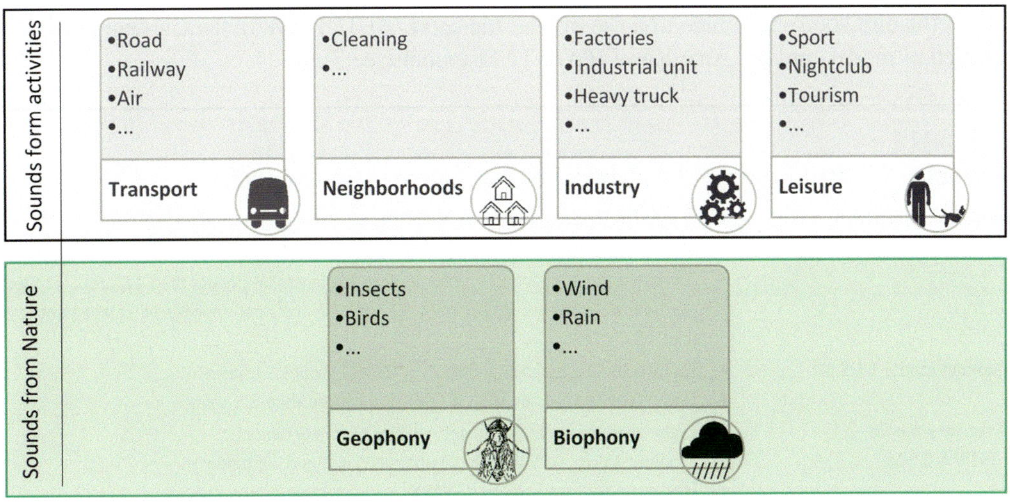

FIGURE 11.1 Sources of sounds/noise in cites.

On the other hand, according to another approach developed in the CRESON research laboratory, the soundscape can have a double meaning, a representative meaning, and another sensitive one (Amphoux 1997).

a. The representative part: To present a landscape, the draftsman draws a painting, the photographer takes photos, while the musician records a sound sequence. This soundtrack represents a soundscape according to CRESSON (Amphoux 1997).
b. The sensitive part: This part is based on the definition of the landscape as "a part of the country that nature presents to an observer." The soundscape is defined "as a sequence of time that naturally present in the ear of a listener"(Amphoux 1997).

In summary, the soundscape is a concept that encompasses all sounds of human and natural origins that allow listeners to have an auditory representation of their environment and to feel the space differently.

11.3.1 Soundscape Components

According to Pijanowski, Villanueva-Rivera, et al. (2011) and Pijanowskii, Farina, et al. (2011) the soundscape consists of three elements (biophony, geophony, and anthrophony). Biophony is the set of sounds made by living organisms such as insects, mammals, and birds. Geophony is the set of sounds coming from natural elements such as wind, rain, thunder, and sea waves. Anthrophony is the sound from human activities such as road traffic, air or rail transport, sporting, and cultural or festive events. We can classify the components of anthrophony into human and mechanical sounds.

For anthrophony, human sounds are all generated by humans, by their instruments and machines, except for mechanical sounds, which are the set of sounds generated mainly through transport (Berkouk et al., 2020). Given the important effects of mechanical sounds on the environment, quality of life, and human health, it has received much attention in the perspectives of international organizations for the protection of health and the environment, state policies, especially in developed countries, as well as in the field of scientific research to combat it (Guastavino 2006; Guastavino et al. 2005).

Indeed, many researchers have proposed classifications of sources of mechanical noise in order to facilitate the study of its impact on the public health and environment, which we can cite among others (Gaulin 2000): the guide to noise in land transport (CETUR 1980), the German noise level prediction model, and the American FHWA TNM model (see Table 11.1).

TABLE 11.1
Example of Classification of Mechanical Noise Sources (Gaulin 2000)

Noise guide (CETUR 1980)	• Light vehicles (vehicles weighing less than 3.5 tonnes) • Heavy vehicles (vehicles weighing more than 3.5 tonnes) • Two motorized wheels: 1) motorcycles (displacement greater than 125 cc). 2) mopeds (including displacement between 50 and 125 cm^3) and mopeds (displacement less than 50 cm^3)
German model RLS 90	• Light vehicles, including the GVWR, less than 2.8 tonnes • Heavy goods vehicles with a GVWR of more than 2.8 tonnes
American model FHWA TNM	• Light vehicles (vehicles weighing less than 4.5 tonnes) • Medium trucks (GVW vehicles between 4.5 and 12 tonnes) • Heavy trucks, road trains (GVWR vehicles over 12 tonnes) • Buses designed to carry nine or more passengers (no indication of total weight) • Motorcycles: any vehicle with two or three tires

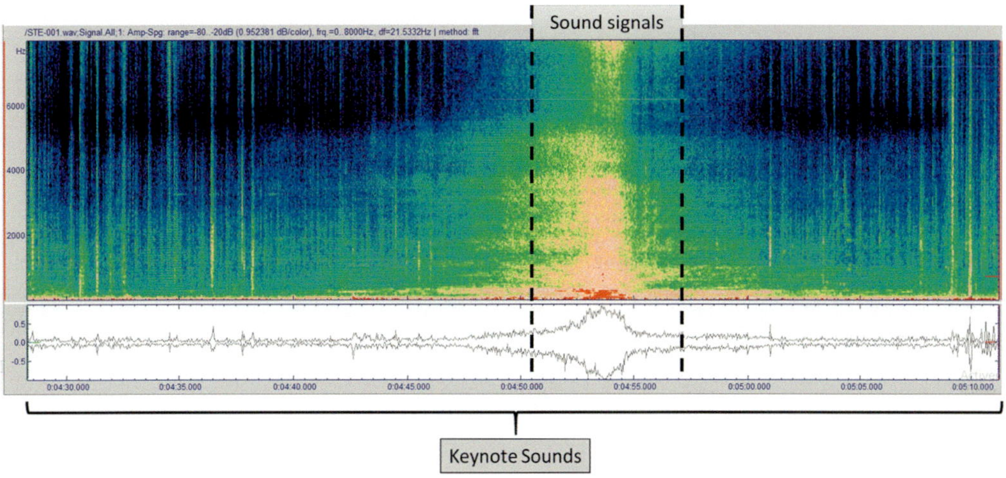

FIGURE 11.2 Relationship between keynote and signal sounds.

11.3.2 Soundscape Structure

The structuring elements of a soundscape are keynote sounds, sound signals, and sound markers.

Keynote sounds are the background of a soundscape; it is the threshold from which we can hear other sounds of the environment. These continuous and homogeneous sounds are only made aware with careful listening because they are ignored by our hearing systems (Tiger 2014), such as the background sounds of a forest or a cafeteria during a discussion with a friend.

Sound signals are the set of sounds in the foreground; it is the sound events that attract attention, like our name in a public space or the horns of cars. They are characterized by a higher intensity than that of the background sound and short duration (Wissmann 2014). The relationship between keynote and signal sounds is presented in Figure 11.2.

Sound markers are the sounds that mark a space and make it different from other spaces in the city. These markers can give a sound identity to urban entities. They can be in the form of the sound of a fountain, a tram station, or even in the form of the usual barking of a neighbor's dog in a residential area (Wissmann 2014).

11.3.3 Soundscape Balance

The harmony and balance between the components of soundscapes depend on the nature of the space: (1) urban, (2) rural, or (3) natural (Pijanowski, Farina, et al. 2011).

In a natural space, for example, we find that the soundscape consists mainly of geophony and biophony; generally in these places, geophony represents the keynote sound while all the sounds of biophony, like the cries of animals and birdsong, represent sound marks and sound signals.

In rural areas, the third component of the "anthrophony" soundscape participates in the sound composition. A certain harmony between the biophony and anthrophony sounds can be observed in these areas; however, in urban spaces, the soundscapes are characterized by the domination of human sounds, particularly mechanical (anthrophony), over the other components of the soundscape (biophony and geophony). The three circles in Figure 11.3 represent the relationship between the soundscape component and their location (Pijanowski, Farina, et al. 2011; Pijanowski, Villanueva-Rivera, et al. 2011).

11.3.4 Types of Soundscapes

Schafer classified soundscapes into two main types according to the type and the relationship between these components (high and low fidelity) (Schafer 2009, 1985; Schafer and Gleize 1979;

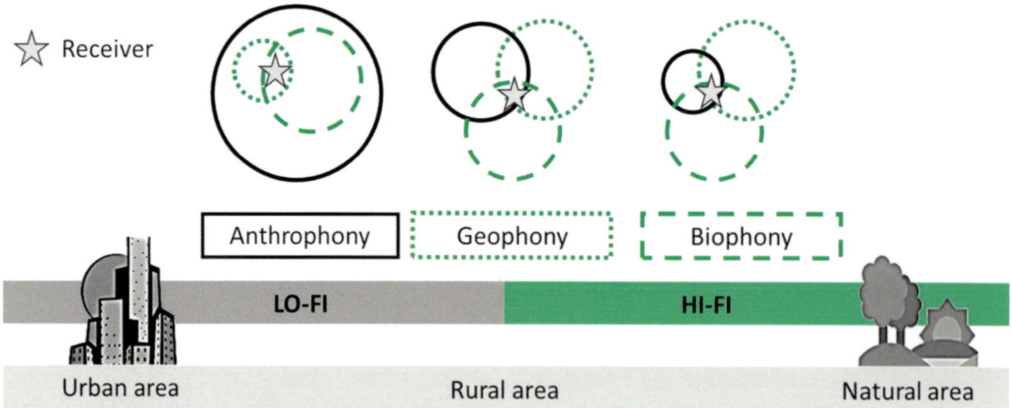

FIGURE 11.3 Soundscape and urbanization.

Schafer 1969). LO-FI (high fidelity) represent the soundscapes where we can clearly identify and hear each component of the sound environment, in particular the sounds of biophony and geophony; it is a panoramic soundscape, we hear further and clearer (Bouzir, Berkouk, and Zemmouri 2019). This type of soundscape is usually found in places where the presence of anthrophony sounds is low, such as natural, rural areas and in the gardens of cities and urban squares (Schafer and Gleize 1979; Schafer 1969; Bouzir, Berkouk, and Zemmouri, 2019; Péneau et al. 1998).

The soundscapes LO_FI (low fidelity) are marked by an immense superposition of sound information, which causes the disappearance of individual sound signals in the general noise (Schafer and Gleize 1979) and influences our ability to understand, reconstruct mental images, and identify spaces from what we hear (Bouzir, Berkouk, and Zemmouri, 2019; Péneau et al. 1998; Wrightson 2000), as it can also be a sign of life, movement and security in some urban places. This type of soundscape has become, among other features, one of the main features of the modern city today.

These two notions represent, according to Schafer, the contrast between pre-industrial and post-industrial sound landscapes (Wrightson 2000). Figure 11.4 shows the contrasted soundscape Lo_Fi and Hi_Fi.

11.3.5 Polluted Soundscape

Starting with the definition of environmental pollution, noise pollution is defined as degradation or alternation of the environment, resulting from human activities, in the form of subsistence, which can endanger the human health and the terrestrial ecosystem like chemical, radioactive, natural subsistence, otherwise in the form of vibrations, heat, or various acoustic and olfactory nuisances (Tairou 2013; Tsagué 2009; European Environment Agency, 2014).

11.4 NOISE POLLUTION

Noise pollution has become one of the main characteristics of modern cities, it is the problem most reported by locals. It mainly depends on the origin, level, and duration of the noise as well as the time of emergence (day/night), and other psychological (non-acoustic) effects such as the capacity to resist, the associated fear the source of the noise is anger (Berglund et al. 1999; Marquis-Favre, Premat, and Aubrée 2005; Villa et al. 2020). It is a term that describes noisy situations where the noise level exceeds the limit values proposed by international environmental and health protection agencies as safety thresholds vis-à-vis for human health and the balance of the ecosystem. This type of pollution is mainly caused by means of transport (road, rail, air), noise from

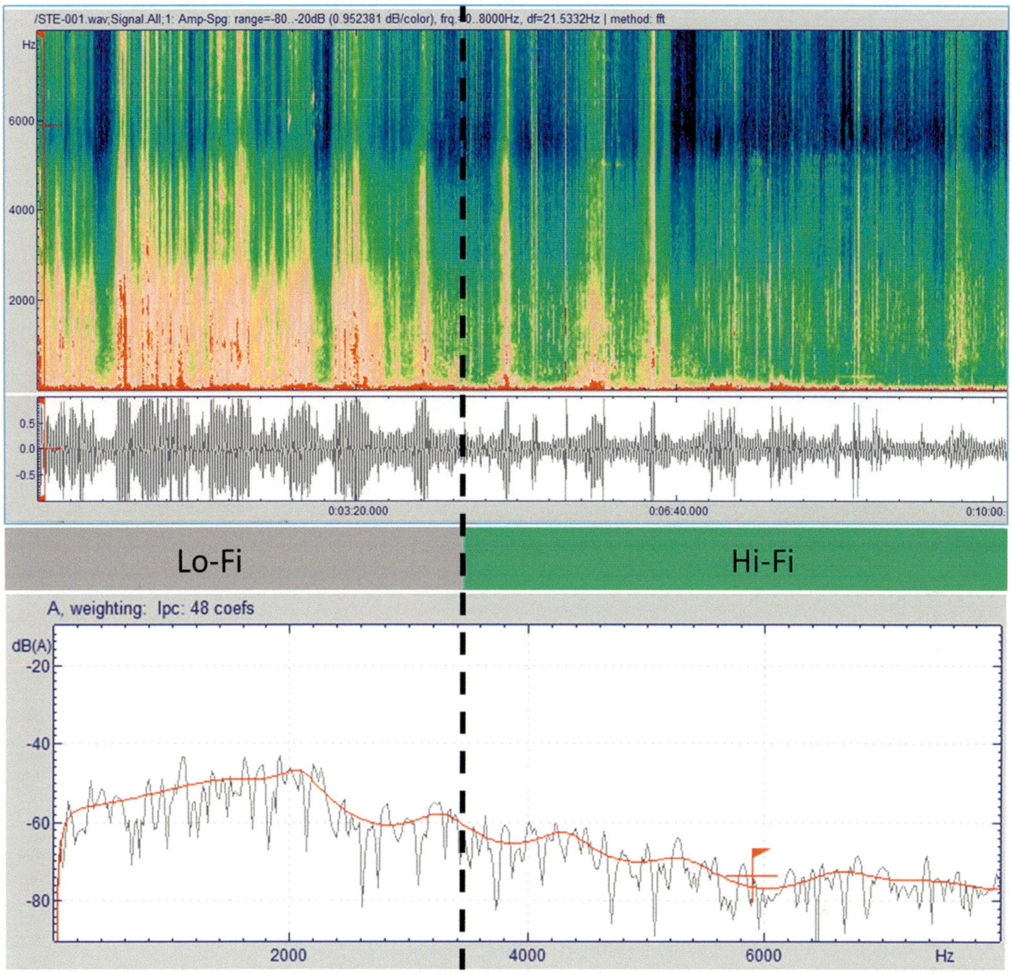

FIGURE 11.4 Contrasted soundscape Lo_Fi/Hi_Fi.

neighborhoods, factories, and other human activities (Maisonneuve et al. 2009; Murphy and King 2014; Singh and Davar 2004).

11.4.1 Effect of Noise Pollution on Health

Beyond these effects on comfort and quality of life, noise can also cause serious and multiple risks to human health, classified into two categories: hearing and other non-hearing effects (Aletta, Oberman, and Kang 2018; Basner et al., 2014; Berglund et al. 1999; Ising and Kruppa 2004; Passchier-Vermeer and Passchier 2000; see Figure 11.5).

Noise has several effects on the hearing system, such as damage to the middle ear due to the impulse of noise at high levels and damage to the inner ear due to prolonged exposure to loud sounds (Kryter 1994; Kryter 2013; Basner et al. 2014; Marquis-Favre, Premat, and Aubrée, 2005).

Regarding the non-auditory effects:

a. **Nuisance:** Considered the most well-known effect of noise on humans, nuisance is a multifaceted psychological concept, which represents all of the negative psychological reactions resulting from exposure to noise (Aletta, Oberman, and Kang 2018; Clark and Stansfeld 2007; Guski, Felscher-Suhr, and Schuemer 1999; Nelson 1987).

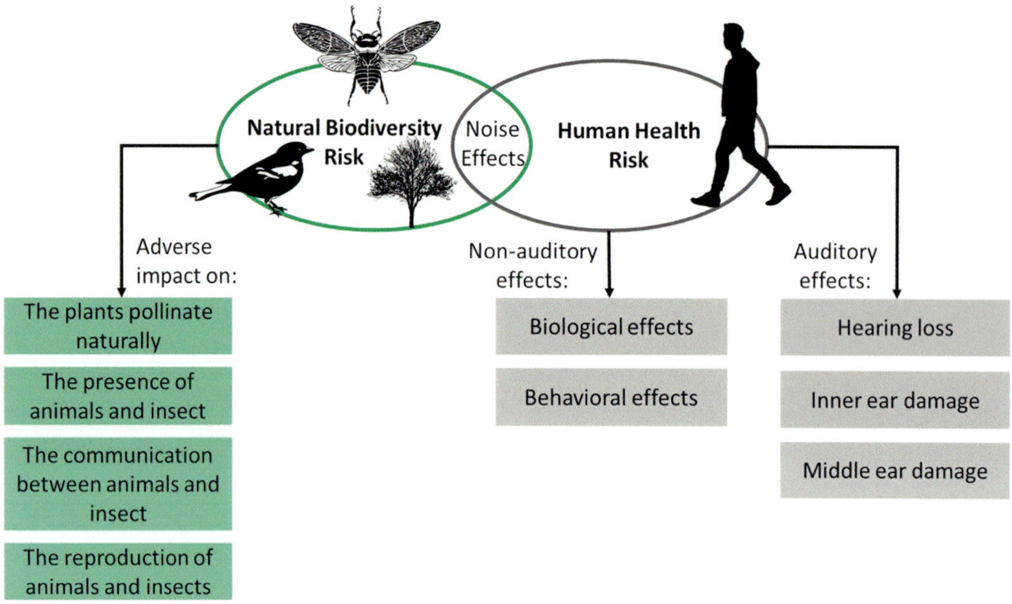

FIGURE 11.5 Effects of noise on human health and biodiversity.

b. **High blood pressure and coronary heart disease:** Considered among the non-hearing effects of sound pollution on human health, it is complicated to determine the parameters that have a direct impact on the human cardiovascular system, due to the difficulty of focusing separately on a single parameter and neglecting others (such as smoking, physical activities, age and diet), but according to recent studies, the relationship between noise and cardiovascular pathologies is approved (Van Kempen et al. 2002; Tomei et al. 2000; Babisch et al. 1993). According to Babisch, noise can cause an increase in diastolic and average blood pressure (Babisch 2000).
c. **Respiratory and digestive systems:** Noise also causes an increase in oxygen consumption, which accelerates the respiratory rate; on the other hand, noise can also cause digestive disorders, such as a decrease in the secretion of saliva and intestinal function (Marquis-Favre, Premat, and Aubrée 2005).
d. **Stress:** One of the main effects of noise pollution on human health, stress represents a concept widely used by scientists and the medical community to define all the physical and psychological reactions resulting from external stimuli and aggression, such as noise (Selye 1976; Faye et al. 2003). These reactions are many and vary from person to person.
e. **Sleep disorder:** Noise, especially from road noise, has become one of the main causes of sleep disorders; night exposure to noise can hinder the ability to fall asleep, the quality, the duration of sleep, and cause repetitive awakenings (Fidell et al. 1995; Jakovljević et al. 2006; Stosic, Belojevic, and Milutinovic 2009).
f. **Psychological health:** A study conducted in Japan around military airports, examining more than 6,000 residents, found that people regularly exposed to noise levels that exceed 70 dB have higher rates of mental instability (Hiramatsu et al. 1997); according to this and other studies (Tarnopolsky et al. 1978; Stansfeld et al. 1993), noise is strongly linked to psychological symptoms such as anxiety and depression.

According to recent statistics concerning the effect of noise, particularly from road noise, on human health, established by the European Environment Agency (European Environment Agency 2014):

a. More than 20 million people living in the European area suffer from noise pollution.
b. More than 8 million people in Europe suffer from noise-induced sleep disturbances.
c. Noise is responsible for more than 10,000 deaths each year in Europe.
d. Noise causes more than 900,000 cases of hypertension in Europe each year.
e. The noise leads to the hospitalization of 43,000 people each year in Europe.

Based on these alarming statistics, we need to change our vision and behavior in the face of noise, a factor that can affect the quality of life and reduce the level of comfort and is a major and serious risk to public health.

11.4.2 Effect of Noise Pollution on Biodiversity

Noise also affects biodiversity and the fragile urban ecosystem (Bouzir, Zemmouri, and Berkouk 2018). It has a harmful impact on insects, birds, and mammals, especially those who use sound signals to communicate, find their way, and move around.

If we take the case of birds, the results of the masking effect caused by traffic noise on their edges are as follows:

a. Escape to other quieter places.
b. Change the singing frequency.
c. Sing higher, earlier (sing at dawn), and/or change the song rhythm.

These changes in the characteristics of sound signals disturb the communication between these living beings, which affects their presence in the urban space as well as their reproduction (Reijnen, Foppen, and Meeuwsen 1996; Reijnen and Foppen 2006; McClure et al. 2013; Summers, Cunnington, and Fahrig 2011; Parris and Schneider 2009).

11.4.3 Fight against Noise Pollution

The strong urbanization as well as the demographic explosion that continues to increase day by day affects the balance of the ecosystem, pollutes the environment, and degrades the quality of life. To limit these harmful effects of humans on nature and restore the balance between the two, each country has proposed a series of laws concerning the protection of the environment and the fight against pollution, including noise. The fight against noise is a very old operation. We can find it in the history of ancient Rome, in the form of a law proposed by Julius Caesar, in order to limit discomfort caused by noise generated by the movement of carts on the stone pavement (Balaÿ 2003; Balaÿ and Arlaud 2000). On the other hand, in the 16th century, Elisabeth I had passed a law banning street music in order to reduce noise pollution outside (Valérie Rozec and Ritter 2003).

In addition, it should also be mentioned that Doctor Robert Koch (Nobel Prize in Medicine) (1843–1910) predicted that the day would come when man would fight against noise in the same way as cholera or the plague (Jaworski 2012). In recent years, the effects of this problem on quality of life have become more evident than ever. According to the EAA, noise is responsible for more than 900,000 cases of hypertension each year" (European Environment Agency 2014). We have approached the day scheduled by Robert Koch. This is why the fight against this phenomenon has become an emergency, and rapid actions must be taken immediately to correct these alarming situations like sensitization, noise mapping, operational actions, and repressive actions.

a. **Sensitization**: Reduces violence by helping police departments locate and arrest suspects that are likely to endanger public safety. A great lack of information and awareness regarding the effects of noise on the environment and especially on public health can be observed even among cultivated classes (Bouzir and Zemmouri 2017). This is why the first action that must be carried out in order to improve the quality of sound environments is the awareness of the population on the serious and multiple risks that can be caused by noise on their health and their environment in general (Ozdemir, Bayramoglu, and Demirel 2014). Through primary schools, associations, and the media, we need to focus on this phenomenon.

b. **Noise mapping:** The second thing and, in accordance with the right of citizens to access information, people must be informed about the level of noise intensity of their living environment. This is why a major project has been carried out in Europe, in order to offer noise maps of major cities to the public and the authorities, with the aim of defining the state of the current sound situations of these cities, the main sources of noise, to determine the underexposed and overexposed areas, in order to have a clear idea on the exposure of the population and sensitive buildings to noise. However, the high cost of these cards and the lack of awareness of their importance represent obstacles to their implementation in developing countries (Bouzir and Zemmouri 2017).
c. **Operational actions:** In order to reduce the noise pollution rate, operational interventions must be applied in these areas of intervention (Brown 2015): (i) Intervene at the source level by reducing the level of noise emitted by the source itself. (ii) Intervene at the transition point: make sure to keep the transmitters away from receivers, use obstacles against the propagation of noise such as noise barriers. (iii) Intervene at the receptor level: protect and isolate the receptors well (Brown 2015).
d. **Repressive actions:** Faced with the phenomenon of noise pollution, legislators in countries as well as international organizations for the protection of the environment and health such as the WHO, EPA USA, have developed laws, regulations, and standards concerning the fight against noise pollution, the application of these regulations, and the respect of these standards vary from one country to another, according to the state will and the awareness of the community (Bouzir and Zemmouri 2018).

11.5 TOOLS AND METHODS FOR STUDYING AND ANALYZING SOUND ENVIRONMENTS

The two main lines of research characterize the field of urban acoustics. The first axis focuses on the sounds of the environment as sources of nuisance against which we must fight and control because of their harmful effects on health, comfort, and the environment.

On the other hand, and after the invention of the concept of the soundscape in the 1970s, another line of research was developed, focusing on the sounds of the environment as an atmosphere. Their quality depends on the nature of their sources and the sensation of human beings who live the sound experience. Sometimes people favor noise, especially in outdoor spaces because they consider it a sign of life, movement, and security (Calleri et al. 2019; Vogiatzis and Remy 2017).

Given the complexity and multidisciplinary of the field of urban acoustics, several researchers have proposed several methods of analysis and evaluation in recent years. These include noise measurement, questionnaires, sound recording, and noise maps, etc.

11.5.1 Noise Measurement

Noise measurement is the classic method for studying a sound environment; it is the operation that allows us to measure the sound level in dB using a sound level meter in accordance with one of the measurement standards (Yang, Aletta, and Kang 2021). We can cite for example, the NF S 31-010, where the sound level meter must be placed at a minimum distance of 2 meters from all reflecting obstacles, and at a height of 1.5 meters from the ground, as there is the NF S 31- 130 which recommends placing the sound level meter at a height of 5 meters and at a distance of 2 meters from the facades (V. Rozec and Moch 2000; Valérie Rozec and Rumeau 2000; Sémidor, Torgue, and Beaumont 2010). But the result of this method does not represent the soundscape as it is perceived by the users of the spaces, and the number in decibels cannot represent the soundscape as a whole especially the subjective part that depends on the feelings of human beings. This is why other methods are proposed by other researchers (Aumond et al. 2018).

11.5.2 Questionnaires

The evaluation of the subjective side of the soundscape depends essentially on the feeling and the feeling of people. It's like music; judgment can vary from person to person. The absence of a measurable physical indicator or a judgment scale that makes it possible to assess the sound quality leads specialists to conduct surveys in situ or on reactivated listening in order to assess this quality (Sémidor, Torgue, and Beaumont 2010; Marry 2011).

11.5.3 Sound Recording

The recording of the soundscape is a new approach used primarily in the science of biodiversity to determine the types of animals and insects that live in the place where the study takes place, to analyze its modes communication, and to characterize its sound signals (Pijanowski, Villanueva-Rivera, et al. 2011; Pijanowski, Farina, et al. 2011; Farina 2013; Farina et al. 2014; Sueur et al. 2014). This new technique has been adopted by Cathrine Semidor for studies of urban acoustics in the form of a method called the sound walk (Semidor 2004; 2006a; 2006b). This method allows you to record the soundscape as it is experienced by the user of the space.

The processing of audio tracks recorded with specialized software such as Seewav (Marry 2011; Sueur, Aubin, and Simonis 2008) will allow us to extract additional information on the sound environment such as the origin of the sounds, the dominant sounds, the frequency and the intensity of the components, in the form of a spectrogram, which is the visual translation of sound landscapes (Raimbault and Dubois 2005; Semidor 2006b; Venot and Sémidor 2006; Adams et al., 2008). On the other hand, the recorded audio tapes can also be used for the execution of the questionnaires in order to assess the quality of an environment from the reactivated listening in the laboratory (Grosjean and Thibaud 2001).

11.5.4 Noise Maps

Noise mapping is a method of analysis, evaluation, and representation of sound environments; it allows us to establish an inventory of sound situations in cities and to identify noisy and quiet areas in the study area to determine the rate of exposure of the population and sensitive buildings such as hospitals and schools to noise (De Coensel et al. 2015; Lavandier et al. 2016). The noise maps are produced on the basis of in-situ data acquisition concerning road traffic (traffic rate per hour, car speed, presence of heavy goods vehicles), rail traffic (speed and type of trains), the presence of airports, and industrial activities (Licitra 2012; Zheng 2019; Murphy and King 2014).

Because of its significant effects on the behavior of sound waves in urban space, meterological conditions such as temperature, wind, and atmospheric pressure as well as the morphological characteristics of the study area like the height of buildings, width of streets, type of paving, etc. are essential for noise maps calculations (Murphy and King 2014; Guillaume et al. 2016).

11.6 CONCLUSION

In this chapter, our documentary research focuses on the notion of soundscape, on its types (Hi_Fi, Lo_Fi), its components (anthrophony, geophony, biophony), as well as its structure, which allows us to define this concept in its broadest sense, by relying on the various scientific and institutional definitions listed in the scientific literature. In addition, we also focused on the concept of noise pollution by emphasizing its definition, its sources, its effects on health and the environment, as well as on the main operations of the fight against this phenomenon, and recent research axes in this theme, as well as the main methods of studying urban acoustics.

Since the study of soundscapes provides valuable and important information on the functioning of our cities, in addition to the information extracted from the luminous, the olfactory, and the landscape; it can open up research perspectives for researchers working on the city and its components (gardens, public places, residential neighborhoods, etc.) to understand how humans affect the quality of life in the urban environment and architectural.

In order to pursue the objective of achieving a sustainable city, especially in developing countries, the study of urban soundscapes has become an essential urgency for future research, for the purpose of protecting existing pleasant soundscapes that may be an intangible preserved heritage for future generations, and for the correction and improvement of those who are polluted.

REFERENCES

Adams, Mags D., Neil S. Bruce, William J. Davies, Rebecca Cain, Paul Jennings, Angus Carlyle, Peter Cusack, Ken Hume, and C. Plack. 2008. 'Soundwalking as a Methodology for Understanding Soundscapes'. *Proc Inst Acoust*; 30(2): 1–8.

Alam, Wazir. 2011. 'GIS Based Assessment of Noise Pollution in Guwahati City of Assam, India.' *International Journal of Environmental Science* 2(2): 731.

Alam, Wazir, Bindiya Aribam, and Waikhom Roshan Singh. 2018. 'GIS Based Assessment of Noise Environment of Imphal City, Manipur (India): A Comprehensive Study.' *Universal Journal of Environmental Research & Technology* 7(1): 1–9.

Aletta, Francesco, Tin Oberman, and Jian, Kang 2018. 'Positive Health-Related Effects of Perceiving Urban Soundscapes: A Systematic Review.' *The Lancet* 392 (November): S3. https://doi.org/10.1016/S0140-6736(18)32044-0

Amphoux, Pascal 1997. *Paysage Sonore Urbain: Introduction Aux Écoutes de La Ville*. IREC, Institut de recherche sur l'environnement construit, Ecole ….

Anomohanran, O., and Jea Osemeikhian. 2005. 'Comparative Noise Pollution Study of Some Major Towns in Delta State, Nigeria.' *Global Journal of Pure and Applied Sciences* 11(2): 285–290.

Aumond, Pierre, Arnaud Can, Leo Jacquesson, and Catherine Lavandier 2018. ''Stochastic modeling for multi-source sound mapping - Modélisation stochastique pour la production de cartes de bruit multi-sources.'Conference: Congrès Français d'Acoustique.

Aziz, Shuokr Qarani, F. A. Lulusi, Nor Azam Ramli, Hamidi Abdul Aziz, Amin Mojiri, and Muhammad Umar 2012. 'Assessment of Traffic Noise Pollution in Bukit Mertajam, Malaysia and Erbil City, Iraq.' *Caspian Journal of Applied Sciences Research* 1(3): 1–11.

Babisch, Wolfgang. 2000. 'Traffic Noise and Cardiovascular Disease: Epidemiological Review and Synthesis.' *Noise and Health* 2(8): 9.

Babisch, Wolfgang, Hartmut Ising, John E.J. Gallacher, Dan S. Sharp, and Ian A. Baker. 1993. 'Traffic Noise and Cardiovascular Risk: The Speedwell Study, First Phase. Outdoor Noise Levels and Risk Factors.' *Archives of Environmental Health: An International Journal* 48(6): 401–5.

Balaÿ, Olivier. 2003. 'Les Chorographies de l'urbanité Sonore.' *Géocarrefour* 78(2): 159–65.

Balaÿ, Olivier, and Blaise Arlaud 2000. 'A Geographical Information System of the Qualitative Sound Environment.' In *Inter. Noise 2000: The 29th International Congress and Exhibition on Nois Control Engineering*.

Basner, Mathias, Wolfgang Babisch, Adrian Davis, Mark Brink, Charlotte Clark, Sabine Janssen, and Stephen Stansfeld 2014. 'Auditory and Non-Auditory Effects of Noise on Health.' *The Lancet* 383(9925): 1325–32.

Berglund, Birgitta, Thomas Lindvall, Dietrich H. Schwela. 1999. 'Guidelines for Community Noise.' World Health Organization (WHO), Geneva, Switzerland.

Berkouk, Djihed, Tallal Abdel Karim Bouzir, Luigi Maffei, and Massimiliano Masullo 2020. 'Examining the Associations between Oases Soundscape Components and Walking Speed: Correlation or Causation?' *Sustainability* 12(11), 4619.

Botteldooren, Dick, Bert De Coensel, and Tom De Muer 2006. 'The Temporal Structure of Urban Soundscapes.' *Journal of Sound and Vibration* 292(1–2): 105–23.

Bouzir, Tallal Abdel Karim. 2018. 'Morphologie Urbaine et Pollution Sonore: Étude de Cause à Effet. Cas de La Ville de Biskra.' PhD Thesis, UNIVERSITE MOHAMED KHIDER BISKRA.

Bouzir, Tallal Abdel Karim, Djihed Berkouk, and Noureddine Zemmouri. 2019. 'Evaluation and Analysis of the Algerian Oases Soundscape: Case of El Kantara and Sidi Okba.' *Acoustics Australia*, 48(3): 131–140.

Bouzir, Tallal Abdel Karim, and Nourdinne Zemmouri. 2018. 'Evaluation of the Sound Environment of the City of Biskra (Algeria).' *Journal of Applied Engineering Science & Technology* 4(1): 7–11.

Bouzir, Tallal Abdel Karim, Nourdinne Zemmouri, and Djihed Berkouk. 2017. 'Assessment of Noise Pollution in the City of Biskra, Algeria.' *World Academy of Science, Engineering and Technology International Journal of Environmental and Ecological Engineering* 11(12): 1052–5.

Bouzir, Tallal Abdel Karim, and Nourdinne Zemmouri. 2017. 'Effect of Urban Morphology on Road Noise Distribution.' *Energy Procedia* 119: 376–85.

Bouzir, Tallal Abdel Karim, Nourdinne Zemmouri, and Djihed Berkouk. 2018. 'Assessment and Analysis of Noise Pollution in Biskra Public Gardens (Algeria).' In *AIP Conference Proceedings* 1968, 030069. AIP Publishing LLC.

Brown, A. Lex. 2015. 'Effects of Road Traffic Noise on Health: From Burden of Disease to Effectiveness of Interventions.' *Procedia Environmental Sciences* 30: 3–9.

Calleri, Cristina, Arianna Astolfi, Anna Pellegrino, Francesco Aletta, Louena Shtrepi, Elena Bo, Martina Stefano, and Paola Orecchia 2019. 'The Effect of Soundscapes and Lightscapes on the Perception of Safety and Social Presence Analyzed in a Laboratory Experiment.' *Sustainability* 11(May): 3000. 10.3390/su11113000.

Carrozza, Maria Luiza. 1996. 'Paysage Urbain: Matérialité et Représentation. Propositions.' *Les Cahiers Du Centre de Recherches Historiques. Archives*;17:1–3.https://doi.org/10.4000/ccrh.2600.

CETUR, Guide du Bruit des Transports. 1980. 'Terrestres–Fascicule.' *Prevision Des Niveaux Sonores.*

Clark, Charlotte, and Stephen A. Stansfeld 2007. 'The Effect of Transportation Noise on Health and Cognitive Development: A Review of Recent Evidence.' *International Journal of Comparative Psychology* 20(2):145–158.

Dahech, Salem, and Fethi Rekik 2012. 'Trafic Routier et Pollution Sonore à Sfax (Tunisie Méridionale): Étude Pluridisciplinaire.' 215:259–274.

Dann, Graham. 2002. *The Tourist as a Metaphor of the Social World.* CABI.

De Coensel, Bert, Kang Sun, Weigang Wei, Timothy Van Renterghem, Matthieu Sineau, Carlos Ribeiro, Arnaud Can, Pierre Aumond, Catherine Lavandier, and Dick Botteldooren 2015. 'Dynamic Noise Mapping Based on Fixed and Mobile Sound Measurements.' 10th European Congress and Exposition on Noise Control Engineering (Euronoise 2015), may 31–june 3, Maastricht.

Donadieu, Pierre, and Elisabeth Mazas 2002. *Des Mots de Paysage et de Jardin.* Educagri éditions.

Dubois, Danièle, Catherine Guastavino, and Manon Raimbault 2006. 'A Cognitive Approach to Urban Soundscapes: Using Verbal Data to Access Everyday Life Auditory Categories.' *Acta Acustica United with Acustica* 92(6): 865–74.

Dufft, Catharina. 2009. *Turkish Literature and Cultural Memory: "Multiculturalism" as a Literary Theme After 1980.* Vol. 16. Otto Harrassowitz Verlag.

Euler, David L., Ajith H. Perera, and Ian Douglas Thompson. 2000. *Ecology of a Managed Terrestrial Landscape: Patterns and Processes of Forest Landscapes in Ontario.* UBC Press.

European Environment Agency. 2014. Noise in Europe 2014.

Farina, Almo. 2013. *Soundscape Ecology: Principles, Patterns, Methods and Applications.* Springer.

Farina, Almo, Philip James, C. Bobryk, Nadia Pieretti, Emanuele Lattanzi, and J. McWilliam. 2014. 'Low Cost (Audio) Recording (LCR) for Advancing Soundscape Ecology towards the Conservation of Sonic Complexity and Biodiversity in Natural and Urban Landscapes.' *Urban Ecosystems* 17(4): 923–44.

Faye, Koumba, L. H. Heng, R. Collomp, and E. Peroux. 2003. 'Hypertension and Stress.' *Journal Des Maladies Vasculaires* 28(1): 4–8.

Fidell, Sanford, Karl Pearsons, Barbara Tabachnick, Richard Howe, Laura Silvati, and David S. Barber. 1995. 'Field Study of Noise-Induced Sleep Disturbance.' *The Journal of the Acoustical Society of America* 98(2): 1025–33.

'Full Text'. n.d. Accessed 14 May 2021. https://hal.archives-ouvertes.fr/hal-01561405/document

Gaulin, David 2000. 'Caractérisation Physique Des Sources Sonores En Milieu Urbain.' PhD Thesis, Le Mans.

Goswami, Sh. 2009. 'Road Traffic Noise: A Case Study of Balasore Town, Orissa, India.' *International Journal of Environmental Research* 3(2): 309–318.

Grosjean, Michèle, and Jean-Paul Thibaud. 2001. *L'espace Urbain En Méthodes*. Editions Parenthèses.

Guastavino, Catherine. 2006. 'The Ideal Urban Soundscape: Investigating the Sound Quality of French Cities.' *Acta Acustica United with Acustica* 92(6): 945–51.

Guastavino, Catherine, Brian F. G. Katz, Jean-Dominique Polack, Daniel J. Levitin, and Daniele Dubois. 2005. 'Ecological Validity of Soundscape Reproduction.' *Acta Acustica United with Acustica* 91(2): 333–41.

Guillaume, Gwenaël, Arnaud Can, Gwendall Petit, Nicolas Fortin, Sylvain Palominos, Benoit Gauvreau, Erwan Bocher, and J. Judicaël Picaut. 2016. 'Noise Mapping Based on Participative Measurements.' *Noise Mapping* 3(1):140–156.

Guski, Rainer, U. Felscher-Suhr, and R. Schuemer 1999. 'The Concept of Noise Annoyance: How International Experts See It.' *Journal of Sound and Vibration* 223(4): 513–27.

Hiramatsu, K., T. Yamamoto, K. Taira, A. Ito, and T. Nakasone 1997. 'A Survey on Health Effects Due to Aircraft Noise on Residents Living around Kadena Air Base in the Ryukyus.' *Journal of Sound and Vibration* 205(4): 451–60.

Hunashal, Rajiv B., and Yogesh B. Patil. 2012. 'Assessment of Noise Pollution Indices in the City of Kolhapur, India.' *Procedia-Social and Behavioral Sciences* 37: 448–57.

Ising, Hartmut, and Barbara Kruppa. 2004. 'Health Effects Caused by Noise: Evidence in the Literature from the Past 25 Years.' *Noise and Health* 6(22): 5.

Jakovljević, Branko, Goran Belojević, Katarina Paunović, and Vesna Stojanov. 2006. 'Road Traffic Noise and Sleep Disturbances in an Urban Population: Cross-Sectional Study.' *Croatian Medical Journal* 47(1): 125–33.

Jaworski, Véronique. 2012. 'Noise and the Law.' *Communications*; 90(1): 83–94.

Krönert, Rudolf, Uta Steinhardt, and Martin Volk. 2001. *Landscape Balance and Landscape Assessment*. Springer Science & Business Media.

Kryter, Karl. 1994. *The Handbook of Hearing and the Effects of Noise: Physiology, Psychology, and Public Health*. Brill.

Kryter, Karl D. 2013. *The Effects of Noise on Man*. Elsevier.

Lavandier, Catherine, Pierre Aumond, Saul Gomez, and Catherine Dominguès 2016. 'Urban Soundscape Maps Modelled with Geo-Referenced Data.' *Noise Mapping* 3(1). 10.1515/noise-2016-0020.

Licitra, Gaetano. 2012. *Noise Mapping in the EU: Models and Procedures*. CRC Press.

Maisonneuve, Nicolas, Matthias Stevens, Maria E. Niessen, Peter Hanappe, and Luc Steels 2009. 'Citizen Noise Pollution Monitoring.' in Proc. 10th Annu. Int. Conf. Digital Gov. Res.: Soc. Netw.: Making Connec. Between Citizens, Data Gov.

Malnar, Joy Monice, and Frank Vodvarka. 2004. *Sensory Design*. University of Minnesota Press.

Marquis-Favre, Catherine, Eric Premat, and D. Aubrée. 2005. 'Noise and Its Effects–a Review on Qualitative Aspects of Sound. Part II: Noise and Annoyance.' *Acta Acustica United with Acustica* 91(4): 626–42.

Marry, Solène 2011. 'Assessment of Urban Soundscapes.' *Organised Sound* 16(3): 245–55.

McClure, Christopher J. W., Heidi E. Ware, Jay Carlisle, Gregory Kaltenecker, and Jesse R. Barber 2013. 'An Experimental Investigation into the Effects of Traffic Noise on Distributions of Birds: Avoiding the Phantom Road.' *Proceedings of the Royal Society B: Biological Sciences* 280(1773): 20132290.

McLean, Kate. 2017. 'Smellmap: Amsterdam—Olfactory Art and Smell Visualization.' *Leonardo* 50(1): 92–3.

Murphy, Enda, and Eoin King. 2014. *Environmental Noise Pollution: Noise Mapping, Public Health, and Policy*. Newnes.

Nelson, Paul M. 1987. *Transportation Noise Reference Book*. Butterworth, London.

Ozdemir, Buket, Elif Bayramoglu, and Oner Demirel. 2014. 'Noise Pollution and Human Health in Trabzon Parks.' *Studies on Ethno-Medicine* 8(2): 127–34.

Ozer, Serkan, Hasan Yilmaz, Murat Yeşil, and Pervin Yeşil. 2009. 'Evaluation of Noise Pollution Caused by Vehicles in the City of Tokat, Turkey.' *Scientific Research and Essays* 4(11): 1205–12.

Parris, Kirsten M., and Angela Schneider. 2009. 'Impacts of Traffic Noise and Traffic Volume on Birds of Roadside Habitats.' *Ecology and Society* 14(1): 4–29.

Passchier-Vermeer, Willy, and Wim F. Passchier. 2000. 'Noise Exposure and Public Health.' *Environmental Health Perspectives* 108 (suppl 1): 123–31.

Péneau, Jean-Pierre, Philippe Woloszyn, Michel Bérengier, and David Gaulin. 1998. 'Caractérisation et Identification Des Sources Sonores En Milieu Urbain.' *Acoustique et Techniques* 16: 7–13.

Pijanowski, Bryan C., Almo Farina, Stuart H. Gage, Sarah L. Dumyahn, and Bernie L. Krause. 2011. 'What Is Soundscape Ecology? An Introduction and Overview of an Emerging New Science.' *Landscape Ecology* 26(9): 1213–32.

Pijanowski, Bryan C., Luis J. Villanueva-Rivera, Sarah L. Dumyahn, Almo Farina, Bernie L. Krause, Brian M. Napoletano, Stuart H. Gage, and Nadia Pieretti 2011. 'Soundscape Ecology: The Science of Sound in the Landscape.' *BioScience* 61(3): 203–16.

Radicchi, Antonella. 2019. 'The Notion of Soundscape in the Realm of Sensuous Urbanism. A Historical Perspective.'*Sound Worlds from the Body to the City: Listen*; 1st ed. Newcastle Upon Tyne: Cambridge Scholars Publishing, UK, 99–125.

Raimbault, Manon, and Daniele Dubois 2005. 'Urban Soundscapes: Experiences and Knowledge.' *Cities* 22(5): 339–50.

Reijnen, R., and Foppen, R. U. U. D. 2006. Impact of Road Traffic on Breeding Bird Populations. In *The Ecology of Transportation: Managing Mobility for the Environment*, (255–74). Springer.

Reijnen, Rien, Ruud Foppen, and Henk Meeuwsen 1996. 'The Effects of Traffic on the Density of Breeding Birds in Dutch Agricultural Grasslands.' *Biological Conservation* 75(3): 255–60.

Roger, Alain. 1995. *La Théorie Du Paysage En France, 1974-1994*. Editions Champ Vallon.

Rozec, V., and A. Moch 2000. 'Towards a Comfortable Outdoor Sound Environment.' In *INTER-NOISE and NOISE-CON Congress and Conference Proceedings, 2000*, 4862–6. Institute of Noise Control Engineering.

Rozec, Valérie, and Philippe Ritter 2003. 'Les Avancées et Les Limites de La Législation Sur Le Bruit Face Au Vécu Du Citadin.' *Géocarrefour* 78(2): 111–9.

Rozec, Valérie, and Michel Rumeau. 2000. 'L'évaluation de l'ambiance Sonore En Quartiers Tranquilles Ou Zones 30.' *Acoustique & Techniques* 20: 30–8.

Schafer, R. Murray. 1985. 'Acoustic Space.' In *Dwelling, Place and Environment*, (pp. 87–98). Springer.

Schafer, R. Murray. 2009. 'I Have Never Seen a Sound.' *Canadian Acoustics* 37(3): 32–4.

Schafer, R. Murray, and Sylvette Gleize. 1979. *Le Paysage Sonore*. J.-C. Lattès Paris.

Schafer, Raymond Murray. 1969. *The New Soundscape*. BMI Canada Limited Don Mills.

Seidman, Michael D., and Robert T. Standring. 2010. 'Noise and Quality of Life.' *International Journal of Environmental Research and Public Health* 7(10): 3730–8.

Selye, Hans. 1976. 'Forty Years of Stress Research: Principal Remaining Problems and Misconceptions.' *Canadian Medical Association Journal* 115(1): 53.

Semidor, Catherine. 2004. 'How to Validate the Urban Soundscape'. *Proc. DAGA-CFA*.

Semidor, Catherine. 2006a. 'Le Paysage Sonore de La Rue Comme Élément d'identité Urbaine.' *Flux*; 66–67 (4): 120–126.

Semidor, Catherine. 2006b. 'Listening to a City with the Soundwalk Method.' *Acta Acustica United with Acustica*, *92*(6), 959–64.

Sémidor, Catherine, Henry Torgue, and Jacques Beaumont. 2010. 'Astuce:(Ambiances Sonores, Transports Urbains, Coeur de Ville et Environnement). Vers l'élaboration d'un Guide Méthodologique à Partir d'étude de Cas'. PhD Thesis, CRESSON, PREDIT, ADEME.

Singh, Narendra, and Subhash C. Davar 2004. 'Noise Pollution-Sources, Effects and Control.' *Journal of Human Ecology* 16(3): 181–7.

Stansfeld, Stephen A., Dan S. Sharp, John Gallacher, and Wolfgang Babisch 1993. 'Road Traffic Noise, Noise Sensitivity and Psychological Disorder.' *Psychological Medicine* 23(4): 977–85.

Stosic, Ljiljana, Goran Belojevic, and Suzana Milutinovic. 2009. 'Effects of Traffic Noise on Sleep in an Urban Population.' *Arhiv Za Higijenu Rada i Toksikologiju* 60(3): 335.

Sueur, Jérôme, Thierry Aubin, and Caroline Simonis. 2008. 'Seewave, a Free Modular Tool for Sound Analysis and Synthesis.' *Bioacoustics* 18(2): 213–26.

Sueur, Jérôme, Almo Farina, Amandine Gasc, Nadia Pieretti, and Sandrine Pavoine. 2014. 'Acoustic Indices for Biodiversity Assessment and Landscape Investigation.' *Acta Acustica United with Acustica* 100(4): 772–81.

Summers, Patricia D., Glenn M. Cunnington, and Lenore Fahrig. 2011. 'Are the Negative Effects of Roads on Breeding Birds Caused by Traffic Noise?' *Journal of Applied Ecology* 48(6): 1527–34.

Tairou, Yafradou Adam. 2013. *Préoccupations Environnementales et Droit de l'entreprise: Dans l'espace OHADA*. Editions L'Harmattan.

Tarnopolsky, Alex, S. M. Barker, R. D. Wiggins, and E. K. McLean 1978. 'The Effect of Aircraft Noise on the Mental Health of a Community Sample: A Pilot Study.' *Psychological Medicine* 8(2): 219–33.

Tiger, Guillaume. 2014. 'Synthèse Sonore d'ambiances Urbaines Pour Les Applications Vidéoludiques.' PhD Thesis, Conservatoire national des arts et metiers-CNAM.

Tomei, Francesco, Sergio Fantini, Enrico Tomao, Tiziana Paola Baccolo, and Maria Valeria Rosati. 2000. 'Hypertension and Chronic Exposure to Noise.' *Archives of Environmental Health: An International Journal* 55(5): 319–25.

Tsagué, Louis. 2009. *La Pollution Due Au Transport Urbain et Aéroportuaire: Caractéristiques et Méthodes de Réduction*. Editions L'Harmattan.

Van Kempen, Elise E. M. M., Hanneke Kruize, Hendriek C. Boshuizen, Caroline B. Ameling, Brigit A. M. Staatsen, and Augustinus E. M. De Hollander. 2002. 'The Association between Noise Exposure and Blood Pressure and Ischemic Heart Disease: A Meta-Analysis.' *Environmental Health Perspectives* 110(3): 307–17.

Venot, Flora, and Catherine Sémidor 2006. 'The Soundwalk as an Operational Component for Urban Design.' Conference on Passive and Low Energy Architecture PLEA, Geneva, Switzerland,; 6–8 Sept.

Villa, Miguel de luque, Andres Camilo Acuña Mendez, Juan Diego Virguez, Mariajose Rubio, and Camila Canchon Triana. 2020. 'Evaluation of the noise impacts on sleep quality in communities near to the international airport El Dorado in Colombia.' *WIT Transactions on Ecology and the Environment* 241: 397–405.

Vincent Jost. n.d. 'Présentation et Analyse d'un Paysage Sonore: La Ville de Montréal.' Accessed 14 May 2021. http://eductice.ens-lyon.fr/EducTice/recherche/geomatique/actualites-et-lettres-geomatiques/articles-lettre-geomatique-13/lettre-18/presentation-et-analyse-d2019un-paysage-sonore-la-ville-de-montreal#_ftnref1

Vogiatzis, Konstantinos, and Nicolas Remy. 2017. 'Soundscape Design Guidelines through Noise Mapping Methodologies: An Application to Medium Urban Agglomerations.' *Noise Mapping* 4(1): 1–19.

Wissmann, Torsten. 2014. *Geographies of Urban Sound*. Ashgate Publishing, Ltd.

Wrightson, Kendall. 2000. 'An Introduction to Acoustic Ecology.' *Soundscape: The Journal of Acoustic Ecology* 1(1): 10–3.

Yang, Tingting, Francesco Aletta, and Jian Kang. 2021. 'Sound Environments in Large Public Buildings for Crowd Transit: A Systematic Review.' *Applied Sciences* 11(April): 3728. 10.3390/app11093728.

Zannin, Paulo Henrique Trombetta, Fabiano Belisário Diniz, and Wiliam Alves Barbosa. 2002. 'Environmental Noise Pollution in the City of Curitiba, Brazil.' *Applied Acoustics* 63(4): 351–8.

Zheng, Yu. 2019. *Urban Computing*. MIT Press.

12 Transportation Sustainability Assessment using an Indicator-Based Method: A Case of Kochi, Kerala, India

Cladia Anna Jose and Firoz C. Mohammed
National Institute of Technology Calicut, Kolkata, India

CONTENTS

12.1 INTRODUCTION

Sustainable development as a concept has been widely recognised since the Brundtland Commission, in both the developing and the developed world. Even though there are several dimensions of sustainability from economic, environmental, and socio-cultural dimensions and studies regarding these, the transport domain and research in this domain can contribute to the three dimensions profusely both in the developed and developing world. The adoption of the UN 2030 new impetus to address the sustainability of transport systems of urban areas has gained

DOI: 10.1201/9781003126195-15

attention across the world. The urban population in India is expected to reach 50% by 2030. Our cities contribute 2% of the land area and 70% of the economic activities (Pucher et al. 2005) (Hiroaki Suzuki, Robert Cervero 2013) and reveals that the transportation sector contributes the maximum to problems of urban areas and contributes 24% of global direct CO_2 emissions in 2016 (Ge 2019). Therefore, the transport sector is one of the most contributing domains to climate change as well. So, it is important to focus on urban transport sustainability, which is gaining the most significance in sustainability research.

Transport is a core component in the domain of socio-economic development (Badassa, Sun, and Qiao 2020). Sustainable transport should meet the mobility needs of the society in the least damaging way to the environment so that current development does not impair the mobility needs of future generations. The domain can act as the link between the three pillars of sustainability that should contribute to improving the standards of living, inclusivity, and quality of life of city dwellers. Currently, abundant research is carried out with the intent to analyse to what extent this domain can be sustainable and how it can be made more sustainable. Therefore, a lot of studies are done for assessing sustainability, monitoring it, and to improve it.

Today, every city regardless of how big or small, economically stable or not, has recognised the need to align the path of development sustainably. To closely monitor the results of initiatives adopted for sustainable development, stakeholders and local government agencies need to derive their data ecosystem and update it periodically. Hence, the key component of implementing sustainable development is the identification of a clear governance structure and appropriate data ecosystem relevant for the city. A sustainable rating system should help to alleviate problems in the planning and management of urban systems and should steer researchers and policy analysts to recommend pertinent strategies for development.

This chapter consists of four parts: literature review, materials and methods, analysis and results, and finally the scope and discussions. The first part deals with the previous research works in the domain of sustainability in general and transport sustainability specifically. This section also accommodates details on various methods used for sustainability assessment and various domains that contribute to sustainable development. The second section is about the methodology adopted for the study, indicators used for measuring sustainability, the process of data collection adopted for this study, etc. Finally, the analysis section compares the results of Kochi city with other Indian cities like Bengaluru and Chennai and discusses strategies and methods to improve the performance of low-performing factors. The limitations and future improvements for the study are discussed in the last section in detail.

12.2 LITERATURE REVIEW

This section discusses the research background that lays out the framework for monitoring the sustainability of the transport domain in the case study city. Accordingly, the literature review is undertaken for the methods of sustainability assessments, indicators used for the assessment, and the construction of a composite index of sustainability.

12.2.1 Methods for Sustainability Assessment

Sustainability assessment is a tool to monitor the progress of sustainable development in countries, cities, neighbourhoods (Dizdaroglu 2017), etc. There are several existing sustainability assessment models like asset-based framework, multi-criteria decision making, impact assessment method, sustainability rating systems, etc (Cohen 2017). Most of these models are already used in practice and are globally acceptable. However, such methods have their limitations. They use universally acceptable variables since they have wider acceptability in various contexts and scales. Most of them are used in studies for comparison of countries and regions. However, research that requires diverse variables and local context-specific variables requires the creation of custom-made sustainability assessment models. Such models do have their advantages like better predictability of results and context relevance. However, such studies do have their own limitations like data availability, measurability, replicability, and quality of data. The global studies and initiatives to assess sustainability focus on issues critical to global sustainability and scientific research methods and statistical data collection techniques are well-framed only in industrialised countries; hence, the concerns and priorities of such countries dominate the existing indicator systems (Dizdaroglu 2017). Hence, to gather accurate, reliable, and accessible data, the geographical scale of the study has to be the smallest independent spatial unit like a neighbourhood.

There are mainly two types of methods used for sustainability assessment: indicator-based methods and rating-based methods. The use of the indicator-based method is more prominent compared to the rating-based method (Cohen 2017). A comparison of the two methods is shown in Table 12.1

Since there are advantages like replicability over areas of similar characteristics, treatment at the local level, and the possibility to constantly monitor and update data, this study proposed to use the indicator-based method for sustainability assessment. This method is also suitable for quantifying sustainability to an index, so that the overall status of sustainability of the area of interest can be reviewed.

Dobranskyte-Niskota et al. (2009) sates that "transport plays a fundamental role in the economy, as its demand is closely linked to economic growth." Hence, sustainable transportation should balance a set of social, environmental, and economic goals. There are negative impacts as well to meet the growing transport demand, like noise and air pollution, traffic congestion, etc. So, the development in the transport domain should be in such a way that it does not disturb the smooth functioning of the environment and socio-economic domain and its sustainability. This calls for the need for sustainable transport. Many institutes and countries have set up an indicator framework for the assessment of transport sustainability like the European Union, Institute for Transportation and Development Policy, Victoria Transport Policy Institute, Canada, etc (Dobranskyte-Niskota et al. 2009), (Badassa, Sun, and Qiao 2020), (Litman and Litman 2007). This study emphasises the indicator-based sustainability assessment of the transport domain.

In the indicator-based method, measurement is done through sustainable development indicators falling in different domains, to assess the overall sustainability of the study area and to

TABLE 12.1
Comparison of Indicator-Based and Rating-Based Methods

Criteria	Indicator Based	Rating Based
Assessment Level	Possible to replicate information over a larger scale of study area	Mainly building-level performances
Generalizing Results	Possible	Site-specific results
Context	Deals with contextual issues	Can assess different domains at once
Precision	Lack of consensus leads to confusion	Possible to precisely examine different cases.
Decision Making	Can lead to better decisions	Decisions are context-specific based on the criterion of interest
Ease of Developing Framework	Easy to develop a framework	Not easy
Updating of Results	Allow timely identification of trends	Do not allow identification of trends
Data	Makes available aggregated information	No aggregated data

Source: (Jose 2020).

analyse the performance of domains by aggregating these indicator scores to their respective domains. The studies using this method begin with the selection of study area and criteria for classifying them (Saville-Smith et al. 2009). Entropy index, land use mix, or areas with a characteristic purpose can be used to distinguish them from others, for example, a transit node can be selected as a study area.

The study area delineation is a key step in the process of indicator-based assessment and such kinds of literature were reviewed to find the most commonly used delineation technique. Land use mix (LU mix) and entropy index (Bahadure 2018)(Kotharkar, Bahadure, and Sarda 2014) and Mix Percentage (Saville-Smith, Dwyer, and Warren 2009) are the most prominently used methods for the selection of the study area. In the absence of clear city limits, area jurisdiction, or criteria for carrying out sustainability assessment, these techniques can be used for the selection of the study area.

The next stage in indicator-based methods is the identification of domains of interest specific to the study area conditions. The selection of critical domains is done through stakeholder consultations, focus group discussions, etc., this is to ensure civic participation at local levels to enhance the transparency of the project objectives. The indicators relevant to the domains are selected based on relevance, previous literature, etc. Indicators are sometimes categorised as quantitative and qualitative indicators.

The Beacon Neighbourhood Sustainability Framework[1] categorised indicators into six domains and then the indicators are given either positive or negative scores (Saville-Smith et al. 2009). Dollar values are assigned in the valuation of the neighbourhood, which is done based on a slender evidential base that mostly presents foreign experiences. According to the NSA tool, all cities that have high- and medium-density areas get a positive dollar sustainability score (D. Bijoux 2007). The Commission for Sustainable Development (CSD) has laid out a variable selection matrix for finalising important variables based on data availability and relevance.

The indicators used for sustainability assessment are common to both the indicator-based and rating-based methods. The process for the selection of indicators and screening, weighing, benchmarking, etc. are given in the subsequent section.

12.2.2 Selection of Indicators

As explained earlier, since the indicator-based method is adopted in this study for the transport sustainability assessment, appropriate indicators are selected from the literature review. There are three steps followed in the selection of indicators: initial selection prepares a comprehensive list of indicators from the literature related to the study; followed by screening based on the variable redundancy, contextual relevance, and scale of the study, and finally; screening based on data availability and expert opinion.

The list of indicators for sustainability assessment can never be exhaustive, but researchers can ensure coverage of the maximum number of domains. Since this study focuses on the sustainability of the transport domain and in this section the process of compiling transport sustainability indicators is discussed. UN guidelines screen indicators based on relevance and data availability on a matrix where most relevant data available and relevant potentially data available indicators are selected for sustainability assessment (UN 2007). All the reviewed studies point to relevance as the key criteria for the selection of indicators for the local context.

The preparation of a holistic list is based on compiling indicators from literature, reports, articles, etc., on sustainability assessment. For this study, a list of over 367 indicators (Indicator list 1) from the literature of urban sustainability, global database for SDGs, NITI Aayog, and relevant institutional documents have been compiled. The screening of a holistic list based on relevance to the transport domain gave the second list of indicators (Dur 2014) (Indicator list 2). Carraro et al. (2009) adopted a relevance-based indicator screening process for the initial stage of indicator screening. The redundancy of variables, data availability, and contextual relevance was checked in the next stage to arrive at 67 indicators (Indicator list 2). The final refinement of the indicator list is done based on

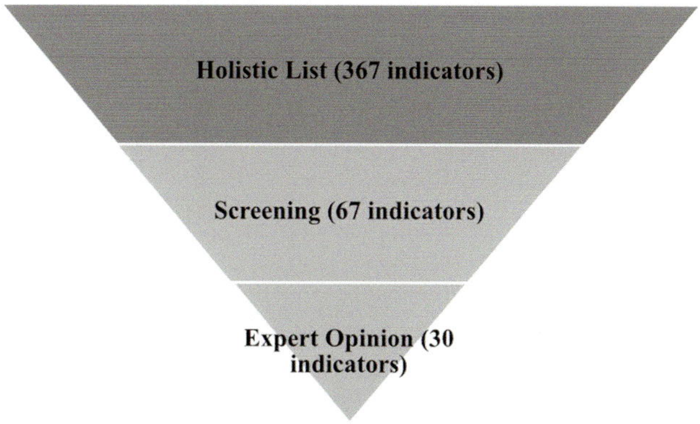

FIGURE 12.1 Indicator screening process.

expert opinion and focus group discussions. (Krishnan and Mohammed 2020). Indicators with 75% agreement can finally be selected as relevant and data available indicators (Indicator list 3). The final list of indicators after deletion/addition from experts were 30 in number. The process of screening is shown in Figure 12.1.

The list of selected indicators through the three levels of screening is shown in Table 12.2.

12.2.3 Tools and Techniques for Index Creation

An index is an amalgam of several indicators in different domains aggregated to quantify a common goal. It can also be called as a composite indicator. The use of indices enables better apprehension and explication of indicators of a given phenomenon in the field of sustainable development, (Tanguay 2009) particularly for the public.Tanguay 2009.

A composite value conveys more information compared to individual indicator values. There are quantitative and qualitative indicators for sustainability assessment, but the creation of an index demands the quantification of all indicators. Hence, qualitative indicators can either be replaced by proxy indicators or can be quantified with the help of binary technique, scaling, etc. (Kotharkar 2015).

The contribution of some indicators may be high while some others may be benign. Therefore, weighting is an important step in the quantification of sustainability indicators. Gan (2017) compares the different methods for weighting the sustainability indicators and describes what to use where and when. Wherever the study is conducted on a larger geographical area and the need of conducting the primary survey is marginal, the equal weighting method can be adopted for weighting the indicators. Studies that focus on sustainability assessment in a smaller geographical area such as a neighbourhood level can use ranking or more sophisticated methods for precision (Bahadure 2012).

The units of indicators vary from each other, which demands the normalization of indicators (Yigitcanlar 2007; Carraro et al. 2009). A scaling technique is used in the study to normalize the indicator values to indicator scores.

The key step in the aggregation of indicators and creation of index is benchmarking. Benchmarking lays down a reference line for assessing the performance of indicators and serve as a touchstone to quantify and collate the efficacy of indicators. Benchmarking aids the appraisal of performance and comparative analysis of neighbourhoods and allows upgrades of the current performance.

Benchmarks established by recognized agencies nationally, globally, etc., can be used as a guideline for the normalization of indicators (MoUD 2013). There are some indicators with already established benchmarked values for sustainability and then there are others without benchmarks;

TABLE 12.2
Selected Indicators

Main Category	Sub Category	Indicators	Desirable Range	Sources
Travel Behaviour	Accessibility	% of income spent on traveling	−ve[2]	(Bahadure et al. 2014)
		Trip length for vegetable market	−ve	(Kotharkar2015) (UN 2007)
		Trip length for college	−ve	(UN 2007) (Kotharkar 2018)
		Trip length for restaurant/theatre	−ve	(UN 2007) (Kotharkar 2018)
		Trip length for health facility	−ve	(UN 2007) (Kotharkar 2018)
		Trip length for park	−ve	(UN 2007), (Kotharkar 2018)
		Trip length for school	−ve	(UN 2007), (Kotharkar 2018)
		Transit service density/ transit service trip length	−ve	(UN 2007), (Kotharkar 2018)
		Parking space for commercial space	−ve	(UN 2007) (Kotharkar 2018)
	Mobility	No. of public buses per 1,000 residents	+ve[3]	(UN 2007) (Aayog 2019) (Kotharkar 2018), (Kotharkar 2015) (MoUD 2013)
		Road network density	+ve	(NITI Aayog Report, 2019)(MoUD 2013) (Aayog 2019)
		Vehicle ownership (PCU)	−ve	Ministry of Housing and Urban Affairs 2013)(Aayog 2019)
	Efficiency	Passengers served by one public bus	+ve	(MoUD 2013)
		Walkability index- availability, rating	+ve	(Bahadure 2012)
		Congestion index	−ve	Bahadure 2012
		Percentage of sustainable mode	+ve	(Kotharkar 2018)

Perception	Safety	Fatal accidents	−ve	(Aayog 2019) (UN 2007) (Carolina Barco 2013) (MoUD 2013)
		Crime rates	−ve	Aayog 2019,Ministry of Housing and Urban Affairs 2013
		Developed area per person	+ve	Aayog 2019,Ministry of Housing and Urban Affairs 2013
	(Aayog 2019) (MoUD 2013) Satisfaction	Wish to shift from current neighborhood	−ve	(D. Bijoux 2007)
		Satisfied with amenities in neighborhood	+ve	(D. Bijoux 2007)
		Part of social group	+ve	(D. Bijoux 2007)
		Ratio of built-up to open spaces	−ve	(Pankaj) (Kotharkar 2015)
		Ratio of population under BPL	−ve	(UN 2007)
	Pollution	Feel air pollution	−ve	Aayog 2019
		Feel traffic pollution	−ve	Aayog 2019
		Feel noise pollution	−ve	Aayog 2019
		Tree density per hectare	+ve	Aayog 2019
		Per capita fossil fuel consumption	−ve	Aayog 2019 (UN 2007)
Landuse	Mix	Entropy index	+ve	(Kotharkar 2015)

Source: (Jose 2020).

we need to combine both and benchmark them for the creation of the index. From the reviewed works of literature, benchmark indicators use a five-point scale or are based on the level of service (LoS). A five-point scale is a more accepted and reviewed technique for data analysis. Hence, this method is used to create the indicator score.

In this study, indicators without benchmarks are quantified by comparison with other Indian cities on a five-point scale using a percentile calculation tool provided by the IBM SPSS software. For indicators without already known benchmarks, the value of the same indicator for different cities is found and the indicator score for such indicators without established benchmarks is calculated using (Reddy et al. 2013) Equation 12.1:

$$Indicator\ \ Score = \frac{ActualValue\ -\ MinimumValue}{MaximumValue\ -\ MinimumValue} \tag{12.1}$$

After comparison with other cities, the value is converted to a five-point scale based on percentile calculation in IBM SPSS. The values less than 20 percentiles correspond to score 1, between the 20th and 40th percentile has score 2, indicators falling between 40 and 60 scores 3, those between 60 and 80 scores 4 and those above 80th percentile scores 5 for those indicators with +ve sign on the desired range in Table 12.2; for other indicators, the scores will be reversed. The benchmarking is done through literature surveys and service-level benchmarks for urban transport laid down by MoUD.

The normalized values of discrete indicators need aggregation to get a perspective on the sustainability scenario of the city. This is done using a composite index that is the summation of discrete indicator scores divided by the number of indicators (Carraro et al. 2009). In this study, the composite value is on a five-point scale, which is converted to an index value using the linear interpolation technique. In the five-point scale, 1 corresponds to low (extremely unsustainable), 2 for medium-low (not preferred but better than low), 3 for medium (discrete level of sustainability), 4 stands for medium-high (satisfactory level of sustainability), and score 5 corresponds to high (target level of sustainability).

The composite indicator score is calculated using the formula (Yigitcanlar 2015; Carraro et al. 2009):

$$Composite\ \ Indicator\ \ Score = \sum_{i=1}^{n} w_i\, i_i \tag{12.2}$$

The transport sustainability index (TSI) is calculated from the composite indicator score using the linear interpolation technique. Index values are usually represented on a 0 to 1 scale. Hence, the composite indicator is linearly interpolated to arrive at the index.

12.3 MATERIALS AND METHODS

This section deals with the selection of the study area followed by the data collection of the selected indicators. The first section explains the criteria for the selection of the study area and the contextual importance of the selected study area for this study. The next section explains the calculation processes and benchmarking methods adopted for the normalization of the selected indicators. The methodology for conducting the study is shown in Figure 12.2.

12.3.1 Study Area

Based on the literature reviews, study areas are selected for sustainability assessment based on the entropy index or mix percentage (Garau and Pavan, 2018) when the assessment is carried is out on a smaller geographical extent. At the city level for urban sustainability assessment, local body jurisdictions can be adopted for the study, considering the availability of data and ease of data collection.

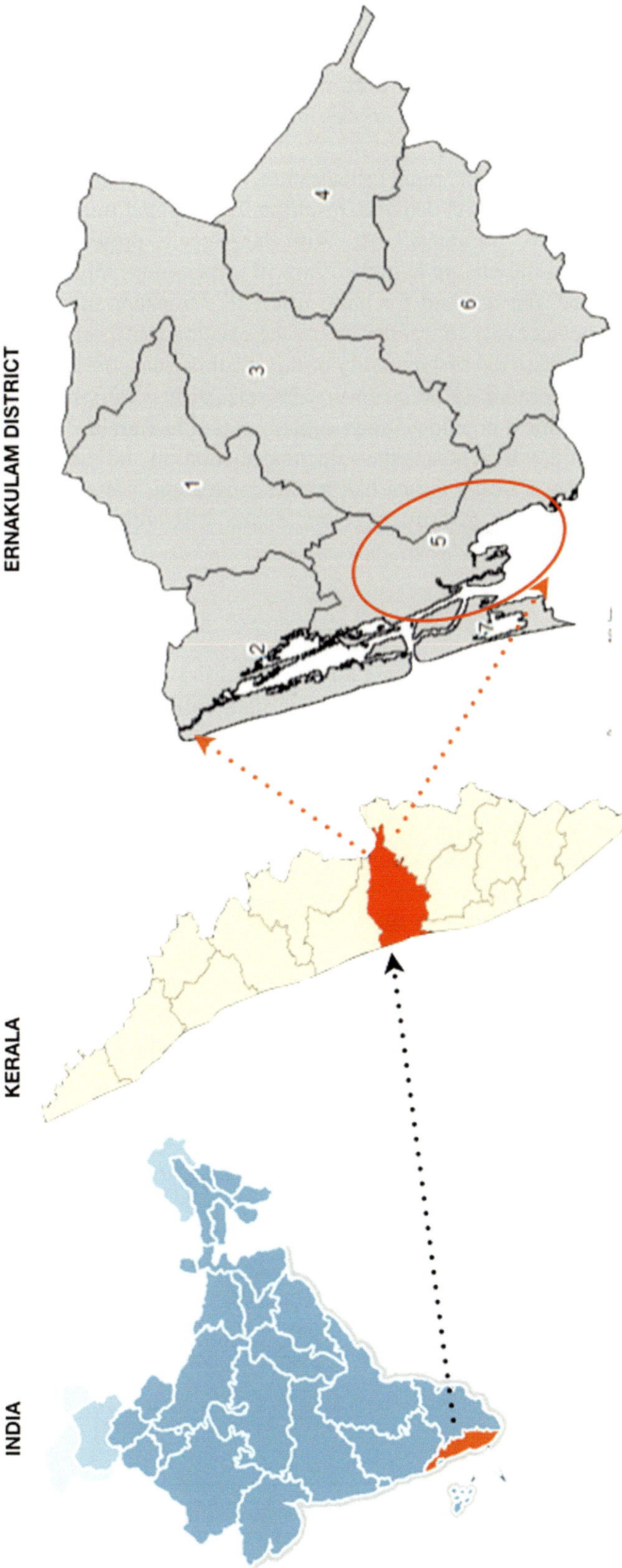

FIGURE 12.2 Study area.

Ernakulam district has the maximum urban population in Kerala. Kochi is the administrative headquarters of the district and houses all the administrative institutions. The city also has the biggest shipyard in the country and a busy port, which is why Kochi acts as the economic hub of Kerala. The city of Kochi offers several modes of transportation, water, road, and metro tail compared to other cities in Kerala.

Intense commercial developments, rapid urbanisation, and high population density in the recent past have caused an increase in travel demand, resulting in a strained transport infrastructure with increasing traffic congestion, accidents, etc. With large-scale projects like smart city and Vallarpadam container terminal etc., in bag, the city will attract more migrant labourers, resulting in more population; hence, the demand for basic needs like transportation is expected to climb sharply, strengthening the necessity for refinement of the existing transport infrastructure in Kochi. This calls for the need to assess the sustainability of the existing transport infrastructure of the city. The Kochi Municipal Corporation (KMC) limits were selected for carrying out the study.

Kochi is the largest and most populous urban agglomeration in Kerala. The urban population in Kochi is steadily increasing, which means the vehicular population and the travel demand also are increasing. The city has been facing issues like traffic congestion, noise pollution, parking difficulties, lack of proper pedestrian infrastructure, etc. Hence, it is important to assess the transport sustainability of the city.

12.3.2 Data Collection

The data collection for the study was initiated after the final list of indicators was prepared. Since the transport-related indicators frame the core of the data collection, primary surveys and secondary data sources were used for data collection. The data collection consists of two sections: variable data collection part and validation.

Variable data collection shows the data sources, the calculation process, and the value corresponding to each transport sustainability indicator. In this study, each indicator is normalized on a five-point scale, as discussed in the literature study; hence, the sources of reference for benchmarking each indicator are shown in Table 12.3.

The three indicators in the satisfaction sub-category of perception indicators, wish to shift from neighborhood, satisfaction with amenities in the neighborhood, and part of social group indicate the quality of life of residents, can be replaced by a proxy variable called the quality of life index. The difference is benign and the result is unaltered. So the final list of indicators was 27. The data collected was validated through a comparison of the study area between the Indian cities Bengaluru and Chennai. This will help to identify where the study area needs to improvise compared to similar cities.

12.3.3 Methodology

The whole process of this study is carried out in three parts: literature review, data collection, and creation of the index. The literature review gives the input for the data collection, i.e., the list of selected indicators. The data collection was carried out from secondary and primary sources. The analysis part was then done by aggregation of indicators to quantify the transport sustainability using the composite score and creation of transport sustainability index (TSI), shown in Figure 12.3.

12.4 ANALYSIS AND RESULTS

The analysis section deals with the aggregation, benchmarking, and creation of the composite indicator score. The first part of this section is about the normalisation of indicators, and then the

TABLE 12.3
Indicator Data Collection

VARIABLE (I)	DATA SOURCE (II)	CALCULATION (III)	VALUE (IV)	SCORE (V)	BENCHMARKING (VI)
Entropy index	Primary Survey (Department of Town and Country Planning, 2017)	The index value of 3 nodes is averaged and compared with the index value of the study area from secondary sources.	0.710.74		
Trip length- school	Primary Survey	NEAR TOOL ArcGIS-Data Required: 1. Mapping the facilities in the study area	620 m	5	(Kotharkar 2015)
Trip length- college			435 m	5	
Trip length- healthcare			405 m	5	
Trip length- market			875 m	5	
Trip length- restaurant			86 m	5	
Trip length- park			1415 m	2	
Trip length- transit			221 m	4	
% Expenditure on traveling	Jose 2018 (Patrick 2015)	$= \frac{(Fare/Km) \times Avg\ Trip\ Length \times 52}{Monthly\ Income}$	16.2%	1	(Kotharkar 2015) ("12 Indian Cities: Transport Indicators" 2010)(Huang et al., 2018)
Road network density	Jose 2018	$= \frac{Road\ Length}{Area}$	35.5 Km of road/ Sq.Km	5	
Percentage of sustainable mode	Jose 2018	$= Percentage\ of\ cycling + Walking$	15%	1	(Kotharkar 2015) ("12 Indian Cities: Transport Indicators" 2010)
Parking space	Anew 2010; S. 2020	$= \frac{Total\ available\ Paid\ Parking}{Total\ available\ Parking}$	44.7%	3	(KMC 2020) (Ministry of Housing and Urban Affairs, 2013)
No.of buses/100 population	KMRL Reports	$= \frac{Fleet\ Size}{Population}$	0.5	5	(Ministry of Housing and Urban Affairs, 2013)
Vehicle ownership	RITES Report August 2001	$= \frac{\Sigma Equivalent\ PCU\ X\ No.\ of\ HH}{No.of\ HH}$	0.35	5	(Kotharkar 2015)

(Continued)

TABLE 12.3 (Continued)
Indicator Data Collection

VARIABLE (I)	DATA SOURCE (II)	CALCULATION (III)	VALUE (IV)	SCORE (V)	BENCHMARKING (VI)
Walkability index	Xavier 2017	$= [(W1 \times Availability\ of\ footpath) + (w2 \times Pedestrian\ Facility\ rating)]$	0.57	2	Min-Max Rule, Linear Interpolation
Congestion index	(Kotharkar 2015), Primary survey	$= 1 - (Average\ Journey\ Speed/Desirable\ Journey\ Speed)$	0.33	1	Min-Max Rule, Linear Interpolation
Passengers served by one bus	(Dennis Jose 2018)	$= \frac{Average\ passenger\ onboard}{No.of\ seats\ in\ Bus}$	0.817	5	(MoUD 2013)
Fatal accidents	(Official Webportal of Police Commissionerate Kochi 2020)	$= \frac{Fatalities\ in\ 2019\ \times 100000}{Total\ population}$	22.88	1	(MoUD 2013)
Crime rates		*Crimes recorded per lakh population*	2034	1	20, 40, 60, 80 percentiles in SPSS linearly compared to 5- point scale
Developed area per capita		$= \frac{Developed\ area}{Total\ population}$	94.11 m^2	4	20, 40, 60, 80 percentiles in SPSS linearly compared to 5- point scale
Per capita open space		$= \frac{Open\ area}{Total\ population}$	39.29 m^2	5	(Wang, 2009)
Ratio of BPL population		$= \frac{BPL\ Population}{Total\ population}$	0.314	2	20, 40, 60, 80 percentiles in SPSS linearly compared to 5- point scale
Tree density	(KSPCB Report2014)	Tree Density per 10 person= Per capita forest land x 10	0.34	1	(Kotharkar 2015)
Per capita fossil fuel consumption		(Proxy Variable) Per Capita Electricity Consumption	544 kWh	5	20, 40, 60, 80 percentiles in SPSS linearly compared to 5- point scale
Air pollution	(Emissions 2009)	PM 2.5 Emissions (Measured in tons/yr/grid)	10-50 tons /yr/ grid	2	(Emissions 2017)

Noise pollution	ENVIS, CPCB, 2014	Ambient Noise levels in dB (Commercial)	78.5 dB	1	20, 40, 60, 80 percentiles in SPSS linearly compared to 5- point scale
Traffic pollution	(Chaudhary, 2018) (KSPCB 2014)	Annual CO_2 Emissions per sq. km	8958.698 Mg km^{-2}	4	20, 40, 60, 80 percentiles in SPSS linearly compared to 5- point scale
Wish to shift from neighborhoodSatisf-action with amenitiesPart of social group	(Numbeo 2020)	Estimation of overall quality of life by using an empirical formula	109.87	3	20, 40, 60, 80 percentiles in SPSS linearly compared to 5- point scale

Source: (Jose 2020).

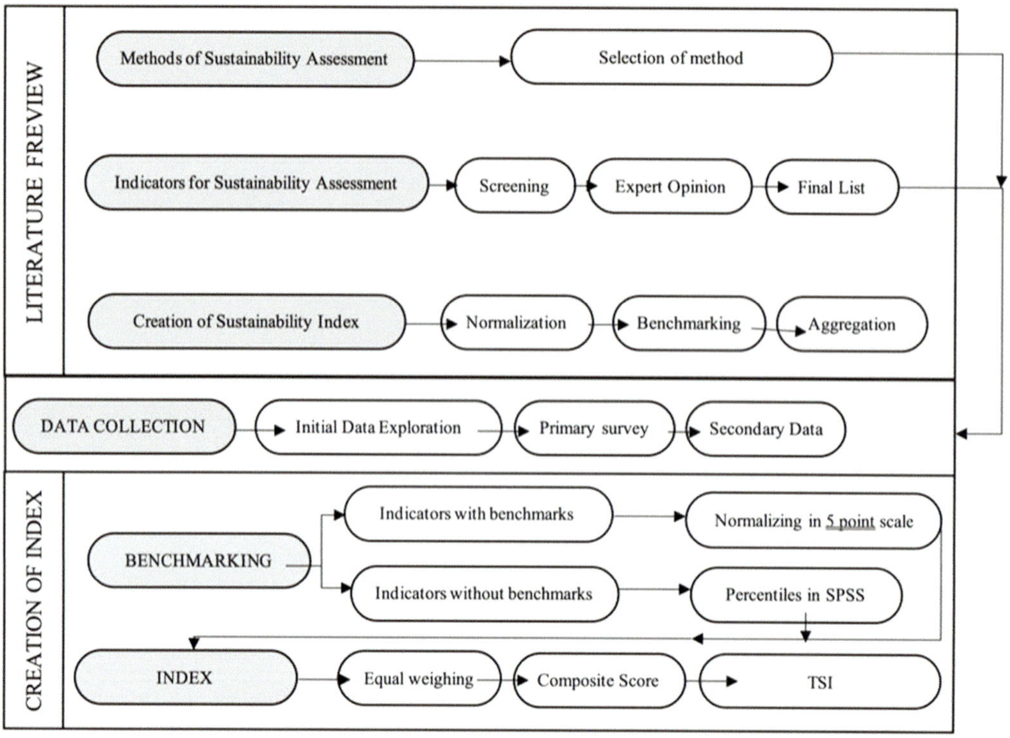

FIGURE 12.3 Methodology of the study.

weighing and aggregation of indicators are discussed. The composite indicator score calculated through aggregation was then used to calculate the TSI for the study area. The last part discusses indicator scores of the Indian cities Bengaluru and Chennai since these also offer similar transit choices like the study area Kochi. Bengaluru and Chennai are the nearest urban agglomerations to Kochi, offering MMT and comparable economic profile compared to other urban areas in Kerala.

12.4.1 Normalization and Benchmarking

The indicator values in Table 12.3 [column IV] are in different units and cannot be aggregated. The process of normalization is carried out based on the process explained in the literature study. The final normalized value of indicators on a five-point scale is shown in column V in Table 12.3. The indicator scores normalized on the five-point scale are now ready to be aggregated to create the composite index. A score of five indicates a more sustainable indicator and a score of one corresponds to the least sustainable indicators.

12.4.2 Weighing and Aggregation

The normalized indicator has to be weighted and aggregated to create the composite indicator score. As explained in literature study section 2.3, the equal weighting method is adopted to weight the indicators. The total number of indicators is 27; each indicator was assigned a weight of 0.037 (1/27). The composite indicator score was then calculated using the formula (Tan Yigitcanlar 2015) (Carraro et al. 2009):-

$$\text{Composite Indicator Score} = \sum_{i=1}^{n} w_i\, i_i$$

where i = 1,2,3,....n, and (n = 27); and w, the weight of each indicator (0.037).

The composite indicator calculated using the above formula accounts to 3.182, which shows a medium discrete level of sustainability, as explained in previous sections.

12.4.3 Transport Sustainability Index

The transport sustainability index (TSI) is calculated from the composite indicator score using linear interpolation. Index values are usually represented on a 0 to 1 scale. Hence, the composite indicator is linearly interpolated to arrive at the index.

$$\boldsymbol{TSI_{(Kochi)} = 0.545}$$

The transport sustainability is close to 0.5, showing medium sustainability according to the benchmarking scale explained in section 12.2.3. This shows the city of Kochi has to improve the transport infrastructure so that it becomes more sustainable and reaches the target score of 5. The recommendations and policy for improving the same are detailed in 12.5.1.

The discrete indicator score for each indicator is given in Table 12.3. The methodology adopted in this study favours a comparison of the indicator scores with other cities. The analysis part of the study does the comparison of indicator scores of Kochi with Bengaluru and Chennai.

12.4.4 Comparison with Other Indian Cities

The comparison of indicator scores gives an idea of issues that are generic to cities. Although all indicator data was not available, the comparison was done for those indicators for which secondary data was collected.

Issues like urban poor, carbon dioxide emissions, crimes, limited developed area per capita are seen in all of the cities. The values of some of the indicators are directly proportional to the total population. Mumbai is the most populous city that has a high below-poverty line population and least developed area per capita. The high crime rate in Kochi may be attributed to the fact that the high literacy rate in Kerala results in maximum reporting of crimes. These types of comparisons can be made using indicator-based methods and the creation of a sustainability index gives an idea about where our cities stand in meeting sustainable development goals and targets.

12.4.5 Categorising Indicators

The indicators are classified into three groups based on their score, as shown in Table 12.3. Indicators with scores 1 and 2 are low performing, 3 are medium performing, and 4 and 5 are high-performing indicators. The proposal and projects have to focus on improving the low- and medium-performing indicators and at the same time maintain high-performing indicators (Table 12.5).

Table 12.4 shows the comparison of indicators with Bengaluru and Chennai. From the indicator scores, it is very evident that the efficiency and safety dimensions are the low-performing ones in Kochi's scenario. The high-performing accessibility dimension and the poor performance of efficiency and safety dimensions exhibit the importance of refining the existing transport quality.

The indicator score of vehicle ownership was calculated based on data from 2004. Vehicle ownership has drastically increased post-2000. The availability of data and a regular monitoring framework has to be laid out to improve the performance of the transport domain. A clear

TABLE 12.4
Indicator Score Comparison with Bengaluru and Chennai

Proxy	Accessibility									Mobility			Efficiency				Safety			Satisfaction			Pollution				
INDICATORS	Trip Length-Market	Trip Length-College	Trip Length-School	Trip Length-Healthcare	Trip Length-Restaurants	Trip Length-Parks/Garden	Trip Length-Transit	% Expenditure on Travel	Parking Space	Road network Density	No. of buses/1000 Population	Vehicle ownership	Percentage of sustainable mode	Walkability Index	Congestion Index	Passengers served by one bus	Fatal Accidents	Crime Rate	Developed Area per Capita	Per Capita Open Space	Ratio of BPL Population	***Quality of Living Index***: Wish to Shift from NH; Part of social group; Satisfaction with amenities	Tree Density per 10 persons	Per capita Fossil Fuel consumption	Air Pollution	Noise Pollution	Traffic Pollution
Kochi	1	2	3	4	5	6	7	8	9	10	11	12	13	14	15	16	17	18	19	20	21	22	23	24	25	26	27
	3	5	5	5	5	2	4	1	3	5	5	5	1	2	1	5	1	1	4	5	2	3	1	5	2	1	4
Chennai	Primary Survey Data Not Available												2	Data Not Available			1	2	3	1	3	2	1	4		1	1
Bengaluru	Primary Survey Data Not Available												2	Data Not Available			1	3	2	4	2	3	1	3		3	2

TABLE 12.5
Categorization of Indicators

Category	Indicators
Low Performing	% Expenditure on Travel
	Percentage of Sustainable Mode
	Congestion Index
	Fatal Accidents
	Crime Rate
	Tree Density per 10 Persons
	Noise Pollution
	Air Pollution
	Trip Length-Parks/Garden
	Walkability Index
	Ratio of BPL Population
Medium Performing	Trip Length-Market
	Parking Space
	Quality of Living Index
Satisfactorily Performing	Trip Length-College
	Trip Length-School
	Trip Length-Health Care
	Trip Length-Restaurants
	Trip Length-Transit
	Road Network Density
	No. of Buses/1,000 Population
	Vehicle Ownership
	Developed Area per Capita
	Per Capita Open Space
	Per Capita Fossil Fuel Consumption
	Traffic Pollution

governance structure has to be established with an indicator framework for assessing the sustainability and efficiency of the transport systems of the city. The categorisation of indicators helps planners and policymakers to concentrate on what needs to improve immediately and what needs to be monitored.

12.5 DISCUSSION

This section is divided into two parts: recommendations and scope for further research. The first part deals with various initiatives in Kochi Corporation limits that can influence the performance of the transport sustainability. The second part discusses the route for further research that can refine similar studies.

The transport sustainability index for the Kochi corporation area is 0.564, which is close to the mean (0.5), so Kochi is neither low nor highly sustainable in the transport domain. The efficiency and safety sub-domains are the most poorly performing divisions as per the indicator scores calculated in the previous sections. Walkability index, congestion index, expenditure on transport, fatal accidents, and crime rate are some of the low-performing indicators in these sub-domains.

The low value of walkability and percentage share of the sustainable node shows that the non-motorized transport infrastructure of the city needs to be improved. The reduction of traffic speed and volume is a prerequisite to steer the focus of urban planning on cars back to people. Researchers underline the importance of low traffic volume and speed in determining which mode of transport people will choose, will they prefer walking/cycling, and how comfortable and safe they feel to let their kids walk to school (Cities 2019). Cities also need to create aesthetic, safe, connected, and continuous pedestrian footpaths and cycle tracks that are viable alternatives to using private vehicles.

Congestion, accidents, and percentage expenditure on transport shows the incapability of the road system to satisfy the motor vehicle users and offer safety to both pedestrians and motor vehicle users. Many cities like Singapore, Stockholm, and London have introduced congestion charging to disincentivising car use in urban areas. Studies point at the inverse relation of road network to traffic congestion, i.e., the more roads we build, the more congestion we get. Reducing road capacity at the same time providing alternative safe and efficient public transport system can help improve the road transport system (Cities, 2019).

The presence of vast areas of wetland surrounding the city ensure air quality in the city. The wetlands act as a natural means to treat the polluted water but the wetlands can filter only so much. These wetlands have to be protected and can be potentially associated with tourism activities. The Kochi Corporation area has a good road network coverage and transit service coverage that ensures accessibility to all parts of the city.

12.5.1 Recommendations

The transport infrastructure of the city of Kochi needs immediate attention on sustainable modes of transport and inclusivity in infrastructure provision for the old and disabled. The Unified Mobility and Transport Authority (UMTA) for Kochi can adapt to meet these needs from the global examples of cities like Curitiba. The single-fare system and bus tube system will enhance the inclusivity and reduce the expenditure on transportation. Scientific and systematic road infrastructure are also key elements in improving the transport infrastructure.

The city of Kochi is performing low on the percentage share of sustainable mode, expenditure on travel, etc. The city already has a proposal for a non-motorised transit plan, the implementation of which is expected to meet last-mile connectivity and increase the sustainable mode of transport. Kochi offers multi-modal transit facilities (rail, air, water, and road); the proposal for water metro by Kochi Metro Rail Ltd. is another initiative for sustainable transport in the city. Once these projects are on the run, the sustainability of the transport domain will increase drastically. The Unified Mobility and Transport Authority for Kochi is looking at integrating all forms of transport and to come up with a more sustainable transport infrastructure.

12.5.2 Scope for Further Research

This study laid out an indicator framework for the study area, where the list of indicators was selected considering data availability, relevance and redundancy, and screening through expert opinion. For practical purposes, the indicator selection process should include one more screening for the addition and omission of indicators through elaborate stakeholder discussions. A participatory approach in the selection process, involving citizens, governmental agencies, planners, experts, NGOs, and CSOs can help to prepare the most precise list relevant for the local context. This can also help to weigh the indicators based on the local demands.

12.6 CONCLUSION

This study assessed the transport sustainability of the study area using the benchmarking method. An indicator-based framework was found to be the most useful method to continuously monitor and update the data ecosystem needed for the assessment. The process of selection of indicators involved two rounds of screening and one expert opinion survey. The holistic list of indicators (Indicator list 1-367 indicators) was prepared by compiling works of previous literatures. The second round of screening was done based on relevance, data availability, and redundancy (Indicator list 2-67 indicators). Finally, the study screened a list of 27 indicators most relevant that can assess the transport sustainability of a city, through expert opinion. The data collection for indicators was done through primary and secondary sources. Normalization was done for the indicators by benchmarking and the scaling technique. This study benchmarks indicators on a five-point scale, where 1 corresponds to low (extremely unsustainable), 2 for medium-low (not suitable but not as bad as previous), 3 for medium (discrete level of sustainability), 4 stands for medium-high (satisfactory level of sustainability), and score 5 corresponds to high (target level of sustainability) on the SPSS Platform. The indicator scores were given by benchmarking indicator values based on service-level benchmarks issued by MoUD and literature reviews. The composite indicator score was then calculated by giving equal weight for all the indicators. The composite indicator score for the study area was found to be 3.182 and, based on the benchmarks, the city fell in the medium discrete level of sustainability category.

The score revealed the need to formulate more action plans and policies to enhance the sustainability of the existing transport infrastructure of Kochi. The individual indicator scores helped to assess the performance of each indicator in the city. The analysis of indicators disclosed the city might not be as pedestrian-friendly as the scores for the percentage share of the sustainable mode of transport (cycling + walking) and walkability index were low. The scores of indicators like congestion index, accidents, and percentage share on transport let out the inadequacy of the existing road transport system in the study area. Concurrently, accessibility indicators and some mobility indicators have high indicator scores, and this indicates that the transport system has efficient coverage within the city.

Calming traffic and improving the capacity can be done by providing a safe, comfortable, and economical public transportation system. Many cities follow a two-step procedure in redefining the transport system: (i) providing connection and (ii) refining quality. In the case of Kochi, indicators show the efficient coverage of road networks, so the city has to focus on refining the quality. Transport planning has to start at the smallest level and be integrated to higher levels to achieve holistic system improvement.

The sustainability of the transport domain is adversely affected by poor land use and urban planning, haphazard growth of settlements, high population and population density, growing income, and increasing travel demand of the residents. This study methodology is a useful guide for policymakers and urban planners to create a tailor-made indicator framework for any city.

ACKNOWLEDGMENTS

The authors wish to thank faculties in the Department of Architecture and Planning at the National Institute of Technology Calicut, India for their valuable inputs. The authors would also like to express gratitude to the Ministry of Education, Government of India, for the necessary financial support during the course work as scholarship. The critical comments of the unknown reviewers are also highly regarded, which have helped improve the manuscript to a great extent.The authors declare that they have no known competing financial interests or personal relationships that could have appeared to influence the work reported in this paper.

NOTES

1 Beacon NSF identifies critical factors of neighborhood life influenced by the built environment and provides a way of quantifying the sustainability of both newly planned neighborhoods and existing neighborhoods considering the social, economic, and environmental aspects of those neighborhoods (Saville-smith, Dwyer, and Warren 2009).

2 −ve shows a lesser value of the indicator the more sustainable it becomes.

3 +ve shows the higher the indicator value, the more sustainable it becomes.

REFERENCES

Anew Zeenab, Parking Space in Kochi: Issues and Solutions, November 2010, 1–40, Centre for Public Policy Research.

Aayog NITI. 2019. United Nations, www.niti.gov.in. SDG India Dashboard 2019-20xx

Badassa, Bayissa Badada, Baiqing Sun, and Lixin Qiao. 2020. "Sustainable Transport Infrastructure and Economic Returns: A Bibliometric and Visualization Analysis." *Sustainability (Switzerland)* 12 (5): 1–24. 10.3390/su12052033.

Bahadure, Sarika, and Rajashree Kotharkar. 2018. "Framework for Measuring Sustainability of Neighbourhoods in Nagpur, India." *Building and Environment* 127 (October 2017): 86–97. 10.1016/j.buildenv.2017.10.034.

Bahadure Pankaj. Compact City Concept: It's Relevance and Applicability for Planning of Indian Cities, PLEA2012 - 28th Conference, Opportunities, Limits & Needs Towards an environmentally responsible architecture Lima, Perú Peru, November 2012, https://www.researchgate.net/publication/265915492_Compact_City_Concept_It's_Relevance_and_Applicability_for_Planning_of_Indian_Cities

Bahadure, Pankaj, Rajashree, Kotharkar, and Neha, Sarda. 2014. "Measuring Compact Urban Form: A Case of Nagpur City, India." *Sustainability (Switzerland)* 6 (7): 4246–72. 10.3390/su6074246.

Carraro, Carlo, Caterina Cruciani, Silvio Giove, and Elisa Lanzi. 2009. "Aggregation and Projection of Sustainability Indicators: A New Approach." *Methodology*, no. October: 1–11. http://www.oecdworldforum2009.org.

Chaudhary, Nikhil (Climate Action Implementation Facility), and Lah, Oliver (Wuppertal Institute). 2018. "Scoping Paper Scoping Paper Kochi - India."

Cities, Natural Walking. 2019. "How to Create Walking Friendly Cities." 2019. http://naturalwalkingcities.com/how-to-make-cities-walking-friendly/

Cohen, Matthew. 2017. "A Systematic Review of Urban Sustainability Assessment Literature." *Sustainability (Switzerland)* 9 (11): 1–16. 10.3390/su9112048.

Department of Town and Country Planning. 2017. "Development Plan Kochi City Region 2031 (Draft)." *Development.*

Dizdaroglu, Didem. 2017. "The Role of Indicator-Based Sustainability Assessment in Policy and the Decision-Making Process: A Review and Outlook." *Sustainability (Switzerland)* 9 (6). 10.3390/su9061018.

Dobranskyte-Niskota, A., A. Perujo, J. Jesinghaus, and P. Jensen. 2009. *Indicators to Assess Sustainability of Transport Activities Part 2: Measurement and Evaluation of Transport Sustainability Performance in the EU27. JRCScientific and Technical Research Reports.* 10.2788/46618.

Dur Fatih. 2014."A Spatial-Indexing Model for Measuring Neighbourhood-Level Land-Use and Transport Integration." *Environment and Planning B: Planning and Design*792–812.

Gan Xiaoyu. 2017. "When to use what: Methods for weighting and aggregating sustainability indicators." *Ecological Indicators* 81: 491–502.

Ge, Mengpin, and Shiying, Wang. 2019. *Everything You Need to Know About the Fastest-Growing Source of Global Emissions: Transport.* World Resources Institute.

Garau, Chiara, and Valentina Maria Pavan. 2018. "Evaluating Urban Quality: Indicators and Assessment Tools for Smart Sustainable Cities." *Sustainability (Switzerland)*10 (3):575. doi:10.3390/su10030575.

Hiroaki, Suzuki, Robert, Cervero, and Kanako, Luchi. Introduction: Critical Challenges Facing Cities and Urban Transport, Transforming Cities with Transit, 1, ISBN: 978-0-8213-9745-9 World Bank, 2013, 25–48.

Huang, Runjie, Anna Grigolon, Mafalda Madureira, and Mark Brussel. 2018. "Measuring Transit-Oriented Development (TOD) Network Complementarity Based on Tod Node Typology." *Journal of Transport and Land Use* 11 (1): 304–24. 10.5198/jtlu.2018.1110.

Jose Dennis. 2018. Integrated Transit System- Case of Kochi, Urban Mobility India Conference.

Jose, Cladia. 2020. Thesis Report, "Report on Transportation Sustainability Assessment of an Urban Area Using Indicator Based Method."

Krishnan, Sruthi, and Firoz Mohammed 2020. "Regional Urban Environmental Quality Assessment and Spatial Analysis." *Journal of Urban Management* 9 (2): 191–204. 10.1016/j.jum.2020.03.001.

Litman, Todd, and Todd Alexander Litman. 2007. "Well Measured Developing Indicators for Comprehensive and Sustainable Transport Planning 4 February 2008." http://courses.washington.edu/cee587/Readings/sustainability.pdf

Ministry of Housing and Urban Affairs. 2013. "SLB in Urban Transport- Phase 2 Cities."

Patrick Martin. Consumption and Saving Patterns in the Households of an Urban setting: A special reference to Fishermen Community, *Working Paper Series CPPR*, 2015, Centre for Public Policy Research.

Pucher, John, Nisha Korattyswaropam, Neha Mittal, and Neenu Ittyerah 2005. "Urban Transport Crisis in India." *Transport Policy* 12 (May): 185–98. 10.1016/j.tranpol.2005.02.008.

Pucher John, Nisha Korattyswaropam, and Neenu Ittyerah 2005. "Urban transport crisis in India." *Transport Policy* 12(3).https://doi.org/10.1016/j.tranpol.2005.02.008.

Ramachandra T. V. 2009. "Emissions from India's transport sector: Statewise synthesis." *Atmospheric Environment.*

Reddy, B. Sudhakara, P. Balachandra, B. Sudhakara Reddy, and P. Balachandra 2013. "Benchmarking Urban Sustainability - Mumbai," no. August. http://www.igidr.ac.in/pdf/publication/WP-2013-008.pdf

Shenbagaraj, N., M. Naresh Kumar, and J. Leo Stalin. 2019. "Assessment of Urban Growth Using Shannon's Entropy Index: A Case Study of Chennai, Detroit of India." *Journal of Applied and Natural Science* 11 (2): 281–4. 10.31018/jans.v11i2.2037.

S. Greeshma. 2020. "Parking Study in M G Road, Kochi." *International Journal of Science, Engineering and Management* 5(4): 108–114.

Saville-Smith, Kay, Moira Dwyer, and Julie Warren 2009. "Valuing Sustainable Neighbourhoods." Wellington, New Zealand. "Valuing Sustainable Neighbourhoods."

Tanguay Georges A. 2009. "Measuring the Sustainability of Cities: A Survey-Based Analysis of the Use of Local Indicators." *Ecological Indicators* 10(2): 407–418.

Wang, Xiao-Jun 2009. "Analysis of Problems in Urban Green Space System Planning in China." *Journal of Forestry Research* 20 (1): 79–82. 10.1007/s11676-009-0014-2

Xavier Jithin. 2017. Kochi Corporation, Walkability Study Kochi, Walkability and Pedestrian Facilities in Kochi 2016–2017.

Yigitcanlar, Tan. 2015. "Measuring and Evaluating Sustainability: Ethics in Sustainability Indexes." *Australian Planner* 52(3): 247–249.

Yigitcanlar Tan. 2007. "A GIS-based land use and public transport accessibility indexing model." *Australian Planner* 44(3): 30–37.

"12 Indian Cities: Transport Indicators." 2010. *EMBARQ – The World Resources Institute Center for Sustainable Transportation*, 15.

13 The Relation between Urban Physical Indicators and Solar Irradiation Availability on Building Envelopes: Using Tehran as a Case Study

Mahshid Ghorbanian and Zahra Chehreghan
Iran University of Science & Technology (IUST), Tehran, Iran

CONTENTS

13.1 INTRODUCTION

Today, large populations live in cities, especially metropolitan areas such as Tehran, growing faster than ever. The energy supply of this population has created numerous environmental challenges for Tehran.

How can urban planning help control the environmental challenges of energy consumption and production in metropolises like Tehran? With the view that urban areas are not a problem, they are the solution.

Today, Tehran's city should be viewed not only as an energy consumer but as an energy producer. Solar energy is an important source of renewable energy, and Tehran has an abundance of it, so it is well suited to harness it. Buildings are one of the biggest energy consumers in Tehran and what is happening in this area is critical in establishing the sustainability of energy usage. The role of urban planners here is crucial. They can optimize energy production in buildings through a range of planning and policies such as urban form planning and selection of urban physical indicators, building codes, and zoning.

13.2 LITERATURE REVIEW

Many studies have specifically focused on how urban form affects solar energy potential.

DOI: 10.1201/9781003126195-16

In 1997, Project ZED examined key indicators of urban form concerning their environmental performance. Based on the results obtained from this project, the processes of radiation exchange and ventilation show a good correlation with urban form indicators. Also, the increase in solar energy absorption in the cities is strongly associated with the volume to surface ratio (Steemers and Nikolopoulou 1998). Based on the project ZED experience, the PRECis project examined the influence of urban form on buildings' energy efficiency aiming to evaluate the capacity for renewable energy production in cities. This project's main focus was to study the effect of geometry, orientation, and layout of buildings on the capacity of renewable energy in urban areas (Compagnon 2004). The SOLURBAN project aimed to harness daylight and sunlight to reduce the demand for light and heat and convert solar radiation into energy and heat. This study evaluated the building's solar energy absorption in three cities of Switzerland (Basel, Geneva, and Lausanne) for different levels of density. Based on comparisons of these three cases, it was found that the solar potential of buildings increases with urban density (Montavon et al. 2005). In a research program on sustainable urban design for Sao Paulo, Brazil, Cheng et al. examined how to maximize plot ratio and the usable floor area without compromising daylight and solar absorption. This study's urban physical indicators included the vertical and horizontal obstruction, site coverage, plot ratio, and the sky view factor (Cheng, Steemers, and Montavon et al. 2006a). They advanced this discussion through holistic analysis of the interactions between solar potential, urban form, and density. This study illustrated the varying impacts of vertical and horizontal randomness on urban solar potential, as well as the relationship between randomness, site coverage, and plot ratio, which could be helpful for renewable energy city planning. (V. Cheng, K. Steemers, and M. Montavon, et al. 2006b). To help architects and urban planners, Kanters et al. analyze solar energy's potential in Swedish urban blocks. Based on the results, the design of the city blocks has a great impact on the amount of solar energy produced (up to 50%). Moreover, the study shows that direct solar energy contributions are considerable even in urban environments. However, shade from adjacent buildings may greatly restrict the amount of energy generated (Kanters, Wall and Duboisa 2014). In 2015, Sarradel et al. examined the relationship between urban morphology and solar energy potential. They examined different urban morphology scenarios in London and tested urban form indicators to increase solar energy utilization. Based on the results of this study, an optimal selection of eight urban form indicators could improve roof solar absorptivity by 9% and facade solar absorptivity by up to 45% (Sarralde et al. 2015). Chatzipoulka et al. examined the relation between urban geometry and building facade solar absorptivity. Based on an investigation of London's 24 urban forms, this study examined a large variety of built density levels within the city. urban physical indicators used in this study included urban density, site coverage, mean building height, the standard deviation of building height, and the standard deviation of building footprint area (Chatzipoulka, Compagnon and Nikolopoulou 2016). Mohajeri et al. explored how urban compactness correlates with solar potential in the 16 neighborhoods of Geneva (Switzerland). Additionally, they introduced a novel parameter, urban entropy, as a measure of building dispersion (Mohajeri et al. 2016). Lee et al. developed a method for assessing solar potential at the urban level. Simulation programs were also used to study the relationship between housing density and urban design. As a result of this research, solar access, which is the amount of solar radiation reaching a building's facade and roof, correlates with housing density. Density-related indicators used in this study included: height, plot ratio, site coverage, typology, and layout of buildings (Lee, Lee, and Lee 2016). Martins et al. tried to determine the most important urban morphological variables for optimizing solar performance in the tropical environment of Brazil. Among all the studied indicators, the aspect ratio, the albedo, and the distance between buildings were the most effective indicators. These three factors may contribute to about 80% of the total influence on a building's solar potential (Martins et al. 2016). Morganti et al. sought to find a collection of urban morphology variables that demonstrate the most significant connections with the solar availability on facades in the Mediterranean climate. The results suggested that facade-to-site ratio, gross space index, and sky factor are highly correlated with solar absorptivity on facades. These results are useful for developing a comprehensive evaluation method of solar efficiency in the urban area (Morganti et al. 2017). In a study in 10 urban areas of Yazd, Aghamolaei et al. evaluated the relationship between solar gain and morphological characteristics of districts in the context of Iran. Based on this study's results, the height of buildings, site coverage, and street width all significantly influence solar gain, with building height contributing the most (Aghamolaei et al. 2018). According to research conducted in Norway, the effect of urban form characteristics and building materials was examined to optimize solar gain in residential areas. The results show that aspect ratio and plot ratio and the shape of buildings significantly affect different components of solar radiation (Lobaccaro et al. 2017). Curreli and colleagues sought to define a method for practical measures to improve urban settlements by analyzing the connection between solar potential and urban morphology. Based on this study, it can be concluded that urban morphological features further affect vertical surfaces' solar potential (Curreli et al. 2016). In their study, Li et al. investigated the potential of solar energy in urban residential buildings based on their density (Li, Liu, and Liao 2015). In a study in Osaka, Japan, the potential for solar energy was assessed on the basis of the connection between solar absorptivity of building roofs and wall surfaces and urban form. Specifically, in this study, the focus was on the effect of shading adjacent buildings on solar energy availability (Takebayashi et al. 2015). Sanaieian et al. provided a research review on the effects of urban form on the environmental performances of buildings and their surroundings. In the part of this study, the effect of urban form on solar access was investigated and based on that, solar neighborhood designs depend on three major points: building orientation, density, and street pattern (Sanaieian et al. 2014). In a study, seven common urban forms in Slovenia were studied in relation to receiving solar energy. According to this study's results, building orientation and the urban layout had the greatest influence on solar energy availability (Kosir et al. 2014). In a Swedish study, the correlation between urban form and solar potential of buildings was investigated. The results showed that by considering solar energy in the process of planning the built environment, it is possible to significantly improve the production of renewable energy on a local scale (Kanters and Horvat 2012). Poon et al., in a study in Singapore, examined the correlation between building solar energy potential and urban morphology. Morphological parameters used in this study included: building orientation, building geometry, average building height, volume area ratio, height to width ratio, site coverage, plot ratio, degree of randomness, compacity, difference between max and min building height, sky view factor, and sky exposure factor (Poon et al. 2020). Zhu et al. explored the correlation of the morphology and solar irradiation gain of dense areas in the dense tropical city, Shanghai. This research introduced two new urban morphology variables, SSU400 and SSU600, which represent the solar energy gain of the building envelopes (Zhu et al. 2020). Shi et al. established a new parametric technique based on local block typologies to examine the relationships between solar energy utilization and urban design. Block typologies consist of a variety of combinations of block dimensions, building patterns, floor area ratio, and site coverage. Singapore's high-density areas are used as a case study to illustrate the method. They discovered that the floor area ratio is the most important factor, followed by site coverage and building pattern (Shi, Fonseca, and Schlueter 2021). According to a study in urban residential blocks in Hangzhou, China, variation in urban block morphology significantly impacts residential urban blocks' solar radiation access. In their study, the plot ratio was found to have an important effect on solar radiation access to urban residential blocks (Pearson correlation –.896) (Xia and Li 2021). Xu et al. provided a technique to measure the problem of block obstruction in solar energy use. Occlusion coefficients are weak for industrial-type blocks (0.01), middle for middle- and high-rise residential areas (0.04), and high (0.34) for commercial types (Xu et al. 2020).

13.3 CONCEPTUAL MODEL

In this part of the research, after reviewing specific literature, the study's conceptual model is represented, which shows the relationship between the research variables (Figure 13.1).

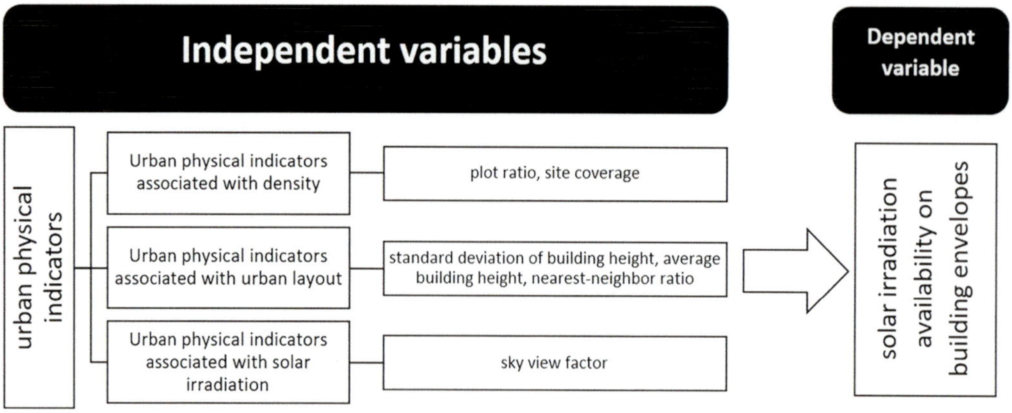

FIGURE 13.1 Conceptual model of the study.

The indicators are explained as follows: plot ratio is the total floor area in a neighborhood divided by the total area. Site coverage is the total built area in a neighborhood divided by the total area. The nearest-neighbor ratio is the average distance between buildings from centroids normalized by the total area of a neighborhood. If the ratio is less than 1, the building configuration indicates clustering; if the ratio is greater than 1, the configuration is more uniformly distributed. The sky view factor is a measure of the openness of a surface; a SVF of 1 means an unobstructed view of the sky, and a SVF of 0 means a completely obstructed view of the sky. One of the most important urban physical variables affecting the availability of solar energy irradiation on building envelopes is urban density. Indicators selected for this variable include plot ratio and site coverage. According to research done in denser built environments due to adjacent buildings' shadowing, solar irradiation on building envelopes decreases. One of the variables selected in the conceptual framework of this research is urban layout. The vertical and horizontal layout of buildings are two influential aspects of urban layout. Selected indicators of this variable include mean building height and standard deviation of building height, representing the vertical layout of buildings, and nearest neighbor ratio, representing the horizontal layout of buildings. The sky view factor is included here, even though it is not an urban form indicator since it directly affects the availability of sunlight on building envelopes.

13.4 DATA AND METHODS

Despite the fact that the methodologies presented and extended in this research are totally universal and applicable to various urban regions, all of the data used and analyzed in this paper is from Tehran, Iran. Considering the objective of this study, that is, to investigate the impact of urban physical indicators on solar irradiation availability on building envelopes, urban forms in Tehran were chosen that show diversity in terms of these indicators to enable evaluation of this effect. On the basis of urban layout (vertical and horizontal) and site coverage, selected urban forms were divided into 16 categories (Table 13.1). The research study adheres to a set of procedures (Figure 13.2).

1. Firstly, for morphological analysis, the selected urban physical indicators are investigated in the 16 urban forms in Tehran by using Arc Map and Excel software.
2. In this research, the hourly solar irradiation on each building surface over a one-year period is calculated using CitySim Pro simulations. CitySim Pro needs two main pieces of information in order to compose the simulation: weather data and geometric data. Several tools are available for evaluating the climate characteristics of a specific location in the world, as requested by CitySim. Among them is Meteonorm, which is used in this study.

TABLE 13.1
Introduction of the Case Study Area

Case	Urban Layout (Horizontal, Vertical)	Site Coverage
1	Uniform, Uniform	> 30
2		
3	Uniform, Uniform	< 30
4		
5		
6	Random, Random	> 30
7		
8		
9	Random, Random	< 30
10		
11	Random, Uniform	> 30
12	Random, Uniform	< 30
13		
14		
15	Random, Random	> 30
16	Random, Random	< 30

(*Source:* By Authors).

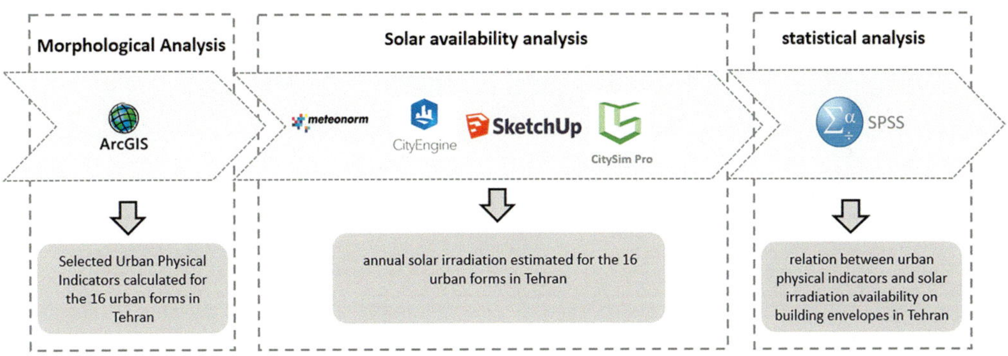

FIGURE 13.2 This figure represents the overall methodology of this study.

Then, CityEngine and Sketchup software were used to simulate 3D and prepare buildings in the area for solar simulation.

3. In this study, multiple linear regression (least-square) models in SPSS software were used to evaluate how urban physical indicators affect solar irradiation availability on building envelopes.

13.5 MORPHOLOGICAL ANALYSIS

In this study, for morphological analysis, spatial information was collected in shapefile format. Then, using ArcMap and Excel software, analytical maps and graphs were produced (Table 13.2; Figure 13.3).

TABLE 13.2
Urban Physical Indicators of the Case Study

ID	Plot Ratio	Site Coverage	Standard Deviation of Building Height	Average Building Height	Nearest-Neighbor Ratio	Sky View Factor
1	191.38	63.79	0	9	1.22	0.55
2	318.97	63.79	0	15	1.22	0.43
3	156.1	31.22	0	15	1.25	0.53
4	192.4	19.66	2.66	28.62	1.13	0.46
5	286.77	20.48	0	42	1.48	0.39
6	57.08	52.44	1.65	3.26	1.40	0.63
7	163.87	42.92	3.69	10.64	1.04	0.52
8	201.89	47.59	7.67	12.35	1.03	0.50
9	288.54	11.51	12.99	75	1.33	0.43
10	291.7	17.82	15.34	53.4	1.94	0.50
11	52.44	52.44	0	3	1.40	0.65
12	70.91	14.18	0	15	1.40	0.53
13	138.19	11.51	0	36	1.33	0.50
14	287.9	11.51	0	75	1.33	0.43
15	201.44	63.79	3.64	9.06	1.22	0.52
16	163.12	17.51	8.36	27.56	0.94	0.50

Source: Authors.

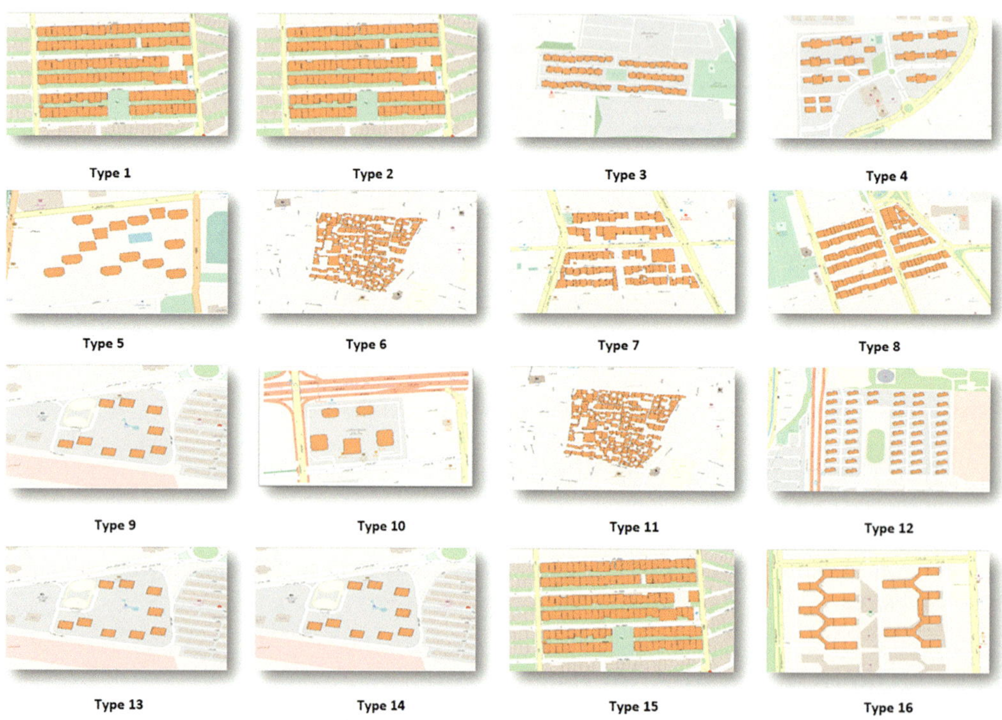

FIGURE 13.3 Building map of the 16 urban forms in Tehran in ArcMap.

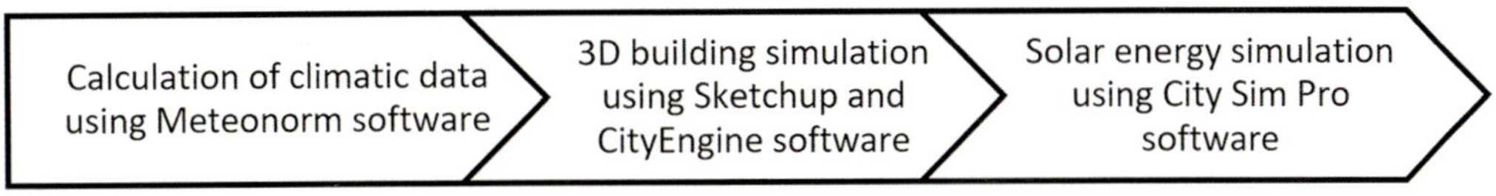

FIGURE 13.4 The figure representing the solar availability analysis of this research.

13.6 SOLAR AVAILABILITY ANALYSIS

In this research, solar availability analysis follows a systematic set of procedures (Figure 13.4). The hourly solar irradiation on each of the building surfaces over a one-year period is calculated using CitySim Pro simulations (Table 13.3) (Figure 13.7). CitySim Pro needs two main pieces of information in order to compose the simulation scene properly. The very first one is represented by the analyzed location weather data and the second one is the geometric information of the buildings you want to simulate.

Location information are composed by some weather information, like the solar irradiance or the wind speed and direction. These kind of data are all collected in a.cli file that must be given as an input to the CitySim Pro GUI. Together with the.cli file, another starting input data is represented by the horizon information. These data are collected in the.hor file and they give to the software the shape of the horizon, according to the direction of our simulation scene (Figure 13.5). Then, CityEngine and Sketchup software were used to simulate 3D and prepare buildings in the area for solar simulation. There are several tools that are able to evaluate the climate and horizon characteristics of a specific location in the world. One among them is Meteonorn, widely used in this industry since it is able to provide hourly data, as requested by CitySim (Figure 13.6).

TABLE 13.3
Annual Solar Irradiation, kWh m2 Estimated Using CitySim for 16 Urban Forms in the City of Tehran

Case	Annual Solar Radiations kWh/m^2
1	941.64
2	752.37
3	921.83
4	869.46
5	779.57
6	1135.13
7	928.06
8	900.2
9	869.96
10	929.69
11	1159.7
12	1023.32
13	976.57
14	856.72
15	922.1
16	934.33

Source: Authors.

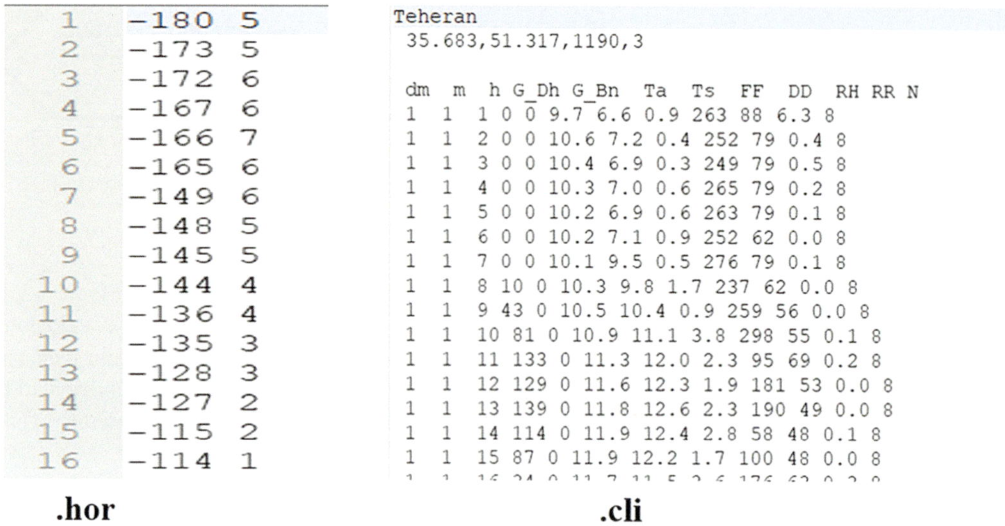

FIGURE 13.5 Meteonorm weather file.

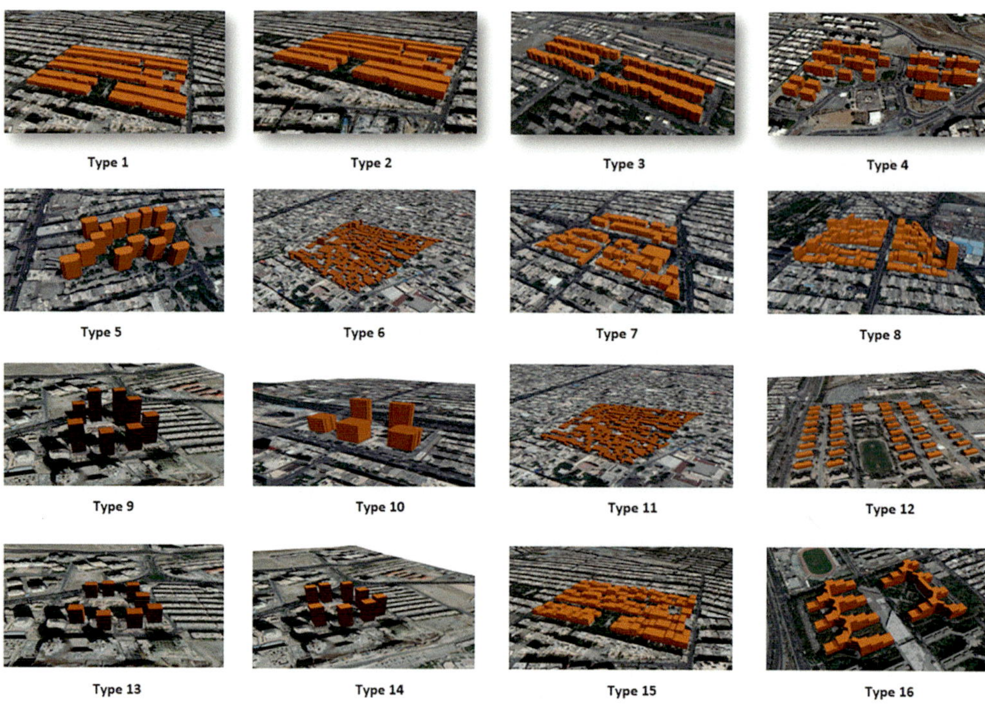

FIGURE 13.6 Simulate 3D of the 16 urban forms in Tehran.

13.7 RESULTS AND DISCUSSION

We compared the six indicators, namely plot ratio, average building height, sky view factor, site coverage, nearest-neighbor ratio, and standard deviation of building height with the annual solar irradiation received by the 16 urban forms in Tehran. We use multiple linear regression (least-square) models in SPSS software to evaluate how urban physical indicators affect solar irradiation

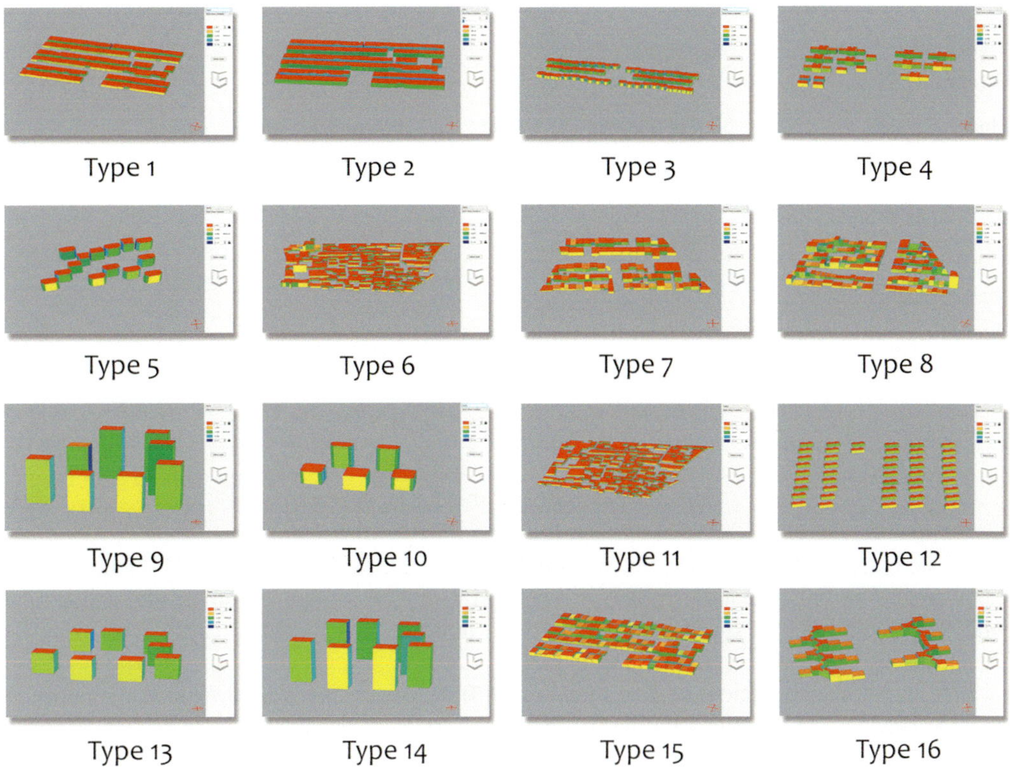

FIGURE 13.7 Annual solar irradiation, kWh m^2 estimated using City Sim for 16 urban forms in the city of Tehran.

availability on building envelopes. Its standard beta coefficient signifies the strength of each independent variable's effect (Table 13.4).

To test whether the presented regression relationship between response (dependent) and predictor (independent) variables is significant, the regression model is defined as below:

$$y_i = \beta_0 + \beta_1 X_1 + \beta_2 X_2 + \cdots + \beta_{\alpha-1} X_{\alpha-1} + \varepsilon_i \tag{13.1}$$

In order to conduct such an analysis, it is necessary to define the assumption that is to be examined: the null hypothesis, H0, and the alternative hypothesis, H1. The null hypothesis is that all coefficients' independent variables are zero. The alternative is that at least one of these coefficients is not zero.

TABLE 13.4
Variables Entered/Removed in SPSS

Model	Variables Entered	Variables Removed	Method
1	sky view factor, nearest neighbor ratio, STD._height, site coverage, average height, plot ratio		Enter

Source: Authors.

TABLE 13.5
F-tests in SPSS

Model		Sum of Squares	df	Mean Square	F	Sig.
1	Regression	172587.253	6	28764.542	235.209	.000[b]
	Residual	1100.641	9	122.293		
	Total	173687.893	15			

Source: Authors.

$$H_0\text{: } \beta_1 = \beta_2 = \cdots = \beta_{\alpha-1} = 0 \quad (13.2)$$

$$H_1\text{: At least one of the } \beta\text{s is not zero} \quad (13.3)$$

The F-statistic, which is the test statistic for F-tests, is 235.2. Due to the test P-value, which is 0.000 and below 0.05, the null hypothesis is refuted with 95% confidence, so the alternative model with 95% confidence is significant. As the data indicate, this model is capable of expressing changes in the dependent variable (Table 13.5).

Here, using the coefficient of determination of 0.99, we can say that 0.99% of the dependent variable changes are explained by the independent variables (Table 13.6).

In order to determine whether the independent variables are necessary for the model, or in other words, to examine the significance of the coefficients of the independent variables, we test the null hypothesis versus the alternative hypothesis.

$$H_0\text{: } \beta_k = 0 \quad (13.4)$$

$$H_1\text{: } \beta_k \neq 0 \quad (13.5)$$

The test statistic of the model is the t-statistic. If the P-value (indicated by the software SPSS with Sig) is below 0.05, the null hypothesis is refuted with 95% confidence, meaning that the variable remains in the model, and if it is greater than 0.05, it can be concluded with 95% confidence that there is no need for that variable in the model.

Given the P-value obtained from the SPSS, all the selected variables remain in the model, with a 95% confidence that the null hypothesis for these variables in the model can be rejected (Table 13.7).

TABLE 13.6
Model Summary in SPSS

Model	R	R Square	Adjusted R Square	Std. Error of the Estimate
1	.997[a]	.994	.989	11.05863

Source: Authors.

Note

[a] Predictors: (Constant), sky view factor, nearest neighbor ratio, STD._height, site coverage, average height, plot ratio.

TABLE 13.7
Coefficients in SPSS

Model		Unstandardized Coefficients		Standardized Coefficients	t	Sig.
		B	Std. Error	Beta		
1	(Constant)	632.152	92.508		6.834	.000
	site coverage	1.530	.498	.295	3.070	.013
	plot ratio	−1.143	.176	−.917	−6.502	.000
	STD._height	2.327	.839	.108	2.773	.022
	nearest neighbor ratio	72.697	17.948	.155	4.050	.003
	average height	2.375	.375	.520	6.326	.000
	sky view factor	595.394	189.410	.385	3.143	.012

Source: Authors.
[a]Dependent Variable: annual solar irradiation.

Given the standardized β value in the coefficient table in SPSS, the effect of the variables on the dependent variable is as follows:

plot ratio, average building height, sky view factor, site coverage, nearest-neighbor ratio, standard deviation of building height.

13.8 CONCLUSION

This chapter examines the relation between several urban physical indicators and solar irradiation availability on building envelopes. For this purpose, 16 urban forms in Tehran (IRAN) are compared to 6 urban physical indicators, including plot ratio, average building height, sky view factor, site coverage, nearest-neighbor ratio, and standard deviation of building height with solar irradiation availability on building envelopes. These findings permit us to address the following questions:

a. Is there a correlation among urban physical indicators and solar irradiation availability on Tehran building envelopes?
   In response to this question, due to the test P-value, which is 0.000 and below 0.05, the null hypothesis is refuted with 95% confidence, so the alternative model with 95% confidence is significant. As the data indicate, this model is capable of expressing changes in the dependent variable.
   By testing this hypothesis, it was found that there is a significant relationship between urban physical indicators extracted from the research literature and solar radiation availability on Tehran building envelopes.
b. What are the most influential urban physical indicators on solar radiation availability on Tehran building envelopes?
   Based on a coefficient of determination of 0.99, the independent variables account for 99% of the changes in the dependent variable. The selected independent variables therefore strongly influence solar radiation availability on Tehran building envelopes.
c. Specifically in Tehran, in what order do urban physical indicators affect solar radiation availability on building envelopes? According to the standardized β value, independent variables influence the dependent variables in the following order: plot ratio, average building height, sky view factor, site coverage, nearest-neighbor ratio, standard deviation of building height.

The main findings are summarized as follows:

- In general, there was a negative relationship between the plot ratio and solar irradiation availability on building envelopes in Tehran, which means that the amount of solar radiation available on building envelopes declined as the plot ratio increased. As can be seen in the areas with the lowest plot ratio (Types 6, 11, 12), we obtain the most solar irradiation availability on building envelopes. However, for Types 5 and 9, although the plot ratio is almost equal in both, the solar irradiation availability on building envelopes is lower in the former, and that is because of higher site coverage in Type 5. So it can be concluded that with the same plot ratio, the lower site coverage causes higher solar absorption by the building envelopes. It is due to the reduction of shading of adjacent buildings.
- According to the results of this study, it has been observed in Tehran that when there is high site coverage, the availability of solar radiation on the building envelope increases with lower average building heights. As can be seen in Types 1, 2, 15, and 6, 15, the site coverage is high in all five ranges, but as the average building height rises in these ranges, we see a significant decrease in the solar irradiation availability on building envelopes. In cases with low site coverage, higher building heights will result in greater solar irradiation available to building envelopes, as seen in Types 13, 14.
- Generally, where the site coverage is low in Tehran, a larger standard deviation in height will result in higher solar absorption by the building envelopes, as seen in Types 9, 14. In cases where the site coverage is high, a lower standard deviation in height will result in higher solar absorption by the building envelope, as seen in Types 1, 2, and 6, 11.

In general, the higher the sky view factor in Tehran, the solar irradiation availability on building envelopes is higher.

13.9 LIMITATIONS AND FURTHER RESEARCH

Nevertheless, it is important to note that the findings given here are more appropriate to increase the solar energy absorption of building envelopes than to be used as a comprehensive strategy to improve neighborhood energy performance. In order to do that, many other factors need to be considered, such as different technologies for generating renewable energy and energy consumption strategies in different layers of a city.

In addition, it should be mentioned that although the use of statistical methods such as design of experiments is outside the area of this study, it can be one of the most important upcoming steps in improving the results of research in this field.

REFERENCES

Aghamolaei, Reihaneh, Mohammad Reza Ghaani, Mohammad Tahsildoost, and Majid Zandi. 2019. "A comprehensive energy-oriented approach for optimization of solar potential in urban contexts: an application study for residential districts." *Advances in Building Energy Research 13(2),* 205–219.

Chatzipoulka, Christina, Raphaël Compagnon, and Marialena Nikolopoulou 2016. "Urban geometry and solar availability on façades and ground of real urban forms: using London as a case study." *Solar Energy 138,* 53–66.

Cheng, Vicky, Koen Steemers, Marylène Montavon, and Raphaël Compagnon. 2006a. "Compact cities in a sustainable manner." *2nd International Solar Cities Congress,* Oxford, 3–6 April 2006.

Cheng, Vicky, Koen Steemers, Marylene Montavon, and Raphaël Compagnon. 2006b. "Urban Form, Density and Solar Potential." *The 23rd Conference on Passive and Low Energy Architecture.* Geneva, Switzerland, 6–8 September 2006.

Compagnon, Raphael. 2004. "Solar and daylight availability in urban areas." *Energy and Buildings* (Ecole d'ingénieurs et d'architectes de Fribourg) 36, 321–328.

Curreli, A., Glòria Serra-Coch, Antonio Isalgue, Isabel Crespo, and Helena Coch 2016. "Solar Energy as a Form Giver for Future Cities." *Energies* 9(7), 544.

Kanters, Jouri, and Miljana Horvat. 2012. "Solar Energy as a Design Parameter in Urban Planning." *Energy Procedia* 1143–1152.

Kanters, Jouri, Maria Wall, and Marie-Claude Duboisa 2014. "Typical values for active solar energy in urban planning." *Energy Procedia 48,* 1607–1616.

Kosir, Mitja, Isaac Guedi Capelutob, Ales Krainer, and Ziva Kristla. 2014. "Solar potential in existing urban layouts—Critical overview of the existing building stock in Slovenian context." *Energy Policy 69,* 443–456.

Lee, Kyung Sun, Jae Wook Lee, and Jae Seung Lee. 2016. "Feasibility study on the relation between housing density and solar accessibility and potential uses." *Renewable Energy 85,* 749–758.

Li, Dapeng, Gang Liu, and Shengming Liao. 2015. "Solar potential in urban residential buildings." *Solar Energy 111,* 225–235.

Lobaccaro, Gabriele, Salvatore Carlucci, Silvia Croce, Rossana Paparella, and Luca Finocchiaro 2017. "Boosting solar accessibility and potential of urban districts in the Nordic climate: A case study in Trondheim." *Solar Energy 149,* 347–369.

de Lemos Martinstins, Tathiane Agra, Luc Adolphe, Leopoldo Eurico Gonçalves Bastos, and Michele Agra de Lemos Martinstins. 2016. "Sensitivity analysis of urban morphology factors regarding solar energy potential of buildings in a Brazilian tropical context." *Solar Energy 137,* 11–24.

Mohajeri, Nahid, Govinda Upadhyay, Agust Gudmundsson, Dan Assouline, Jerome Kampf, and Jean-Louis Scartezzini 2016. "Effects of urban compactness on solar energy potential." *Renewable Energy* 469–482.

Montavon, Marylène, Darren Robinson, Jean-Louis Scartezzini, and R. Compagnon 2005. *Solurban Project, Solar Utilisation Potential of Urban Sites*. Bern: Swiss Federal Office for Energy.

Morganti, Michele, Agnese Salvati, Helena Coch, and Carlo Cecere 2017. "Urban morphology indicators for solar energy analysis." *Energy Procedia 134,* 807–814.

Poon, K.H., J.H. Kämpf, S.E.R. Tay, N.H. Wong, and T.G. Reindl. 2020. "Parametric study of URBAN morphology on building solar energy potential in Singapore context." *Urban Climate 33,* 100624.

Sanaieian, Haniyeh, Martin Tenpierik, Kees van den Linden, Fatemeh Mehdizadeh Seraj, and Seyed Majid Mofidi Shemrani. 2014. "Review of the impact of urban block form on thermal performance, solar access and ventilation." *Renewable and Sustainable Energy Reviews 38,* 551–560.

Sarralde, Juan Jose, David James Quinn, Daniel Wiesmann, and Koen Steemers. 2015. "Solar energy and urban morphology: Scenarios for increasing the renewable energy potential of neighbourhoods in London." *Renewable Energy 73,* 10–17.

Shi, Z., Jimeno A. Fonseca, and Arno Schlueter. 2021. "A parametric method using vernacular urban block typologies for investigating interactions between solar energy use and urban design." *Renewable Energy 165,* 823–841.

Steemers, Koen, and Marialena Nikolopoulou. 1998. "Assessing the Urban Microclimate: Introducing innovative modelling techniques." *Environmentally Friendly Cities: Proceedings of Plea 98,* 157–158.

Takebayashi, Hideki, Etsuko Ishii, Masakazu Moriyama, and Ai Sakaki. 2015. "Study to examine the potential for solar energy utilization based on the relationship between urban morphology and solar radiation gain on building rooftops and wall surfaces." *Solar Energy 119,* 362–369.

Xia, Bing, and Zhihao Li. 2021. "Optimized methods for morphological design of mesoscale cities based on performance analysis: Taking the residential urban blocks as examples." *Sustainable Cities and Society 64,* 102489.

Xu, S., Zhixin Li, Chen Zhang, Zhaojian Huang, Jia Tian, Yongqiang Luo, and Hu Du. 2021. "A method of calculating urban-scale solar potential by evaluating and quantifying the relationship between urban block typology and occlusion coefficient: A case study of Wuhan in Central China." *Sustainable Cities and Society 64, 102451.*

Zhu, Dan, Dexuan Song, Jie Shi, Jia Fang, and Yili Zhou. 2020. "The effect of morphology on solar potential of high-density residential area: A case study of Shanghai." *Energies 13(9),* 2215.

14 Urban Water Quality Index of the Commercial Capital City of Bangladesh

Prabal Barua
Jahangirnagar University, Dhaka, Bangladesh

CONTENTS

14.1 INTRODUCTION

The water quality is important because it not only accelerates the uses for daily household purposes, but also reduces the water crisis for urban dwellers. For the efficient water quality management through suitable organize actions, unremitting monitoring of the different important water quality components are essential. The water quality index (WQI) is one of the effectual utensils to communicate information on the quality of water to the concerned citizens and policy makers and it is a unitless, single dimensional number between 0 and 100 (Barua and Rahman, 2020).

Bangladesh is a developing city and one of the most dense population countries on Earth and the country has experienced speedy and poor management of urban development escorted by solemn environmental degradation. Because of the increased urban augmentation, however, the urban area is a veteran of the solemn degradation of environmental perspectives and a different level of ecological troubles (Hasan et al., 2013). Approximately 56% of the total land area had completely shifted due to the extension of the developed places and different human actions for more than 36 years for the urban city increased by the 618%, while the standard mean annual tempo of amplifying of 17.5% (Hassan 2013, Chatterji 2002). The second largest and most important city of Bangladesh is Chittagong metropolitan city according to the household number, area of the city, and community living condition (Rahman, 2012). According to world urbanization Prospective Report of 2018, Chittagong is the 40th urban agglomeration and 7th fast-growing city in the world. The busiest sea port of the country makes the city the main international business hub, as well as the commercial capital of the country (Barua and Rahman, 2021).

Urban water bodies (UWBs) recognized as a micro-morphological component of the urban aquatic bodies where the most indication of different categories of water bodies such as the river, canal, pond, *dighi*, *doba*, *khal*, lake, humid fallow land, and different classes of reservoirs existing in the urban areas (Francis, 2012). Generally, urban water bodies (UWBs) comprise various structures of the water sources such as step wells (*baoris*), storm water drains, trenches surrounding as old forts, and man-made aquatic environment such as ponds inside temples, mosques,

DOI: 10.1201/9781003126195-17

and other different community locations that are together, generally known as the "green architecture" of the urban city (CPHEEO, 2013). Yet, urban water bodies are at many times neglected, although they are used as alternate water sources for keeping the micro-climate saturated and also providing water for fire service, fishing, aquaculture, holding flood water, and so on. Besides, the urban supply water has become a critical condition and key community health issue in urban Bangladesh, particularly in addressing the quality and availability. In this situation, the urban poor directly or indirectly get their demanding water from this water body. The availability and extent of the pure and safe drinking water was a significant indicator of the No. 6 goal of sustainable development goals (SDGs). Chittagong Water Supply and Sewerage Authority (CWASA) are working for ensuring water supply and management for the 0.5 million inhabitants of the Chittagong city through 600 water street hydrants and also through a pipeline for 25,000 household connections. CWASA has the capability of supplying only 30% total demand (585 million litters, but fulfill 175 million liters waters per day; MLD in 2016) produced by more than 5 million people (CWASA, 2010), although the capacity of supplying has increased 38% in 2017 (CWASA, 2017).

There are 5 million inhabitants living on the 770 square kilometer Chittagong metropolitan city. The speedy expansion of urbanization, population, and industrialization created an incredible heaviness on land use changes in the urban city. Urban water bodies are in harsh intimidation: vanishing; changing of depth, shape, and size swiftly because of man-made and natural actions. The approach towards urban water bodies is shifting; besmirched approaches of modest concentration, but as more industrious ecosystems along with inherent values in their personal rights (Francis, 2012), that build noteworthy assistance to the local, regional, and national biodiversity as well as conservation actions. The function of the urban pond and other water sources in contributing significant modifiable and edifying ecosystem services is also progressively more predictable (Voelker and Kistemann, 2014).

Due to this situation, citizens have been distressed from the uneven, insufficient, and insecure water supplies mostly due to the incompetent management practices and this circumstance is inferior in low-earning residential places. In this circumstance, citizens especially from the lower-class income-generating group (urban poor: low income and slum people) directly used water from different urban water bodies, namely *dighis* and ponds for household consumption purposes and middle-class income-generating groups were practically using water from these water bodies (Rahman et al., 2011). So, the author presented a case study documentation in this book chapter on the condition of the water quality index (WQI) of Chittagong city urban water bodies (UWBs) regarding swap water points for the purpose of community consumption.

14.2 PROFILE OF THE COMMERCIAL CAPITAL CITY OF BANGLADESH

The study area of Chittagong city, which is a famous place as the commercial capital city of the nation, is located between 22°15′ and 22°25′ North latitudes and among the 91°45′ and 91°55′ East longitudes along the southeastern coast of Bangladesh, surrounded by the river Karnaphuli and its branch of the river Halda to the south and east, through the mighty Bay of Bengal to the west and north side is enriched with a continuous range of hilly area. Chittagong city has different industrial organizations that formed the 10 miles (16 km) to the north and northeast of the urban city. This commercial capital city is also recognized for large areas of commercial Bangladesh export processing zone and sister concern offices of various foreign banks and commercial offices (Uddin, 2016). There are more than 5 million people living in this urban city and and 0.5 million inhabitants receive water from the 600 water points that were developed and operated by the Chittagong Water Supply and Sewerage Authority (CWASA). Chittagong city consists of a narrow shred of the coastal area surrounded by the Bay of Bengal and a series of the low hills segmented by the productive valleys (Figure 14.1). The speedy increasing rate of population, commercialization, development, and urbanization process created an incredible heaviness on land use changes in the Chittagong city. Chittagong city is a veteran of a speedy decline in urban poverty in recent

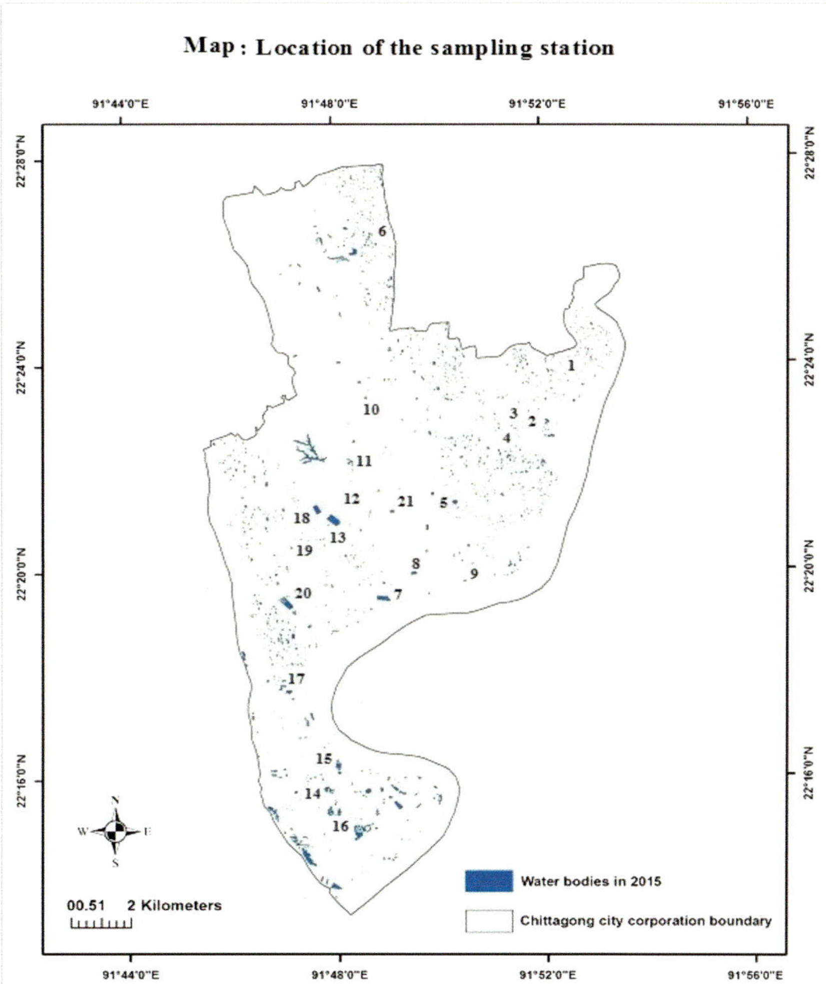

1. Master Colony Pond [Mohara ,**05**]
2. Baitul salat jame mosque Pond [Chandgaon, **04**]
3. Bahharhar Bari Pond [East Sholashahar, **06**]
4. Miar Baper Barir Pukur [Bakolia, **17**]
5. Munshi Pukur [Chawkbazar, **16**]
6. Fateabad Dighi [South Pahartali, **01**]
7. Asker Dighi [Jamalkhan, **21**]
8. Lal Dighi [Lal Dighi, **32**]
9. Kola-Bagisa Pond [Patharghata, **34**]
10. Olima Dighi [Jalalabad, **02**]
11. Baizid Bostami Pond [Jalalabad, **02**]
12. Sheer-Shah Dighi [Sulakbahar, **08**]
13. Agrabad Deba Dighi [Agrabad, **28**]
14. Korno Mohon Sheal Bari Pond [South Patenga, **41**]
15. Hindu Para Pond (Durga Bari) [South Patenga, **40**]
16. Raja Pond, South Patenga [South Patenga,**41**]
17. Boro Pukur or Pond (Hadu Serang Bari) [South-Middle Halishar, **34**]
18. Kazir Dighi (Sharaipara) [North Kattali, **10**]
19. Voluar Dighi [Sharaipara, **19**]
20. Jora Dighi [Sharaipara, **19**]
21. Aladi jumadar Wafkup state mosque Pond [Dampara, **14**]

FIGURE 14.1 Geographical location of the study area.

times that is expected at 15% in 2018 (Uddin, 2018). Inhabitants in slums and squatter communities settlement, where about one-fourth of this urban city's inhabitants live, are impacted the worst in terms of superiority and accessibility to different basic services and facilities. Furthermore, inhabitants countenance various categories of local environmental lumbers such as noise pollution, traffic congestion, air pollution, and surface water pollution. Conversely, Chittagong city is now under pressure to ensure housing and accommodation for their increasing populations and tackle the different dimensional challenges such as transportation, communication, and urban slump developments (Soyinka et al., 2016).

14.3 DATA AND METHODS

The author took 21 urban water bodies (UWBs) or surface water samples for water quality analysis. The profile of the selected water bodies will presented in Table 23.1. Water samples were collected two times on the basis of seasons from 2019–2020, respectively. Firstly, samples were collected from November to December (winter season) during 2019 and June to July (rainy season) of 2020 (Table 14.1).

The collected samples were analyzed by the Industrial Microbiological Research Division and Chemistry lab, Bangladesh Council of Scientific and Industrial Research, Chittagong (BCSIR, Chittagong). UWBs were selected on the basis of frequent uses, familiar with dwellers, permanent water retention ability, and water bodies in lower-class residential areas (because they directly used these water bodies for household purposes, especially bathing, cooking, dishwashing, ablution, cleaning, and somewhat drinking). Table 14.2 shows the parameters of water quality, analytical methods, and units utilized for determination of exterior water assessment in the Chittagong metropolitan city.

The water quality index (WQI) has been assessed by applying the drinking water quality standards that are suggested by the World Health Organization (WHO, 2014) and Bangladesh Standard Testing Institute (BSTI). The method of the weighted arithmetic index (Brown et al., 1991) has been utlized to find out the value of the WQI of the selected water bodies. Further, the water quality ranking or sub index (q_n) was assessed through utilizing the following expression:

$$q_n = \frac{100[V_n - V_{io}]}{[S_n - V_{io}]}$$

where

n= water quality components and quality ranking or sub-index, corresponding to n^{th} parameters is a number sparking the relative range of these components in the degraded water esteem to their standard acceptable concentration.

q_n = water quality ranking for the *nth* water quality parameter

V_n= probabled range of the *nth* parameter at a provided sampling station

S_n = typical allowable range of the *nth* parameter

V_{io} = perfect range of *nth* parameter in pure water

Idyllic concentration in most of the events Vio = 0 apart from the convinced components like pH and dissolved oxygen. The assessment of water quality rating for pH and DO (Vio ≠ 0) is 7.0 and 14.6 mg/l correspondingly. Unit weight was assessed through a range inversely comparative to the suggested standard ranges Sn of the corresponding components.

The standard value of the pH is 7.0 where 8.5 is the allowable range of water; therefore, pH quality is found from the following relation.

$$\mathbf{qpH = 100[(VpH - 7)/(8.5\text{–}7)]}$$

TABLE 14.1
An Introduction to Collection of Water Samples from Aquatic Water Bodies of Chittagong

Sampling Station	Local Name of Sampling Ponds	Ward No: Ward Name	Geographical Location	Area (sq. ft.)	Users (Apr.)	Using Purposes	Ownership	Pollution Status
S 1	Master Colony Pond	05: Mohara (Near the Rail station of Mohara)	22°23'46.1"N 91°52'26.7"E	400 X 400 sq. ft.	1,000	Bathing, clothing, washing dishes, and fishing	Personal	Households and entrance tidal water (Polythin)
S 2	Baitul salat jame mosque Pond	04:Chandgaon (West Faridapara, (Block-A)	22°22'24.8"N 91°50'43.5"E	200 X 150 sq. ft.	1,500	Ablution, commercial washing cloth shop, bathing, clothing, washing dishes, and fishing	Community	Household solid waste
S 3	Bahharhar Bari Pond	06:East Sholashahar	22°22'05.7"N 91°50'47.5"E	150 X 150 sq. ft.	1,300	Bathing, clothing, washing dishes, and fishing	Personal (Bahharhar Bari)	Household solid waste
S 4	Miar Baper Barir Pukur	17: Bakolia	22°21'09.1"N 91°50'27.3"E	90 X 90 sq. ft.	1,500	Bathing, clothing, washing dishes	Personal	Municipal drain emitting and housing waste (Polythin)
S 5	Munshi Pukur	16: Chawkbazar (Kapashgola)	22°21'43.4"N 91°50'22.7"E	120 X 80 sq. ft.	800	Bathing, clothing, washing dishes, and fishing	Community	Household waste
S 6	Fateabad Dighi	01:South Pahartali	22°26'51.4"N 91°49'08.5"E	8 acor	500	Ablution, bathing, clothing, washing dishes, and fishing	Community	Surface runoff
S 7	Asker Dighi	21: Jamalkhan	22°20'50.8"N 91°49'46.6"E	650 X 200 sq. ft.	2,500	Bathing, clothing, washing dishes, and fishing	Personal	Household waste and shop
S 8	Lal Dighi	32: Lal Dighi	22°20'16.6"N 91°50'16.7"E	120X 50 sq. ft.	1,000	Ablution (Beside Mosque) and fishing	Chittagong City Corporation	Summer season (algae bloom)
S 9	Kola-Bagisa Pond	34: Patharghata	22°19'47.0"N 91°50'28.4"E	250 X 200 sq. ft.	2,000	Bathing, clothing, washing dishes, and fishing	Community	Entering tidal water and household waste
S 10	Olima Dighi	02: Jalalabad	22°23'41.6"N 91°48'58.5"E	2.5 acor	1,500	Bathing, clothing, washing dishes, and fishing	Community	Household solid waste
S 11	Baizid Bostami Pond	02: Jalalabad (Baizid, Jalalabad)	22°23'21.1"N 91°48'36.4"E	3.5 acor	Useless	Holy place	Mazar Authority	End of the year (summer) water has been polluted
S 12	Sheer-Shah Dighi	08: Sulakbahar	22°22'52.3"N 91°48'50.4"E	120 X 8 sq. ft.	1,500	Bathing, Clothing, washing dishes and fishing	Community	Households waste

(Continued)

TABLE 14.1 (Continued)
An Introduction to Collection of Water Samples from Aquatic Water Bodies of Chittagong

Sampling Station	Local Name of Sampling Ponds	Ward No: Ward Name	Geographical Location	Area (sq. ft.)	Users (Apr.)	Using Purposes	Ownership	Pollution Status
S 13	Agrabad Deba Dighi	28: Agrabad	22°19′31.1″ N91°48′47.6″E	19.75 Or 20 acor / 50 kany.	100,000[1]	Everything (i.e., bathing, clothing, washing dishes) and 200 times of water connect by electric motor	Bangladesh Railway	Households (Polythin) waste
S 14	Korno Mohon Sheal Bari Pond	41: South Patenga (South Patenga, Del Para)	22°15′11.5″N 91°47′45.8″E	0.5 acor	100	Everything (i.e., bathing, clothing, washing dishes, and fishing)	Personal	Households waste and entrance tidal water
S 15	Hindu Para Pond (Durga Bari)	40: South Patenga	22°16′11.5″N 91°47.5′45.8″E	1 acor	300	Everything (i.e., bathing, clothing, washing dishes, and fishing)	Personal	Households solid waste (uses lime but didn't know proper amount)
S 16	Raja Pond, South Patenga	41: South Patenga (Chowdhury Para)	22°15′13.0″N 91°48.5′10.9″E	2 acor	500	Everything (i.e., bathing, clothing, washing dishes, and fishing)	Personal	Households solid waste
S 17	Boro Pukur or Pond (Hadu Serang Bari)	34: South-Middle Halishar	22°18′06.4″N 91°47.5′16.7 E	3 acor	200	Everything (i.e., bathing, clothing, washing dishes, and fishing)	Personal	Households solid waste (plastic and solid waste)
S 18	Kazir Dighi (Sharaipara)	10: North Kattali	22°21′14.0″N 91°47′00.6″E	3 acor	50,000[2]	Everything (i.e., bathing, clothing, washing dishes, and fishing)	Personal (16/36 person)	Households solid waste (plastic and solid waste)
S 19	Voluar Dighi	12: Sharaipara	22°21′17.2″N 91°47′39.4″E	Data not found	50,000[3]	Everything (i.e., bathing, clothing, washing dishes, and fishing)	Bangladesh Railway	Households solid waste (plastic and solid waste)
S 20	Jora Dighi	12: Sharaipara	22°20′57.5″N 91°47′53.5E	24 acor	20,000[4]	Everything (i.e., bathing, clothing, washing dishes, and fishing)	Bangladesh Railway	Households solid waste (plastic and solid waste)
S 21	Aladi jumadar Wafkup state mosque Pond	14: Dampara	22°21′08.4″N 91°49′22.2″E	Data not found	Beautification	Beautification	Aladi jumadar Wafkup state mosque Pond	Static water

TABLE 14.2
Water Quality Parameters, Units, and Analytical Methods Used for Determination of Surface Water Evaluation

Parameters	Units	Analytical Methods
1. Temperature	°C	Thermometer
2. pH	----	pH meter (HANNA HI 8424 pH meter) (made in Romania)
3. Electrical conductivity (EC)	$\mu S\ cm^{-1}$	Combo meter, Model HI 98129 (HANNA Instruments, Inc., Woonsocket, RI)
4. Total dissolved solids (TDS)	$mg\ L^{-1}$	TDS meter (HANNA DiST 1 HI 98301, made in Mauritius)
5. Total suspended solids (TSS)	$mg\ L^{-1}$	Reference 1
6. Dissolved oxygen (DO)	$mg\ L^{-1}$	DO meter (HANNA HI 9146, made in Romania)
7. Biological oxygen demand (BOD)	$mg\ L^{-1}$	Manometric Method: Reference 1
8. Chemical oxygen demand (COD)	$mg\ L^{-1}$	Titrimetric method (Dichromate Reflux Method: Reference 1)
9. Turbidity	NTU	Turbidity meter (HANNA HI 98703 Turbidity Meter)
10. Chloride	$mg\ L^{-1}$	Titrimetric method (Mohr method): Reference 1
11. Salinity	$mg\ L^{-1}$	Chloride Concentration and Salinity
12. Ammonia (as nitrogen) ($NH^{-}{}_{3}$)	$mg\ L^{-1}$	Direct Nesslerization Method, Reference 1
13. Free chlorine	$mg\ L^{-1}$	Reference 1
14. Copper (Cu)	μg/l	Heavy metal analysis was carried out on all samples by using atomic absorption spectrophotometer (AAS) after wet digestion. Instrumentation: Atomic absorption spectrophotometer (AAS) (Type: iCE 3,300 AA system, Thermo Scientific, designed in UK) was used to determine Cu, Cd, Cr, Fe, As, Pb, Hg, Mn in water samples. The analysis was carried out using respective hollow cathode lamps under standard instrumental conditions.*Reference Book for digestion technique*: Reference 1
15. Cadmium (Cd)	μg/l	
16. Chromium (Cr)	μg/l	
17. Iron (Fe)	μg/l	
18. Arsenic (As)	μg/l	
19. Lead (Pb)	μg/l	
20. Mercury (Hg)	μg/l	
21. Manganese (Mn)	μg/l	
22. Total coliform (TC)	MPN- 100 ml^{-1}	MPN method
23. Fecal Coliform (FC)	MPN- 100 ml^{-1}	MPN method

where

VpH = observed value of pH

DO calculation through the water quality rating equation:

$$\mathbf{qDO = 100[(VDO - 14.\ 6/(5\text{–}14.\ 6)]}$$

The unit weight was assessed by a value inversely proportional to the suggested standard range vSn of the analogous component.

$W_n = \frac{K}{S_n}$

where

W_n = unit weight for the *nth* parameters

S_n = standard value for *nth* parameters

TABLE 14.3
Range of Water Quality Index and Quality of Water

Water Quality Index Level	Water Quality Status
0–25	Excellent water quality
26–50	Good water quality
51–75	Poor water quality
76–100	Very poor water quality
>100	Unsuitable for drinking

K = constant for proportionality (Vs = Sn)

$$K = \frac{1}{\frac{1}{Vs1} + \frac{1}{Vs2} + \frac{1}{Vs3} + \ldots\ldots\ldots\ldots\ldots + \frac{1}{Vsn}}$$

The overall water quality index was intended through a cumulative quality rating with the linear unit weight.

$$WQI = \sum q_n \frac{W_n}{W_n}$$

Table 14.3 explores the value of the water quality index as well as water condition of the aquatic water body that was proposed by Chatterji and Raziuddin, 2002. Due to the unavailability of the sources of unit weight data, the following parameters have not been analyzed [turbidity, salinity, free chlorine, total coliforms (TC), fecal coliforms (FC), copper (Cu), chromium (Cr), cadmium (Cd), lead (Pb), iron (Fe), arsenic (As), mercury (Hg) and manganese (Mn)] in this section. The quantitative data were analyzed using the SPSS software (version 20 for Windows).

14.4 RESULTS

To investigate the scenario of the surface water condition of UWBs regarding of alternate water sources for city dwellers, the author collected twenty-one (21) samples from the whole metropolitan area. Sample sizes of the pond and other water bodies were assessed on the basis of a few indicators, mostly used for alternate water purposes for households; a minimum of two thousand (~ 2000) urban dwellers directly use these water bodies. Besides, a total of 23 selected parameters in terms of physiochemical, biological, and trace metals were determined for calculating the quality of water in selected UWBs in CMC. Table 14.4 illustrates that categories of water quality for various sampling points in UWBs apply the water quality index in the Chittagong metropolitan city.

The author found that in the rainy season, almost six physiochemical parameters, such as temperature, electrical conductivity (EC), biological oxygen demand (BOD), chemical oxygen demand (COD), turbidity, and nitrite crossed the permissible limit among 13 parameters. During the winter season, nearly five parameters, such as electrical conductivity (EC), chemical oxygen demand (COD), biological oxygen demand (BOD), turbidity, and nitrite, crossed the permissible limit. Basically, physiochemical parameters are the indicating parameters of water quality because these are represented by the presence of exotic materials in water.

TABLE 14.4

Drinking Water Standards Recommending Agencies and Unit Weights (All Values Except pH and Electrical Conductivity Were in mg/l)

Parameters	Standard[5]	Recommended Agencies[6]	Unit Weight
1. Temperature	25–30	WHO	0.0866
2. pH	7–8.5	ICMR/BIS	0.2190
3. Electrical conductivity (EC)	300	ICMR	0.371
4. Total dissolved solids (TDS)	500	ICMR/BIS	0.0037
5. Total Suspended Solids (TSS)	500	WHO	0.0037
6. Dissolved oxygen (DO)	5.0	ICMR/BIS	0.3723
7. Biological oxygen demand (BOD)	5.0	ICMR	0.3723
8. Chemical oxygen demand (COD)	4.0	WHO	0.08266
9. Turbidity	5.0	WHO	0.16533
10. Chloride	250	ICMR	0.0074
11. Nitrite	<1	ICMR/BIS	0.0412

The temperature of water depended on different variables and its limit showed the presence of exotic materials in water. In the rainy season, the maximum limit was 34 °C, which was detected in S 6 (Fateabad Dighi) and it was situated on 01 under the South Pahartali ward and a minimum limit of 26.5 °C was detected in four different locations, such as S2 (Baitul salat jame mosque Pond), S9 (Kola-Bagisa Pond), S12 (Sheer-Shah Dighi), and S21 (Aladi jumadar Wafkup state mosque Pond), which were situated in no 04 in Chandgaon, 34 in Patharghata, 08 in Sulakbahar, and 14 in Dampara, respectively.

The electrical conductivity (EC) parameter was degraded in both seasons. In the rainy season, a maximum EC (841 μS cm^{-1}) was detected in S15 [Hindu Para Pond (Durga Bari)], which is situated in no 40 (South Patenga), and a minimum EC (3.28μS cm^{-1}) was detected in S21 (Aladi jumadar Wafkup state mosque Pond), which is situated in no 14 (Dampara). In the winter season, a maximum EC (640 μS cm^{-1}) was detected in S1 (Master Colony Pond), which is situated in no 05 [Mohara (near the rail station of Mohara)], and a minimum EC (160 μS cm^{-1}) was detected in S10 (Olima Dighi), which is situated in no 02 (Jalalabad), respectively.

The biological oxygen demand (BOD) parameter was crossing the permissible limit in both seasons. In the rainy season, a maximum BOD (64 mg/l) was detected in S4 (Miar Baper Barir Pukur), which is situated in no 17 (Bakolia) and a mean BOD was detected at 19.6148 mg/l, where the permissible limit is 5 mg/l. In the winter season, a maximum BOD (31 mg/l) was detected in S15 [Hindu Para Pond (Durga Bari)], which situated in no 40 (South Patenga) and a mean BOD detected was 9.55 mg/l.

The chemical oxygen demand (COD) parameter was crossing the permissible limit in both seasons. The limit of COD was in the worst condition, because the detected limit of COD was crossed in both seasons and every sample from the different water points in the study area. A maximum COD and minimum COD limit were exiting the permissible limit. In the rainy season, a maximum COD detected was 170 mg/l and in the winter season 150 mg/l where the permissible limit is 4 mg/l in drinking water.

The turbidity parameter was crossing the permissible limit in both seasons. The limit of turbidity was in the worst situation, because the detected limit of turbidity was crossed in both seasons and every sample in the rainy season and most of the samples in the winter season in the Chittagong metropolitan city. Almost every sample crossed the permissible limit in the rainy season. Besides, maximum turbidity (75.80 NTU) was detected in S1 (Master Colony Pond), which is situated in no 05 [Mohara (near the rail station of Mohara)], but the mean turbidity limit was 25.15 NTU in the winter season of selected urban water points in the city.

The parameter nitrite was found to have crossed the permissible limit in both seasons. In the rainy season, maximum nitrite (5.22 mg/l) was detected in S7 (Asker Dighi), which is situated in no 21 (Jamalkhan) and a mean nitrite was detected at 1.8057 mg/l. However, the mean value shows the maximum samples were crossing the permissible limit.

The water pollution level and detected limits were in worse conditions in the rainy season than the winter season in Chittagong city. The aesthetic views of water bodies of water were good and the dwellers used this water for household purposes, although the permissible quality was unsuitable for drinking purposes. Moreover, two biological water quality parameters, such as total coliform and fecal coliform, were analyzed for justification or determination of the biological condition of water. According to the WHO water quality guideline, two parameters and every sample were crossing the permissible limit for drinking purposes and detected 1100^{+} MPN- 100 ml^{-1} in water bodies.

Table 14.5 explores the trace metals determination of selected water bodies in the Chittagong metropolitan city. Although only one parameter [lead (Pb)] crossed the permissible limit, the presence of other trace metals was alarming for drinking purposes. Copper (Cu) and cadmium (Cd) were nil in the water of the selected water bodies and arsenic (As) was found in below detected level (BDL). Mercury (Hg), chromium (Cr), manganese (Mn), and iron (Fe) were detected in the water of these water bodies, although those were safe for drinking purposes. During the field survey, it was observed that a number of water bodies were linked with municipal drain and water bodies situated near the polluting industry. However, the water leached below that and caused the industrial liquid pollutant to easily enter the nearby water reservoir or water sources. These processes made it easier for the mixing of industrial pollutants with water near water bodies, although water bodies did not detect any link with any polluting industrial liquid in the Chittagong metropolitan city (Table 14.5).

The present research found that a number of parameters crossing the permissible limit and a small number of parameters were permissible for drinking purposes. Although water is a universal solvent, for drinking purposes every parameter should keep a permissible limit. Water is a heterogeneous mixture and also one parameter not only degraded the water quality, but rather accelerated the permissible condition for drinking.

A total of twenty-three (23) water quality components were identified to determine urban water bodies' water quality, including physiochemical, biological, and trace metals. Due to the unavailability of unit weight data, the following parameters were not taken into condition for analysis [turbidity, salinity, free chlorine, total coliforms (TC), fecal coliforms (FC), copper (Cu), arsenic (As), mercury (Hg), cadmium (Cd), chromium (Cr), iron (Fe), lead (Pb), and manganese (Mn)] in this section. Tables 14.6 and 14.7 present the drinking water values, suggesting different agencies and unit weights. The water quality index was used in two different reasons: rainy and winter seasons.

Table 14.8 illustrate the water quality index (WQI) in the rainy season. Chatterji and Raziuddin (2002) mentioned that if the water quality index (WQI) is 0–25 it represented the water quality as excellent condition, good water quality when 26–50, 51–75 represented water quality as a poor condition, and very poor water quality condition during 76–100 and >100 represented unsuitable for drinking. A total of ten components were analyzed for assessing the water quality index (WQI) at selected ponds and other water points in the Chittagong urban city and the index gained from the different water bodies in the various seasons for the study period i.e., winter and rainy seasons were 237.11 and 99.62, respectively, which indicated the unsuitability for drinking (Chatterji and Raziuddin, 2002;Table 14.8).

In the winter season, Table 14.9 stated that the water quality index was better than the rainy season, but unsuitable for drinking, which detected 99.62 values for ten selected parameters among

TABLE 14.5
Determination of Physiochemical and Biological Parameters of Water Quality of UWBs

Parameters	Units	Standards	Rainy Season					Winter Season				
			Max^{m}	Min^{m}	Mean	Std.dev^{n}	Suitability	Max^{m}	Min^{m}	Mean	Std.dev^{n}	Suitability
			Physiochemical Parameters									
Temperature	°*C*	25–30	34.00	26.50	30.6805	2.45711	*NS*	25.70	25.20	25.3429	0.12071	S
pH	----	6.5–8.5	8.80	7.10	8.0838	0.41722	S	6.60	5.70	6.3143	0.22646	S
Electrical conductivity (EC)	µS cm^{-1}	300	841.00	3.28	481.452	272.1082	NS	640.00	160.00	352.382	12.25932	NS
Total dissolved solids (TDS)	mg L^{-1}	500	529.00	2.00	283.002	168.8832	S	390.00	96.00	21.1712	74.26791	S
Total suspended solids (TSS)	mg L^{-1}	500	139.00	13.00	62.7143	402.2951	S	359.00	15.00	16.0862	95.79991	S
Dissolved oxygen (DO)	mg L^{-1}	4–6	7.90	2.98	5.6943	1.25351	S	6.02	1.15	3.6643	1.44667	S
Biological oxygen demand (BOD)	mg L^{-1}	5.0	64.00	0.61	19.6148	209.1991	NS	31.00	0.55	9.5500	8.70847	NS
Chemical oxygen demand (COD)	mg L^{-1}	4.0	176.00	15.89	64.1448	436.8481	NS	105.00	5.00	37.8048	28.43981	NS
Turbidity	NTU	5	92.30	29.00	55.7500	186.3081	NS	75.80	4.75	25.1471	16.62801	NS
Chloride	mg L^{-1}	250	145.00	10.00	75.7900	305.1841	S	70.00	25.00	35.9048	9.13184	S
Salinity	mg L^{-1}	250	270.00	19.00	143.192	560.1611	S	126.40	45.25	64.9733	16.47281	S
Nitrite	mg L^{-1}	<1	5.22	0.10	1.8057	1.31222	NS	16.80	0.00	3.8295	5.54616	NS
Free chlorine	mg L^{-1}	0.3	0.20	0.00	0.0543	0.05853	S	0.80	0.00	0.3000	0.21909	S
			Biological Parameters									
Total coliforms (TC)	MPN- 100 ml^{-1}	50	1100^{+}				NS	1100^{+}				NS
Fecal coliforms (FC)	MPN- 100 ml^{-1}	50	1100^{+}				NS	1100^{+}				NS

a WHO suggested water quality standards (WHO 2004).
b Values are averaged from at least three consecutive measurements. SD: standard deviation.
c Suitability for drinking as compared with WHO suggested water quality standards, "S," suitable; "NS," not-suitable.

TABLE 14.6
Determination of Trace Metals of Urban Water Bodies in Chittagong Metropolitan City

Parameters	Units	Standards	Rainy Season					Winter Season				
			Max^{m}	Min^{m}	Mean	Std.dev^{n}	Suitability	Max^{m}	Min^{m}	Mean	Std.dev^{n}	Suitability
Copper (Cu)	µg/l	2	*Nil*					*Nil*				
Cadmium (Cd)		0.003	*Nil*					*Nil*				
Chromium (Cr)		0.05	0.04	00.00	0.0062	0.01244	S	0.04	0.00	0.0095	0.01499	S
Iron (Fe)		0.3	1.20	00.00	0.2176	0.35417	S	1.18	0.00	0.2133	0.34907	S
Arsenic (As)		0.01			*BLD (Below Detected Level)*					*BLD (Below Detected Level)*		
Lead (Pb)		0.01	0.09	0.01	0.0481	0.01861	NS	0.09	0.01	0.0533	0.02058	NS
Mercury (Hg)		0.006			*BLD (Below Detected Level)*					*BLD (Below Detected Level)*		
Manganese (Mn)		0.4	0.27	0.00	0.0348	0.07229	S	0.60	0.00	0.0633	0.14242	S

TABLE 14.7
Drinking Water Standards Recommending Agencies and Unit Weights (All Values Except pH and Electrical Conductivity Were in mg/l)

Parameters	Standard[7]	Recommended Agencies[8]	Unit Weight
1. Temperature	25–30	WHO	0.0866
2. P^H	7–8.5	ICMR/BIS	0.2190
3. Electrical conductivity (EC)	300	ICMR	0.371
4. Total dissolved solids (TDS)	500	ICMR/BIS	0.0037
5. Total Suspended Solids (TSS)	500	WHO	0.0037
6. Dissolved oxygen (DO)	5.0	ICMR/BIS	0.3723
7. Biological Oxygen Demand (BOD)	5.0	ICMR	0.3723
8. Chemical Oxygen Demand (COD)	4.0	WHO	0.08266
9. Turbidity	5.0	WHO	0.16533
10. Chloride	250	ICMR	0.0074
11. Nitrite	<1	ICMR/BIS	0.0412

TABLE 14.8
Seasonal Variations of the Physiochemical Parameters of the Selected Water Bodies

Parameters	Rainy Season (Mean of Results; N = 21)	Winter Season (Mean of Results; N = 21)
1. *Temperature*	30.6805	25.3429
2. *pH*	8.0838	6.3143
3. *Electrical conductivity (EC)*	481.452	352.382
4. *Total dissolved solids (TDS)*	283.002	21.1712
5. *Total suspended solids (TSS)*	62.7143	16.0862
6. *Dissolved oxygen (DO)*	5.6943	3.6643
7. *Biological oxygen demand (BOD)*	19.6148	9.5500
8. *Chemical oxygen demand (COD)*	64.1448	37.8048
9. *Turbidity*	55.7500	25.1471
10. *Chloride*	30.6805	35.9048
11. *Nitrite*	1.8057	3.8295

23 parameters. In the winter season, water was usually not influenced by the urban flood (Table 14.10).

However, the water became polluted due to the unauthorized linkage of water bodies with a municipal drain, unfortunate discharge of industrial wastes and throwing of municipal or household wastes on water bodies. Although physicochemical parameter quality was good or moderately good, the biological parameters were crossing the acceptance level. Both biological parameters, such as total coliform and fecal coliform, were detected 1100^{+} in every water body in Chittagong metropolitan city. Besides, trace metals were also detected in water bodies, although these were found in the permissible level in the Chittagong metropolitan city. However, the water quality index (WQI) was detected for drinking purposes but not detected for household purposes.

TABLE 14.9

Calculation of Water Quality Index (WQI) in Rainy Season

Parameters	Observed Values	Standard Values (Sn)	V_{io} = Ideal Value of nth Parameter	Unit Weight (W_n)	Quality Rating (q_n)	W_n q_n
1. Temperature	30.6805	25–30	0	0.0866	102.27	8.86
2. pH	8.0838	7–8.5	7	0.2190	72.00	15.77
3. Electrical conductivity (EC)	481.452	300	0	0.371	160.48	59.53
4. Total dissolved solids (TDS)	283.002	500	0	0.0037	56.60	0.21
5. Total suspended solids (TSS)	62.7143	500	0	0.0037	12.54	0.046
6. Dissolved oxygen (DO)	5.6943	5.0	14.6	0.3723	92.81	34.55
7. Biological oxygen demand (BOD)	19.6148	5.0	0	0.3723	392.29	146.04
8. Chemical oxygen demand (COD)	64.1448	4.0	10	0.08266	1002.4	82.86
9. Chloride	30.6805	250	0	0.0074	12.27	0.09
10. Nitrite	1.8057	<1	0	0.0412	180.00	7.41
				$\Sigma W_n = 1.5598$	$\Sigma q_n = 2083.66$	$\Sigma W_n q_n = 355.366$

Water Quality Index = $\Sigma q_n W_n / \Sigma W_n$
= 355.66/1.56 = 237.11 (Unsuitable for drinking)

TABLE 14.10

Calculation of Water Quality Index (WQI) in Winter Season

Parameters	Observed Values	Standard Values (Sn)	Vio = Ideal value of nth Parameter	Unit Weight (Wn)	Quality Rating (qn)	Wn qn
Temperature	25.3429	25–30	0	0.0866	101.37	8.78
pH	6.3143	7–8.5	7	0.2190	– 45.71	–10.01
Electrical conductivity (EC)	352.382	300	0	0.371	117.46	43.58
Total dissolved solids (TDS)	21.1712	500	0	0.0037	4.23	0.01
Total suspended solids (TSS)	16.0862	500	0	0.0037	3.22	0.01
Dissolved oxygen (DO)	3.6643	5.0	14.6	0.3723	–13.91	–5.18
Biological oxygen demand (BOD)	9.5500	5.0	0	0.3723	191.00	71.11
Chemical oxygen demand (COD)	37.8048	4.0	10	0.08266	378.04	31.25
Chloride	25.1471	250	0	0.0074	10.06	0.07
Nitrite	3.8295	<1	0	0.0412	382.95	15.77
				Σ Wn =1.5598	Σ qn =1128.71	Σ Wn qn =155.39

Water Quality Index = $\Sigma q_n W_n / \Sigma W_n$

= 155.39/1.5598 = 99.62 (Unsuitable for drinking)

Although in both seasons, water quality was unsuitable for drinking purposes in the Chittagong metropolitan city. So, selected water bodies were prohibited for drinking purposes, but it may use other household purposes of dwellers.

14.5 DISCUSSION

In this book chapter, the author mentioned that mismanagement of municipal and household wastes and industrial liquid waste were the prime causes of surface water pollution in Chittagong metropolitan city. In the rainy season, urban flood had accelerated the surface runoff and this runoff was mixing the polluted water (municipal or household wastes and industrial liquid) and stagnant water bodies water in Chittagong metropolitan city. As a result, the water quality was easily degraded during the rainy season. But mismanagement of household wastes and illegal linkage of drain water with water bodies were the major causes for water pollution in the urban Chittagong city. Although the water pollution level and detected limits were the worst condition in the rainy season than the winter season in Chittagong city. The aesthetic views of water bodies were good and dwellers used this water for household purposes, although the permissible quality was unsuitable for drinking purposes.

Total twenty-one (21) samples and twenty-three (23) parameters were selected for assessing the water quality of selected ponds and other water sources in whole urban city area. A total of 13 physiochemical parameters, including temperature (°C), pH, electric conductivity (EC), total dissolved solid (TDS), dissolved oxygen (DO), biological oxygen demand (BOD), turbidity, chloride (Cl_2), salinity, total suspended solid (TSS), chemical oxygen demand (COD), free chlorine (Cl^-), nitrite (NO_2), and two biological components, such as total coliform and fecal coliform, and eight trace metals involve chromium (Cr), copper (Cu), arsenic (As), cadmium (Cd), iron (Fe), lead (Pb), mercury (Hg), and manganese (Mn), respectively.

For determination of the permissible limit of water, two types of methods were used, such as suitability analysis (SA) and water quality index analysis (WQIA). For determination of suitability analysis of selected water quality, the limit of World Health Organization (2004) was used and categorized including "S," suitable; "NS," not-suitable on the basis of this standard.

In the rainy season, almost six physiochemical parameters, such as temperature, biological oxygen demand (BOD), turbidity, electrical conductivity (EC), chemical oxygen demand (COD), and nitrite, crossed the permissible limit among the 13 parameters. In the winter season, nearly five parameters, such as biological oxygen demand (BOD), turbidity, electrical conductivity (EC), chemical oxygen demand (COD), and nitrite, crossed the permissible limit. Besides, total coliform and fecal coliform were dangerous situations because every sample was deleted 1100^+ MPN in both seasons and one trace metal (lead, Pb) was detected in a hazardous condition of this water.

In the rainy season, water quality index was high, which detected 237.11 values for ten selected parameters among 23 parameters. In the rainy season, Chittagong city was affected by urban flooding and six polluted industrial zones that have been established around metropolitan city area. Due to tidal fluctuation, mismanagement of municipal wastes, blockage of the municipal drain by municipal wastes and siltration, encroachment of tidal creeks, channels and streams, and low-lying topography were the main causes for urban flooding. As a result, industrial polluted liquid, municipal wastes, and drain wastes spread up the whole city area of urban flooding and these entered the water bodies and finally polluted the water in the pond water of Chittagong city.

In addition, biological parameters were in dangerous conditions, because some bacterial species were detected in high levels (1100^+). So, in the rainy season water from water bodies was totally prohibited for drinking purposes in the Chittagong metropolitan city. Moreover, trace metals were also detected in these water bodies, because industrially polluted water entered the water bodies during the rainy season by urban flooding. It threatened the human health due to the changes it brought to the internal metabolism of human health.

The water quality index (WQI) obtained from the water bodies in different seasons of the study period i.e., rainy and winter were 237.11 and 99.62, respectively, indicated the unsuitableness for drinking. In the rainy season, the water quality index was so high, it detected 237.11 values for ten selected parameters among 23 parameters. In the rainy season, Chittagong city was affected by urban flooding and six polluted industrial zones have been established around the metropolitan city area. Due to tidal fluctuation, mismanagement of municipal wastes, blockage of municipal drain by municipal wastes and siltration, encroachment of tidal creeks, channels, and streams, and low-lying topography were the main causes for urban flooding. As a result, industrial polluted liquid, municipal wastes, and drain wastes spread up the whole city area of urban flooding and these entered the water bodies and finally polluted the water in water bodies in Chittagong metropolitan city.

The author found that in the winter season, the water quality index was better than the rainy season but unsuitable for drinking, which detected 99.62 values for ten selected parameters among 23 parameters. In the winter season, water was kept undisturbed or out of the influences of urban flooding. But unplanned connection of water bodies with municipal drain, unfortunately discharging industrial wastes and throwing municipal or household wastes on water bodies. As a result, water was polluted. Although the physicochemical parameter quality was good or moderately good, biological parameters were crossing the acceptance level. Both parameters i.e., total coliform and fecal coliform were detected 1100^{+} in every water body in Chittagong metropolitan city. Besides, trace metals were also detected in water bodies, although these were found in the permissible level in Chittagong metropolitan city.

14.6 CONCLUSIONS

Chittagong city has now become a very busy and lucrative place for the people of Bangladesh due to urban facilities and commercial activities of the country. So, urbanization and population of this commercial city's are increasing significantly among the country. Enormous population and urban autonomous bodies failed to supply the basic amenities for city dwellers, particularly drinking water or potable water or supply water. Due to inadequate supply of supply (piped) water, urban water bodies are used as alternate water sources in the Chittagong City Corporation. Water from aquatic environments is used for household purposes, mainly in lower-class residential areas and partially middle- and higher-class residents used for bathing and washing of personal vehicle purposes in Chittagong metropolitan city.

The existing water bodies are sufficient as alternate sources of water in case of a shortage of water supply from CWASA in Chittagong city. Due to the absence of proper management with the protection and conservation of the existing water bodies, they were not used for drinking and cooking purposes. So, CWASA and related soul agent, particularly DoE, should carry out the quality-based monitoring of water in familiar water bodies and set up permanent quality assessment meters that will refer to the quality of water for household purposes. Although DoE continuously determines the water quality of the prominent water bodies in the urban city, it did not consider the sampling to ensure the superiority for the utilizers of water in this aquatic environment. The techniques not only ensure the quality of water but also act as safeguards for water users because there is a possibility for the creation of waterborne diseases.

The polluting industry was been introduced in this city before the liberation war (1971). So, "*The Building Construction Act, 1996*" and "*Bangladesh National Building Code 2006*" should be established properly, because these acts directly take into account the provision of industrial settings and infrastructural development in any city area. The laws and enforcement authority should ensure the establishment of this for the city to meet the demands of planned industrial development. Planned industrial development includes the proper management of industrial wastes, discharge of the liquid after treatment, establishment of the ETP (effluent treatment plant). Unfortunately, unplanned industrial development is the main cause of water pollution in this city.

A number of laws, rules, and policies have been established for management of water resources and pollution control in Bangladesh, but there are few laws, rules, and policies directly designed for the preservation, conservation, and management of UWBs in Bangladesh. Among them "*All Playgrounds of Municipal Area, Open Area, Park and natural water reservoir including Municipal Area of City, Divisional Town & District Town, Conservation Act, 2000,*" "*The Rivers, Flood Plains and Water Bodies Conservation, Development and Reclamation and Filling Restriction Act 2005*" and "*Jaladhar Songrokkhon Aain, 2000*" are prominent. So, if the above-mentioned laws are effectively established, then the preservation, conservation, and management of UWBs in Chittagong city would be easier.

Whereas 38% of the demand of water for city dwellers is fulfilled by WASA (CWASA, 2017), the dwellers must use the surface water for household purposes against their wish. In this issue, the study prescribes that dwellers should use effective mechanisms to purify surface water before household purposes. Basically, boiling, filtering (manually and digitally), and potassium alum [$KAl\ (SO_4)_2.12H_2O$] (fitcary), a water purification tablet used for purification of water, have been recommended. The mentioned techniques would reduce the risks of waterborne diseases by the users from UWBs.

NOTES

1 100,000 (whole citizens in Ctg. Lalkhan Bazar, Chawmuhuny, 2 No Gate, Patenga, Dampara, and Madar Bari) all types of income-generating groups; adjoining hotels and restaurants.
2 50,000 (this area is industrial and iron cutting industry here) adjoining with heterogeneous types of labor are bathing activities here.
3 50,000 (this area is industrial and iron cutting industry here) adjoining with heterogeneous types of labor are bathing activities here.
4 20,000 (adjoining people and neighbors do bathing activities here (Motizona, Batali hill, and Pahartali)).
5 Standard values have been selected by WHO (2004). *Guidelines for Drinking-Water Quality*, Third Edition, Volume-1, Geneva and Department of Environment, Bangladesh.
6 ICMR –Indian Council for Medical Research / BIS – Bureau of Indian Standard and WHO – World Health Organization cited by Yogendra and Puttaiath, 2008.
7 Standard values have been selected by WHO (2004). Guidelines for Drinking-water Quality, Third Edition, Volume-1, Geneva and Department of Environment, Bangladesh.
8 ICMR –Indian Council for Medical Research / BIS – Bureau of Indian Standard and WHO – World Health Organization cited by Yogendra and Puttaiath, 2008.

REFERENCES

Chatterji, C., and M. Raziuddin. "Determination of water quality index (WQI) of degraded river in Asnol Industrial area, Raniganj, Burdwan, West Bengal." *Nature, Environment and Pollution Technology*, 1 (2002): 181–189.

CPHEEO, N. "Advisory on conservation and restoration of water bodies in urban areas." *Journal of Environmental Conservation*, 10 (2013): 250–275.

CWASA, H. "Preparation of Master plan for water supply and wastewater Management of the detailed planned area of Chittagong." *Urban Management*, 10 (2010): 80–95.

CWASA, H. "Situation of water supply and sanitation in the context of rainy season." *Sustainability*, 20 (2017): 75–90.

Francis, R. "Positioning urban rivers within urban ecology." *Urban Ecosystem*, 15 (2012): 15–29.

Hasan, A. B., S. Kabir, H. M. Reza, M. N. Zaman, M. A. Ahshan, M. A. Akbar, and M. Rashid. "Trace Metals pollution in seawater and groundwater in the ship breaking areas of Sitakund upazila, Chittagong, Bangladesh." *Marine Pollution Bulletin*, 71 (2013): 317–324.

Hassan, M. M., and M. N. Nazem. "Examination of land use/land cover changes, urban growth dynamics, and environmental sustainability in Chittagong city, Bangladesh." *Environment Development and Sustainability*, 50 (2013): 45–65.

Rahman, M. M., M. N. Islam, M. S. Hossain, Z. A. Begum, and H. Hasegawa. "Stagnant surface water bodies (SSWBs) as an alternative water resource for the Chittagong metropolitan area of Bangladesh: physicochemical characterization in terms of water quality indices." *Environmental Monitoring and Assessment*, 173 (2011): 669–684.

Rahman, M. S. “Quantifying Urban Form-Compactness versus Sprawl: An Analysis of Chittagong and Sylhet Metropolitan Cities.” *Jahangirnagar University Planning Review*, 10 (2012): 39–50.

Soyinka, O. K., K. Siu, T. K. Lawanson, and A. Olufemi. “Assessing smart infrastructure for sustainable urban development in the Lagos Metropolis.” *Journal of Urban Management*, 5 (2016): 52–64.

Uddin, N. “Paradox of conceptualizations, measurements and causes of urban poverty: Context evidence from Bangladesh.” *International Journal of Social and Economic Research*, 7 (2016): 54–73.

Uddin, N. “Assessing urban sustainability of slum settlements in Bangladesh: Evidence from Chittagong city.” *Journal of Urban Management*, 7 (2018): 32–42.

Voelker, J., and N. Kistemann. “Developing the urban blue: Comparative health responses to blue and green urban open spaces in Germany.” *Health Place*, 35(2014): 196–205.

WHO. “Emerging issues in water and infectious disease.” Techical Report 45 (2004), World Health Organization, Geneva, Switizerland.

World Health Organization (WHO). “Protecting surface waters for health – Managing the quality of drinking-water sources.” Technical Report No 50 (2014), World Health Organization, Geneva, Switzerland.

Section IV

Urban Sprawl, Resource Consumption, Management, and Smart Cities

15 Urban Sprawl, Blight, and the COVID-19 Pandemic

Anzhelika Antipova, Ehsan Momeni, and Reza Banai
University of Memphis, Memphis, TN, United States

CONTENTS

15.1 INTRODUCTION

Urban sprawl is identified by the spread of population and jobs from the city center to the urban and suburban edge, disproportionate land consumption relative to population, leapfrog development pattern contributing to many current urban and environmental problems including increased vehicle-miles traveled, gridlock on highways and major roads, green space reduction, and conversion of green space to impervious land prone to hazardous urban flooding. To promote sustainable development and mitigate negative outcomes of urban sprawl, it needs to be efficiently monitored as well

DOI: 10.1201/9781003126195-19

as controlled using various measures and alternatives to growth commonly referred to as "smart growth". The importance of these movements became especially evident during the current COVID-19 pandemic due to their ability to improve the quality of life as cities across the world increasingly rely on teleworking, online commerce, and education.

The wide-ranging dimensions of the urban sprawl phenomena motivated this chapter to provide an expansive review of the literature. Regarding spatial variation of sprawl and blight, its manifestation is different in different cities due to the city-specific contexts and empirical analyses. Despite the different definitions, sprawl and its consequences are measurable. Often, the sprawl footprint is mapped at an aggregate scale (city-region, urbanized area, metropolitan statistical area: see Galster et al., 2001; Lopez, 2014; Laidley, 2016) allowing sprawl comparisons across metropolitan regions, and hiding the different internal urban morphologies that contribute to that sprawl (Ewing and Hamidi, 2014). For that reason, city-specific case studies of urban sprawl add insights on socio-spatial impacts within the city empirically. A common measure, entropy is described in Chapter 19, but at a scale not commonly applied in the literature. Antipova, Banai, Momeni (Chapter 17) of a city in the southeastern region of the United States is a case in point, using the standard census definition of metropolitan subareas (block groups) with readily available socio-spatial attribute data, such as land use and income data used in this study. Other available census block-group attributes, including population, housing units, and employment (not used here), can extend the scope of investigation. Despite the unique socio-spatial impacts of spawl within cities, general patterns are discernible globally in cities of the north and south. The universal pattern of sprawl in U.S. cities motivated movements since the 1980s to counter the largely negative consequences. We note the movement of new urbanism, new regionalism, and smart growth in our comprehensive review of the literature. Since urban sprawl is a universal phenomenon, the movements to provide alternatives spread to cities globally.

Due to its global nature, we discuss sprawl drivers in developed and developing countries (section 15.2), and how sprawled development differs from compact development providing examples of urban sprawl by mapping two metropolitan areas with nearly the same population but different spatial extent in the USA, and discuss sprawl's various consequences, including blight (sections 15.3, 15.4). Blight and sprawl are among the key indicators that plague the metropolitan region, also called "twin problems" of the regional city (subsections in 15.5). The connection between sprawl and blight is relatively understudied, however. Accordingly, we test this hypothesis and explain how blight and sprawl are related, reviewing the nexus of the blight and sprawl literature. This chapter includes blight definitions, direction of blight causation, consequences of blighted areas, and sprawl and blight policy implications. Next, it discusses differences between urban growth and sprawl (section 15.6), and ways to halt sprawl (section 15.7). This chapter concludes with the impacts of various disasters including the COVID-19 pandemic on cities (section 15.8). This chapter adds to literature on sustainable planning in smart cities.

15.2 WHAT DRIVES URBAN SPRAWL?

Knowing what causes urban sprawl is critical in preventing this undesirable urban development and making appropriate plans (Gouda et al., 2016). Research identifies various drivers of urban sprawl. Conventional (Euclidean) zoning supports segregation by class and race with the effect of exclusion of many from desirable areas, it promotes low-density patterns causing urban sprawl (Antipova, 2018b). Some natural drivers of urban sprawl include the rise of income, population growth, diversity in the choice of users, and competition for lands, while taxation, crimes, damaged infrastructures, and the number of educational centers are other drivers (Mieszkowski and Mills, 1993). Land value, consumer preference, and technological innovations are other drivers (Ewing, 1997; Pendall, 1999). Similar findings of sprawl-causing factors resulted from an examination of the urban form of the mid-sized metropolitan area comprising Memphis in western Tennessee by studying trends in land cover and land use mix by computing a Simpson's index for both measures over for 1990s–2010s where the share of developed land use has increased by almost 4% since the early 1990s to meet the demand of housing and jobs for the growing population, while planted area and forest decreased significantly due to sprawl and urban development like in other metropolitan areas (Momeni and Antipova, 2018).

Due to differences in socio-economic characteristics and planning systems and approaches in different regions, intensity, extent, and speed, urban sprawl varies from region to region, and it may be more intense, faster, and its extent may be more inclusive in some regions (Gouda et al., 2016). A study based in North African and Middle Eastern region noted that factors driving urban sprawl in the Middle East are different from those in the West, included are the urbanizing peripheral rural areas and the rural-to-urban migration.

Administrative and planning reasons also drive urban sprawl the strongest in developing countries including Egypt and Iran (Gouda et al., 2016). Inadequate administrative and planning strategies on blight can be found in the developed world. To illustrate, Memphis and Shelby County officials used to address blight (vacant and abandoned properties) on an individual basis by demolishing or improving individual houses ignoring underlying causes. Since 2015, blight was made a major issue and the city and the county developed various anti-blight programs.

Urban sprawl is associated with cars and the freeway era; the U.S. cities rapidly grew in the post–World War II period (Antipova, 2018a). In a sprawled development, land uses are segregated, leapfrog, or scattered (poor land-use mix) causing auto dependence, vacant land lies between developed lands; and commercial development is in the form of a "strip" with commercial uses located along busy arterial roads (Ewing, 1997), while features are lacking that make neighborhoods vibrant including walkable "town centers" and public open spaces.

The opposite of sprawled development is compact development. *Compactness* is typically measured with five variables known as *D-variables* (e.g., density, diversity, design, destination accessibility, and distance to transit) (Stevens, 2017). Built environments that are high on the D-variables (except for distance to transit, which is low) are compact, and sprawling environments are low on the D-variables (Ewing and Cervero, 2017). Compact development typically has multistoried and higher-density development.

We provide an example of urban sprawl at the metropolitan scale in the United States by mapping Milwaukee-Waukesha, Wisconsin, and Jacksonville, Florida, metropolitan areas (shown on the left and right in Figure 15.1, respectively). While population is about the same in both areas in 2019 (1.58 million people in Milwaukee-Waukesha and 1.56 million in Jacksonville), the area of Milwaukee-Waukesha is less than half (1,454.9 versus 3,201.7 square miles), while its population density/sq. mile is larger (1,082.7 versus 487.1 people per square mile), as well as its composite (total) sprawl score is higher (134.18 versus 80.85 according to Measuring sprawl, 2014). The Milwaukee-Waukesha, WI, metropolitan area is more compact, while the Jacksonville, FL, metropolitan area is sprawled.

Poor residential accessibility (e.g., mean travel time and length) is also indicative of sprawl. To provide an example for the above metropolitan areas, people in Milwaukee-Waukesha-West Allis, WI have an average one-way commute time of 23.0 minutes, mean travel time to work is 26.9 in Jacksonville, FL, metro area using 2018 American Community Survey one-year estimates. Longer commute times in sprawling areas can decrease the social capital (Pohanka and Fitzgerald, 2004).

15.3 CHARACTERISTICS OF URBAN SPRAWL

Sprawl occurs as large low-density urban areas under market conditions are expanding into the surrounding rural lands where land subdivision has little planning control and coordination. The physical pattern of sprawling land can be characterized as patchy, scattered, and discontinuous

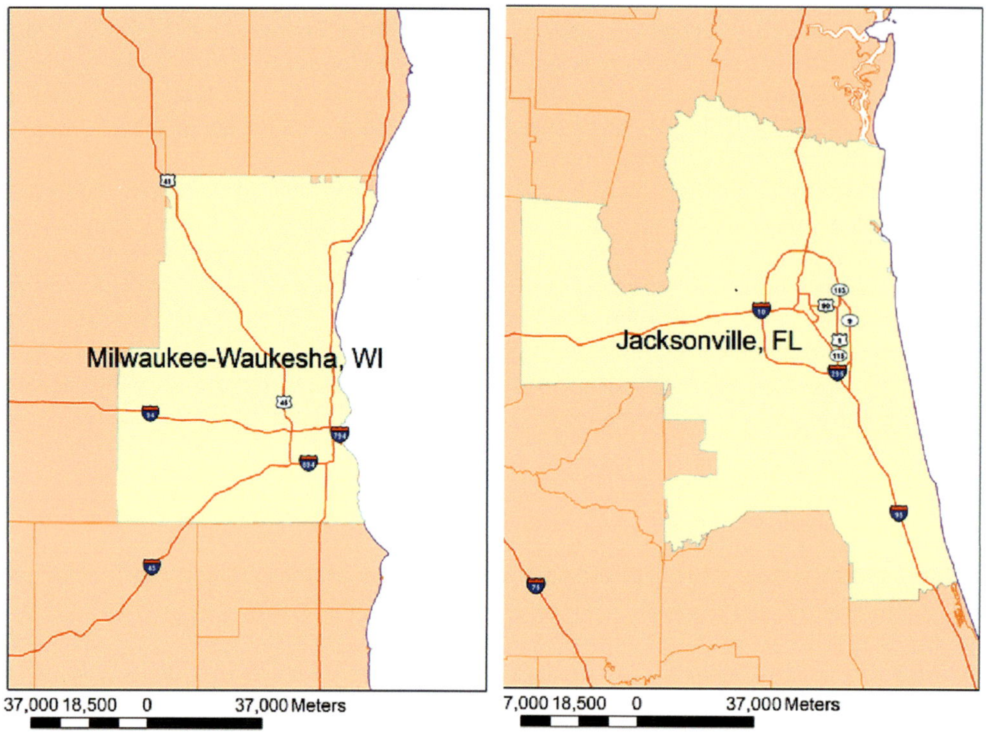

	US metropolitan area	
Location	Milwaukee-Waukesha, WI	Jacksonville, FL
Population (in 1,000s)	1,575,179	1,559,514
Area, sq mile	1454.9	3,201.70
Population density/sq.mile	1,082.70	487.1
Composite (total) sprawl score (Measuring sprawl, 2014)	134.18	80.85
Mean one-way commute time, min	23	26.9

FIGURE 15.1 An example of urban sprawl.

(European Environment Agency, 2006), while essential places including work, homes, schools, and stores are segregated.

Sierra Club (1998) characterized spawl as a "low-density development beyond the edge of service and employment, which separates where people live from where they shop, work, recreate and educate." Angel et al. (2007) defined key characteristics of urban sprawl as "endless cities, fuzzy boundaries between city and countryside, a polycentric urban structure, ribbons, and commercial strips, scattered development, and the fragmentation of open space, among others." Income and population growth, low price of lands, and new centers for jobs are other important characteristics (Habibi and Asadi, 2011).

Sprawl is a particular form of suburban growth, not any form (Downs, 1999). Ten characteristics include unlimited outward development, low-density settlements, leap-frog development, fragmentation of powers over land uses, private-vehicle-oriented neighborhoods, no plan for control of land uses, strip commercial development, fiscal disparities among localities, segregation of land uses, and filtering process to provide housing to low-income households (Downs, 1999).

Other characteristics associated with urban sprawl include spatial disintegration, informality, gated communities, upmarket residential areas, elite communities (Gouda et al., 2016), a polycentric urban structure (Sat, 2018), high impervious surfaces, and fragmentation of habitats.

15.4 CONSEQUENCES OF URBAN SPRAWL

Mostly, negative effects have been noted (Galster et al., 2001; Heirman and Coppens, 2013). Sprawl reduces farming lands and threatens open spaces (Kahn 2001). Below, the specific consequences of urban sprawl are listed.

15.4.1 Health Impacts

Sprawl can decrease life quality in the city center and suburbs, increase center-city poverty, car dependency, and congestion on suburban roads (Kahn, 2001). Sprawling development commonly lacks alternatives for private cars and housing options discouraging neighborhood walking and biking. Auto-dependency shapes pockets of isolated housing (Brunner, 2012). Urban sprawl is linked with public health issues including overweight and obesity. Neighborhood sprawl requires more driving to schools, shops, parks, and entertainment and promotes sedentary activity (Lumen Learning, 2020). Higher body mass index increases injuries; vehicle and pedestrian accidents result in fatalities (Pohanka and Fitzgerald, 2004). The car-dependent lifestyle increases the risk of mortality, cardiovascular disease, and cancer. Other negative consequences include increasing hypertension rates and chronic diseases (Urban Sprawl, 2013). Sprawl-caused air pollution increases respiratory diseases. Higher air pollution and more roadways and rooftops increase the heat island effect, which causes respiratory issues, non-fatal heat stroke, heat cramps, and heat-related mortality (Cool Roofs, 2014). Other human health issues include mental health: living in disconnected suburbs can lead to social isolation which decreases social interactions (Habibi and Asadi, 2011; Ewing, 1997) causing psychological consequences for individuals and making communities more fragmented reducing the trust among citizens (Pohanka and Fitzgerald, 2004). More driving is associated with spending less time with family and friends, and contributing to less civic and religious activities. In compact neighborhoods with a school or a corner shop just a few blocks away from homes, the sense of belonging to a community is higher. More response time is required for public serices services including fire, police, and ambulance (Pohanka and Fitzgerald, 2004).

15.4.2 Natural Habitats

Sprawl reduces farming lands and threatens open spaces (Kahn, 2001), and sustainable development. Urban landscape consumes forests, meadows, and wetlands, decreasing, fragmenting, and degrading natural habitats. Proximity of urban activities to natural and protected areas stresses ecosystems and species through air and noise pollution. Loss of agricultural and wetlands, forest fragmentation, loss of natural corridors for migration of wildlife species, and isolated population reduce the natural habitat (Lumen Learning, 2020). Many European cities have grown on former agricultural lands. Its loss negatively impacts biodiversity. Urban sprawl causes soils to lose their essential properties becoming compact and impenetrable, causing loss of biodiversity: 52% of soils in developed areas in Germany have lost water permeability and became sealed (Lumen Learning, 2020).

15.4.3 Higher Costs

Compared with high-density areas, providing services (building new highways, streets, bridges, schools, sewer and water systems, street lighting, gas, electric lines, libraries, and parks) is costlier in sprawling developments as homes and jobs are placed farther apart (Judd and Swanstrom, 2006; Brunner, 2012). Maintaining urban facilities, e.g., water, electricity, and infrastructure is costlier in sprawling urban areas: road costs are 25–33%, utilities costs are 18–25%, and municipal and school district operating costs are 3–11% higher in sprawling areas than in sprawl-free areas (U.S. Department of Housing and Urban Development, 1999). Services including mail delivery, street cleaning, waste control, police, and fire protection are costlier in low-density settlements (Bhatta, 2010).

Property taxes are higher to cover service costs. Children and people with disabilities experienced more transportation costs in sprawling neighborhoods (Brunner, 2012). There is higher commuting, travel, congestion, costs of infrastructure (highways), utilities (electricity), energy consumption, and air pollution, as well as a reduction of agricultural lands (Habibi and Asadi, 2011). Moving toward more compact neighborhoods versus sprawled ones in the United States can decline costs by an average of 9.7% (McGuire and Sjoquist, 2003).

15.4.4 Energy and Materials Consumption, Air Pollution

Compact urban areas with higher population density are more energy-efficient, while sprawling areas consume more energy and materials, including metal, concrete, and asphalt for development (Brunner, 2012). Sprawl has other negative impacts on the environment (Galster et al., 2001), including increased use of vehicles, energy consumption, and greenhouse emissions (Barrington-Leigh and Millard-Ball, 2015). By increasing the consumption of energy in sprawled urban areas, CO_2 emission increases.

Traffic jams are more common among commuters of sprawling neighborhoods with gridlocks that can cause air and water pollution (Judd and Swanstrom, 2006). In sprawled cities, transportation-related CO_2 emissions tend to be higher because of higher automobile dependency and greater travel; while higher NO_2 concentrations occur in sprawl-like urban areas including less contiguous built-up areas and isolated developments (Bechle et al., 2011). Sprawl consumes vegetation, contributing to a heat island effect (Pohanka and Fitzgerald, 2004). In sprawling cities, its formation is enhanced due to decentralized land uses generating more surface heat than denser urban forms, potentially leading to higher ozone exceedances than in compact cities (Stone, 2008), with public health implications.

15.4.5 Water Pollution and Floods

Among a myriad of environmental problems associated with urban sprawl, such as water and air pollution, soil degradation, and urban heat islands (Banai and DePriest, 2014), water-related issues are of great importance since water quality and quantity problems resulting from growing urban areas occur in large and small cities (Depriest and Antipova, 2013). Much farmland, wetland, and open space converts to developed area due to sprawl: more concrete and paved parking lots and roads can pollute water through run-off oil/gas, metal, nutrients, and organic waste, degrading water quality (Lumen Learning, 2020). A sprawling area produces 43% more urban run-off than denser populated areas; run-offs are a source of water pollution (Pohanka and Fitzgerald, 2004) in rivers and streams (Judd and Swanstrom, 2006). Depriest and Antipova (2013) investigated the relationship between land use change, population growth, and changing urban form and related the changes to the frequency of local flood events in the mid-sized city of Jackson, Tennessee, finding that changes in flood frequency reflected in a steady flood increase over the last four decades may be related to population growth in the area while urban form may also change and affect local flood patterns in new or different ways. Despite the different definitions, sprawl and its consequences are measurable (Banai and DePriest, 2014), including a common measure of entropy and at a finer scale than commonly applied in the literature (see Chapter 19).

15.4.6 Socio-Economic Impacts

Sprawl has negative impacts on economy, society, and ecological development. Sprawl can segregate residential developments based on income. Sprawl increases household expenditures by adding more costs to their commuting, utilities, and services. Therefore, there are more middle- and upper-income families living in suburban and peripheral areas (Lumen Learning, 2020). Sprawl negatively affects social capital since social capital is related to behavior and self-related health. Sprawl does not impact all people equally and can bring social injustice. Older people, minorities, poor individuals, and groups with lower socio-economic status may not have access to proper housing and may end up living in areas with higher crime or environmental exposures (Pohanka and Fitzgerald, 2004). Residents of a compact development have lower commuting time and distance (Brunner, 2012).

15.4.7 Impact of Sprawl in Other Countries

The negative impacts of sprawl on the environment are documented in many countries worldwide. The Dutch version of the American dream motivated the large construction of commercial and industrial facilities in urban fringes in the Netherlands and caused the loss of agricultural lands for decades (Van Der Valk, 2002; Tjallingii, 2000). Impacts of urban sprawl on the environment were detected in Japan, particularly in major cities including Tokyo and Osaka (Sorensen, 1999), Canada (Zolnik, 2004), and Israel (Razin, 1998).

15.4.8 Positive Effects

Studies find positive impacts of sprawl (Chin, 2002; Cox and Utt, 2004). Kahn (2001) believes urban sprawl can increase housing affordability in both suburbs and city centers, and thus decrease the white/black housing consumption gap. He concluded that the number of black homeowners is higher in sprawled areas. A high-sprawled area was defined as that "whose share of jobs outside the 10-mile ring is 44 percent or higher." Other positive consequences include improving the local economic growth (Urban Sprawl, 2013). Similarly, it allows construction of bigger houses and provides a diverse range of housing preferences and prices (Heirman and Coppens, 2013).

15.5 THE NEXUS OF BLIGHT AND SPRAWL

We provide a brief review of the nexus of the blight and sprawl literature including definitions of blight, direction of causation, its consequences, data for measuring spawl, and policy implications to mitigate sprawl.

15.5.1 Definitions of Blight

In the early 1900s, the term *blight* was used to describe slums. By the 1910s, the blighted areas and districts became a distinctive part of urban environment. Blight is rarely defined with any precision in federal and state urban renewal policies. It was believed that expansion of blighted districts over time may turn them into a slum district, and therefore, blighted areas should be condemned, replanned, sold off, or redeveloped (Fitzgerald and Bartlett, 1912). In 1912, blighted districts were defined as where "land values after a period of increase are stationary or falling" (Fogelson, 2001; Fitzgerald and Bartlett, 1912). In contrast with slums, which were considered a social problem, the latter definition considered blight an economic problem. Still later, the Comprehensive Plans Committee of Philadelphia in 1918 broadly defined a blighted area as "a district which is not what it should be" (Fogelson, 2001). Definitions of blight changed among the U.S. governments for many decades: during and before the Great Depression the term "slums" meant blights (Terry and

A.I.C.P., 2012), while the Hoover Administration at a housing conference in 1930 defined slums as "a residential area where the houses and conditions of life are of such a squalid and wretched character and which hence has become a social liability to the community," and a blighted area as an area that "has become an economic liability to the community" (Garfield, 1931), and during the 1950s–1960s, blight was identified as an economic problem that can destroy a neighborhood at a micro-scale, but seen as an opportunity for building a better urban area with a better economy at a macro scale (Schilling and Pinzón, 2016).

In Tennessee, blighted areas were defined in 2019 as "areas, including slum areas, with buildings or improvements that, by reason of dilapidation, obsolescence, overcrowding, lack of ventilation, light and sanitary facilities, deleterious land use, or any combination of these or other factors, are detrimental to the safety, health, morals, or welfare of the community" (Tennessee Code 13–20-201).

Generally, in defining urban blight, vacant land and abandoned structures are commonly used interchangeably, including the terms *blighted, vacant, abandoned*, or *derelict* (Mallach, 2018). However, Newman et al. (2016) make a distinction through an examination of the underpinning causes. Vacant land is a consequence of the expanding city boundary, whereas abandoned structures are the outcome of a declining city population. Concomitantly, vacant land is not responsive to improving the local economy, while abandoned (blighted) structures are linked to the urban economy.

Factors causing blighted environments include economic restructuring, urban disinvestment, mortgage foreclosures, and environmental and engineering disasters. These factors increase poverty, population turnover rates, and a disproportionate amount of social and physical disorders to the neighborhood, while decreasing housing quality, local services, and level of social cohesion in the neighborhoods (Kondo, 2018). An example of natural causes of blight is Hurricane Katrina in 2005, which damaged New Orleans. After the hurricane, many areas lost population and resources and turned to blight with an increasing amount of vacant or abandoned properties (Kondo, 2018).

15.5.2 Causation: Which Comes First, Sprawl or Blight?

The earliest observation of the nexus of sprawl and blight is from the Chicago school of urban sociology (Burgess, 1925; Park et al., 1925). Its concentric zone theory (CZT) of urban expansion identified various rings of the urban growth. Blight was in "transitional" zone near the factory. The CZT observed the outward growth of the city as an essentially unfettered market economy (Banai, 2019). However, Batchis (2010) argues the case for sprawl as a consequence of the regulation of the land market through legislation (zoning). Although the "amorphous" urban outcome is observed, there is no mention of blight as a feature of sprawl. Brueckner and Helsley (2011) come the closest to the connection between sprawl and blight. Urban sprawl and blight share similar contributing factors: "market failures." New suburban and older central-city properties are in competition for the same residents. The declining "cost" of suburban location results in suburban expansion. Similarly, the declining central-city property values reduce the incentive to reinvest resulting in blight. To abate blight, targeted policies are needed to draw population back to the city from suburbs to reinvest in housing in the central city. What are the drivers of the shift from city to suburb? Frey (1979) identifies racial and economic and ecologic conditions and motivation.

Hwang and Woo (2020) provide a perspective on the connection of sprawl and urban decline. Regarding employment, a decline at the urban core correlates with an increase in the "hinterland." For population, the result appears as counter-intuitive. The reduction of the urban core's population density is associated with the decline of the density in the hinterland.

Vacant urban areas, residential and business land use, are a manifestation of urban expansion. Newman et al. (2016) shed some light on the nexus of blight and urban expansion in a longitudinal (decade) observation across 20 U.S. cities. They conclude that when the city expands extending its boundaries, and increases in size, its residential land vacancy increases. In contrast, in cities that do not extend boundaries or shrink in size, infill development of vacant properties is observed.

Observing two European countries, Nuissl et al. (2007) conclude that decline is not limited to sprawl. The automobile is commonly regarded as a culprit for sprawl. However, Wassmer (2008) finds "natural evolution," "flight from blight," and "local revenue reliance" as more important than auto ownership. Per capita income and proportion of poor show a greater sensitivity to both urban area size and population density. Recall "natural evolution" is at the kernel of the Chicago school's conception of outward urban expansion, noted above.

15.5.3 Consequences of Blight

Urban blight and decay are a problem across the United States. In the early 20th century, the term "blight" was used by social reformers to bring attention to unhealthy housing and low-quality living conditions of immigrants since blight includes vacant lots, abandoned buildings, and houses that are in dangerous shape and contaminate the environment, while overgrown lawns, uncontrolled litter, and inappropriate street lighting are characteristics of blighted properties that have signs of neglect. Blighted properties usually have conditions that interfere with the general public's use of those properties (Schilling and Pinzón, 2016).

The negative effects of blight include significant community costs associated with blighted properties and structures (Terry and A.I.C.P., 2012). A blight drains resources and harms the city neighborhood by increasing public service costs (police services). Vacant lands and buildings, and abandoned properties drain value, reduce the revenue of the local government, and increase the need for fire and police services, code enforcement, and property maintenance and reduce the quality of life and the value of surrounding properties. In Philadelphia, vacant properties drop 20% of the property value in the neighborhood and the city spends over $20 million for their maintenance annually. Blight slows down economic growth of the area by stopping the creation of a modern city (Gordon, 2004). (Robinson and Cole, 2007).

Besides the community-level effect, blighted properties negatively impact individual homeowners and residents where residents often have higher insurance premiums. Having a large number of vacant properties in a neighborhood decreases house values and decreases life quality (Terry and A.I.C.P., 2012).

15.5.4 Methodology of the Blight and Sprawl Connection

Wassmer (2008) uses regression for the connection of auto ownership, per capita income, and proportion of poor residents in decentralization. He concludes auto dependence contributes to urban decentralization. However, income and poverty contribute even more than automobile reliance. The new suburban and central city properties compete for mobile residents, showing similar market failures contributing to urban sprawl and blight (Brueckner and Helsley, 2011).

The city-to-suburb movement of whites is determined by race, central city decline, and demographic structure in the literature. However, Frey's (1979) methodology applied to 39 large SMSAs considers this movement as outcome of two distinct stages: the push from the city (origin) and the pull from the suburb (destination). The racial and non-racial factors impact the push from the city more compared to the pull from the suburb. Metropolitan area fiscal and ecological features offer clues in explanation, though racial effects are not discounted.

Newman et al. (2016) provide a quasi-experimental methodology to explain the impacts of urban expansion and population change on vacant land. A longitudinal analysis of vacant addresses from 2000 to 2010 compares 20 cities with expanding boundaries with 20 cities with contracting boundaries. A "fixed effects panel" observes the changes in total residential and business land use over time. The conclusion: "aggressive" urban expansion can spur increased urban vacancies, particularly residential land uses. A related Newman et al. (2018) survey of cities makes a distinction between vacant land and abandoned structures. Primary variables are employment, fiscal position, elasticity, population alteration, and regional location. Interestingly, abandoned structures are sensitive to city economy, whereas vacant land is linked to city administrative boundary. Deng and Ma (2015) explicitly associate sprawl and blight focusing in vacant residential land. High resolution, multispectral satellite imagery facilitated by GIS aides in the analysis of economic, social, and environmental determinants of vacant residential land at both block group and parcel level. The aerial mapping is useful for capturing vegetation changes that reflect blighted residential land.

15.5.5 Data on Spawl-Related Urban Blight

In the above-mentioned survey, longitudinal vacant address data from 40 U.S. cities of over 100,000 persons from 2000 to 2010 compare the property vacancies impact of expanding cities with contracting cities, observing the total change in residential and business land use (Frey, 1979).

Sprawl-related blighted parcel-level property data are collected directly or indirectly. Case studies may use an existing, direct survey of city properties including a 12-week parcel-level survey conducted during September–December 2015, assessing the condition of a city-wide land including industrial, residential, and vacant lots (Bluff City Snapshot Survey, 2016). In situations where a direct, and likely costlier and time-consuming, survey is not feasible, an indirect approach is an alternative (described in Banai and Ploderer, 2018): Shelby county assessor of property GIS data have a parcel ID, size, land use codes, zoning, tax status, potential electricity disconnections, code enforcement to determine vacant or blighted property liability available from the Memphis Property Hub collection. A site-specific inspection of the physical conditions of the blighted properties is facilitated with Google street maps. For a typology of the urban and suburban physical form of sprawl revealed with aerial imagery, see Hayden (2004).

15.5.6 Sprawl and Blight Policy Implications

The discussions of the causes, methodologies, and theories in the literature of the nexus of sprawl and blight commonly conclude with some policy implications to remediate blight and control sprawl. Newman et al.'s (2018) policy recommendation for vacant urban areas is regional planning that strategically locates new industries and jobs, and phased regulations of population/density. Policies that attract population from suburb to the city abate blight through reinvestment in housing (Brueckner and Helsley, 2011). Vacancy is not just an indicator of urban blight, it is the legacy of the social, economic, and environmental conditions with transformations of the city in history, from industrial to post-industrial (Nassauer and Raskin, 2014). They are better addressed as "socio-ecologic systems" in a "transdisciplinary" approach to planning and design.

Urban sprawl and neighborhood blight are thought of as an unintended consequence of public policy or local legislative activity. The National Interstate and Defense Highways Act is a well-known example, regarded as a contributor to decentralization (or suburbanization) of population and businesses and central city decline. The National Environmental Policy Act is also examined in the context of urban sprawl and neighborhood decline (Babcock, 2008). Batchis (2010) attributes urban sprawl to the "permissive zoning jurisprudence" enabled by a landmark Supreme Court decision (1926): *Euclid v. Ambler*.

Unlike the U.S. cities with the state-enabled policy to curtail urban sprawl, like Portland, OR, in the 1970s, with an Urban Growth Boundary, the Memphis and Shelby County's 2000 Policy Plan in the 1980s outlined an Urban Service Boundary for the city and suburbs with water, sewer, and roads. The Memphis 2000 Policy Plan's (1981) Urban Service Boundary is regarded as a driver of Memphis and Shelby County's sprawl, particularly with a disconnect with land use and zoning regulations. The current comprehensive planning strategy for growth favors "built up not out," albeit belated.

15.6 DIFFERENCE BETWEEN URBAN GROWTH AND URBAN SPRAWL

Both urban growth and urban sprawl represent urbanization process (Heirman and Coppens, 2013). However, the processes are different. Urban sprawl implies excessive growth compared with usual growth. When urban growth proceeds without resident needs, many lands can be utilized for construction as a result (Habibi and Asadi, 2011). Sprawl represents the leading edge of urban growth (European Environment Agency, 2006), with residential, commercial, and industrial lands extending into areas beyond city boundaries. To differentiate between the two processes, many publications portray urban sprawl as fast and uncontrolled urban growth, while some studies refer to this phenomenon as "horizontal urban growth" or "uncontrolled urban development" (Gouda et al., 2016). While urban growth implies healthy urban development, urban sprawl implies undesirable and dysfunctional growth, recognized primarily by encroachments upon agricultural lands. In addition, urban sprawl can be identified as an outlying city expansion.

Density and spatial configurations are sprawl characteristics identified by different scholars. While density can vary from low to high, a spatial configuration can vary from dispersed to compact. Based on these two factors, Harvey and Clark (1965) noted the most common types of urban sprawl as low-density continuous, ribbon, and leap-frog development. In this concept, a low-density continuous development (occurs when the development proceeds at a lower density. The ribbon development (also strip development), is a linear urbanization alongside infrastructures. The leap-frog development (also scattered or discontinuous development), happens by small individual developments at further distances from a city requiring the highest capital expenditures. Yet another development is poly-nucleated, which happens at the crossing of different infrastructures (Figure 15.2).

In the United States, urban sprawl affects some places where different land uses tend to be kept separate, while other places develop in compact and connected ways with a mix of homes, shops, and offices and where homes and jobs tend to be closer together. Examples of the most sprawling U.S. metropolitan areas are Kingsport/Bristol/Bristol, TN-VA and Augusta/Richmond County, GA-SC, while New York/White Plains/Wayne, NY-NJ and San Francisco/San Mateo/Redwood City, CA, are the most compact and connected (Measuring Sprawl, 2014). The lives of millions of Americans are affected by these two development strategies, resulting in either ability to walk, ride a bicycle, and use public transportation due to more transportation options, or compelled to driving to get around places in their community (Measuring Sprawl, 2014). Outcomes of development strategies include differences in combined costs of housing and transportation, time spent commuting, economic opportunities, and individual health outcomes including life expectancy. In car-

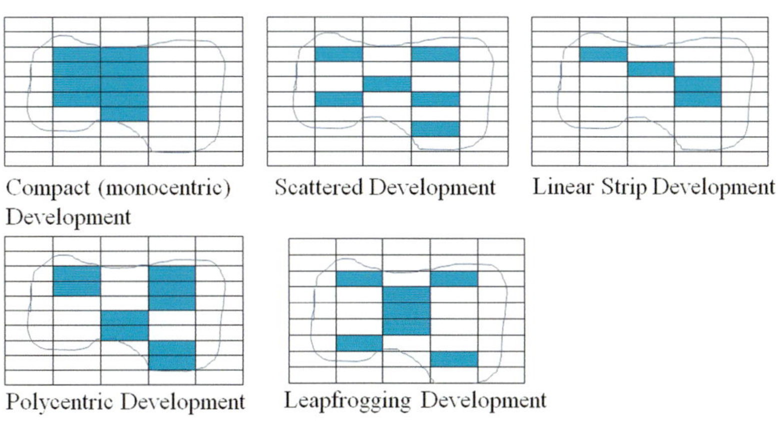

FIGURE 15.2 Different types of urban sprawl.

oriented communities, some population segments are especially at a disadvantage including people in poverty, the elderly, and children due to inability to drive, buy, and maintain automobiles (Antipova, 2018b).

15.7 WAYS TO HALT SPRAWL

Managing urban growth and providing sustainable development are among key urban strategies. Antipova (2018b) provides an example of urban area regeneration as one way to halt urban sprawl used in the United Kingdom. Area regeneration occurs when already urbanized lands are reused. In the United Kingdom, area regeneration is a key tool in preserving greenfields and rural areas: 60% of new housing development occurs in already built-up urban areas and not in the countryside. This approach is especially useful in post-industrial areas which experienced economic decline after traditional manufacturing industries had been closed and high unemployment and dereliction set in. An example of an area regeneration is the Isle of Dogs in the East End of London, a part of the London Docklands, which became dilapidated after the docks closed in 1980 followed by increasing unemployment and growing social deprivation. After the area was redeveloped in the early 1980s using the Battery Park City in Manhattan as a model, it became the prestigious Canary Warf development, attracting many financial and business services and becoming one of the largest office complexes in Europe. A relaxed, simplified planning was adopted in the area, attracting large-scale developments (versus then-restrictive planning in the city of London), and financial incentives were used together with transport infrastructure improvement such as the new Docklands Light Railway, London City Airport, providing an easier access into the Canary Wharf business complex and better integrating the Isle of Dogs with other parts of London (Antipova, 2018b). Thus, area regeneration is an approach for sustainable development.

In the United States, this form of infill development is known under the term of *urban revitalization*. Various factors such as a project location, design, financing, entrepreneurship, and time may contribute to a success or failure of an urban planning initiative. One example shows that not all infill development schemes are successful. While revitalization was successfully implemented in one of the communities in Savannah, GA, in the 1960s, a similar initiative to restore the city's Victorian District, which contained vacant and deteriorating structures failed in the early 1990s because of an insufficient market demand (Antipova, 2018b).

Another approach to contain sprawl and check urban growth is a "greenbelt," which has been used in the United Kingdom since 1955. Additionally, this approach allows to preserve a community character. Local authorities designate greenbelts around their towns so that the created greenbelts effectively halt urban sprawl and prevent cities and towns from fusing into one another to form continuous agglomerations (Antipova, 2018b). Greenbelts comprise about 12% of land in England, promoting regenerated urban land and reuse abandoned land.

To stop the consequences of urban sprawl, strategies including new urbanism and growth management were proposed (Brunner, 2012). In the United States, urban growth management occurs through various planning strategies including "urban growth boundaries" and "form-based codes" administered by state and municipal governments protect natural areas and control growth of urban zones and especially peripheral growth by allowing urban development and public infrastructure and services to occur only within these boundaries (Antipova, 2018b).

The "new urbanism" and "smart growth" approaches emerged in Europe and the United States in response to suburban sprawl to address land use separation, long commuting times, traffic congestion, and air pollution. Smart growth emphasizes balanced regional growth of transportation, community, and environmental planning, and new urbanism advocates healthy neighborhoods and communities achieved by urban design and architecture (Judd and Swanstrom, 2006). The smart growth approach advocates compact urban forms, higher density, and mixed-use developments. King County, Washington, adopted a comprehensive growth management plan in 1964 to provide affordable housing, public facilities, and economic growth while controlling the growth

(Robinson et al., 2005). Additionally, residential development was allowed in rural areas at a lower density (one dwelling unit per 2.5–10 acres) in 1985. To minimize land conversion, Washington State adopted the growth management act (GMA; Chapter 36.70A RCW) in 1990 to concentrate growth in urban areas.

Smart growth approach also encourages multiple modes of transportation including public transport, walking, and cycling. Transit-oriented development (TOD) achieves the objectives of higher population and housing density and mixed-use land uses around the stations, while mass transit improves accessibility.

Smart growth avoids negative consequences of urban sprawl and fulfills economic, social, and environmental balance (Robinson et al., 2005). In King County, Washington, smart growth was accomplished by zoning in which urban areas were zoned for higher residential density (minimum 1–12 dwelling per acre) and rural areas were zoned for lower residential density (1 dwelling per 2.5–10 acres).

15.8 HOW COVID-19 IMPACTS CITIES

15.8.1 Smart Growth, Implementation of Smart Technologies, and COVID-19

In the past decades, especially since 1990s, movements toward smart cities improved the efficiency of urban operations and raised the life quality. The current pandemic motivates these movements by increasing the reliance on teleworking, and online commerce, and education. Also, advanced information and communication technologies (ICTs) and big data analytics minimize person-to-person interactions (Sharifi and Khavarian-Garmsir, 2020).

ICT- and and big data analytics-assisted smart solutions improve life quality by making urban operations more efficient and efficacious. Smart city movements might be boosted during the COVID-19 due to greater reliance on smart technologies minimizing human-to-human interaction (teleworking, telemedicine, surveillance systems, and online commerce and education) (Kunzmann, 2020). The smart solutions can be also adjusted during the humanitarian and health crises to locate infected individuals, estimate diffusion patterns, and take appropriate containment measures (Sharifi and Khavarian-Garmsir, 2020). Overall, multiple benefits of smart solutions have been demonstrated.

Cities may learn from each other valuable lessons much needed during disruptive events. For example, pre–COVID-19, an urban observatory in Newcastle, UK, was used for real-time data collection and storage. This recalls Pattrick Geddes's Outlook Tower in the late 19th-century England the purpose of which was similarly for the general public to gain information about the regional context holistically while planning the city and the neighborhod (Geddes, 1968). The live data feeds included vehicular traffic, pedestrian mobility patterns, and air quality metrics. After pandemic hit, a data dashboard was developed so that local authorities and different stakeholders could be informed in a timely manner about changes in people's behaviors allowing for a fast decision making based on the live data feeds and allowing to adapt initial decisions based on evidence. To illustrate, abnormal changes in movement and activity patterns could be immediately revealed requiring attention (James et al., 2020).

Cities utilize smart technologies and various initiatives to become more resilient and sustainable during COVID-19. Cities in China used drones to autonomously deliver medical and commercial supplies during the total lockdown which otherwise may have major socioeconomic implications, while using artificial intelligence helped to prevent healthcare workers from direct contact with patients (Chen et al., 2020). Based on different social-political contexts, Chinese cities adopted a "techno-driven," top-down approach whereby the pandemic is contained through citizen discipline and free flow information control, overall demonstrating great success in containing COVID-19 spread, while a more "human-driven" approach was utilized by Western societies (Kummitha, 2020). In the former example, a "colorcoded ranking" program used in smartphone applications based on recent health records for a person and their relatives in China allowed to control people movement patterns. In yet another example, in Russia, the central government promoted a smartphone application enabled to enforce and track compliance with social distancing and quarantine rules. In the latter example, when the Western world deploys a "human-driven" approach, the pandemic is controlled via citizen education and information provision while promoting two-way communication between citizens and the government. Citizens are also able to solve other socioeconomic and environmental issues, both existing and emerging, benefitting from a combination of both approaches and using smart solutions to contain COVID-19, but also addressing and mitigating privacy concerns, while allowing for efficient coordination and information sharing and preventing fake news and misinformation from spreading. Thus, combining two approaches that raise citizen awareness, cities might easier adapt to future events.

15.8.2 Emerging Infections and Cities

Until recently and before the COVID-19 spread, while much was published on the impacts of various man-made and natural disasters on cities including planning, recovery, and mitigation measures when dealing with disasters, there was a relative lack in studies about the impacts of a pandemic on cities (Sharifi and Khavarian-Garmsir, 2020). Urban studies related to previous pandemics and impacts on cities tended to focus on more vulnerable to infections categories including poor and marginalized groups. The COVID-19 pandemic brought this opportunity for urban planners to understand how urban areas might be affected by a global pandemic. After the first confirmed case of COVID-19 was detected in Wuhan, Hubei Province, China, in late 2019, the potential vulnerability of cities to contiguous disease and pandemics become a topic of discussions again.

Cities are a hotspot of COVID-19 infection as they concentrate population and economic activities. To understand the impacts of the pandemic on urban areas, scholars study the dynamics of the pandemic in urban areas. Overall, early studies focused on four major themes, including socio-economic impacts, briefly highlighted next (others are environmental quality, management and governance, transportation, and urban design).

The earlier view of the global epidemic representing a systematic disadvantage that may equally affect and limit everyone's economic activity, with any socioeconomic status or from any geographic location, was rejected while finding that certain factors may either increase or decrease people's vulnerability to the financial stress related to COVID-19 (Qian and Fan, 2020). In China's context, these factors include education, family income, membership in Communist Party, and state-sector employment.

Socio-economic conditions and the built environment characteristics affect health-related outcomes. Factors associated with social disadvantage including crowded housing conditions, lower education and income can make people less resistant and more vulnerable to the infection. In the USA context, to visually illustrate the connection between population density and health, we used COVID-19 morbidity and mortality data from the New York City, USA. Figure 15.3 shows the NYC boroughs of Brooklyn and Queens (in purple and dark blue, respectively, in the upper left panel) have more people per household, and more renters residing in overcrowded conditions, while characterized with higher infection rates measured by total cases per 100,000 people, while the wealthy borough of Manhattan (shown in brown in Figure 15.3) characterized with higher population density, and a greater share of population with college degrees, had lower infection rates (see also Hamidi et al., 2020, for the discussion of density and coronavirus).

Not all cities and regions are affected similarly by the COVID-19 epidemic. A recent study examined factors increasing vulnerability of the city in a pandemic from the urban economics perspective. Cities with an undiversified economic structure, including those with special economic functions with industries where many workers are shoulder-to-shoulder and share cramped spaces for a prolonged time (e.g., meat-packing and poultry processing plants, or mining-oriented municipalities where it is not always possible to maintain the sanitary regime in mines), and cities

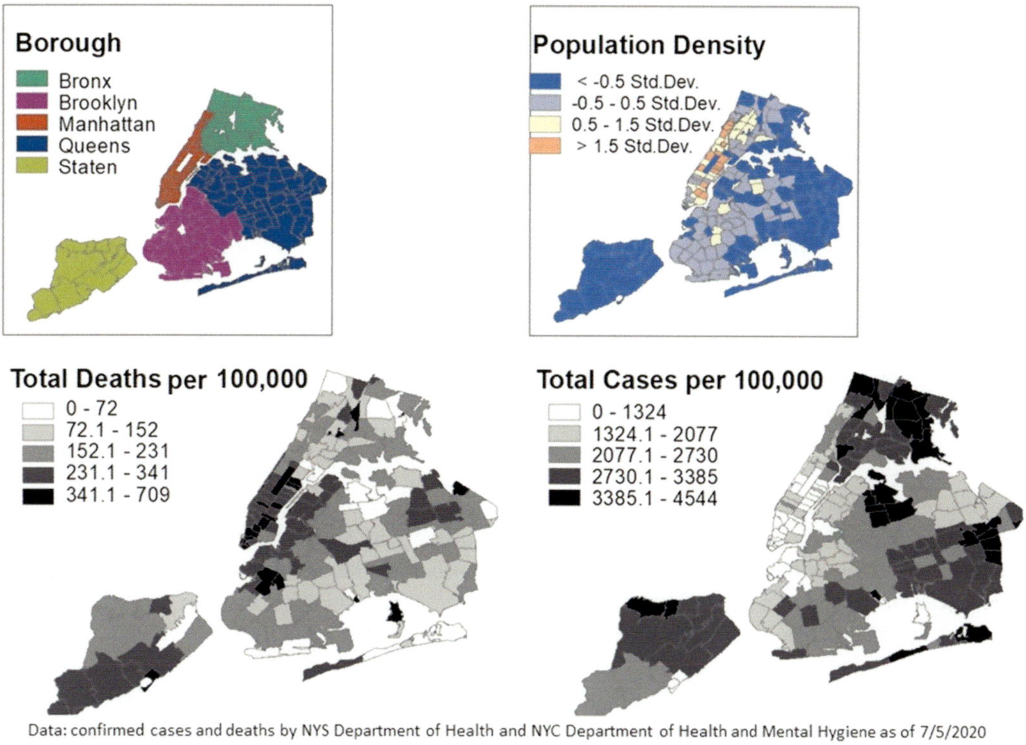

FIGURE 15.3 Population density, morbidity, and mortality rate in New York City.

relying on tourism experience steep declines of international and domestic tourists. Also, cities that have large care centers, polycentric cities, and shrinking cities, are the most vulnerable to negative impacts on urban economy including the urban hotel market; city tax revenues; citizens' income, tourism, and hospitality; small- and medium-sized firms; urban food supply chain; and migrant workers (Krzysztofik et al., 2020; Banai, 2020).

15.8.3 Sprawl, Blight, and COVID-19

The urban studies literature is given considerable attention to the subject of sprawl and blight, although not as commonly in combination as noted in subsection 15.5 above. How might the features of sprawl and its related phenomenon, blight, be considered in the context of the COVID-19 pandemic?

An emerging concern is related to the decreases in the city's budget due to COVID-19, which has further urban development implications where implementation of some plans may be considered less priority, such as environmental and cultural and be delayed or cancelled (Sharifi and Khavarian-Garmsir, 2020; Kunzmann, 2020).

A fundamental consequence of sprawl is regional inequality (Calthorpe and Fulton 2001), manifested by the provision of infrastructure in city vs suburb and exurban areas. The pandemic revealed the unequal access to a 21st-century infrastructure regarded at par with the infrastructure of water, sewer, and road: cyberspace. When physical space proved infectious, virtual space provided a safer alternative that was not accessible to all, however. That meant unequal access to jobs, education, and services.

While low-density urban or exurban is regarded as a negative or wasteful feature of sprawl, it turns out, low density is viewed as a positive feature for a pandemic that is exacerbated by compact living and commuting (Hamidi et al., 2020, Banai, 2020).

Even urban blight provided a practical alternative to non-blight urban space. Who could have anticipated the blight that is caused by sprawl, observed by the sea of parking space in commercial land use, some of which is boarded up, or bankrupt, or that all too familiar auto-centric structure, the drive-in outdoor cinema would find a second life, particularly during a pandemic alongside the perennial drive-in restaurants (for further elaboration, see Banai, 2020).

To sum up, blight is a consequence of urban expansion, as noted above. However, blight is also a cause of urban expansion, with depopulation and decline of the central city, a source of urban and regional inequality of a wide-ranging variety, including household income, municipal revenue, expenditure, and services. A manifestation of the urban-regional inequality caused by sprawl and blight is job-housing imbalance, limited regional mobility, particularly with inequality of access to jobs and services, including food deserts. While the consequences of sprawl and blight are known, less recognized are the disproportionate impacts on population distinguished by class, race, gender, and ethnicity revealed during the coronavirus pandemic.

15.9 CONCLUSION

We have provided a comprehensive overview of urban sprawl by pulling together its various features and wide-ranging impacts recorded in vast urban studies literature. We have highlighted the nexus of urban sprawl and blight that is given inadequate attention in the literature with also wide-ranging dimensions that are characteristic of sprawl itself.

Because of the concentration of population and economic activities, cities are a hotspot of the COVID-19 infection. However, the urban form sheds particular light on both the vulnerability and resilience of cities during the pandemic. It is too early to state whether COVID-19 exacerbated the negative sprawl and blight impacts; future studies will examine spatial variations of impacts if any. Population density and compact communities usually regarded as desirable features exhibited vulnerabilities of the city in a pandemic. While the air-quality impact of the pandemic initially improved due to the lockdown and reduced tail-pipe pollution, the increased goods shipment via trucks did not sustain air quality in a dispersed urban form of residences and businesses. And the socio-economic impacts of the pandemic proved uneven across groups distinguished by class, race, gender, and ethnicity.

Although local government is arguably an ideal locus of decision making in the city, the pandemic overwhelmed the resources of the city, and in the U.S. case, required federal and state guidance for effective coping. Policies using techno-driven and human-driven approaches incorporating smart technologies render cities more resilient and sustainable during COVID-19. Smart growth alternatives to the auto-dependent sprawl, with pedestrian-friendly land use mix, convenient access to shops and services, and proximity to green space provided some relief for city residents vying for a sense of community in a pandemic. Further work plausibly extends studies on four major themes: environmental quality, socio-economic impacts, management and governance, transportation, and urban design.

REFERENCES

Angel, S., Parent, J., and Civco, D. May 2007. "Urban Sprawl Metrics: An Analysis of Global Urban Expansion Using Gis." ASPRS 2007 Annu. Conf. Tampa, Florida, 1–12.

Antipova A. 2018a. Chapter 1: Introduction. In: *Urban Environment, Travel Behavior, Health, and Resident Satisfaction*. Cham: Palgrave Macmillan. 10.1007/978-3-319-74198-7_1.

Antipova A. 2018b. Chapter 2: Urban Environment. In: *Urban Environment, Travel Behavior, Health, and Resident Satisfaction*. Cham: Palgrave Macmillan. 10.1007/978-3-319-74198-7_1

Babcock, H. 2008. "The National Environmental Policy Act in the Urban Environment: Oxymoron or a Useful Tool to Combat the Destruction of Neighborhoods and Urban Sprawl?" *Journal of Environmental Law and Litigation*, *23*(1), 1–33.

Banai, R. 2019. *Concentric Zone Theory*. The Wiley Encyclopedia of Urban and Regional Studies, Wiley and Sons Ltd.

Banai, R. 2020. "Pandemic and the Planning of Resilient Cities and Regions." *Cities: The International Journal of Urban Policy and Planning*, *106*, 102929.10.1016/j.cities.2020.102929

Banai R., and DePriest, T. Dec. 2014. "Urban Sprawl: Definitions, Data, Methods of Measurement, and Environmental Consequences." *Journal of Sustainability Education*, 7(12), 1–15.

Banai, R., and Ploderer, L. 2018. The Geography of Industrial Blight: Neglected Options for Sustainable Urban Revitalization, Memphis and Shelby County. Paper presented at North American Meetings of the Regional Science Council International 2018, San Antonio, Texas 65th Annual Meeting November 7–10. Retrieved from https://blogs.memphis.edu/rbanai/files/2019/09/The-Geography-of-Blight.pdf

Barrington-Leigh, C., and Millard-Ball, A. 2015. "A Century of Sprawl in the United States." *Proceedings of the National Academy of Sciences of the United States of America*, 112(27), 8244–8249.

Batchis, W. 2010. "Enabling Urban Sprawl: Revisiting the Supreme Court's Seminal Zoning Decision Euclid v. Ambler in the 21st Century." *Virginia Journal of Social Policy and the Law*, 17(3), 373–403.

Bechle, M. J., Millet, D. B., and Marshall, J. D. 2011. "Effects of Income and Urban Form on Urban NO2: Global Evidence from Satellites." *Environmental Science and Technology*, 45 (11), 4914–4919.

Bhatta, B. 2010. "Causes and Consequences of Urban Growth and Sprawl." *In: Analysis of Urban Growth and Sprawl from Remote Sensing Data. Advances in Geographic Information Science*. Springer, Berlin:Heidelberg.17–36.

Bluff City Snapshot Survey. 2016. The Department of Neighborhood Improvement, Division of Public Works, City of Memphis, TN.

Brueckner, J. K., and Helsley, R. W. 2011. "Sprawl and Blight." *Journal of Urban Economics*, 69(2), 205–213. 10.1016/j.jue.2010.09.003

Brunner, A. 2012. "The Effects of Urban Sprawl on Daily Life." *53rd Annual Transportation Research Forum,* TRF 2012, 2, 855–874.

Burgess, E. W. 1925. "The Growth of the City." In E. P. Robert, E. W. Burgess, and R.D. McKenzie (eds.), *The City*. Chicago: University of Chicago Press.

Calthorpe, Peter, and William B., Fulton. 2001.*The Regional City: planning for the end of sprawl*. Washington, DC: Island Press.

Chin, N. 2002. *Unearthing the Roots of Urban Sprawl: A Critical Analysis Of Form, Function And Methodology*. (CASA Working Papers 47. Centre for Advanced Spatial Analysis. London, U.K.

Cool Roofs. Everything Connects. 2014. [Online]. Retrieved from https://www.everythingconnects.org/cool-roofs.html#/

Cox, W., and Utt, J. 2004. The Costs of Sprawl Reconsidered: What the Data Really Show. Backgrounder, 1770,10. Washington, D.C.

Deng, C., and Ma, J. 2015. "Viewing Urban Decay from the Sky: A Multi-scale Analysis of Residential Vacancy in a Shrinking U.S. City." *Landscape and Urban Planning*, 141, 88–99. 10.1016/j.landurbplan.2015.05.002.

Depriest, T., and Antipova, A. 2013. Urban Sprawl and Its Impact on Flood Events in Jackson, Tennessee. Paper presented at Annual Meeting of the Association of American Geographers (AAG), April 9–13, 2013. Los Angeles, CA.

Downs, A. 1999. "Some Realities about Sprawl and Urban Decline." *Housing Policy Debate*, 10(4), 955–974.

European Environment Agency. 2006. "Urban Sprawl in Europe, the Ignored Challenge." *European Commission: Joint Research Center*, 6 (23), 24–25.

Ewing, R. 1997. "Is Los Angeles-Style Sprawl Desirable?". *Journal of the American Planning Association*, 63 (1): 107–126.

Ewing, R., and Cervero, R. 2017. "Does Compact Development Make People Drive Less? The Answer Is Yes." *Journal of the American Planning Association*, 83 (1), 19–25.

Ewing, R., and Hamidi, S. 2014. "Smart Growth America: Measuring Sprawl." Retrieved from http://gis.cancer.gov/tools/urban-sprawl/ (accessed 25 April 2014).

Fitzgerald, J., and Bartlett, D. 1912. *Proceedings of the Fourth National Conference on City Planning*. American Planning Association.

Fogelson, R. 2001. *Downtown: Its Rise and Fall, 1880–1950, 3rd Printing Edition*. Yale University Press.

Frey, W. 1979. "Central City White Flight: Racial and Nonracial Causes." *American Sociological Review*, 44(3), 425–448. Retrieved from http://www.jstor.org/stable/2094885 (accessed 13 November 2020).

Galster, G., Hanson, R., Ratcliffe, M. R., Wolman, H., Coleman, S., and Freihage, J. 2001. "Wrestling Sprawl to the Ground: Defining and Measuring an Elusive Concept." *Housing Policy Debate*, 12(4), 681–717.

Garfield, A. 1931. *Slums, Large-scale Housing and Decentralization: Reports of the Committees on Blighted Areas and Slums*. Washington, D.C.

Geddes, P. 2004. "Blighting the Way: Urban Renewal, Economic Development, and the Elusive Definition of Blight." *Fordham Urban Law Journal, 31*(2): 305–337. Available at: https://ir.lawnet.fordham.edu/ulj/vol31/iss2/2

Gouda, A. A., Hosseini, M., and Masoumi, H. E. 2016. "The Status of Urban and Suburban Sprawl in Egypt and Iran." *GeoScape*, 10(1), 1–15.

Habibi, S., and Asadi, N. 2011. "Causes, Results and Methods of Controlling Urban Sprawl." *Procedia Engineering*, 12, 133–141.

Hamidi, S., Sabouri, S., Ewing, R. 2020. "Does Density Aggrevate the COVID-19 Pandemic?" *Journal of the American Planning Association,* 86(4), 495–509.

Harvey, R. O., and Clark, W. A. V. 1965. "The Nature and Economics of Urban Sprawl." *Land Economics*, 41(1), 1. 10.2307/3144884

Hayden, D. 2004. *A Field Guide to Sprawl*. New York: W. W. Norton and Company.

Heirman, S., and Coppens, S. Nov. 2013. Causes, Consequences and Affordability of Urban Sprawl in the Caribbean: Case Causes, Consequences and Affordability of Urban Sprawl in the Caribbean: Case Paramaribo. Caribb. Urban Forum 2013.

Hwang, U., and Woo, M. 2020. "Analysis of Inter-Relationships between Urban Decline and Urban Sprawl in City-Regions of South Korea." *Sustainability*, 12(4), 1656. 10.3390/su12041656

James, P., Das, R., Jalosinska, A., and Smith, L. 2020. "Smart Cities and a Data-driven Response to COVID-19." *Dialogues in Human Geography*, 10 (2), 255–259. 10.1177/2043820620934211.

Judd, R. D., and Swanstrom, T. 2006. *City Politics: The Political Economy of Urban America*, 5th ed. Pearson.

Kahn, M. E. 2001. "Does Sprawl Reduce the Black/White Housing Consumption Gap?" *Housing Policy Debate*, 12(1), 77–86.

Kondo, M. C. 2018. "Blight Abatement of Vacant Land and Crime in New Orleans." *Public Health Reports*, 133(6), 650–657.

Krzysztofik, R., Kantor-Pietraga, I., and Spórna, T. 2020. "Spatial and Functional Dimensions of the COVID-19 Epidemic in Poland." *Eurasian Geography and Economics*, 61(4–5), 573–586. Retrieved from https://www.tandfonline.com/doi/full/10.1080/15387216.2020.1783337

Kummitha, R. K. R. 2020. "Smart Technologies for Fighting Pandemics: The Techno- and Human- Driven Approaches in Controlling the Virus Transmission." *Government Information Quarterly*, 37 (3), 101481.

Kunzmann, K. R. 2020. "Smart Cities After Covid-19: Ten Narratives." *DISP*, 56(2), 20–31. 10.1080/02513625.2020.1794120

Laidley, T. 2016. "Measuring Sprawl: A New Index, Recent Trends, and Future Research." *Urban Affairs Review*, 52(1), 66–97.

Lopez, R. 2014. "Urban Sprawl in the United States: 1970–2010." *Cities and the Environment (CATE)*, 7(1). Retrieved from https://digitalcommons.lmu.edu/cate/vol7/iss1/7

Lumen Learning. 2020. *Environmental Biology*. Albany, NY: SUNY Press.

Mallach, A. 2018. *The Empty House Next Door: Understanding and Reducing Vacancy and Hypervacancy in the United States*. Cambridge, MA:Lincoln Institute of Land Policy.

McGuire, T. J., and Sjoquist, D. L. 2003. Urban Sprawl and the Finances of State and Local Governments. *State and Local Finances under Pressure*. Edward Elgar Publishing Ltd., 299–326.

Measuring Sprawl. 2014. Smart Growth America. April. Retrieved from https://smartgrowthamerica.org/app/uploads/2016/08/measuring-sprawl-2014.pdf (accessed 6 March 2021).

Memphis 2000 Policy Plan Memphis. 1981. Memphis City Council Adoption (September), Shelby County Board of Commissioners Adoption (October).

Mieszkowski, P., and Mills, E. S. 1993. "The Causes of Metropolitan Suburbanization." *Journal of Economic Perspectives*, 7(3),135–147.

Momeni, E., and Antipova, A. Nov 2018. A time-series study of socio-demographic and land use/cover factors and travel behavior in Memphis and Shelby County, TN. Paper presented at South-Eastern Division of the Association of American Geographers (SEDAAG). November 18–19, 2018, Johnson City, TN.

Nassauer, J. I., and Raskin, J. 2014. "Urban Vacancy and Land Use Legacies: A Frontier for Urban Ecological Research, Design, and Planning." *Landscape and Urban Planning*, 125(2014), 245–253, 10.1016/j.landurbplan.2013.10.008

Newman, G., Gu, R., Kim, J. H., Bowman, A., and Li, W. 2016. "Elasticity and Urban Vacancy: A Longitudinal Comparison of U.S. Cities." *Cities*, 25(2016), 143–151, 10.1016/j.cities.2016.05.018.

Newman, G., Yunmi, P., Bowman, A., and Jung Lee, R. 2018. "Vacant Urban Areas: Causes and Interconnected Factors." *Cities*, 72(Part B), 421–429. 10.1016/j.cities.2017.10.005.

Nuissl, H., Rink, D., Couch, C., and Couch, K. 2007. "Decline and Sprawl: Urban Sprawl is not Confined to Expanding City Regions, Urban Sprawl in Europe." *Landscapes, Land-Use Change and Policy*, John Wiley & Sons, 136–162. 10.1002/9780470692066.ch5

Park, R. E., Burgess, E.W., and McKenzie, R.D. eds. 1925. *The City: Suggestions for Investigation of Human Behavior in the Urban Environment*. Chicago: University of Chicago Press.

Pendall, R. 1999. "Do Land-use Controls Cause Sprawl?" *Environment and Planning B Planning and Design*, 26(4), 555–571.

Pohanka, M., and Fitzgerald, S. Jan. 2004. "Urban Sprawl and You: How Sprawl Adversely Affects Worker Health." *American Association of Occupational Health Nurses Journal*, 52(6), 242–246.

Qian, Y., and Fan, W. 2020. "Who Loses Income during the COVID-19 Outbreak? Evidence from China." *Research in Social Stratification and Mobility*, 68, 100522. 10.1016/j.rssm.2020.100522

Razin, E. 1998. Policies to Control Urban Sprawl: Planning Regulations or Changes in the 'Rules of the Game'? *Urban Studies*, 35(2), 321–340.

Robinson, L., Newell, J. P., and Marzluff, J.M. 2005. "Twenty-Five Years of Sprawl in the Seattle Region: Growth Management Responses and Implications for Conservation." *Landscape and Urban Planning*, 71, 51–72.

Sat, N. A. 2018. "Polycentricity in a Developing World: A Micro-regional Analysis for Morphological Polycentricity in Turkey." *GeoScape*, 12(2), 64–75.

Schilling, J., and Pinzón, J. 2016. "The Basics of Blight: Recent Research on Its Drivers, Impacts, and Interventions." *VPRN Research & Policy Brief*, 2(2016). https://vacantpropertyresearch.com/wp-content/uploads/2016/03/20160126_Blight_FINAL.pdf

Sharifi, A., and Khavarian-Garmsir, A. R. 2020. "The COVID-19 Pandemic: Impacts on Cities and Major Lessons for Urban Planning, Design, and Management." *Science of The Total Environment*, 749, 1–3.

Sierra Club. 1998. *The Dark Side of the American Dream: The Costs and Consequences of Suburban*. San Francisco, CA:The Sierra Club. https://vault.sierraclub.org/sprawl/report98/

Sorensen, A. 1999. "Land Readjustment, Urban Planning and Urban Sprawl in the Tokyo Metropolitan Area." *Urban Studies*, 36(13), 2333–2360.

Stevens, M. R. 2017. "Does Compact Development Make People Drive Less?" *Journal of the American Planning Association*, 83 (1), 7–18.

Stone, B. 2008. "Urban Sprawl and Air Quality in Large US Cities." *Journal of Environmental Management*, 86, 688–698.

Tennessee Code 13–20-201 – Blighted areas and dilapidation defined » LawServer. [Online]. Retrieved from https://www.lawserver.com/law/state/tennessee/tn-code/tennessee_code_13–20-201 (accessed 18 March 2021).

Terry, B., and A.I.C.P. 2012. *Dealing with Blight: Strategies for Tennessee's Communities*. Nashville.

Tjallingii, S. P. 2000. Ecology on the edge: Landscape and ecology between town and country. *Landscape and Urban Planning*, 48(3–4), 103–119.

Urban Sprawl. 2013. Everything Connects. [Online]. Available: https://www.everythingconnects.org/urban-sprawl.html.

U.S. Department of Housing and Urban Development. 1999. The State of the Cities 1999. Washington, DC.

Van Der Valk, A. 2002. "The Dutch Planning Experience." *Landscape and Urban Planning*, 58(2–4), 201–210.

Wassmer, R. 2008. "Causes of Urban Sprawl in the United States: Auto Reliance as Compared to Natural Evolution, Flight from Blight, and Local Revenue Reliance." *Journal of Policy Analysis and Management*, 27(3), 536–555. 10.1002/pam.20355

Zolnik, E. J. 2004. "The North American City Revisited: Urban Quality of Life in Canada and the United States." *Urban Geography*, 25(3), 217–240.

16 Improving Food Security in African Cities towards Smartness: A Bibliometric Analysis

Joan Nyika
Technical University of Kenya, Nairobi, Kenya
University of Johannesburg, South Africa

Megersa Olumana Dinka
University of Johannesburg, South Africa

CONTENTS

16.1 INTRODUCTION

Globally, measures to alleviate hunger have been taken up, although undernutrition, malnutrition, and food insecurity remain enormous challenges of the contemporary society (Sibhatu & Qaim, 2017; Nyika et al., 2021a). The situation has escalated globally following the emergence and persistence of the COVID-19 pandemic, which has negatively affected the food value chain, particularly the production, access, affordability, and transport capacity (Workie et al., 2020). Realizing food security is

DOI: 10.1201/9781003126195-20

therefore a desirable high-priority worldwide, irrespective of the socioeconomic status and political systems of a given region. Globally, today's era is characterized by a growing population, urbanization, high demand for natural and man-made resources, and extreme weather among other environmental problems such as pollution and land degradation (Jerzak & Smiglak-Krajewska, 2020). With increased food demand amidst low crop productivity due to soil degradation, prices of food have risen and its distribution, access, and availability have become income dependent. In the scenario, poor households suffer in favour of the affluent, as Ahmed et al. (2017) noted. Workie et al. (2020) also noted the trend and suggested that developing countries are affected most since their vulnerability is high despite low preparedness for the ongoing challenges of environmental degradation, disease emergence and climate change. Therefore, poverty, climate change, natural disasters, conflicts, and war exacerbate the malnutrition and hunger state of the world (Prosekov & Ivanova, 2018; Pawlak & Kolodziejczak, 2020). It is for these reasons that the Food and Agricultural Organization noted that 13% of the poor developing countries of the world experience undernourishment (Roser & Ritchie, 2013) while Palwak and Kolodziejczak (2020) noted that feeding the world has been a pre-existent problem that is likely to worsen in future. Additionally, the growing global population at 7.6 billion as of 2018 and projected at 9.2 billion by 2050 will result to an increased food demand up from 59% to 102% (Fukase & Martin, 2017; Silva, 2018). In view of this challenge, both urban and rural centres must be proactively involved in food production to double the production as suggested by Tilman et al. (2011), as this will meet the ever rising demand and bridge the existent food security gap.

In Africa, for instance, majority of the population survive below the global poverty line and are adversely affected by hunger, malnutrition, famine, undernourishment and the region manifests extreme food shortages (Ngcamu & Chari, 2020). The food insecurities in the continent have been exacerbated by factors such as diseases (including tropical diseases, COVID-19 and HIV/AIDS) (Workie et al., 2020), poor governing policies and poor governance, political-economic issues, civil wars, extreme weather patterns, and prolonged dry spells. Assoumana et al. (2016) in putting this issue in perspective claimed that majority of African countries depend on agriculture and the economic activity employs over 80% of the workforce. In named countries of Africa, such as Kenya (Nyika, 2020a) and South Africa (Nyika, 2020b), the situation is escalating and cases of food insecurity are now a common phenomenon in the regions. With the apparent challenge in food insecurity and the factors promoting it, African countries will continue to be poorer (Rankoana, 2016). The situation is therefore a wakeup call for the continent to revamp its food production systems and adopt approaches towards sustainability (Chakona & Shackleton, 2019).

There is a strong conviction from research that food insecurity in Africa is largely a rural problem and proposed solutions are skewed towards a green revolution that advocates for massive production of food by small scale farmers (Ejeta, 2010; Otsukaa & Kijimab, 2010; Crush & Frayne, 2011a; Ejeta, 2012; Smit, 2016). However, this view can be disputed considering countries such as South Africa that produce almost enough food for its population yet more than 60% of its population dwells in urban regions (Crush et al., 2011). Additionally, the country experiences a high prevalence of undernutrition and malnutrition diseases compared to less productive countries of the continent (Crush et al., 2012). In another study, Walsh and Van Rooyen (2014) dispelled the suggestions that food poverty is largely a rural but an urban problem considering that the former is less likely to be poorer even when resources to avert poverty are limited compared to the latter. According to the UN-HABITAT (2010), it is projected that all African cities, just as South Africa, will see a surge in urban dwellers compared to a rural population. Of concern with the trend is the fact that new urbanites seeking for better opportunities in cities live in deplorable conditions characterized by overcrowding at informal settlements and have low-income jobs or are even unemployed (Chihambakwe et al., 2019). Additionally, they will have limited access to water for consumption or even basic agricultural activities, as is evident in Kenya (Nyika, 2020a).

The characteristics and challenges aforementioned therefore beg the question of how the expected new urbanites will be fed towards making urbanization sustainable and in improving their food security. This chapter sought to explore the studies that have been done on improving food security in African cities towards the smartness and sustainability of the urban centres by employing a bibliometric analyses methodology. The scientometric approach in this context will inform on the pre-existent research activities regarding improved food security for smart urbanization, the institutions and countries involved, and the priority themes that inform future research (Nyika et al., 2021a). Bibliometric analysis also provides insight on the key scientific actors contributing to food solutions in urban areas of developing countries using empirical simulations, comparisons, and evidence-based descriptions (Nyika et al., 2021b). Additionally, the chapter proposes measures that the continent must adopt towards improved food security and economic development of its towns and cities.

16.2 METHODOLOGY

16.2.1 Database Selection

The Web of Science (WOS) database was used in this study to retrieve relevant publications on improving food security in African cities towards smartness and sustainability. The database has several advantages that make it appropriate for scientometric analysis. It is a very expansive database covering a wide range of publications. Its coverage is rated as the most consistent with publications dating back to the beginning of the 20th century. According to Chadegani et al. (2013), searches done on the WOS have open access options, have details on citations and authors, and are not limited to the English language alone. Additionally, Mongeon and Paul-Hus (2015) noted that the database gives preference to journal archiving and hence is the best for bibliometric researches and can provide adequate empirical evidence.

16.2.2 Search Strategy

One of the prerequisites of bibliometric analyses is generating an accurate search query, which will produce valid and comprehensive results for precise analysis. This study developed queries on the topic of improving food security in African cities or towns to enhance smartness or sustainable urbanisation in a preview of both scientific and grey literature publications. A prior compilation of search phrases as Sweileh and Mansour (2020) did in a bibliometric analysis studying on antimicrobial resistance was done. In this study, three study scenarios were generated for the search in WOS and joined by the Boolean operator "or." The specific searchers were "food security in African cities" or "smart food secure African urban areas" or "food security in African towns." The search was on topic basis.

16.2.3 Refining Retrieved Results of the Search

This search included all the obtained results without filtering the document types. The searched results were rechecked to remove any false negatives through an eligibility analysis. This was done to ensure all the documents were related to the search topic and had enough information regarding the query. The study period was set between 1990 and 2021 though preliminary assessments showed slow growth in publications prior to the year 2000. No language restrictions were imposed to ensure a holistic search was done.

16.2.4 Data Export and Analysis

The data from the searched results was downloaded from the database and transferred to Microsoft Excel for graphical or tabular representation. The VOSviewer software was used to generate the visualization maps (Van Eck & Waltman, 2011). Using lines, which represented link strengths from the generated maps, dissimilar associations of the publications, their original countries and institutions, and co-citations of involved authors were established. The thickness of the line corresponded to the association so that thicker lines had higher correlations and vice versa (Van Eck & Waltman, 2011). A number of bibliometric indicators were used in establishing the associations in the publications. These included: 1) publication growth in the searched years; 2) research themes and WOS categories and research areas related to the search query; 3) most active sources (journals), institutions, funding agencies, and regions; as well as 4) co-citations. The information obtained in the most-cited publications with regards to measures of improving food security were also discussed to devise a way forward towards sustainable development in African cities.

16.3 RESULTS AND DISCUSSION

16.3.1 Features of Publications

In the current study, the total documents retrieved were 130, and out of this total 124 (95.4%) were articles, 4 (3.1%) were reviews, 1 (0.8%) was a proceeding paper, 2 (1.5%) were early access, and 2 (1.5%) were editorial materials. The majority of the publications at 96.9% (n = 126) were written in English while French and Afrikaans contributed 2.3% (n = 3) and 1 (0.8%) of the total searches, respectively. Approximately 40% (n = 52) of the retrieved publications were available on open access.

16.3.2 Growth in Publications and Citations

The growth in publications related to food security enhancement in African cities towards smartness has been exponential since the mid-1990s. Over the last five years (2016-to-date), this growth was more pronounced as 53% of the total searched results were published in this period. Similarly, the citations have grown over the last years to a record count of 222, 331, 386, 501, and 493 from 2016–2020, respectively. A representation of the growth in publications and citations is as shown in Figure 16.1. The growth in publications and their citations is attributable to the growing concern of food insecurity in Africa and globally, as well as the need to shift the focus to smart cities and towns of the continent that are sustainable and can adequately feed their population (Smit, 2016; Nkrumah, 2018). From the concerns, there is a need to understand the governance of urban food systems and ensure residents of the areas are involved in food production and animal husbandry

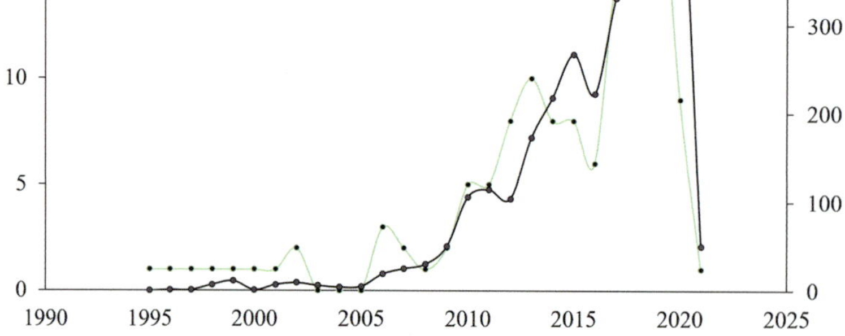

FIGURE 16.1 Growth trend in number of publications and citations on food security enhancement towards smart African cities.

actively as Smit (2016) and Nkrumah (2018) recommended. Therefore, the adoption of intensified urban agriculture in African cities must transit from a statement of the possible into action, as Nkrumah (2018) advocated. This could be the reason why some authors perceive urban agriculture to have low impact on urban food security (Crush et al., 2011; Frayne et al., 2014; Battersby, 2017, 2018) since its intensification is limited and the practice occurs on an ad hoc basis on a small scale.

16.3.3 Subject and Category Analysis

The results of the search query were analysed in two forms of classification: 1) WOS categories and 2) research areas. Research areas referred to subject classes shared by product databases of WOS while categories are mapped research areas. In this research, 44 WOS categories were identified and out of this total, 8 had more than 10 publications. The top 10 categories are shown in Table 16.1. The total research areas identified were 37 and out of this total, 8 had more than 10 publications. Ten of the research areas with the majority of the publications are shown in Table 16.1. From both classifications, most of the studies of the research query were derived from environmental science fields. However, the resultant publications covered a wide scope of fields including urban studies, agriculture, economics, science technology, and nutritional dietetics just to mention a few.

16.3.4 Keyword Analysis

Previous researchers such as Zhang et al. (2017) have used keyword analysis to categorize trends and issues in scientometrics. In this study, a total of 810 keywords were identified by the VOSviewer software. Using the all keyword options, words with a minimum number of occurrences of 3 were selected and out of the total, 85 met the threshold. Their co-occurrence via VOSviewer mapping is shown in Figure 16.2. The keywords were categorised into five conspicuous groups based on their colours. The red cluster had keywords associated with the causes of food insecurity in urban areas including climate change, issues of land and water resources management, and green space depletion. Additionally, the cluster had keywords on solutions to smart urban agriculture such as green infrastructure and peri-urban agricultural growth. The blue cluster had keywords associated with the problem of food security in cities of Africa and provided

TABLE 16.1
Top 10 WOS Categories and Research Areas Identified in the Research Query

No.	Web of Science Category	Record Count	%	No.	Research Area	Record Count	%
1.	Environmental Science	33	25.4	1.	Environmental Sciences Ecology	43	33.1
2.	Environmental Studies	28	21.5	2.	Science Technology Other Topics	22	16.9
3.	Green Sustainable Science Technology	19	14.6	3.	Agriculture	17	13.1
4.	Geography	17	13.1	4.	Geography	17	13.1
5.	Development Studies	15	11.5	5.	Development Studies	15	11.5
6.	Public Environmental Occupational Health	12	9.2	6.	Public Environmental Occupational Health	12	9.2
7.	Urban Studies	11	8.5	7.	Urban Studies	11	8.5
8.	Economics	10	7.7	8.	Business Economics	10	7.7
9.	Agriculture Multidisciplinary	8	6.2	9.	Nutrition Dietetics	7	5.4
10.	Nutrition Dietetics	7	5.4		Public Administration	7	5.4

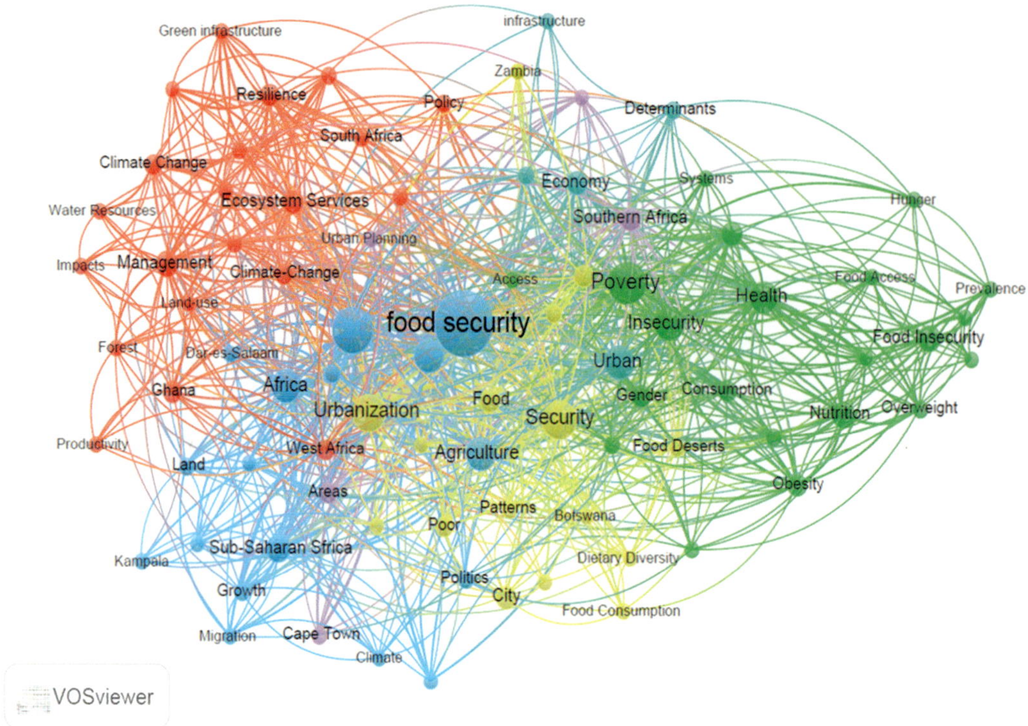

FIGURE 16.2 Co-occurrence of keywords related to food security enhancement in African cities towards smartness.

examples such as Cape Town of South Africa and Kampala of Uganda. This cluster showed the highest linkage to other keywords based on the strength of keywords (represented in curved lines) and their occurrences (represented by the size of the circle). The yellow cluster had keywords related to urban food system patterns that make it vulnerable to food security. The specific urban areas focused on in the analysed studies were clustered together in purple. The green cluster outlined keywords of a host of challenges in urban areas that depict food insecurity. Such challenges deal with the rise in prevalence of overweight and obese conditions among urban residents, rise in poverty, limited food access, and the existence of food deserts in the towns.

16.3.5 Geographical Distribution of Publications, Active Countries, and Institutions

The countries that were most actively involved in publishing on food security enhancement in African cities are shown in Table 16.2. From the total 43 countries identified by WOS, South Africa, the USA, and Canada led with a record count of 33.8, 22.3, and 16.9%, respectively. The top 10 countries published 55.4% of all the publications. The countries were mainly drawn from developing countries with the exception of fast-developing African countries including South Africa, Ghana, and Kenya. This trend where developed countries are more involved in resolving problems of developing Africa could be associated with their research and development, financial, and human resource capability, as noted in other bibliometric analyses by Wang et al. (2018) and Izuchukwu et al. (2020) where developed countries published more. The dominance of South Africa in the publications could be attributable to its fast economic growth related to the ability to do more research on its problems and the growth in awareness of food security in many urban areas

TABLE 16.2
Top 10 Countries and Institutions Involved in Research on Food Security Enhancement in African Cities

Rank	Country	Record Count	%	Rank	Institution	Record Count	%
1.	South Africa	44	33.8	1.	University of Cape Town	17	13.1
2.	USA	29	22.3	2.	University of Waterloo	13	10.0
3.	Canada	22	16.9	3.	University of the Western Cape	7	5.4
4.	England	13	10.0	4.	CGIAR	6	4.6
5.	Germany	11	8.5	5.	Stellenbosch University	6	4.6
6.	France	8	6.2	6.	University of Guelph	6	4.6
7.	Ghana	7	5.4	7.	CIRAD	5	3.8
8.	Australia	6	4.6	8.	John Hopkins Bloomberg School of Public Health	4	3.1
9.	Kenya	5	3.8	9.	John Hopkins University	4	3.1
10	Netherlands	5	3.8	10	Queens University Canada	4	3.1

of the country, as noted by Jonah and May (2019). The dominance in the countries was also evident in the institutions, which were actively involved in publishing on the search query. The University of Cape Town and University of the Western Cape from South Africa were ranked first and third with 13.1 and 5.4% of total publications, respectively, while the University of Waterloo, Canada, was second, with 10% of the total record count.

A similar trend was also evident in the VOSviewer analysis of co-authorship interrelationship among countries, as shown in Figure 16.3. The analysis was done after setting a minimum number of citations and documents to 1 in the VOSviewer software and 42 of the 43 countries met the threshold. In this case, South Africa and the USA had the strongest interrelationships, corresponding to high output and inter-collaborations of authors.

16.3.6 Active Journals

Of the 130 sources reviewed, 83 of the total were derived from various journal sources. Only 3 of the 83 had more than 5 publications on the research query. Table 16.3 shows the most productive of the sources. *Sustainability, World Development*, and *African Geographical Review* journals had the majority of publications at 10.7, 5.4, and 3.8% of the total, respectively. The activity of the various journals was also evident from their bibliographic coupling using the VOSviewer software (Figure 16.4). In the software, the 83 journals were subjected to thresholding by setting the minimum documents from a source to 1 and the minimum citations per source as 5, in which 60 journals met these conditions. Evidently the *Journal of Sustainability and World Development* had the highest output based on the size of the circle and the strongest linkages based on the size of the curved line compared to other sources.

16.3.7 Author Analysis

The top 10 most active authors are shown in Table 16.4. The frequency of authors corresponds to their dominance in the specific field, as Wang et al. (2018) noted. From the database, 395 authors were affiliated with the research query and out of this total, 3 had more than 5 publications. This trend corresponds to the limited research on the topic and the sluggish growth of the subject.

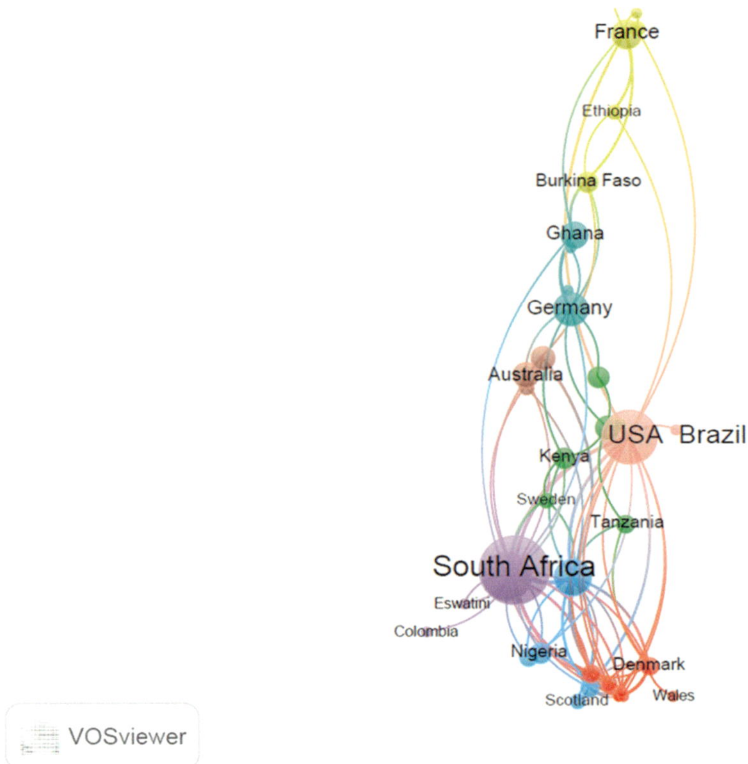

FIGURE 16.3 Interrelationship of countries involved in authorship on food security enhancement in urban areas of Africa.

TABLE 16.3
Top 10 Publishing Journals on Food Security Enhancement in African Cities

Rank	Source Title	Record Count	%
1.	*Sustainability*	14	10.8
2.	*World Development*	7	5.4
3.	*African Geographical Review*	5	3.8
4.	*Development Southern Africa*	4	3.1
5.	*Land Use Policy*	4	3.1
6.	*Cities*	3	2.3
7.	*Environment and Urbanization*	3	2.3
8.	*Environmental Research Letters*	3	2.3
9.	*Journal of Hunger Environmental Nutrition*	3	2.3
10.	*Public Health Nutrition*	3	2.3

Jonathan Crush, who is a professor at Wilfrid Laurier University and the Founder of Hungry Cities Partnership and Southern African Migration Programme, was the most outstanding author with 8 publications. He is actively involved in research on food security challenges in African cities, particularly those of southern Africa (Crush & Frayne, 2011b; Crush, 2013; Crush & Battersby, 2016). Bruce Frayne, who is a professor at the University of Waterloo, was the second most productive

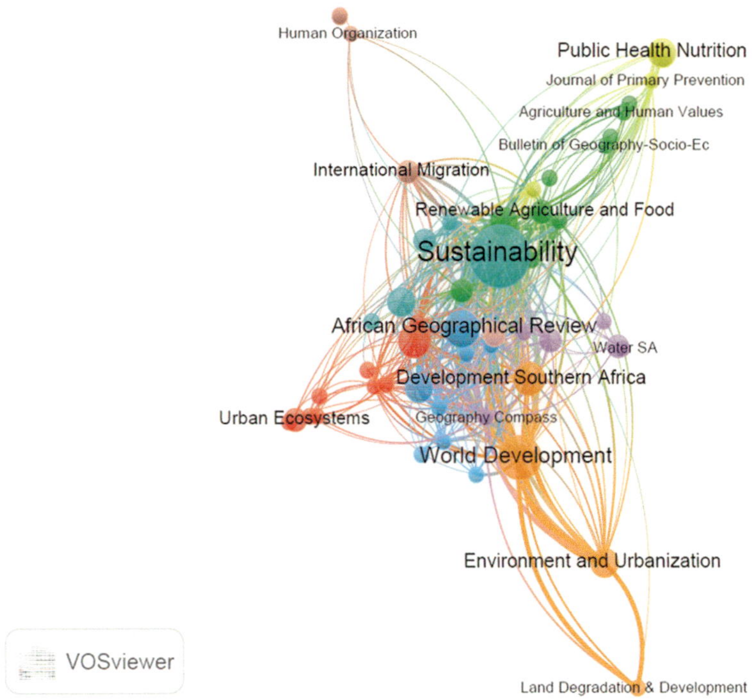

FIGURE 16.4 Bibliographic coupling of journals resulting from the search query.

TABLE 16.4
Most Active Authors on Food Security Improvement in African Cities

Rank	Author	Record Count	%
1.	Crush J	8	6.2
2.	Frayne B	7	5.4
3.	Battersby J	6	4.6
4	Binns T	4	3.1
5.	McCordic C	4	3.1
6.	Buerkert A	3	2.3
7.	Gittelsohn J	3	2.3
8.	Legwegoh AF	3	2.3
9.	Olivier DW	3	2.3
10.	Shackleton CM	3	2.3

author. As an urban geographer and planner, he has been and is involved in research on food security, urbanization, and human migration in Africa (Frayne et al., 2014; Frayne & McCordic, 2015; Sgro et al., 2019). Jane Battersby, who is an urban geographer and a professor at the University of Cape Town, South Africa, was third in the rank of productive authors. She has published widely on urban food security theories, policies, and systems (Battersby, 2013; Battersby & Watson, 2018; Battersby & Haysom, 2018). The relationship of these and other top authors were also presented in their bibliographic coupling, as shown in Figure 16.5. Using the VOSviewer software, 371 authors were involved in publication of the search query and this number was narrowed down by setting the

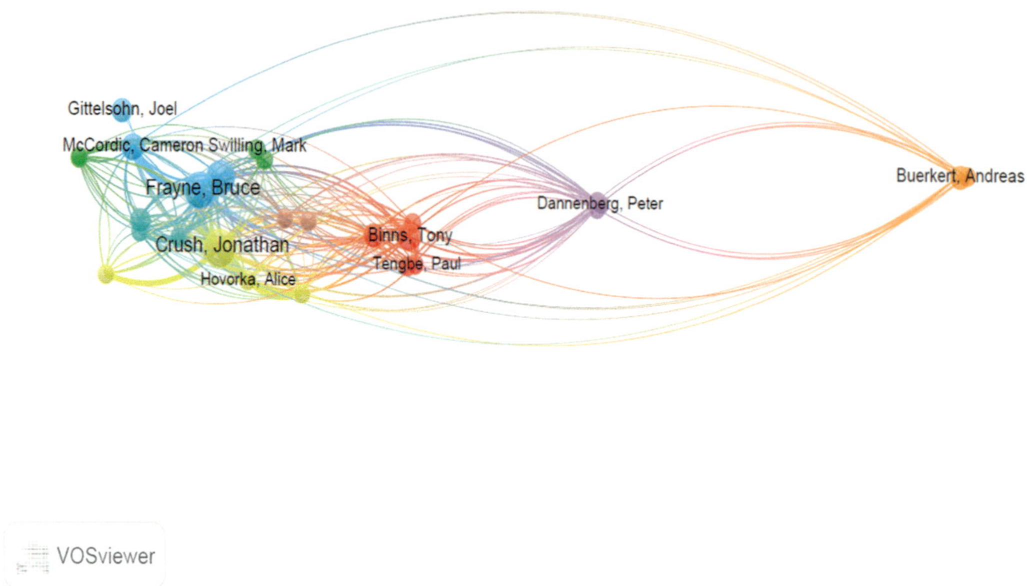

FIGURE 16.5 Bibliographic coupling of authors with the highest output and citations.

minimum number of documents and citations per author as 2 in the software, where 27 authors met these conditions. Evidently, the top 10 authors shown in Table 16.4 were involved in various collaborations based on the clustering of their coupling. Similar colours were indicative of possible co-authorship, co-citations, and collaborations.

16.4 SUGGESTED MEASURES TO IMPROVE FOOD SECURITY IN AFRICAN CITIES

Rapid and expansive urbanization in Africa results in the invisible crises of food insecurity. The negative effects of food insecurity have an overall effect on the smartness and economic development of the cities, as is evident in urban and peri-urban areas of Mozambique, South Africa, and Botswana (Crush et al., 2011). The problem is categorized as an emerging challenge of the modern day that requires urgent multi-stakeholder attention according to Crush and Frayne (2011b). Sub-Saharan African cities have also been reported to be food insecure at endemic levels by Battersby (2013). The top authors in this bibliometric analysis agree that food insecurity is a major impediment in the quest for smart cities in Africa. They, however, propose some measures to reverse the apparent deplorable economic and food security state of African cities. Some of the suggestions include:

1. The need to rework the framing to urban food security using an integrated food security strategy (IFSS) supported by effective policies. This will ensure food production in the areas expands from the usual safety nets and household production systems to a greater connectivity of drivers to insecurity including the exclusion of urban food deficiency during planning (Battersby, 2012).
2. Improved spatial planning, urban governance, and regulation is advocated for in African cities. The aspects will enhance food retail formalization and eradicate informal outlets associated with negative health and environmental effects and the unwarranted hike of food prices (Battersby & Watson, 2018; Battersby, 2018). Crush et al. (2012) also had similar views highlighting the importance of super-marketization of foods towards their

formalization, claiming that such a measure would alleviate food insecurity if coupled with extensive urban agriculture.

3. There is a need to adopt the new urban agenda (NUA), which is a shared vision among cities on how to push towards realization of sustainable development goals and, in particular, improved access to appropriate food and nutrition. Using the NUA, food security improvement is prioritized as indispensable towards developing smart cities according to Battersby and Watson (2019).
4. The need to revamp the four pillars of food security stability, utilization, accessibility, and availability, has been emphasized through devising better planning and policy interventions (Battersby & Haysom, 2020).
5. Urban-rural or cross-border migration to urban areas is evidently discouraged because it is positively correlated to urban food insecurity. The trend was established in an evaluation of southern African cities by Crush (2013).
6. The three authors (Crush, Battersby, and Frayne) also advocate for a shift from urban agriculture, suggesting that it has little contribution to smart cities and food security enhancement. Instead, they advocate for improved supply chain of available food to ensure access and affordability for all and regulate the associated food prices (Crush & Frayne, 2011a). Other authors, however, have disagreed with this suggestion, claiming that urban agriculture must be intensified and expanded to increase food productivity for the population in the towns (Nkrumah, 2018; Chihambakwe et al., 2019).

16.5 FUTURE PERSPECTIVES

From this bibliometric analysis, it is evident that research on food security enhancement in African cities is growing, as publications in the last five years have grown exponentially. The trend is associated with increased awareness of the challenge of food insecurity despite the growing trends in urbanization, the rise in awareness of the drivers to food insecurity particularly climate change, depleting water resources, and land, soil, and environmental degradation. Many authors evaluating the food security situation in Africa unanimously agree that it is one of the greatest challenges of the 21st century (Oke et al., 2017; Gassner et al., 2019; Ngcamu & Chari, 2020). As new mitigation measures are sought to improve food production and availability in the rising cities, research is expected to grow as is evident in this research. Similarly, the fields in which these studies are evaluated are expected to grow from the traditional environmental science and ecology research areas and scope to being multidisciplinary. Therefore, the evaluation of food security in African cities toward smartness will accommodate studies from the science technology, economic, development studies, public health, and geography fields among others. This will eventually lead to the hybridisation and overlap of research on food security in urban areas among various disciplines and research areas, as predicted by Bordons et al. (2004) in an evaluation of cross-disciplinary scientific research of today.

Although growth on the research query publication was shown to be on the rise, it was established that the rate is sluggish, as is evident from the low number of publications, the limited involvement of developing countries particularly those of Africa in researching on their own problems, and the low co-authorship and collaboration rates from the VOSviewer interrelationships. To bridge this gap, developing African countries must actively engage in research on food insecurity eradication in their cities for sustainable growth. This suggestion comes from the precognition that the countries are severely affected by food prices, particularly urban areas are at high risk of malnourishment and have a poor urban food infrastructure (Szabo, 2015; Nyika, 2020a). They are, therefore, the least capable to satisfy the growing urban production with food considering that their vulnerability to drivers of food insecurity, such as climate change, land, and environmental degradation, is equally higher and they are the least prepared (Nyika, 2020b). Additionally, the countries better understand the root causes of their food insecurity challenge both in urban and rural areas and are, therefore, best suited to find the solutions to the problem that they can best implement in the region.

Since agriculture in urban regions has been found to have a minimal contribution to urban food security (Crush et al., 2011), going forward, rural agriculture should be revamped and intensified to supply urban residents with enough food. Such advances were also supported by Ahmed et al. (2017), who suggested that small-scale rural farming plays a significant role in contributing to food security in Pakistan, which is a developing country. This can be done through the use of wastewater for agricol activities and adoption of technologies that improve crop productivity. The use of wastewater for agriculture was touted to confront water shortages amidst the growing population, even in urban areas, which has led to increased demand for resources (Jaramillo & Restrepo, 2017). Using treated wastewater for agriculture will also redirect fresh water for other high-priority consumptive uses, considering the finite nature of the resource and the rise in climate change effects such as prolonged drought spells (Nyika, 2020a). Adoption of technology to expand agricultural capacity, enhance efficient and effective land and water resources through precision agriculture, micro-irrigation, and use of desalinated water are also a future prospects that African countries should shift to for enhanced food security (Lavee et al., 2019). Developing countries in areas of Africa experiencing water scarcity, such as Tunisia, Morocco, and Egypt, have tried the adoption of technology and reuse of desalinated water and wastewater in agriculture towards sustainable growth and food security successfully (Molle et al., 2019). It is worth noting that if rural agriculture is improved for enhanced urban food security, then the logistics of the produce in the two areas must be improved to converge the demand and supply, as proposed by Fukase and Martin (2017). Similarly, Knorr et al. (2018) pointed out that viable urban food systems must address supply factors such as production, access, distribution, processing, consumption, and preparation patterns in the food loop.

From this research, it is therefore evident that food security will remain a growing challenge for the ever-rising urban areas of developing countries of Africa. However, the situation could be reversed if the focus shifts from assessing the problem, which has been established in literature, to solution-based research and knowledge sharing. The focus can be intensified through research and development and collaborations of institutions and authors from both developed and developing countries. The collaborations were found limited in this bibliometric analysis and, therefore, there is a need for affirmative action. Prospects such as the adoption of an integrated food security strategy and the new urban agenda should be taken up as they promote the pillars of food security (stability, utilization, accessibility, and availability) and improve planning, governance, and regulation of urban regions in all aspects, including the management of food systems.

16.6 CONCLUSIONS

The aim of this study was to evaluate the various studies that have been conducted regarding food insecurity in urban regions of Africa and their inherent characteristics in a scientometric approach. Relationships of institutions, keywords generated, scientific actors involved, and growth trends in citations and publications in the searched query were assayed using the VOSviewer software. It was evident that the studies spanned across different research areas and categories, hence multidisciplinary in nature. In addition, research on the topic had realized exponential growth in recent times due to the awareness of the problem and its relationship to poverty levels in Africa. Collaborations among authors and countries was found to be limited, particularly in Africa, despite the continent being the greatest bearer of food insecurity. Sustainability was the most active journal in reference to the searched results. A number of suggestions were made towards better food security and sustainable urbanization in Africa. The includes the adoption of the new urban agenda and the integrated food security strategy with an aim to revamp agriculture and better nutritional approaches in both rural and urban areas. The need for collaborative research involving developed countries as well as developing countries of Africa was emphasized to make advancements and progress on the searched subject holistically. Overall, food insecurity is a growing challenge in urban areas of Africa and finding viable solutions to overcome it should be prioritized.

REFERENCES

Ahmed, U.I., L. Ying, M.K. Bashir, M. Abid and F. Zulfigar. "Status and determinants of small farming households' food security and role of market access in enhancing food security in rural Pakistan." *PLoS ONE* 12 (2017): e0185466.

Assoumana, B.T., M. Ndiaye, G. Van Der Puije, M. Diourte, and T. Graiser. "Comparative assessment of local farmers' perceptions of meteorological events and adaptations strategies: Two case studies in Niger Republic." *Journal of Sustainable Development* 9 (2016): 118–135.

Battersby, J. "Urban food security and urban food policy gap". Presented at *Towards Carnegie III Conference*, University of Cape Town, South Africa, 3rd September, 2012.

Battersby, J. "Hungry cities: A critical review of urban food security research in Sub-Saharan African cities." *Geography Compass* 7(7), (2013): 452–463.

Battersby, J. "MDGs to SDGs-new goals, same gaps: the continued absence of urban food security in the post 2015 global development agenda." *African Geographical Review* 36(1), (2017): 115–129.

Battersby, J. "Urban food security in developing countries: shifting policy trajectories." *The Sage Handbook of Nature* 2 (2018): 561–582.

Battersby, J. and G. Haysom. *Linking Urban Food Security, Urban Food Systems, Poverty and Urbanization*. New York: Routledge Publishers (2018).

Battersby J. and G. Haysom. "Urban Food Security." In: Massey, R. and Gunter, A. (eds), *Urban Geography in South Africa*. GeoJournal Library. Cham: Springer Publishers (2020).

Battersby, J. and V. Watson. "Addressing food security in African cities." *Nature Sustainability* 1(4), (2018): 153–155.

Battersby, J. and V. Watson "The planned 'city region' in the New Urban Agenda: an appropriate framing for urban food security." *The Town Planning Review* 90(5), (2019): 497–518.

Bordons M., F. Morillo, and I. Gomez. "Analysis of cross-disciplinary research through bibliometric tools." In: Moed, H.F., Glänzel, W., and Schmoch, U., (eds.), *Handbook of Quantitative Science and Technology Research*. Dordrecht: Springer (2004).

Chadegani, A., H. Salehi, M. Yunus, H. Farhadi, M., Fooladi, M. Farhadi, and N. Ebrahim. "A comparison between two main academic literature collections: Web of Science and Scopus databases." *Asian Social Science* 9(5), (2013): 18–26.

Chakona, G. and C. Shackleton. "Food insecurity in South Africa: To what extent can social grants and consumption of wild foods eradicate hunger?" *World Development Perspectives* 13 (2019): 87–94.

Chihambakwe, M., P. Mafongoya, and O. Jiri. "Urban and peri-urban agriculture as a pathway to food security: A review mapping the use of food sovereignty." *Challenges* 10(6), (2019): 1–12.

Crush, J. "Linking food security, migration and development." *International Migration* 51(5), (2013): 61–65.

Crush, J. and J. Battersby. *Rapid Urbanization, Urban Food Deserts and Food Security in Africa*. Switzerland: Springer International Publishing (2016).

Crush, J. and B. Frayne. "Supermarket expansion and the informal food economy in Southern African cities: implications for urban food security." *Journal of Southern African Studies* 37(4), (2011a): 781–807.

Crush, J. and B. Frayne. "Urban food insecurity and the new international food security agenda." *Development Southern Africa* 28 (2011b): 527–544.

Crush, J., B. Frayne, and W. Pendleton. "The crisis of food insecurity in African cities." *Journal of Hunger and Environmental Nutrition* 7 (2012): 271–292.

Crush, J., B. Frayne, and W. Pendleton. "The crises of food insecurity in African cities." *Journal of Hunger and Environmental Nutrition* 7 (2012): 271–292.

Crush, J., A. Havorka and D. Tevera. "Food security in Southern African cities: the place of urban agriculture." *Progress Development Studies* 11(4), (2011): 285–305.

Ejeta, G. "African green revolution needn't be a mirage." *Science* 327(5967), (2010): 831–832. 10.1126/science.1187152.

Ejeta, G. "African green revolution needn't be a mirage." *Science* 327 (2012): 831–832.

Frayne, B., J. Crush, and M. McLachan. "Urbanization, nutrition and development in Southern African cities." *Food Security* 6(1), (2014): 101–112.

Frayne, B. and C. McCordic. "Planning for food secure cities: Measuring the influence of infrastructure and income on household food security in Southern African cities." *Geoforum* 65 (2015): 1–11.

Fukase, E. and W. Martin. "*Economic Growth, Convergence, and World Food Demand and Supply*; Policy Research Working Paper 8257." Washington, DC, USA: World Bank Group, Development Research Group Agriculture and Rural Development Team (2017).

Gassner, A., D. Harris, K. Mauscch, A. Terheggen, C. Lopse, R. Finlayson, and P. Dobie. "Poverty eradication and food security through agriculture in Africa. Rethinking objectives and entry points." *Outlook on Agriculture* 48(4), (2019): 309–315.

Izuchukwu, J., M. Ebenezer, and M. Ngadi. "Two decades of eco-efficiency research: A bibliometric analysis." *Environmental Sustainability* 3(1), (2020): 155–168.

Jaramillo, M. and I. Restrepo "Wastewater reuse in agriculture: A review about its limitations and benefits." *Sustainability* 9 (2017): 1734.

Jerzak, M. A. and M. Smiglak-Krajewska. "Globalization of the market for vegetable protein feed and its impact on sustainable agricultural development and Food Security in EU Countries illustrated by the example of Poland." *Sustainability*, 12 (2020): 888.

Jonah, C. and J. May. "The nexus between urbanization and food insecurity in South Africa: does the type of dwelling matter? *International Journal of Urban Sustainable Development* 12(1), (2019): 1–13.

Knorr, D., C. Khoo, and M. Augustin. "Food for an urban planet: challenges and research opportunities." *Frontiers in Nutrition* 4(73), (2018): 1–6.

Lavee, D., E. Feitelson, and H. Joseph-Ezra. "Israel." In: Molle, F., C. Sanchis-Ibor, and L. Avella-Reus (eds), *Irrigation in the Mediterranean. Global Issues in Water Policy, vol. 22*. Cham: Springer Publishers (2019).

Molle, F., C. Sanchis-Ibor, and L. Avella-Reus. "Irrigation in the Mediterranean. Technologies, institutions and policies." *Global Issues in Water Policy* 22, Cham, Switzerland: Springer Nature (2019).

Mongeon, P., and A. Paul-Hus. "The journal coverage of Web of Science and Scopus: a comparative analysis." *Scientometrics* 106 (2015): 213–228.

Ngcamu, B. and Chari, F. "Drought influences on food security in Africa: A systematic literature review." *International Journal of Environmental Research and Public Health*, 17 (2020): 5897.

Nkrumah, B. "Edible backyards: climate change and urban food (in) security in Africa." *Agriculture and Food Security* 7 (2018): 45.

Nyika, J. "Climate change situation in Kenya and measures towards adaptive management in the water sector." *International Journal of Environmental Sustainability and Green Technologies* 11(2), (2020a): 34–47.

Nyika, J. "Understanding water-food-energy nexus in the climate change era and the roadmap to implementation in South Africa." In: Karmaoui, A., Barrick, K., Reed, M., and Baig, M. (eds.), *Impacts of Climate Change on Agriculture and Aqualculture*. USA: IGI Global Publishers (2020b).

Nyika, J., J. Mackolil, E. Workie, C. Adhav, and S. Ramadas. "Cellular agriculture research progress and prospects: Insights from bibliometric analysis." *Current Research in Biotechnology* 3 (2021a): 215–224.

Nyika, J., F. Mwema, R. Mahamood, E. Akinlabi, and T. Jen. "A five-year scientometric analysis of the environmental effects of 3D printing." *Advances in Materials and Processing Technologies* (2021b): 1–12.

Oke, D., K. Bokana, and G. Uddin. "Food insecurity in selected African countries: Effect of food imports among other predictors." *SPOUDAI Journal of Economics and Business* 67(3), (2017): 18–31.

Otsukaa, K. and Y. Kijimab. "Technology policies for a green revolution and agricultural transformation in Africa." *Journal of African Economies* 19(2), (2010): 60–76.

Pawlak, K. and M. Kolodziejczak. "The role of agriculture in ensuring food security in developing countries: Considerations in the context of the problem of sustainable food production." *Sustainability* 12 (2020): 5488.

Prosekov, A. and Ivanova, S. "Food security: the challenge of the present."*Geoforum* 91, (2018):73–77. 10.1016/j.geoforum.2018.02.030

Rankoana, S. A. "Rainfall scarcity and its impacts on subsistence farming: The role of gender and religious rituals in adaptation to change."*Agenda* 30(3), (2016):124–131. 10.1080/10130950.2016.1259867.

Roser, M. and H. Ritchie. "Hunger and undernourishment." https://ourworldindata.org/hunger-and-undernourishment#what-share-of-people-are-undernourished (2013).

Sgro, J., B. Frayne, and C. McCordic. "Linking the sustainable development goals through an investigation of urban household food security in Southern Africa." *Sustainability* 10(12), (2019): 4425.

Sibhatu, K. and M. Qaim "Rural food security, subsistence agriculture, and seasonality." *PLoS ONE* 12, (2017): e0186406.

Silva, G. "Feeding the World in 2050 and Beyond–Part 1: Productivity Challenges." Michigan State University Extension–3 December 2018. https://www.canr.msu.edu/news/feeding-the-world-in-2050-and-beyond-part-1 (2018).

Smit, W. "Urban governance and urban food systems in Africa: Examining the linkages."*Cities* 58, (2016): 80–86. 10.1016/j.cities.2016.05.001.

Sweileh, W. and A. Mansour. "Bibliometric analysis of global research output on antimicrobial resistance in the environment (2000–2019)." *Global Health Research and Policy* 5(37), (2020): 1–11.

Szabo, S. "Urbanization and food insecurity risks: assessing the role of human development."*Oxford Development Studies* 44(1), (2015):28–48. 10.1080/13600818.2015.1067292.

Tilman, D., C. Balzer, J. Hill and B.L. Befort. "Global food demand and the sustainable intensification of agriculture." *Proceedings of the National Academy of Sciences of the United States of America* 108 (2011): 20260–20264.

United Nations Human Settlement Programme (UN-HABITAT). *The State of African Cities, 2010: Governance, Inequalities and Urban Land Markets.* Nairobi, Kenya: UN Centre for Human Settlements (2010).

Van Eck, N. and L. Waltman. "Text mining and visualization using VOSviewer." In: *Centre for Science and Technology Studies*. The Netherlands: Leiden University (2011).

Walsh, C. and F. Van Rooyen. "Household food security and hunger in rural and urban communities in the Free State province, South Africa." *Ecology of Food and Nutrition* 54(2), (2014): 118–137.

Wang, Z., Y. Zhao, and B. Wang. "A bibliometric analysis of climate change adaptation based on massive research literature data." *Journal of Cleaner Production* 199 (2018): 1072–1082.

Workie, E., J. Mackolil, J. Nyika, and S. Ramadas. "Deciphering the impact of COVID-19 pandemic on food security, agriculture and livelihoods: A review of the evidence from developing countries." *Current Research in Environmental Sustainability* 2 (2020): 100014.

Zhang, Y., K. Huang, Y. Yajuan, and B. Yang. "Mapping of water footprint research: a bibliometric analysis during 2006–2015." *Journal of Cleaner Production* 149 (2017): 70–79.

17 Analysis of Urban Sprawl and Blight Using Shannon Entropy Index: A Case Study of Memphis, Tennessee

Anzhelika Antipova, Ehsan Momeni, and Reza Banai
University of Memphis, Memphis, TN, United States

CONTENTS

17.1 INTRODUCTION

Several factors, including the way land is utilized, how people travel, and how cities enlarge over vast geographic areas contribute to sprawl (Frumkin, Frank, and Jackson, 2004). Sprawl is an unintended consequence of a lifestyle that wastes land, water, air, and energy. Experts in different fields, e.g., architects, planners, real estate agents, and bankers, have their point of view on sprawl that makes it difficult to have a cohesive definition. However, we review the various definitions of urban sprawl.

In a sprawling development, urbanization is patchy and scattered; there are leap-frogs and a lack of continuity in urbanization (Couch et al., 2008). A broad definition of sprawl was

DOI: 10.1201/9781003126195-21

offered by Nelson and Duncan (1995) as "unplanned, uncontrolled, and uncoordinated single-use development that does not provide for an attractive and functional mix of uses and/or is not functionally related to surrounding land uses and which variously appears as low density, ribbon on the strip, scattered, leapfrog or isolated development" (Nelson and Duncan, 1995).

Urban sprawl is defined as a greater rate of consumption of agricultural or natural land for urbanization than population growth rate (Fulton et al., 2001; Pohanka and Fitzgerald, 2004). By this definition, most U.S. metropolitan areas are sprawling faster today than before. Additionally, sprawl often occurs more rapidly than the development of infrastructures including schools, roads, and sewer systems (Pohanka and Fitzgerald, 2004). Traditionally, sprawl in the U.S. cities is considered due to auto dependency, which makes the cities less dense and thus difficult to provide public transit alternatives. Metropolitan areas consume lands at a much greater rate than they add population. Thus, their marginal density is extremely low.

Hayden (2004) considered sprawl as "a process of large scale real estate development resulting in low-density, scattered, discontinuous car-dependent construction, usually on the periphery of declining older suburbs and shrinking city centers" (Hayden, 2004). Bourne (2001) defined sprawl as disorganized, poorly planned serviced, and largely unplanned development of the suburbs. Habibi and Asadi (2011) considered sprawl as an American phenomenon whose level depends on environmental, economic, social, and political context. In a planned urban development, urban growth is in proportion with urban population growth.

Heirman and Coppens (2013) defined urban sprawl as a low-density or ribbon development. Barrington-Leigh and Millard-Ball (2015) define sprawl as low densities, spatially segregated land uses, and a street network with low connectivity.

Overall, Galster et al. (2001) recognize the ambiguity in the definition of urban sprawl, as it is "one name for many conditions" from patterns of land use, to process of urbanization, to cause of particular land use, and to consequences of them. Galaster et al. consider sprawl as "scattered or low-density patterns of urban development" and noted Los Angeles and Atlanta as as examples of urban sprawl. Density, continuity, concentration, clustering, centrality, nuclearity, mixed uses, and proximity are defined as eight dimensions of sprawl (Galster et al., 2001).

Despite the various definition, urban sprawl is considered an unsustainable form of urban growth. It is usually identified by population and jobs moving from the downtown area orcity center to the suburbs and the urban edge, disproportionate land utilization compared with population growth, and leapfrog development leading to various urban and environmental problems such as more vehicle miles traveled, traffic jams, reduced green space, and the conversion of the latter to impervious land susceptible to urban flooding.

Antipova, Momeni, and Banai (2022, chapter 15) review a vast literature to outline the various features of sprawl. Gordon and Richardson (1997) questioned the desirability of the compact city compared to low density, spread-out city. The availability of housing and neighborhood choice for the consumer outside of the central city is regarded as a positive feature of urban development that spreads into suburban and even exurban areas, also the location of jobs and services. School quality in the suburb versus central city is also a centrifugal force. The spread of urban development is itself a natural solution to the metropolitan congestion and housing costs (and the perception of crime) in the central city. Consumers trade-off transportation for housing with a bigger lot and lower density suburban living. In an essentially unfettered real estate market economy, developers strive responding to the demand for housing and neighborhood alternatives in a polycentric metropolitan region.

However, Ewing (1977) and, more recently, Ewing, Bartholomew, and Nelson (2011), counter the argument in favor of the compact city. Increasing public health and, above all else, climate change, has altered the costs of sprawl since the initial calculation by Gordon and Richardson (1997); for a discussion of sprawl and public health, see also Frumkin, Frank, and Jackson (2004). We address blight as a consequence of sprawl, that is rarely considered jointly in the discussion of

TABLE 17.1
Characteristics of Urban Sprawl

Physical pattern	Patchy, scattered, discontinuous development	Galster et al., 2001
Type of development	Ribbon development along corridors, strip commercial development, continuous strip development	Heirman and Coppens, 2013; Nelson and Duncan, 1995; Galster et al, 2001
Land use patterns	Spatially segregated land uses, leap-frog, discontinuous, fragmentation of open space, disorganized	Ewing, 1997; Barrington-Leigh and Millard-Ball, 2015; Nelson and Duncan, 1995; Hayden, 2004; Angel, 2007
Density	Low density	Nelson and Duncan, 1995; Hayden, 2004; Heirman and Coppens, 2013
Street network	Low connectivity	Barrington-Leigh and Millard-Ball, 2015
Urbanization speed	Greater land consumption of land than population growth, more growth than usual, disproportionate consumption of land	Fulton et al., 2001; Habibi and Asadi, 2011
Planning type	Unplanned/poorly planned, uncontrolled, uncoordinated development	Bourne, 2001; Nelson and Duncan, 1995

sprawl. The references cited above are not exhaustive. Table 17.1 summarizes characteristics of urban sprawl.

17.2 WHERE URBAN SPRAWL CAN BE FOUND

Nearly all metropolitan areas in the U.S. contain a large number of detached single-family homes with large yards. After all, the house and a private yard is an American dream (Hayden, 2004). The low-density, mainly single-family developments are a uniquely U.S. residential development pattern, compared to other cities globally (Judd and Swanstrom, 2006). The development was concentrated in the United States before the 1960s (Robinson et al., 2005). In many industrial cities in the United States, urban sprawl began after World War II, particularly post-national interstate highway construction and contributed to environmental deterioration, traffic congestion, air pollution, crime, poverty, racial tension, poor schools, and poor public services (Brunner, 2012).

The demand by middle- and high-income households for larger and less expensive lands, mostly available outside of central cities, and the preference of spatial separation based on class and race were among the primary reasons for urban expansion and decline of central city population in the United States, so higher income residents were leaving the inner city , where lot sizes are restricted, to urban fringe and city outskirts (Gouda et al., 2016). The lower taxes on gas, housing policies, and other subsidies encouraged homeowners in the United States to move more frequently and into larger homes (Judd and Swanstrom, 2006). After many rich people initiated the process and left their residences of inner cities to suburban places in order to get a higher quality of life, this pattern of population suburbanization continued during several decades and caused job and commerce suburbanization (Brunner, 2012). More than 95% of the U.S. population growth occurred outside cities during the 1970s and 1980s with the land development growth at commonly higher rate than population growth. For example, population growth was 38% in the Chicago metro area from 1950 to 1990, however, the land development growth was 124% in the same period (Robinson et al., 2005).

Other reasons accelerating urban sprawl were larger households' income, governmental tax, expenditure, and zoning policies (Gouda et al., 2016). To illustrate, nearly 50% of the suburbanization during 1950–1980 was related to the increase in people's income (Margo, 1992). Racial discrimination is yet another reason behind urban sprawl, with suburbanization of white residents escaping the problems of crime and social disorder of the central city called "flight from blight," or "white flight." Sprawl in the United States is mainly a post-war, post-interstate highway urban development associated with mass car ownership (Barrington-Leigh and Millard-Ball, 2015). Los Angeles is commonly cited as an urban area where the construction of federally subsidized highways combined with low cost of personal vehicles facilitated population suburbanization. Transportation networks shape how cities evolve and change from a traditional monocentric to a polycentric urban form. Increasingly "strip" and "ribbon" patterns are the features of many European and U.S. cities where urban development occurs along arterial roads (Antipova, 2018, Chapter 2; Banai, 2019). Americans drive more than people in other countries, and their commute distance is greater than in other countries and increasing (Judd and Swanstrom, 2006). As a result of this travel pattern, American residents consumed gasoline four times as much as European residents in the 1990s. Even within the United States, residents of sprawling areas (such as Houston, TX), consume much more gasoline than residents of highly populated areas (such as New York City) (567 versus 335 gallons annually, respectively) (Judd and Swanstrom, 2006).

Baum-Snow (2007) found the structural effect of highways on suburbanization of population utilizing a land use and commuting model. Population of the inner city decreases after building a new highway through the center. Accordingly, to indicate sprawl, we can use the distance at which the population is located from the downtown area (the distance-effect). A peak of sprawled construction happened in the mid-1990s and then declined since 2000 to the level of 1960s. More connected and grid-like streets developed in the United States over the past two decades. Today's urban development in the United States seems to be less sprawling than before. Sprawl is still a current dominant pattern of development in the United States with more people who live and work in the suburbs than in cities (Robinson et al., 2005). Besides lower commuting costs, other factors may influence people's choices of a residential place. The motivating push and pull factors attracting residents from central cities to urban peripheries include crime rates, air pollution, school qualities, access to public services, and others.

Urban sprawl is a de facto and growing phenomenon in different world regions. Various studies based in different countries provide evidence of sprawl. Generally, greater sprawl is found in developed countries than the developing areas of either Asia or Latin America, where cities are denser, more compact, and more regular in shape than the U.S. region (Huang et al., 2007). However, besides the U.S. cities, e.g., Chicago and New York City, cities in many countries in Europe, Latin American, India, and China have experienced sprawl (Barrington-Leigh and Millard-Ball, 2015).

A "good city form" debate considers a sprawling urban form that is commonly found in the United States as undesirable while contrasting it with a dense compact form found in Europe (Ewing, 1997). However, similarly to the United States, large-scale suburbs are also increasingly found in most European cities. Urban sprawl is a significant land use change in Europe. Despite many more people in Europe live in small- and medium-sized cities in larger city-regions, many cities are spatially extending and create large, single, continuous conurbations. These extensive urban formations can comprise several cities and towns fused into a single developed area. There are about 50 conurbations in Europe, such as Frankfurt-Stuttgart and Rhine-Ruhr in Germany, London-Newcastle in England, and Randstad Holland in the Netherlands. The studies on sprawl found two major high-sprawl hotspots in Europe, one cluster occupies northeastern Belgium, France, the Netherlands, and a big part of Western Germany and the second high-sprawl hotspot is located in the United Kingdom (Antipova, 2018, Chapter 2). Urban sprawl is observed in Spain and Portugal (Barrington-Leigh and Millard-Ball, 2015). Attributed to urban sprawl, some parts in Europe experience life quality decreases including segregation, lifestyle changes, and neglected urban centers.

Other world regions, including the Middle Eastern region, experience unsustainable growth. A 2016 study set in Egypt and Iran observed that urban sprawl is not only the phenomenon of large metropolitan areas. Urban and suburban sprawl became an inclusive pattern observed in various-sized cities including mid-sized and small cities in the Middle Eastern region (Gouda et al., 2016). As evidence, all six large cities and many mid-sized cities of Iran experience severe urban sprawl, reflected in low-density residential places, and rapid rate of physical urban expansion exceeding that of population growth, accompanied by lacking public amenities in the suburbs (Gouda et al., 2016).

China is the world's most populous country that experienced a remarkable urbanization in a short time, when urban areas rapidly expanded utilizing agricultural lands and substantially degrading environment. Xu and Zhang (2017) note that significant urbanization occurs in some cities in China whereby the rural population moves to urban areas, but also that people relocate from the inner areas of a city to the suburbs. To lessen urban sprawl and prevent cities from overspreading and reduce high dependency on cars, many cities in China are imposing a rigid urban growth boundary, while promoting compact communities and intermodal transportation (Tong et al., 2016).

17.3 HOW TO MEASURE URBAN SPRAWL

Despite urban sprawl being defined differently, it can be measured using various methods. Simple to complex techniques have been developed that measure different aspects of sprawl. Population density is a generally recognized as a sprawl feature computed by dividing urban population by urban area. Accordingly, sprawl can be measured using residential density.

Ewing et al. (2003) used principal component analysis and developed urban sprawl index based on four urban form measures including land use mix, residential density, street accessibility, and degree of centering. Other methods quantifying sprawl include index methods such as "density balance" sprawl index, which uses geographic census data in computing metropolitan-area sprawl (El Nasser and Overberg 2001; Lopez and Hynes, 2003; Lopez, 2014); and multivariate indicators of "urbanized area" sprawl (Galster et al., 2001). Often, to map the sprawl footprint, a regional scale is used, e.g., a metropolitan statistical area, city-region, and urbanized area (Galster et al., 2001; Lopez, 2014; Laidley, 2016). These are aggregate scales. It is useful for comparative evaluation of sprawl across several metropolitan areas; however, aggregate scale likely masks the various internal structural factors, contributing to that sprawl urban (Ewing and Hamidi, 2014; Laidley, 2016).

Sprawl can be measured using a mixture of jobs, services, and homes in a neighborhood; and street network accessibility. Regarding the latter, sprawl is measured by low connectivity in the street network (Barrington-Leigh and Millard-Ball, 2015). Low connectivity and intersection density are among commonly used measures of sprawl in urban planning and transportation studies. Street connectivity is associated with vehicle travel and incidents of diabetes, asthma, and similar health issues. Less connectivity of streets increases the network distance to Euclidean distance ratio, which makes the neighborhood less pedestrian-oriented.

Strengths and weaknesses of the various sprawl measures used by contemporaneous research have been noted by Laidley (2016). Certain morphological factors applied in the calculation of a composite sprawl indicator at the aggregate scale, including overall density, present a problem when interpreting it for ranking of urban areas. To illustrate, some urban areas may be ranked high in this category but receive a lower ranking score regarding other sprawl aspects. Prior research revealed that misleading results might be obtained when studies use various scales for urban forms (Ewing and Hamidi, 2014; Laidley, 2016). Therefore, fine variations in urban morphology might be hidden when the aggregate scale, e.g., the entire metropolitan level, is applied to measure urban sprawl.

Lopez and Hynes (2003) use a comparative framework as they calibrate and assess urban sprawl across metropolitan areas and describe a threshold-level sensitive nature of a sprawl index that is context-specific and based on multivariate indicators such as density, thus, presenting a limitation. In contrast, prior research (El Nasser and Overberg, 2001; Lopez and Hynes 2003) found using spatial units that are based on a standard definition, e.g., U.S. Census–based, is preferred also due to availability of many socio-spatial characteristics that is in public domain including population,

TABLE 17.2
Urban Sprawl Measures

Urban Sprawl Measures		Sprawl	Compact
Density	Residential density, overall density	Low density	High
Land use	Existence of land uses (e.g., housing units, employees) within the same area, land use mix/mixture of homes, jobs, services, land use segregation	Poor land use mix	Good
Centrality, location near the CBD	Degree of centering, average distance of a land use (e.g., housing units) from CBD, weighted average distance from CBD	Lower values reflect more sprawl	Higher values reflect less sprawl
Accessibility	Accessibility of the street network		High
Street connectivity	Connectivity in street network, intersection density		High
Continuity	Unbrokenness of development of developable land		
Concentration	Very high density (housing units or employees) grids (2 Standard Deviations above the mean), coefficient of variation, Delta index	Lower values reflect more sprawl	Higher values reflect less sprawl
Clustering	Clustered versus spread evenly development within an area	Lower values	Higher values
Nuclearity (a measure of mononuclear pattern of development)	Housing or employment nuclearity: nodes or nuclei in housing units density and employees density	Lower values	Higher values
Proximity	Interuse measure (average distance between any two different land uses, e.g., between households, jobs), intrause measure (average distance between any two randomly chosen observations of same land use (between households and jobs) observations of same land use, and (weighted) average across uses	Lower values	Higher values
Composite score (urban sprawl index)		Lower values	Higher values

housing, land use to calculate a sprawl index. Other measures include contiguity of the built-up area, and segregation of land uses. Table 17.2 summarizes urban sprawl measures.

17.4 THE URBAN AND SUBURBAN NEIGHBORHOOD SPATIAL STRUCTURE AND SPRAWL MEASUREMENT: A CASE STUDY OF MEMPHIS, TENNESSEE

17.4.1 Introduction

As a case study, urban sprawl and blight were examined in Memphis, Tennessee, located in the southeastern United States. The case study also tests the blight decay hypothesis. Our case study used an existing survey of blighted properties. For the study, we extracted land data from the county assessor of property GIS including parcel ID, size, land use codes, zoning categories, and tax status to establish vacant (or blighted) property liability (Banai and Ploderer, 2018). We used this approach to map the whereabouts of industrial blight in Memphis and Shelby County.

Shannon entropy is used to efficiently monitor urban sprawl. Accordingly, the Shannon entropy index was used in the case study to measure urban sprawl and blight. This index is commonly used at the metropolitan regional scale. This allows the comparison of urban sprawl across different regions, including the magnitude and extent. The case study of Memphis and Shelby County's urban expansion calibrates the shape of the function that relates blight to sprawl.

Previous urban sprawl-related research commonly relied on Shannon entropy and Moran statistics (Rahman, 2016). As was shown in early studies, entropy measures the spatial distribution of a geographic phenomenon (Batty, 1972; Thomas, 1981). Entropy has found applications in a research on urban development phenomena. For example, based on land cover and use data, entropy computes dispersion and concentration of built-up (that is, developed land) area. Another spatial metric, Moran statistic, is used to examine spatial correlation. Normalized entropy measures the degree of sprawl in spatial units or different-sized spatial features, and is scale invariant. Moran index varies with the distance band used to determine the spatial weights (Musakwa and Van Niekerk, 2014).

An alternative to sprawl is provided by new urbanism movement in its definitions of a neighborhood both individual parcels including residential, commercial, and open space, and the expected values of mixed land use and density needed for the neighborhood to encourage walkability (Calthorpe, 1993; Katz, 1994; Duany et al, 2000). Thus, land use mix and land use diversity are the desired features of new urbanism. Accordingly, land use mix and diversity were mapped using the land use parcel data at the U.S. Census block group level to capture the degree of "disorder" or departure from the desired order.

Entropy measures a mixture of land use regularly used in urban sprawl studies to reveal if parcels form cluttered or dispersed patterns. Previous studies used the National Land Cover Data (NLCD) to examine spatial composition of urban development (Bereitschaft and Debbage, 2014). Similarly, the case study relied on various land cover categories including developed (built-up) and non-developed land (2011). Figure 17.1 illustrates the distribution of eight categories of land cover across our study area. Studies on urban sprawl need to explain both state and spatial process (Bourne, 2001). Accordingly, to understand if there were conversions of land cover types within the block groups during a decade, and thus to study the process, the change in entropy was examined, paying attention to concentration or dispersion.

Next, the case study focuses on the vacant to built-up land transition using 2010 data to calculate block group entropy to understand the "state." Thus, the case study considers both what causes sprawl (i.e., the process) and what effects sprawl causes (the state) in mapping urban sprawl. During the process of urban development, unused land and greenfields convert to built-up land causing urban sprawl, while sprawl causes the excessive land use consumption, much higher compared with population growth; thus, this state is indicative of unsustainable urban growth, or sprawl.

Previous studies that measured the amount of sprawl also accounted for the spatial closeness effect (Baum-Snow, 2007). Similarly, to incorporate the proximity effect (also referred to as the distance decay effect), the distance from each centroid of a census block group to the city center is measured and averaged to test the blight decay hypothesis.

For areal units, census-defined block groups were used in the case study as the building blocks of neighborhoods and to compute an entropy index at the level that offers readily obtainable spatial data from the U.S. Census. In addition, sprawl at block group scale is computed using parcel information, similarly publicly extractable in GIS format.

While commonly used, density is applied for the metropolitan region using the population or housing density, the threshold of density is determined in a subjective way. However, the parcel does not depend on the subjectivity of the categorization and is classified without ambiguity such as residential, commercial, or open space. Similarly, when sprawl is determined using proximity to

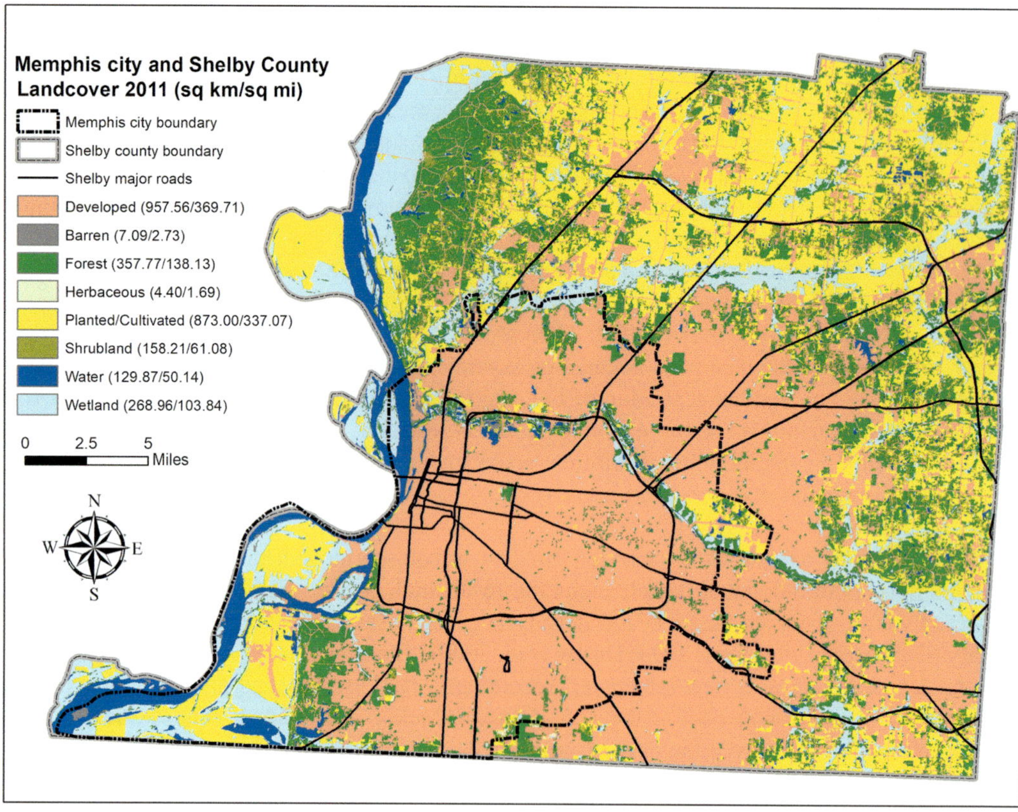

FIGURE 17.1 Memphis and Shelby County Land Cover, 2011.

urban center(s), the fine differences in land use mixture with distance to center(s) are overlooked. To overcome this issue, for the case study measures distances of Census block groups to the center, and, thus, incorporates the land use mixture differences.

17.4.2 Hypothesis to Test

Previous research on sprawl measurement incorporates the spatial closeness and centrality effects (Baum-Snow, 2007). Similarly, this case study measures the distances from block groups to the city center (the CBD) within the study area (Shelby County) to test the blight decay hypothesis. Calthorpe and Fulton (2001) and later Mock (2017) refer to the major metropolitan problems of bight and sprawl as "twin problems." Specifically, this case study tests a hypothesis that these key problems are related at the neighborhood level using the block group scale for the statistical analysis of correlation of sprawl and blight.

17.4.3 Study Objectives

Previous studies looked at the various sprawl aspects, linking urban sprawl to accessibility of public transit, consumption of energy use, air quality, and public health (Clark, 2013). Similarly, the first objective of this case study is to measure the relationships between sprawl, blight, the CBD distance, and income by using the Shannon entropy. The second objective is to examine the distribution of entropy values at the block group level to study the variation in the block group urban pattern within the city and the county. The third objective is to establish whether the calculated entropy changes overtime (2001–2011) indicating that the urban patterns resemble a greater or less amount of sprawl from the block group level to the metropolitan scale. For this, the entropy index is computed for land use and cover data. The data on conversions for all categories of land cover over the entire period provide additional information regarding the sprawl configuration and land utilization, especially state transitions from greenfields to developed/built-up lands. We compute the values of the Shannon entropy index for land use and land cover using the scale of block groups.

17.4.4 Study Area

Shelby County, which contains the city of Memphis, is located in the state of Tennessee. Besides Memphis, the greater metropolitan area includes nine counties, consisting of several suburban towns. Since 2000, the economic growth of this metropolitan area has been impacted by sprawl as it has been spreading to adjacent areas . The Memphis tri-state metro area (TN-MS-AR) is one of the most sprawling large metropolitan regions (a large metro area is defined when a population exceeds one million) (Ewing and Hamidi, 2014).

Memphis and Shelby County, TN, commonly known as a sprawling metropolitan region, offer a good testing ground for the case study to answer the above-mentioned research questions. Specifically, how sprawl impacts the intra-city land use and land cover at the neighborhood scale, and whether sprawl correlates with the urban blight. The case study specifically determines the magnitude of urban sprawl.

17.4.5 Study Rationale

The region that the case study focuses on is burdened with urban sprawl; however, the overall sprawl value measured at the metropolitan area may mask substantial variation across geographic urban and suburban areas, while the variation in the sprawl magnitude within the metropolitan region is rarely measured. The case study provides a more granular, block group scale, measurement of sprawl. It is different from the prior sprawl studies in that they are commonly applied on a wider scale including a metropolitan region consisting of many counties, or the entire urbanized area (Masek et al., 2000; Galster et al., 2001), while we provide a variation in sprawl among block groups within the central city and county. Studying sprawl at the finer-grain, block group area approximates the local community level, enabling assessments of other phenomena while supported by readily publicly available census block group data. The case study both uses entropy to measure sprawl and relates sprawl to other outcomes inherent in urban environment, the latter is rarely implemented by previous research (Laidley, 2016).

17.4.6 Materials and Methods

This study applies the GIS capabilities (geographic information systems) to assimilate parcel information obtained from the local assessor of property, and a fine-scale resolution (30 meters) raster maps from the NLCD into the GIS environment for mapping and computations of block group entropy of land use and land cover. Statistical analyses are used for the correlations of blight and sprawl with other phenomena including household income and the CBD distance. The results indicate blight follows the distance decay function. Measured as the block group proportion of blighted parcels, it decreases exponentially as the CBD distance from the downtown area increases. A correlation analysis shows an association of blight and sprawl.

17.4.7 Theory and Calculations

17.4.7.1 Mapping the Morphology of Urban Sprawl with Shannon Entropy

Per information theory, the most probable state is reflected by large values of entropy, however it may also result in disorder due to low predictability (Theil, 1967; Thomas, 1981). Since urban sprawl represents a phenomenon characterized by "disorder" and the challenges of "predictability," to estimate urban sprawl, entropy can be used (Bhatta et al., 2010). Based on the theory, the case study uses Shannon's entropy to measure the extent of cluttering or scattering of developed land using data of both land use and cover. Higher entropy values indicate a continuous scattering of developed land reflecting urban sprawl while lower entropy is indicative of cluttering or lower fragmentation of developed land signaling a less likelihood of sprawl. Shannon's entropy is calculated using the formula below:

$$H_j = \sum_i^s p_i \; log_e\left(\frac{1}{p_i}\right) \tag{17.1}$$

where p_i is the probability or share of occurrence of *ith* category (e.g., built-up land) in the *jth* spatial feature across the total J spatial features, s is the total number of the category of interest (here, total built-up land), the probability is given by:

$$p_i = x_i / \sum_i^s x_i \tag{17.2}$$

where x_i is the observed value of the *ith* category in the *jth* spatial unit.

To illustrate, the phenomena here are represented by the different land categories of uses and covers. There are seven categories of land use ($s = 7$), including commercial, residential, etc., while land cover is represented by eight categories ($s = 8$), e.g., developed, forest, water bodies (Table 17.3). A total number of block groups within the county (J) is 656. To calculate p_i, the area of *ith* category (e.g., residential) is normalized by the total block group area. $p_i$is the proportion of a category of land use or cover xi of a spatial feature. When there is 0 land use or land cover among all land use or land cover categories in the spatial feature, $p_i = 0$.

TABLE 17.3
Land Cover Change from 2001 to 2011 (rounded up to the nearest decimal)

Change Percent in Land Cover		To 2011								
		Developed	Barren	Forest	Herbaceous	Planted/ Cultivated	Shrub	Water	Wetland	Total
`From 2001	Developed	**40.9**	0	0	0	0	0	0	0	40.9
	Barren	**0.06**	0.14	0	0	0	0	0.01	0	0.21
	Forest	**0.74**	0.03	12.6	0.08	0.03	0.06	0	0	13.5
	Herbaceous	**0.004**	0	0	0.06	0	0	0	0	0.06
	Planted/ Cultivated	**2.07**	0.03	0.04	0.01	23.84	0.04	0.05	0.09	26.2
	Shrub	**0.3**	0.02	0.04	0.02	0.01	4.57	0	0	5
	Water	**0.05**	0.05	0	0	0.01	0.02	4.6	0.02	4.7
	Wetland	**0.19**	0	0	0	0	0	0	9.2	9.44
	Total	44.3	0.3	12.7	0.16	23.9	4.7	4.6	9.4	100.00

Entropy ranges from 0 and log(s). The value of 0 indicates a concentrated pattern and the value of log(s) indicates a dispersed pattern. To bound entropy Hj value between 0 and 1, it has to be normalized using the relative entropy H'_j:

$$H'_j = \frac{H_{nj}}{log_e(s)} \tag{17.3}$$

$$\text{Thus,} \quad 0 \leq H'_j \leq 1.$$

The relative entropy index H'_j has a range between 0 and 1 indicating a lower or greater mixture of land use or cover, thus, serves as an indicator of the urban form. The speed at which a land converts to other land categories can be determined by measuring entropy over time providing policy makers with useful information.

The following formula is used to compute the temporal (t) change in entropy during a period m:

$$\Delta H'_j = H'_j(t + m) - H'_j(t) \tag{17.4}$$

The entropy change for a decade (m) is computed for land cover data for the period of 2001–2011 (while for 2003–2010 for land use data), to understand if land cover and land use patterns convert to a more or less concentration or dispersion at the block groups level.

17.4.7.2 Block Group Land Cover and Land Use Transitions

In total, eight land cover types are used (Figure 17.1 presents these categories), while land use is presented by six types consisting of commercial, industrial, residential, exempt public, mixed-use, and farming/agricultural. Land cover data were extracted from the NLCD (here, 2001 and 2011 data were used for land cover), and land use data was obtained from the county tax assessor parcel GIS which provides 2010 land use classification as the georeferenced shapefiles of parcels. The survey of blighted properties was a determining factor for using Census data that approximated the date the survey was administered. The U.S. Census TIGER (NHGIS) was the source for the boundaries of the city and block groups.

Figure 17.2 presents the land use entropy measured by the Shannon relative land use index which was computed for developed land at block group level (2010). Low entropy values reflect low mix of land uses and as a result more concentration, while less fragmentation regarding land use types. This concentrated land use is common found in zones with a single land use type, e.g., a regional open space area such as the Shelby Farms Park), shown in the central-eastern part in the figure in the form of a white pentagon-shaped area where an entropy index is less than 0.2. To provide some context, the median land use entropy of built-up areas within the block groups for 2010 is 0.73. Similarly, we calculated the 2003 land use entropy values for developed areas with a median of 0.62, thus, built-up areas became more fragmented as developed parcels spread out in 2010 than in 2003. In the same way, entropy was determined for eight categories of land cover for 2001 and 2011 to see if land covers followed a more concentrated or more fragmented (spread out) pattern during these years. The median land cover entropy value is slightly lower in 2011 compared with the 2001 value (0.07 versus 0.08), indicating less mix in land cover types and less fragmentation, while more concentrated by 2011 compared with 2001.

Applying equation (17.4) for Shannon entropy change using land cover data, we studied conversion of various categories over 2001–2011 (Figure 17.3 presents these transitions). Table 17.3 complements this visual information. Open green space area (Shelby Farms Park) has a low transitional value (0–0.1), reflecting the stability of the primary land cover, further characterized by low land cover diversity index value, discussed below, of less than 0.2.

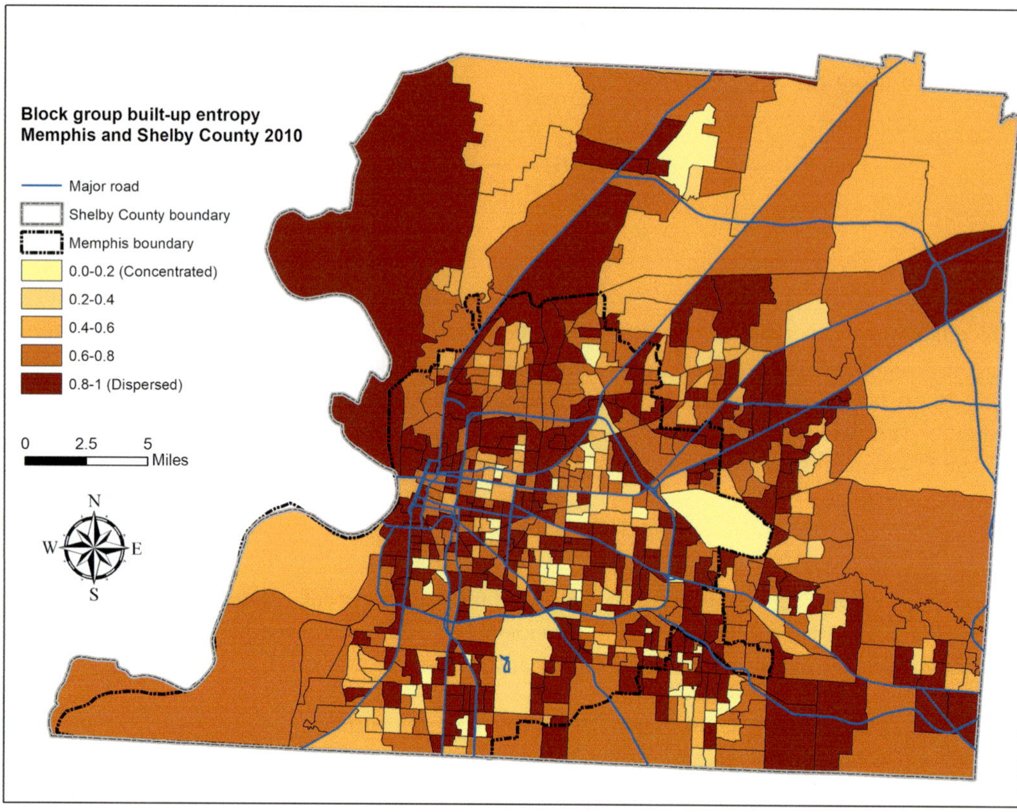

FIGURE 17.2 Land use entropy for the built-up areas (Shannon relative index for land use), 2010.

Despite the extension of suburban and exurban areas of Memphis into greenfields of Shelby and surrounding counties, it has not been quantified . Thus, the mapped extent of land cover conversions over 2001–2011 using the Shannon relative index shows that the area classified as "planted/cultivated" is the largest proportion of area that became developed. In total, over 1.7% of natural land has been developed and became urban built-up. For Memphis and Shelby County together, the largest proportion of total land transitioned from nature to urban development is represented by planted/cultivated, and forest.

Simpson's diversity index (*D*) also measures diversity. It is defined as the likelihood that any randomly selected two components are parts of the same group. This diversity indicator ranges 0–1, where low values of *D* reflect lower diversity, while the higher the *D*, a greater diversity is implied (Bhatta et al., 2010). Simpson's diversity index *D* is computed for developed areas. Applied for the categories of land use, it is helpful in understanding if developed land, follows a more or less diverse regarding land uses, using the equation (17.5):

$$D = 1 - \sum_i^s p_i^2 \tag{17.5}$$

where p_i is the percent of a certain land use type. Thus, the entropy measured by the relative Shannon index is a sprawl indicator, while Simpson's diversity index reflects if built-up land is less or more diverse. These two measures were used in a correlation analysis, resulting in a positive association (shown in Figure 17.4).

For Memphis and Shelby County together, the values of Simpson's and Shannon (0.75–1.00) indices reveals significant sprawl than diversity regarding land use in 2010 (Figure 17.5a).

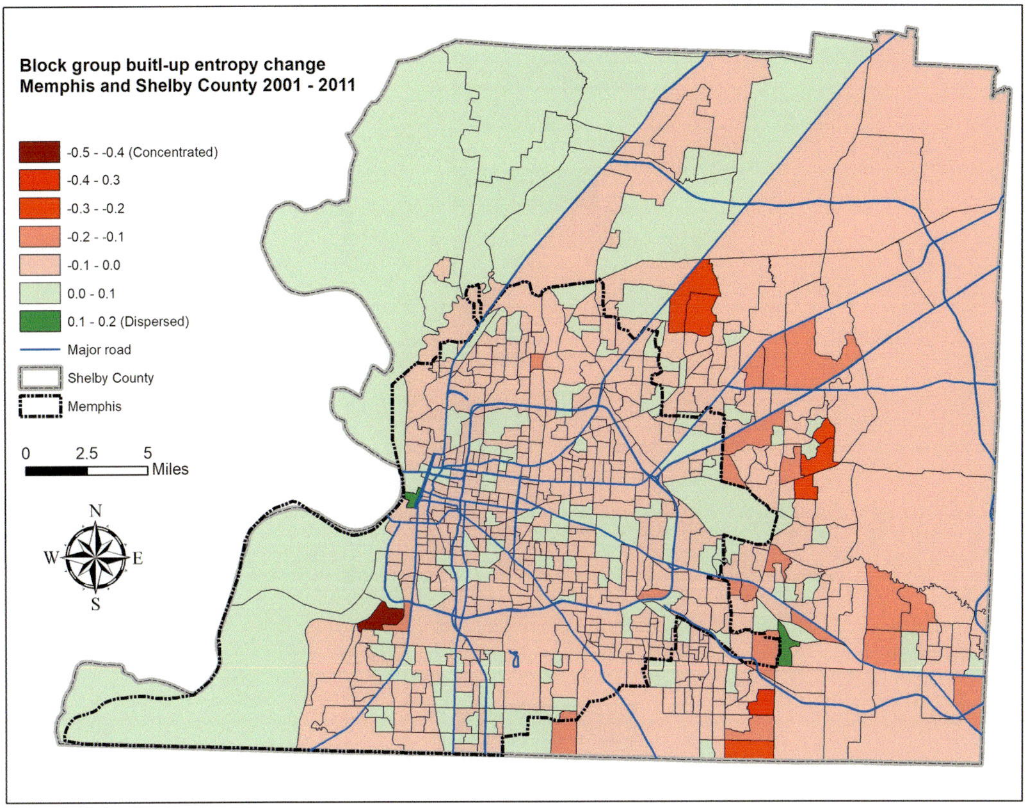

FIGURE 17.3 Land cover entropy for land cover transitions (Shannon relative index for land cover), 2001–2011.

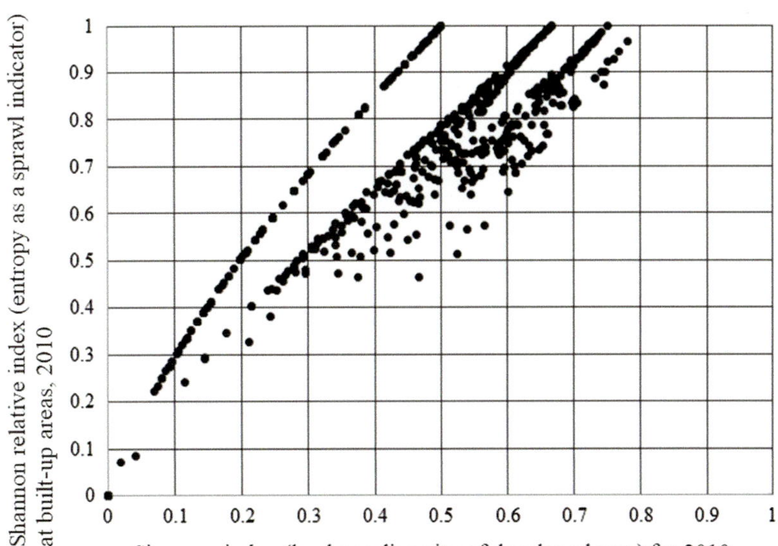

FIGURE 17.4 Simpson versus Shannon relative index at built-up areas, 2010.

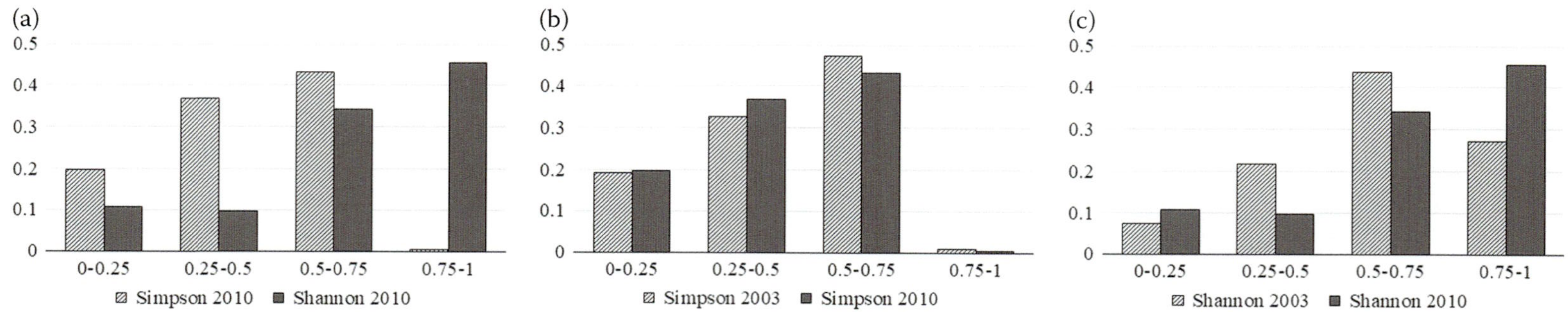

FIGURE 17.5 a) Distribution of Simpson (diversity) and Shannon (sprawl) index of land use, 2010; b) Simpson index 2003–2010, and c) Shannon index, 2003–2010.

Figure 17.5b reports changes in land use between 2003 and 2010 with the Simpson's index, diversity decreases by 2010. Land conversions are presented in Figure 17.5c, a greater magnitude of Shannon index in 2010 (over 0.75) compared with 2003 indicates substantial sprawl.

17.4.7.3 Correlation of Sprawl and Blight

There is ample evidence of issues due to sprawl including environmental, social, and economic. Research provides a compelling documentation of a systemic correlation between urban sprawl and income inequality. However, lacking in debates of these twin problems is an establishment of a correlation of sprawl and urban blight. This case study measures the relationship by using entropy (measured by the relative Shannon index) and blight measured by socio-spatial variables defined below. Included is the Simpson's index as an indicator of diversity of developed area (Figure 17.4). Figure 17.6 shows how blighted area is distributed in the study area in 2016.

Thus, we used the following variables in regression (Model 1): the Shannon relative index (land use mix), as an explanatory variable x and as a response variable y we used the percent blighted properties per block group for 2016.

To increase the model's fit, we applied a log-linear function (17.6):

$$\log(y) = \beta_0 + \beta_1 * \log_e(x1) + e \tag{17.6}$$

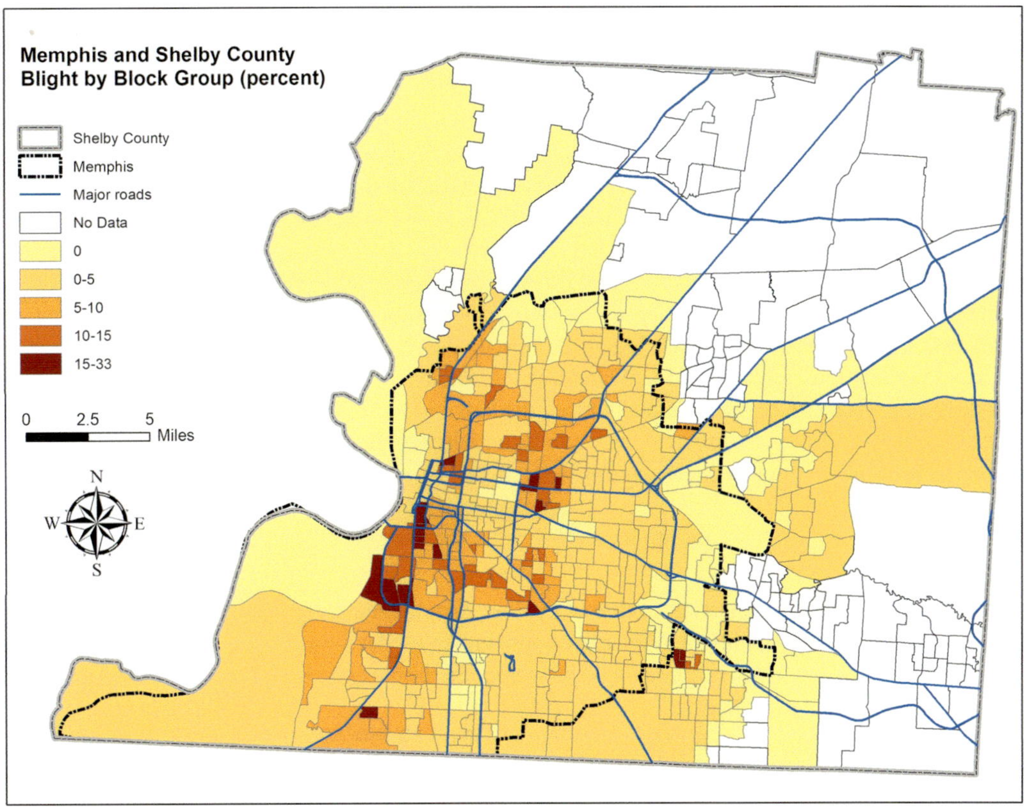

FIGURE 17.6 Distribution of blighted area, 2016.

Source of property blight data: Bluff City Snapshot survey, 2016.

Solving for *y*:

$$y = e^{\beta_0+\beta_1 * \log_e(x1)+e} \tag{17.7}$$

To get the marginal effect we need to differentiate with respect to *x*:

$$dy/dx_1 = \beta_1 * y/x_1 \tag{17.8}$$

Solving for β_1 (which is an elasticity) we get:

$$\beta_1 = dy/dx_1 x_1/y \tag{17.9}$$

Plugging in the variables and coefficients in Model 1, we get the following equation:

$$\text{percent\_blight} = e^{-3.62+1.003* \log_e(\text{Shannon Index})+e} \tag{17.10}$$

Since both dependent (response) and independent (predictor) variables have been log-transformed, we interpret the estimated coefficients as the percentage changes. The value of elasticity ($\beta1$) = 1.003, which can be interpreted that by increasing the Shannon index by 10% (when land use has a greater mix), the share of blight per block group also increases by 10%. In a real world, in the U.S. inner-city area, there are more blighted and abandoned properties while land use mix is similarly high, and with the distance from the CBD (measured in meters) increasing, the amount of blight decreases.

We studied how blight and income are related. The reason for the variable selection is the reflection of the bigger picture of urban sprawl, namely regional inequality. Income is a logical indicator when used to study inequality, spatial, or otherwise (other indicators are noted in the discussion section). Model 2 estimates a statistical relationship between the block group–based per capita income *x* as an explanatory variable *x* and blight (an indicator of blight using the Shannon entropy) as a response variable within the study area for 2016.

In Model 3, we used land use mix as a predictor (explanatory variable) and a percentage of blighted properties per block group as an outcome (response variable), using 2016 data. Both predictor and response have been log-transformed, then we fitted a log-linear function in both regression equations (equations 17.11 and 17.12). Tables 17.2 and 17.3 report the results of the model fitting exercise using Shannon index, median income, and CBD distance as independent (explanatory) predictors in bivariate regressions, and the coefficients with 95% confidence interval, and measures of the model fit (R^2, and RMSE).

$$\text{prcblight} = e^{13.02-1.7_* \log\ (\text{median income})+e} \tag{17.11}$$

In Model 2, the estimated elasticity value of $\beta_1 = -1.7$, indicating a 10% increase in median income results in a 17% drop in blight. The regression indicates declining blight with rising (median) income. Since median (block) income is considered, the impact on other income groups is masked.

$$\text{prcblight} = e^{4.44-0.911_* \log_e(\text{CBD distance})+e} \tag{17.12}$$

In Model 3, which tests the distance-decay relationship, the estimated value of $\beta_1 = -0.911$, interpreted as the distance to the city center increases by 10%, on average, blight decreases by 9.1% per block group. Model 3 results support a distance-decay proposition as the percent of blight decreases log-linearly as the CBD distance increases. We also regressed blight as a response variable against three explanatory factors (land use mix measured by the Shannon index, median household income, and the city center distance) implemented separately for block groups in the study area, for 2010, leading in the best fit for Model 2 (R^2 = 0.04; 0.31, and 0.17, respectively).

Next, to establish the simultaneous effect of multiple variables on blight, a stepwise multiple regression modeling was used (results are reported in Table 17.4). Model 4 explores the relationship between percentage of blighted properties, land use mix measured with the Shannon relative index, and the central city distance. The best fit was achieved with a normal linear regression modeling specified in Model 4:

$$y = \beta_0 + \beta_1 * x_1 + \beta_2 * x_2 + e \qquad (17.13)$$

Plugging in the variables, and then the estimated coefficient values from Model 4, we get equations (17.14) and (17.15), respectively:

$$\text{prcblight} = \beta_0 + \beta_1(\text{Shannon Index}) + \beta_2(\text{Distance to the CBD}) + e \qquad (17.14)$$

$$\text{prcblight} = 0.054 + 0.015 * (\text{Shannon Index}) - 0.00000247 * (\text{Distance to CBD}) + e \qquad (17.15)$$

Model 5 estimates the relationship between blight and land use mix (the Shannon relative index), and median household income. Model 6 analyzes the impact of land use mixShannon relative index), the CBD distance, and income, and blight. Model 7 estimates the association between blight, the CBD distance, and income. To increase model fit, a log-linear function has been used for the three models.

Equations (17.16), (17.17), and (17.18) specify Models 5, 6, and 7, respectively:

$$\text{prcblight} = e^{12.56+0.57*\log_e(\text{Shannon})-1.634*\log_e(\text{median income})+e} \qquad (17.16)$$

(R^2 = .323)

$$\text{prcblight} = e^{15.14+0.36*\log_e(\text{Shannon})-0.57*\log_e(\text{Distance to CBD})-1.38*\log_e(\text{med. income})+e} \qquad (17.17)$$

(R^2 = .382)

$$\text{prcblight} = 0.054 + 0.015 * (\text{Shannon Index}) + 00000247 * (\text{Distance to the CBD}) - 0.00000247 * (\text{median income}) + e \qquad (17.17a)$$

$$\text{prcblight} = e^{15.67-0.573*\log_e(\text{Distance to CBD})-1.435*\log_e(\text{med.income})+e} \qquad (17.18)$$

(R^2 = .37)

While implementing regression exercise, we obtained the best fit in Model 6 (R^2 = 0.38), and lower performance is observed in Models 4, 5, and 7 (R^2 = 0.27; 0.32, and 0.37, respectively) (Table 17.5).

We observe a consistence of the signs across all models (Table 17.5). The share of blight decreases with the CBD distance. But as the CBD distance increases, values of both income and Shannon index increase, not surprisingly. The role of both income and distance on blight is significant at all levels, but land use mix (indicated by the Shannon index) is no longer significant when the CBD distance is added in Model 4, and in Model 6 with distance and income included in the model.

Due to the revealed distance-decay function between blight and the CBD distance, we constructed a semivariogram which includes the information on the spatial locations of the pairs of

TABLE 17.4

Model Fitting of the Relationship between Blight and Sprawl (Shannon Relative Index), OLS Regression Results

		Dep. Variable	Ind. Variables			Constant	R^2	F	RMSE	n
			log_e(Shannon_re index)	Log_e(medIncome)	Log_e(dist2CBD)					
Model 1	Log-Log	log_e _blighted area %	1.003***	N/A	N/A	−3.62***	0.04	15.79	1.37	627
Model 2	Log-Log	log_e _blighted area %	N/A	−1.7***	N/A	13.02***	0.31	184.48	1.16	627
Model 3	Log-Log	log_e _blighted area %	N/A	N/A	−0.911***	4.44***	0.17	86.24	1.27	627

TABLE 17.5

Model Fitting of the Relationship between Blight, Sprawl, Distance to CBD, and Income, Multiple Regression Results

		Dep. Variable	Ind. Variables			Constant	R^2	F	n
			$\log_e$ (Shannon_re index)	$\log_e$ (medIncome)	$\log_e$ (dist2CBD)				
Model 4	Multiple	blighted area %	0.015 (p-value=.056)	N/A	−2.47E-6***	0.054***	0.269	107.73***	588
Model 5	Multiple	$\log_e$ _blighted area %	0.57***	−1.634***	N/A	12.56***	0.32	90.26***	588
Model 6	Multiple	$\log_e$ _blighted area %	0.358	−1.376***	−0.569***	15.14***	0.382	77.87***	588
Model 7	Multiple	$\log_e$ _blighted area %	N/A	−1.435***	−0.573***	15.67***	0.373	120.99***	588

Note: *: = $p \leq 0.05$, **$p \leq 0.01$ level, ***$p \leq 0.001$ level.

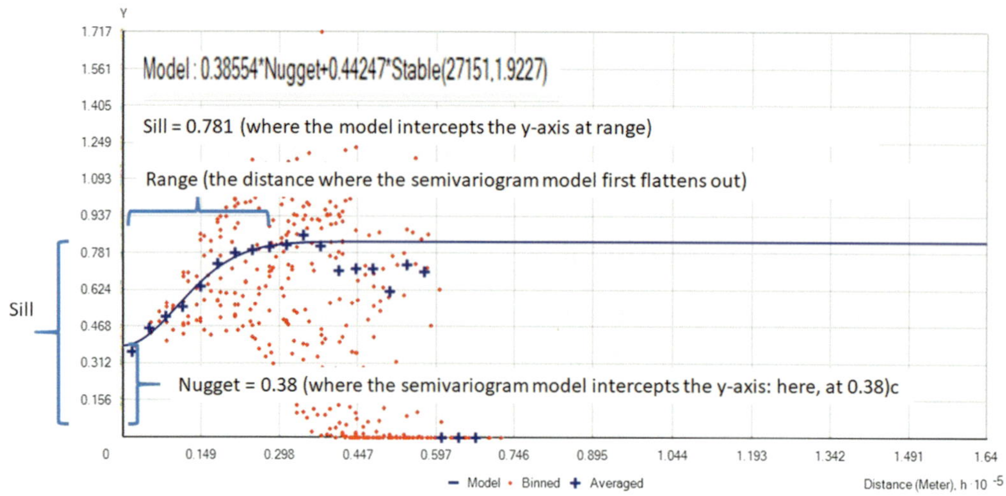

FIGURE 17.7 A semivariogram of the spatial continuity of blighted property.

observations to illustrate spatial variations within the study area regarding blight using the 1-km lag distances separating the pairs of observations and to measure spatial autocorrelation of a variable (Figure 17.7).

17.4.8 Discussion

The case study uniquely contributes to the sprawl literature in substance and procedure. The case study's scale of block group entropy complements analysis of urban expansion commonly done at the higher scale of the metropolitan region or the metropolitan statistical area (MSA). The case study also provides an empirical evidence for analysis of sprawl and its consequence blight. Empirical investigation of the relation of blight and sprawl particularly with statistical models are limited in urban studies literature.

Shannon entropy is used as an indicator of the extent of the sprawling area. Additionally, as we note here, sprawl is too complex of a multifaceted phenomena to be reduced to a single indicator. For that reason, Simpson's diversity index is used as well as Shannon's entropy. Due to a substantial masking of both cluttering and scattering patterns of land cover and land use of the sprawl if a single entropy value for the entire metropolitan area is used, a finer-scale analysis is needed to establish what occurs to the morphology of land cover and land use when a city spreads outward. This case study uses entropy to measure sprawl, median household income as a regional inequality and blight measure, and land use mix as a measure of the cluttered and scattered patterns of land use and land cover, and the CBD distance commonly used to indicate urban expansion. It investigates the links among entropy, income, land use mix, and the CBD proximity.

The results indicate the dependence of urban blight on sprawl and the decay of blight with the CBD distance, supported by a theoretical and empirical discussions of sprawl and blight in the literature (Calthorpe and Fulton, 2001; Mock, 2017). Time and space are the key variables in an investigation of urban sprawl due to sprawl's inherently dynamic nature. The time is incorporated by including land use and land cover transitions. This case study examined and mapped conversions with the change in land use and land cover entropy values using land use and land cover data at a block group scale. The results indicate block group's developed lands spread out over 2003–2010, while less fragmentation occurred in land covers over 2001–2011.

17.4.9 Limitations of the Study and Scope for Further Research

The U.S. Census block group provides a finer areal unit of the metropolitan region. However, it still masks the variability of land cover and land use at an ever finer scale of the pedestrian shed, critical for sustainable urbanism. Additionally, while entropy has been commonly used as an indicator of sprawl, its suitability in dealing with a multidimensional urban sprawl phenomena in entirety is questioned, calling for still other metrics of urban sprawl (Nazarnia et al., 2019).

The case study may be extended by adding other readily available Census-based attributes including racial and ethnic membership, employment, and other socio-economic data, as well as incorporating built-environment measures to add to an analysis of urban form particularly at the scale of the neighborhood in future investigations.

Memphis is a shrinking city, losing more that 5% of population over 2001–2011, while Shelby County's population increased by almost 4%. Over the same period, the amount of developed land grew in both Memphis and Shelby County, by 3.3% and 8.3%, respectively. Population density decreased in both city and county, more so in Memphis, decreasing by over 8% (from 12.6 to 11.6 people/hectare), while in Shelby County population density decreased by a lower amount of 4.7% (from 10.2 to 9.8 people/hectare) by 2011, and land consumption per capita became much higher in 2001 in Memphis and Shelby County compared with other U.S. places (Calthorpe and Fulton, 2001).

The case study observes land cover transitions over the decade (2000–2011) in Memphis and Shelby County finding substantial transitions from not developed land cover to developed land over 2000–2011, that is urban development. Regarding sufficiency of the observed patterns to base policy recommendations, findings on the spatial internal structure of the city with concentrated versus dispersed within city, block group by block group provide a basis to target policy with the aim of achieving a desirable land use mix and diversity that reflects neighborhood residents preferences. As such, our Shannon's entropy–based analysis combined with Simpson's diversity measure provide practical tools planners and policy makers can use. Methodologically, we have also noted a further extension of our study in a spatial and temporal investigation of urban expansion. Further, regarding policy implications, the administration of Memphis is considering the sewer service extension policy to Shelby County. However, both sewers and roads are the key drivers of urban growth, as infrastructural elements of a comprehensive plan , together with zoning regulations, or enforcement of urban growth (service) boundary (Kelly, 2010). Tennessee municipality is using code enforcement, administrative inspection warrant, administrative hearing officer, housing authorities, tax sales, and land banking as possible remedies to combat blight (Combating Blight in Tennessee Communities: Preliminary Report, 2011). Inner-city blight remediation addresses the issue of an improved infrastructure supply and more sustainable urban growth especially when challenged by increasing budgetary constraints. Other policy implications include planning and zoning regulation of land use mix and diversity to achieve a more sustainable urban form.

REFERENCES

Antipova, A. "Chapter 2: Urban Environment: The Differences between the City in Europe and the United States." In *Urban Environment, Travel Behavior, Health, and Resident Satisfaction*. Cham: Palgrave Macmillan (2022). 10.1007/978-3-319-74198-7_2

Antipova, A., E. Momeni, and R. Banai. "Urban Sprawl, Blight, and the COVID-19 Pandemic." In *Advances in Urbanism, Smart Cities and Sustainability*. Taylor and Francis (2022).

Banai, R., and Ploderer, L. "The Geography of Industrial Blight: Neglected Options for Sustainable Urban Revitalization, Memphis and Shelby County." In *North American Meetings of the Regional Science Council International*. San Antonio, Texas (2018). Accessed June 9, 2021. https://blogs.memphis.edu/rbanai/files/2019/09/The-Geography-of-Blight.pdf

Barrington-Leigh, C., and A. Millard-Ball. "A Century of Sprawl in the United States." *Proceedings of the National Academy of Sciences of the United States of America* 112, no. 27 (July 7, 2015): 8244–8249. Accessed June 9, 2021. https://pubmed.ncbi.nlm.nih.gov/26080422/

Batty, M. "Entropy and Spatial Geometry." *Area* 4, no. 4 (1972): 230–236. Accessed June 10, 2021. https://www.jstor.org/stable/20000695

Baum-Snow, N. "Did Highways Cause Suburbanization?" *The Quarterly Journal of Economics* 122, no. 2 (May 1, 2007): 775–805. Accessed March 29, 2021. https://academic.oup.com/qje/article-lookup/doi/10.1162/qjec.122.2.775

Bereitschaft, B., and K. Debbage. "Regional Variations in Urban Fragmentation Among U.S. Metropolitan and Megapolitan Areas." *Applied Spatial Analysis and Policy* 7, no. 2 (September 8, 2014): 119–147. Accessed June 10, 2021. https://link.springer.com/article/10.1007/s12061-013-9092-9

Bhatta, B., S. Saraswati, and D. Bandyopadhyay. "Urban Sprawl Measurement from Remote Sensing Data." *Applied Geography* 30, no. 4 (December 1, 2010): 731–740.

Bourne, L. "The Urban Sprawl Debate: Myths, Realities and Hidden Agendas." *Plan Canada* 41, no. 4 (2001): 26–30. Accessed February 25, 2021. https://www.researchgate.net/publication/294564221_The_urban_sprawl_debate_Myths_realities_and_hidden_agendas

Brunner, A. "The Effects of Urban Sprawl on Daily Life." *53rd Annual Transportation Research Forum, TRF 2012* 2 (2012): 855–874.

Calthorpe, P. *The Next American Metropolis Ecology, Community, and the American Dream. Princeton Architectural Press, New York. - References - Scientific Research Publishing.* New York: Princeton Architectural Press (1993). Accessed March 29, 2021. https://www.scirp.org/(S(i43dyn45teexjx455qlt3d2q))/reference/ReferencesPapers.aspx?ReferenceID=1570938

Calthorpe, P., and W. Fulton. *The Regional City: Planning for the End of Sprawl. Undefined.* Washington, D.C.: Island Press (2001). Accessed June 10, 2021. https://www.semanticscholar.org/paper/THE-REGIONAL-CITY%3A-PLANNING-FOR-THE-END-OF-SPRAWL.-Calthorpe-Fulton/2aa352d89570a33047266e96a48c1c81891066f1.

Ciscel, D. H. "The Economics of Urban Sprawl: Inefficiency as a Core Feature of Metropolitan Growth." *Journal of Economic Issues* 35, no. 2 (2001): 405–413. Accessed June 10, 2021. https://www.tandfonline.com/doi/abs/10.1080/00213624.2001.11506374

Clark, T. A. "Metropolitan Density, Energy Efficiency and Carbon Emissions: Multi-Attribute Tradeoffs and Their Policy Implications." *Energy Policy* 53 (February 1, 2013): 413–428.

Combating Blight in Tennessee Communities, Preliminary Report, 2011. 2011. At: https://www.tn.gov/content/dam/tn/tacir/commission-meetings/2011-december/Combating%20Blight%20in%20Tennessee%20Communities%20-%20Preliminary%20Report%20.pdf.

Couch, C., L. Leontidou, and G. Petschel-Held (eds.). *Urban Sprawl in Europe: Landscapes, Land-Use Change & Policy. Urban Sprawl in Europe: Landscapes, Land-Use Change & Policy.* Wiley-Blackwell: Oxford. (2008).

Duany, A., E. Plater-Zyberk, and J. Speck. *Suburban Nation: The Rise of Sprawl and the Decline of the American Dream* (2000). Accessed June 10, 2021. https://www.amazon.com/Suburban-Nation-Sprawl-Decline-American/dp/0865477507

Ewing, R. "Is Los Angeles-Style Sprawl Desirable?" *Journal of the American Planning Association* 63, no. 1 (1997): 107–126.

Ewing, R., K. Bartholomew, and A. C. Nelson. "Compactness vs. Sprawl" from Companion to Urban Design. In *Companion to Urban Design* 17. 1st Edition. Taylor and Francis (2011). Accessed June 30, 2021. https://www.taylorfrancis.com/chapters/edit/10.4324/9780203844434-50/compactness-vs-sprawl-reid-ewing-keith-bartholomew-arthur-nelson

Ewing, R., and Hamidi, S. "Measuring Sprawl." *Smart Growth America* 45 (2014): 51. http://www.ncbi.nlm.nih.gov/pubmed/24946764

Ewing, R., R. Pendall, and D. Chen. "Measuring Sprawl and Its Transportation Impacts." In *Transportation Research Record*, 175–183. National Research Council (2003). Accessed June 10, 2021. https://journals.sagepub.com/doi/10.3141/1831-20

Frumkin, H., L. Frank, and R. Jackson. "Urban Sprawl and Public Health: Designing, Planning, and Building for Healthy Communities." *Environmental Health Perspectives* 113, no. 3 (2004): A202. Accessed March29, 2021. https://www.ncbi.nlm.nih.gov/pmc/articles/PMC1253792/

Fulton, W., R. Pendall, M. Nguyen, and A. Harrison. *Who Sprawls Most? How Growth Patterns Differ Across the U.S.* Washington, D.C. (June 2001). Accessed February24, 2021. https://www.brookings.edu/wp-content/uploads/2016/06/fulton.pdf

Galster, G., R. Hanson, M. R. Ratcliffe, H. Wolman, S. Coleman, and J. Freihage. "Wrestling Sprawl to the Ground: Defining and Measuring an Elusive Concept." *Housing Policy Debate* 12, no. 4 (2001): 681–717.

Gordon, P., and H. W. Richardson "Are Compact Cities a Desirable Planning Goal?" *Journal of the American Planning Association* 63, no. 1 (1997): 95–106. Accessed June30, 2021. https://www.tandfonline.com/doi/abs/10.1080/01944369708975727

Gouda, A. A., M. Hosseini, and H. E. Masoumi. "The Status of Urban and Suburban Sprawl in Egypt and Iran." *GeoScape* 10, no. 1 (June 1, 2016): 1–15.

Habibi, S., and N. Asadi. "Causes, Results and Methods of Controlling Urban Sprawl." *Procedia Engineering* 21 (2011): 133–141. Elsevier Ltd.

Hayden, D. *A Field Guide to Sprawl*. New York: W. W. Norton and Company (2004).

Heirman, S., and T. Coppens . "Causes, Consequences and A Ordability of Urban Sprawl in the Caribbean: Case Paramaribo." *Caribbean Urban Forum* 2013, no. November (2013). https://www.researchgate.net/publication/309609893_Causes_Consequences_and_A_ordability_of_Urban_Sprawl_in_the_Caribbean_Case_Paramaribo

Huang, J., X. X. Lu, and J. M. Sellers. "A Global Comparative Analysis of Urban Form: Applying Spatial Metrics and Remote Sensing." *Landscape and Urban Planning* 82, no. 4 (October 17, 2007): 184–197.

Judd, R. D., and T. Swanstrom. *City Politics: The Political Economy of Urban America*. 5th ed. Pearson (2006).

Katz, P. *The New Urbanism: Toward an Architecture of Community*. 1st Ed. New York: McGraw-Hill (1994). Accessed June 10, 2021. https://www.amazon.com/New-Urbanism-Toward-Architecture-Community/dp/0070338892

Kelly, E. D. *Community Planning: An Introduction to the Comprehensive Plan*. Washington: Island Press (2010). Accessed June 10, 2021. https://www.amazon.com/Community-Planning-Introduction-Comprehensive-Second/dp/1597265535

Laidley, T. "Measuring Sprawl: A New Index, Recent Trends, and Future Research." *Urban Affairs Review* 52, no. 1 (January 1, 2016): 66–97. Accessed June 10, 2021. https://journals.sagepub.com/doi/10.1177/1078087414568812.

Lopez, R. "Urban Sprawl in the United States: 1970-2010." *Cities and the Environment (CATE)* 7, no. 1 (February 24, 2014). Accessed March 29, 2021. https://digitalcommons.lmu.edu/cate/vol7/iss1/7

Lopez, R., and Hynes, H. P. "Sprawl in the 1990s: Measurement, Distribution, and Trends." *Urban Affairs Review* 38, no. 3 (January 18, 2003): 325–355. Accessed March 29, 2021. http://journals.sagepub.com/doi/10.1177/1078087402238805

Margo, R. A. "Explaining the Postwar Suburbanization of Population in the United States: The Role of Income." *Journal of Urban Economics* 31, no. 3 (May 1, 1992), 301–310.

Masek, J. G., F. E. Lindsay, and S. N. Goward. "Dynamics of Urban Growth in the Washington DC Metropolitan Area, 1973–1996, from Landsat Observations." *International Journal of Remote Sensing* 21, no. 18 (2000): 3473–3486. Accessed June 10, 2021. https://www.tandfonline.com/doi/abs/10.1080/014311600750037507

Mock, B. "The Meaning of Blight." *Bloomberg*. Last modified 2017. https://www.bloomberg.com/news/articles/2017-02-16/why-we-talk-about-urban-blight.

Musakwa, W., and A. Van Niekerk. "Monitoring Urban Sprawl and Sustainable Urban Development Using the Moran Index: A Case Study of Stellenbosch, South Africa." *International Journal of Applied Geospatial Research* 5, no. 3 (July 1, 2014): 1–20.

El Nasser, H., and P. Overberg. "What You Don't Know about Sprawl: Controlling Development a Big Concern, but Analysis Has Unexpected Findings." *USA Today*, February 22, 2001.

Nazarnia, N., C. Harding, and J. A. G. Jaeger. "How Suitable Is Entropy as a Measure of Urban Sprawl? *Landscape and Urban Planning* 184 (April 1, 2019): 32–43. Accessed June 10, 2021. https://app.dimensions.ai/details/publication/pub.1111059394.

Nelson, A. C., and J. B. Duncan. *Growth Management Principles and Practices*. 1st Edition. Chicago, IL: Planners Press (1995).

Pohanka, M., and S. Fitzgerald. "Urban Sprawl and You: How Sprawl Adversely Affects Worker Health." *AAOHN Journal: Official Journal of the American Association of Occupational Health Nurses* 52, no. 6 (June 23, 2004), 242–246. Accessed June 9, 2021. http://biology.usgs.gov/luhna/chap5.html.

Rahman, M. T. "Detection of Land Use/Land Cover Changes and Urban Sprawl in Al-Khobar, Saudi Arabia: An Analysis of Multi-Temporal Remote Sensing Data." *ISPRS International Journal of Geo-Information* 5, no. 2 (February 1, 2016): 15–32. doi:10.3390/ijgi5020015.

Robinson, L., J. P. Newell, and J. M. Marzluff. "Twenty-Five Years of Sprawl in the Seattle Region: Growth Management Responses and Implications for Conservation." *Landscape and Urban Planning* 71, no. 1 (February 28, 2005), 51–72.

Theil, H. *Economics and Information Theory*. Amsterdam: North-Holland (1967). Accessed June 10, 2021. https://www.worldcat.org/title/economics-and-information-theory/oclc/710718565.

Thomas, R. W. *Information Statistics in Geography (Concepts and Techniques in Modern Geography)*. Norwich, United Kingdom: GeoAbstracts, University of East Anglia (1981). Accessed June 10, 2021. https://www.amazon.com/Information-statistics-geography-Concepts-techniques/dp/086094090X.

Tong, X., Y. Wang, and E. H. W. Chan. "International Research Trends and Methods for Walkability and Their Enlightenment in China." *Procedia Environmental Sciences* 36 (January 1, 2016): 130–137.

Xu, Y., and X. Zhang. "The Residential Resettlement in Suburbs of Chinese Cities: A Case Study of Changsha." *Cities* 69 (September 1,2017): 46–55.

18 A Geospatial Analysis on Effects of Wetland Changes in the Coastal Urban Area in Ampara District

A.L. Iyoob
Land Use Policy Planning Department, District Secretariat, Ampara, Sri Lanka

R.M.K. Ratnayake
University of Sri Jayewardenepura, Nugegoda, Sri Lanka

CONTENTS

18.1 INTRODUCTION

Wetlands are the most important ecosystems on Earth's surface, carrying out the Earth's ecological balance as the Earth's kidneys, while it plays an important role in maintaining the functioning of environmental services. However, the wetlands are affected by rapid population growth due to the indiscriminate activities of human beings. In this context, wetland changes have a potential to impact on biodiversity, human life, regional climate change, and environmental conservation (Junhong et al., 2013). Earlier, despite considerations on the wetland given, the most common definition of the wetland is "the areas of marsh, fen, peat land or water, whether natural or artificial, permanent or temporary, with water that is static or flowing, fresh, brackish or salt, including areas of marine water the depth of which at low tide does not exceed six meters" (Ramsar handbook 5th Edition, 2016, p. 9).

The reported global inland and coastal wetlands cover an area of approximately 12.1 million km^2, of which 54% is permanently submerged and 46% is seasonally submerged (Ramsar Convention on Wetlands, 2018). Natural wetlands are noted to have had the longest decline worldwide between 1970 and 2015, with both inland and coastal wetlands declining by nearly 35%. This is three times more to the rate of deforestation. Moreover, the man-made wetlands, mostly paddy fields and reservoirs have almost doubled during this period. Presently, it has formed 12% wetlands, however these increases have not compensated for the natural wetland loss.

The primary cause of wetland loss worldwide is considered to be agricultural development. Accordingly, 27% of the land area in Asia, 6% in South America, and 2% in Africa (Gallant et al.,

DOI: 10.1201/9781003126195-22

2007) have been lost. An International Indigenous Government Agreement, the 1971 Ramsar Conference, helped 160 countries to conserve the most important remaining wetlands (Zedler and Kercher, 2005).

Wetlands are a treasure trove of nature with their richness of biodiversity. Studies on wetland management and conservation are being conducted in order to efficiently conserve and manage wetland resources using state-of-the-art techniques. Although the best mechanism to protect wetlands in developed countries is through technology and conservation investment programs, due to improper protection of capacity in developing countries, difficulties in enforcing security laws, unfitting tourism activities, industry development, and behavior of the people play a major role in the deterioration of wetlands.

Urbanization poses significant threat to the wetland environment. In the wake of development, wetlands may be completely lost or cut off to the extent that their environmental services are sacrificed as a result of human development activities. Increased impervious surface in nearby areas increases the amount of runoff entering wetland areas. Filtering wetlands to change farmland, excavating them to make stream/river diversions, or diverting their flows are part of a range of aquifer conversion activities that can degrade wetlands. Loss of wetlands is driven by other factors such as the introduction of invasive species and human impacts such as animal grazing or charcoal extraction (Environmental Protection Agency, 2001).

When wetlands are degraded, the broad range of benefits they produce begins to deteriorate and eventually disappear. Wetland degradation is defined as the alteration of a current or intact wetland resulting in simplification or disruption in its structure, function, and composition and, in turn, a loss of biodiversity and ecosystem services. Not only have population pressures and other human-induced stressors resulted in the degradation of wetlands across the globe, but the effects of climate change (e.g., sea-level rise, temperature increases, and changes in flood and drought patterns) also increasingly impact the quality and flow of wetland services. The continued loss and degradation of wetlands will result in a further reduction of benefits and thus negatively impact human health and wellbeing of the future, particularly for the poor and disenfranchised who often depend disproportionately on these public goods and services.

According to Van Zon (2003), a massive 68% of the internationally important sites in Sri Lanka were reported to be under moderate or high threat. It was indicated that especially the coastal lagoons and the marshes of the wet zone were under high risk, combined with low protection status.

Around 50% of the total area (120 million hectares of wetlands, excluding permanent rice paddies) in Southeast Asia, is considered moderately or seriously threatened. At the ecosystem level, specific threats become even more apparent. Many types of wetlands in Southeast Asia, including the freshwater swamp forests, mangrove forests, and peat swamp forests, are most seriously threatened. Consequently, wetland conservation and management are now a global issue with significant implications and are now receiving attention worldwide (Ananda et al., 2003). yet, developing countries often have considerable development pressures associated with poorly regulated resource extraction and management, rapid human population growth, poverty and social hardship, and technological advancement (Newmark and Hough, 2000; Lynch et al., 2016).

Swamps act as a barrier against coastal erosion, tsunamis, and sea level rise. Therefore, the map of wetlands would be valuable for landowners to implement better coastal management practices to mitigate climate impacts. The swamps along the coast were seen as part of the spread. Thus, it would be valuable to combine coastal vegetation with swamps and dunes (Madurapperuma et al., 2019).

Three types of wetlands have been identified in Sri Lanka: inland freshwater wetlands and saltwater land and man-made wetlands. There are about 4,500 km^2 of 103 rivers in Sri Lanka. More than 10,000 man-made ponds have been designated as wetlands (IUCN Sri Lanka, 2004). The mangrove class suffered significant losses in both the marsh and settlement classes. In *Negombo* Lagoon and *Muthurajawela* Marsh areas, swamps decreased in 2017 compared to 2007 (Athukorala et al., 2021). According to Kaleel (2017), due to the loss of wetland in these areas, many natural spaces, especially the sections, are declining. It is noteworthy that many wetlands have been filled with sand for construction activities. Following the tsunami disaster, much of the wetland was filled up for resettlement purposes and to provide temporary shelter for the affected. All construction activities should take place considering environmental issues. According to a study focusing on *Lahugala,Pottuvil*, and *Thirukovil* areas, agricultural land increased by 9.4% in 1991 and 16.4% in 2017. Construction land increased by 0.1% in 1991, 2.1% in 2017, and forest land decreased to 80.3% in 1991 and 72.2% in 2017 (Zahir and Nijamir, 2018).

The main reseason for the decrease in wetland in Sri Lanka is urbanization and introduction of new development projets in coastal areas. Most of the urban centers in Sri Lanka are concentrated in coastal areas. In addition, most of the large urban centers and fast-growing centers are situated along the coastal belt of the country as a result of popularity and demand of coastal tourism industry. The salinity of the lowland areas in the coastal belt also promote alternative use with high demand for spread of urban and non-agricultural activities. Also, most of the highways and other infrastructure facilities are being developed in coastal region of the country.

The previous situation gradually increased the threat to wetland areas of the coastal belt as a result of the high demand of land for many purposes, including fast-growing infrastructures, introduction of many development projects related tourism the industry, concentration of urban centers and spread of urban activities along the coastal area, and more generation of waste from urbanization, industrialization, domestic activities, and other sources, etc. This can be seen on average within 5 km from the coastal line to land areas in all districts in Sri Lanka, Colombo, Kalutara, Galle, Matara, Hambantota, Ampara, Batticaloa, Trincomalee, Gampaha, Puttalam, Mannar, Jaffna, Mullaitivu, and Kilinochchi Districts. The Eastern Tourism Bureau will introduce mega projects for tourism development in Ampara, Batticaloa, and Trincomalee Districts. In addition, the eastern coastal area is rapidly developing following the end of the war. At present, these districts are more crucial regions in the country for perspective changes.

The Ampara Administrative District is a selected area for the study. The *Ampara* District is located in the southeastern part of Sri Lanka. The district covers an area of 449,551 hectares and is viewed as an agricultural district in Sri Lanka. This is a place where paddy fields and water bodies can be found in addition to marshes, swamps, and many wetlands.

The Ampara District consists of 19 divisional secretariats with 2 municipal councils, 1 urban council, and 17 *Pradeshiya Sabhas.* According to statistics, the population of the Ampara District coastal area in 2012 was 392,302. This area covers 64% of the population and 42% of the land area of the Ampara District. The boundaries of the study area in the north - Batticaloa District; in the east - Indian Ocean (Bay of Bengal); in the south - Hambantota District; and in the west and southeast – part of the Ampara District area. The Ampara District coastal area comprises 13 divisional secretariat areas Figure 18.1.

The case of the study is to identify the extent of reduction of wetland in the Ampara District during last 15 years by analyzing satellite images. Therefore, the objective of this study focuses on the reduction of wetland in the Ampara District using new technological tools.

18.1.1 The Methology Applied

The wetlands in the Ampara District coastal areas are being decreased due to various reasons. The study aimed at identifying these wetlands using the Landsat satellite images and to identify the causes for the extinction from 2005–2019. This was generated to identify the water levels, vegetation index, wetlands, and other land use features found in the area and to identify the causes of the interconnected destruction.

In order to achieve the desired objective, both spatial data and non-spatial data were used in the study. The basic data for this study were obtained as non-spatial data. Many thematic maps have been obtained from the Department of Land Use and Disaster Management unit. In addition, data has been obtained from the Ampara District secretariat database, geo-portal in the Sri Lanka Database, and risk info. Data were also obtained from books, regional reports, and articles. Spatial

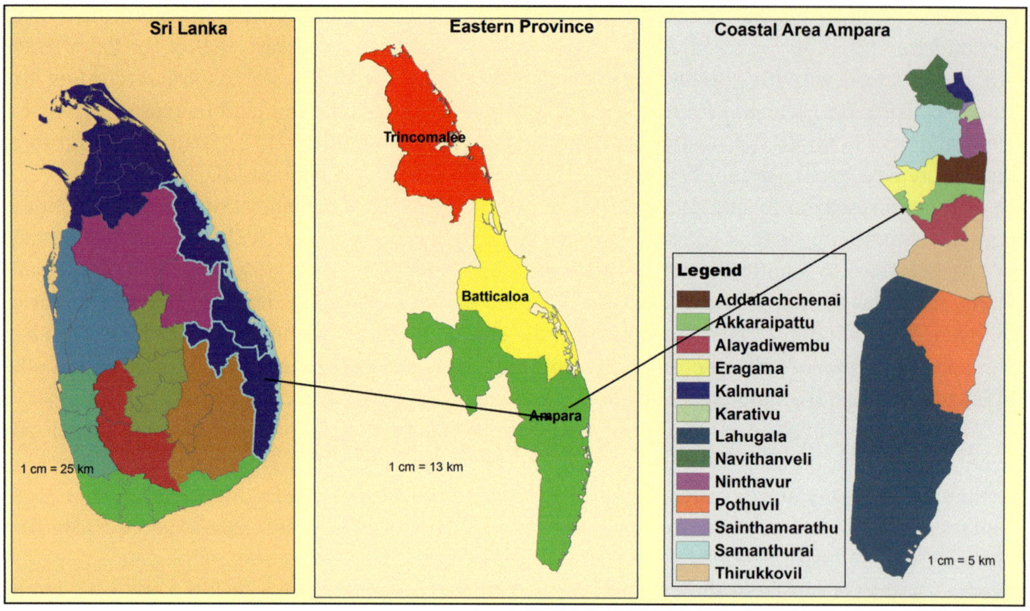

FIGURE 18.1 Study area.

Source: Department of Survey in Sri Lanka, 2001.

data were also obtained from Landsat satellite images, government organizations, previous studies, books, and journals. Landsat images such as advanced Themed Mapper Plus (ETM +), Operational Land Imager (OLI), and Infrared Sensor (TIRS) US Geological Survey (USGS) deposits from the study period 2005, 2010, 2015, and 2019 were also used.

The entire wetland system in the study area based on the Ramsar wetland were not considered for the analysis. Only natural wetlands such as inland water bodies, marshes, and mangroves are considered as wetlands in this study. In addition, the entire area of the Ampara District was not considered for this research. It is noteworthy that only the densely populated coastal areas are considered, regardless of the classification of local councils in the Ampara District. The data analytical flow is shown (Figure 18.2).

18.2 EXISTING WETLANDS IN THE STUDY AREA

According to the national wetland directory, the wetlands were selected based on the selection criteria they explained in order to fine-tune the site consideration. The following wetlands in the district are included in the national wetland directory as they met all the criteria given in the directory.

Arugam lagoon is a shallow, brackish water body consisting of mangroves and marshy areas. It supports the locals to improve their socio-economic conditions and provide shelter for a large number of the water birds. Lahugala and Kitulana National Parks are surrounded by the dry zone with the flat terrain as grazing areas for elephants to move to this area from nearby places. Part of the wetland in the Maduru-Oya National Park is also located in the Ampara District, another feeding site for the elephants and water birds. Pottuvil Lagoon is a coastal lagoon consisting of brackish water surrounded by mangroves, salt marshes, coconut plantations, home gardens, and sand dunes. Rainfall and drainage of several streams are the means of freshwater input for this wetland (Figure 18.3).

Kumana wetland cluster has two sites: Kumana National Park and Panama Kudumibigala Sanctuary. These sites have been declared as Ramsar wetlands in 2010. Coastal wetlands, lagoons,

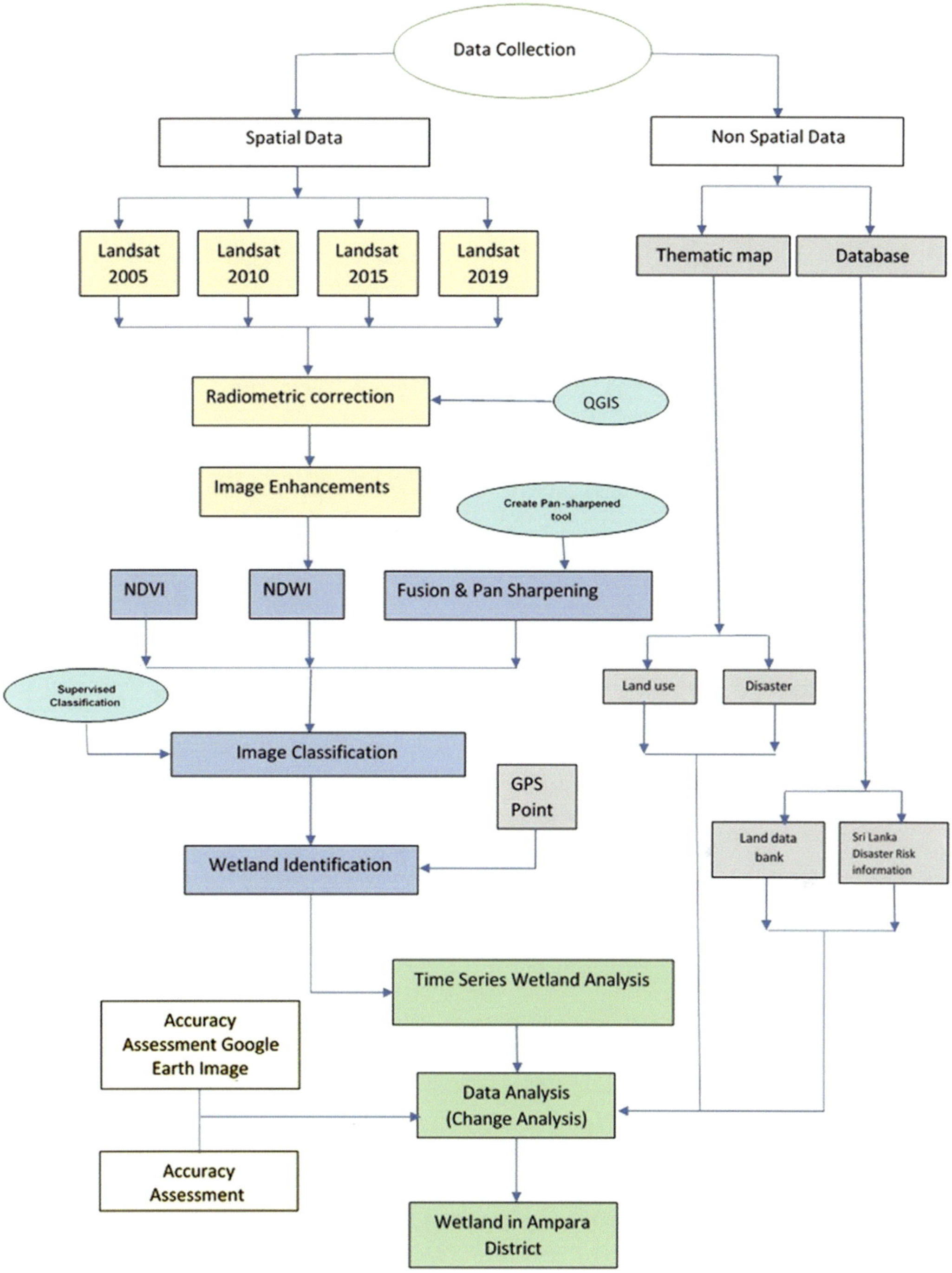

FIGURE 18.2 Analytical flows.

Source: Create by Authors (2020).

mangroves, estuarine areas, and reservoirs are the different wetlands in Kumana that support threatened wetland species: turtles and wetland birds (Ramsar, 2014). All wetlands are located in the coastal urban area in the Ampara District.

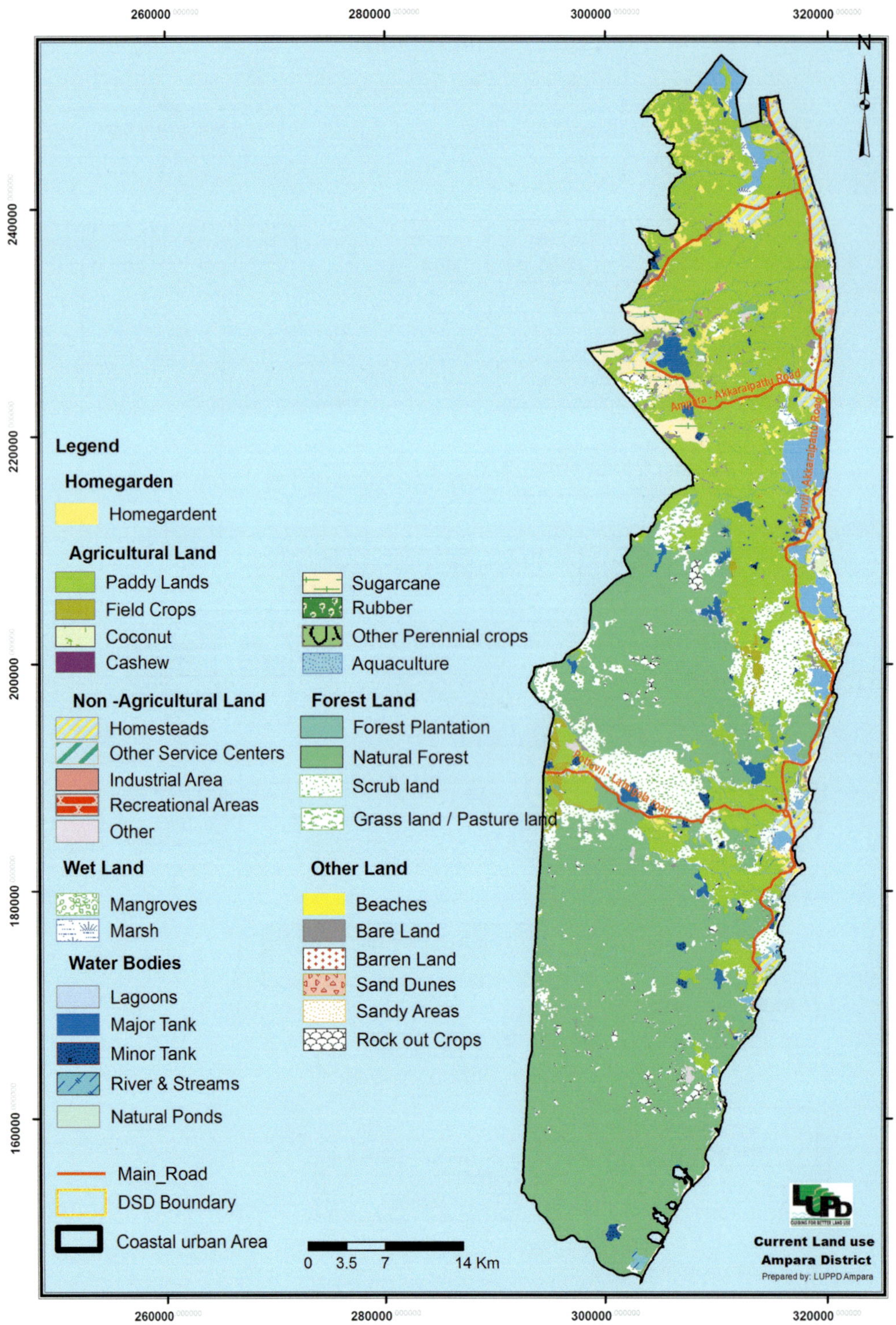

FIGURE 18.3 Land use map of the coastal areas, Ampara District (2016).

Source: Land use Policy Planning Dapartment, *Ampara* (2016).

TABLE 18.1
Existing Land Use Classes in 2016

Type of Land Use	Extant (Ha)
Agriculture	59,820
Forest	100,702
Homestead/Urban	11,008
Other	5,938
Wetland	13,490
Total	190,959

Source: Land Use Policy Planning Department, Kachcheri, Ampara.

The present land use of the study area has been categorized mainly as a homestead, agricultural land, forest land, wetland, and others. Here, forest area is a dominant land use in the study area that consists of about 52.7% (100,702 ha) of the total area of the Ampara District. As well, agriculture, urban or homestead, wetland and others are specified as 31.3% (59,820 ha), 5.8% (11,008 ha), 7.1% (13,490 ha), and 3.1% (5,938 ha), respectively (Table 12.1). The main land use is classified as subclasses of forest lands: natural forest, a forest plantation, grassland/pasture land, and scrubland; agricultural land: paddy, field crops, coconuts, cashew, sugar land, rubber, other perennial crops, and aquaculture; homestead: residential, home gardens, service centers, commercial and industrial area; wetland: lagoons, major tanks, minor tanks, natural tanks, rivers and streams, marshes and mangroves; others: bare lands, barren lands, rockout crops, beach, sandy areas, sand, and recreational areas (Table 18.1).

Wetlands such as lagoons, water bodies, marshes, and mangrove areas have been examined in this study. There are lagoons of 5,552 ha. Likewise, water bodies, marshes, and mangroves areas are 5,986 ha, 1,848 ha, and 155 ha, respectively. Therefore, the total extent of the existing wetland in the study area is 13,490 ha, which is about 7.1% of total land in the study area.

According to the study, the identified wetland reclamation for the settlements, agricultural activities, and other development activities are causing many ramifications for the existence of wetlands. Thus, a few wetland sites have become dump yards, which finally lead to socio-environmental issues. The major causes for the gradual disappearance of wetlands in the Ampara District are urbanization, agricultural activities, and tourist promotion activities.

18.3 CHANGES IN WETLANDS DURING FIFTEEN YEARS (FROM 2005 TO 2019)

Monitoring wetlands using conventional methods is a difficult and time-consuming task. The remote sensing technique is an efficient way to do so. In this sense, Landsat 7ETM+ and Landsat 8 OLI/TIRS satellite images have been used for the time-series analysis for this study from 2005 to 2019. Even though challenges existed during the analysis with the existing data, the available facilities have been used for the analysis purposes. Based on 2005, 2010, 2015, and 2019 satellite images obtained in this manner, the results of the study obtained were a supervised classification of the studies.

The existing wetlands have been analyzed in order to find the periodical change caused by many means. Identified were the seasonal droughts, development of urban activities, and reclamation of the wetlands as the major factors for the decline of the wetlands in the study area. Time series analysis is an excellent method to find the periodical change of the wetlands using satellite imagery (Figures 18.4).

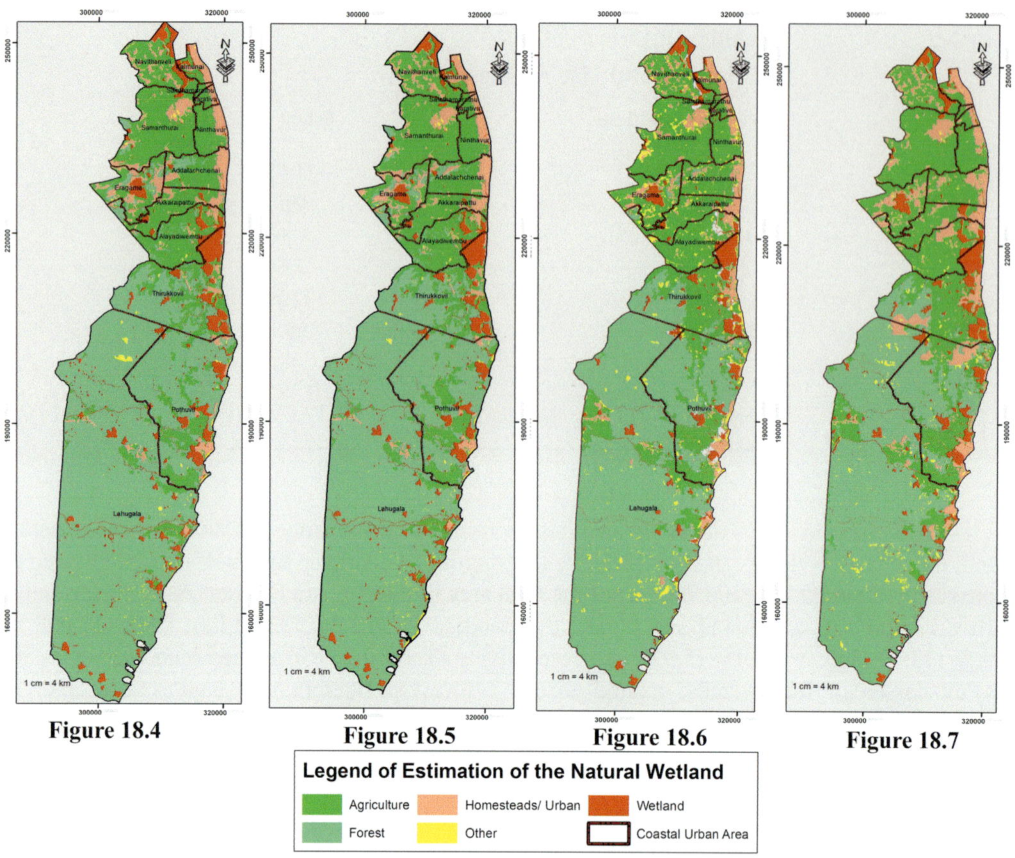

FIGURE 18.4–18.7 Maps of wetland change.

Source: Created based on Landsat Image (from 2005–2019).

Figures 18.4 to 18.7 indicate the changes of wetlands in Ampara. In 2019, the wetland area was 12,447 hectares. According to compare with data from landuse Dapertment in 2016 and satellite data from 2019, 1043 hectares of wetland was deduct. This is due to the fact that the decline of wetlands is occuring more than previous years. The 2019 trend data are comparable to 2015, 2010, and 2015 data, with a declining trend. Compared to 2015 and 2019, the wetland area has decreased by 1,065 hectares (Figures 18.8).

Compared to Figures 18.3 and the output of analysis from 2005 to 2019, the wetlands have decreased by 2,263 hectares. In addition to that, natural wetland changes are shown in Figure 18.9.

The depletion of wetlands in the Ampara District is more prevalent in the coastal areas. It is clear from this study that these wetlands are being used for various needs of the people with a population growth in the Ampara District.

The extent of wetlands available in the years of 2005, 2010, 2015, and 2019 was taken into consideration for the study and clearly identified by overlay analysis as follows in Figures 18.4 to 18.7. The maps clearly show the spatial location of wetlands once every five years from 2005 to 2019. This will help in locating wetlands from time to time.

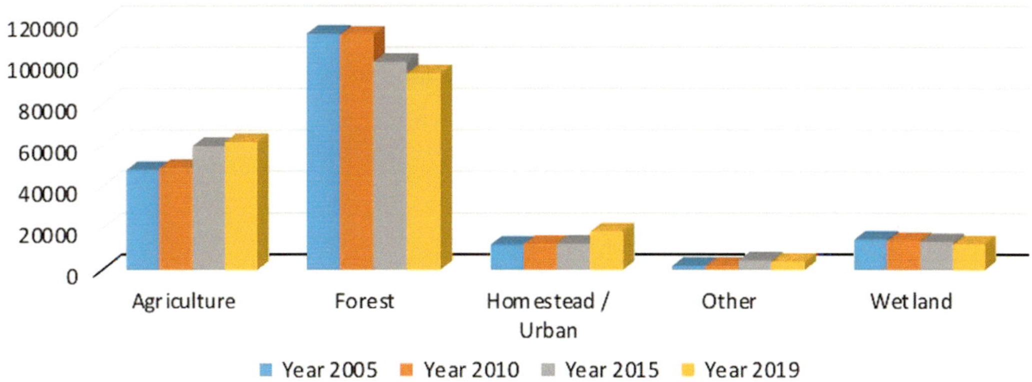

FIGURE 18.8 Land use changes in Ampara from 2005 to 2019.

Source: Created based on Landsat Image (from 2005–2019).

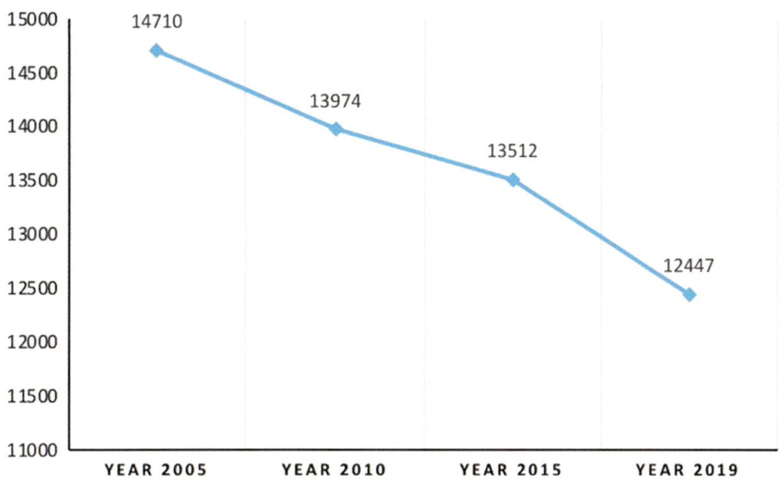

FIGURE 18.9 Natural wetland changes from 2005–2019.

Source: Created Based on Landsat Image (from 2005–2019).

18.4 SPATIAL CHANGES OF WETLANDS IN THE AMPARA COASTAL AREA FROM 2005 TO 2019

A decline of the wetlands in the Ampara District can be observed from 2005 to 2019. A spatial comparison of them would have been even better. Wetlands of the Ampara District with spatial and regional changes have been detected. Their current status has been identified as spatial and the causes have been explored (Figure 18.10).

Wetlands in the Kiddanki area on the border of Kalmunai and Navithanvli outlying areas are being encroached on for residential and general needs of the people of the area. Encroachment has been continuous since 2005, but an increase in encroachment after 2015 is noticeable. Similarly, the lake in the north of the Sammanthurai region has been dry since 2015.

The wetlands in Karaitivu, which have been declared protected wetlands by the government, are also under threat and have been decreasing from 2010 to 2015. The area is being encroached on for the needs of the people and refilled for setting up a cemetery. Paddy lands that have long been abandoned by the Gal-Oya Reservoir are being found as wetlands in the Nintavur Area. They are

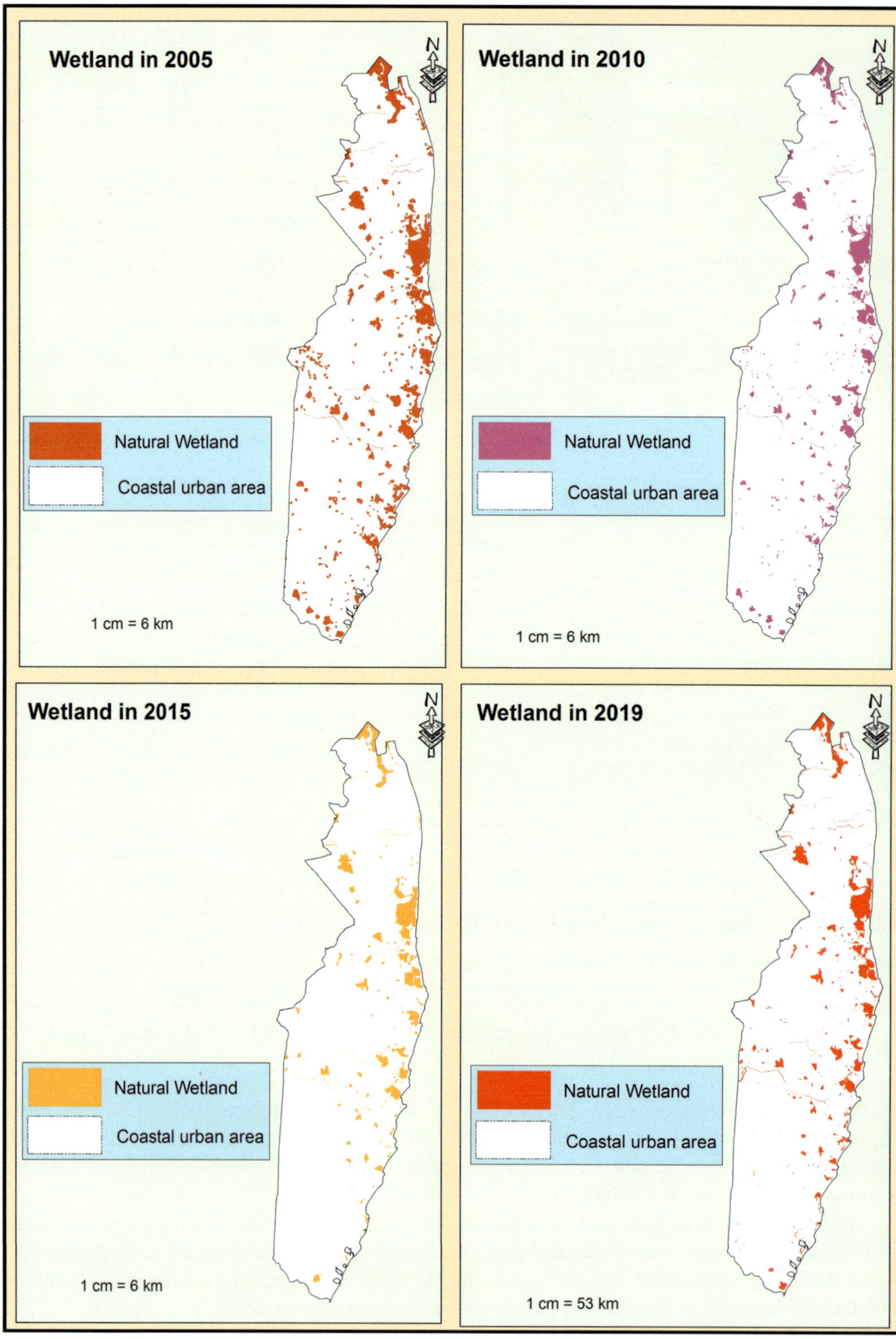

FIGURE 18.10 Spatial changes in natural wetlands 2005 and 2019.

Source: Created based on Landsat Image (2005 and 2010).

currently being filled with wetlands and used for industrial and agricultural activities. Similarly, the lake in the Addalaichenai divisional secretariat is found to be dry. It is also observed that the marshes in the Akkaraipattu area are being filled up rapidly. It is also noteworthy that the area was turned into a marsh by the Galoya Reservoir.

The wetland in the Alayadiwembu fringe has been highly encroached. Encroachment is being carried out for the residential needs of the people in the area and for setting up a playground. The Ambalan Oya Reservoir, which is located within the Damana Divisional Boundary, is being encroached upon by the people for paddy cultivation. Thus, the wetlands in the area are declining.

The Thirukkovil area is considered as having the most number of lagoons in the district. These lagoons are found in shallow areas and often cause dehydration in many means. Mangroves in the area are being destroyed due to tourism development activities, fishing, and gathering of firewood in the particular area. Due to this, the wetlands of the Thirukkovil area have been declining.

As a popular tourist destination, Pottuvil has many diverse wetland ecosystems, such as mangroves and marshes. Komari Lagoon is one of the most affected areas by fishermen and tourists alike. The mangroves there have been destroyed by fishing (shrimp) activity. Urani and Kotukkal are the most important tourist destinations in the Ampara District. These are very dense areas and rich in biodiversity. These areas are being polluted by tourist sites, dumping of waste in wetlands, boat services, and replenishment of water bodies.

The Arugam Bay is a famous surfing bay in Sri Lanka where the international meets of surfing take place. The availability of wetlands in the area has become impossible as wetlands are being filled with soil for agricultural purposes. Development activities for the tourist resort and hotels have consumed wetlands in these areas.

The Lahugala area, which has abundant forests and a section of Kumana wetland clusters, Ramsar wetland is also under threat. Migratory birds and endemic species depend on the wetland where the safari vehicles enter the area for bird and animal watching. Unfortunately, according to the Department of Wildlife, decreasing water levels in the area are a matter of concern for the reduction of wetlands.

It can be observed that water bodies have dried up after 2012 due to insufficient water in the lakes in the area. In some places, the forest is covered with water bodies, making it difficult to identify using satellite images. However, based on the available data, water levels in the Lahugala area are declining.

Main reasons are the impact of the urbanization process, such as development of tourism industry, dumping sites, infrastructure development, peri-urbanization and human settlement, and other activities related to an urban lifestyle spreading along the beachside as urban fringe.

18.5 CONCLUSION

Wetlands are important in the Ampara coastal area despite the various land use features. The last 15 years have seen large-scale changes in the land use in the Ampara coastal area and they have been found to be decreasing over a period of 10 years based on the analysis. By conserving them, we can protect the biodiversity in the coastal areas in the Ampara District.

During the 15-year period from 2005–2019, the forest cover has decreased to 19,414 hectares. Also, 6,287 hectares have been converted to urban land during the same period. In addition, the figures show the increased rate of agricultural use during the same period for 13,385 hectares. These figures indicate the urbanization and the agricultural development land areas have increased more than 19,672 hectares.

Wetlands are 2,263 hectares less in 2019 than it in 2005. The reasons of this include natural factors such as drought, agricultural activities, human settlement, and other related needs. Due to the increase in population in the Ampara District, wetlands are being cleared and converted into residential areas with a view to urban fringes. Post-war tourism growth has increased in areas such as Pottuvil and Thirukovil. Tourist sites have been set up in wetlands in the region, and natural wetlands are being decimated by factors such as boat services and boat lanes for tourists. In addition, wetlands are affected by the dumping of plastic waste from urban and tourism industries in the area.

The Oluvil Harbor, which has been constructed in the southeastern part of the Ampara District coastal area, has caused increased erosion since 2010. As a result, much of the mangroves and marshes in the region have been destroyed. Wetlands formed in low-lying areas by natural water currents are now depleted. Instead of natural water currents, the drain is made of concrete so that the water reaches the river directly as runoff water without going to the wetlands. In addition, areas with marshes and mangroves are being filled for the purpose of setting up industrial activities, cultivation activities, housing, and commercial establishments.

Not only human factors but also natural factors have impacted the depletion of wetlands. The sand eroded by the floods is deposited in the marshes, mangroves, and water bodies, causing the area to become elevated and the wetlands to be destroyed. Wetlands on both sides of the river are eroded by river floods.

The population growth rate of the Ampara District in 2018 is 22 per 1,000 people. The Ampara District is next to Trincomalee, compared to other provinces of Sri Lanka. The population of the Ampara District is found in the coastal areas. Thus, there is an increased demand for land in the area. The people who do not have the money to buy land are setting up their locations in wetlands, water bodies adjoining, and lowland areas. It can be seen that these people are also encroaching on wetlands for their children, considering the future land needs.

Due to the lack of a proper solid waste disposal system in this densely populated area and the improper behavior of the people, daily waste products are being dumped in the water bodies running in the urban areas. In some places, house debris and plastic waste are also dumped. The best example of this is the dumping of waste in the Sainthamaruthu Tona area. This Tona area is covered with a water hyacinth plant and the water bodies are polluted. Closure of wetlands causes flooding in the area where water is not drained.

After the commencement of the Galloya River Project in 1948, the low-lying coastal areas of the Ampara District stagnated without adequate access to the sea. Thus, after 1948, new waters formed in the coastal areas and the lowlands became wetlands. Thus, the area developed in harmony with the natural environment. Due to the increasing population and urbanization since 2000, these lands are being plundered for residential and commercial purposes.

Not only human factors but also natural factors contribute to the depletion of wetlands. Sand and debris eroded by floods are deposited in swamps and water bodies. The area becomes shallow and degraded over time. Wetlands on both sides of the river are destroyed when rivers flood.

In addition, the region experiences a prolonged drought every year. During the months from February to November, the water bodies dry up due to the increased heat and the wetlands also become dehydrated. People are taking advantage of this situation to convert it into residential land and, over time, these lands are being turned into fallow lands due to the lack of water.

18.6 RECOMMENDATION

It is better to maintain a database for wetlands in the study area. This will be an opportunity for future researchers to continue their work. The database will help government and non-government organizations take necessary actions to protect wetlands.

Presently, the application of unmanned aerial vehicles (UAVs) is the best method to find the micro-level changes in the wetlands. It can be used in this study as well in order to derive efficient findings. In addition, high-resolution satellite imagery is required to make this analysis even better. Obtaining them now is not an easy task for researchers. The results of studies on wetlands would be better when there is an opportunity to use high-resolution images for research purposes.

In order to protect the wetland vertical housing schemes, apartments should be built instead of individual houses to meet the demand for housing. This will meet the growing demand for housing and pave the way for sustainable development. The survey suggests that rental housing schemes should be developed to change the individual housing practices in the area.

Water discharged from river basins should be regenerated in protected areas to prevent stagnation in wetlands or low-lying areas without unnecessarily reaching the sea as run-off water.

The study found that people living in nearby wetlands do not know enough about the importance of these wetlands. Awareness seminars should be conducted to make them aware of the importance of wetlands and the benefits they can bring to humans. In addition, events and environmental clubs should be set up within the study area with the participation of the youth. Competitions should be organized among these environmental organizations with due recognition. This will enhance the awareness about wetlands and provide an opportunity to protect these wetlands in the future.

In addition, wetlands should be identified by the Land Survey Department and the extent of the areas should be measured. Action should be taken by the Ministry of Lands and the Environment Authority to declare "this area is protected." This will prevent encroachment of the people and give legal recognition to wetlands.

Surface water is polluted by alkaline and other cover plants. In order to prevent this, local organizations can encourage farmers to create organic manure by building small barriers to prevent cover crops in selected areas of the river. In addition, awareness programs should be conducted for farmers to prevent unwanted plants from being removed from their fields and thrown into water bodies. This can be done with the assistance of the Agrarian Service Center.

Steps should be taken to form divisional and rural environmental committees. In this way, future generations will gain knowledge about the importance of wetlands. In addition, awareness can be raised by the local people to stop the activities against wetlands.

Local councils must step in to reduce bogus land prices in these areas, and government and private organizations must develop housing schemes that will enable the poor people to get housing. Action should be taken to evacuate people from areas encroaching on wetlands, and also, local bodies should place fences and nameplates to protect wetlands.

The issuance of land title deeds to encroached lands in certain areas should be stopped completely. The divisional secretariat processes and the registrar general's departments should not give permission for the legal sale or purchase of these lands. Legislation should be enacted to prosecute violators at the state's expense.

Urban and divisional councils should take action to clean water bodies and wetlands. Water hyacinth plants that have been trapped in water bodies should be removed to reduce the chance of debris being dumped. This requires the creation of entertainment sites and sports sites in areas such as Tona. CCTV cameras can be set up in addition to them.

Areas of declining wetlands have been identified. Steps should be taken to replace the extinct wetland plants in the identified area with the same type of vegetation in those areas. In addition, safety zones should be created to regenerate fish species that were lost or depleted in these water bodies.

There should be an understanding between private and non-governmental organizations on wetland conservation. To this end, actions should be taken by implementing the environmental police program developed by the police.

REFERENCES

Ananda, Joshi R. and J. Kunjani. *Wetland Conservation: A Vision for Sustainable Management, Environmental Management and sustainable Development*, pp. 92–105 (2003).

An Introduction to the Ramsar Convention on Wetlands. 7th ed. Ramsar Convention Secretariat, Gland, Switzerland. 09–10 (2006).

Athukorala, D., R.C. Estoque, Y. Murayama, and B. Matsushita. Impacts of Urbanization on the Muthurajawela Marsh and Negombo Lagoon, Sri Lanka: Implications for Landscape Planning towards a Sustainable Urban Wetland Ecosystem. *Remote Sensing* 13, 316. Available at: https://doi.org/10.3390/rs13020316 (2021).

Environmental Protection Agency. *Threats to Wetlands* (Publication Record EPA843-F- 01-002d). Washington, DC (2001).

Gallant, A. L., R. W. Klaver, G. S. Casper, and M. J. Lannoo . "Global Rates of Habitat Loss and Implications for Amphibian Conservation." *Copeia* (4): 967–979. Available at: https://earthexplorer.usgs.gov/ (2007).

IUCN Sri Lanka. Wetland Conservation in Sri Lanka. Proceedings of the National Symposium on Wetland Conservation and Management: Sri Lanka, iii+75pp (2004).

Lynch, J. A., J. Kalumanga, A. Elikana, and Guillermo, Ospina. "Socio-Ecological Aspects of Sustaining Ramsar Wetlands in Three Biodiverse Developing Countries." *Marine and Freshwater Research,* (2016).

Joy, B. Z. and K. Suzanne. "Wetland Resource: Status, Trends, Ecosystem Services, and Restorability." *Annual Review of Environment and Resources* 30:39–74 (Volume publication date 21 November 2005), First published online as a Review in Advance on July 6 (2005), Available at: (10.1146/annurev.energy.30.050504.144248 (2005).

Junhong, B., C. Baoshan, C. Huicong, L. Ainong, and Z. Baiyu. *Wetland Degradation and Ecological Restoration.* Hindawi Publishing Corporation. Volume 523632 (2013).

Kaleel, M. I. M. "The Impact on Wetlands: A Study Based on Selected Areas in Ampara District of Sri Lanka." *World News of Natural Sciences*, 716–725 (2017).

Madurapperuma, B. D., I. L. M. Zahir, K. Nijamir, and A. L. Iyoob. *Mapping and Change Detection Of Mangroves along the Coastline Of Ampara District From 2004 To 2019*, Proceedings, South Eastern University International Arts Research Symposium -2019, 18th December 2019, pp. 330–336 (2019).

Newmark, W. D., and J. L. Hough. "Conserving wildlife in Africa: Integrated Conservation and Development Projects and Beyond." *Bioscience* 50, 585–592. Available at: (doi:10.1641/0006-3568(2000)050[0585:CWIAIC]2.0.CO;2) (2000).

Ramsar Convention on Wetlands. *Global Wetland Outlook: State of the World's Wetlands and their Services to People.* Ramsar Convention Secretariat, Gland, Switzerland (2018).

Ramsar, https://www.ramsar.org/news/sri-lanka-designates-kumana-wetland-cluster-ramsar-site-as-its-5th-wetland-of-international. (2014).

Shaw, S. P., and C. G. Fredine. Wetlands of the United States: Their extent and values to Waterfowl and other wildlife. Washington D. C. Department of the Interior, Fish and Wildlife Service, Office of River Basin Studies. *Circular* 39 (1956).

Van Zon, J. C. J. Wetland Conservation and Management, Sri Lanka: A Status Paper, *Proceedings of the National Symposium on Wetland Conservation and Management,* IUCN SriLanka PP02 (2004).

Zedler, Joy B, and Suzanne, Kercher. "Wetland Resources:Status, Trends, Ecosystem Services, and Restorability." *Annual Review of the Environment and Resources* 30, 39–74 (2005).

Zahir, I. L. M., and K. Nijamir. "Application of Geospatial Technology for Wetlands' Mapping and Change-Detection: A Case Study in Selected Areas of South Eastern Coast in Ampara District, Sri Lanka." *Sustainable Geoscience and Geo tourism* 1, 25–32, doi:10.18052/www.scipress.com/SGG.1.25, SciPress Ltd., Switzerland (2018).

19 Geospatial Analysis of Solid Waste Management in Badulla Municipality—Uva Province, Sri Lanka

S.A. Sudusinghe, R.M.K. Ratnayake, and D.K.D.A. Ranaweera
University of Sri Jayewardenepura, Nugegoda, Sri Lanka

CONTENTS

DOI: 10.1201/9781003126195-23

19.1 INTRODUCTION

Waste and waste management is a pressing issue in most of the developing countries, including Sri Lanka. It has become a major global concern that should be addressed immediately. As a result of industrialization, globalization, rapid population expansion, and economic development, the volume of waste generated has increased. Hence, waste management has grown into a global issue due to its improper management. This poses a threat to the existence of humans and animals. It also causes the degradation of the environment, which cannot be reversed.

According to Karunarathne (2015), daily, over 6,400 tons of solid waste are generated in Sri Lanka. Waste collection and disposal is a serious issue in most of the urban areas in Sri Lanka. As cited by Bandara and Hettiaratchi (2010), "In Sri Lanka, the majority of the Municipal solid waste management cost is allocated for waste collection and transportation rather than for waste disposal and treatment." Based on the rules and regulations that have been implemented by various acts and ordinances in Sri Lanka, waste collection and disposal is handled by municipal councils and urban councils.

Open dumping is the most usual practice used in Sri Lanka instead of open burning; 85% of collected waste is subjected to open dumping (Karunarathne, 2015). Municipal solid waste (MSW) is the most acute environmental issue in urban Sri Lanka. It is a result of swift urbanization, industrialization, and population growth. Its effects on human health are a severe problem associated with MSW dump sites.

Currently, with the development, the Badulla District also faces the waste management problem. In the future, this will become a major issue in the area. Collected from 11 Grama Niladhari divisions in the municipality area, the Badulla Municipal Council dumps nearly 30 tons of solid waste per day.

In order to manage this situation, selection of proper sites for waste disposal is significant. Many factors should be integrated into one system and should be analyzed properly before selecting a site as a solid waste disposal site. The geographic information system (GIS) has the potential to handle and simulate the necessary data collected from various sources. GIS combines spatial data (maps, aerial photographs, and satellite images) with quantitative, qualitative, and descriptive information databases, which can maintain a wide range of spatial queries. All of these factors have made GIS an essential tool for location studies (Al-hanbali et al., 2011).

19.1.1 Research Problem

There are two main types of issues correlated with solid waste management. These two are with environmental effects and economic effects. Surface water contamination, soil contamination, air pollution, and leachates can be identified as environmental effects. And when considering economic effects, it has an impact on municipal wellbeing and it creates recycling revenue.

Disposal of garbage as solid wastes is a common problem in both urban and rural areas in many developing countries. Due to the lack of continuous garbage-collection systems and convenient landfills, it creates many environmental hazards. Open canals and drains are being blocked by waste. This garbage waste is mostly plastics, papers, and low toxic materials. However, such toxic materials represent a hazardous impact on the environment due to the breakdown of their degradable constituents, a matter that adds significant loads to the biological oxygen demand (BOD) of the local ecosystem. People dispose of garbage solid waste and untreated effluent into the nearby drains because they are not aware about the consequences. There are not any considerable financial incentives to stop them from such practices and to encourage them to alter their habits. The fact is small volumes of effluent induce pollution to a very large volume of water bodies.

With the development, the Badulla Municipality also faces waste management problems. Badulla is the capital of the Uva Province. Around 100,000 people reach the city daily for employment, education, administrative, health, commercial, and other services. The majority of visits to the city are for employment. The average population growth rate of the Badulla District is 0.37%

per annum. Migration to the city is also increasing significantly. With the population growth and migration, waste generation and accumulation also increases day by day.

According to statistics, the Badulla Municipal Council (BMC) dumps 30 tons of solid waste daily, collected from the municipality area. Badulla MC collects around 70% of its total solid waste in the area. The residential sector is the main contributor to the waste generation. In addition, contribution of commercial, industrial sectors, and hospitals are also high. The open dumping and open burning are the frequent current disposal methods used by the BMC, which creates numerous environmental problems.

The Badulla Municipal Council is faced with a severe problematic situation during the solid waste management process. Twenty percent of the solid waste they collect is mixed waste. The Municipal Council is unable to separate the 20% as biodegradable and non-biodegradable waste due to capacity issues. This has created collected residual waste that cannot be sold or separated from the year 2014.

The issue is increasing day by day as the municipality doesn't have a suitable site for waste disposal. Hence, they dispose collected waste in the Badulupitiya area near the Badulla town. The waste heap is increasing gradually, creating a nuisance to the public and generating several environmental issues. Subsequently, the dumping yard is located between Vincent Dias Stadium, the only ground with the necessary facilities in Badulla, and the Botanical Garden of Badulla. This has reduced the utility, efficiency, and productivity of these resources.

There is no available approach to manage leachate generation in the city. These wastewaters flow directly to common drains and then flow to Badulu Oya, adding polluted wastewater stream. Since the Badulu Oya is the main source of pipe-born water to Badulla city, this situation has to be considered critically.

Therefore, this research is mainly focused on recommending a suitable solution to waste management issues to abate social and environmental problems and to safeguard human health and the surrounding environment in a sustainable manner using the GIS technology within the Badulla Municipality. The main objective of the study is to identify suitable locations for solid waste disposal in the municipality. This research study was conducted during the February 2020–November 2020 time period.

19.2 LITERATURE REVIEW

19.2.1 Solid Waste Issues in the Urban Sector

Solid waste is produced as a by-product of all the resource usage, including resource-intensive, consumer-based economic lifestyles (Bhada-Tata and Hoornweg, 2012).

Municipal solid waste (MSW) is a term that refers to a diverse collection of waste generated in urban areas, the type of which varies by region. Normally MSW are considered non-hazardous wastes, but sometimes it can be considered toxic or hazardous wastes with the presence of toxic components in waste such as inks, batteries, paints, fabrics, and lamps (Karunarathne, 2018).

Most of the urbanizing townships have been recognized by municipal solid waste management as a problem in the developing world. With the urban population and accelerated population density, this problem creates a critical situation (Glawe et al., 2006).

In South Asian countries, solid waste management is a major issue. Although there are some formulated policies for environmental protection, the implementations are limited. Thus, in remote areas, open dumping is the preferred form of disposal. In the waste management process, avoidance, minimization, reuse, recycling, treatment, and disposal are the important processes. But in the sustainable waste management system, disposal should be the final step. If we can't manage wastes in other methods, we should move into the disposal stage.

According to Bhada-Tata and Hoornweg (2012), countries in the world use different SWM practices such as source reduction, collection, recycling, composting, incineration, and landfilling or dumping and the level of these practices depend on their income level.

Technical, environmental, socio-cultural, legal, and institutional considerations all play a significant role in the proper implementation of solid waste management systems (Guerrero et al., 2013).

Although the issue of solid waste is problematic the world around, it creates a special situation in developing countries in the Asian region, though they still generate much less waste than developed countries when compared to per capita figures. The most popular waste disposal method in developing countries in Asia is the landfill. With the development and the growth in the population, availability of land will be a major issue for landfilling practices (Abeynayaka and Werellagama, 2007). The above is also influenced by a lack of adequate resources, poor planning, and poor solid waste management procedures.

Al-Hanbali et al. (2011) stated that when considering the solid waste management process, direct waste for a solid waste disposal site is the last step that should be be taken in the solid waste management process. Selection of a solid waste management site is complex, whether it is municipal or hazardous waste. It must take into account social, environmental, technological, and economical factors.

19.2.2 Use of Geospatial Technology for Site Selection

To finalize a solid waste landfilling location, environmental considerations such as land use, geology, settlement areas, surface waterways, population density, slope, and protected areas as well as economic factors such as airports, solid waste transfer stations, property values, and roads are evaluated. The recognized factors are divided into sub-categories based on the suitability of a solid waste landfill, and values are assigned. For each factor, a score between 0 and 5 is assigned. To identify the suitable locations for a decentralized wastewater treatment plant (Deepa and Krishnaveni, 2012) the analytical hierarchy principle (AHP) method with the help of the GIS process has been used. Thematic layers were used as follows: land use or land availability, slope, soil, population density, cost, and technology to carry out the analytical part. Saaty (2008) conducted a study using the analytical hierarchy principle (AHP), and a paired comparison matrix was prepared for the selected seven criteria and individual class weights (rank) and map scores (weight) were worked out. Then, the linear summation equation was created by applying the weights equation to gain a unified weight map with due weights of all input variables, which will be further reclassified to create a suitable area map. The key concepts for that research were to break down the problem, pair-wise comparison of the numerous alternatives, and synthesis of the preferences.

The geographic information system is an effective, robust, and powerful management tool that can be used for environmental management by supporting decision making, problem solving, and the planning process. It has the capability to associate spatial data, perform numerous analyses, and to display large volumes of data. And it is a cost-effective and less time-consuming tool that functions as an inventory for geo-referenced data (Zulu and Jerie, 2017).

The GIS has the capability to manage spatial information with overlaying and integrating multiple layers and derive the requirement. Today, GIS experts are a help to decision makers for selecting the most suitable sites using modern technologies (Fernando, 2014).

The aim in a site selection exercise is to find the best location with preferred conditions that fulfil preset selection criteria. There are usually two stages to site selection. Those are site screening and site evaluation. Site screening leads to the discovery of a small number of potential sites from a large geographic area and a range of selection factors. Site evaluation leads to an in-depth investigation of each candidate site to determine which is the most suitable (Fernando, 2014).

Since 1960, multi-criterion analysis (MCA) has been used successfully in deferent domains. It has been combined with geographical information systems since the early 1990s for improved decision making (Ekanayake, 2010).

The incorporation of GIS and multi-criteria evaluation (MDE) has been shown in studies related to site determination in various subjects, including urban-regional planning, ecological sciences, waste management, hydrology and water resource, agriculture, forestry, natural hazards, recreation/tourism, housing/real estate, geological sciences, manufacturing, and cartography (Malczewski, 1999).

It is primarily concerned with how to aggregate information from several criteria into a single evaluation index. It is used to address the challenges that decision-makers face when dealing with enormous amounts of complex information (Nas et al., 2010).

Attempts have been made to identify appropriate landfill sitings using multi-criteria decision analysis (MCDA) or the multi-criteria decision making method (MCDM) by combinations with overlay analysis using GIS (Babalola and Busu, 2011).

The principle of MCDA and MCE is to break down the decision issues into smaller units that are more understandable, analyze each unit separately, and then combine the units in a logical manner. It has been used to overcome the challenges that decision-makers face when dealing with large amounts of complex information and, as a result, it has evolved into an efficient, effective, and powerful tool for solving site selection problems that arise during planning and decision-making when combined with GIS (Nas et al., 2010).

Sharifi et al. (2009) employed GIS and MCDA to execute an initial screening procedure to exclude inappropriate sites and identify the most eligible sites based on information from regional experts and newly established criteria. MCDA employs a collection of procedures for assigning values to alternatives that are assessed for a particular purpose.

According to Malczewski (2004), one of the most extensively used MCE approaches for land suitability analysis is weighted linear combination. It entails standardizing the suitability maps, assigning relative relevance weights to the maps, and then combining the weights and standardized suitability maps to arrive at an overall suitability score.

The selection of solid waste disposal sites requires numerous factors that should be incorporated into one system to be analyzed properly. The geographic information system (GIS) provides the ability to handle and simulate data received from a variety of sources. GIS combines spatial data (aerial pictures, maps, and satellite images) with qualitative, quantitative, and descriptive information databases to support a wide range of spatial queries (Al-Hanbali et al., 2011).

The use of GIS to evaluate and select a suitable location for a landfill site is more practical and economical, which has become a suitable tool for land use analysis. It is helpful to distinguish between the most suitable and unsuitable lands in the selection procedure (Yazdani et al., 2015).

A case study of the Sakkottai-block, Sivagangai District of Tamil Nadu, India has used GIS technology through a weighted overlay analysis to select the possible sites for solid waste disposal and the sites have been classified into three categories: good, moderate, and poor (Tamilenthi et al., 2011).

Akbari et al. (2008) have used GIS and fuzzy multi-criteria decision analysis (FMCDA) for landfill site selection. As the first stage, the GIS digital map overlay technique has been used to find the suitable sites and as the second stage FMCDA has been used to rank the various landfill sites based on the decisions of experts.

19.3 METHODOLOGY

19.3.1 Study Area

Municipal solid waste is the most serious environmental problem in Sri Lanka, especially in urban areas. It is an outcome of rapid urbanization, industrialization, and population growth. We can observe this situation in various magnitudes around the country.

The situation is critical in Colombo and other metropolitan areas, due to the massive amount of municipal solid wastes generated and lack of sustainable waste disposal options. Every day, the Colombo Municipal Council produces almost 1,000 tons of solid waste. Each day, the Kolonnawa Urban Council, Sri Jayawardenapura Kotte Municipal Council, and Moratuwa Municipal Council gather between 350 and 400 tons. The Western Province generates more than 3,200 tons of trash daily (EML consultants, 2017).

The issue of waste generation and waste management issue severe in above areas, when compared to the Badulla Municipal Council. Even though the waste management problem is very common to the whole country, it is essential to select a suitable area for the necessary data collection due to limited time for the study. Hence, the Badulla municipality area located in the Uva Province of Sri Lanka was selected as study area. Another reason to select the Badulla Municipal Council (BMC) as the study area is the fact that many studies on waste management have been conducted covering the location. Several government and non-government organizations are also involved in that process. When compared to other urban councils and municipalities, the waste management issue in Budulla municipality area has received less attention.

During previous years, the issue of waste management in the Badulla Municipality has increasingly paved the way for a severe environmental issue. Mixed garbage, such as paper, bottles, cans, plastic containers, and occasionally electronic items, is found together with decomposable waste from dead animals, food, building debris, and even industrial waste.

The main waste dumping site of the Badulla Municipality is Badulupitiya. We identified a number of issues due to mixed waste disposal at the site. Many incidences were reported during the past years due to disposal of solid wastes in open spaces. In 2016, a fire occurred in the waste dumping site. When a fire erupted in the Badulupitiya municipal dump yard, it quickly spread, posing a threat to nearby areas. The fire consumed thousands of tons of garbage, polluting the air with poisonous fumes. Eight persons were hospitalized due to inhalation of hazardous fumes from the burning landfill (Daily news, 2016).

Medical waste is another problem. There are no any proper clinical waste disposal methods at the Badulla General Hospital. In 2019 Augus,t an incident connected to waste generated by the hospital was reported. According to reports, a stock of hazardous medicine intended for cancer patients at the Badulla General Hospital was being stored in an unsafe manner at a storage unit owned by Sathosa. It was also alleged that the Badulu Oya flows just behind the Sathosa warehouse, and if the hazardous medicines were to mix with the water stream it would create a disaster (Sri Lanka News – Newsfirst (2020)).

During rainy days, leachates created from waste dumping sites move through natural drainages and finally mix with water bodies, which accelerates water pollution. Since Badulla is an elevated area, the situation will increase. With the rapid development and population growth, waste generation also will increase in the future. The situation will be worsened if we are unable to address waste management issues.

Open dumping and open burning are the present waste disposal methods of the BMC, which creates numerous environmental problems such as land and surface water pollution, spreading of vector borne and communicable diseases, emission of toxic gases and leachates, odor, and damaging the aesthetic beauty of the area. These are the main factors to select the Badulla Municipality area as the study area.

Being the main city in the Badulla District, the Badulla Municipal Council consists of 13 Grama Niladhari divisions located in western part of the Badulla divisional secretary division. The total area of Badulla city is 1,056 ha. Accordingly, the population density within Badulla city limits is 44.06 people per hectare. Badulla is a multi-ethnic city. At the present, the tertiary sector service provision is prominent in Badulla, surpassing agriculture sector. Although there are places that attract more tourists, tourism has not been well developed yet in Badulla. The Badulla Municipal Council area is located between 6.5–7.1 latitude and 81.2–81.4 longitude. It is bounded by Soranathota Pradeshiya Sabha in north, Badulla Pradeshiya Sabha in the east, and Hali Ela Pradeshiya Sabha in the east and south. Badulla belongs to a wet and dry intermediate climatic zone and the average annual temperature is about 24 degrees Celsius. The average annual rainfall is around 1,885 mm. It is shaped like a basin and the middle area is in plain nature topographically. The study area is shown in Figure 19.1.

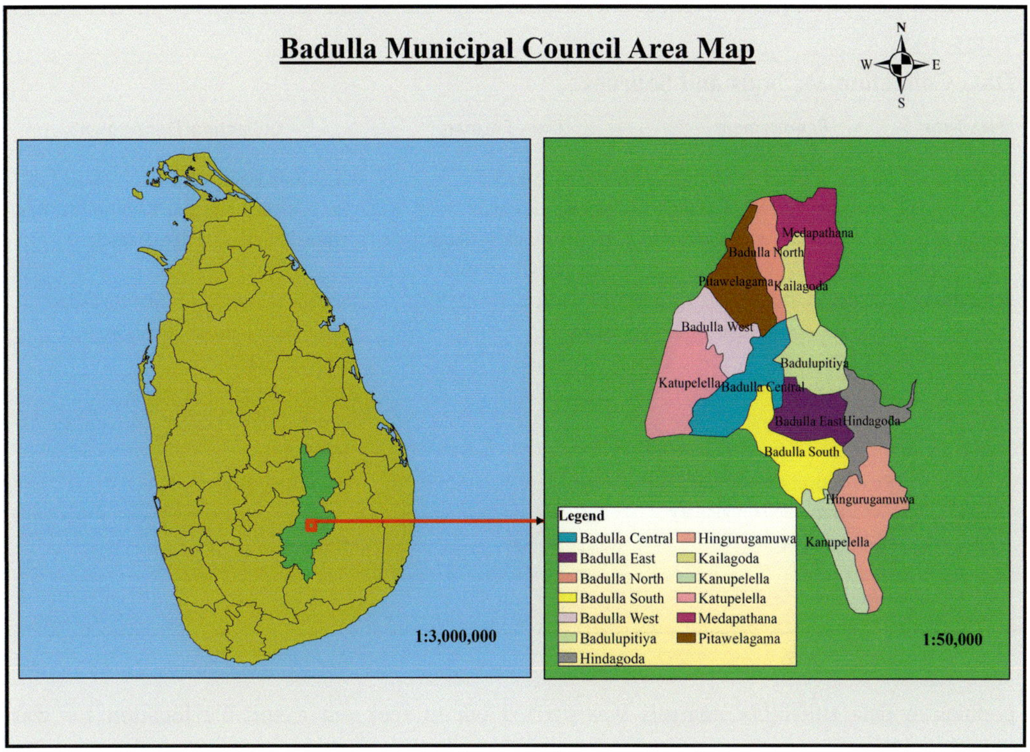

FIGURE 19.1 Map of the study area.

Source: Author generated map based on survey department data, 2020.

19.3.2 Data Source and Types

To order to achieve the objective, primary data and secondary data were used for the study. Literatures revealed some important requirements on this waste disposal site selection and spatial criteria were elaborated in some cases. The following table shows the way data was collected and types of data with respective authorities. Primary data were collected through formal and informal discussions and observations. Separately, town planning officers of the Urban Development Authority, CEA officers, president of the Badulla local authority, and respective officers of Divisional Secretariat office participated in these formal and informal discussions. In some cases, required data were collected via telephone conversations (due to COVID-19 pandemic situation). The governing criteria and their weights were identified through those discussions with expertise officers and literatures. The data collection period was limited to 20th April to 15th July in 2020. Field surveys were arranged for getting a real experience of the Badulla Municipal Council limits, but the unexpected COVID-19 pandemic situation made it hard due to social distancing. But, the current status of a waste disposal site of the Badulla MC was observed in this field visit. Table 19.1 shows the data collection methods and sources.

19.4 DATA ANALYSIS

As a GIS technique, suitability analysis was mainly used in this study; 1:5,000 digital data collected in Esri shape file format was used for the analysis.

Considering the hydrological network, land use pattern (Classified by UDA), transport network and built-up areas, classified hazard layer (National Building Research Organization –NBRO), and

TABLE 19.1
Data Collection Methods and Sources

Data Type	Requirement	Data Formats	Collection/Departments
Primary	Identification of governing criterions for waste site selection and weightages of them	Formal, informal discussions and observations. – Semi-structured Interview	Local authorities-Badulla, CEA-Badulla, Divisional Secretariat Badulla MC limits, UDA-Badulla & RDA-Badulla
Secondary	Population data	MS Excel	Department of Census and Statistics
	Land use map (Digital/ 1:5,000)	Shape file	Urban Development Authority-Badulla (UDA)
	Hazards map	Shape file	National Building Research Organization–Badulla district office (NBRO)
	Road network maps, build-up area map, GND boundary	Shape file	Survey Department
	DEM (SRTM)	Raster format	Internet-USGS site

Source: Author generated, 2020.

population data suitability analysis was carried out to seek out a suitable location for waste management.

Selection of a suitable waste disposal site depends on geospatial factors. Therefore, in order to achieve the main objective, which was to identify a suitable waste disposal site, the GIS-integrated multi-criteria decision making (MCDM) analytical approach was selected.

In this study, the thematic map layers were imported to GIS for analysis. The main analysis part of this study was a GIS-integrated multi-criteria analysis-based model for determining the suitable waste disposal site.

Data analysis was conducted primarily on GIS multi-criteria decision making (MCDM) analysis approach, as introduced in the methodology section. The collected data in the personal geodatabase was analyzed using the model builder technique in ArcGIS spatial analyst tool and analysis was conducted on the main three steps.

1. Create the geo-spatial database.
2. Develop the model using a multi-criteria analysis approach to identify relevant criteria.
3. Identify the suitable site for waste disposal under the selected criteria.

19.4.1 Create the Geospatial Database

Taking into account data type, number of the data layers, and access limitation to the database, a personal geodatabase was used to store all the data,. The geodatabase was used to store all collected data layers and attributes with a common environment in the GIS software. The collected data from various sources were in different formats and different coordinate systems. Therefore, all the various coordinated data were required to be converted into common database environments. Then, the geodatabase technique was chosen to store the data due to many advantages of the model. The special advantage of using a personal geodatabase in this type of study is the possibility to convert a different-layered coordinate system and different spatial reference system into one coordinate and reference system that is set in the geodatabase.

19.4.2 Develop the Model Using the Multi-Criteria Analysis Approach to Identify Relevant Criteria

In this study, mainly all analyses were conducted as raster analysis. Therefore, all the vector files were required to be converted into a raster format. In this case, the ArcGIS euclidean distance tool was used to calculate distances from the hydrological network and distance from roads. Other pre-classified land use layers, hazard layers, population layers, and building layers were converted into raster layers prior to raster analysis.

19.4.3 Identify the Suitable Site for Waste Disposal under the Selected Criteria

All the layers were reclassified except the building layer. The building layer was underwent a kernel density function and the resulting layer was reclassified. Then, after by using calculated weights for each criterion, all six reclassified raster layers were used as inputs for a weighted overlay function. To develop a suitability map, it should be combined with all selected map layers together to have a single ranked map of potential sites for waste disposal. The final resultant map was created by considering all the factors with their priorities. The analytical method for this study is shown in Figure 19.2.

19.5 RESULTS AND DISCUSSION

19.5.1 Geospatial Analysis as a Solution for Solid Waste Issues in the Badulla Municipality

To date, there are no specific spatial criteria used for selecting a solid waste disposal site in Sri Lanka. The criteria that have been used in this research were derived from the literature review based on the criteria used in other countries and other districts of Sri Lanka. It has been used with modifications and alterations to local desired priorities and requirements.

In order to find out the suitable solid waste disposal site for the Badulla Municipality area, the following evaluation criteria were determined and classified into three main categories according to the considerable impact of the disposal site on them.

1. Hydrological network
2. Land use pattern
3. Transport network

Under these three main categories, five reclassified raster layers, including distance to hydrological network, distance to roads, pre-classified land use layer, population layer, and building layer were used in this study. Other than these layers, the pre-classified hazard layer produced by NBRO-Badulla was engaged for this analysis.

19.5.2 Hydrological Network Map

In this study, the hydrological network map was extracted from SRTM DEM, which was downloaded from the USGS Earth Explorer site for free. All rivers and channels were categorized as surface water. Badulu Oya was the main surface water body present in the Badulla Municipality area.

Disposal of solid wastes near the river may cause ecological problems that have an extended impact for humans and animals who utilize this contaminated water source for various activities. Therefore, the landfill site should have to maintain a considerable distance from the surface water sources.

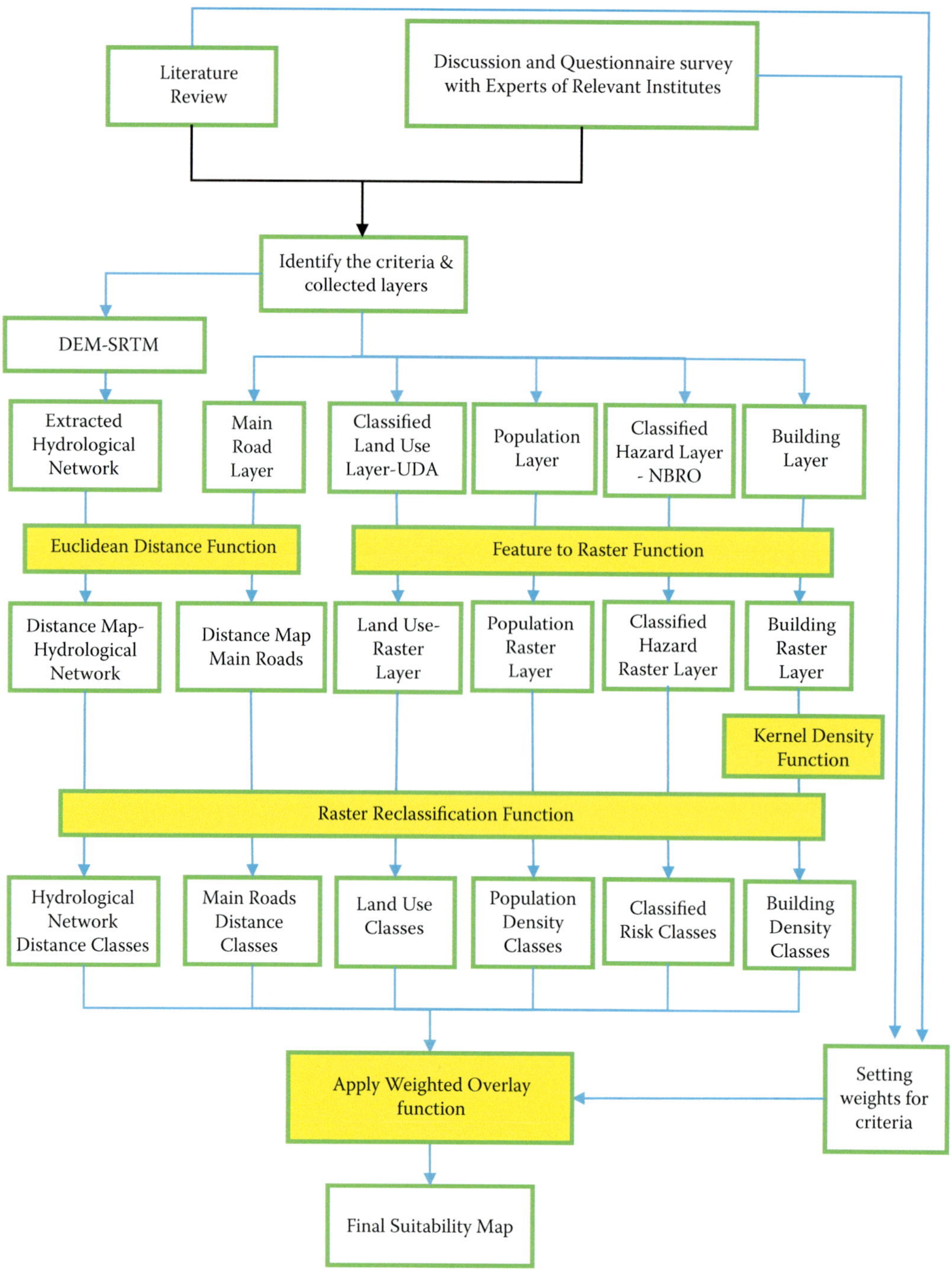

FIGURE 19.2 Analytical techniques.

Source: Author generated, 2020.

The distance from 0–50 m was considered restricted, 50–150 m was considered unsuitable, 150–250 m was considered suitable, and a distance greater than 250 m was considered highly suitable. Accordingly, four different zones were specified, considering the relative distance from surface water Figure 19.3, Figure 19.4 and Table 19.2

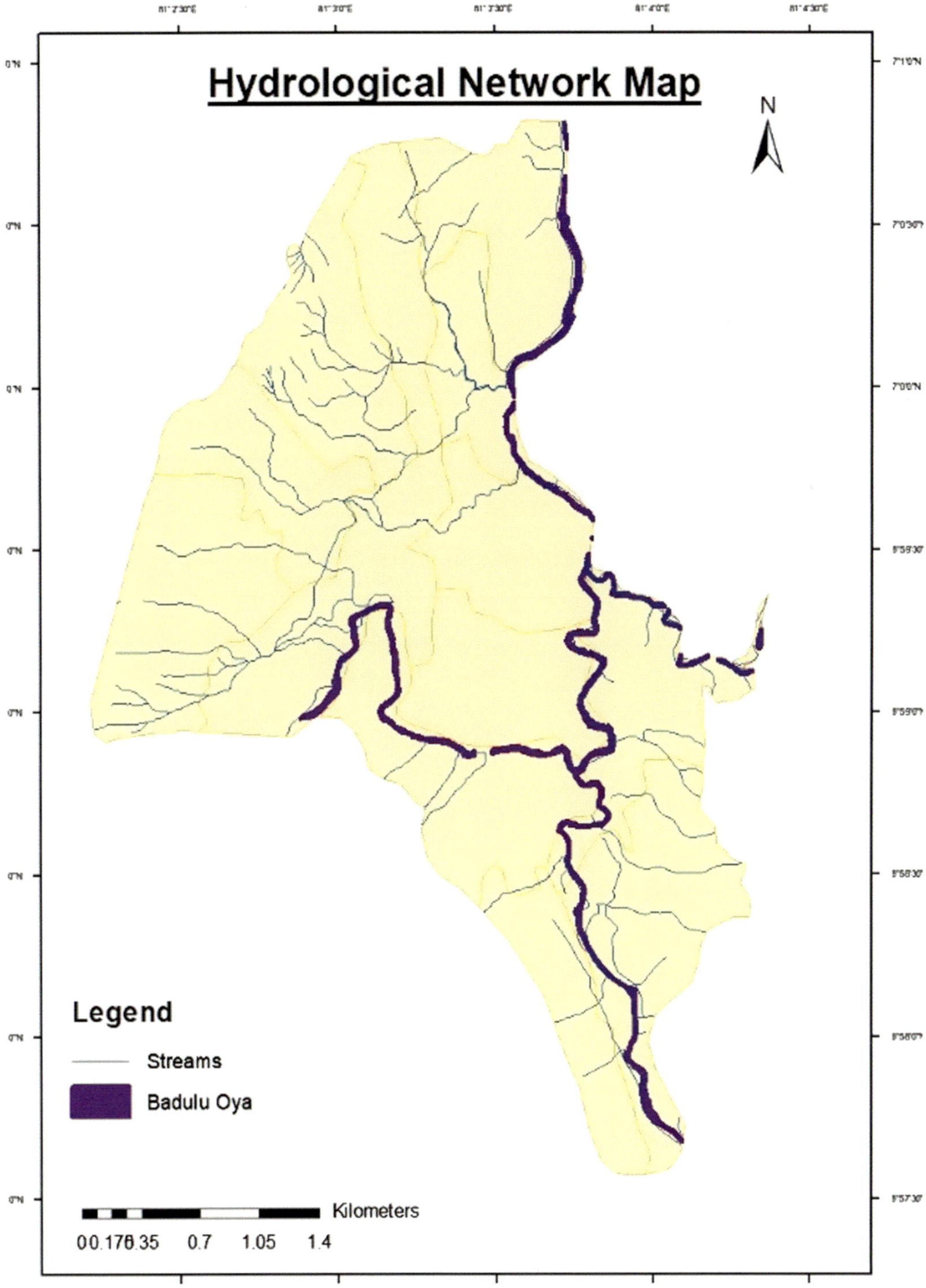

FIGURE 19.3 Distribution of the hydrological network of the Badulla municipality.

Source: Author generated map using DEM, 2020.

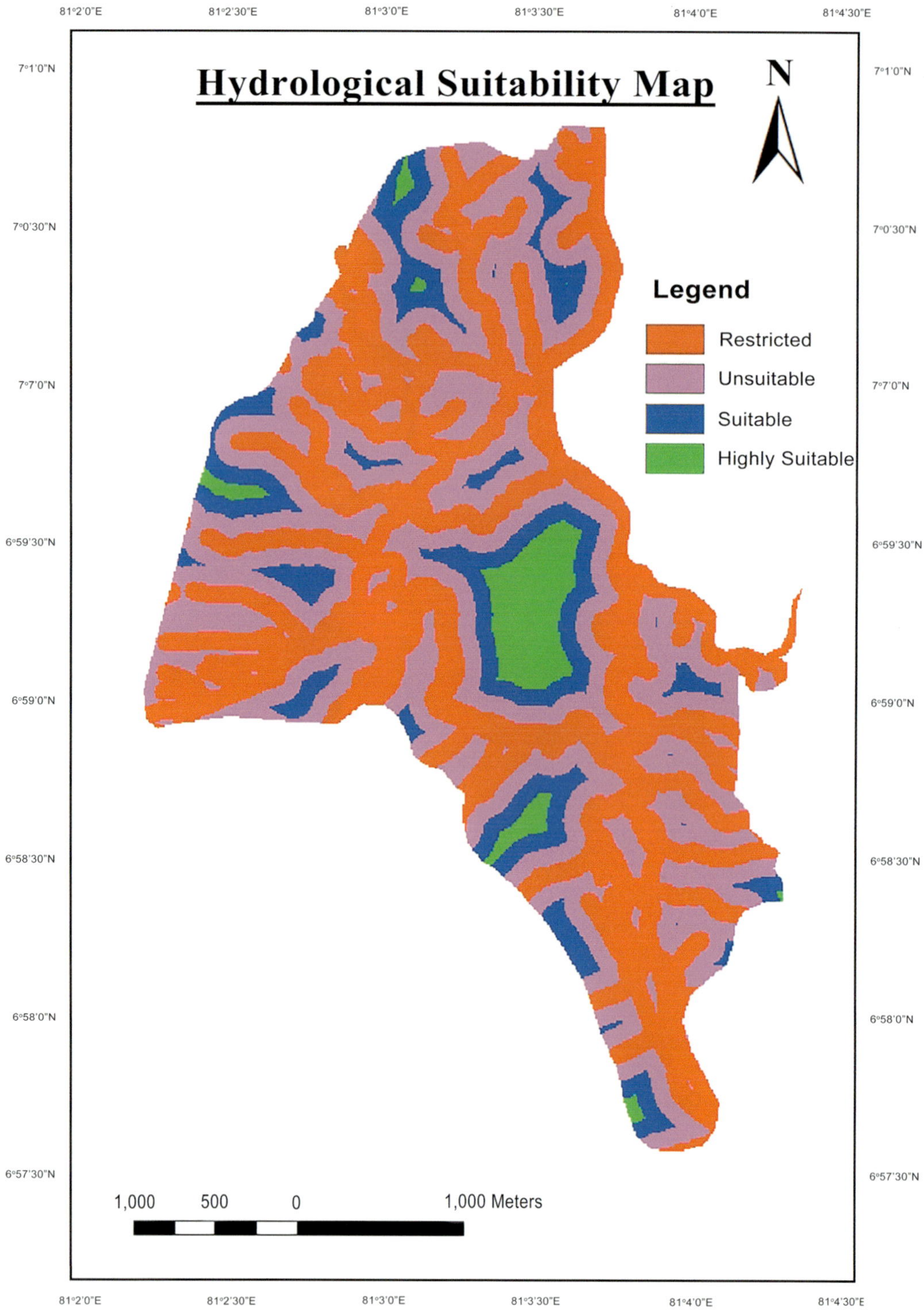

FIGURE 19.4 Map shows suitability base of hydrology of the Badulla municipality.

Source: Author generated map using DEM, 2020

TABLE 19.2
Distance from Surface Water and Its Suitability for Solid Waste Disposal Site

Distance (m)	Class	Score	Classification
0–50	1	1	Restricted
50–150	2	2	Unsuitable
150–250	3	3	Suitable
> 250	4	4	Highly Suitable

Source: Author generated, 2020.

19.5.3 Land Use Pattern

A land use map was an important thematic map required for this analysis. This map displays the utilization of the land by humans and the natural cover of the Badulla Municipality area. Land use data was collected from the Urban Development Authority of Sri Lanka.

A collected land use pattern shape file was classified under several map layers. Those were archeological sites, cemeteries, religious sites, recreational areas, commercial areas, institutions, residential areas, road reservations, health facilities, water bodies, forests, paddy areas, scrub teas, and other cultivations. The land use pattern of Badulla had been studied under four map layers, called agricultural land, built-up areas, land cover, and forests (Figure 19.5).

Paddy lands, water bodies, and residential areas were categorized under development-restricted area. Teas, forests, scrub, other cultivations, and utilities were categorized as low-developed areas. Archeological sites, road reservations, and cemeteries were categorized as developed areas. Commercial areas, institutes, health, transportation, religious sites, and recreational sites were categorized as highly developed areas. Within these four categories, the low-developed area was considered as suitable land for locating waste disposal (Figure 19.6 and Table 19.3).

19.5.4 Built-Up Areas

A disposal site should not be placed near a residential or an urban area. It should be placed far enough to avoid or mitigate the adverse effects on land value, the future development, for the health and safety and the well-being of the general public from environmental hazards caused by the disposal sites (Nas et al., 2010). A high weight should be assigned to settlements while selecting a waste disposal site. It is a very important factor that has a direct effect from the disposal site and hence the priority should be given to it (Al-Hanbali et al., 2011; Nas et al., 2010). The building density map for the study area was prepared by using a built-up area map obtained from the survey department. In this study, building density was classified under four categories. Those were very low density, low density, high density, and very high density. The areas which have very low building were the most suitable areas for the waste disposal (Figure 19.7 and Table 19.4).

19.5.5 Road Networks

In the Badulla Municipality, the transport routes are highly important due to their geographic location. The transport network, which is distributed through the study area, can be categorized as RDA roads and MC roads.

To avoid the unnecessary difficulties and health effects, it is required to decide the distance between waste disposal sites and main roads. On other hand, the waste disposal site should not be located in a faraway location from the road network. It is necessary to maintain a proper distance between the main

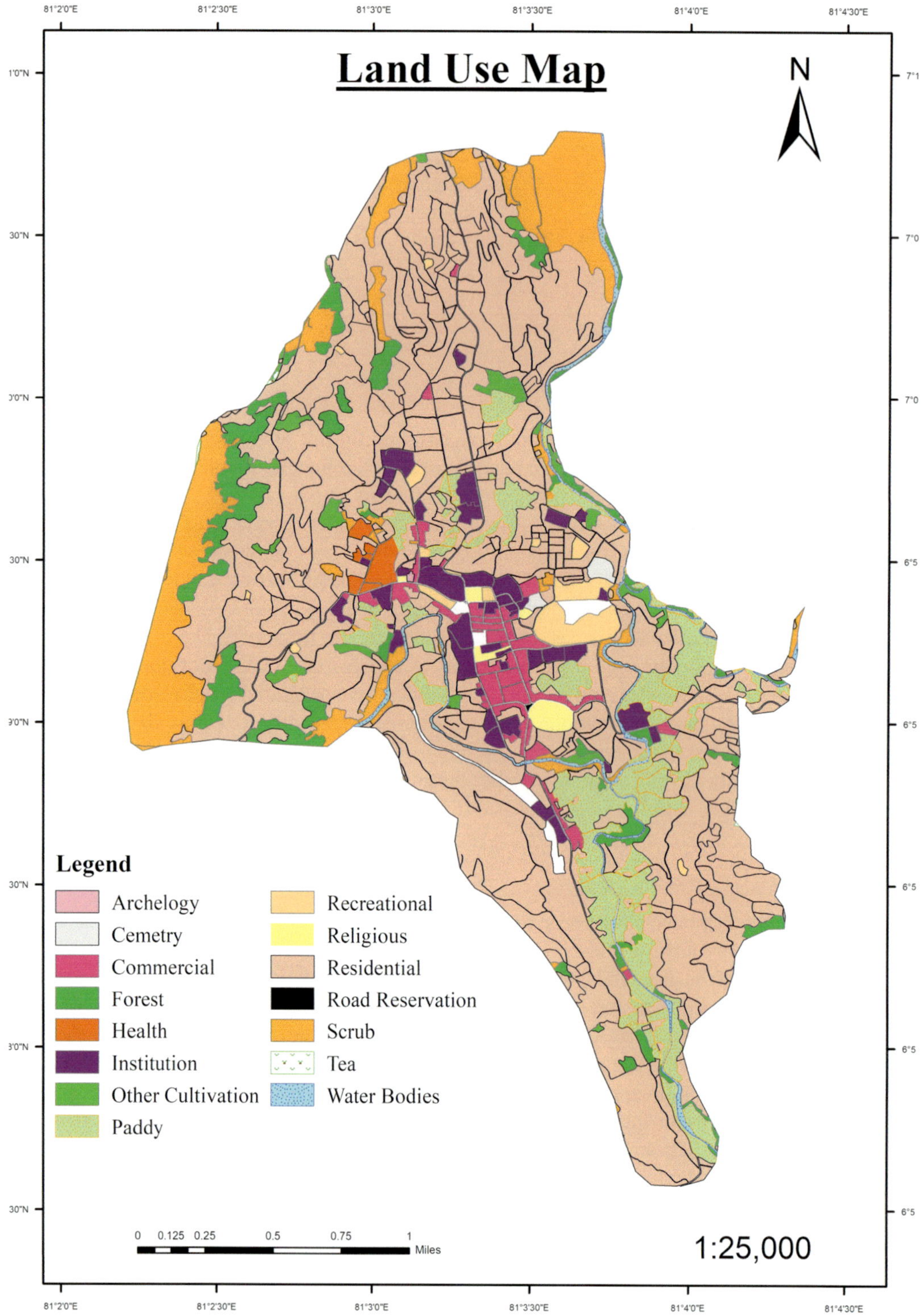

FIGURE 19.5 Land use of Badulla Municipality.

Source: Author generated map based on Urban Development Authority data, 2020.

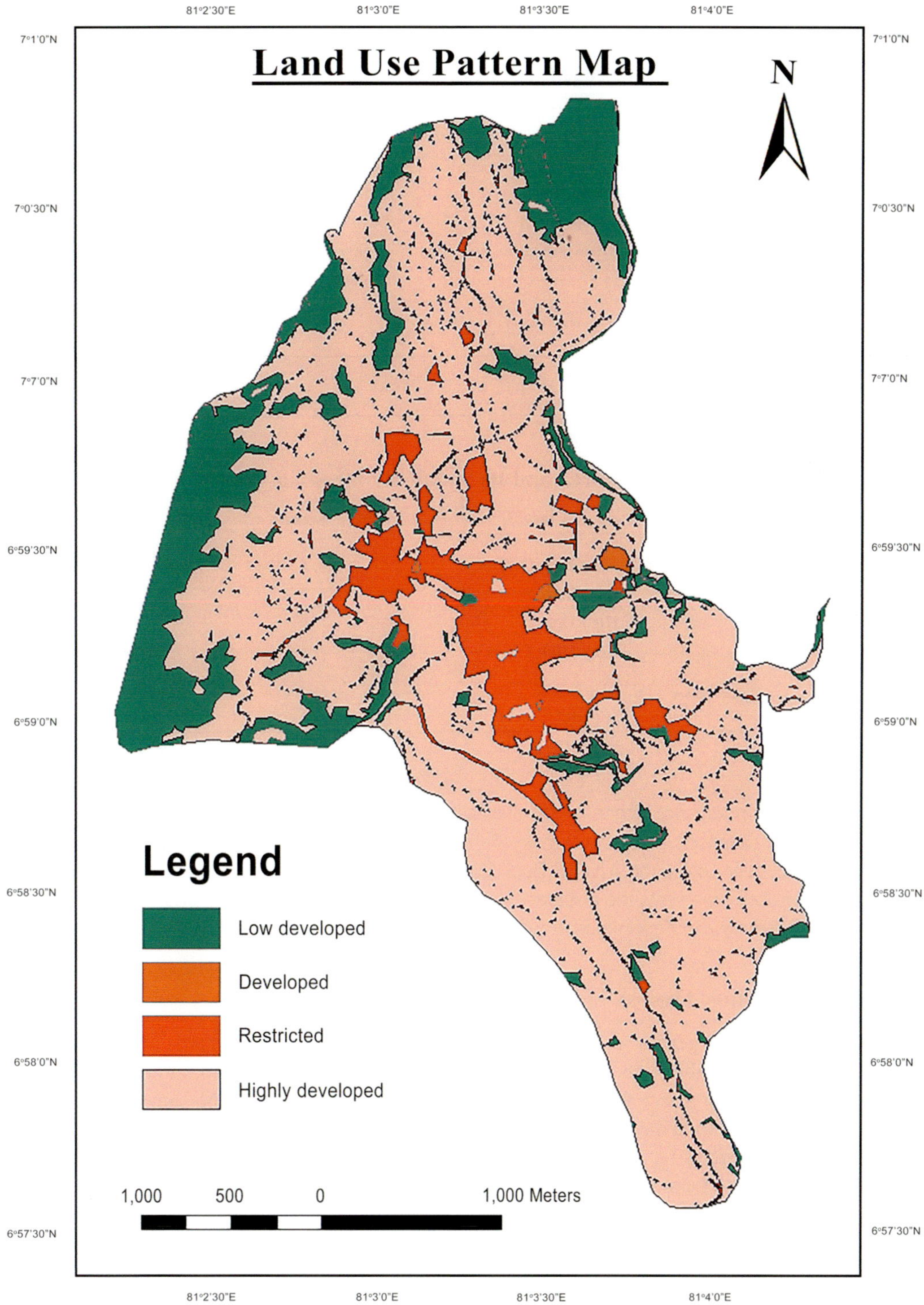

FIGURE 19.6 Land use pattern map in study area.

Source: Author generated map based on Urban Development Authority data, 2020.

TABLE 19.3
Land Use Suitability for Solid Waste Disposal Site

Criteria	Class	Score	Classification
Paddy lands, water bodies, residential	Restricted	1	Highly unsuitable
Teas, forests, scrub, other cultivations, utilities	Low-developed areas	2	Unsuitable
Archeological sites, road reservations, cemeteries	Developed areas	3	Suitable
Commercial areas, institutes, health, transportation, religious sites, recreational sites	Highly developed areas	4	Highly suitable

Source: Author generated, 2020.

TABLE 19.4
Building Density of the Study Area and Its Suitability for Solid Waste Disposal Site

Density (units/m^2)	Class	Score	Classification
0–200	Very Low Density	4	Highly Suitable
200–1,000	Low Density	3	Suitable
1,000–1,900	High Density	2	Unsuitable
> 1,900	Very High Density	1	Highly Unsuitable

Source: Author generated, 2020.

road and waste disposal site. Hence, waste disposal sites that are near to the main roads were decided not suitable. The distance between 100 m to 450 m was considered most suitable. In order to calculate the proximity to main roads, the ArcGIS Euclidean distance tool was used. The result was a raster data set where every cell represents the distance to the main roads (Figure 19.8). Then this raster layer was reclassified. Based on the importance, a weight was assigned for this layer (Table 19.5).

19.5.6 Population Density

In order to protect the general public from the potential environmental hazards of waste disposal sites, the waste disposal site should not be located near an urban or residential area. If the site is close, it will adversely affect the land value and future development. At the same time, it should not be placed too far to avoid additional transportation costs and environmental pollution. Hence, to reduce adverse effects on human health and social condition, a waste disposal site should have considerable distance from populated areas.

Jayawardhana et al. (2015) used the following mentioned criteria in their study for a weighted analysis process. A population density greater than 400 per km^2 was weighted as a high risk (weight = 1) area and population density and less than 400 per km^2 was weighted as low-risk areas (weight = 4).

The Budulla Municipality area was not too large an area. And, when compared with the other GN divisions in the Uva Province, the population was also somewhat high in the municipality area. So in this study base on population density suitability for waste disposal, four categories were studied and mentioned in Figure 19.9 and Table 19.6.

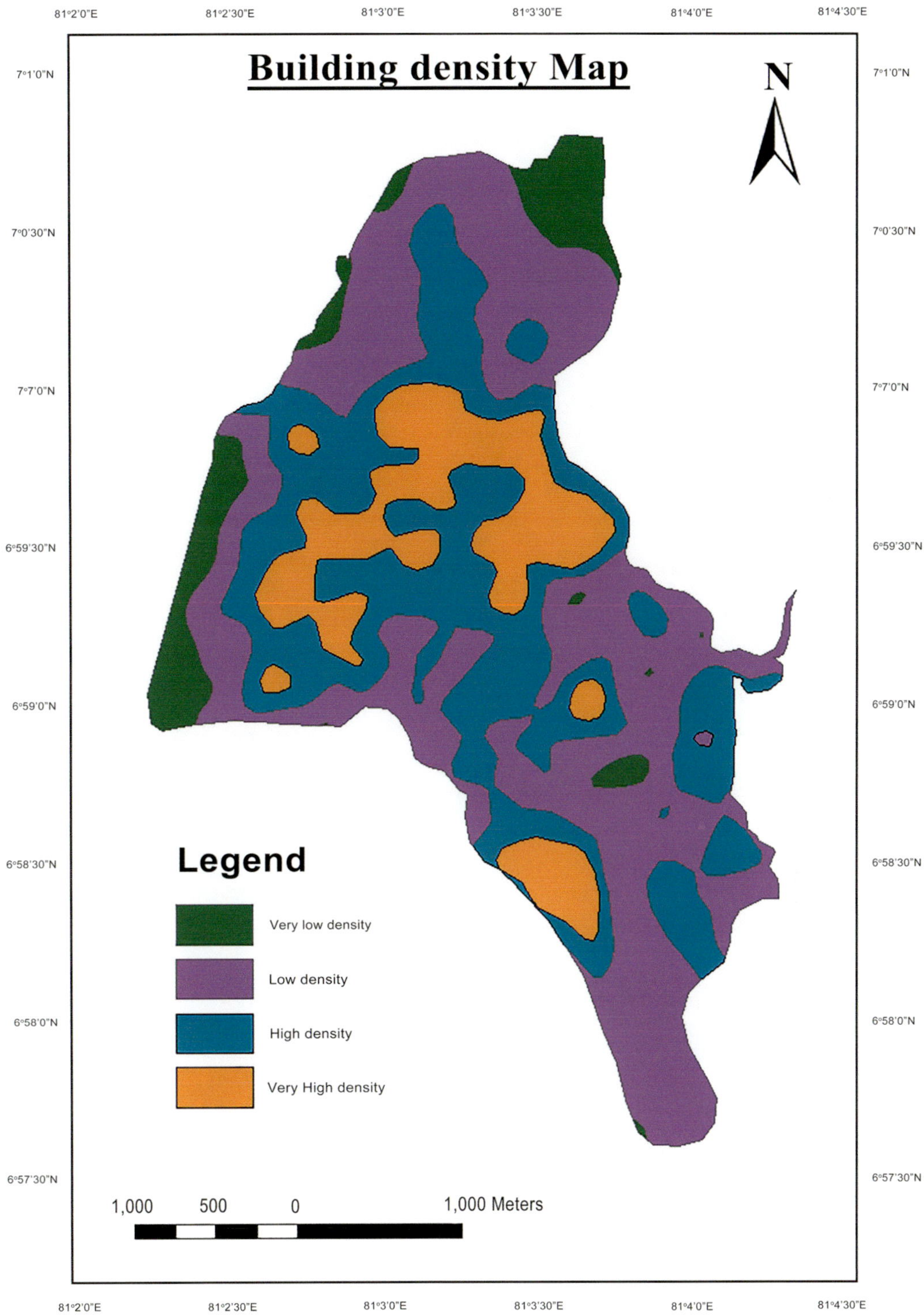

FIGURE 19.7 Map shows building density of the study area.

Source: Author generated map based on survey department data, 2020.

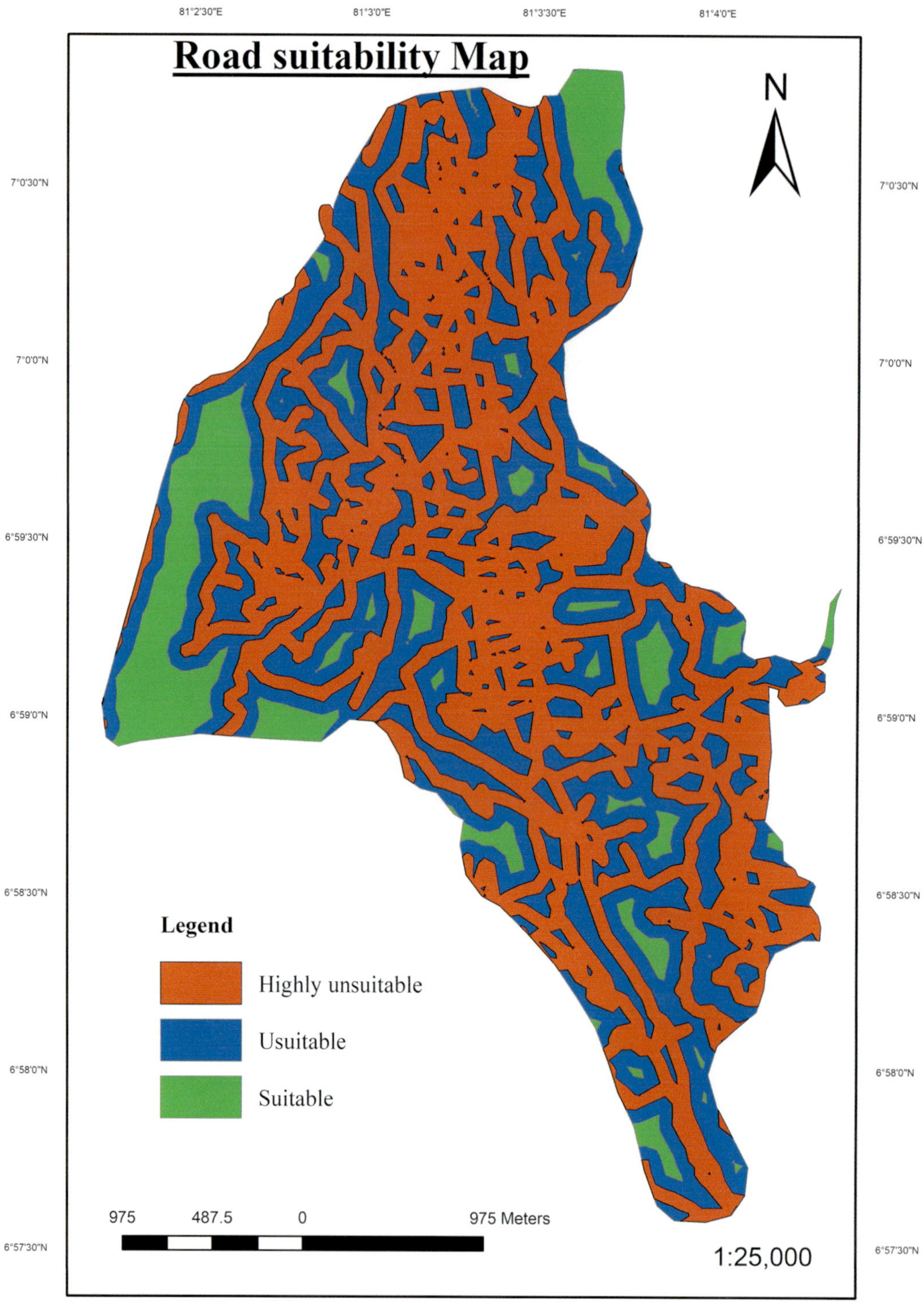

FIGURE 19.8 Map shows suitability based on road distribution of the study area.

Source: Author generated map based on survey department data, 2020.

TABLE 19.5
Distance from Major Roads and Their Suitability for Solid Waste Disposal Site

Distance (m)	Class	Score	Classification
0–30	1	1	Highly Unsuitable
30–100	2	2	Unsuitable
100–450	3	4	Suitable
> 450	4	1	Highly Unsuitable

Source: Author generated, 2020.

19.5.7 Hazards

Slope is one of the key criteria to be considered in a solid waste disposal site section. According to Akbari et al. (2008), areas with high altitude or high slopes are not suitable landfill sites. The ideal places for solid waste are medium altitudes surrounded by no more than a 20% slope. The amount of water in the soil, the rate of erosion, surface runoff, and groundwater pollution are all influenced by the slope.

In this study, the hazard shape file created by NBRO-Badulla was used for selecting the better site. NBRO considered all severity factors that have a positive effect on landslides and natural disasters in the region. Therefore, considering slope as a single factor for this study was replaced by adding a hazard shape file. A hazard map is a map that highlights areas that were affected by or were vulnerable to a particular hazard. The Landslide Research and Risk Management Division of NBRO has implemented a landslide hazard zone map of Badulla. The map depicts the intensity of landslide danger potential throughout the area. Based on the vulnerability for landslides, the study area is categorized under four categories (Figure 19.10 and Table 19.7).

19.5.8 Assigning Weights

A weight for each map layer was assigned based on the literature modifications and upon the discussion with respective officers who were experts in those fields. The reclassified map layers score and assigned weighs are indicated below.

Generally, it is inappropriate to give equal significance to every criterion being consolidated. The criteria should be weighted, relying upon its significance. The weights were evaluated by considering the likelihood of adjusting the normal states of the locations by proper designing intercessions, in order to increase their suitability (Nas et al., 2010).

The final composite suitability map was created by combining all the weighted suitability maps together. The weighted values are assigned using the ArcGIS weighted overlay tool (Table 19.8).

Based on the analyzed criteria, the findings have shown that 0.21% of the total area was identified as highly suitable, 35.58% as moderately suitable, 62.82% as less suitable, and 1.39% as unsuitable to locate a solid waste disposal site in the Badulla Municipality (Figure 19.11).

19.6 CONCLUSION

The analysis has taken the hydrological network, distance to roads, land use, pre-classified hazard map, population density, and density of buildings as determining factors in order to find a suitable site for solid waste disposal while considering the priorities of pre-determined factors.

Appropriate sites for solid waste disposal have been identified through the analysis of this study. They were classified into "highly suitable," "suitable," "unsuitable," and "highly unsuitable." The

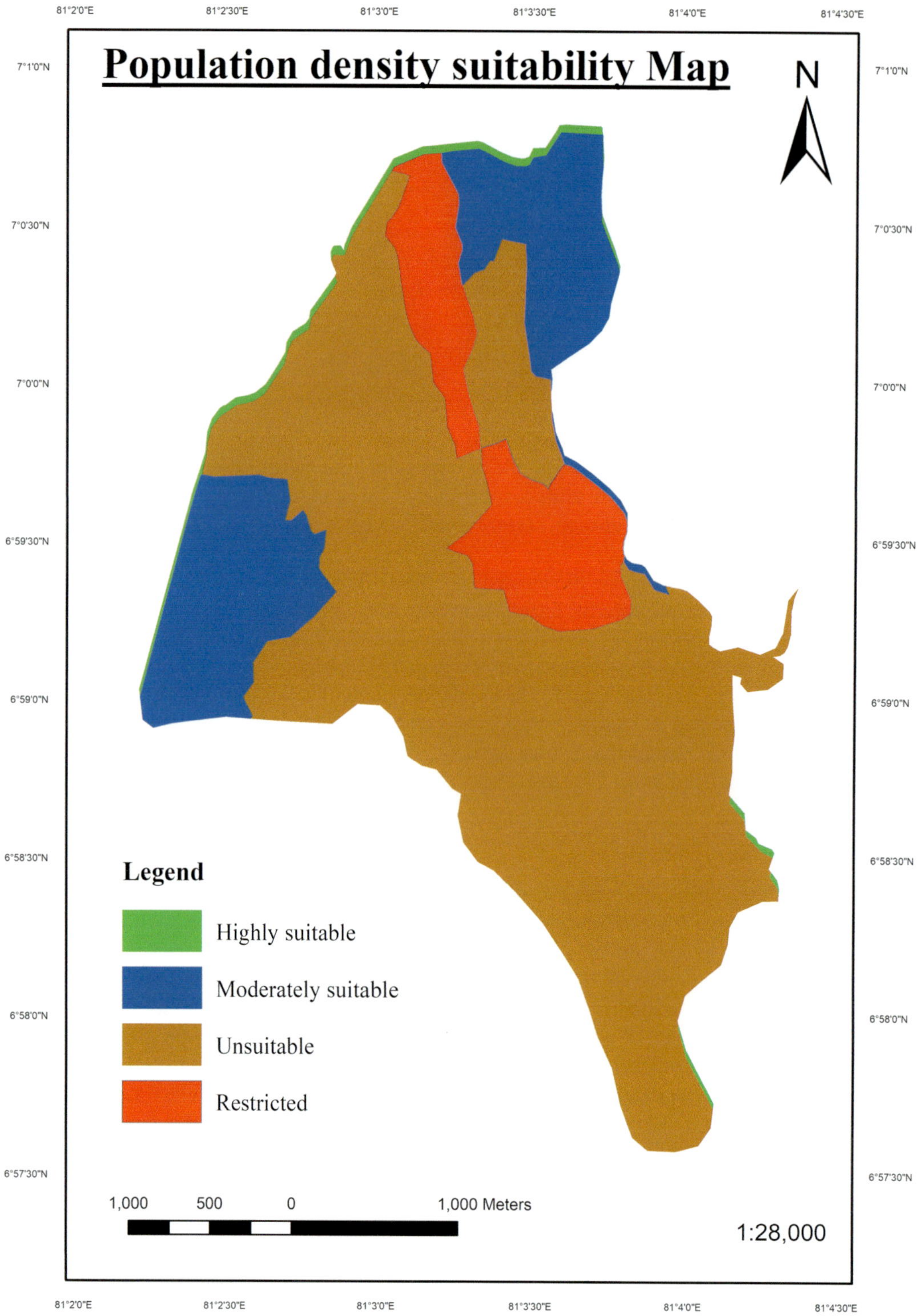

FIGURE 19.9 Map shows suitability based on population density of the study area.

Source: Author generated map based on survey department data, 2020.

TABLE 19.6
Population Density and Its Suitability for Solid Waste Disposal Site

Density (heads/km^2)	Class	Score	Classification
0–1,500	Highly suitable	4	Highly Suitable
1,500–3,000	Moderately suitable	3	Suitable
3,000–6,000	Unsuitable	2	Unsuitable
> 6,000	Restricted	1	Highly Unsuitable

Source: Author generated, 2020.

first two categories could be used to locate a solid waste disposal site after a proper in-depth study and a field evaluation of the area by experts.

The study reveals that 5.06 acres of the study area were highly suitable for waste disposal. While 292.28 acres were suitable, 1,452 acres were unsuitable, and 885.106 acres of the study area were highly unsuitable. When taking it as a percentage from the whole municipality area, 0.19% of the total area was identified as highly suitable, 11.09% as suitable, 55.13% as unsuitable, and 33.59% as highly unsuitable to locate a solid waste disposal site in the Badulla Municipality.

The findings have shown that the GIS could be used as an effective tool to aid in the effective identification and selection of suitable sites for solid waste disposal. It can be used to investigate different data sets and to create a new data set according to the required criteria.

The integration of multi-criteria decision analysis is a useful tool in solving the landfill site selection problem, because it provides efficient spatial data manipulation and presentation. And the findings have shown the application of the GIS and AHP methods as a viable tool for analyzing the multi-criteria for decision making.

The GIS has a high significance when there is a need for a rapid analysis with a proper visualization of the outcomes. This will minimize the environmental risk and the human health hazards that could be caused by the solid waste disposal site.

The GIS model is less time consuming and more productive than the traditional approaches to potential site selection for waste disposal. But field verification should use this with further analytical tests. Badulla is an environmentally sensitive elevated area. Water sources such as rivers and streams are highly distributed all over the area. So, further analysis about groundwater tables and soil types is important and required to be done prior to the site selection.

For this study, collecting reliable, precise, and up-to-date statistics, demographics, and socioeconomic information regarding the Badulla Municipality, as well as information on waste generation, was a challenge.

The lack of sufficient literature was one of the major setbacks for clearly identifying a criterion, especially Sri Lankan studies about the criterias used in waste management or dumping site selection was not available yet in publications or in written media.

Other than these limitations, the prevailing COVID-19 pandemic was the main constraint for primary data collection. Therefore, the filed surveys and questionnaire surveys were unable to be performed as planned.

Due to a profusion of environmental laws and regulations, as well as a lack of public awareness and involvement in zoning and environmental issues, the site selection process has become increasingly complicated. The GIS is a very vital efficient tool for solving siting issues. Its special capability for multi-criteria analysis was very useful in developing the model discussed in this research. Selection of the criteria by the expertise is very important to get the best decisions. A team of experts should be represented from economic, social, and environment fields to fulfil this process.

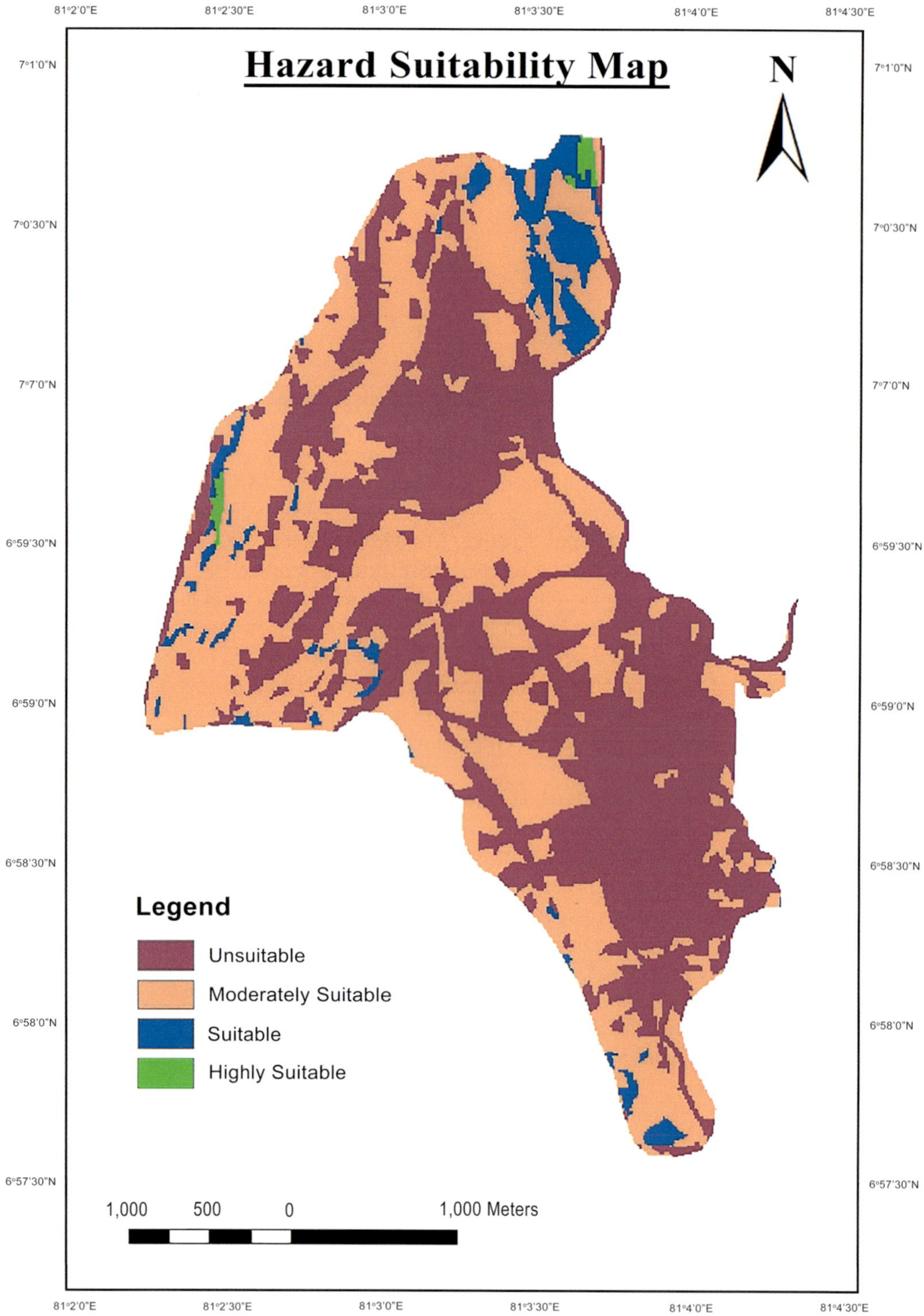

FIGURE 19.10 Map shows suitability based on hazard vulnerability of the study area.

Source: Author generated map based on NBRO data, 2020.

TABLE 19.7
Hazard Criteria and Their Suitability for Solid Waste Disposal Site

Categories	Class	Score	Classification
1	Unsuitable	1	Highly Unsuitable
2	Moderately suitable	2	Unsuitable
3	Suitable	3	Suitable
4	Highly Suitable	4	Highly Suitable

Source: Author generated, 2020.

TABLE 19.8
Weights Assigned

No.	Criteria	Percentage %	Ranking the Criteria
1	Distance to the Main Road	10	4
2	Distance to the Surface Water Bodies	30	1
3	Building Density	10	4
4	Land use Categories	25	2
5	Hazard Zones	15	3
6	Population Density	10	4

Source: Author generated, 2020.

19.7 RECOMMENDATIONS

In the case of a future increase in population size in the district, construction of a sanitary landfill or engineered landfill can be considered as a suitable site for establishing a better solid waste management strategy, in the case a selected site is not adequate for the construction.

Hence, this is a preliminary study, and these sites generally satisfy the basic and the minimum requirements of the selection of the solid waste disposal site, especially considering the spatial factors. This study further requires a geological and hydrological in-depth analysis to incorporate the soil types and the groundwater table. Field verification is also important prior to selecting the disposal site.

In this study, six criteria were used to select the potential solid waste disposal sites, but there are several other factors that influence the solid waste disposal site selection and should be included, such as evaluating criteria like cost of construction, aspects, and others.

As the final recommendation, there are several responsible authorities in Sri Lanka for solid waste management, but the active participation is not at a satisfactory level when conducting studies or research. As a main responsible government body, the Central Environmental Authority has a right to be involved in further studies by engaging new technology with their knowledge to solve the existing issues that arise in urban cities. And the Urban Development Authority and urban and municipal councils have an important task to identify the respective lands for waste disposal. Involvement of these authorities will make a better understanding of a waste disposal site with the best fit for waste disposal or treatment methods that will suit relevant regions.

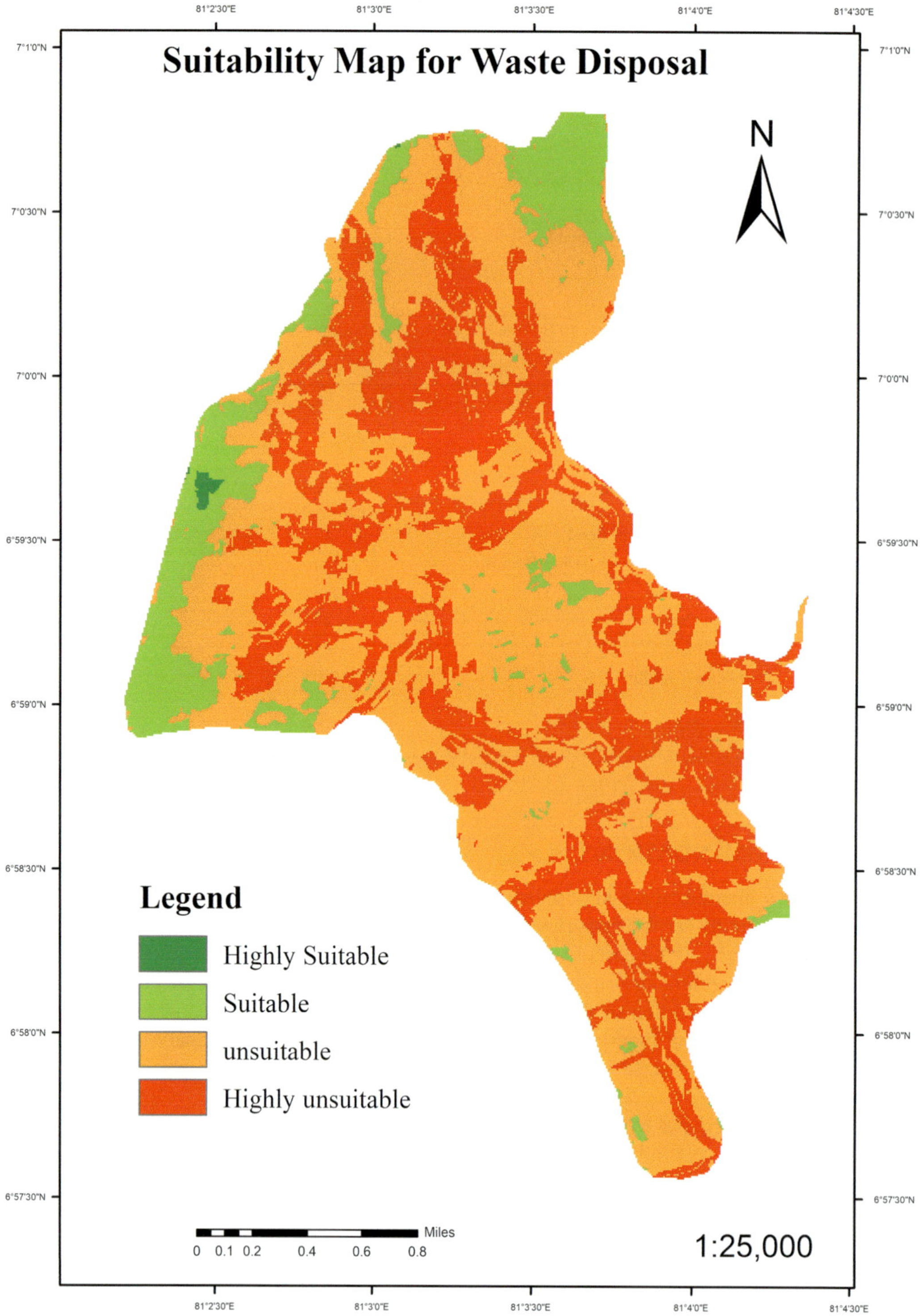

FIGURE 19.11 Suitability map for solid waste disposal.

Source: Author generated map, 2020.

REFERENCES

Abeynayaka, A. and D. R. Werellagama. "Efficiency improvement of solid waste management systems with load reduction: A case study in Kandy City, Sri Lanka." International conference on Sustainable Solid Waste Management, Chennai, India. pp. 126–133 (2007).

Akbari, V., M. A. Rajabi, S. H. Chavoshi, and R. Shams. "Landfill site selection by combining GIS and fuzzy multi criteria decision analysis. Case study: Bandar Abbas, Iran." *World Applied Sciences Journal, 3*(1), 39–47 (2008).

Al-Hanbali, A., B. Alsaaideh, and A. Kondoh. "Using GIS-based weighted linear combination analysis and remote sensing techniques to select optimum solid waste disposal sites within Mafraq City." Jordan. *Journal of Geographic Information System, 03*(04), 267–278 (2011).

Babalola, A., and I. Busu "Selection of landfill sites for solid waste treatment in Damaturu Town-using GIS techniques." *Journal of Environmental Protection*, *2*(01), 1–10 (2011).

Bandara, N. J., and J. P. A. Hettiaratchi. "Environmental impacts with waste disposal practices in a suburban municipality in Sri Lanka." *International Journal of Environment and Waste Management*, *6*(1–2), 107–116 (2010).

Bhada-Tata, P., and D. H. A. P. Hoornweg. *What a Waste: A Global Review of Solid Waste Management*. Washington: World Bank's Urban Development and Local Government Unit of the Sustainable Development Network (March 2012).

Deepa, K., and M. Krishnaveni. "Suitable Site selection of decentralised treatment plants using multicriteria approach in GIS." *Journal of Geographic Information System*, *4*, 254–260. 10.4236/jgis.2012.43030 (2012).

Ekanayake, E. W. M. L. R. K. GIS based multi criteria evaluation for locational suitability of residential development in Colombo sub urban area (Special Reference to Kaduwela Pradeshiya Sabha) (2010).

Fernando, G. "Development of GIS based model for site selection of industrial zone" (A case study on Kesbewa Divisional Secretariat Division) (2014).

Glawe, U., C. Visvanathan, and M. Alamgir. "Solid waste management in least developed Asian Countries – A comparative analysis." *International Conference on Integrated Solid Waste management in Southeast Asian Cities* (2006).

Guerrero, L. A., G. Maas, and W. Hogland. "Solid waste management challenges for cities in developing countries." *Waste Management*, Elsevier, *33*(1), 220–232 (2013).

Jayawardhana, B. A. Y. B., M. Vithanage, K. Kawamoto, J. Hara, and M. Zhang. "Vector based GIS applications to select suitable land for landfill sitting in Kandy." *Sri Lanka*; 3rd International Symposium on Advances in Civil and Environmental Engineering Practices for Sustainable Development (ACEPS – 2015). 194–200 (2015).

Karunarathne, H. M. L. P. "Municipal solid waste management (MSWM) in Sri Lanka." In 1st National Symposium on Real Estate Management and Valuation (2015).

Karunarathne, H. M. L. P. "Municipal solid waste management (MSWM) in Sri Lanka" (2018).

Malczewski, J. *GIS and Multicriteria Decision Analysis*. New York: John Wiley & Sons (1999).

Malczewski, J. "GIS-based land-use suitability analysis: A critical overview." *Progress in Planning*, Elsevier, *62*, 3–65. 10.1016/j.progress.2003.09.002 (2004).

Nas, B., T. Cay, F. Iscan, and A. Berktay. "Selection of MSW landfill site for Konya, Turkey using GIS and multi-criteria evaluation." *Environmental Monitoring and Assessment*, *160*(1–4), 491–500 (2010).

Saaty, T. L. "Decision making with the analytic hierarchy process." *International Journal of Services Sciences*, *1*(1), 83–98 (2008).

Sharifi, M., M. Hadidi, E. Vessali, P. Mosstafakhani, K. Taheri, S. Shahoie, and M. Khodamoradpour. "Integrating multi-criteria decision analysis for a GIS-based hazardous waste landfill sitting in Kurdistan Province, western Iran." *Waste management*, *29*(10), 2740–2758 (2009).

Sri Lanka News – Newsfirst. "Badulla Hospital Waste Storage: Catastrophe If Toxic Waste Mixes With Badulu-Oya." [online] Available at: (https://www.newsfirst.lk/2019/08/15/badulla-hospital-waste-storage-catastrophe-if-toxic-waste-mixes-with-badulu-oya/) (October 2020).

Tamilenthi, S., M. K. Chandra, P. L. Vijaya, and R. R. S. Suja. "The data base, land use and land cover and solid waste disposal siteusing remote sensing and GIS: A case study of Sakkottai-block, Sivagagai District, Tamil Nadu, India." *Advances in Applied Science Research*, *2*(6), 379–392 (2011).

Wang, G., L. Qin, G. Li, and L. Chen. "Landfill site selection using spatial information technologies and AHP: a case study in Beijing, China." *Journal of Environmental Management*, Elsevier, *90*(8), 2414–2421 (2009).

Yazdani, M., S. M. Monavari, G. A. Omrani, M. Shariat, and S. M. Hosseini. "Landfill site suitability assessment by means of geographic information system analysis." *Solid Earth*, *6*(3), 945–956 (2015).

Zulu, S., and S. Jerie. "Site suitability analysis for solid waste landfill site location using geographic information systems and remote sensing: A case study of Banket Town Board, Zimbabwe." *Review of Social Sciences*, *2*(4), 19–31 (2017).

Section V

Urban Smart Building, Modern and Geospatial Technology, and Smart Cities

20 Building a Sustainable Green Space System in Bhubaneswar City, Odisha, Using Space Inputs

Ashis Chandra Pathy and Gopal Krishna Panda
Utkal University, Bhubaneswar, Odisha, India

CONTENTS

20.1 INTRODUCTION

In Urban areas green space plays a vital role in providing environmental, recreational and economic benefit to city dwellers. According to Jim and Chen (2003) "urban green spaces can be defined as outdoor places contain with varied vegetation species and exist mainly as semi-natural area which are accessible for public''. Urban green space connectivity offers habitats and corridors which mainly led to the contribution of nature conservation. By citing some researches of different urban areas, many studies adopt different methodology to know the nature of green spaces. One of the main factors in determining the nature of green spaces is their quantity in the city., (Avtar, Tripathi, Kumar Aggarwal, and Kumar, 2019). Secondly, existing qualities like activities and experiences, and perceived benefits to the users determine the utilization of green spaces. Thirdly, the functionality of those green spaces is equally influenced by the location and distribution (accessibility) in the whole city.

Urban green spaces supply to cities with ecosystem services ranging from maintenance of biodiversity to the regulation of urban climate. Comparing with rural areas, differences in solar input, rainfall pattern and temperature are usual in urban areas. Solar radiation, air temperature, wind speed and relative humidity vary significantly due to the built environment in cities. (Sadashivam and Tabassu, 2006). Urban heat island effect is caused by the large areas of heat

DOI: 10.1201/9781003126195-25

absorbing surfaces, in combination of high energy use in cities. Urban heat island effect can increase urban temperatures by 5°C (Andrea, 2015).

Due to rapid urbanization process, the area and extent of green spaces are gradually decreasing. In the near future, a plan for the effective conservation of green space will be needed for Bhubaneswar city, because the increase of green spaces can mitigate the negative impact of urbanization. Therefore, in the present research emphasis was given to analyse the present condition of urban green spaces of Bhubaneswar city along with the site selection for further extension, conservation, preservation etc. This research was carried out by using GIS and Remote Sensing to analyse the status of urban green space over time and space and evaluate the green areas for further extension and development.

This chapter deals with the green spaces' availability in the city, green spaces change over time, and generation of land suitability model for development of green space. First the chapter examines the desirable environmental quality of the city from two aspects i.e current situation and greening indices. Second stakeholder analysis for land suitability, five suitability factors were taken by the method of weighted score and certainty score to generate suitability model.

20.2 STUDY AREA

Bhubaneswar city is bounded by Bhubaneswar Development Authority (BDA) limits. This is in fact a part of a greater urban complex formed by Cuttack Municipal Corporation, Khurda Municipality, Jatni Municipality and Pipili NAC located at boundary corners with Bhubaneswar being at centre. It is located between latitude 20° 12'46" to 20° 22'03" N and longitude 85° 45'24" to 85° 54'21" E in the eastern part of Odisha Figure 20.1 and Table 20.1.

20.3 RESEARCH OBJECTIVE

1. To study the current status of landuse and specificaly green space in the city.
2. To derive land suitability classification and assessment for identification for green space.
3. To generate suitability model for identification of green space in the city.

20.4 GREEN SPACE STATUS INSIDE BHUBANESWAR DEVELOPMENT AREA (BDA) AREA

The built-up area in BDA is 7223 hectare (2011). The greening coverage rate in the city is 4629 hectare which is about 18% of the area (excluding agricultural Land) and Green space per capita is 52 meter square (excluding agricultural land), as devised by Remote sensing and GIS method Table 20.2.

By looking into the density of green space in Bhubaneswar city, there are huge differences between green spaces proportion from the year 1974-2011. In 1974 there were green space per capita about 799 m2 which reduces to 223 m2 and 52 m2 in the year 1990 and 2011 respectively. When focussing on green space per 1000 persons, in 2011 the ratio is only 5.2 ha per 1000 persons.

The Greening coverage rate of Bhubaneswar city during 1974-2011, indicates there was loss of 11% and 17% of green space in the two time periods i.e 46% in 1974 which is comes down to 35% in 1990.. In the year 2011, the greening coverage rate is confined to only 18% (Table 6.2). As per the standards suggested by UDPFI guidelines of ITPI, New Delhi, the greening coverage rate should be more than 30% in the city for good environmental condition. Bhubaneswar city is far behind the standards of UDPFI/ITPI.

From the green space land use distribution of the city indicate that the tree cover areas consist of only two percent of the total BDA area. The major permanent green spaces are Dense scrubs/ bush

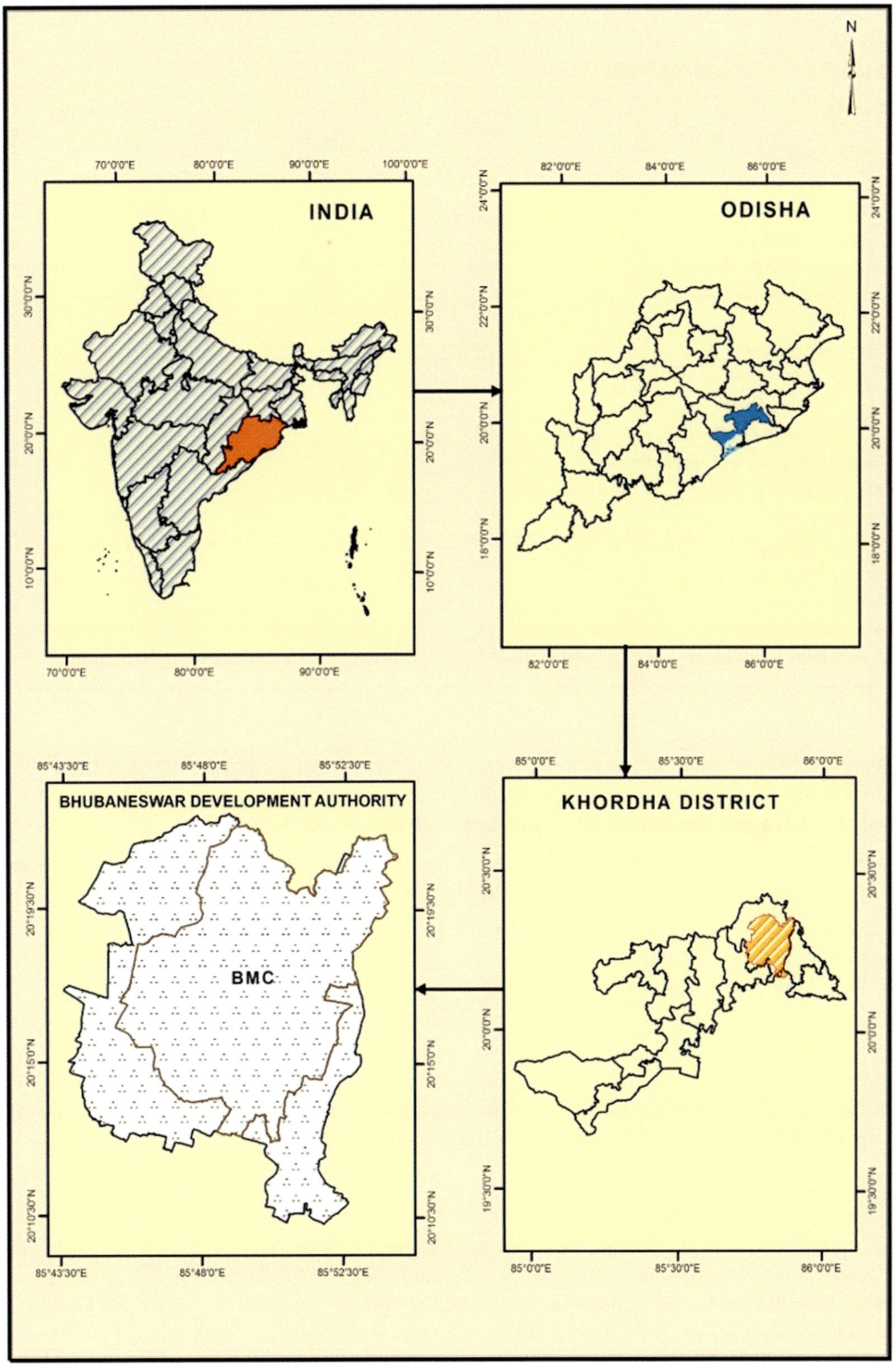

FIGURE 20.1 Study area.

TABLE 20.1
Information Regarding Study Area

District	**Khordha**
Demography	
Total Population 2001 (nos)	647,302
Total Population 2011 (nos)	840,834
Population Density	2131
Number of Households	201873
Avg Household size (nos)	4
Sex Ratio	892
Slum Information	
Number of Slum Settlements	436
Slum Population 2011 (nos)	301611
Slum Population as a Percentage of total Population (%)	35
Location, Climate & Topography	
Area in Sq km	186
Climatic Zone	Tropicalavanna Climate
Soil Characteristics	Deltaic Alluvial
Ground water level	7 m below ground level
Avg Max Temp	37.2 degree C.
Avg Min Temp	15.6 degree C.
Annual mean Rainfall (mm)	1436.1

TABLE 20.2
Green Space per Population and Coverage Rate during 1974–2011

Year	Population	Green Space in (ha)	Green Space per Capita	Green Space/1000 Person (ha)	Greening Coverage Rate
1974	145000	11589	792	79.2	46%
1990	392000	8773	223	22.3	35%
2011	881988	4629	52	5.2	18%

lands (5%) and Seasonal green spaces are grasslands (8%) and agricultural lands (21%). The Parks are only confined to 1% of the total BDA area Figure 20.2.

20.5 DATABASE AND METHODOLOGY

Cartosat II PAN (2011) Satellite data were used to produce Land use and land cover analysis & Water system influence map. SRTM Digital Terrain Model (DTM) was created to prepare slope map. Groundwater prospects map was obtained from ORSAC, Bhubaneswar and Land Ownership data was obtained from BDA, Bhubaneswar. All these databases were combined and processed in GIS Figure 20.3.

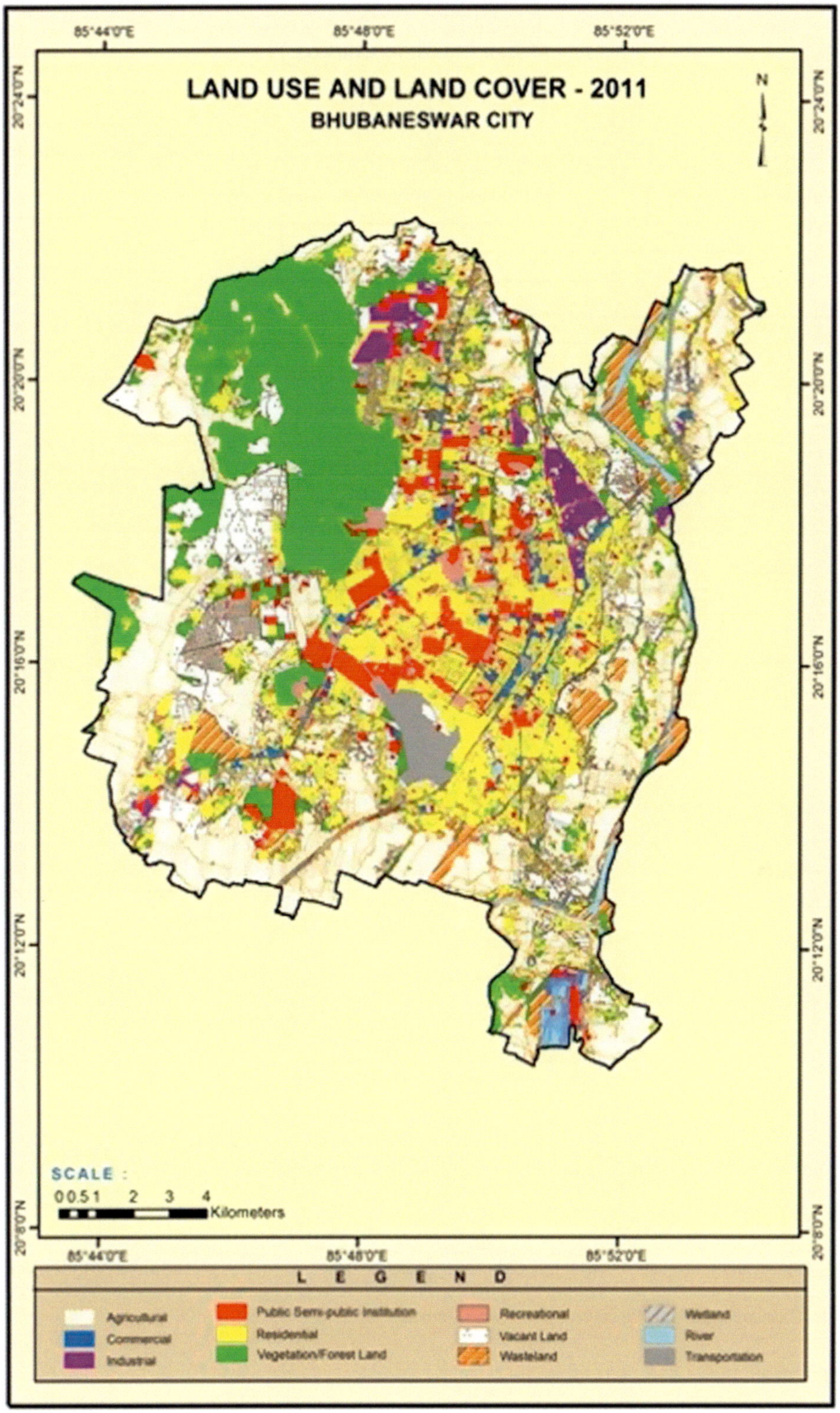

FIGURE 20.2 Land use & Land cover.

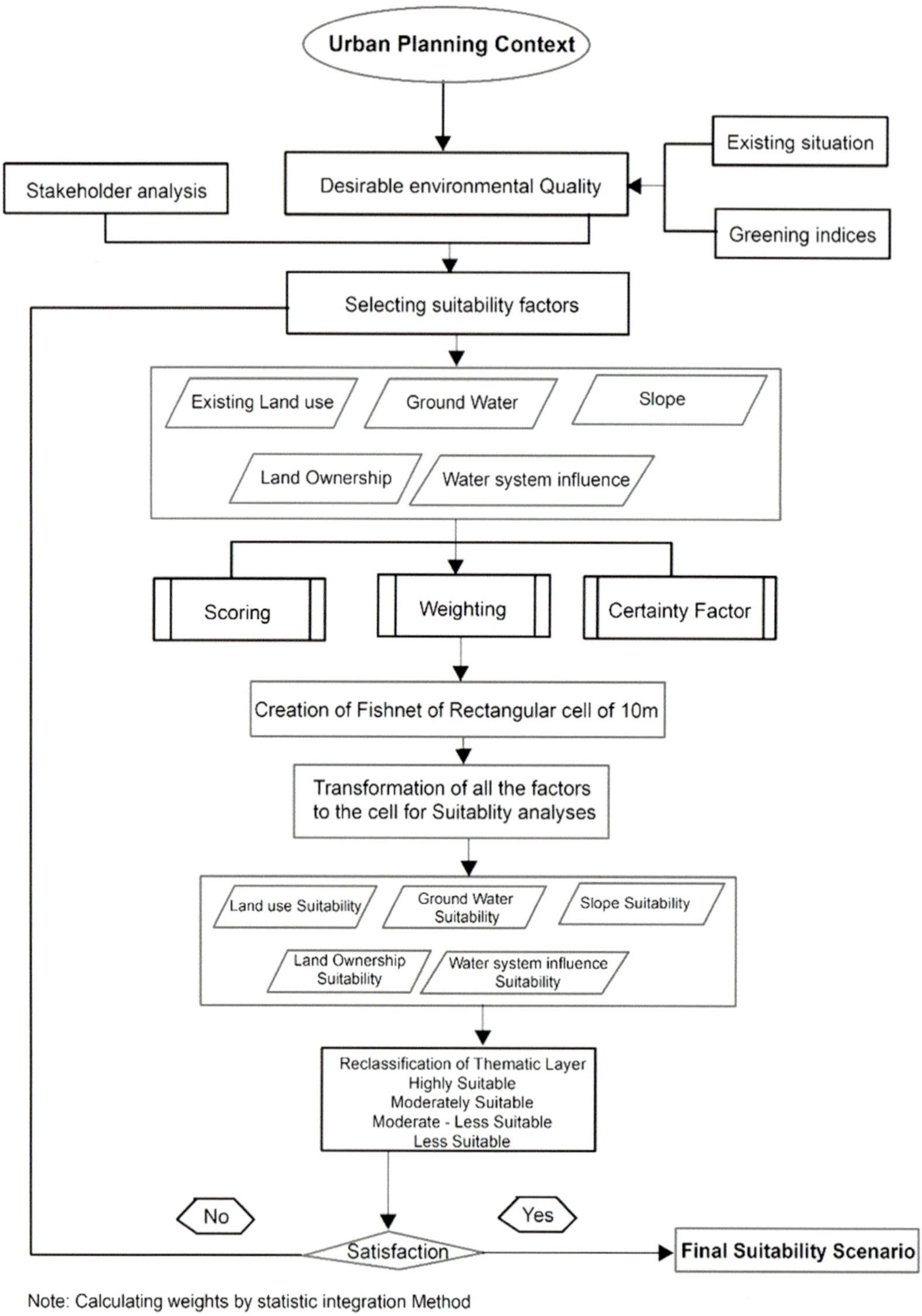

FIGURE 20.3 Flow chart of Methodology.

20.5.1 Scoring/Ranking of Criteria

For Suitability analysis it is necessary to use some score to each of the criteria as per their suitability for Green space development. The parameter used for the suitability analysis are Luse (existing land use), Wsystem (water system influence), Gwater (Ground Water), Slope (Slope), Ownership (Land Ownership). These data, which can get the certainty factor arranging from '0.1' to '0.9' score.

20.5.2 Derivation of Weights by Statistic Integration

Twenty-six stakeholders including 7 urban planners, 5 environmentalists,10 urban dwellers and 4 local public servants were asked to give their viewpoints about the parameters and their importance in green space suitability. The investigating information of this people were taken for statistic integration Table 20.3.

From Table 20.3, it is found that, stakeholders about 65% says that existing land use was the 1st importance, which is suitable for green space, 2nd with 13%, 3rd with 5%. fourth with 8%. Likewise other factors have certain importance. By using the formula, the weights were determined as under Table 20.4.

After the normalization, the original weighting factor, W = (4.17, 2.59, 3.5, 2, 94, 1.8), is converted into the final weighting factor, W = (.278, .172, .23, .196, .12). As such, each factor weight is showed in Table 20.4 Table 20.5.

20.6 SUITABILITY SCENARIO

For each parameter such as Existing land use, slope, Water System influence, Ground water and land ownership weights and certainty factor are determined. And five suitability map has been generated and by aggregating all the suitability map, one composite suitability map was generated Figures 20.4 and 20.5.

TABLE 20.3
Investigating Information

Parameter	1st Importance	2nd Importance	3rd Importance	Fourth Importance	Last Importance
Existing Land use	65%	13%	5%	8%	9%
Slope	13%	8%	9%	65%	5%
Water System Influence	5%	65%	13%	9%	8%
Ground Water	8%	9%	65%	5%	13%
Land Ownership	9%	5%	8%	13%	65%

TABLE 20.4
Matrix for Statistic Intrgration

$$\bar{W} = [D \cdot C^T]^T = \left(\begin{pmatrix} 0.65 & 0.13 & 0.05 & 0.08 & 0.09 \\ 0.13 & 0.08 & 0.09 & 0.65 & 0.05 \\ 0.05 & 0.65 & 0.13 & 0.09 & 0.08 \\ 0.08 & 0.09 & 0.65 & 0.05 & 0.13 \\ 0.09 & 0.05 & 0.08 & 0.13 & 0.65 \end{pmatrix} \cdot \begin{pmatrix} 5 \\ 4 \\ 3 \\ 2 \\ 1 \end{pmatrix} \right)^T$$

$$= 4.17,\ \ 2.59,\ \ 3.5,\ \ 2,\ \ 94,\ \ 1.8$$

TABLE 20.5
Factors Weight by Statistic Integration

Factor	Existing Land Use	Slope	Water System Influence	Ground Water	Land Ownership
Weight	0.278	0.172	0.23	0.196	0.12

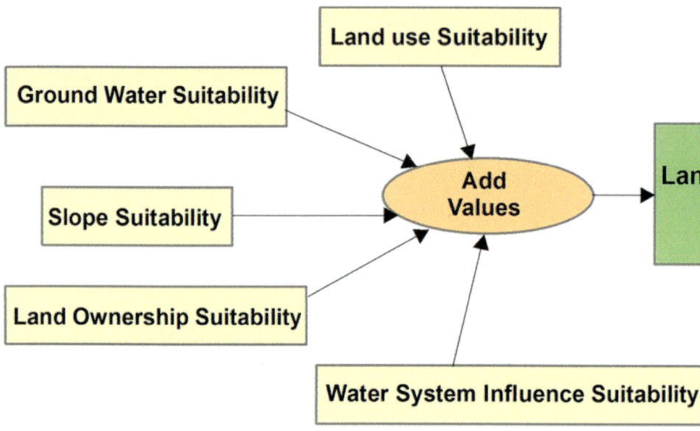

FIGURE 20.4 Composite Suitability Model.

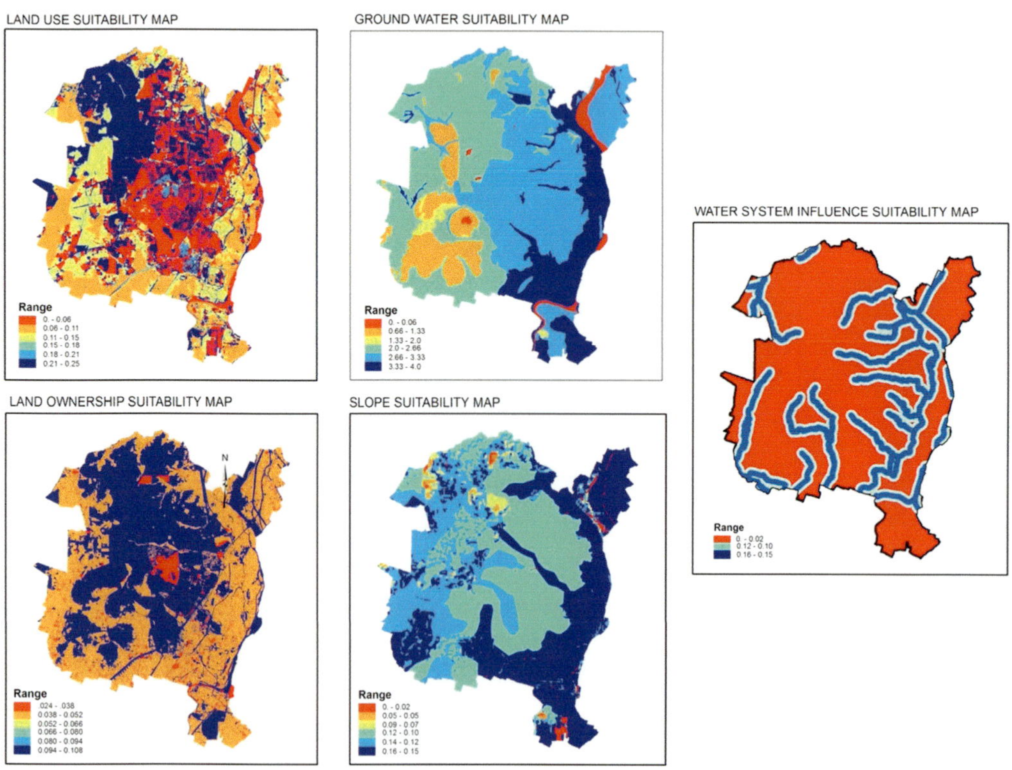

FIGURE 20.5 *Single Factor* Suitability Model.

Formula – Final Suitability

$$\text{Scenario} = \text{Luse} * \text{Wa1} + \text{Wsystem} * \text{Wa2} + \text{Gwater} * \text{Wa3} + \text{Slope} * \text{Wa4} + \text{Lownership} * \text{Wa5}$$

For final suitability model the composite suitability score was grouped into 4 classes by using histogram in Arc GIS 10 Table 20.6.

20.7 FINDINGS

The results from this study provide the First comprehensive and integrated land suitability assessment of all the five factors for development of green space in Bhubaneswar City. It is estimated most parts of Bhubaneswar is coming under less suitability class with an area of 8644 hectare or 35% of the total area. It is also observed that highly suitable class with an area of 6415 hectare or 26% of the total area and moderately suitable area of 2683 hectare or 10% of the total area can be use for green space. considering the environmental condition of the city. The highly suitable areas were mainly identified in the North west part of the city. The areas are Bharatpur Reserved forest area, Jagannath Prasad and Sundarpur area considered as the Green belt of the city. Furthermore the highly suitable was identified in Malipada, Nuagaon, Bidyadharpur, Pandara, Naharkantia and in the middle of the city i.e inside the Institutional, Industrial, Heritage or conservation area, Residential, Road and Rail side corridor, Drainage corridor etc.

Moderately suitable areas were identified in Raghunathpur, Koradakanta, Haridaspur, Patharagadia and dumduma area. The central part of the study site mainly been classified as Less suitable area with an area of 7015 hectare, which is 29% of the total area,because this region is mostly under built up area and other land use where there is no scope for any green space development according to the suitability analysis Table 20.7.

From the analysis of the Land suitability, it is observed that, the Bharatpur Reserve Forest area covering approximately 25 Sq Km of area under High Suitability land and considered as the Green belt of the city Figure 20.6.

TABLE 20.6
Suitability Class Based on Histogram

Suitability	Group
High suitability	$0.67 \leq Vs \leq 0.87$
Moderate suitability	$0.57 \leq Vs < 0.67$
Moderate-Less suitability	$0.36 \leq Vs < 0.57$
Less suitability	$0.20 \leq Vs < 0.36$

TABLE 20.7
Land Suitability for Green Space

Suitable Zones	Area in Ha	% of total	Suitability Score
Less Suitability	7015	29	1
Moderate -Less Suitability	8644	35	2
Moderate Suitable	2683	10	3
Highly Suitable	6415	26	4
Total	**24757**	**100**	

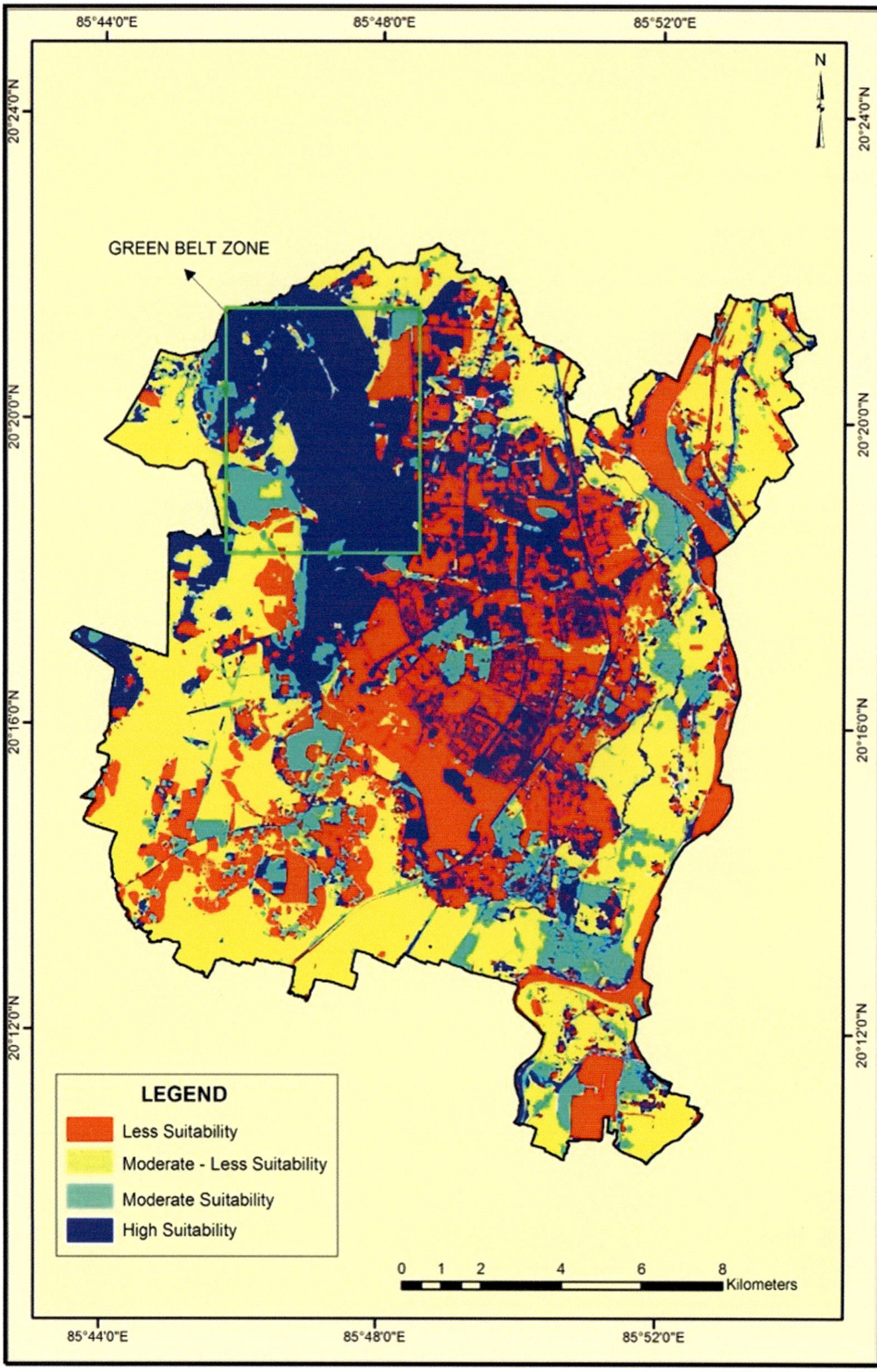

FIGURE 20.6 *Final* Suitability *Scenario*.

20.8 CONCLUSION

The proposed aims to identify the suitable zone for development of green space in the city. The Proposed suitability model says that most of the area are not found to be suitable and comes under the less to moderate suitability for green space development. Development restriction is the main cause behind it. High and Moderate Suitability areas are coming under the vacant areas and Government reserved areas are suitable for green space development. The Bhubaneswar development Authority is continuing plantation in some of the areas. But It is hardly meet the requirement of the city. Due to widening of the road, most of the trees are cut down. For Sustainable development of green space in the city, BDA should take strict regulation for city dwellers to plant at least 20% in the residential land and 40% in the commercial areas as suggested in the BDA Regulation.

REFERENCES

Andrea, E. P. 2015. *Study on impact of urbanization and rapid urban expansion in Java and Jabodetabek Megacity, Indonesia*. Ph.D. Thesis, Kyoto, Japan: Kyoto University.

Avtar, R., Tripathi, S., Kumar Aggarwal, A., and Kumar, P. 2019. Population-Urbanization-Energy Nexus: A Review. *Resources*, *8*, 136.

Jim, C. Y., and Chen, S. S.2003. Comprehensive greenspace planning based on landscape ecology principles in compact Nanjing city, China. *Landscape and Urban Planning*, *65*(3), 95–116.

Lingjun, L., Zong, H., Yan, H.2008. Study on Land use Suitability Assessment of Urban-Rural Planning based on Remote Sensing. A case Liangping in Chongqing. *The International Archieves of the Photogrammetry, Remote Sensing and Spatial Information Sciences*, *37*(Part-II).

Pham Duc Uy. 2008. Application of Land Suitability analysis and Landscape ecology to urban green space planning in Honoi, Vietnam. *Urban Forestry & Urban Greening*, *7*, 25–40.

Sadashivam, T., and Tabassu, S.2006. Trends of Urbanization in India: Issues and Challenges in the 21 St Century. *Int. J. Inf. Res. Rev.*, *3*, 2375–2384.

Yang, M.2003. Suitability analysis of Urban Green space system based on GIS. Masters in Geoinformation Science thesis submitted to the International Institute for *Geo-information Science and Earth Observation, Netherland.*

Xiaolu, Z., and Wang, Y. C.2011. Spatial-temporal dynamics of urban green space in response to rapid Urbanization and greening policies. *Landscape and Urban Planning Elsevier*, *100*, 268–277.

21 Identification of Landslide Hazard Zones of Gangtok Urban Area in Sikkim Himalayas with the Help of the Multi-Criteria Evaluation Method Using Geospatial Techniques

Bappaditya Koley and Nilendu Chatterjee
Bankim Sardar College, West Bengal, India

Uday Chatterjee
Bhatter College, Dantan, Paschim Medinipur, West Bengal, India

Anindita Nath, Subhajit Saraswati, and Bidhan Chandra Ray
Jadavpur University, Kolkata, West Bengal, India

CONTENTS

DOI: 10.1201/9781003126195-26

21.1 INTRODUCTION

Mountainous terrains are affected by the occurrence of landslides throughout the world (Roy and Saha, 2019). In India, most of the mountainous terrain areas face numerous landslide disasters (Bhandari, 2004). Landslides are very frequent natural events in the Himalaya mountainous terrain (Bhasin et al., 2002; Sarma et al., 2011; Kaur et al., 2019; Koley et al., 2019). Hosseini et al. (2011) observed that most of the slope failure occurs along the roads. Two factors are mainly responsible for landslide occurrences, such as triggering factor and preparatory factors (Koley et al., 2019). The triggering factors (rainfall, earthquake) are external stimuli responsible for the actual occurrences of landslides. On the other side, preparatory factors are cumulative events, such as geology, slope morphology, aspect, topography, river alignment, distance to fault or thrust line, road alignment, and land use are responsible for initiating landslides. The the last decade, quantitative methods have significantly been applied for landslide hazard zonation (LHZ) mapping on the basis of the relationship between preparatory factors and occurrence of landslide (Banerjee et al., 2018; Kannan et al., 2015; Chen et al., 2014; Glade and Crozier, 2005; Van Westen et al., 2008; Samia et al., 2018). A landslide hazard zonation (LHZ) study is most significant for prevention of landslide disasters and to develop the mitigation strategies.

Several approaches, such as qualitative (knowledge-driven) and quantitative (statistical), were applied for landslide hazard evaluation (Reichenbach et al., 2018; Kaur et al., 2017). Based on the qualitative (knowledge-driven) approach, the landslide hazard zones can be identified by expert knowledge (Gupta et al., 2018). The expert can evaluate the hazard zones or location basis of the characteristics of geomorphological and geological with the help of inventory maps of the landslide (Zhu et al., 2014; Pathak, 2016; Ayalew and Yamagishi, 2005). The geospatial-based multi-criteria evaluation (MCE) method is the most significant pathway for the analyses and predications of landslide hazards. Remote sensing and GSI technologies are useful to identify the landslide locations with areas using a proper database (Feizizadeh and Blaschke, 2012; Kannan et al., 2015; Anbalagan et al., 2015). This study has considered the geospatial-based multi-criteria evaluation approach for the identification of landslide hazard areas. This approach is applied to sample data based on the relationship between the independent and dependent variables.

The aim of the present study is to apply the multi-criteria evaluation approach for the LHZ mapping in the Gangtok urban area, Sikkim. The multi-criteria evaluation method through the weighted overlay method is considered for this study because this method is widely applied in LHZ mapping in the present time (Ahammad, 2009; Feizizadeh and Blaschke, 2012; Park et al., 2013; Senouci et al., 2021). The outcomes of the present study can be helpful for prevention and mitigation of landslide hazards, planning for the tourism industry, management of land-use planning, and sustainable development in the Gangtok urban area, Sikkim.

21.2 STUDY AREA

21.2.1 Geomorphological Characteristics

The Gangtok urban area (GUA) geographic area is 76.32 sq. km extended between 27°17′30′′N to 27°22′30′′N latitude to 88°35′E to 88°40′E longitude, and is situated in the East Sikkim (Figure 21.1) with an elevation of 826 to 2,855 m (Figure 21.2) and flanked by two rivers, Rorochu and Ranikhola, in the eastern and western side, respectively. The Gangatok urban area (GUA) is mostly urbanized and populated (Figure 21.3) among the other places of Sikkim State, whereas the total urban population is 79.55% (Kaur et al., 2019). The GUA area is dominated by a south-facing slope of the Sikkim Himalayas (Kaur et al., 2019). The Sikkim Himalayas receive excessive rainfall during monsoons. Several rain-induced landslides were documented in the present study area (GSI, 2016). The maximum parts of the Sikkim Himalayas Mountains received a high amount of rainfall throughout the year (GSI, 2016) because it is very close to the Bay of Bengal basin and the obstruction of the path of monsoon clouds by mountains. The months of October to March are comparatively drier in the present study area. Based on the distribution of the average rainfall, Thangu received minimum rainfall (82 mm) and the study area (Gangtok) received maximum rainfall (3,580 mm) (GSI, 2016). May to early October contributes heavy rainfall well distributed and the month of July is the wettest. During monsoons (June–September), rainfall intensity differs from 150 to 300 mm within a day (24 hours), which is known as a cloud burst in the meteorological parlance (GSI, 2016). The increasing trend of urbanization is observed in the surrounding area of Gangtok because it is the capital city of East Sikkim. This area faced excessive pressure on the hill slope, which has been initiated to occreanvce of landslides in the Gangtok urban area. The aerial view of the urbanization of the Gangtok urban area is shown in Figure 21.3.

21.2.2 Geological Characteristics

Geologically, the Darjeeling-Sikkim Himalayas are comprised of intra-thrusted rock slices of the fold thrust belt (FTB) of the Eastern Himalayas (GSI, 2016). This region shows a complex geological and tectonically milieu, in which rocks of the precambrian to quaternary age's area are juxtaposed along certain E–W trending tertiary regional thrusts (GSI, 2016). The district of East Sikkim is a part of the Eastern Himalayas and revealed homogeneous geological features as in other parts of the Eastern Himalayas. Geological features are the most significant attributes to consider in hazard zonation (landslide and seismic). Mainly four geological formations are encountered in the study area, such as Darjeelin/Kanchenjunga gneiss, Chungthang Formation, Gorubathan Formation (Daling group of rocks), and Lingtse Granite Gneiss. Two thrust formations have been flanked due to the geological setup of coarse-grained garnet mica schist of Daling group rests over Gangtok. The eastern part (Main Central Thrust) separates the Daling group from the Darjeeling Gneiss of CCGC and the western part (Main Central Thrust) separates Lingste Gneiss from the Daling Group (Figure 21.4).

The present study area mainly contributes the Kanchenjunga/Darjeeling Gneiss rocks, which is 27.17 sq. km (35.60%). Phyllite and schist with inter-bends of quartzite rocks (Gorubathan Formation) contribute 12.27 sq. km (16.21%). Coarse-grained garnet mica schist and garnet mica schist with phyllite rocks also contribute 11.37 sq. km (14.90%) and 11.42 sq. km (14.96%) in the study area. Garnet kyanite sillimanite boitite schist and quartzite rock (Chungthang Formation) contribute 10.41 sq. km (13.64%) and lingtse granite gneiss rocks only contributes 3.58 sq. km (4.69%) in the Gangtok urban area. Due to heavy rainfall, weathered and eroded rocks are observed of the study areas, which increase the landslide frequency, respectively. Table 21.1 shows the different geological rock units in the Gangtok urban area.

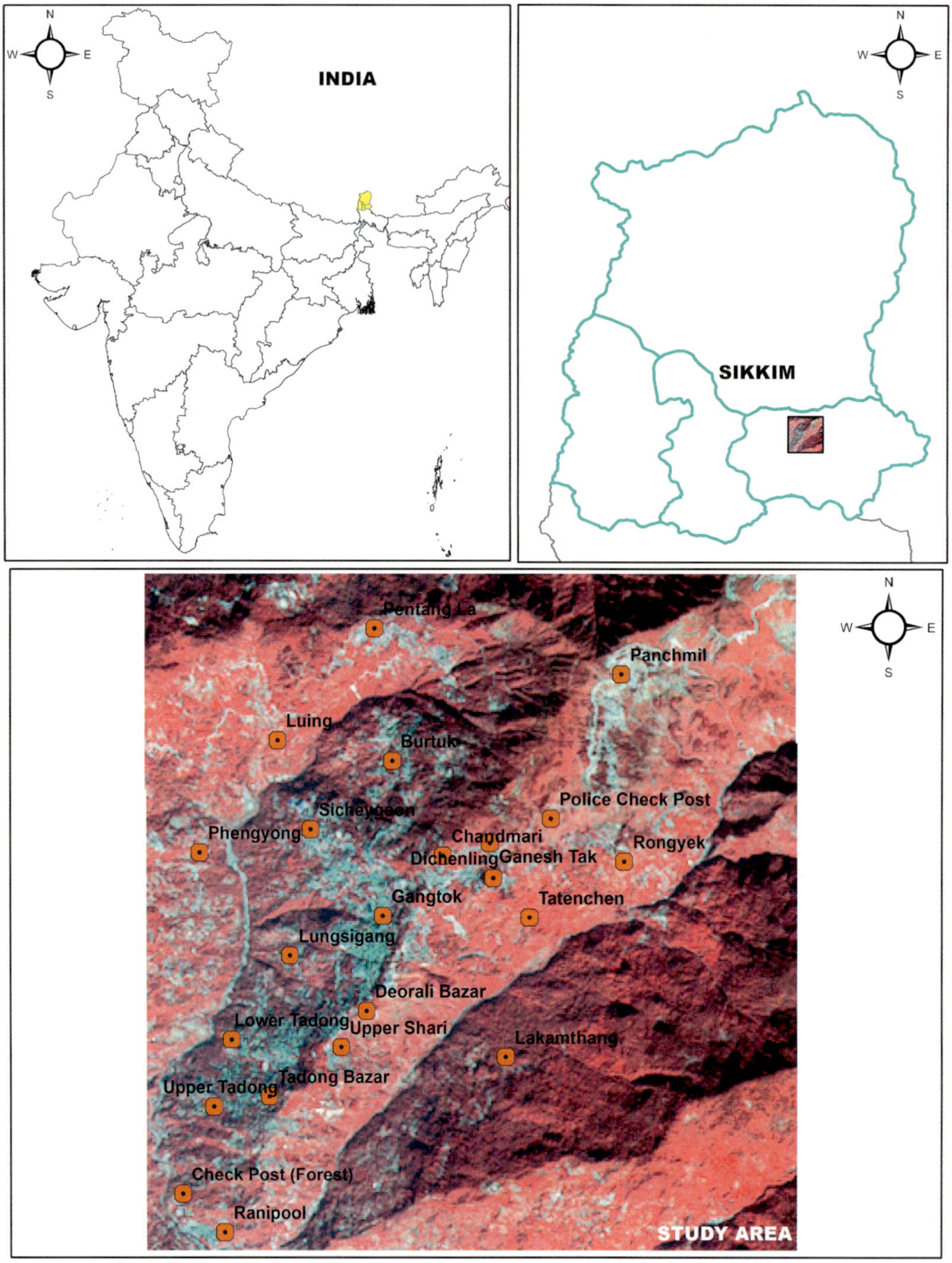

FIGURE 21.1 Location of the study area.

21.2.3 Seismological Characteristics

A seismic zonation map of India indicates that the Sikkim Himalayas belong to seismic zones IV and V, zones of considerable highly vulnerability to seismic activities (BIS, 2002). The

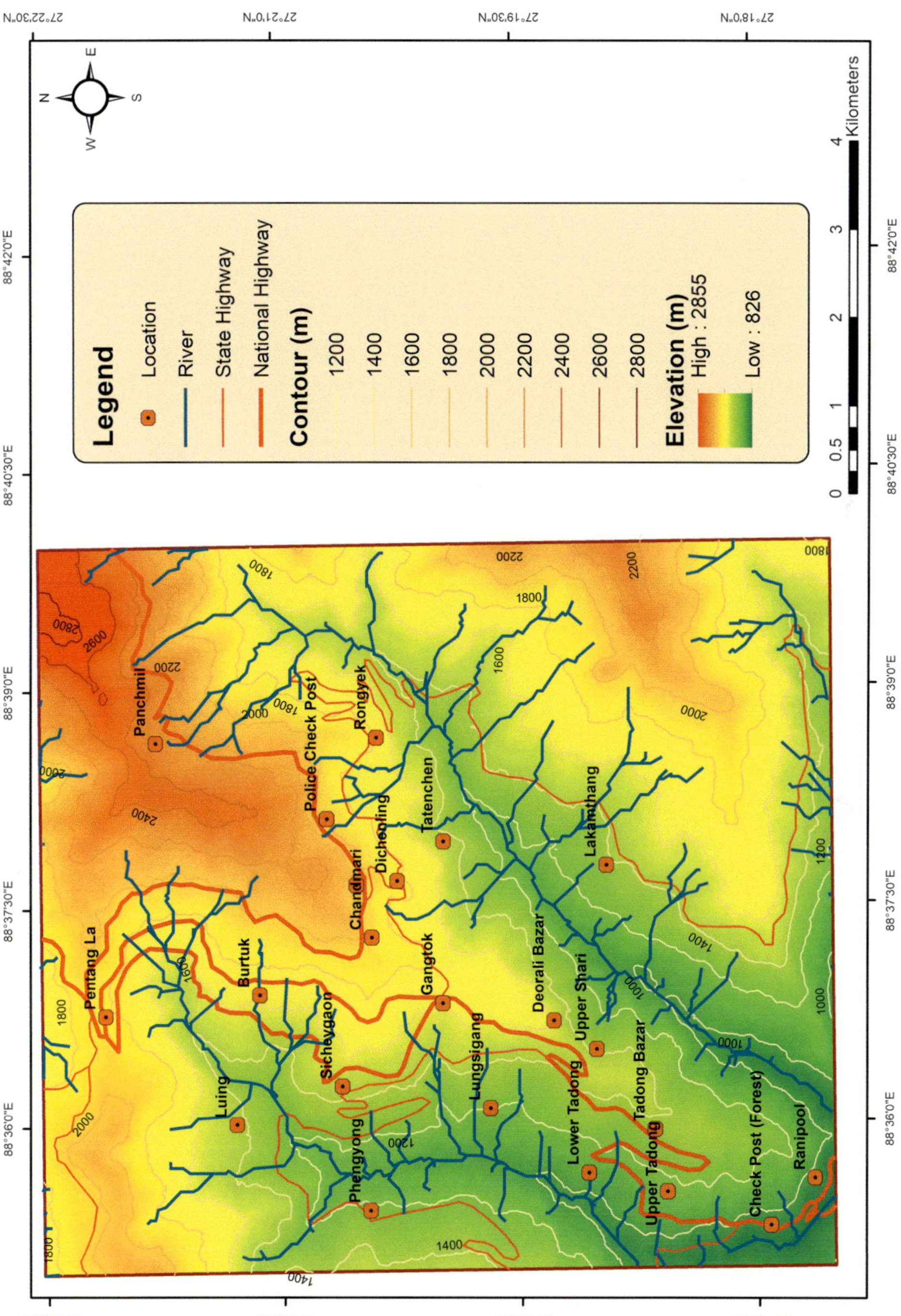

FIGURE 21.2 Terrain elevation in the Gangtok urban area (GUA).

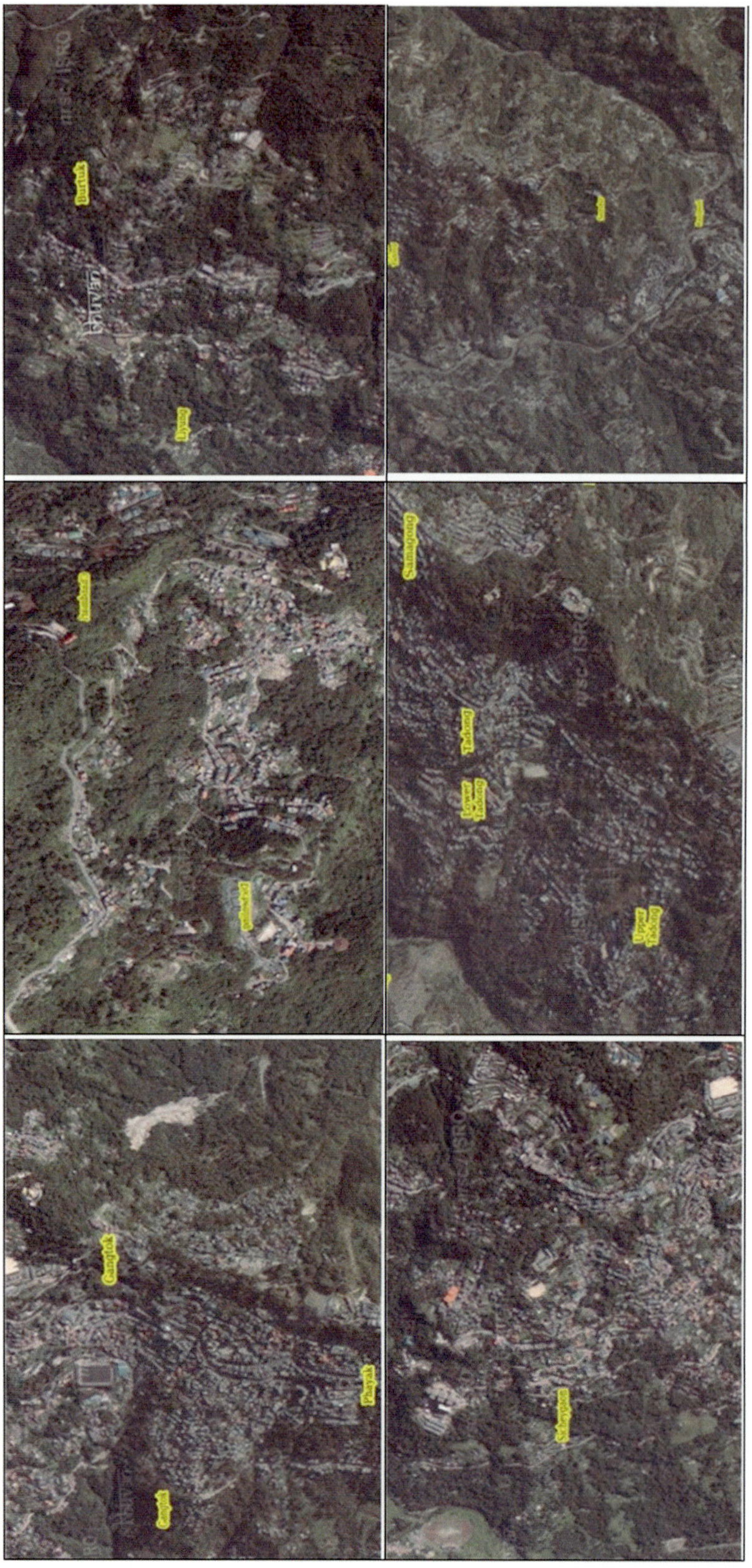

FIGURE 21.3 Aerial view of urbanized area surrounding the Gangtok city.

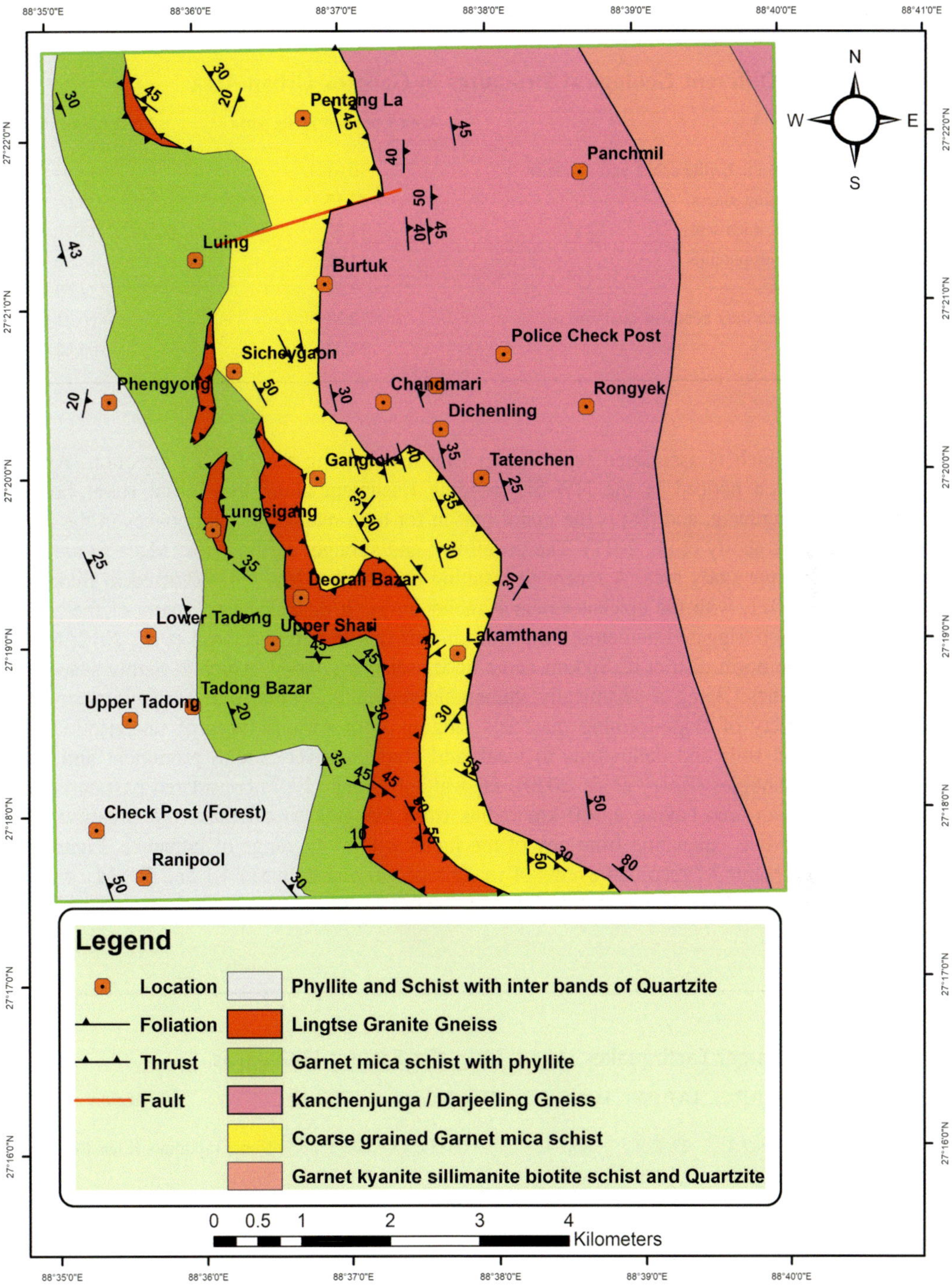

FIGURE 21.4 Different geological structure of the Gangtok urban area (GUA).

majority of the previous seismic activities occurred on shallow focus (<40 km) and intensity between 4.5 to 5.5 magnitude ranges on the Richter scale (Ghosh et al., 2012). As per GSI (2000), it has been stated that the distribution pattern of earthquakes in the Sikkim Himalaya indicates the clustered form of earthquakes are found in medium to high (Mw –5.0 to 5.9) magnitude on a

TABLE 21.1
Distribution of Different Geological Structures in Gangtok Urban Area

Rock Type	Area Covered in sq. km	Percentage of Area
Garnet kyanite sillimanite boitite schist and quartzite	10.41	13.64
Kanchenjunga/Darjeeling gneiss	27.17	35.60
Coarse grained garnet mica schist	11.37	14.90
Garnet mica schist with phyllite	11.42	14.96
Lingtse granite gneiss	3.58	4.69
Phyllite and schist with inter bends of quartzite	12.37	16.21
Total	**76.32**	**100.00**

regional scale, which is associated with Teesta Lineament along the NW-SE direction. Another fault line has been noticed in the NW-SE trending lineament along the Teesta River between Lachen and Chungthang, and that is the major reason for high-magnitude earthquakes in the region (GSI, 2000; Chakraborty et al., 2011). The prominent and stronger earthquakes ($M_w \geq 5$) are listed in Table 21.2 in the study area. A recent devastating earthquake (Mw 6.9) occurred in Sikkim on September 18, 2011, with the epicenter near Kanchenjunga. It damaged large parts of the Sikkim Himalayas and also triggered numerous landslides in this fragile terrain (Ghosh et al., 2012; Martha et al., 2014). The north district of Sikkim came under seismic zone-V, which is highly susceptible to seismic activities. Being a seismically vulnerable region that falls under seismic zone-IV, it comprises a variety of slope-forming materials ranging from various types of unconsolidated to semi-consolidated soils and colluviums to weak and competent rocks with prominent and active structural discontinuities (Koley at al., 2020). Jaiswal and Sinha (2007) considered past earthquake distributions for an area having a 300 km radius from Gangtok to calculate site response to all possible future events emanating from any of the faults within this range of influence. Figure 21.5 (GSI, 2015) represents 81 recorded events of magnitude varying between 4.1 and 7.8 M_w within a 300 km radius circle from Gangtok city.

TABLE 21.2
List of Some Stronger Earthquakes ($M_w \geq 5$) in the Eastern Himalayas

DATE	TIME (UTC)	LAT (°N)	LONG (°E)	Depth (km)	Magnitude	Region
03/02/2006	1:57:47.2	27.4°N	86.7°E	31.5	5.3	Nepal (Sikkim - Bihar Border)
14/02/2006	0:55:18.2	27.7°N	88.8°E	33.0	5.7	Sikkim
20/05/2007	14:18:16.5	27.5°N	88.3°E	15.0	5.0	South Sikkim
18/09/2011	12:40:47	27.7°N	88.2°E	19.7	6.9	Sikkim-- Nepal Border Region
03/10/2013	06:12:39	27.4°N	88.5°E	9.7	5.0	South Sikkim
25/04/2015	06:11:25	28.1°N	84.6°E	10	7.5	Nepal
03/01/2016	04:35:16	24.8 N	93.5°E	17	6.7	Tamenglong, Manipur. (Tremor was felt in Sikkim also)

Source: Sikkim State Disaster Management Authority.

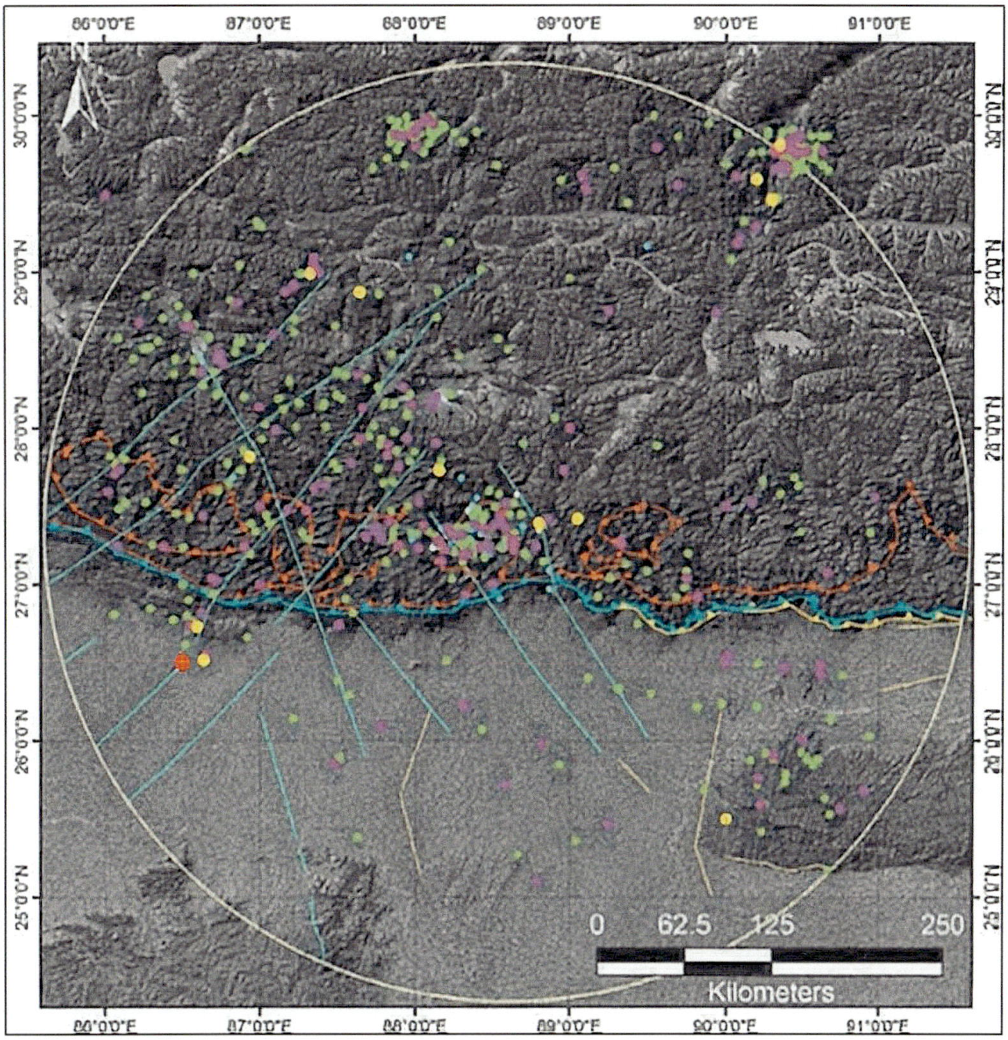

FIGURE 21.5 Spatial distribution of earthquake epicentres for 300 sq. km area, Gangtok is at the centre of the circle.

21.3 DATA USED AND METHODOLOGY

21.3.1 Data Collection and Processing

Hazard zonation of landslides is important for defining spatial relationships and previous historical landslide data and different preparatory factors such as slope, aspect, relative relief, geology, distance from the river, distance from the road, distance from the fault, and land use. Landslide preparatory factors depend on surface topography, geology, and environmental parameters (Chen et al., 2017). This study has considered eight preparatory parameters based on research area conditions (Phong et al., 2019) like slope, aspect, relative relief, geology, proximity to river, road, fault, and land use. Those factors can be helpful to identify the hazard area of landslide. Spatial landslide data were collected from different organizations such as the Geological Survey of India (GSI) and the Global Landslide Catalog Downloadable Products Gallery (Cooperative Open Online Landslide Repository (COOLR, NASA). Based on the ground truth verification, those data were computed and verified through the global positioning system (GPS). Slope, aspect, relative relief, and stream order maps were extracted and prepared from the ASTER Digital Elevation Model (DEM) (30 m), which is collected from the USGS (https://earthexplorer.usgs.gov/). The geological structure was digitized from the Geological Survey of India (GSI) geology map of 1:50,000 scales and then converted from Shapfile to raster. LISS III image (Acquired date: 06 Jan 2019, 24 m resolution) was utilized for location map which was collected for Bhuvan (ISRO, https://bhuvan-app3.nrsc.gov.in/data/download/index.php). Distance to river, thrust/fault, and road raster layer were prepared using Euclidean distance tools in the ArcGIS environment. The supervised classification method has been used for preparation of land use mapping with the help of Landsat 8 ODI (30 m) satellite imagery that is collected from USGS (Acquired date: 05.01.2019). Ground control points have been used through Google Earth for the improvement of planimetric accuracy of the satellite imageries. For the processing of the various raster data set (30 m × 30 m), UTM projection and WGS84 datum have been maintained. ArcGIS platform has been applied for the preparation of all thematic layers and images. The study's eight thematic layers like slope, aspect, geology, relative relief, distance to road, distance to river, distance to thrust/fault, and land use have been used for prediction of landslide hazard zones. A landslide incident database was also created for validation of landslide hazard zones. For this, it is most significant to record previous landslide incidents for the prediction of future landslide initiations. Past landslide data has been compiled and documented from the Geological Survey of India (Special Publication 103, 2016 and N. Kumar, 2015), GSI Bhukosh gateway (https://bhukosh.gsi.gov.in/Bhukosh/MapViewer.aspx), and Global Landslide Catalog Downloadable Products (NASA) (https://maps.nccs.nasa.gov/arcgis/apps/MapAndAppGallery/index.html?appid=574f26408683485799d02e857e5d9521). This landslide incident map indicates the extension of spatial location and typology of landslide induced by rainfall and earthquakes (triggering factors). Finally, 55 landslide locations (previously occurs) were used for the ground truth validation of landslide hazard zones in the Gangtok urban area. The collection of data and sources are described in detail in Table 21.3.

21.3.2 Multi-Criteria Evaluation Method

The multi-criteria evaluation (MCE) method is mostly applied for landslide hazard zonation (LHZ) studies (Carver, 1991; Othmana et al., 2012; Banerjee et al., 2018; Feizizadeh et al., 2014; Ahmed, 2014; Kavzoglu et al., 2013; Bhat et al., 2019; Abija et al., 2020). To execute this method, various processes have been used by past researchers: analytical hierarchy process (AHP) (Chimidi et al., 2017; Ahmed, 2014; Bera et al., 2019; Saaty, 2008), fuzzy logic (FL) (Razifard et al., 2018; Meten et al., 2015; Lee, 2007), and the weighted overlay method (WOM) (Prakasam et al., 2020; Shano et al., 2020; Bera et al., 2019; Ayele et al., 2014). After a review of various literature (Eastman,

TABLE 21.3
Data Used for the Present Study

Data Layers	Data Obtained	Scale/Resolution	Source
Location map	Toposheet 78 A/11, LISS III	1:50000, 24 m	SOI, Bhuvan
Slope angle, Aspect slope, Relative relief, Distance to river	ASTER DEM	30 m	USGS
Geological map, Thrust or Fault	Geology Map	1:50000	GSI 2002, 2015
Road network	Toposheet 78 A/11	1:50000	SOI, Kolkata
Land use	Landsat 8 OLI and TIRS	30 m, PAN 15 m	USGS
Landslide (ground truth data for validation)	GSI SP 103, Bhukosh gateway, GLCDP	–	GSI, NASA

2001, 2009; Ayele et al., 2014; Kanungo et al., 2006; Shano et al., 2020; Bera et al., 2019; Ahmed et al., 2014), the present study has followed the WOM, which is a direct and simple method to predict the hazard zones of landslide risk of the study area. This approach is based on the prediction, the condition which has been carried out into the previous landslide records if reactivated in the future in another location and once more landslides can be initiated (Shano et al., 2020). The weighted values of each factor layer has been estimated by the weighted overlay method (WOM) (Shit et al., 2016; Ahmed et al., 2014). Evaluation of landslide hazard areas needs the factor to be in order according to their importance. A rating system has been applied to perform the entire method, whereas those causative factors and their classes are providing numerical value (Shit et al., 2016). The assigned weights are improved on the basis of the associated preparatory factors for landslide field survey and on the expert knowledge on landslide initiation causes from past literature (Ghorai et al., 2015; Pathak, 2016; Shit et al., 2016).

The MCE method is very effective using geospatial techniques to identify the landslide vulnerable areas of the Gangtok urban area. For the present study area, geomorphological, topographical, and anthropogenic factors (preparatory) are most significant to the hazard area. Multicriteria evaluation (MCE) through WOM was applied to identify and estimation of the hazard zone of the present study area. Present study was considering eight preparatory factors for WOM in the present study. The preparatory factor was assigned the numerical value, called its weight and its respective factor classes were assigned the numerical value known as the rating (Kanungo et al., 2006; Shano et al., 2020). Each preparatory factor layer was assigned a weight based on its vulnerability (Table 21.4). Each raster layer of the preparatory factor was reclassified different classes and a rank of 0–9 was assigned on each class based on its vulnerability (Table 21.4) (Bera et al., 2019; Shano et al., 2020). The higher value of weight or rating to a preparatory factor or its

TABLE 21.4

Distribution of Weight and Rating of Various Preparatory Factors and Factor Classes

Sl. No.	Factors Layers	Weight (%)	Subclasses (reclassified)	Rating
1	Slope Angle (in °)	20	0–15	1
			15–25	3
			25–35	5
			35–45	7
			> 45	9
2	Geological Structure	20	Garnet kyanite sillimanite biotite schist and quartzite (Chungthang Formation)	8
			Kanchenjunga/Darjeeling gneiss	9
			Coarse grained garnet mica schist	7
			Garnet mica schist with phyllite	6
			Lingtse granite gnesiss	4
			Phyllite and schist with inter-bends of quartzite	5
3	Aspect Slope (in °)	10	Flat (–1 - –0. 01)	0
			North (–0.01 - 22.5, 337.5 – 360)	2
			Northeast (22.5 - 67.5)	3
			East (67.5 - 112.5)	5
			Southeast (112.5 - 157.5)	7
			South (157.5 - 202.5)	8
			Southwest (202.5 - 247.5)	9
			West (247.5 - 292.5)	6
			Northwest (292.5 - 337.5)	4

(Continued)

TABLE 21.4 (Continued)
Distribution of Weight and Rating of Various Preparatory Factors and Factor Classes

Sl. No.	Factors Layers	Weight (%)	Subclasses (reclassified)	Rating
4	Relative Relief (m)	10	<300	1
			300–400	3
			400–500	5
			500–600	7
			>600	9
5	Distance to River (m)	10	0–100	9
			100–200	7
			200–300	5
			300–400	3
			400–500	2
			>500	1
6	Distance to Road (m)	10	0–100	9
			100–200	7
			200–300	5
			300–400	3
			400–500	2
			>500	1
7	Distance to Thrust/ Fault (m)	10	0–100	9
			100–200	7
			200–300	5
			300–400	3
			400–500	2
			>500	1
8	Land Use	10	Dense Vegetation	1
			Sparse Vegetation	3
			Rocky Waste	5
			Built-up	7
		100		

corresponding factor classes shows the greater influences for initiation of landslide (Preuth et al., 2010; Ayele et al., 2014; Shit et al., 2016; Shano et al., 2020; Nath et al., 2020). After the weights were assigned based on their susceptibility and each raster layer has been multiplied by the weight values for extracting the final output map (Michael and Samanta, 2016; Nath et al., 2020). All preparatory raster layers were integrated in ArcGIS by equation 21.1 of WOM (Shano et al., 2020; Shit et al., 2016).

$$S = \frac{\Sigma W_i S_{ij}}{\Sigma W_i} \tag{21.1}$$

where S represent the value of the spatial unit in the output map (LHZ)

W_i represent the weight of ith factor map,

S_{ij} represent the ith spatial class weight of 'jth' factor map,

These preparatory factor layers were overlaid and prepared a single layer map that has been generated by obtaining weight values to each factor attribute. The LHZ map has been prepared, including five hazard classes (very low to very high). The hazard zonation of landslide has been

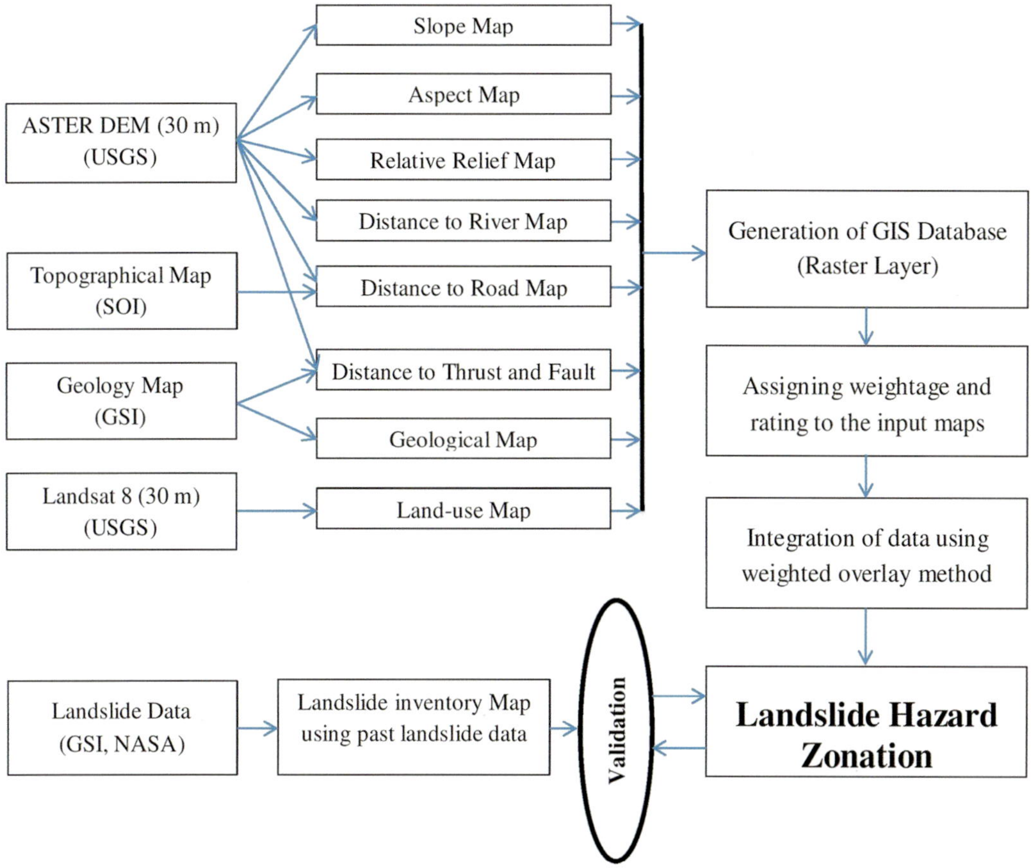

FIGURE 21.6 Flow chart of methodology adopted for landslide hazard zonation using the MCE method (WOM).

validated with past landslide locations (ground truth verification) of the present study area. A flow chart of adopted methodology for landslide hazard zonation using the MCE method is shown in Figure 21.6.

21.4 RESULTS AND DISCUSSION

The present outcome of the study is discussing three different aspects: i) spatial distribution of various landslide preparatory factors classes are also analysed as part of the present study, ii) preparation and evaluation of the LHZ map, and iii) validation of hazard zones of landslides using past landslide locations. The outcome in the present study has been discussed in the following parts.

21.4.1 Spatial Distribution of Various Preparatory Factors

21.4.1.1 Slope Angle

Slope angle is a major preparatory factor of landslide hazard zonation mapping. Several researchers consider slope angle an important factor (Yalcin et al., 2011; Kavzoglu et al., 2013; Shahabi et al., 2014; Youssef et al., 2014; Phong et al., 2019;). Slope angle has been obtained from DEM (30 m resolution) and divided into five equal classes with 10° intervals, such as 0–15°, 15–25°, 25–35°, 35–45°, and above 45° (Figure 21.7). Based on the spatial analysis, slope angle zones 0–15° cover 11.52 sq. km (15.10%), 15–25° covers 26.86 sq. km (35.19%) area, 25–35°

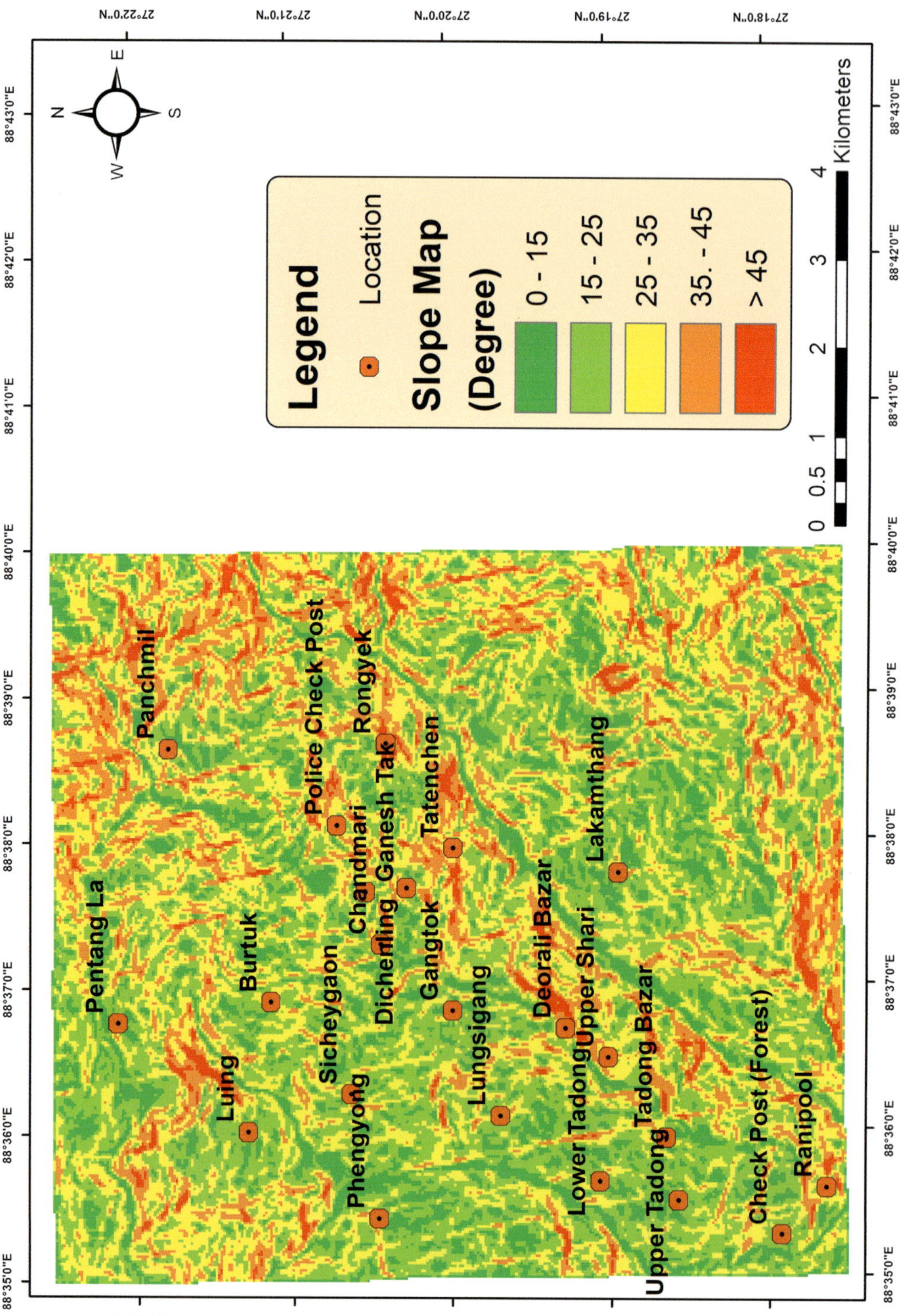

FIGURE 21.7 Slope map of the Gangtok urban area (GUA).

covers 23.67 sq. km (31.01%), 35–45° covers 11.35 sq. km (14.87%), and above 45° slope zone contributes only 2.92 sq. km (3.83%) area of the total area of the study. Slope angle zones 15–25° and 25–35° are the mostly dominated slopes that contribute 50.53 sq. km (66.20%) in the Gangtok urban area.

21.4.1.2 Slope Aspect

Slope aspect may control landslide initiation because several aspects can affect meteorological parameters, like sunlight, rainfall, and discontinuities (Dai et al., 2002; Capitani et al., 2013). Aspect also influences the vegetation cover and moisture content that can affect soil strength and landslide imitation (Banerjee et al., 2018). Several studies has been considered aspect angles as preparatory factors for LHZ mapping (Capitani et al., 2013; Kavzoglu et al., 2013; Phong et al., 2019; Kaur et al., 2019). In the present study, the aspect slope has been classified into nine classes (Figure 21.8) such as northwest (292.5°–337.5°), west (247.5°–292.5°), southwest (202.5°– 247.5°), south (157.5°–202.5°), southeast (112.5°–157.5°), east (67.5°–112.5°), northeast (22.5°–67.5°), north (0°–22.5° and 337.5°–360°), and flat (−1). Based on the spatial analysis, the entire south (southeast, south, southwest) and west aspect facing area are mostly dominated in the Gangtok urban area, which contributes 46.71 sq. km (61.20%) of the total area. The entire north (northeast, north, northwest) and east aspect facing contributes only 29.61 sq. km (38.80%) area in the study area.

21.4.1.3 Geological Structures

Geological structures carried out a significant part in landslide initiation (Phong et al., 2019; Bhat et al., 2019). The strength of rocks and soil permeability has been changed due to lithological and structural variations (Kavzoglu et al., 2013). Lithological thrust, fault, joints, and fractures can influence instability in rock structures and initiate landslides (Pham et al., 2019). Geological structures serve major functions in landslide hazard analysis because various units of geological structures have different susceptibilities to active geomorphic processes (Youssef et al., 2014). Various authors (Bhat et al., 2019; Phong et al., 2019; Wang et al., 2009; Youssef et al., 2014; Pham et al., 2019) have considered geological structures as preparatory factors to determine landslide hazard zonation mapping. A geological map of the Gangtok urban area has been prepared (Figure 21.9) with six lithological units and several thrusts or faults. Based on geological mapping, six different rock structures have been observed (Figure 21.9) of the present study area such as garnet kyanite sillimanite biotite schist and quartzite (Chungthang Formation), Kanchenjunga gneiss, coarse-grained garnet mica schist, garnet mica schist with phyllite, Lingtse granite gneiss, phyllite, and schist with inter-bends of quartzite. Base on the spatial distribution, Kanchenjunga/ Darjeeling gneiss is mostly dominated rock structures contributing 27.17 sq. km (35.60%) of the study area. On the other side, the rock type of garnet kyanite sillimanite biotite schist and quartzite (Chungthang Formation) have contributed 10.41 sq. km (13.64%), Coarse-grained garnet mica schist contributes 11.37 sq. km (14.90%), garnet mica schist with phyllite contributes 11.42 sq. km (14.96%), phyllite and schist with inter-bends of quartzite contribute 12.37 sq. km (16.21%), and Lingtse granite gneiss contributes 3.58 sq. km (4.69%).

21.4.1.4 Relative Relief

Relative relief plays an important role of absolute maximum difference in altitude at a particular location (Psomiadis et al., 2020). Amplitude of relief in terms of relative relief represent actual variation of elevation in a particular area with respect to local base level. Compared to slopes with similar geometric and geo-mechanical parameters, those with a high altitude deficit are more vulnerable to landslides. A very high amount of runoff and lower infiltration rates have been noticed in greater elevation landscapes (Foumelis et al., 2018). Relative relief has been derived from ASTER DEM (30 m resolution) by using the GIS environment and classified into five classes (Figure 21.10) such as < 300 m, 300–400 m, 400–500 m, 500–600 m, and above 600 m. Such categories indicate that various relative relief zones occupied a particular area like below 300 m

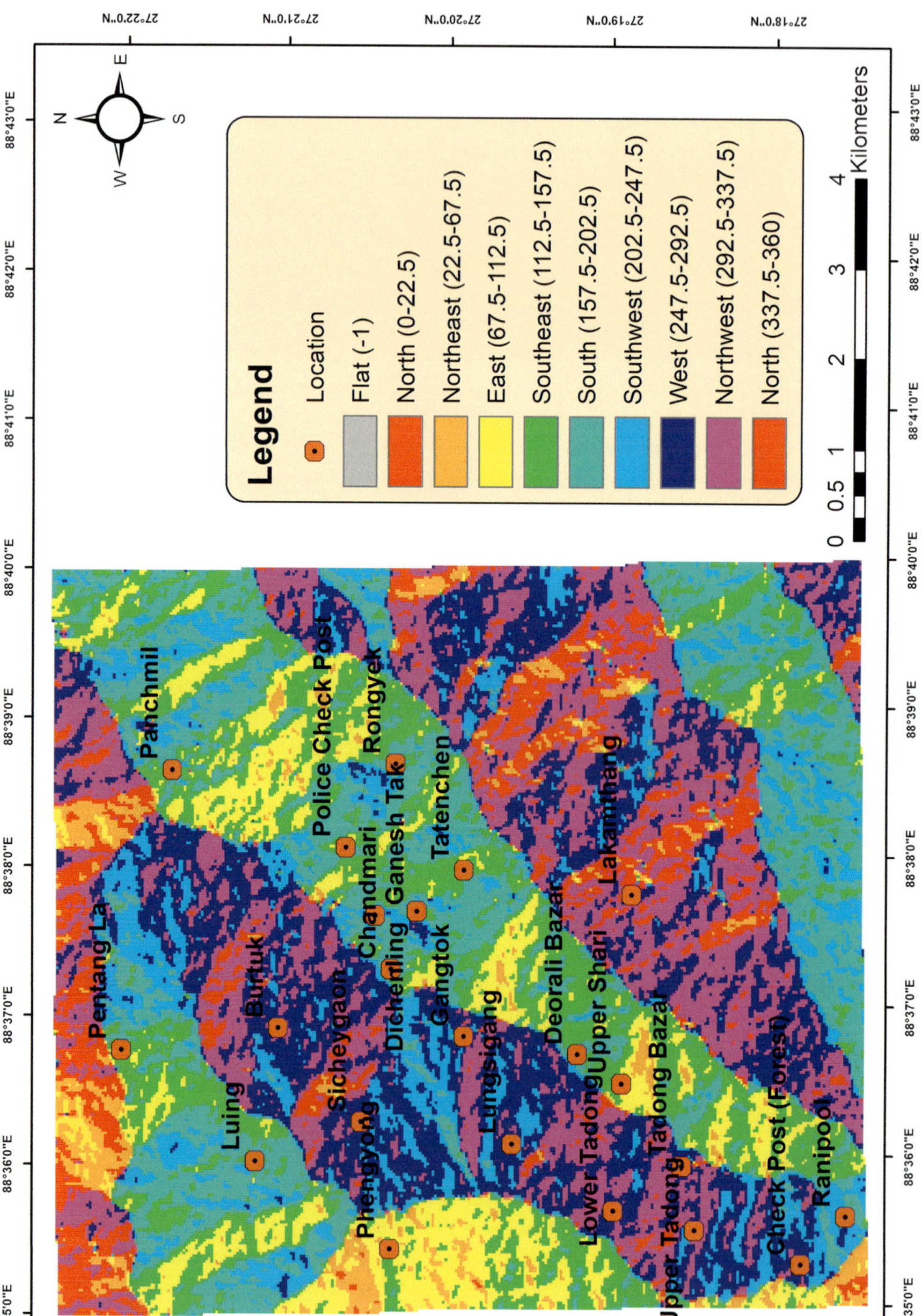

FIGURE 21.8 Aspect map of the Gangtok urban area (GUA).

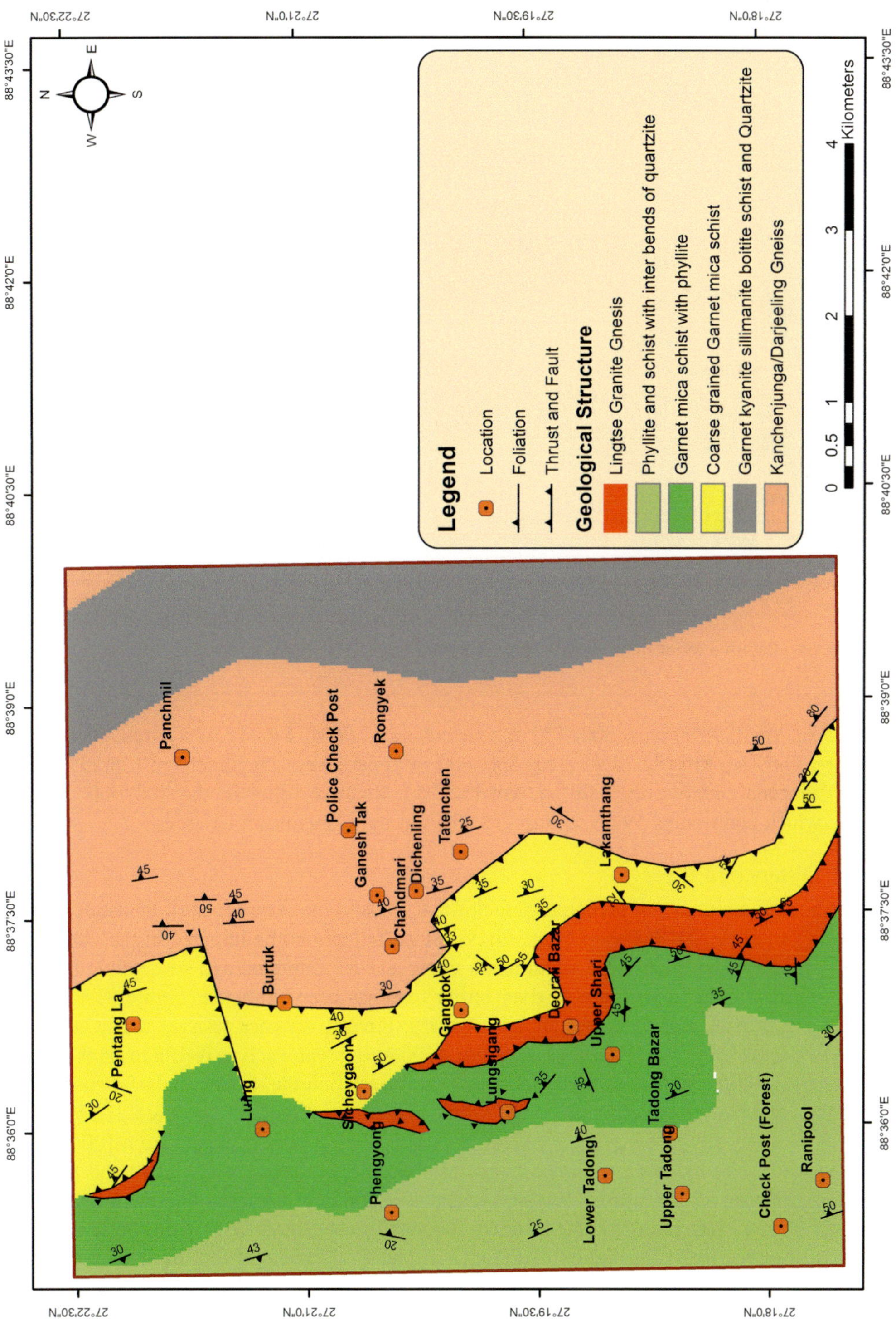

FIGURE 21.9 Geological map of the Gangtok urban area (GUA).

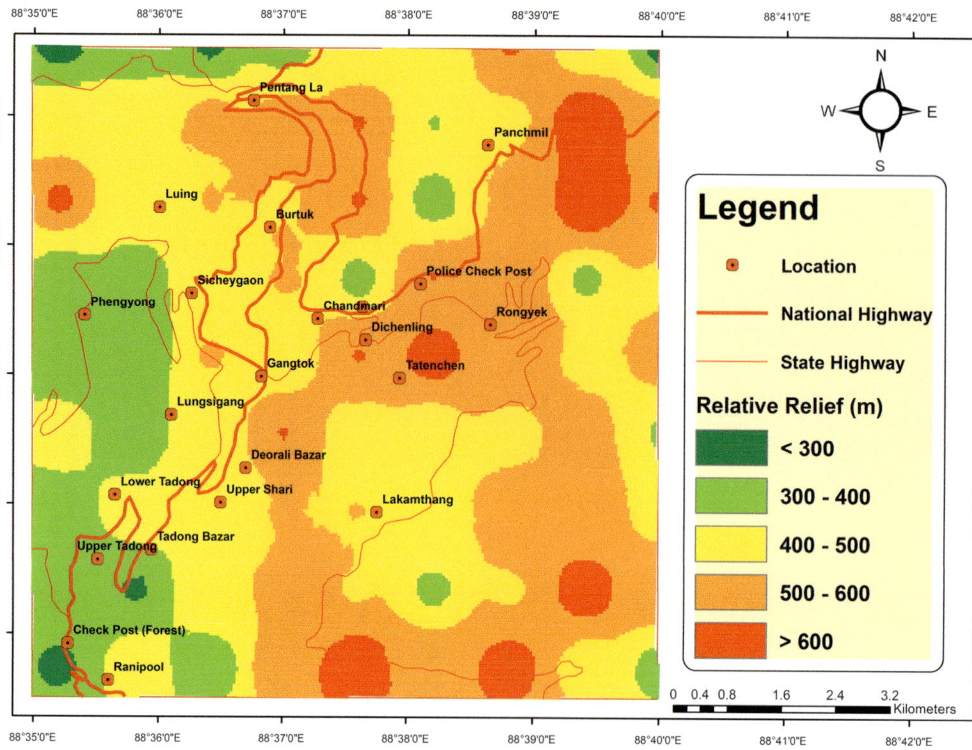

FIGURE 21.10 Relative relief map of the Gangtok urban area (GUA).

covers 0.75 sq. km (0.98%) area, 300–400 m zone covers 11.96 sq. km (15.67%) area, 400–500 m zone covers 32.65 sq. km (42.78%) area, 500–600 m zone covers 26.90 sq. km (35.25%), and above 600 m zone covers only 4.06 sq. km (5.32%). Relative relief in the 400–600 m zone dominates, which contributes 59.55 sq. km (78.03%) in the Gangtok urban area.

21.4.1.5 Distance to River

Distance to road is a significant preparatory factor that leads to the occurrence of landslides in the hilly region (Yan et al., 2018; Phong et al., 2019). Slope failure can be initiated in the vicinity to rivers because materials of the slope accumulate water and get saturated and susceptible to slope failure (Phong et al., 2019). Distance to river buffer map has been extracted (Figure 21.11) from the ASTER DEM using Euclidean distance in ArcGIS. Finally, distance to river raster layer has been classified into six classes (Figure 21.11) with a 100 m interval, such as 0–100 m, 100–200 m, 300–400 m, 300–400 m, 400–500 m, and above 500 m. Based on the spatial analysis, distance to river map indicates that most dominated areas within 100 m from the river occupied 21.15 sq. km (27.70%) of the study area. Otherwise, 17.49 sq. km (22.92%) has been occupied from 100–200 m, 13.21 sq. km (17.31%) has been occupied from 200–300 m, 10.02 sq. km (13.13%) and 8.14 sq. km (10.67%) has been occupied from 300–400 m and 400–500 m of the river alignment. Only 6.31 sq. km (8.27%) area has been occupied above 500 m from the river bed of the present study. Finally, it is observed that contribution of the area gradually decreased from the river bed.

21.4.1.6 Distance to Road

Road proximity is on of the most important preparatory factors to landslide initiation, which has a deep relation with occurrence of landslides (Shirzadi et al., 2011). Road networks create negative impacts on the slope of hilly terrain due to the changing surface morphology and slope stability of

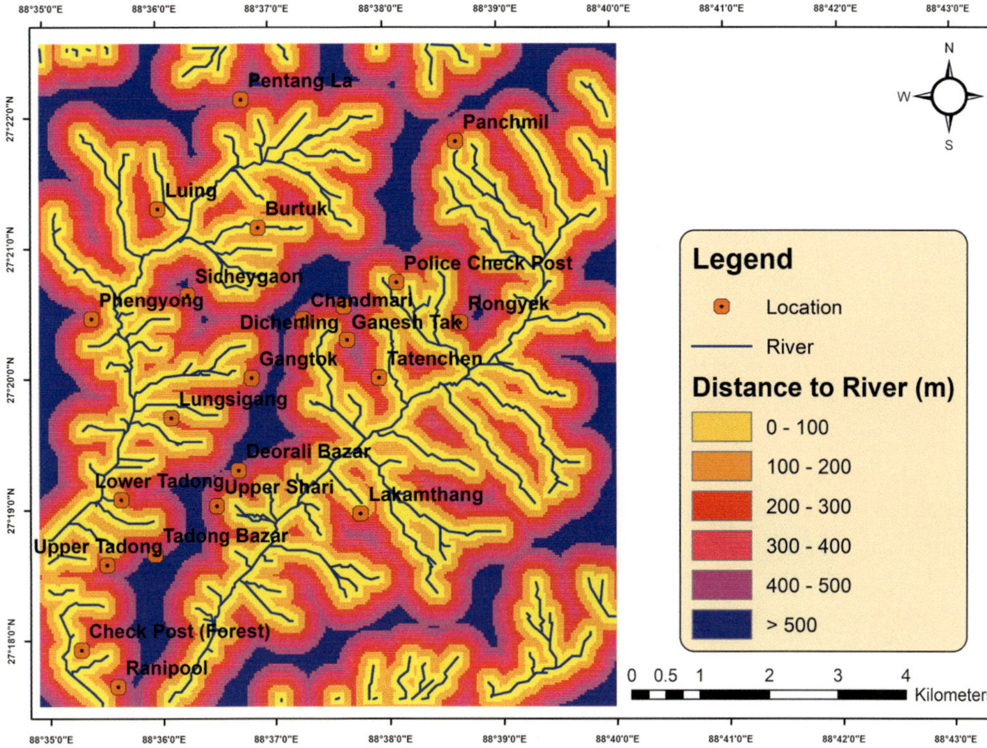

FIGURE 21.11 Distance to river map in the Gangtok urban area (GUA).

mountain ranges (Yan et al., 2018). The slope stability can be changed due to road construction and movement of vehicles (Kavzoglu et al., 2013; Collins, 2008). Several researchers consider proximity to the roads for the identification of landslide susceptibility zones (Youssef et al., 2015; Banerjee et al., 2018; Kaur et al., 2019). Distance to road map has derived from DEM using Euclidean distance in the GIS platform. Finally, distance to road layer has been classified into six classes with a 100 m interval, such as 0–100 m, 100–200 m, 200–300 m, 300–400 m, 400–500 m, and above 500 m (Figure 21.12). Distance to road map indicates that close proximity of the road from 0–100 m covers 15.68 sq. km (20.55%) area. On the other side, it has been observed that 10.07 sq. km (13.19%) area covers 100–200 m; 8.43 sq. km (11.05%) covers 200–300 m; 7.00 sq. km (9.17%) and 6.12 sq. km (8.02%) covers 300–400 m and 400–500 m of the study area, respectively. It is observed that 29.02 sq. km (38.02%) areas have been occupied above 500 m from the road.

21.4.1.7 Distance to Thrust and Fault

The thrust and fault lines are the weaker zones of the geological structure that naturally decrease strength of the rock (Banerjee et al., 2018). Due to the seismic activities, the dislocation of the thrust and fault line is responsible for several numbers of landslides. So, distance to the thrust and fault line was considered a factor of LHZ mapping (Van Westen et al., 2008; Banerjee et al., 2018). A distance to thrust/fault map has been prepared using the Euclidean distance tools in the GIS platform (Figure 21.13). This map is classified into six classes (Figure 21.13) with 100 m intervals, such as 0–100 m, 100–200 m, 200–300 m, 300–400 m, 400–500 m, and above 500 m. Distance to thrust and fault map indicates that 7.09 sq. km (9.29%) area covers the distance of 100 m from the thrust and fault line. Otherwise, 6.54 sq. km (8.57%) covers the distance 100–200 m, 5.65 sq. km (7.40%) covers 200–300 m, 3.96 sq. km (5.19%) covers 300–400 m, 3.78 sq. km (4.95%) covers 400–500 m, and 49.30 sq. km (64.60%) area also covers the distance above 500 m from the thrust and fault line.

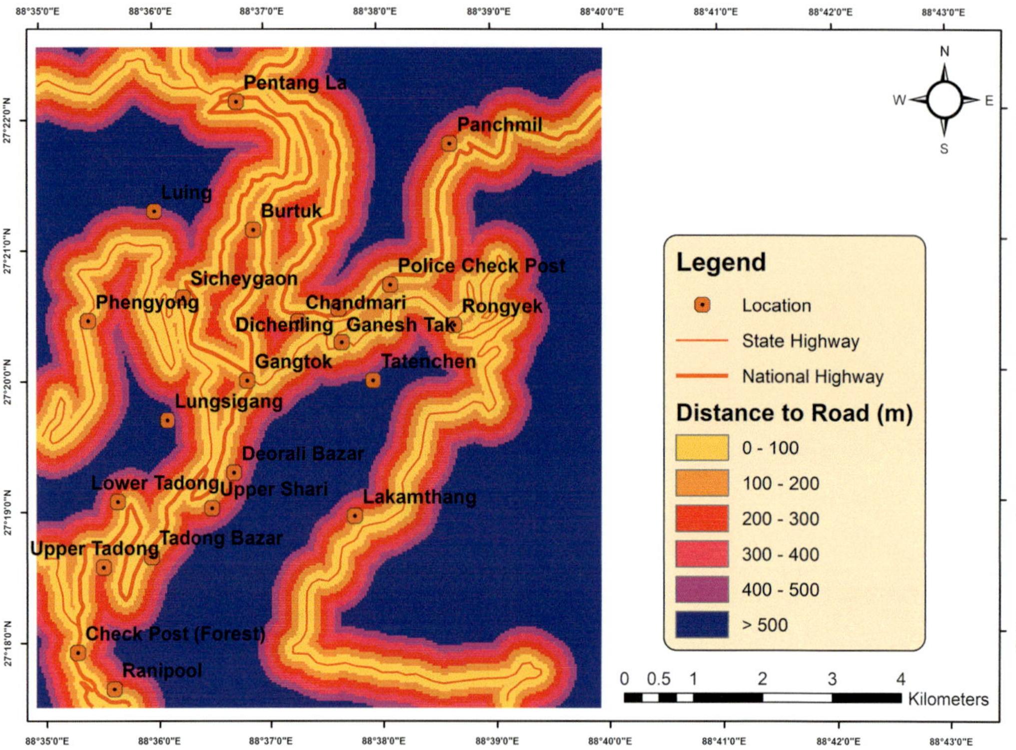

FIGURE 21.12 Distance to road map in the Gangtok urban area (GUA).

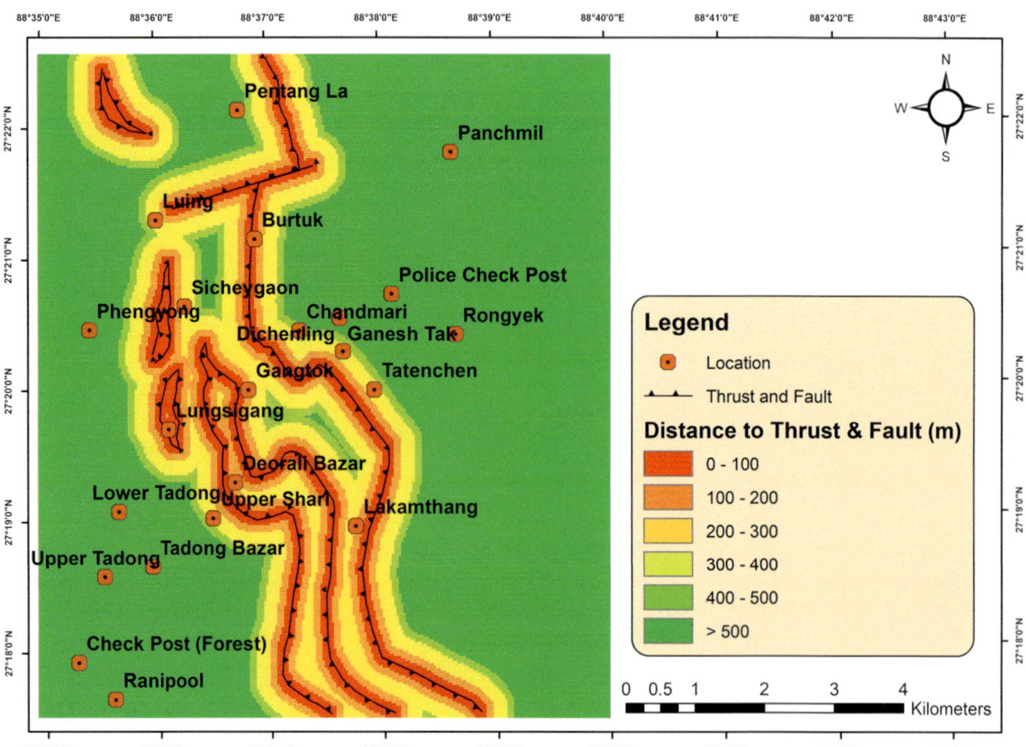

FIGURE 21.13 Distance to thrust and fault map in the Gangtok urban area (GUA).

21.4.1.8 Land Use

Land use has been considered an important preparatory factor for landslide initiation and many researchers consider it (Raghuvanshi et al., 2015; Shit et al., 2016; Bera et al., 2019). Land areas that are sparsely vegetated, rocky waste, or barren and urbanized or weathered are prone to slope instability (Raghuvanshi et al., 2015). Densely vegetated slope areas indicate stable conditions of the land surface because vegetation prevents water seepage into the slope. The large root systems of vegetation increase the shear strength of the soil mass, which can be help to improve stability of the slope area (Greenway, 1987). In the present study, land use has been classified into four categories (Figure 21.14), such as densely vegetated area, sparsely vegetated area, rocky waste, and built up. In the present study, the land use map (Figure 21.14) indicates that 33.28 sq. km (43.61%) and 15.41 sq. km (20.19%) area have been occupied by the densely and sparsely vegetated area. On the other side, 19.62 sq. km (25.71%) and 8.01 sq. km (10.49%) areas have been occupied by rocky waste and built-up areas.

21.4.2 Preparation and Evaluation of LHZ Map

The weighted overlay method (WOM) has been applied for generating LHZ mapping using the ArcGIS environment. Selected landslide preparatory factors layers have been combined on the ArcGIS platform and output and a final map (LHZ) has been prepared (Figures 21.15 and 21.16). According to the landslide hazard index (LHI), a final output map has been classified into five hazard classes based on their vulnerability, such as very low hazard zone (LHI:2-3), low hazard zone (LHI:3-4), moderate hazard zone (LHI:4-5), high hazard zone (LHI:5-6), and very high hazard zone (LHI:6-8). The area of landslide hazard zone has been calculated using the zonal

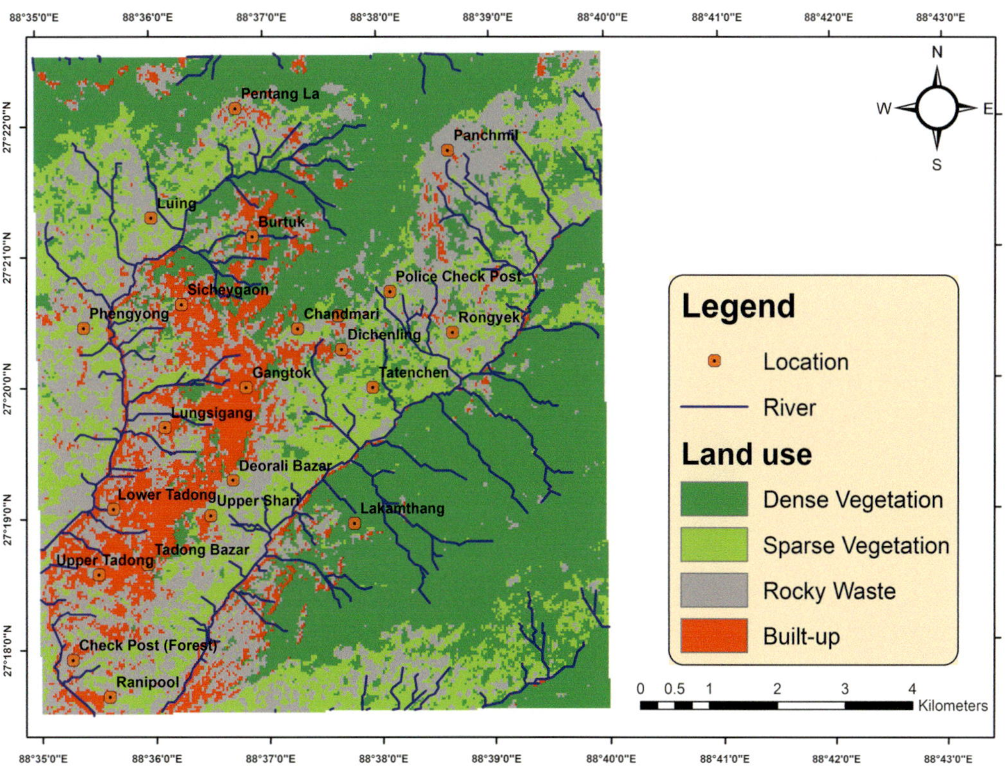

FIGURE 21.14 Land use map in the Gangtok urban area (GUA).

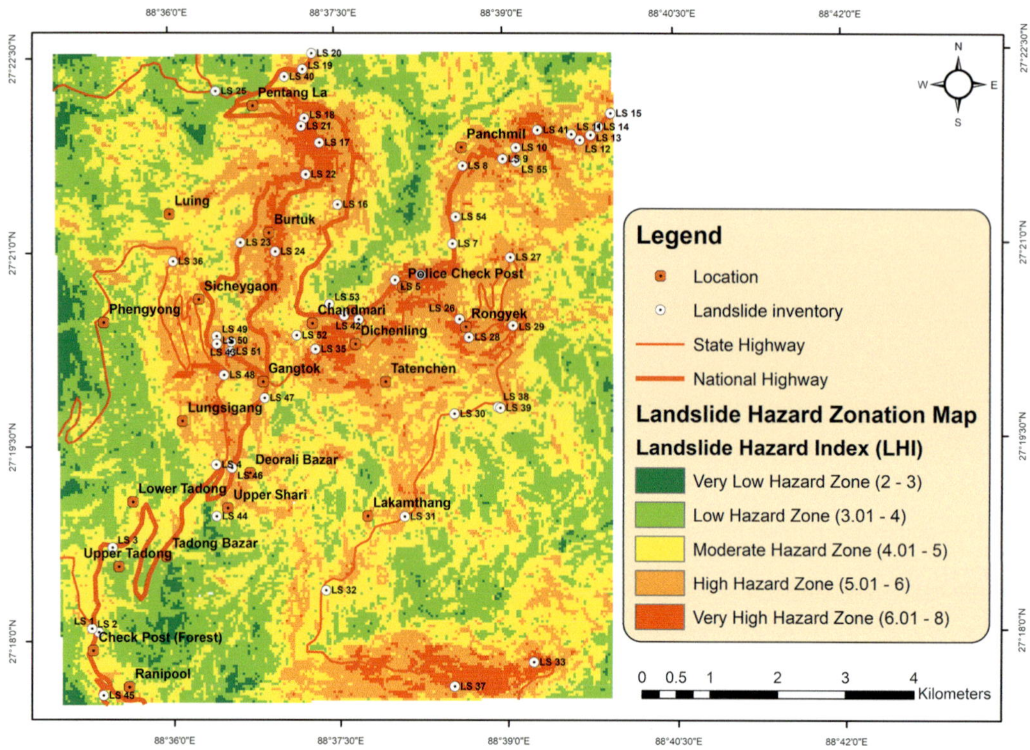

FIGURE 21.15 Landslide hazard zonation mapping with landslide locations.

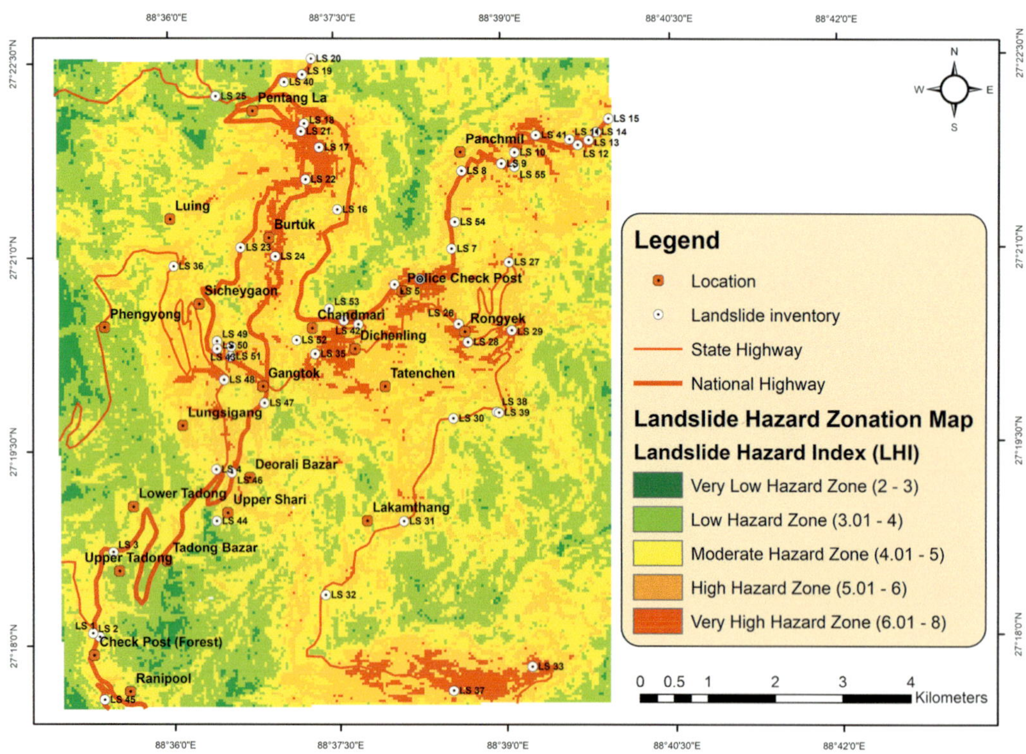

FIGURE 21.16 Landslide hazard zonation mapping with hill shade.

TABLE 21.5
Area Distribution of Landslide Hazard Zones

LHZ Classes	Area in sq. km.	Percentage of Area	Cumulative Area (%)
Very low hazard zone	2.19	02.87	2.87
Low hazard zone	20.79	27.24	30.11
Moderate hazard zone	30.77	40.32	70.43
High hazard zone	18.66	24.45	94.88
Very high hazard zone	3.91	05.12	100.00

statics method and the area is represented in Table 21.5 where 3.91 sq. km (5.12%) areas under very high hazard zone, 18.66 sq. km (24.45%) areas under high hazard zone, 30.77 sq. km (40.32%) areas under moderate hazard zone, 20.79 sq. km (27.24%) areas under low hazard zone, and only 2.19 sq. km (2.87%) areas under very low hazard zone.

21.4.3 Validation of Landslide Hazard Zones

Validation of landslide hazard zonation (LHZ) mapping in the Gangtok urban area has been performed using spatial past landslide data and GIS-based analysis. Based on the collected data, a landslide incident map has been prepared of the present study area. A total of 55 landslides data (location) have been considered for the validation of hazard zones in the study area (Table 21.6; Figures 21.15 and 21.16). The locations points of the landslide overlap on the LHZ map to find out their relation with different hazard zones. Based on the overlay analysis, a very high frequency of landslide (**61.08%**) has been observed in very high hazard zones (Figure 21.17). On the other hand, high hazard zones also contribute **26.66%** landslide frequency, moderate hazard zone covers **10.35%** landslide frequency, and only **1.91%** landslide frequency contributes in a low hazard zone (Figure 21.17). A very low hazard zone has no contribution for landslide occurrence. The validation of LHZ indicates that the percentage of landslide frequency gradually increases from very low to very high hazard classes (Figure 21.17). Based on the validation, it is proved that the adopted methodology has been successfully applied for evaluating landslide hazard zoning.

TABLE 21.6
Validation and Landslide Frequency Distribution of the Study Area

Landslide Hazard Index	Landslide Hazard Zones	Area (sq. km.)	No. of Landslides	Landslide Frequency /per sq.km	Percentage (%) of Landslide Frequency
2–3	Very low hazard zone	2.19	0	0.000	**0.00**
3.01–4	Low hazard zone	20.79	2	0.096	**1.91**
4.01–5	Moderate hazard zone	30.77	16	0.520	**10.35**
5.01–6	High hazard zone	18.66	25	1.340	**26.66**
6.01–8	Very high hazard zone	3.91	12	3.069	**61.08**
Total		**76.32**	**55**	**5.025**	**100.00**

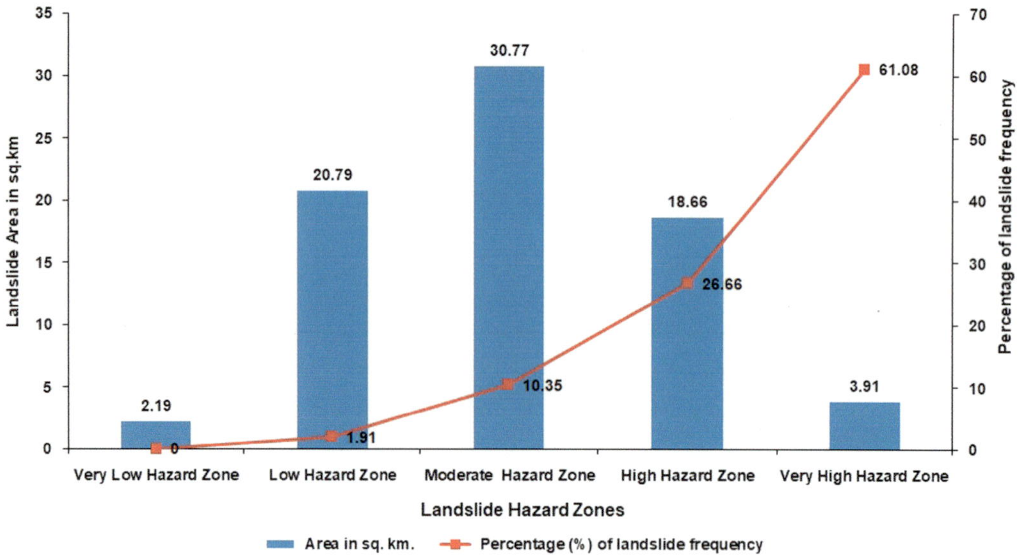

FIGURE 21.17 Distribution of different hazard zones and percentage of landslide frequency.

21.5 CONCLUSION

The Gangtok urban area (GUA) is a part of the Sikkim Himalayas and prone to landslides. Heavy rainfall and earthquakes are the major triggering factors for landslide initiations. The multi-criteria evaluation method through the weighted overlay method has been adopted for the preparation hazard zonation mapping of landslides using geospatial techniques. Based on the weighted overlay analysis, the landslide hazard map has been prepared and a final output map has also been classified into five zones of hazard classes, such as very low (2.87%), low (27.24%), moderate (40.32%), high (24.45%), and very high hazard zone (5.12%) of the study area. The landslide hazard zone has been validated through past landslide incident data in the study area and the validation indicates that the landslide frequency percentage gradually decreases from very high hazard to very low hazard zones, whereas the very high hazard zone covers 61.08% of landslide frequency, high hazard zone also contributes 26.66% landslide frequency, moderate hazard zone covers 10.35% landslide frequency, and low hazard zone covers only 1.91% landslide frequency. Based on the urbanized location, Pentang La, Upper Burtuk, Burtuk, Chandmari, Panchmil, Gangtok, Dichenling, Rongyek, and Lakamthang belong to high to very high hazard zones and Upper Tadong, Lower Tadong, Lungsigang, Deorali Bazar, Upper Shari, Tadong Bazar, Sicheygaon, Phengyong, Luing, Tatenchen, Ganesh Tak, Check Post (Forest), and Ranipool belong in the low to moderate hazard zone in the Gangtok urban area (GUA). Preparation of the landslide hazard zonation map is the initial attempt to the minimisation of landslide hazards which are developed for disaster management and sustainable development. Moreover, creating awareness of people is the most significant basis of the predicted landslide hazard map.

REFERENCES

Abija, F.A., Nwosu, J.I., Ifedotun, A.I., and Osadebe, C.C. "Landslide susceptibility assessment of Calabar, Nigeria using geotechnical, remote sensing and multi-criteria decision analysis: implications for urban planning and development." *SDRP Journal of Earth Sciences & Environmental Studies* 4, no. 6 (2020): 774–788. DOI:10.25177/JESES.4.6.RA.617

Ahammad, R. Understanding institutional changes for reducing social vulnerability to landslides in Chittagong City, Bangladesh. Dissertation, Stockholm University, Sweden (2009).

Ahmed, B. "Landslide susceptibility mapping using multi-criteria evaluation techniques in Chittagong Metropolitan Area, Bangladesh." *Landslides* 12 (2014): 1077–1095. 10.1007/s10346-014-0521-x

Ahmed, M.F., Rogers, J.D., and Ismail, E.H. "A regional level preliminary landslide susceptibility study of the upper Indus river basin." *European Journal of Remote Sensing* 47, no. 1 (2014): 343–373. 10.5721/EuJRS20144721

Anbalagan, R., Kumar, R., Lakshmanan, K., Parida, S., and Neethu, S. "Landslide hazard zonation mapping using frequency ratio and fuzzy logic approach, a case study of Lachung Valley, Sikkim." *Geoenvironmental Disasters* 2 (2015): 6. doi:10.1186/s40677-014-0009

Ayalew, L., and Yamagishi, H. "The application of GIS-based logistic regression for landslide susceptibility mapping in the Kakuda-Yahiko Mountains, Central Japan." *Geomorphology*, 65 (2005): 15–31.

Ayele, S., Raghuvanshi, T. K., and Kala P. M. "Application of remote sensing and GIS for landslide disaster management—A case from Abay gorge, Gohatsion– Dejen section, Ethiopia." In: Singh M., Singh R. B., Hassan M. I. (eds) *Landscape Ecology and Water Management, Proceedings of International Geographical Union (IGU) Rohtak Conference*. Advances in Geographical and Environmental Science, (pp. 15–32). Springer, Japan (2014).

Banerjee, P., Ghose, M. K., and Pradhan, R. "Analytic hierarchy process and information value method based landslide susceptibility mapping and vehicle vulnerability assessment along a highway in Sikkim Himalaya." *Arabian Journal of Geosciences* (2018). 11:139.doi:10.1007/s12517-018-3488-4.

Bera, A., Mukhopadhyay, B. P., and Das, D. "Landslide hazard zonation mapping using multi-criteria analysis with the help of GIS techniques: A case study from Eastern Himalayas, Namchi, South Sikkim." *Natural Hazards* 96 (2019): 935–959. DOI: 10.1007/s11069-019-03580-w

Bhandari, R. K. "Landslide hazard zonation: Some thoughts." In K. S. Valdiya (ed.), *Coping with Natural Hazards: Indian Context* (2004): 134–152.Orient Longman: Hyderabad.

Bhasin, R., Grimstad, E., Larsen, J., Dhawan, A. K., Singh, R., Verma, S. K., and Venkatachalam, K. "Landslide hazards and mitigation measures at Gangtok, Sikkim Himalaya." *Engineering Geology* 64 (2002): 351–368. DOI:10.1016/S0013-7952(01)00096-5

Bhat, I. A., Shafiq M., Ahmed, P., and Kanth, T. A. "Multi-criteria evaluation for landslide hazard zonation by integrating remote sensing, GIS and field data in North Kashmir Himalayas, J&K, India." *Environmental Earth Sciences* 78 (2019): 613. 10.1007/s12665-019-8631-3

BIS. 1983 "Criteria for earthquake resistant design of structures: General provisions and buildings", Bureau of Indian Standards (Part-1) (2002).

Capitani, M., Ribolini, A., and Bini, M. "The slope aspect: A predisposing factor for landsliding? *Comptes Rendus Geoscience* 345, no. 11–12 (2013): 427–438. DOI: 10.1016/j.crte.2013.11.002

Carver, S. J. "Integrating multi-criteria evaluation with geographical information systems." *International Journal of Geographical Information Systems* 5 (1991): 321–339. 10.1080/02693799108927858

Chakraborty, I., Ghosh, S., Bhattacharya, D., and Bora, A. "Earthquake induced landslides in the Sikkim-Darjeeling Himalayas - An aftermath of the 18th September 2011 Sikkim earthquake." Earthquake Report, Govt. of Sikkim (2011), 1–8.

Chen, T., Niu, R., Du, B., and Wang, Y. "Landslide Spatial Susceptibility Mapping by Using GIS and Remote Sensing Techniques: A Case Study in Zigui County, the Three Georges Reservoir, China." *Environmental Earth Sciences* 73, no. 9 (2014): 5571–5583. DOI:10.1007/s12665-014-3811-7

Chen, W., Shirzadi, A., Shahabi, H., Ahmad, B. B., Zhang, S., Hong, H., and Zhang, N. "A novel hybrid artificial intelligence approach based on the rotation forest ensemble and naïve Bayes tree classifiers for a landslide susceptibility assessment in Langao County, China." *Geomatics, Natural Hazards and Risk*8, no. 2 (2017): 1955–1977.

Chimidi, G., Raghuvanshi, T. K., and Suryabhagavan, K. V. "Landslide hazard evaluation and zonation in and around Gimbi town, western Ethiopia – a GIS-based statistical approach." *Applied Geomatics* 9, no. 4 (2017): 219–236.

Collins, T. K. "Debris flows caused by failure of fill slopes: early detection, warning, and loss prevention." *Landslides* 5, no. 1 (2008): 107–120.

Dai, F. C., Lee, C. F., and Ngai, Y. Y. "Landslide risk assessment and management: an overview." *Engineering Geology* 64, no. 1 (2002): 65–87. DOI: 10.1016/S0013-7952(01)00093-X

Eastman, R. J. "IDIRISI Andes; Guide to GIS and Image Processing." Clark Labs, Clark University, USA, 7 (2001).

Eastman, R. J. "IDIRISI Andes; Guide to GIS and Image Processing." Clark Labs, Clark University, USA, 135 (2009).

Feizizadeh, B., and Blaschke, T. "Comparing GIS-Multicriteria Decision Analysis for landslide susceptibility mapping for the lake basin, Iran." 2012 IEEE International Geoscience and Remote Sensing Symposium (2012). DOI: 10.1109/igarss.2012.6352388

Feizizadeh, B., Jankowski, P., and Blaschke, T. "A GIS based spatially-explicit sensitivity and uncertainty analysis approach for multi-criteria decision analysis." *Computers & Geosciences* 64 (2014): 81–95. DOI: 10.1016/j.cageo.2013.11.009

Foumelis, M., Lekkas, E., and Parcharidis, I. "Landslide susceptibility mapping by GIS-based qualitative weighting procedure in Corinth area." *Bulletin of the Geological Society of Greece* 36, no. 2 (2018): 904–912. DOI:10.12681/bgsg.16840

Ghorai, D., Maiti, S., and Paul, A. K. "Landslide susceptibility mapping: a case study of cauvery basin and east flowing rivers south of Cauvery basin, India." *Journal of Remote Sensing and GIS* 6, no. 1 (2015): 24–36.

Ghosh, S., Chakraborty, I., Bhattacharya, D., Bora, A., and Kumar, A. "Generating fields-based inventory of earthquake induced landslides in the aftermath of the 18 September 2011 Sikkim Earthquake." *Indian Journal of Geosciences* 66, no. 1 (2012): 27–38.

Glade, T., and Crozier, M. J. "The nature of landslide hazard impact." In T. Glade, M. G. Anderson, and M. J. Crozier (eds.), *Landslide Hazard and Risk*. Chichester: Wiley (2005): 43–74. DOI:10.1002/97804 70012659.ch2

Greenway, D. R. "Vegetation and slope stability." In: M.G. Anderson, and K.S. Richards (eds.), *Slope Stability*. Wiley, New York (1987): 187–230.

GSI. "A report on Modelling Seismic Susceptibility of Gangtok City, Sikkim." *Geological Survey of India, Kolkata, Bulletin Series – B*, no. 67 (2015): 1–79.

GSI. "A report on macro-scale (1:50,000) landslide susceptibility mapping in parts of toposheets nos.78a /11, *12*, 8 &7 in east, south and west districts, Sikkim." *Geological Survey of India* (2016): 1–95.

GSI. *Seismotectonic Atlas of India and Its Environs*. Geological Survey of India Publication (2000).

Gupta, S., Kaur, H., Parkash, S., and Thapa, R. "Landslide susceptibility zonation of Gangtok city, Sikkim using knowledge driven method (KDM)." *Disaster Advances* 11, no. 11 (2018): 34–43.

Hosseini, S. A., Lotfi, R., Lotfalian, M., Karina, A., and Parsakhoo, A. "The effects of terrain factors on landslide features along forest road." *African journal of Biotechnology* 10, no. 64 (2011): 14108–14115. DOI: 10.5897/AJB11.856

Jaiswal, K., and Sinha, R. "Probabilistic seismic-hazard estimation for Peninsular India." *Bulletin of the Seismological Society of America* 97, no. 1B (2007): 318–330.

Kannan, M., Saranathan, E., and Anbalagan, R. "Comparative Analysis in GIS-based landslide hazard zonation – A case study in Bodi–BodimettuGhat Section, Theni District, Tamil Nadu, India." *Arabian Journal of Geoscience* 8 (2015): 691–699. DOI:10.1007/s12517-013-1259-9

Kanungo, D. P., Arora, M. K., Sarkar, S., and Gupta, R. P. "A comparative study of conventional, ANN black box, fuzzy and combined neural and fuzzy weighting procedures for landslide susceptibility zonation in Darjeeling Himalayas." *Engineering Geology* 85, no. 3–4 (2006): 347–366. DOI: 10.1016/j.enggeo.2 006.03.004

Kaur, H., Gupta, S., and Parkash, S. Comparative evaluation of various approaches for landslide hazard zoning: A critical review in indian perspectives. *Spatial Information Research* 25 (2017): 389–398. DOI:10.1007/s41324-017-0105-7.

Kaur, H., Gupta, S., Parkash, S., Thapa, R., Gupta, A., and Khanal, G. C. "Evaluation of landslide susceptibility in a hill city of Sikkim Himalaya with the perspective of hybrid modelling techniques." *Annals of GIS* 25, no. 2 (2019): 113–132, DOI:10.1080/19475683.2019.1575906.

Kavzoglu, T., Sahin, E. K., and Colkesen, I. "Landslide susceptibility mapping using GIS-based multi-criteria decision analysis, support vector machines, and logistic regression." *Landslides* 11, (2013):425–43. doi:10.1007/s10346-013-0391-7

Koley, B., Nath, A., Saraswati, S., Bandyopadhyay, K., and Ray, B. "Assessment of Rainfall Thresholds for Rain-Induced Landslide Activity in North Sikkim Road Corridor in Sikkim Himalaya, India." *Journal of Geography, Environment and Earth Science International* 19, no. 3 (2019): 1–14. DOI: 10.9734/ jgeesi/2019/v19i330086

Koley, B., Nath, A., Saraswati, S., and Ray, B. C. "Assessment of 2016 Mantam Landslide at Mangan, North Sikkim Himalayas using Geospatial Techniques." *Journal of Scientific Research* 64, no. 2 (2020): 1–9. 10.37398/JSR.2020.640201

Kumar, N. "Macro-scale (1:50,000) landslide susceptibility Mapping in parts of topo-sheets no. 78A/7, 8, 11, 12, East, South and West districts, Sikkim." Unpublished, GSI report of FS 2015-2016 (2015).

Lee, S. "Application and verification of fuzzy algebraic operators to landslide susceptibility mapping." *Environmental Geology* 52 (2007): 615–623. 10.1007/s00254-006-0491-y

Martha, T. R., Govindharaj, K. B., and Kumar, V. "Damage and geological assessment of the 18 September 2011Mw 6.9 earthquake in Sikkim, India using very high-resolution satellite data." *Geoscience Frontiers* 6, no. 6 (2014): 793–805. 10.1016/j.gsf.2013.12.011

Meten, M., Bhandary, N. P., and Yatabe, R. "Application of GIS-based fuzzy logic and rock engineering system (RES) approaches for landslide susceptibility mapping in Selelkula area of the lower Jema River gorge, Central Ethiopia." *Environmental Earth Sciences* 74, no. 4 (2015): 3395–3416. 10.1007/s12665-015-4377-8

Michael, E. A., and Samanta, S. "Landslide vulnerability mapping (LVM) using weighted linear combination (WLC) model through remote sensing and GIS techniques." *Modeling Earth Systems and Environment* 2(2016): 88. 10.1007/s40808-016-0141-7

Nath, A., Koley, B., Saraswati, S., and Ray, B. C. "Identification of the coastal hazard zone between the areas of Rasulpur and Subarnarekha estuary, east coast of India using multi-criteria evaluation method." *Modeling Earth Systems and Environment* 7, (2020):2251–2265.doi.org/10.1007/s40808-020-00986-5

Othmana, A. N., Naim, W. M., and Noraini S. "GIS based multi-criteria decision making for landslide hazard zonation." *Procedia – Social and Behavioral Sciences* 35 (2012): 595–602. doi: 10.1016/j.sbspro.2012.02.126

Park, S., Choi, C., Kim, B., and Kim, J. "Landslide susceptibility mapping using frequency ratio, analytic hierarchy process, logistic regression, and artificial neural network methods at the Inje area, Korea." *Environmental Earth Sciences* 68 (2013): 1443–1464. DOI: 10.1007/s12665-012-1842-5

Pathak, D. "Knowledge based landslide susceptibility mapping in the Himalayas." *Geoenvironmental Disasters* 3 (2016): 8. DOI:10.1186/s40677-016-0042-0.

Pham, B. T., Shirzadi, A., Shahabi, H., Omidvar, E., Singh, S. K., Sahana, M., Asl, D. T., Ahmad, B. B., Quoc, N. K., and Lee, S. "Landslide susceptibility assessment by novel hybrid machine learning algorithms." *Sustainability* 11, no. 16 (2019), 4386. 10.3390/su11164386

Phong, T. V., Phan, T. T., Prakash, I., Singh, S. K., Shirzadi, A., Chapi, K., Ly, H., Si Ho, L., Quoc, N. K., and Pham, B. T. "Landslide susceptibility modeling using different artificial intelligence methods: a case study at Muong Lay district, Vietnam." *Geocarto International* (2019). vol 36 no 15:1685 –1708. 10.1080/10106049.2019.1665715

Prakasam, C., Aravinth, R., Kanwar, V. S., and Nagarajan, B. "Landslide Hazard Mapping Using Geo-Environmental Parameters—A Case Study on Shimla Tehsil, Himachal Pradesh." In: J. Ghosh, and I. da Silva (eds.), *Applications of Geomatics in Civil Engineering*. Lecture Notes in Civil Engineering, Springer, Singapore, *33* (2020). 10.1007/978-981-13-7067-0_9

Preuth, T., Glade, T., and Demoulin, A. "Stability analysis of a human-influenced landslides in eastern Belgium." *Geophysical Journal of the Royal Astronomical Society* 120 (2010): 4–98. 10.1016/j.geomorph.2009.09.013

Psomiadis, F., Charizopoulos, N., Efthimiou, N., Soulis, K. X., and Charalampopoulos, I. "Earth observation and GIS-based analysis for landslide susceptibility and risk assessment." *International Journal of Geo-Information* 9 (2020): 552. doi:10.3390/ijgi9090552

Raghuvanshi, T. K., Negassa, L., and Kala, P. M. "GIS based grid overlay method versus modelling approach – A comparative study for landslide hazard zonation (LHZ) in Meta Robi District of West Showa Zone in Ethiopia." *The Egyptian Journal of Remote Sensing and Space Sciences* 18 (2015): 235–250. 10.1016/j.ejrs.2015.08.001

Razifard, M., Shoaei, G., and Zare, M. "Application of fuzzy logic in the preparation of hazard maps of landslides triggered by the twin Ahar-Varzeghan earthquakes." *Bulletin of Engineering Geology and the Environment* 78 (2018): 223–245. 10.1007/s10064-018-1235-4

Reichenbach, P., Rossi, M., Malamu, B. D., Mihir, M., and Guzzetti, F. "A review of statistically-based landslide susceptibility models." *Earth-Science Reviews* 180 (2018): 60–91. 10.1016/j.earscirev.2018.03.001

Roy, J., and Saha, S. "Landslide susceptibility mapping using knowledge driven statistical models in Darjeeling District, West Bengal, India." *Geoenvirontal Disasters* 6 (2019): 11. 10.1186/s40677-019-0126-8

Saaty, T. "Decision making with the analytical hierarchy process." *International Journal of Services Sciences* 1, no. 1 (2008): 83–98.

Samia, J., Temme, A., Bregt, A. K., Wallinga, J., Stuiver, J., Guzzetti, F., Ardizzone, F., and Rossi, M. "Implementing landslide path dependency in landslide susceptibility modeling." *Landslides* (2018): 1–16. DOI:10.1007/s10346-018-1024-y

Sarma, A. K., Josi, V., and Kumar, K. "Landslide hazard zonation of Gangtok area, Sikkim Himalaya, using remote sensing and GIS techniques." *Journal of Geometrics* 5, no. 2 (2011), 85–90.

Senouci, R., Taibi, N. E., Teodoro, A. C., Duarte, L., Mansour, H., and Yahia Meddah, R. "GIS-based expert knowledge for landslide susceptibility mapping (LSM): Case of Mostaganem Coast District, West of Algeria." *Sustainability* 13 (2021): 630. 10.3390/su13020630

Shahabi, H., Khezri, S., Ahmad, B. B., and Hashim, M. "Landslide susceptibility mapping at central Zab basin, Iran: A comparison between analytical hierarchy process, frequency ratio and logistic regression models." *Catena* 115 (2014): 55–70. 10.1016/j.catena.2013.11.014

Shano, L., Raghuvanshi, T. K., and Meten, M. "Landslide susceptibility evaluation and hazard zonation techniques – a review." *Geoenvironmental Disasters* 7 (2020): 18. 10.1186/s40677-020-00152-0

Shirzadi, A., Bui, D. T., Pham, B. T., Solaimani, K., Chapi, K., Kavian, A., Shahabi, H., and Revhaug, I. "Shallow landslide susceptibility assessment using a novel hybrid intelligence approach." *Environmental Earth Sciences* 76, no. 2 (2011): 60. 10.1007/s12665-016-6374-y

Shit, P. K., Bhunia, G. S., and Maiti, R. "Potential landslide susceptibility mapping using weighted overlay model (WOM)." *Modeling Earth Systems and Environment* 2 (2016): 21. DOI 10.1007/s40808-016-0078-x

Van Westen, C. J., Castellanos, E., and Kuriakose, S. L. "Spatial Data for Landslide Susceptibility, Hazard, and Vulnerability Assessment: An Overview." *Engineering Geology* 102, no. 3–4 (2008): 112–131. DOI:10.1016/j.enggeo.2008.03.010

Wang, W. D., Xie, C. M., and Du, X. G. "Landslides susceptibility mapping based on geographical information system, GuiZhou, south-west China." *Environmental Geology* 58, no. 1 (2009): 33–43. 10.1007/s00254-008-1488-5

Yalcin, A., Reis, S., Aydinoglu, A. C., and Yomralioglu, T. "A GIS-based comparative study of frequency ratio, analytical hierarchy process, bivariate statistics and logistics regression methods for landslide susceptibility mapping in Trabzon, NE Turkey." *Catena* 85, no. 3 (2011): 274–287. DOI: 10.1016/j.catena.2011.01.014

Yan, G., Liang, S., Gui, X., Xie, Y., and Zhao, H.. "Optimizing landslide susceptibility mapping in the Kongtong district, NW China: comparing the subdivision criteria of factors." *Geocarto International* (2018): 34, 13 :1–19. doi.org/10.1080/10106049.2018.1499816

Youssef, A. M., Pradhan, B., Jebur, M. N., and El-Harbi, H. M. Landslide susceptibility mapping using ensemble bivariate and multivariate statistical models in Fayfa area, Saudi Arabia." *Environmental Earth Sciences* (2014). DOI: vol. 73 no. 7: 3745–3761. DOI 10.1007/s12665-014-3661-3

Zhu, A. X., Wang, R. X., Qiao, J. P., Qin, C. Z., Chen, Y. B., Liu, J., Du, F., Yang, L., and Zhu, T. X. "An expert knowledge-based model to landslide susceptibility mapping using GIS and fuzzy logic." *Geomorphology* 214 (2014): 128–138. DOI: 10.1016/j.geomorph.2014.02.003

Youssef, A. M., Pradhan, B., Pourghasemi, H. R., and Abdullahi S. "Landslide susceptibility assessment at Wadi Jawrah Basin, Jizan region, Saudi Arabia using two bivariate models in GIS." *Geosciences Journal*, 19 no. 3 (2015). 449–469. DOI 10.1007/s12303-014-0065-z

22 Designing Sustainable Urban Blocks: An Effort to Optimizing 3D Form and Achieving Maximum Amount of Solar Radiation

Amir Shakibamanesh and Omid Veisi
Art University, Tehran, Iran

CONTENTS

22.1 URBAN BLOCK: FROM THEORETICAL APPROACHES TO PRACTICAL CONCEPTS

A block has been one of the main concerns of the charter of the new urbanism. Designers of this era have always emphasized the recapture of houses, blocks, streets, parks, neighborhoods, cities, and the environment (Urbanism 2000). The charter pays special attention to "blocks, streets and buildings" and proposes solutions that are normatively used like "form-based code" and the use of transects to shape policies (Duany and Talen 2002). Form-based codes cope with existing conditions by providing instructions for dividing huge blocks. The block proposed by the new urbanists, Moule and Polyzoides (1994), is a rectangle that is 76 meters wide and 183 meters long. Form-based codes examine dimensions and consider blocks larger than 152 m or with a circumference of less than 488 m optimal (Parolek, Parolek, and Crawford 2008).

DOI: 10.1201/9781003126195-27

The shape of the contemporary city has been identified as a source of environmental, social, and economic problems (Pakzad and Salari 2018). Urban sprawl resulting from human activities is directly related to global energy consumption. Small and scattered urban forms lead to an increase in personal mobility and will have a direct impact on the lifestyle and consumption patterns of households in various spatial configurations. The result is that current urban planning is not a process that ensures energy efficiency across cities, and depends entirely on fossil fuel energy. On the other hand, more concise and integrated urban models are an important pillar for efficient and sustainable use of energy resources, especially in transportation of local production-consumption chains (Amado, Poggi, and Amado 2016). Now the question that can be posed in this area is: What size, shape, orientation, and characteristics of the urban block can create the most optimal conditions to reduce energy consumption in a city?

22.1.1 Urban Block: The Challenge

Urban physical-geographical approaches besides land use analysis play an essential role in tackling the complexity of cities. Many of these approaches are exploited in analysis of various aspects of urban development in spatial macro-scales such as urban shape and distribution of the city growth or population density. This comprises many interrelated methods and tools (Amado et al. 2017). In initial design stages, urban designers combine and manipulate mass models in order to operate a rapid test on different urban morphologies. Data type varies in mass models depending on the designers; it can include a various range of building type, architectural type, land use, and infrastructural data. Mass models with geometrical data can provide qualitative and quantitative feedback for the designers. From a quantity viewpoint, mass models can be used to present descriptive data of some design aspects like density and building height calculation (Chen and Norford 2017; Table 22.1).

Typological attitude (spatial configuration) investigates the basic structures of the city as usable patterns in the urban structure. Hence, a study of these structures offers some patterns and general schemes of the amount of energy consumption related to other patterns, as well as optimization of forms according to their totality. So, in this chapter of the book, spatial configuration is used simultaneously in order to obtain general indicators and optimization of energy consumption regarding the initial block patterns and their general structures. In the following, the structure and variables of usable urban blocks in energy calculations are studied.

22.1.2 Urban Block: Definitions and History

Cities, whether they are planned or organic, produce a broad spectrum of blocks and buildings that are different from each other in terms of size and shape. These are the results of different attitudes in urban design, but they are all produced based on the main elements of building a city: building, plot, block, and street (Vialard 2013). A block is defined when its boundaries are clearly defined and then this definition is challenged. Moreover, a block is initially a piece of land that is defined everywhere by a mass of roads and also planned and unplanned streets (Pakzad and Salari 2018). In order to understand an urban housing, it is essential to understand the concept of a complex relationship between a residential unit and urban form. A city structure cannot be evaluated without any idea about how habitable units work in a significant city block. On the other hand, urban shape influences the type of residential units and requires some rules to design blocks, sizes, shapes, and their directions and also street dimensions (Kamell 1996; Table 22.2).

22.1.3 Sustainable Urban Block

An urban environment consists of buildings with a number of floors with a range of variables that are separated from each other via streets. From the point of view of solar energy evaluation, urban

TABLE 22.1
Urban Morphological Attitudes

Schools	Principles	Parameters	Parameters of Block Analysis
Historical-geographical attitude	Investigation of how and why the cities are built	City plan (streets and their organization, land plots and the way they are gathered in a block and the block design), building forms, and functions	City plan (streets and their organization, land plots and the way they are gathered in a block and the block design), building forms
Spatial analysis attitude	Interactions between the components	Adding visual elements (three-dimensional urban landscape studies) and perceptional elements (perception of residents and beneficiaries)	
Spatial configuration attitude	Process and attitude of typology and how the cities are built	Elements (buildings), building of the elements (urban fabric), and system structures and organism systems (urban area or districts)	Elements (buildings)
Process typology attitude	Activities and programs inside of the buildingsDistricting and zoning of the buildings according to the activity	Elements (buildings), schedule of changes	Elements (buildings)

Source: (Shi, Fonseca, and Schlueter 2017).

TABLE 22.2
Classification of Research in terms of Urban Blocks

Data Analysis	Analytical Methods	Center of Attention
Sustainability of urban block	Image processing technique	Environmental issues specifically energy consumption
	Case study	Sustainability of urban shape
Quantitative evaluation of urban shape	Quantitative evaluation of indicators	Connection and density of urban block
Geometry of urban block	Qualitative evaluation	Urban block and morphological specifications
	Analytical method, comparative study	Investigation of the impact of size and block form on urban development
	Comparative study	Size, shape, and configuration of urban blocks
Urban form codes	–	Ideal values for urban blocks
Urban form	Theory of diagram	Relationships between the connections of the built forms, surrounding environment, and the transport network

Source: (Pakzad and Salari, 2018).

objects can be classified as land, buildings, and trees (Redweik, Catita, and Brito 2013). Discussions about ideal or desired urban form dates back to the late 1900s and Howard's suggestions (Jabareen 2006). Traditionally, morphology of the urban block has been shaped by some issues like land use, transportation, financial affairs, and globalization. Therefore, many of the recent urban blocks have been planned inattentively to improving the urban variables, study of open space conditions, respect to the neighbors, and enhancement of social relationships. Apparently, the process of urban block formation is long and complicated (Oikonomou 2015). Furthermore, despite the studies done on various aspects, still there is a little knowledge on specifications and function of different block sizes, shapes, and arrangements in terms of rotation, land use, building form, and some other aspects (Siksna 1997).

In order to understand the planning of an energy-efficient city, an extensive study has been conducted in Europe on the evidence about the relationship between energy consumption and urban form, solar potentials and urban morphology, energy performance of the buildings, and projects developed in various European cities. Recently, some research has been done to initiate a move towards a sustainable and low-carbon society, which shows that energy efficiency in urban areas is more cost-effective than optimizing each building individually (Amado, Francesca, and Amado 2016). According to sustainable development, strategies should mainly focus on local level and micro-scale rather than macro-scale. It sounds trivial that one of the main reasons of this fact is that the existing urban structures are very much permanent and applying changes in a macro-level is really difficult. Thus, in a micro-level, implementing strategic arrangements in an urban block level is fairly easier (Pakzad and Salari 2018). Urban shape changes in a block scale directly affects outdoor climate, including the impact of heat islands and air pollution emission; and it indirectly influences the quality of indoor environments and energy consumption via demands for artificial lighting, heating, and air ventilation (Osmond 2008). Therefore, designing a sustainable block according to a study of different variables and optimizations of each variable can lead to an optimized state and designing a sustainable city.

22.2 INTRODUCTION TO SOLAR ENERGY: A FRIENDLY RENEWABLE ENERGY

Energy production and specifically electrical energy production is one of the major problems to be solved in our world. One of the solutions is to use environmentally friendly energy resources. The use of renewable energy resources is a potential solution to this problem. Among all kinds of renewable energy resources, solar energy is the most abundant and unlimited one (Karathanasis 2019). Radiation is defined as the amount of solar energy that reaches a surface in the unit of time and unit of surface. In other words, radiation is density of the emitted flux or it is simply called flux (Iqbal 2012). Moreover, it is important to note that solar performance in every city should be measured via different methods according to the climate (Chen and Norford 2017). Solar radiation travels through the space from the sun to the space-atmosphere interface, where the ionization layer of the atmosphere ends, and finally enters the atmosphere. Then the atmosphere, clouds, and existing particles of the atmosphere absorb a specific amount of solar radiation or photons; the space reflects a specific amount and the ground absorbs a specific amount of it. In addition, the ground surface, due to its temperature, reflects a specific amount of energy by radiating it through various wavelengths. Around 50% of the total solar radiation remains in the ground atmosphere and surface. Direct sunshine can be diffused in two different ways: reflected on the ground surface or return to the outside of the atmosphere (Sen 2008; Figure 22.1).

Although solar energy is one of the renewable energies and is the cleanest one, its huge potentials have extensively remained unused. In order to develop low-energy buildings in sustainable cities, reduce carbon emission, or maximize passive solar heating, it is essential to increase the knowledge of exploiting solar energy (Bizjak, Žalik, and Lukač 2015). Accordingly, not only some fundamental changes need to be applied to reduce the amount of energy we use, but also to the way this energy is produced. Recent statistics have revealed that all of the renewable energy resources may provide

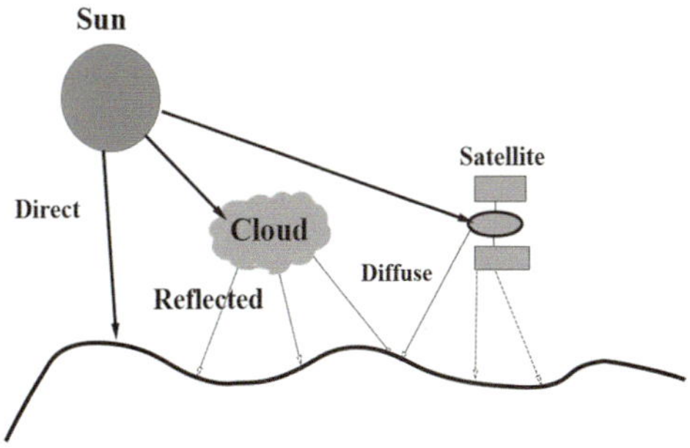

FIGURE 22.1 Solar radiation paths. a Direct. b Diffuse. c Reflected (Sen, 2008).

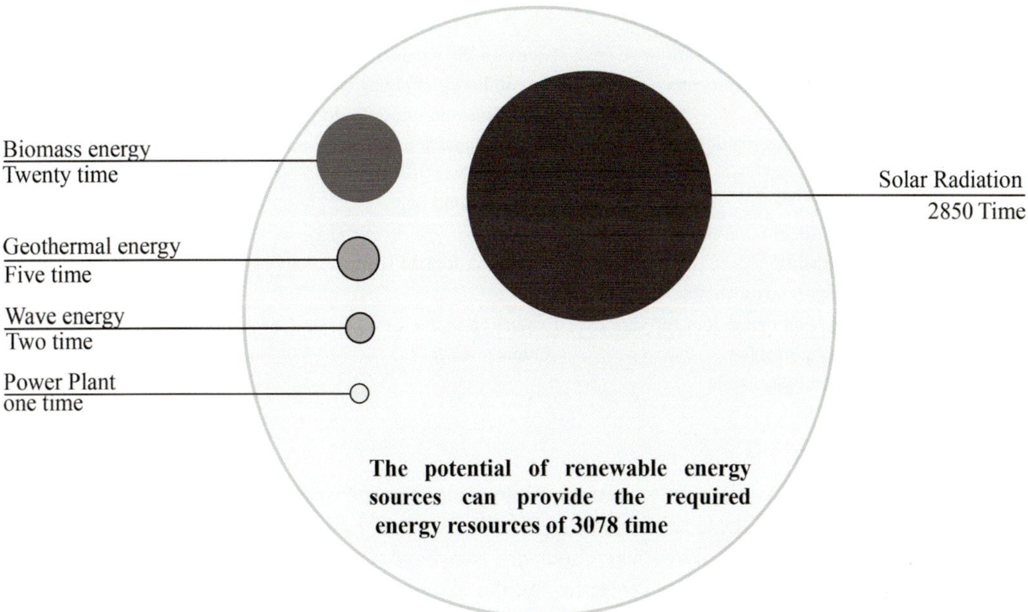

FIGURE 22.2 Theoretical potential of renewable energy resources in comparison with global energy requirements (Horvat and Wall 2012).

3,078 times more energy than the current global energy requirement. Among all renewable energies, solar energy has the greatest potential, as shown in Figure 22.2. This energy in itself ensures 2,850 times more energy than the annual global required energy (Horvat and Wall 2012).

22.2.1 Solar Radiation: Modeling and Simulation

Energy system modeling of the buildings and the cities is often considered an open or closed energy system. It deals with internal procedures and energy or some materials and interactions in the system border (Yang and Yan 2016). The high level of accuracy that can be obtained by the vector-based method offers appropriate conditions to study of the smaller areas; for instance, a building at a district scale. Moreover, adding the necessary level of details to obtain solar fluxes in a broad and complicated area (for instance at a city scale) has a relatively high cost of calculation. Besides, this method is vector based and improves the reflection network approaches for large-scale functions. Most of the aforementioned models estimate the sky radiation based on a clear and bright sky and also evaluation of resolution. There are some other methods to use solar radiation observation in order to increase the accuracy while evaluating the surface radiation (Lindberg et al. 2015).

TABLE 22.3
Different Tools for Analysis of Energy Models in Urban Scale

Tools	Function	Analyzable Scales	Reference
GIS	• Study of the Geographical Information System (GIS) evaluation of the energy usage • Using 2.5D data Freely available	Evaluation of energy consumption in the urban scale with the statistical method of urban criteria	(Groppi et al. 2018)
EnergyPlus	• Modeling, heating, cooling, lighting, and ventilation This software is available freely.	Evaluation in the building scale	(Fesanghary et al. 2012)
Ladybug	• Energy analysis in various scales • Parametric analysis and optimization • Currently available	Focus on the parametric method and the possibility of applying different methods of optimization in order to provide a direct connection to Python program in the city block scale and neighborhood unit	(Roudsari 2017)
Citysim	• Main focus is on urban energy calculation • Not currently available	Evaluation in the district scale using 3D models in limited scales	(Vermeulen, Kämpf, and Beckers 2013)
simscale	• This is an online tool for various climatic analysis • Currently available	Evaluation in the district scale for various climatic analysis	(Crahmaliuc)

In order to perform a solar analysis in an urban scale, experts exploit some specialized recently developed tools. Some of these tools are: CitySim, DIVA, and Ladybug. These tools enhance solar analysis for design purposes. However, there are two factors that confine the implementation of these tools to urban design and planning; firstly, the expertise for simulation in a required time for creation of a model in the urban scale and secondly, the required software applications for some of these analysis in large scales (Morganti et al. 2017). Table 22.3 indicates some of the tools and their functions concisely.

22.3 A REVIEW OF OPTIMIZATION ALGORITHM

Evaluation of the quality of calibration models to determine the best possible calibration method is available to the experts. These features have a variety of approaches ranging from manual graphical methods to statistical analysis and optimization-based methods. The second type usually requires less judgment from the users; therefore, it offers more opportunities for automation of the calibration process. Considering time limitations, for many buildings there is no possibility for manual calibration; hence, in the field of urban energy simulation, automation is an essential issue (Sokol 2015). The first comprehensive review of calibration methods was conducted by Reddy et al. as part of the ASHRAE 1051 research project. Reddy combined the most successful methods and obtained a multi-step partially automated method based on sensitivity analysis and two-step optimization (Reddy, Maor, and Panjapornpon 2007a, b). Following Reddy's analysis, many other studies have been conducted on calibration, which are categorized into three divisions: optimization, Bayesian calibration, and meta modeling (Sokol 2015). In this study, the optimization method has been adopted for calibration of the urban block model.

In the next investigations, a collection of optimization algorithms has been studied. Many articles and books have reviewed and introduced optimization algorithms from various viewpoints

TABLE 22.4
Population Methods for Optimization

Algorithms	Variable	Analysis	Source
Differential Evolution	Continuous parameters	• Optimization of height dimension and glass ratio according to the thermal dimensions of urban buildings • Optimization of radiation calculation on buildings • Tools used Citysim, RADIANCE oconv	(Vermeulen, Kämpf, and Beckers 2013, Kämpf and Robinson 2010)
Genetic Algorithms	Continuous parameters	• Optimization urban block • Optimization process with the Grasshopper tool and Ladybug plug-in	(Xu et al. 2019)
Particle Swarm Optimization	Continuous parameters multi-objective	• Optimization of parameter energy models in building scale	(Hamdy et al. 2016)

(Andreasson, Patriksson, and Evgrafov 2020; Baldick 2006; Arora 2015). Some of them, which are broadly used, are the evolutionary optimization family such as genetic algorithm (Affenzeller et al. 2009, Caldas and Norford 2002), swarm of intelligence, and hybrid family (Kämpf et al. 2010). According to the recent studies, among all optimization methods based on simulation for analysis, some of them are more popular. The most popular optimization algorithms are PSO, GA (particle swarm optimization), differential evolution, firefly algorithm, cuckoo search, and hybrid methods (Kochenderfer and Wheeler 2019). In this research, GA (genetic algorithms) optimization method has been used, which has been already examined in many other previous studies in the field of urban studies and architecture and the results have been accurate (Table 22.4).

22.4 METHODOLOGY: OPTIMIZATION PROBLEMS

Throughout the time, different types of urban modeling techniques have been proposed for space energy demand patterns in buildings. They are known in two main categories (Cerezo Davila 2017). General "top-down" models link urban energy consumption in a national, regional, or urban scale with statistical variables such as population procedure and economical activities (Howard et al. 2012). The top-down approach comprises the use of energy consumption of an area in a specific period of time (usually annually) and dividing it into sections assigned to specific groups of buildings. The bottom-up approach adopts the reverse path and creates models in the level of individual buildings with identical energy consumption. Then an appraisal is operated for the entire existing buildings in a complex (Sokol 2015). However, statistical models require a great collection of data from calculated energy consumption, which are rarely available to modelers other than annual data; therefore, they are unable to assess lower time scales or predict the impact of the new technologies. In order to address these shortages, some bottom-up "engineering" models that are "physic-based" are presented in which building requirements are estimated analytically via specific properties of fundamental models (Firth, Lomas, and Wright 2009). There are two bottom-up methods as following: firstly, engineering method (EM) which creates building engineering models with the BEM software or simplified thermal models and secondly, statistical method (SM) that uses black box modeling (Swan and Ugursal 2009). Figure 22.3 indicates the analysis of methods used for residential energy consumption modeling. These are comparable with urban energy modeling for every building type.

The common method to obtain the best urban variables parameterizes the relevant variables in description of the buildings and probably the existing spatial relationships among the buildings. It

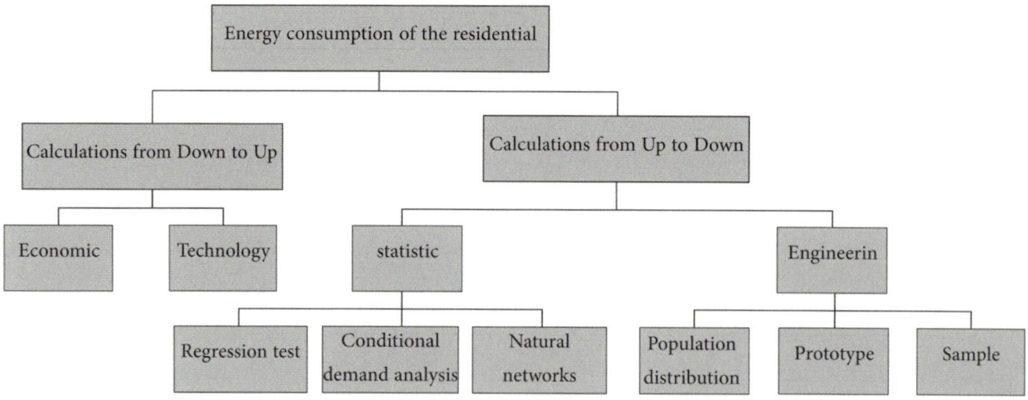

FIGURE 22.3 Techniques used to estimate the residential energy consumption in the regional or national scale (Swan and Ugursal 2009).

also determines which of these parameters maximizes the potential for solar energy usage. In the case of some discrete variables, it is probably possible to examine all of the available facilities congregationally. However, when the parameter space for exploration becomes large and very large, it is desired to use optimization algorithms. Using such algorithms, we should be able to find the universal maximum (maximum possible amount) of function f, which is dependent on independent decision-making variables (Kämpf and Robinson 2010; Figure 22.4).

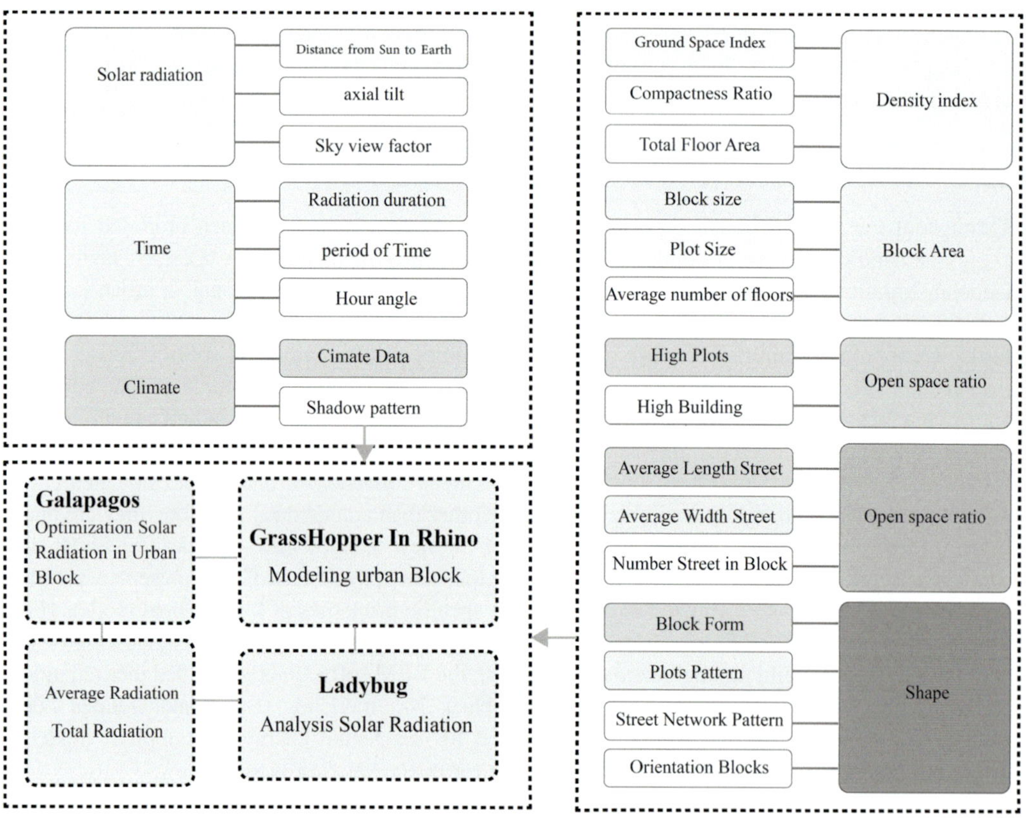

FIGURE 22.4 Graph of the influential variables and the procedure of urban block form optimization.

22.4.1 Genetic Algorithms: Simulated Annealing

A genetic algorithm is an advanced algorithm used in optimization of urban cells. This algorithm is based on a population of individuals evolving over generations to enhance the received value by target performance (Eiben and Smith 2015). There are three main reasons for choosing this algorithm: (i) due to the similarity, various geometries can collect the same amount of solar radiation. Thus, there can be several local solutions. Evolutionary algorithms are appropriately adaptable to solve these kinds of non-convex problems. (ii) These algorithms are able to manage continuous variables. (iii) These documents are potential to be arranged properly, easily executed, and parallelized (Nguyen, Reiter, and Rigo 2014). The main properties of the algorithm are summarized below (Figure 22.5).

This algorithm uses an initial unit of population and the evaluation of the individuals or the usage of genetic operators occurs in a parallel way. Accordingly, every person may compete or pair with any other person. The most common parallel operation is the evaluation of the individuals, because the fitness of an individual is independent from the rest of the population and there is no need for communication in this stage. The evaluation of the individuals becomes parallel by specifying a fraction of the population to every available processor (Sivanandam and Deepa 2007).

In this research, developing an urban data algorithm has been adopted using a genetic algorithm in the Galapagos plug-in to optimize solar energy data in the urban block. This is illustrated in Figure 22.6. In the preliminary research, there is a need for an initial population. In this research,

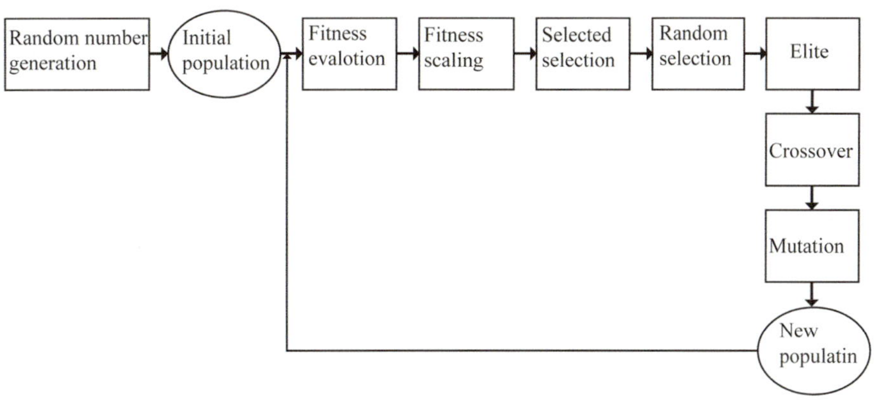

FIGURE 22.5 Flow chart of genetic algorithm (Pham and Karaboga 2012).

```
produce an initial population of individuals
for all individuals do in parallel
        evaluate the individual's fitness
end parallel for
while not termination condition do
        select fitter individuals for reproduction
        produce new individuals
        mutate some individuals
        for all individuals do in parallel
                evaluate the individual's fitness
        end parallel for
        generate a new population by inserting some new good individuals
        and by discarding some old bad individuals
end while
```

FIGURE 22.6 Pseudocode of genetic algorithm.

the initial population comprises 50 cases. Among these 50 people, some of them, usually 5% of the whole population, are known as the best choices. Therefore, these choices are identified as parents and are paired with each other to produce another particle known as a child. The selected people are kept in the population for the next generation. In order to ensure the accuracy of selection and research, a term called a mutation is exploited. It optimizes a number of random search samples in the whole process and in the searchable environment, while every stage of the genetic optimization algorithm is operated. If a visible sample is detected as the maximum sample, it will be added to the research as a testable sample. Then it will go to the next stage alongside with the newborn children, who are the winners of the competition. The process of optimization is repeated until the maximum number of generations is achieved or until the convergence criterion is attained. The maximum number of generations for the target performance is set according to the annual direct and diffused radiation of a day in a bright sky. If 50 generations are successful and the amount of the function target is evaluated as less than the current evaluation, the search will stop. This amount increases the search time practically. In this research, up to ten generations of the search have been stopped by the researcher, manually depending on the search conditions and whether variables remain constant or not.

22.4.2 Simulation and Analysis Solar Radiation in Urban Block

Generally, the field of study comprises three stages: model production, analysis, and optimization. In the first stage, simulation of the environment has been created via the Grasshopper parametric modeling tool in the Rhinoceros3D software (McNeel 2010). In the second stage, Ladybug plug-ins (Roudsari 2017) are used in Grasshopper to study and analyze the solar radiation energy. Finally, in the third stage, the model optimization has been done by genetic algorithm. This workflow includes an optimization via Galapagos tool, modeling of the three-dimensional building parameters and embodiment of the results in a unified way. Meteorological data from the Kermanshah Province in Iran has been used as an input for solar radiation in the form of EPW file (EnergyPlus_Development_Team 2020; Figure 22.7).

22.5 CASE STUDY: MODEL DEVELOPMENT OF URBAN BLOCK

Six general urban layouts have been studied according to the building prototype shapes in cold and mountainous weather. Potentials of solar radiation absorption have been surveyed in this study. According to the obtained calculations from digital elevation models (DEM), the operated studies revealed that the type of central courtyard commonly used in this kind of regional climate is more advantages than the other types in thermal and daylight performances (Zhang et al. 2019). Moreover, the impact of the urban block type on the usage of energy and heat facilitation have been studied by Taleghani et al. They have found that the ratio of surface to volume is a considerable geometrical factor and the central courtyard model performs better compared with singular and linear models (Taleghani et al. 2013). However, it has been unknown that how and under which conditions in these forms enhancement of the heat facilitation can be achieved. Rode et al. in their survey of urban architectural style have studied various patterns and shapes of the initial patterns; consequently, they have found that urban morphological factors can influence the efficiency of thermal energy up to six times. They have also found that in an urban neighborhood scale, compact and high buildings are more energy efficient compared with detached houses (Rode et al. 2014).

Different urban blocks which are analyzed in this study that have various geometrical parameters (height, surface area, and surface-to-volume ratio) in different patterns. Each urban block as a pattern is assumed as a representative of a special kind of urban block in the city fabric of the city of Kermanshah. These blocks are shaped by a number of ordinary buildings seemingly representing the most common building types in Kermanshah. This study has adopted a typological approach for evaluation of the urban block energy in the Farhangian-Faz1 district of the city of

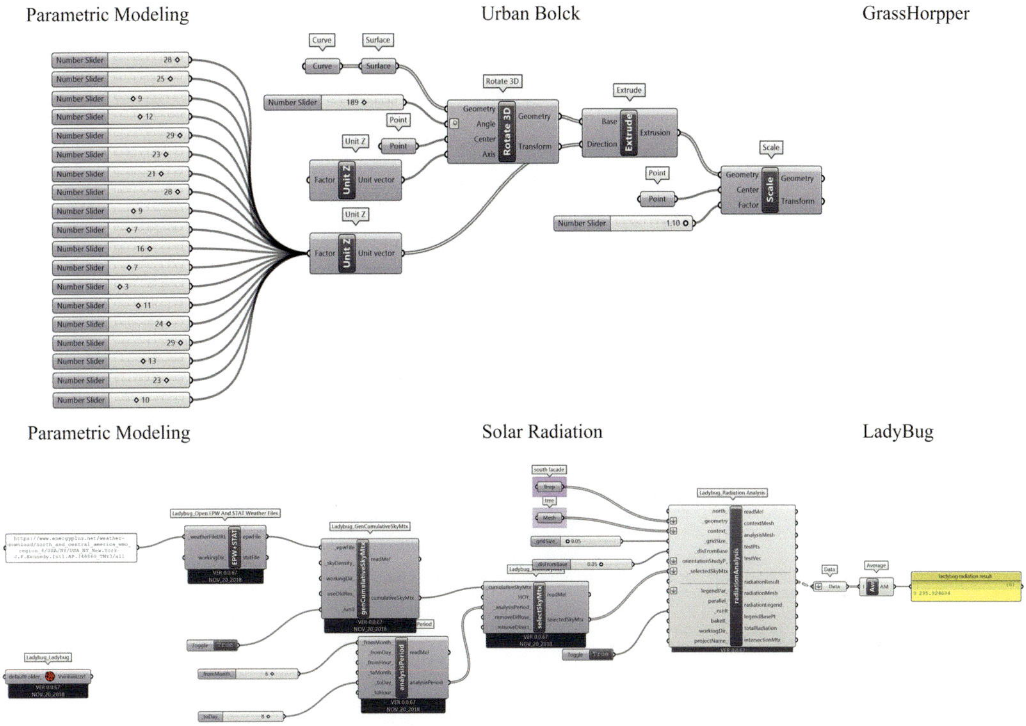

FIGURE 22.7 Parametric algorithm of urban blocks and solar radiation.

Kermanshah. This is achieved by a simulation based on realities and previous studies in the field of thermal energy consumption evaluation in the city scale.

Figure 22.8 indicates that this analysis in district 2 of the city of Kermanshah comprises the following four morphological indicators of the urban blocks: 1) building height, 2) volume-to-area ratio, 3) building dimension proportions, and 4) urban block direction. It has been already proved that the aforementioned indicators have a causative relationship with energy performance in the city scale. Therefore, a typology is manually defined providing the following conditions: 1) the configuration patterns correspond to various types of urban blocks, 2) the size of the blocks is displayed differently and corresponds to the real world, 3) the built volume of every configuration is exactly equal to one of the optimization cases with a different orientation in the scale of .9 to 1.1; scale variation in this interval is for measuring the amount of urban block tendency to compact or spread block.

Investigation of the block maps of the Farhangian District indicates that the site is divided into six categories (tower kind, segmental, courtyard, interconnected, centralized, and peripheral) in terms of prevailing types. Figure 22.9 categorizes the urban block patterns of the previous studies (Zhang et al. 2019), which will be analyzed and optimized on behalf of the prevailing site patterns. These patterns are selected from 224 urban blocks in 602,380 square meters in the Farhangian-Fazl District.

22.6 RESULT AND DISCUSSION: OPTIMIZATION ALGORITHMS BETWEEN URBAN BLOCK AND SOLAR RADIATION

In this study, a block is assumed as an integrated element with a constant form surrounded by the streets. The dimension height of the blocks is supposed to be within the maximum local standards; namely, 10 floors or 30 meters. Therefore, the height range varies from 0 to 30 meters. It should be noted that in this study, the dimension height of the parts resulted from the height data of Google Earth and field visits and is simulated from the real perceptions of the environment. An important

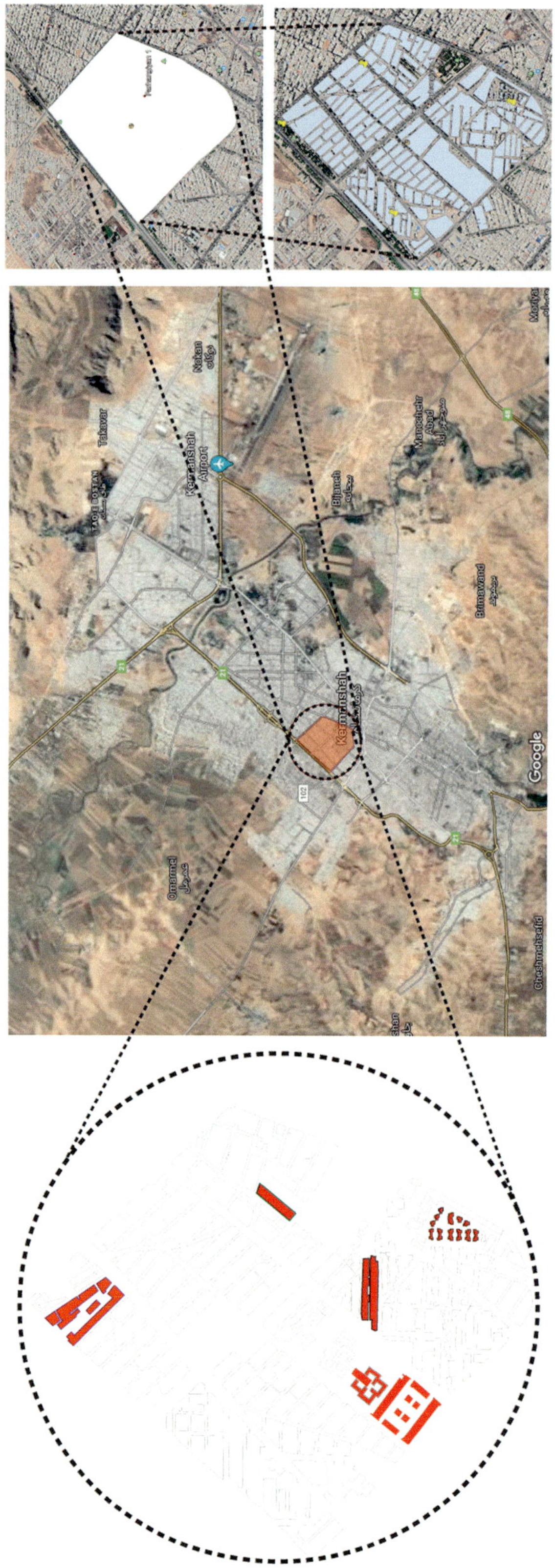

FIGURE 22.8 Location Kermanshah, Farhangian-Faz1.

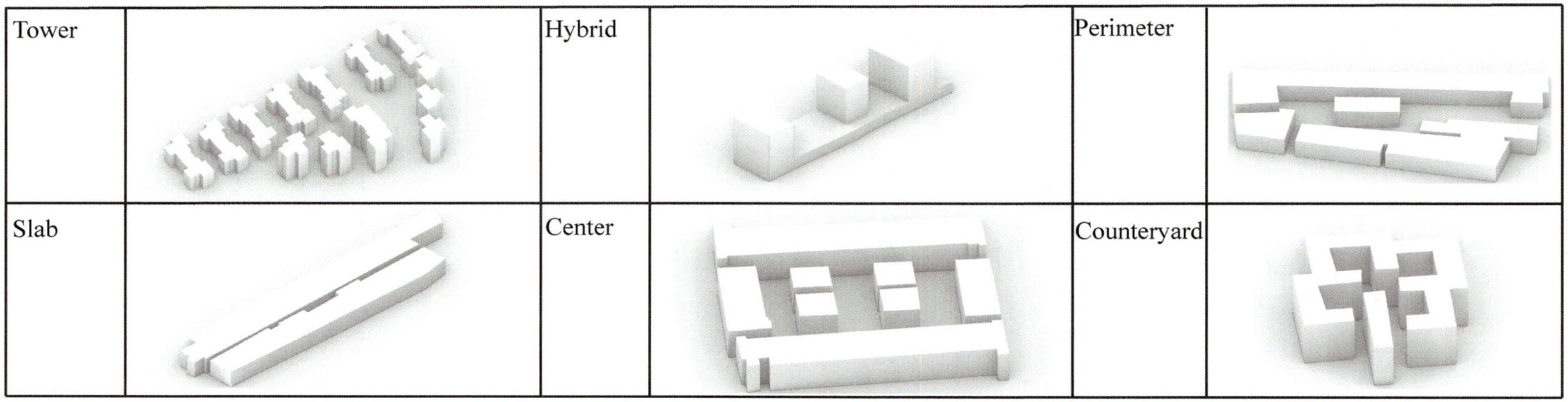

FIGURE 22.9 A pattern of urban blocks.

consideration in this research is to preserve the block integrity and to prevent from any changes on the identity of the shapes and forms via variation in nature and disconnection between the blocks.

The annual analysis of urban blocks in the Farhangian-Fazl District is illustrated in Figure 22.10. The presented numbers in this scale are in the unit of kilowatt hour per square meter. In the following, the research data are analyzed to reveal the fact that which of the research patterns absorb the radiation most and how the other patterns can be optimized in terms of orientation and other searchable variables. In general terms, what will be the behavior of the form when confronting with different variables in the optimization algorithm in order to achieve the maximum radiation absorption.

Furthermore, Figure 22.10 provides a considerable amount of data about the impact of geographical orientation on surface radiation and also urban elevation codes compared with adjacent surfaces and even roof surfaces in some cases such as block E, which is the hybrid mode. These figures indicate that in all cases, the roof has the most amount of radiation. Then the south facades of the building and finally, the western parts have the most amount of radiation. Considering the area of each block, it is expected that the block A has the highest amount of radiation absorption and the block E has the lowest amount. This is proved by the research results. Hence, the priority is to influence the block area in absorbing radiation. Another important concern in this research is the height, which creates the amount of wall surfaces. This needs to be examined by various tests and volumetric optimizations.

Analysis of the solar radiation pattern in various urban block patterns reveals an important point. That is the grading of the components, which forms the urban block, is effective on the amount of solar radiation absorption, while maintaining the integrity of the urban block. Research data investigation displays that the perimeter pattern and the center pattern with the approximate radiation absorption rate of respectively 43 and 30 have the highest amounts. This is shown in Table 22.5 as Radiation Year_ Block B and Radiation Year_ Block A. This data is based on the area of each pattern in accordance with the initial expectation. In spite of this correspondence, Figure 22.13 clearly indicates that a factor different than the coefficient of the areas is influential in this radiation. On the other hand, calculation of different seasons shows that summer and spring have the highest and winter has the lowest amount of radiation absorption (Figure 22.11).

Table 22.6 shows that Chi-square tests have been used to investigate the relationship between urban block pattern variables and the amount of radiation absorption. The statistics show a significant relationship between the block types and the radiation amount. In these statistics, Sig = .000, which shows a strong relationship between the research variables (Figure 22.12).

In this stage, the blocks are optimized via the genetic algorithm in the Galapagos plug-in. All the block grading is parametrically designed and is capable of height change in the domain of 30 meters. Therefore, the blocks can change in an integrated way in a two-dimensional scale along the Y and X vectors from .5 to 1.1. This is the amount in which the volumes can be moved into the streets.

In this research, the SPSS software has been used for complicated statistical analysis and the collection of Office Excel software has been exploited to depict data and graphical statistics. In order to show a significant relationship among a set of data, two options need to be studied: I) The first option is the normality of data. In this investigation, the process of data change is studied to check whether data follows a certain procedure or not. As it is illustrated in Figure 22.13, to check the normality of data, the Normal P-P plot test has been used. It has revealed that the data follows a certain increasing procedure in all the block patterns and its relative variables such as average height changes, the amount of solar radiation absorption, scale, and orientation. Therefore, apparently the data has been in a normal condition. II) The next option is to study the relationship between the data via correlations analysis in the bivariate mode. If Sig≤.05, the zero assumption is rejected and a significant statistical difference is shown in the average of the results from the case study variables. Otherwise, if in the statistical test .07 ≤ Sig > .05, there is a weak relationship between the research variables. This means that it is not possible to confirm or reject the assumption, which regards the relationship between the research variables as zero. For Sin>.07, the

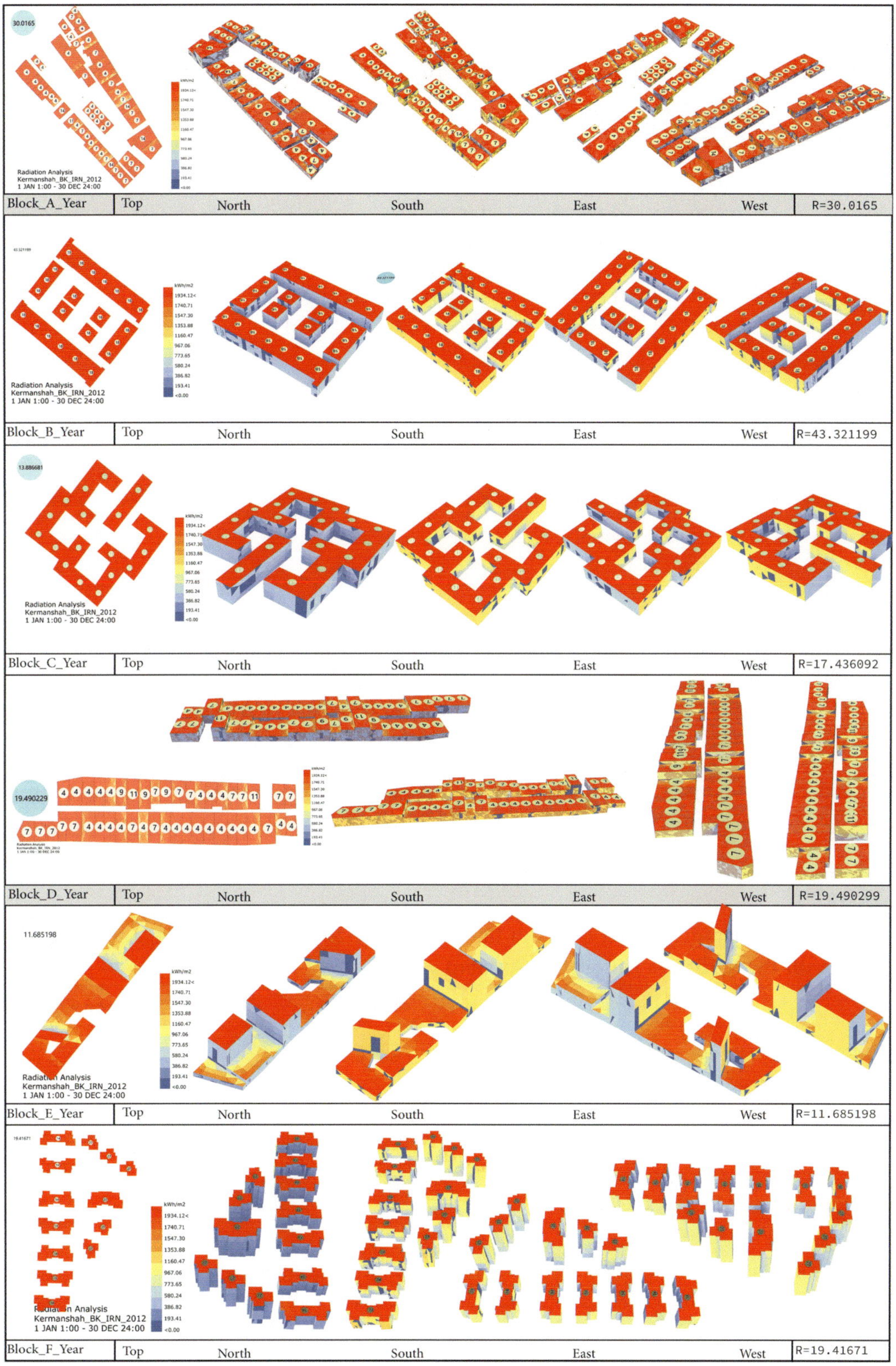

FIGURE 22.10 Analysis solar radiation in the urban block.

TABLE 22.5
The Amount of Radiation Received by the Urban Block Based on Different Years and Seasons

Type Block	Area	R*_Year	R_Winter	R_Spring	R_Summer	R_Fall
Block_A	12280	30.0165	5.33564	9.617231	9.788241	5.17654
Block_B	14420	43.321199	7.951957	13.53`6491	13.856385	7.833853
Block_C	4449	13.886681	2.460906	4.144908	4.244689	2.428385
Block_D	8479	19.490229	3.552495	6.119825	6.267189	3.486423
Block_E	3781	11.685198	2.140941	3.666019	3.731633	2.108606
Block_F	4067	19.41671	3.835915	5.718233	5.966015	3.831523

Note
* Radiation

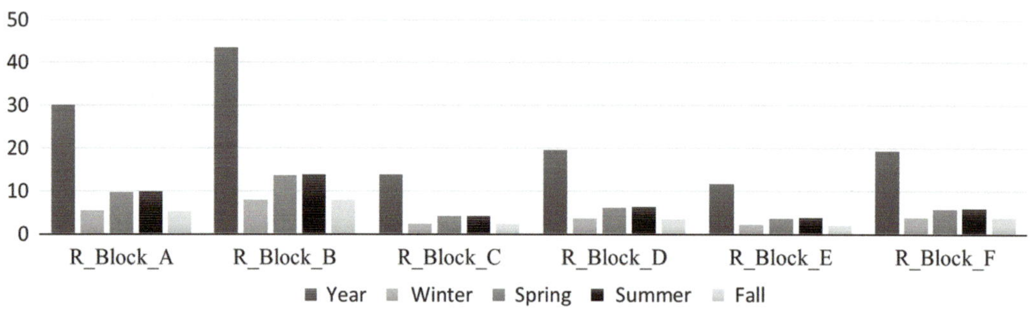

FIGURE 22.11 The graph of comparison between solar radiation absorption in various urban block patterns in different seasons of the year.

TABLE 22.6
Analysis of a Significant Test between the Block Type and the Block Area, and the Block Type with the Radiation Absorption Amount

	Value	df	Asymptotic Significance (2-sided)
Pearson Chi-Square	120.000[a]	25	.000
Likelihood Ratio	79.954	25	.000
N of Valid Cases	24		

Note
[a] 36 cells (100.0%) have expected count less than 5. The minimum expected count is .17.

average results of the laboratory are not significantly different from each other and a significant assumption between the variables is rejected. In the study of the Block_A pattern, solar absorption variables and the block orientations have a significantly weak relationship with each other because, according to the statistical calculations, Sin = .071, which is a value greater than 0.5. Moreover, while examining the rest of the variables, all of the available patterns of the research show Sig = .000, and that indicates a strong relationship between the research variables. As is shown in

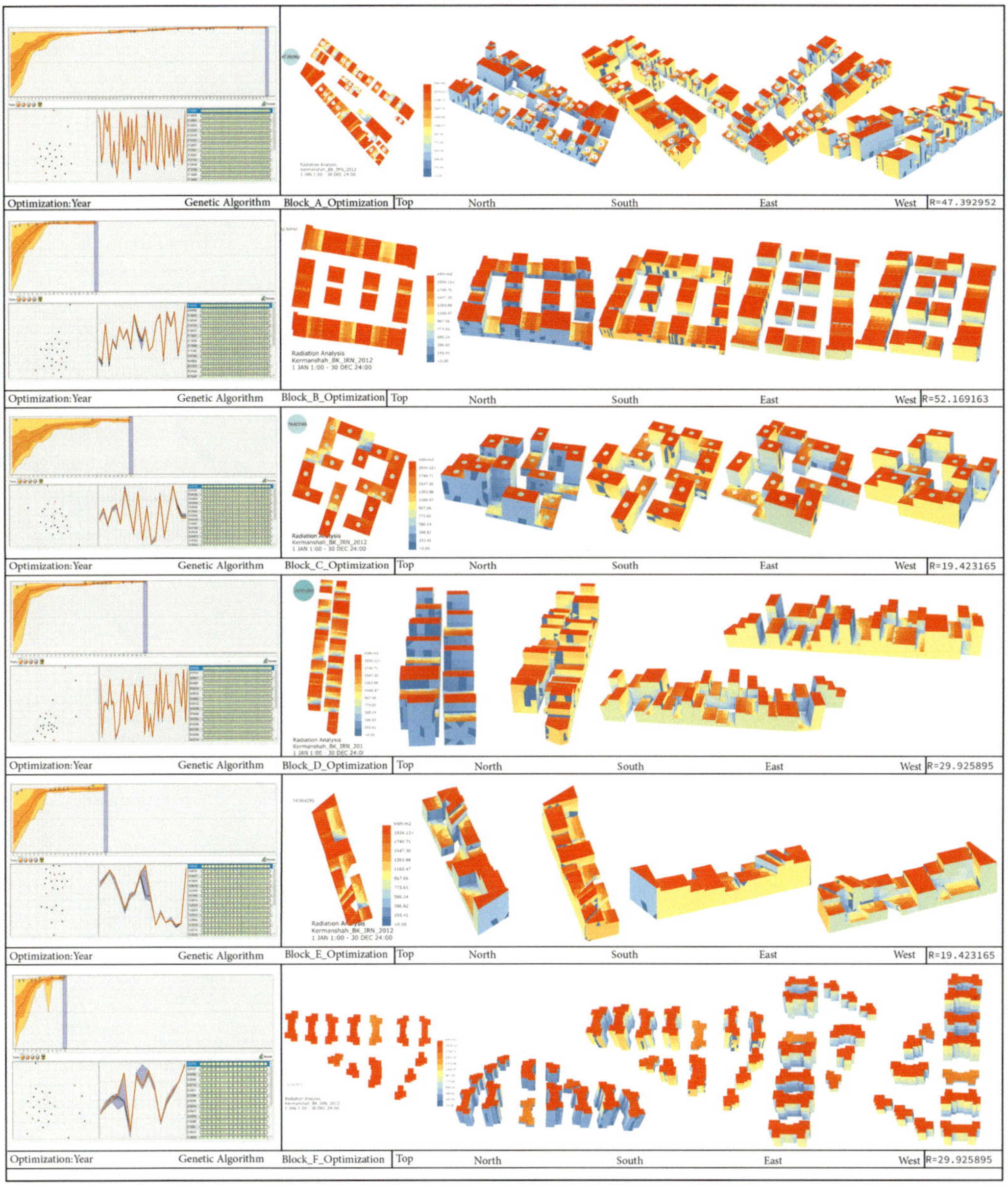

FIGURE 22.12 Optimization solar radiation in urban block.

Figure 22.13 and Table 22.7, there are two factors that indicate the effectiveness of the research variables on the radiation amount; namely, normality of the data and the significant relationship between the variables. Later in this research, the effectiveness assumption and the predictability of research data, which have been examined using genetic algorithm are studied via regression statistics. From one hand, this has determined the effectiveness of research variables and from another hand, the predictability of this data has been examined.

As is shown in Table 22.8, investigation of the predictability of relationships between the variables has been operated using the ANOVA test. This relationship shows that in the regression of all the research variables, Sig = .000. Accordingly, the predictability of research data is shown.

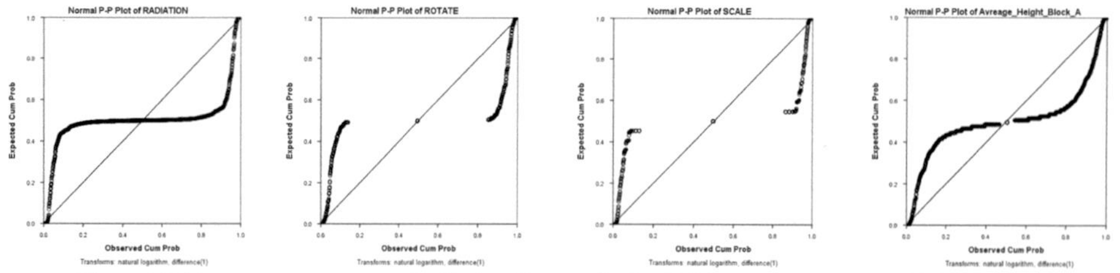

Normal P_P | Radiation_Rotate_Scale_Height | Urban Block_A

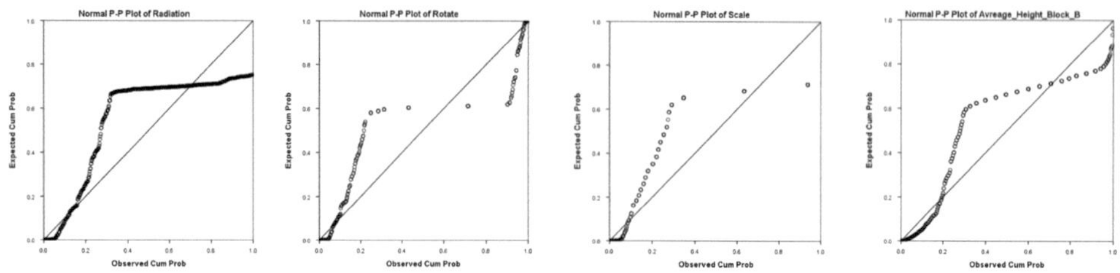

Normal P_P | Radiation_Rotate_Scale_Height | Urban Block_B

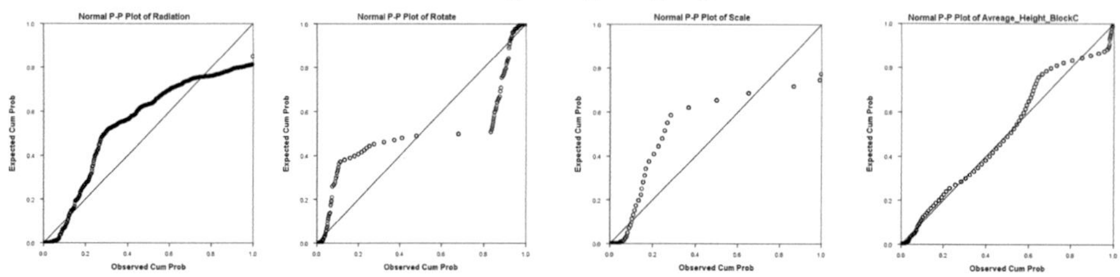

Normal P_P | Radiation_Rotate_Scale_Height | Urban Block_C

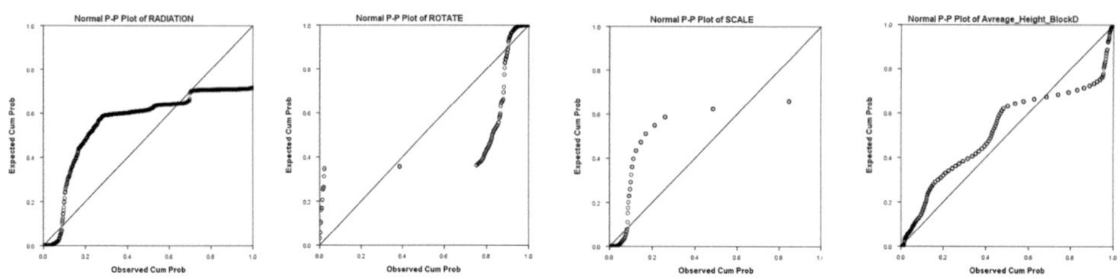

Normal P_P | Radiation_Rotate_Scale_Height | Urban Block_D

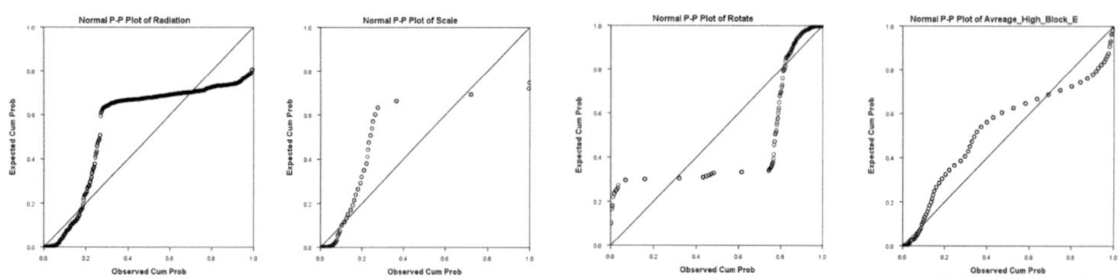

Normal P_P | Radiation_Rotate_S cale_Height | Urban Block_E

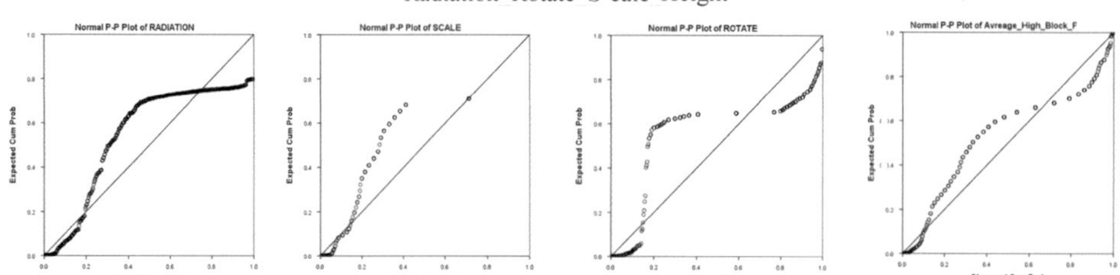

Normal P_P | Radiation_Rotate_Sale_Height | Urban Block_F

FIGURE 22.13 Graph Normal P_P Plot of radiation, rotate, scale, and height in pattern urban block E_F.

TABLE 22.7
Analysis Correlations for Significant Relationship between Variable Effective on Urban Block Patterns

Block_pattern		Radiation	Rotate	Scale	Avreage_Height
Radiation	Pearson Correlation	1	.042**	.984**	.736**
Block_A	Sig. (2-tailed)		.071	.000	.000
	N	1861	1861	1861	1861
Radiation	Pearson Correl`ation	1	.355**	.987**	.699**
Block_B	Sig. (2-tailed)		.000	.000	.000
	N	579	579	579	579
Radiation	Pearson Correlation	1	.172**	.971**	.368**
Block_C	Sig. (2-tailed)		.000	.000	.000
	N	761	761	761	761
Radiation	Pearson Correlation	1	-.598**	.985**	.213**
Block_D	Sig. (2-tailed)		.000	.000	.000
	N	841	841	841	841
Radiation	Pearson Correlation	1	.981**	-.729**	.425**
Block_E	Sig. (2-tailed)		.000	.000	.000
	N	623	623	623	623
Radiation	Pearson Correlation	1	.974**	-.625**	.401**
Block_F	Sig. (2-tailed)		.000	.000	.000
	N	372	372	372	372

Note
** Correlation is significant at the 0.05 level (2-tailed).

In addition, the F statistics in each test are big enough to confirm the assumption of inequality of averages and this shows a significant relationship between the variables.

Referring to Figure 22.14, the procedure of the optimization of data and its variations show the normality of data according to the statistical changes. This shows the capability of predicting data normalization, a significant relationship between the block types, variation in height density, scale, and orientation of the blocks according to the absorption of the solar radiation energy. These are all confirming the research results. Table 22.9 indicates that by optimizing the form of the urban blocks (scale variation, density, and orientation), the rate of the increase in solar radiation absorption on the surfaces ranges from 20 to 56% (Chatzipoulka, Compagnon, and Nikolopoulou 2016). Furthermore, in order to increase these percentages considerably, paying attention to the following factors are essential: the principles of optimization and production of the optimizers that enable the user to have more control and acceleration of the process and also developing some models to lead the user to the optimal solutions faster.

The form pattern variables, height changes, and scale variations evolve the form entity towards its maximum volumetric value. Therefore, the larger the scale of the form, the more radiation it will absorb and this amount needs to be controlled via other functions. However, study of the height changes via genetic algorithm in the parametric environment of the Rhino software with the Grasshopper plug-in indicates some different results. It shows that the form optimization intends to keep the optimized state in the average height range and achieve the desired results in that range. Thus, as these research results believe, densifying and high-rise buildings are in a contradiction with efforts to maximize the use of sunlight in the facades and roofs (Figure 22.15 and Table 22.10).

TABLE 22.8
Analysis Regression for Predictions Relationship between Variables by the ANOVA[a] Test

Model		Sum of Squares	df	Mean Square	F	Sig
Block A	Regression	75450.708	3	25150.236	37881.707	.000 [b]
	Residual	1232.890	1857	.664		
	Total	76683	1860			
Block B	Regression	49500.414	3	16500.138	18734.580	.000 [b]
	Residual	506.421	575	.881		
	Total	50006.835	578			
Block C	Regression	8151.772	3	2717.257	13594.676	.000 [b]
	Residual	151.307	757	.200		
	Total	8303.076	760			
Block D	Regression	17773.631	3	59243544	22110.355	.000 [b]
	Residual	224.277	837	.268		
	Total	17997.908	840			
Block E	Regression	4702.991	3	1567.664	10508.443	.000 [b]
	Residual	92.343	619	.149		
	Total	4795.335	622			
Block F	Regression	7157.992	3	2385.997	8413.251	.000 [b]
	Residual	104.365	368	.284		
	Total	7262.375	371			

Notes
[a] Dependent Variable: Radiation
[b] Predictors: (Constant), Avreage_Height, Scale

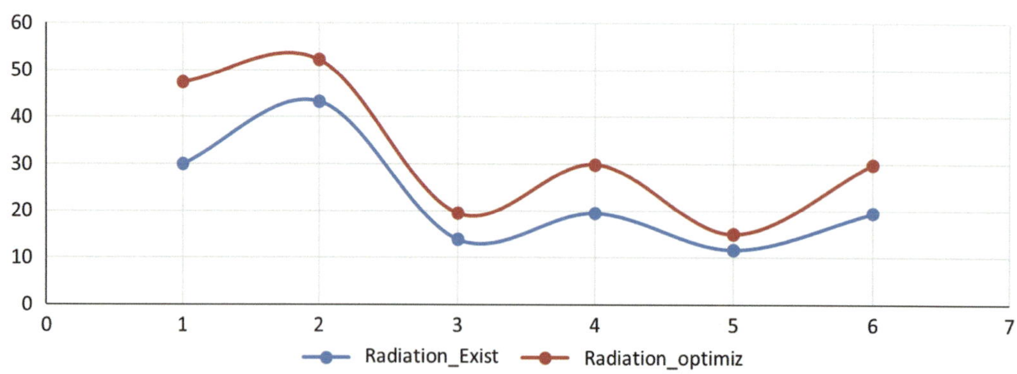

FIGURE 22.14 Comparison of the amount of solar radiation absorption in the existing and optimized situations.

Investigation of the variables shows that the scale variable has the most variation among the other variables. The scale variable also has the most impact on increasing the amount of radiation absorption of the surfaces by exploring the urban block patterns. As is shown in Table 22.11, the initial analysis of the entire patterns show that Scale=1; while, the final optimization of the genetic algorithm shows that scale=1.1, which is the maximum state. In addition, rotation of the block and aligning it to the northeast-southwest direction can significantly enhance the amount of solar absorption. The A and D modes have the maximum amount of variation in the process of

TABLE 22.9
Comparison of the Amount of Solar Radiation Absorption in the Existing Optimized State

	Block_A	Block_B	Block_C	Block_D	Block_E	Block_F
Radiation_Exist	30/0165	43/32119	13/886681	19/49029	11/68518	19/4161
Radiation_optimiz	47/392952	52/16913	19/423165	29/92585	14/95423	29/9255
POO[a]	%56	%20	%23	%52	%27	%52

Note
[a] Percentage of optimization

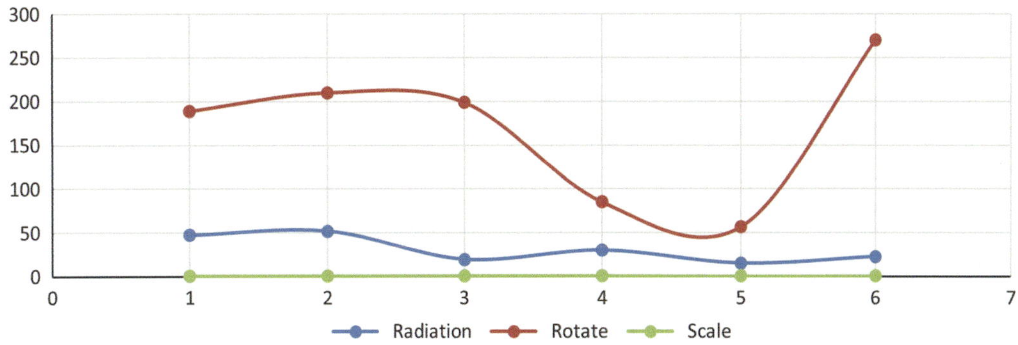

FIGURE 22.15 The number of changes in the two variables of the scale and rotation in the form of the urban blocks and their impacts on the solar radiation absorption.

TABLE 22.10
The Existing Variables of the Block Patterns in Calculation of the Solar Radiation Energy

Group	Radiation	Rotate	Scale	Avrege_High	Max_High	Min_High	Count_Plot
Block_A	30/0165	0	1	5/9	14	4	53
Block_B	43/3212	0	1	18	18	18	23
Block_C	13/88668	0	1	11	11	11	19
Block_D	19/49023	0	1	5/68	11	4	44
Block_E	11/6852	0	1	8/12	24	4	16
Block_F	19/41671	0	1	20	27	14	13

optimization. Therefore, it is understood that there are some conditions that can improve the solar absorption on the surfaces in the Farhangian-Fazl District of the city of Kermanshah. These conditions are variation in scale at its maximum state; variation in the height pattern in the range of 50% of the final state, which is 15 to 20 meters; and also rotation in the prevailing west to east direction or inclined to it. Finally, it is perceived that the impact of the height density variables, orientation and scale block, have significant impacts on the different types of urban blocks.

The findings of this research are capable of being used for optimization of the urban block forms before and after construction. This research does not require much data for optimization. Hence, it can be used by urban designers and planners for the purpose of determining the codes of the urban

TABLE 22.11
Optimization of the Block Pattern Variables in Calculation of the Solar Radiation Energy

Group	Radiation	Rotate	Scale	Avr_High	Max_High	Min_High	Count_Plot
Optimiz A	47/39295	189	1/1	16/67	30	1	53
Optimiz B	52/16916	210	1/1	17	27	7	23
Optimiz C	19/42317	199	1/1	14/57	28	2	19
Optimiz D	29/9259	85	1/1	15/2	29	2	44
Optimiz E	14/95429	57	1/08	16/93	30	5	16
Optimiz F	22/62748	270	1/09	17	27	3	13

block heights, parts, and optimal orientations. Considering different aspects of the research, as well as optimization of urban block forms, can be beneficial in some other areas, such as considering the minimum or maximum absorption of radiation, installation of solar cells, and also using daylight in reduction of the energy consumption in interior spaces.

22.7 CONCLUSION

This chapter deals with the relationships between different urban block patterns and the variables that form a block: height density, orientation, and scale with the maximum amount of radiation absorption. Generally, during the research stages, six initial categories are extracted based on the previous calculations and studies. Calculation of the radiation in these categories has shown that there is a considerable difference between the different categories in terms of radiation absorption of the surfaces. In order to optimize these categories, a design algorithm has been exploited, which uses the following factors: the three independent variables of height, orientation, and scale, and also genetic algorithm. In this section, it is possible to optimize every urban block pattern in terms of radiation; this can be achieved via genetic algorithm and the Galapagos plug-in that is used in the field of optimization in the parametric space of Grasshopper. The calculations of the patterns show that naturally the pattern of the urban block has a significant impact on the radiation absorption of the surfaces; so, it is important for the patterns to be selected accurately in planning and design. Moreover, it is emphasized that the patterns that absorb more radiation in the initial investigation show more capability in solar energy absorption after optimization.

In this research, optimization of the form has indicated that it is possible to increase the amount of energy absorption in the block surfaces from 20 to 50%; this can be achieved via optimization of the categories with a genetic algorithm. The optimization results in height, scale, and orientation via genetic algorithm have shown some priorities; namely, receiving the maximum solar radiation according to the maximum scale, optimization of the orientation variables, and average of the height dimension and constant orientation. Under this circumstance, the categories that had the maximum energy absorption again showed the maximum energy absorption and revealed a better performance in optimization. It is important to note that the optimized state of the data is not conclusive and the results are likely to change throughout the time; although the relative changes might be very little and negligible. Therefore, in order to achieve the optimum solar energy among the urban blocks, it is important to take some qualitative and quantitative factors into consideration, such as block dimensions, categories, orientation, scale height, the distance between the blocks, and shading. Investigation of these factors and the way they can be optimized are proper proposals for future studies.

The results highlight the necessity and importance of having an optimized targeted design in urban planning and architectural design strategies in a cold and mountainous city context. Some significant planning and geometrical parameters related to solar potentials and energy efficiency in the urban blocks have been investigated in this study; all of these findings can be a reference for strategic guidance for passive design, as well as being a model for urban planning, management, and design.

REFERENCES

Affenzeller, Michael, Stefan Wagner, Stephan Winkler, and Andreas Beham. 2009. *Genetic algorithms and genetic programming: Modern concepts and practical applications*. CRC Press.

Amado, Miguel, Francesca Poggi, and António Ribeiro Amado. 2016. "Energy efficient city: A model for urban planning." *Sustainable Cities and Society* 26: 476–485. doi: 10.1016/j.scs.2016.04.011.

Amado, Miguel, Francesca Poggi, António Ribeiro Amado, and Sílvia Breu. 2017. "A cellular approach to net-zero energy cities." *Energies* 10(11): 1826. doi:10.3390/en10111826.

Amado, Miguel, Poggi, Francesca, Ribeiro Amado, António, & Breu, Sílvia (2017). A Cellular Approach to Net-Zero Energy Cities. Energies, 10, 182610.3390/en10111826.

Andreasson, Niclas, Michael Patriksson, and Anton Evgrafov. 2020. *An introduction to continuous optimization: foundations and fundamental algorithms*. Courier Dover Publications.

Arora, Rajesh Kumar. 2015. *Optimization: Algorithms and applications*. CRC Press.

Baldick, Ross. 2006. *Applied optimization: Formulation and algorithms for engineering systems*. Cambridge University Press.

Bizjak, Marko, Borut Žalik, and Niko Lukač. 2015. "Evolutionary-driven search for solar building models using LiDAR data." *Energy and Buildings* 92: 195–203. doi: 10.1016/j.enbuild.2015.01.051.

Caldas, Luisa Gama, and Leslie K. Norford. 2002. "A design optimization tool based on a genetic algorithm." *Automation in Construction* 11(2): 173–184.

Cerezo Davila, Carlos. 2017. *Building archetype calibration for effective urban building energy modeling*. Massachusetts Institute of Technology.

Chatzipoulka, Christina, Raphaël Compagnon, and Marialena Nikolopoulou. 2016. "Urban geometry and solar availability on façades and ground of real urban forms: using London as a case study." *Solar Energy* 138: 53–66.

Chen, Kian, and Leslie Norford. 2017. "Evaluating urban forms for comparison studies in the massing design stage." *Sustainability* 9(6). doi: 10.3390/su9060987

Congress for the New Urbanism 2000. "Charter of the new urbanism." *Bulletin of Science, Technology & Society* 20: 339–341.

Crahmaliuc, R. 2021Open-source or proprietary software-what is best for users? SIMSCALE blog website.https://www.simscale.com/blog/2017/06/open-source-vs-proprietary-software/.

Duany, Andres, and Emily Talen. 2002. "Transect planning." *American Planning Association. Journal of the American Planning Association* 68(3): 245.

Eiben, Agoston E., and James E. Smith. 2015. *Introduction to evolutionary computing*. Springer.

EnergyPlus_Development_Team. 2020. "Weather Data for EnergyPlus." (File, EnergyPlus Weather): https://energyplus.net/weather

Fesanghary, Mohammad, Somayeh Asadi, and Zong Woo Geem. 2012. "Design of low-emission and energy-efficient residential buildings using a multi-objective optimization algorithm." *Building and Environment* 49: 245–250.

Firth, Steven K., Kevin J. Lomas, and A. J. Wright. 2009. "Investigating CO2 emission reductions in existing urban housing using a community domestic energy model." *Building Simulation* 9:2098–2105

Groppi, Daniele, Livio de Santoli, Fabrizio Cumo, and Davide Astiaso Garcia. 2018. "A GIS-based model to assess buildings energy consumption and usable solar energy potential in urban areas." *Sustainable Cities and Society* 40: 546–558. doi: 10.1016/j.scs.2018.05.005.

Hamdy, Mohamed, Anh-Tuan Nguyen, Jan L. M. Hensen. 2016. "A performance comparison of multi-objective optimization algorithms for solving nearly-zero-energy-building design problems." *Energy and Buildings* 121: 57–71.

Horvat, M., and Maria Wall. 2012. "Solar design of buildings for architects: Review of solar design tools." Report. 41.

Howard, B., L. Parshall, J. Thompson, S. Hammer, J. Dickinson, and V. Modi. 2012. "Spatial distribution of urban building energy consumption by end use." *Energy and Buildings* 45: 141–151.

Iqbal, Muhammad. 2012. *An introduction to solar radiation*. Elsevier.

Jabareen, Yosef Rafeq. 2006. "Sustainable urban forms: Their typologies, models, and concepts." *Journal of Planning Education and Research* 26(1): 38–52.

Kamell, Elizabeth Natanya. 1996. *Building, block, street: residential block design*. Massachusetts Institute of Technology.

Kämpf, Jérôme Henri, Marylène Montavon, Josep Bunyesc, Raffaele Bolliger, and Darren Robinson . 2010. "Optimisation of buildings' solar irradiation availability." Solar Energy 84(4): 596–603.

Kämpf, Jérôme Henri, and Darren Robinson. 2010. "Optimisation of building form for solar energy utilisation using constrained evolutionary algorithms." *Energy and Buildings* 42(6), 807–814. doi: 10.1016/j.enbuild.2009.11.019.

Karathanasis, Stavros 2019. *Linear Fresnel reflector systems for solar radiation concentration*. Springer.

Kochenderfer, Mykel J., and Tim A. Wheeler 2019. *Algorithms for optimization*. MIT Press.

Lindberg, Fredrik, Per Jonsson, Tsuyoshi Honjo, and Dag Wästberg. 2015. "Solar energy on building envelopes – 3D modelling in a 2D environment." *Solar Energy* 115: 369–378. doi: 10.1016/j.solener.2015.03.001

Morganti, Michele, Agnese Salvati, Helena Coch, and Carlo Cecere . 2017. "Urban morphology indicators for solar energy analysis. *Energy Procedia* 134: 807–814.

Nguyen, Anh-Tuan, Sigrid Reiter, and Philippe Rigo. 2014. "A review on simulation-based optimization methods applied to building performance analysis." *Applied Energy* 113: 1043–1058.

Oikonomou, M. 2015. "The urban block as a potential for sustainable urban design." *The Sustainable City X, 194*, 69.

Osmond, P. 2008. *An Enquiry in to New Methodologies for Evaluating Sustainable Urban Form. Unpublished Ph. D. Thesis*, University of New South Wales.

Pakzad, Erfan, and Newsha Salari. 2018. "Measuring sustainability of urban blocks: The case of Dowlatabad, Kermanshah city." *Cities* 75: 90–100. doi: 10.1016/j.cities.2018.01.005

Parolek, Daniel G., Karen Parolek, and Paul C. Crawford. 2008. *Form based codes: A guide for planners, urban designers, municipalities, and developers*. John Wiley & Sons.

Pham, Duc, and Dervis Karaboga. 2012. *Intelligent optimisation techniques: genetic algorithms, tabu search, simulated annealing and neural networks*, Springer Science & Business Media.

Reddy, T. Agami, Itzhak Maor, and Chanin Panjapornpon. 2007a. "Calibrating detailed building energy simulation programs with measured data—Part I: General methodology (RP-1051)." *Hvac&R Research* 13(2): 221–241.

Reddy, T. Agami, Itzhak Maor, and Chanin Panjapornpon. 2007b. "Calibrating detailed building energy simulation programs with measured data—Part II: Application to three case study office buildings (RP-1051)." *Hvac&r Research* 13(2), 243–265.

Redweik, P., C. Catita, and M. Brito. 2013. "Solar energy potential on roofs and facades in an urban landscape." *Solar Energy* 97: 332–341. doi: 10.1016/j.solener.2013.08.036.

Rode, Philipp, Christian Keim, Guido Robazza, Pablo Viejo, and James Schofield. 2014. "Cities and energy: urban morphology and residential heat-energy demand." *Environment and Planning B: Planning and Design* 41(1): 138–162.

Roudsari, M. Sadeghipour. 2017. "What is Ladybug Tools." *Availabe online*: http://www.ladybug.tools/ (accessed on 18 November 2017).

Scott, D. 2010. "Grasshopper generative modeling for Rhino." *Computer Software* (Version 6)McNeel. http://www.grasshopper3d.com.

Sen, Zekai. 2008. *Solar energy fundamentals and modeling techniques: atmosphere, environment, climate change and renewable energy*. Springer Science & Business Media.

Shi, Zhongming, Jimeno A. Fonseca, and Arno Schlueter. 2017. "A review of simulation-based urban form generation and optimization for energy-driven urban design." *Building and Environment* 121: 119–129. doi: 10.1016/j.buildenv.2017.05.006.

Siksna, Arnis. 1997. "The effects of block size and form in North American and Australian city centres." *Urban Morphology* 1(1): 19–33.

Sivanandam, S. N., and S. N. Deepa. 2007. *Introduction to genetic algorithms*. Springer Science & Business Media.

Sokol, Julia Alexandrovna. 2015. *Deriving archetype templates for urban building energy models based on measured monthly energy use*. Massachusetts Institute of Technology.

Swan, L. G., and V. I. Ugursal. 2009. "Modeling of end-use energy consumption in the residential sector: A review of modeling techniques", *Renewable and Sustainable Energy Reviews* 13: 1819–1835.

Taleghani, Mohammad, Martin Tenpierik, Andy Van Den Dobbelsteen, and Richard De Dear. 2013. "Energy use impact of and thermal comfort in different urban block types in the Netherlands." *Energy and Buildings* 67: 166–175.

Vermeulen, Thibault, Jérôme Henri Kämpf, and Benoît Beckers. 2013. "Urban form optimization for the energy performance of buildings using Citysim." *EPFL Solar Energy and Building Physics Laboratory (LESO-PB)*: 915–920.

Vialard, Alice. 2013. *A typology of block-faces*. Georgia Institute of Technology.

Xu, Xiaodong, Yifan Wu, Wei Wang, Tianzhen Hong, and Ning Xu. 2019. "Performance-driven optimization of urban open space configuration in the cold-winter and hot-summer region of China." *Building Simulation* 12(3):411–424

Yang, Perry Pei-Ju, and Jinyue Yan. 2016. "Modeling urban design with energy performance." *Energy Procedia* 88: 3–8. doi: 10.1016/j.egypro.2016.06.002.

Zhang, Ji, Le Xu, Veronika Shabunko, Stephen En Rong Tay, Huixuan Sun, Stephen Siu Yu Lau, and Thomas Reindl. 2019. "Impact of urban block typology on building solar potential and energy use efficiency in tropical high-density city." *Applied Energy* 240: 513–533. doi: 10.1016/j.apenergy.2019.02.033.

23 Rethinking Disaster-Resilient Cities: A Close Integration of Planning with Geospatial Technology

Navneet Munoth
Maulana Azad National Institute of Technology, Bhopal, India

Divya Jain, Apurva Deshmukh, and Nirmoha Mandal
School of Planning and Architecture, New Delhi, India

CONTENTS

23.1 INTRODUCTION

Cities are an intricate system of socio-economic and ecological elements. However, they are susceptible when any of these subsystems are damaged or unable to adjust to any different or new problem (Coaffee 2010). The two major indeterminate factors, climate change, and natural disasters, have a noteworthy role in intimidating urban growth. The occurrence of natural disasters like drought, landslides, floods, and desertification are sometimes due to humans interfering with nature. For example, flash floods due to deforestation in the higher catchment areas of the rivers change the

DOI: 10.1201/9781003126195-28

hydrological pattern. Land degradation and unsustainable land use practices ultimately increase in disaster-prone areas. The reduction of green cover due to overgrazing in dry areas results in dust storms that may result in desertification and increase the risk of drought. The fast rate of population growth acts as a catalyst in increasing the existing problem areas. Due to population growth, people have started settling in areas that were previously unoccupied (along the unstable steep slopes, river flood plains, and marginal arid lands) and fall in high disaster-prone zones.

Some of the disasters are classified as unexpected emergency conditions because of a misjudged hazard with unusual conditions. Like in the case of drought, which basically starts with the signs of shortage and uneven rainfall patterns, but its extreme effect occurs when dilapidation of the land and other resources happens due to desertification. Likewise, the pollution and degradation of rivers and water bodies are slow processes; however, the subsequence in a decrease of fisheries may be a fast and disastrous process. The assessment and evaluation of the impact of a disaster are not easy, different dimensions like the loss of life, financial losses, and environmental degradation need to be considered (Bello and Aina 2014). But with the advancement of geospatial technology and using modern tools like remote sensing and GIS, the process of predicting the risks and hazards is further accurate and uncomplicated in comparison to the conventional methods.

For a long time, these threats of disaster existed and since the 19th century, a few of the big cities have been abandoned or permanently destroyed. Some of the renowned cities worldwide, such as Berlin, Warsaw, Hiroshima, Beirut, Tokyo, and Dresden, rebuilt themselves and are more vibrant than before, even after being destroyed by the natural disasters (Zhang and Li 2018). Geospatial data always plays an important role in building and supporting a better resilient urban plan. GIS performs a crucial role in tracking risks and hazards, but its utilization in emergency situations needs to be fast-tracked to make sure the upcoming disasters become less devastating. Using GIS technology, advanced planning with risk assessment, situational responsiveness, rescue and recovery procedures, better collaboration, and disaster response will improve, progress, and eventually deliver a safer and healthier environment for people to live in.

23.2 DISASTER AND CITIES

Disasters are combined with primary consequences that are directly associated, like loss of life and property, damage to infrastructure, cultural values, ecosystems, roads, and bridges, and secondary consequences, like outbursts of diseases, famine, and poverty (Amoako and Sun 2018). As per the world's demographic trends, the growth of the future population will happen mostly in small and medium-sized cities of the developing countries of Africa and Asia that are already vulnerable to numerous types of disasters. A report by United Nations regarding disaster risk reduction, reveals that the number of disasters related to climate change is increasing at a much faster rate since the late 1970s (Nations United 2007). With the increase in haphazard and unplanned urban populations, geographically concentrated communities are prone to more large-scale disasters. This makes it important to understand the perspective of people, human-environment interaction, and social processes to clarify why the resilience of some cities are better and other cities are still at risk to hazards and disasters. Resilience capability of any community is briefly explained as its reaction and response mechanism towards disaster. As per different research, it is suggested that resilience can be explained as the flexibility, the ability to adjust during uncertainty, and the capability to capitalize on a positive moment in the coming future (Surjan and Shaw 2008).

23.2.1 Impact of Disaster

There are several adverse impacts of disasters on both the social and economic development of a country. In India, during the 2018 Kerala flooding, around 1.4 million people were evacuated, the piped water supply was disconnected to over 6.7 million people, and the shallow wells of six majorly affected districts became contaminated and inoperable (United Nations Development Programme 2018). Positively no considerable epidemic outbreak took place, but it should be kept in mind that events like these have the potential to worsen the occurrence of diseases like diarrhea and cholera because of contamination of water due to washed-up waste. Similarly, it impacts the household economy, especially those families living in poverty with fewer assets and access to withstand the impacts of disaster by worsening their conditions. During the 2004 tsunami, more than 2.7 million jobs in agricultural and coastal fisheries were lost, affecting the whole economy of the state (UNDRR 2020).

Disasters and hazards lead to an increase in poverty as it severely affects the education system of the area. In 2018, during the Kerala flooding, approximately 1,700 schools were transformed into relief centers, and even after reopening, due to stress, trauma, and family needs, the attendance was only 20% for quite a long period (United Nations Development Programme 2018). To end poverty, education programs are organized by governments worldwide, but disasters lead to a major discontinuity into such programs, thus forming a continuous loop where access to school gets disrupted, leading to poverty in the long run.

Disasters also affect the health sectors by impacting the health delivery services due to a sudden increase in the number of casualties beyond the capacity or by losing critical infrastructure. After the Indian Ocean Tsunami, a huge amount, USD$30 million, was estimated for the reconstruction of the affected healthcare infrastructure (UNDRR 2020). Though it not only causes the finances of the state it also severely affects the productivity and well-being of the people, especially after the disaster when the need for health care increases rapidly.

Further, due to less productivity, loss of assets, and infrastructures, the economic growth is hindered and gets compromised. These combined damages and losses, with the recovery and reconstruction, may disturb the whole budget of the state, affecting future development projects for years. In India, as per the Ministry of Home Affairs, between 1991 and 2005 due to hazards and 431 major disasters, India's GDP was reduced by 2% (Kumar, Walia, and Chaturvedi 2011). In 2018, in the Kerala floods and landslides, more than 5.4 million people were affected and crops, livestock, transport network, housing, power supply, and other infrastructures were severely damaged. The initial estimation to the post-disaster needs was around USD$4.4 billion, in which 38% damage was in the infrastructure sectors, 27% in the cross-cutting, and 17% damage in the production industry sectors, and this led to a drop in the GDP of Kerala, which was estimated to be 2.6% (United Nations Development Programme 2018). Events like these emphasize the need for rethinking disaster-resilient cities to avoid and minimize immense losses and economic slowdown. This becomes more important to the developed and the fast-developing countries like India, where 63% of the nation's GDP is contributed by the urban regions and the cities that are still exposed to hazards (National Disaster Management Authority; Government of India 2019).

23.2.2 Disaster-Resilient Cities

By the year 2050, more than 70% of the world's population is expected to live in urban areas and eventually, cities will become the hub for economic opportunity. However unplanned growth and impact of climate change and social distress can cause a disruptive impact on the development of the urban systems. A resilient city has the capability to absorb and recover from any shock and stress without affecting its necessary services, structures, and identity by adapting and sustaining constant rearrangements (Bizzotto, Huseynova, and Estrada 2019). A disaster-resilient city has a low risk to disasters due to its capability to respond to climate change, disasters, and financial shocks (Bansal, Mukherjee, and Gairola 2017). Building a resilient city requires the identification and assessment of hazard risks, reduction to exposure and vulnerability, and adaptive capacity, increasing resistance, and emergency preparedness.

23.3 GEOSPATIAL TECHNOLOGIES AND DISASTER MANAGEMENT

Global navigation satellite systems including the global positioning system (GPS), remote sensing (RS), and geographic information systems (GIS) are all part of geospatial technologies. The technology gives location-based data that can be used in disaster management. It also plays a significant role in the disaster management cycle. Natural events like earthquakes and tsunamis use geospatial technology in post-disaster responses. Remote sensing provides detailed data required for emergency and post-disaster responses (Westlund 2010).

The GIS with spatial data has many preconditions to be integrated reasonably for giving precise outputs for implementing it in the disaster risk reduction cycle. The most significant of all data is the high-resolution data that is required for the assessment of risks, and evaluation of mitigation, preparedness, and response and recovery operations. The contribution of GIS accelerates the workability of complex analyses by combining analysis tools with innovation for generating hazard, exposure, vulnerability, and risk maps that assist public, private authorities, stakeholders, decision makers, or policymakers with required and relevant information that is easy to apply and use. The generic methodological workflow depicted in Figure 23.1 shows the contribution of geospatial information to escape the adverse impact of disasters, consequently making the cities resilient (Der Sarkissian, Zaninetti, and Abdallah 2019).

Case Study (India): The cyclones Hud-Hud, Gaja, Amphan, and Nisarga, which occurred around 2019 and 2020, had many lives saved through preparedness and planning using GIS technology. It has improved environmental understanding, tracking the change due to climate impact, strategic decision making, and finding out the future risks. The technology was facilitated in various stages of the disaster management cycle; which started with identifying locations to construct shelters for flood and weak points in the flooding area to initiate repair; after which efforts were made to prepare grid analysis that would be used to set up the automated weather stations. The process involves preparing various maps, like a base map with the location and operation of boats for various districts and gram panchayat for the easy movement of rescue officers. There is a phase in any crisis or disaster that gives a chance to build resilience. With integration of GIS into disaster management, the planning

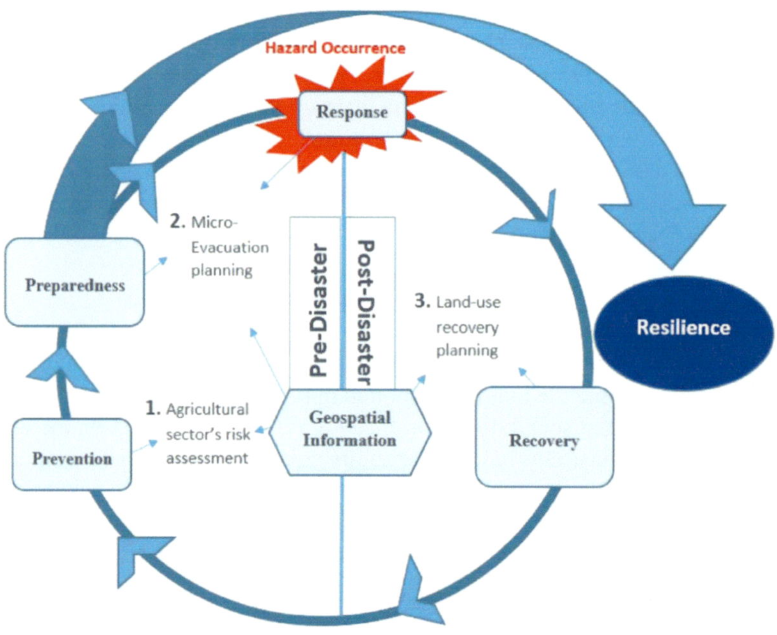

FIGURE 23.1 General workflow adopted in disaster risk reduction cycle.

process can be improved for a responsive framework. GIS gives an idea about the aftermath of potential damage and predicts the utilization of resources during the emergency, whereas departments like front-line workers can gain real-time information to monitor the situation and later share up-to-date data with other departments as well as the public (India TV Tech Desk 2021).

23.3.1 Geospatial Technology

The term "geospatial" recently gained recognition and has been utilized to establish the relationship between the aggregated information and connected technology with a locational/geographical aspect incorporated within. A glance at Google's Ngram Viewer displays that the word has been used in literature studies in the late 1980s and from then it acquired the ascend in the frequency of its use. Geospatial technology calls attention to the technology accustomed to acquiring, manipulating, and storing spatial data. GPS, GIS, Google Earth, remote sensing, aerial photography, drone capturing, and geo-fencing are other samples of geospatial technology. In geospatial data, geospatial is used to the word geospatial to spot data features that have a geographic component associated with them. This suggests that the information in an exceeding data set has spatial data linked to them like coordinates in different projection systems. Geospatial technology or data plays an extremely vital part in disaster management due to the fact that the features that are vulnerable to be impacted by disaster can be geographically located. GIS and remote sensing are dependable tools that are employed within the evaluation of natural or man-made disasters by presenting a kind of synoptic coverage of a broad area in a very low-cost manner (Dempsey 2014).

23.3.2 Remote Sensing in Disaster Management

The applications of remote sensing in disaster management have become popular, especially with the integration of GIS. The requirements for hazard reduction and tracking are high on the list of priorities in the development of most new Earth Observation Satellite Programmes. It enables the inclusion of many types of data by using different models. The inclusion of various types of geographic data includes integration of spatial information with non-spatial information, attribute data, and the utilization of this information is relevant at different levels of disaster management. Similarly, GIS can be also used in the management of large information, which is collected at the time of disaster for vulnerability and hazard assessment through remote-sensing applications such as satellite imagery, etc. It serves as a crucial tool that can be used at the disaster mitigation and preparedness stage for planning evacuation routes, designing operational emergency centers, and for the analysis of space-based information with other relevant data in the design. Further, for the relief phase, GIS linked with GPS is very useful in search and rescue operations where devastation has taken place (Dr. Geetha Srikanth 2021; Sharma and Joshi 2010). How the remote sensing data can be used for emergency and disaster management by assisting the government actions has been shown through flowchart in Figure 23.2.

23.3.3 GIS and Disaster Management

Today, many cities are described by low-density urban sprawl, fragile infrastructure, and low resilience to disasters. Due to rapid population growth and unplanned urbanization with poorly managed urban infrastructures, tainted ecosystems, and poverty, the frequency and impact of disasters have increased massively. As cities are a combination of different urban systems like housing, water supply, sanitation, transportation, etc. strengthening every system will automatically uplift the resilience capability of the city (Mausom and Choudhary 2017). Smart cities with advanced planning and information and communication technologies improve the city services and boost urban systems which further increases disaster resilience of the city. Social, economic, and environmental

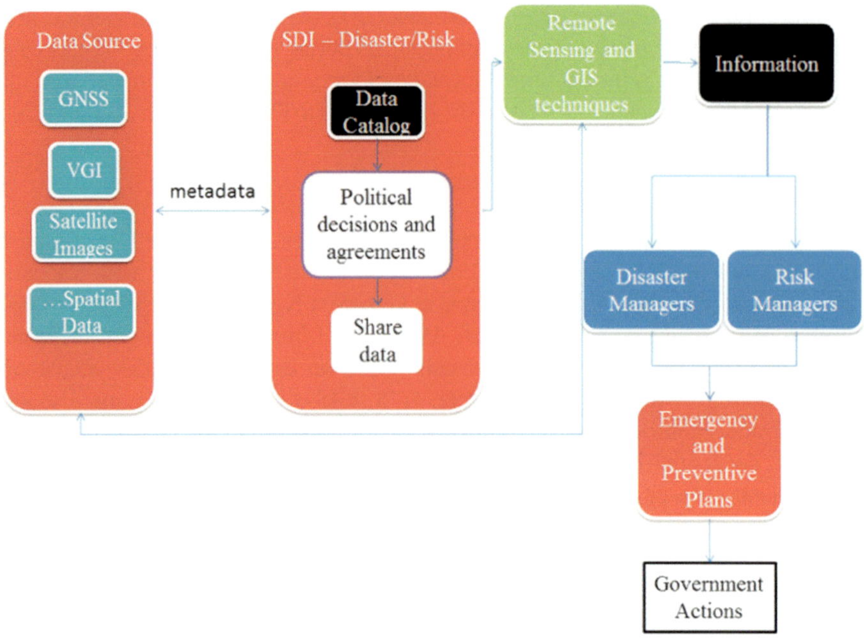

FIGURE 23.2 Scheme for space-based data use for risk and disaster risk.

sustainability; better quality of life; and digital inclusion are contemplated to be crucial factors in designing smart cities. Due to the increased frequency of disasters, resilience and emergency response systems are the crucial dimensions of smart and future city planning (Alazawi et al. 2014).

Advanced planning and geospatial tools help in assessing the risk and minimizing the impact of the disaster by solving complex planning and management problems. The disaster management system includes three crucial stages: the pre-disaster stage consisting of planning, preparedness, and mitigation; the on-disaster stage consisting of response, recovery, and evacuation; and the post-disaster stage consisting of damage assessment, rehabilitation, and providing medical facilities. All the stages of emergency management, reduction, readiness, response, and recovery, can benefit from GIS (Shrivastava 2014).

The role of GIS in the three crucial stages of disaster management system can be summarized:

- **Pre-Disaster Stage –** For some, disaster prevention and mitigation is not possible, and the time for protective actions, warnings, and evacuations may be possible just before the disaster hits. During such situations, activities like vulnerability assessment and potential risk mapping can be prepared in GIS, which will help in early preparedness and awareness of the health staff, local authorities, and communities.
- **On-Disaster Stage** – This stage consists of the time when the disaster hits, causing damage, injury, and death. The moment after the impact is the time for rescue and relief operations. In this situation, GIS can be utilized to figure the shortest route for emergency evacuation and analyze the damage.
- **Post-Disaster Stage** – After the disaster, leads to damage assessment, rehabilitation, and providing medical facilities. To analyze the total damage aftermath and data from satellite imageries can be incorporated with GIS to prepare thematic maps. Based on those maps, rehabilitation centers and available resource allocation can be done (Shrivastava 2014).

The common approach for modeling the concepts of disaster and risk associated with it can be adopted with GIS for generating risk maps for hazards that show the areas that are more vulnerable

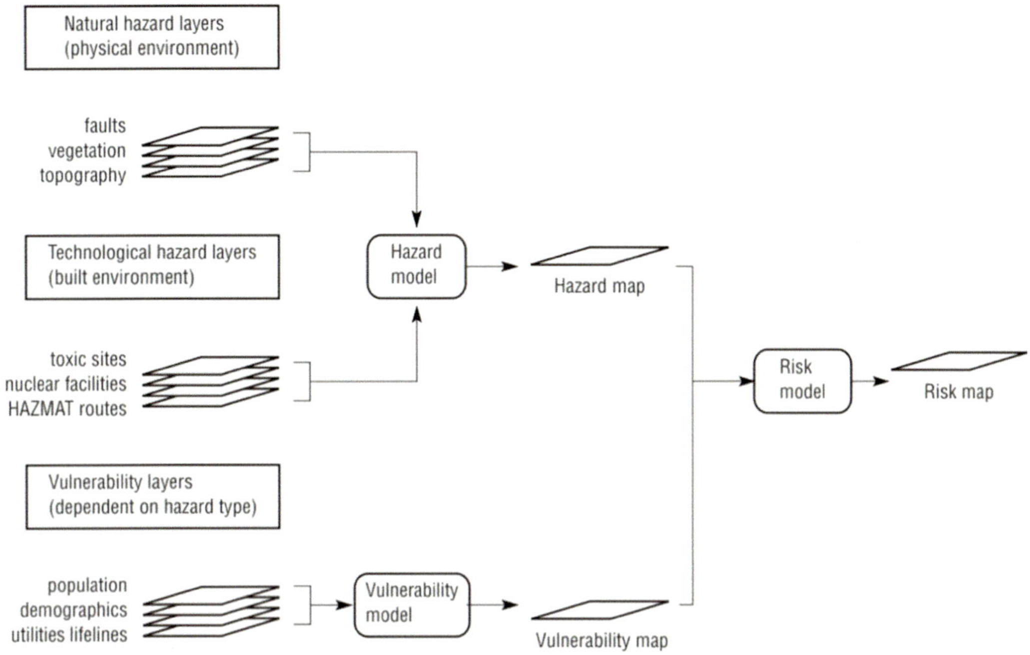

FIGURE 23.3 Approach for modelling the concepts of disaster risk in GIS.

and can be most impacted by disaster. The general requirements and integrated models for producing a risk map of any particular natural hazard that can be further used for making strategies to prevent the damage is shown in Figure 23.3.

23.3.4 Land Use and Hazard Vulnerability Assessments

Land use and urban planning are acknowledged as solutions to non-structural risk reduction measures with the potential to avoid exposure in the most hazardous zones and to decrease overtime exposure and vulnerability in already urbanized areas. The land use plans provide relevant information about environmental features including natural hazards of the areas to be developed or redeveloped. For this, the land use and hazard vulnerability are assessed to develop integrated land use vulnerability maps, indicating the site location of people, surrounding natural environment, or property that are at risk due to a possible disastrous event resulting in injury, pollution, death, or other destruction (Magotra et al., 2019). These maps can help planners and decision-makers in developing appropriate strategies for risk reduction and mitigation and build upon a robust knowledge base on different components of the risk function – hazards, exposure, vulnerability, and resilience, where these integrated maps provide data for achieving safety and environmentally intended land use management. With the use of this information, planners and local authorities can improve their land use policies and practices while considering the vulnerability of different areas such as coastal zones (Sowmya, John, and Shrivasthava 2015).

23.4 APPLICATION OF GEOSPATIAL TOOLS IN DISASTER RISK REDUCTION

With time, disasters whether natural or man-made, have arisen as global issues and concerns. The population residing in the assorted built environment (specifically in urban areas) has been increasing continuously and subsequently the risk of exposure to the disaster of high frequency and magnitude is also surging. Evolving geospatial technologies including remote sensing (RS), geographic information system (GIS), and global navigation satellite system (GNSS) have been doing substantial work in managing various disasters including flooding, cyclones, drought, landslides, forest fires, earthquakes, etc. Out of these technologies, RS has been utilized particularly in the early stages of preparedness and responses while handling disasters (Bello and Aina 2014).

Many disasters have occurred in the past year that drove out the need for technology involvement, such as Hurricane Andrew in 1992, where the lack of fast and reliable situation or damage assessment tools obstructed the deployment of federal resources post-disaster for providing relief consequently highlighted the urgent need of real-time estimation methodologies; whereas in the Northridge Earthquake in 1994, GIS was involved in the initial stage, advancing the crucial spatial and visual information on disaster management functions during the response and recovery periods; and Hurricane Charley in 2004, the operation of field survey based on GIS technology helped to identify the damage and destruction of the occurred disaster so that research could be carried out to study the impact of hazards in a comprehensive and inclusive way. All such disastrous events demonstrate the window that emerges when real-time data can be delivered more easily and effectively to stakeholders making important decisions during the disaster (Eguchi et al. 2008).

The significance of applied geospatial technologies is emerging rapidly in real-world phenomena, notably because of the level of reliability, accessibility, and effectiveness in allocating accurate models and simulation techniques in disaster management. These innovations are proficient enough to address both spatial and temporal aspects of disasters, making them constructive tools for efficient decision making. The ease of handling the tools of geospatial analysis provides the accountable authorities making decisions with the implanted data in the decision-making process through the modelled geospatial data (Abdalla and Li 2010). The use of RS, GIS, and GNSS tools and techniques based on spatial data becomes necessary for the management of disasters and discussions regarding the deployment and methodologies will allow the gap identification in practicality and possibility to access information for applicability (Manfré et al. 2012). This section of this chapter will highlight some geospatial tools that can be utilized in disaster management for reducing the risk and impact of the disaster in urban areas.

23.4.1 Floods and Coastal Systems

Floods of coastal areas are supposed to be reoccurring and devastating natural hazards that have their impact on countries worldwide. These hazards eventually result in social vulnerabilities, affecting infrastructure, buildings, and people. Further, the increasing population living along the coastal areas is recognized as a catalyst component, elevating the heights of vulnerability (Rumson, Hallett, and Brewer 2017) The prospect of using the data that is obtainable in cartographic forms shows its remarkable role in dealing with urban flood mapping at the local level of planning in urban areas. Moreover, the information that is accessible from geospatial technologies has contributed to a significant level in flood mapping and planning. High-resolution satellite imagery, land use maps, hydraulic characteristics of river channels and flood-plain surveys, and probable water levels are the prerequisite information that can be used for predictive flood hazard mapping (Singh and Sharma 2009). These data can act as input to analyze the existing situation or the probable flooding areas, by which appropriate measures could be taken before or on-disaster phase.

The application of GIS as a mapping tool can give diverse output in the form of flood hazard mapping, flood hazard management, and hydrological data storing and management. The estimation process is beneficial in detailing and marking the potential flood hazard areas with additional information such as stream drainage patterns, slope, rainfall intensity, elevation, flow accumulation, and aspect ratio (Ozkan and Tarhan 2016) The integration of multi-criteria decision making (MCDM) with the geospatial technology can also be used to generate the risk map that shows the spatial distribution of flood risk besides providing its extremity level by incorporating the factors of risk assessment considering various vulnerabilities of socio-economic or environmental concerns. An example of required layers and data sets for generating a flood shelter suitability map is shown in Figure 23.4.

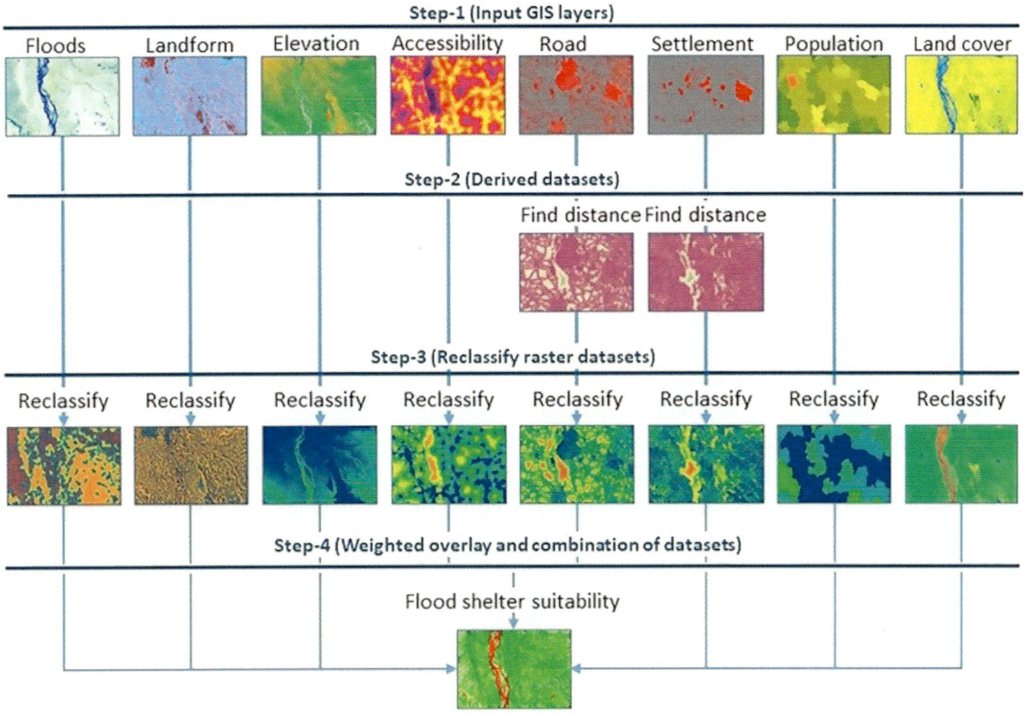

FIGURE 23.4 Example of methodological steps followed for the flood emergency suitability mapping using different factors.

GIS-based modeling methods, which are part of the synthesis of threshold, proved an efficient tool in the comprehensive planning and decision-making process in cities to recognize the flooding areas (Rincón, Khan, and Armenakis 2018). A rational flood risk analysis is another important spatial analysis tool that can be turned towards urban planning by assimilating land use and urban design component for controlling the floods and for emergency response (Tomar 2020). Although there are some challenges to implementing these tools and gathering the required information, GIS continues to gain recognition as a dynamic tool for furnishing, integrating, and analyzing varied spatial and geo-referenced data sets indispensable for planning and flood management. The sharing of geospatial technology with relevant stakeholders in the city effectively integrates different systems for a better result of GIS in flood management, reducing the damages (Arinabo 2020).

23.4.2 Earthquakes

Earthquakes are one of the rampant disasters bringing damage to a certain larger scale, particularly in urban areas and cities (Xu et al. 2008). Presently, the most pivotal task for estimating and evaluating the possibility of occurrence is mapping of risk for prevention purposes in predicting the earthquake (Jena et al. 2021). The risk of earthquake or potential damage of certain land in a city is due to the compounding of hazard, vulnerability of the built environment, and its exposure. The forecasting of the impact of earthquakes using a complex scientific evaluation approach innately provides convenient information for decision-making and formulation of policies and implementing the earthquake management initiatives for risk reduction. Multiple attempts have been devised worldwide to establish software networks that help in the quantification of the losses that were caused due to earthquakes. Some of the tools are well renowned for the evaluation and estimation of damage linked with earthquakes: HAZUS, RADIUS, HAZ-Taiwan, RISK-UE, etc (Sinha, Aditya, and Gupta 2008).

Earthquake data from concerned agencies such as digital elevation model (DEM), demarcated boundary, property details, and land cover/use maps and related information of the urban area can be used for probability, vulnerability, coping capacity, and risk map generation through the use of manifested databases present in GIS. Several calculations including inverse distance weighting (IDW), spline, Euclidean distance, kernel density, and buffer can be utilized to produce multiple layers for the assessment of risk in earthquake-prone areas. The resulting impacted areas can be used by the planners, administrators, and decision-makers to develop a framework for management purposes for reducing anticipated damage, subsequently lessening future risk in urban areas (Jena et al. 2021). Also, by using remote sensing, damage accumulation in cities can be located quickly in comparison to conventional ground survey techniques as satellite images and damage maps show the spatial distribution of destruction eventuate. These details can be used in search and rescue operations (SAR) and emergency actions like identifying damaged areas and escape routes, reckoning casualties, and formulating and implementing strategies for recovery and relief work including redefining locations for temporary housing (Mamoona Saher 2010). Some of these analyses of earthquake-prone areas can be done prior to the formation of the development plan of the city so that these areas can be marked susceptible to disaster and appropriate developmental controls can be applied for reducing the future uncertainty to damage.

23.4.3 Landslides

Landslides are considered as a dominant and serious risk in mountain regions where human impact is more (Audisio et al. 2017). The occurrence of landslides can be due to natural ecosystem processes or human anthropogenic activities or a combination of both. In most of the instances, human actions can trigger or accelerate the dynamics of natural processes by modifying the threshold of occurrence of landslides subsequently increasing the risks for human life and settlement. Land-use conversion and unsuitable land management practices usually interact with the natural factors influencing the hydrological response of soil, thus increasing the probability of hazard and risk associated with it (Moresi et al. 2020). However, proper planning and management can minimize socio-economic losses due to landslides. Landslide-prone areas can be mapped using geospatial technology for land use planning and disaster management for urban areas at the local level (Bayes Ahmed 2015).

Landslide inventory can be prepared by using the remote sensing systems that produce much useful land use information in the form of images to integrate them with additional spatial aspects directing the phenomenon of landslide in GIS. This formed inventory becomes rudimentary for landslide analysis focusing on the spatial zoning of specified areas. The images collected through the RS application from LANDSAT ETM+, IRS P6, ASTER, etc. with the topographical sheets of the specified area form the rationale for deriving elementary information on multiple aspects (Rai, Mohan, and Kumra 2014). The intense need to mitigate and prevent landslides results in the development of landslide susceptibility (LS) assessment techniques. An LS map has been prepared through the assessment, which details out probable places with the propensity of future landslide occurrences by considering some of the relevant aspects that are related to landslides and taking into account the prior spatial distribution of landslide occasions as inputs. Furthermore, landslide hazard (LH) evaluation comprises an important function in the damage risk controlling approximation. The principal and most significant level for LH assessment is denoted by the correlation of the landslide inventory with the geodatabase (Alexiou and Charalampopoulos 2020). The contemporary geospatial technologies covering the satellite-based remote sensing can be used for qualitative (heuristic approach) and quantitative (inventory/base-probability, statistical, base/geotechnical approaches) landslides prediction. The prospective high-resolution sensors create a way for the preparation of a better-quality landslide hazard zonation (LHZ) (Safaei and Omar 2010). Drainage map, contour map, digital elevation model, slope angle map, land use/cover map, a relative relief map, buffer map, photo lineament map, and geological map of cities are an

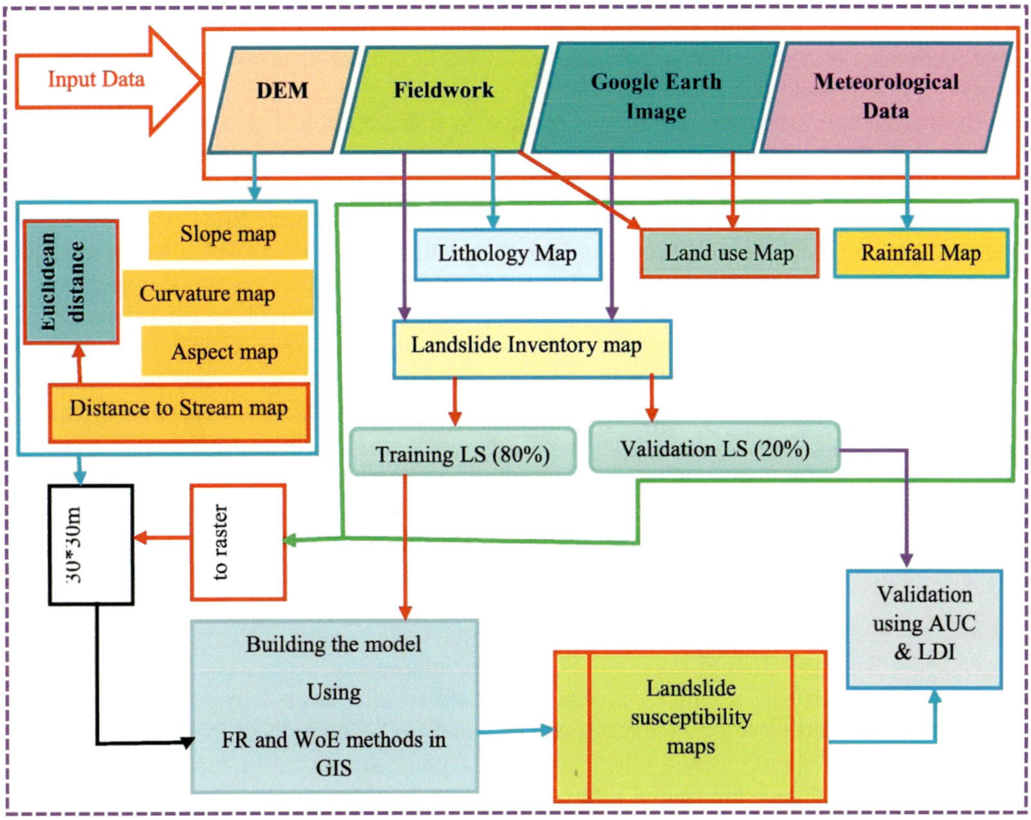

FIGURE 23.5 Example of method adopted for preparation of landslide susceptibility map.

elementary necessity for the zonation of landslides or for identifying landslide-prone areas, which can be identified with the help of GIS and RS information (Rai, Mohan, and Kumra 2014). With this above-mentioned information and recommended spatial analysis methods, landslide risk can be curtailed to a certain level in urban areas by accommodating required strategies in the developmental framework. An example of the method is adopted for the preparation of the land susceptibility map from various data sets and analysis is shown in Figure 23.5.

23.4.4 Cyclones

Cyclones are an inexorable hazard culminating from nature's ferocity that is beyond people's influence. It eventually leads to the destruction of the lives of people as well as livestock, agricultural fields, infrastructure, amenities, and telecommunication services in cities. Another major aspect to manage cyclones is the collection of information and mapping its spatial distribution (Nayak 2014). Cyclone is conditional and based upon location, therefore various tools and techniques can be used for evaluating and determining its susceptibility. The GIS is one of the vital tools that has been used so far for technical research of disaster, its impact assessment, and its management through the involvement of progressive planning and mapping techniques by urban development authorities in cities that can be taken into account for the conceptualization of weighted scores for hazard, vulnerability, and risk assessment based on intensities of occurred cyclones, their magnitudes, casualties, and current coping capacities (Hossain, Karlson, and Neset 2019). Low-resolution weather satellites can be equipped to help in the monitoring or tracking of cyclones with early warning systems to reduce apparent damage to humans and the built environment as a part of disaster preparedness. One such example is Global Emergency Observation and Warning (GEOWARN) by ESA and NASA, which has been developed by the integration of satellite communications and remote-sensing systems, consisting of a system for warning and relief aid in disaster management, particularly in the case of cyclones worldwide (Bello and Aina 2014).

To analyze and assess the damages, a method to procure satellite data before and after the disaster with the cooperation of an early warning system and analyzing them hand in hand for change detection and also images captured through satellites of certain areas prior to the cyclone and after the cyclone can be collected for mapping the situation (Nayak 2014). This could give a fair perception of the damages that occurred and destruction that happened and will help to identify the areas which need an urgent response in terms of force, food, or rescue. Researchers keep developing models based on tools and algorithms of geospatial technology for better real-time application. Correspondingly, a storm surge model has been developed that integrates past-occurring cyclone information with a digital elevation model (DEM) generating the cyclone risk maps for different periods, further assessing the risk correlating with urban environment factors to estimate the socio-economic vulnerability in cities that can be involved for giving signs of awareness to the local community and the responsible authorities to avail planning for the management of the cyclone at the grassroots level (Rana et al. 2010).

23.4.5 Forest Fire

Forest fires have affected millions of area units of forests all over the globe every year, eventually engendering the destruction of trees, plants, animals, atmosphere, ecosystem, biodiversity, structures, and environmental resources (Kanga et al., 2014). GIS technology can be used for the analysis of fire hazards and for the forecasting and managing of incidents of forest fires. It supports the integration of algorithms and other models to control the spread of fire. The optimal distribution of fire hydrants, fire station locations, delineation of fire regions as per the type of fire, and preparation of early region-specific intervention plans is very crucial for fire management while planning and taking preventive steps. Combined with remote-sensing data and machine learning techniques, GIS is also used to evaluate forest-fire vulnerability and provide hazard zonation maps. Some regularly used thermal sensors are appropriate, genuine, accurate, and cost-effective; still, they cannot be used in the identification of an actual forest fire from stretch (Mangiameli, Mussumeci, and Cappello 2021). Here, geospatial technology becomes a vital tool for forest fire hazard detection and mapping using satellite images of different brands.

Forest fire risk modeling techniques through multiple criteria analysis with the integration of distinctive layers led to the development of fire risk zonation mapping of specified areas using geospatial technology. Weights are allocated to different layers according to their susceptibility for the assessment of the probable forest fire vulnerable areas. Slope analysis, aspect ratio, elevation, settlement, type of fuels, roads, and agricultural areas can be suitably chosen as per their vulnerability and their function in fire activities. Then weights are assigned to these factors as per their importance in the fire susceptibility. FARSITE (fire area simulator) can be utilized for the study of forest fire spread and behavior using different aspects such as topography, forest type, height, density, etc. (Kanga et al. 2014). If a forest fire continues for more than a month, then the vegetation anomaly index can be used to delineate affected areas through preliminary identification. The vegetation anomaly index is created every 10 days and published in the early warning system (Ayanz et al. 2011).

23.4.6 Epidemic/Pandemic

Infectious diseases have antimicrobial and transmission characteristics, which slowly turn into a pandemic/epidemic. It has been demanded to unravel the disease's virulence by the local health organizations while considering the environmental and demographic aspects that support the propagation of infectious virus or bacteria through the spatial and temporal domains (Saran et al.

2020). Geospatial technologies are widely used in the fight against the pandemic/epidemic. Various GIS and remote-sensing tools are being utilized to integrate and manage the public health system, which has contributed to tackling the pandemic and/or epidemic (Sarfo and Karuppannan 2020). The earliest evidence of tracing the linkage between disease and location for producing maps for visualization can be tracked down plague epidemic in Italy in 1694 (McMichael 2018). In 1854, John Snow made a historic and remarkable contribution in the field of health and epidemiology by integrating cartographic applications with geographic visualization to fight cholera. Even after 160 years, maps are recognized as an effective application to understand and track infectious diseases like the 1918 influenza pandemic, yellow fever, cholera, and now COVID. Since then, web-based applications and cartographic techniques are used in the public health system (Boulos 2004).

GIS-RS systems come up with effective maps that help in understanding the geographical spread of disease for analyzing frequency of cases, disease mapping, contact tracing, disease association with environmental factors, spatial cluster of diseases, network analysis, etc. The consolidation of GIS with real-time databases related to infectious disease through mapping techniques result in the development of a geospatial dashboard and geospatial service framework, which helps in surveillance and monitoring of infectious disease. The integration of surveillance data (confirmed or active cases) with healthcare system data such as a number of hospitals, availability of emergency services, availability of nurses/doctors/ICU/beds, etc. (Saran et al. 2020) produces a holistic information that can be further used by the decision-makers, administrators, and executives to look upon the existing situation and to take and prepare strategies to prevent the spread of disease and ensure the availability of healthcare facilities to all people residing in cities as well as the people coming from rural areas. In this way, the lives of the people can be saved and spread can be minimized.

For example, the Bengaluru Municipal Corporation in India set up a centre, which integrates GIS technology with real-time data to monitor the existing operations and spread of the coronavirus disease (COVID-19) cases by generating maps, apps, and dashboards that display information about hospital capacity, ICU beds, and ventilators that subsequently helped in the management of the pandemic. The officials had the accessibility to real-time information from concerned organizations and authorities such as the health and police department for analysis of the situation, insights of established measures, as well as disseminating data to people residing in urban areas (India TV Tech Desk 2021).

23.5 CHALLENGES WITH GEOSPATIAL TECHNOLOGIES IN DISASTER MANAGEMENT

In this generation of increasing demand, the easy and fast approach to geospatial data sources becomes imperative. For emergency management, decision-making authorities rely greatly on geospatial technology that has the capability to generate and utilize precise, updated, and real information for disaster prevention and response events (National Research Council 2007). The application of geospatial technology in disaster management faced considerable challenges, too, which are mostly related to the operation, application, and management. However, upcoming challenges only stimulate more advanced research for easy applicability of geospatial technology for providing effective solutions (Abdalla and Li 2010) for disaster management and community strengthening by developing resilience in urban areas. Some of these challenges are described below:

i. **Spatial Data Acquisition:** A notable challenge in disaster management is the accessibility to the relevant data to the required individual/agency/organization in a functional form. "Functional form" here refers to the scale, accuracy, and details of the provided information (Esri and White Paper 2000). Various sources provide different information for the same data set that question its accuracy and applicability and impact output while integrating it with other data.

ii. **Geographic Data and GIS-Based Analysis:** The algorithms involved in the models of GIS analysis become more complex during operation. Multiple data sets endure temporal adjustments that subsequently induce uncertainty to the performed analysis resulting in inaccuracy and reconsideration (Esri and White Paper 2000).

iii. **Data Quality:** Geospatial information is only good when the information is available. The lack of quality assurance and control standards and testing processes lead to inconsistent and inaccurate data giving contrary effect to the analyses performed by the decision makers. Finding out whether differences operated analysis is the result of inconsistent or inaccurate information becomes a cumbersome task (National Research Council 2007).

iv. **Infrastructure and Data Security:** The infrastructural issues include the data security from illegal data acquisition and the protection of buildings where all the equipment is stored. The well-grounded power supply system, availability, and speed of the Internet, proper hardware system is another requirement that if not met properly can lead to disturbances and can significantly reduce the feasibility of spatial data infrastructure (UNCTAD 2012).

v. **Participatory GIS and Crowdsourcing:** Verification of the reliability and originality of data supplied by the crowdsources is one of the major challenges. Several crowdsourcing applications, such as Open Street Map, have they're own built-in verification process (Haklay 2010), but many other platforms don't have any such provisions; thus, the accuracy of the data acquired from these platforms is still uncertain.

vi. **Coordination Among Authorities:** Several efforts have been made to integrate geospatial data by agencies, and proved to be futile. At the local, state, and federal levels, coordination among the private sector and public sector is still not achieved in this regard (Folger 2011). Many authorities are somehow unwilling to share their information or make it public results in duplication of observations. Interoperability and data sharing are major challenges that need to be eliminated (UNCTAD 2012).

vii. **Scale:** Many elevation models do not have the appropriate resolution and hence these are not feasible on many applications of risk management. Present risk simulation works on small areas with large grids and are very lagged. Developing codes should focus on fine data grids that involve surrounding areas with their risk profile. Even finer resolution data will be required for cities to model the movement of natural, man-made, chemical, and biochemical disasters (Esri and White Paper 2000).

viii. **Cost-Efficient Data:** Geospatial technologies have a financial value related to them as per one's requirements. The operation of open-source software also requires highly skilled software professionals, which is lacking in certain developing and underdeveloped countries. The effective adoption and use of geospatial technologies require the advancement of applications that can cater to the determined demands of the organization. These challenges have a high cost associated for the effective integration of geospatial technology in development (UNCTAD 2012). The challenges with the use of geospatial and remote sensing technology have been shown in Figure 23.6.

Major challenges within the operational side is the low level of interoperability, lower data integration capabilities, and conflict between stakeholders' needs and expectations. These challenges are among many that put a hurdle in the integration of geospatial technology in disaster management. It is the present need to integrate geospatial technology in development plans and disaster management to get desired results. It is an emerging field as web geospatial applications have begun their operations globally and they supply their series to decision-makers and other stakeholders, which helps in accessing situational awareness models and real-time data at multiple locations, simultaneously. In

FIGURE 23.6 Some challenges with geospatial technology in disaster.

the future, authorities can overcome these challenges through a consultative process with various stakeholders and professionals engaged in the field of disaster management (Abdalla and Li 2010).

23.6 CONCLUSION

As an estimate, 2.5 billion more people are expected to live in cities by 2050. According to research by the United Nation's world population prospects, around 890 million people, which accounts for nearly 60% of the population of the world, are currently reside in cities and are vulnerable due to the frequent occurrence of various natural disasters like floods, cyclones, earthquakes, or drought. Some of the recent occurring disasters, such as the Sumatra-Andaman earthquake (2004), Cyclone Nargis (2008), Haiti earthquake (2010), and East Africa Drought (2011), have devastating impacts on the lives of people. Such disasters occur when our preparedness is not sufficient to prevent the impact of hazards on infrastructural development and human civilization. It takes years to develop infrastructure in cities, but even a single disaster can devastate the whole and take many countries to the level from where they started developing. As the world is full of uncertainty, socio-economic and environmental setbacks can take place at any time. To survive such shocks, our cities must be developed in a resilient way. The successful integration of geospatial technologies has proved to be a boon in handling recent disasters such as Cyclone Fani, Cyclone Amphan, Columbia Landslide, Florida floods, etc. that had fewer fatalities. This became a reality with the use of data analysis and precautionary measures with real-time surveillance and operation.

Remote sensing (RS) and geographic information system (GIS) have the ability to revolutionize the planning process in urban areas through improvement in the distribution of important services, optimization of supplies, and reduction in the cost of operation, maintenance, and monitoring. The application of geospatial technology can be significantly used in the integration of data acquired from space to real-time ground operations. These technologies can help in collecting the required data and mapping the disaster-prone areas by analyzing them. In developing countries, where the sources of resource mapping are limited, these technologies can be the savior. The prior mapping of the potential disaster-impacted areas will assist in the rescue and relief operations in pre-disaster and post-disaster periods. Developing a resilient city and infrastructure is the need of the current time, which can be achieved by proper preparedness, awareness, and planning. Adoption of an emergency management framework by the responsible authorities can be an appropriate step towards prevention and mitigation of uncertain hazards and their impact. During the impact phase of disaster when every minute counts, it becomes of prime importance to identify the disaster-affected regions. "Geospatial technology" can be used for the prevention, preparedness, response, and recovery phases of disaster management. Real-time and precise geospatial data with requisite tools have the capability to reconstruct the information into more relevant data to facilitate decision making to planners and disaster management officials that can be proved transformative for cities and will help in safeguarding the vulnerable from disaster and its impact for attaining sustainable development and establishing urban resiliency through sound technology and smart data planning and management of cities.

REFERENCES

Abdalla, Rifaat, and Jonathan Li. 2010. "Towards Effective Application of Geospatial Technologies for Disaster Management." *International Journal of Applied Earth Observation and Geoinformation* 12(6): 405–7. doi:10.1016/j.jag.2010.09.003.

Ahmed, Bayes. 2015. "Landslide Susceptibility Mapping Using Multi-Criteria Evaluation Techniques in Chittagong Metropolitan." Springer, no. March 2014, 1077–95. doi:10.1007/s10346-014-0521-x

Alazawi, Zubaida, Omar Alani, Mohmmad B. Abdljabar, Saleh Altowaijri, and Rashid Mehmood. 2014. "A Smart Disaster Management System for Future Cities." *WiMobCity 2014 - Proceedings of the 2014 ACM International Workshop on Wireless and Mobile Technologies for Smart Cities, Co-Located with MobiHoc 2014*, 1–10. 10.1145/2633661.2633670

Psomiadis, Emmanouil, Alexiou, Despoina-Simoni, X. Soulis, Konstantinos, Papazachariou, Andreas, and Charalampopoulos, Ioannis. 2020. Landslide Mapping and Susceptibility Assessment Using Geospatial Analysis and Earth Observation Data. *Land.*

Amoako, Emmanuel Oduro, and Lin, Sun. 2018. "Application of Remote Sensing Technique and Geographic Information Science for Flood Risk Mapping-A Case Study of the Offinso District, Kumasi-Ghana." *Journal of Remote Sensing & GIS* 07(01): 1–3. doi: 10.4172/2469-4134.1000224.

Arinabo, Denis. 2020. "The Contribution of GIS in Urban Flood Management. Research Gate.

Audisio, C., G. Nigrelli, A. Pasculli, N. Sciarra, and L. Turconi. 2017. "A GIS Spatial Analysis Model for Landslide Hazard Mapping Application in Alpine Area." *International Journal of Sustainable Development and Planning* 12(5): 883–93. doi:10.2495/SDP-V12-N5-883-893

Ayanz, Jesus San-Miguel, Ioannis Gitas, Andrea Camia, and Sandra Oliveira. 2011. Advances in Remote Sensing and GIS Applications in Forest Fire Management From Local to Global Assessments. JRC Scientific and Technical Report

Bansal, Neha, Mahua Mukherjee, and Ajay Gairola. 2017. "Smart Cities and Disaster Resilience." In *From Poverty, Inequality to Smart City*, edited by Fumihiko Seta, Joy Sen, Arindam Biswas, and Ajay Khare, (pp. 109–22). Singapore: Springer Singapore.

Bello, Olalekan Mumin, and Yusuf Adedoyin Aina. 2014. "Satellite Remote Sensing as a Tool in Disaster Management and Sustainable Development: Towards a Synergistic Approach." *Procedia - Social and Behavioral Sciences* 120: 365–73. doi:10.1016/j.sbspro.2014.02.114

Bizzotto, Matteo, Ayan Huseynova, and Victoria Vital Estrada. 2019. *Resilient Cities, Thriving Cities: The Evolution of Urban Resilience*. ICLEI.

Boulos, Maged N. Kamel. 2004. "Descriptive Review of Geographic Mapping of Severe Acute Respiratory Syndrome (SARS) on the Internet." *International Journal of Health Geographics* 3: 1–12. doi: 10.11 86/1476-072X-3-2

Coaffee, J. O. N. 2010. "Protecting Vulnerable Cities: The UK's Resilience Response to Defending Everyday Urban Infrastructure." *International Affairs* 4(July 2010): 939–54.

Dempsey, Caitlin. 2014. "GIS Lounge: What Is the Difference Between GIS and Geospatial?." https://www.gislounge.com/difference-gis-geospatial/

Eguchi, Ronald T., Charles K. Huyck, Shubharoop Ghosh, and Beverley J. Adams. 2008. "The Application of Remote Sensing Technologies for Disaster Management." *The 14th World Conference on Earthquake Engineering 14th World Conference on Earthquake Engineering*, no. November 2014, pp. 17.

Esri, An, and White Paper. 2000. "Challenges for GIS in Emergency Preparedness and Response." *Challenges for GIS in Emergency Preparedness and Response*, no. May: 29.

Folger, Peter. 2011. "Geospatial Information and Geographic Information Systems (GIS): Current Issues and Future Challenges." Geospatial Information and GIS: Background and Issues 1–34.

Haklay, Mordechai. 2010. "How Good Is Volunteered Geographical Information? A Comparative Study of OpenStreetMap and Ordnance Survey Datasets." *Environment and Planning B: Planning and Design* 37(4): 682–703. doi:10.1068/b35097

Hossain, M. S., M. Karlson, and T.-S. Neset. 2019. "Application of Gis for Cyclone Vulnerability Analysis of Bangladesh." *Earth Science Malaysia*, no. March, 25–34. doi:10.26480/esmy.01.2019.25.34.

India TV Tech Desk. 2021. "Here's How GIS Helps in Better Disaster Management." India TV. https://www.indiatvnews.com/technology/gadgets-how-gis-helps-in-better-disaster-management-691394

Jena, Ratiranjan, Biswajeet Pradhan, Sambit Prasanajit Naik, and Abdullah M. Alamri. 2021. "Earthquake Risk Assessment in NE India Using Deep Learning and Geospatial Analysis." *Geoscience Frontiers* 12(3). Elsevier B.V.: 101110. doi:10.1016/j.gsf.2020.11.007.

Kanga, Shruti I, Laxmikant Sharma II, Prem Chandra Pandey III, and Mahendra Singh Nathawat. 2014. "Gis Modeling Approach for Forest Fire." *International Journal of Advancement in Remote Sensing, GIS and Geography* 2(2014): 30–44.

Kumar, K.J. Anandha, Walia Ajinder, and Chaturvedi Shekher. 2012. "Disaster Report 2011". NIDM.

Magotra, Rohit, Parikh Jyoti K., Shaw Moumita, and Kaushik Asha. 2019. MOHUA. "Sustainable and Disaster Resilient Urban Development: Assessment of 10 Cities in India".

Manfré, Luiz A., Eliane Hirata, Janaína B. Silva, Eduardo J. Shinohara, Mariana A. Giannotti, Ana Paula C. Larocca, and José A. Quintanilha. 2012. "An Analysis of Geospatial Technologies for Risk and Natural Disaster Management." *ISPRS International Journal of Geo-Information* 1(2): 166–85. doi:10.3390/ijgi1020166

Mangiameli, Michele, Giuseppe Mussumeci, and Annalisa Cappello. 2021. "Forest Fire Spreading Using Free and Open-Source GIS Technologies." *Geomatics* 1(1): 50–64. doi:10.3390/geomatics1010005.

Mausom, Mayank, and Ankita Choudhary. 2017. *Urban Poverty: Trends, Assessment, and Inclusive Planning as a Solution BT – From Poverty, Inequality to Smart City*. Springer.

McMichael, Celia. 2018. "Cartographies of Disease: Maps, Mapping, and Medicine." *The Cartographic Journal* 55(4): 403–4. doi:10.1080/00087041.2018.1545461.

Moresi, Federico Valerio, Mauro Maesano, Alessio Collalti, Roy C. Sidle, Giorgio Matteucci, and Giuseppe Scarascia Mugnozza. 2020. "Mapping Landslide Prediction through a GIS-Based Model: A Case Study in a Catchment in Southern Italy." *Geosciences (Switzerland)* 10(8): 1–22. doi:10.3390/geosciences10080309.

National Disaster Management Authority; Government of India. 2019. National Disaster Management Plan, 2019. A Publication of the National Disaster Management Authority, Government of India. November 2019, New Delhi. *International Journal of Co-Operative Accounting and Management*, no. Volume 2, Number 1.

National Research Council. 2007. *Successful Response Starts with a Map: Improving Geospatial Support for Disaster Management. Successful Response Starts with a Map: Improving Geospatial Support for Disaster Management*. National Research Council. doi:10.17226/11793.

Nations United. 2007. "Disaster Risk Reduction: 2007 Global Review." *Global Platform for Disaster Risk Reduction, First Session Geneva*. United Nations.

Nayak, Ashok Kumar. 2014. "*Significance of GIS and Remote Sensing in Cyclone Management*." no. Indian Institute of Water Management, 52–6.

Ozkan, Sevim Pelin, and Cigdem Tarhan. 2016. "Detection of Flood Hazard in Urban Areas Using GIS: Izmir Case." *Procedia Technology* 22: 373–81. doi: 10.1016/j.protcy.2016.01.026

Rai, Praveen Kumar, Kshitij Mohan, and V. K. Kumra. 2014. "Landslide Hazard and Its Mapping Using." *Journal of Scientific Research*. 58(ii): 1–13.

Rana, S., K. Gunasekara, M. K. Hazarika, L. Samarakoon, and M. Siddiquee. 2010. "Application of Remote Sensing and GIS for Cyclone Disaster Management in Coastal Area: A Case Study at Barguna District, Bangladesh." *International Archives of the Photogrammetry, Remote Sensing and Spatial Information Sciences – ISPRS Archives* 38: 122–6.

Rincón, Daniela, Usman T. Khan, and Costas Armenakis. 2018. "Flood Risk Mapping Using GIS and Multi-Criteria Analysis: A Greater Toronto Area Case Study." *Geosciences (Switzerland)* 8(8). doi:10.3390/geosciences8080275

Rumson, Alexander G., Stephen H. Hallett, and Timothy R. Brewer. 2017. "Coastal Risk Adaptation: The Potential Role of Accessible Geospatial Big Data." *Marine Policy* 83(March). Elsevier Ltd, 100–10. doi:10.1016/j.marpol.2017.05.032

Safaei, Mehrdad, and Husaini Omar. 2017. "Applying Geospatial Technology to Landslide Susceptibility Assessment." *Electronic Journal of Geotechnical Engineering*, 8. 677–96.

Saher, Mamoona. 2010. "Disaster Assessment of Earthquake Using GIS and Remote Sensing." *Geospatial World*. https://www.geospatialworld.net/article/disaster-assessment-of-earthquake-using-gis-and-remote-sensing/.

Saran, Sameer, Priyanka Singh, Vishal Kumar, and Prakash Chauhan. 2020. "Review of Geospatial Technology for Infectious Disease Surveillance: Use Case on COVID-19." *Journal of the Indian Society of Remote Sensing* (8). Springer, India, 1121–38. doi:10.1007/s12524-020-01140-5

Sarfo, Anthony Kwabena, and Shankar Karuppannan. 2020. "Application of Geospatial Technologies in the COVID-19 Fight of Ghana." *Transactions of the Indian National Academy of Engineering* 5(2). Springer, Singapore, 193–204. doi:10.1007/s41403-020-00145-3

Sarkissian, Rita Der, Jean Marc Zaninetti, and Chadi Abdallah. 2019. "The Use of Geospatial Information as Support for Disaster Risk Reduction; Contextualization to Baalbek-Hermel Governorate/Lebanon." *Applied Geography* 111(September). Elsevier Ltd: 102075. doi:10.1016/j.apgeog.2019.102075

Sharma, A. K., and Varun Joshi. 2010. "Use of Remote Sensing and GIS in Disaster Management in Gangtok Area, Sikkim." *Geospatial World*. https://www.geospatialworld.net/article/use-of-remote-sensing-and-gis-in-disaster-management-in-gangtok-area-sikkim/

Shrivastava, Rajesh. 2014. "Remote Sensing and GIS in Disasters Management-in Special Reference to Asian Countries." *Recent Research Science and Technology* 6(1): 153–6.

Singh, Anupam K., and Arun K. Sharma. 2009. "GIS and a Remote Sensing Based Approach for Urban Flood-Plain Mapping for the Tapi Catchment, India, IAHS-AISH Publication, 331(October): 389–94.

Sinha, Ravi, K. S. P. Aditya, and Achin Gupta. 2008. "GIS-Based Urban Seismic Risk Assessment Using RISK.Iitb.' *ISET Journal of Earthquake Technology* 45(3–4): 41.

Sowmya, K., C. M. John, and N. K. Shrivasthava. 2015. "Urban Flood Vulnerability Zoning of Cochin City, Southwest Coast of India, Using Remote Sensing and GIS." *Natural Hazards* 75(2): 1271–86. doi:10.1007/s11069-014-1372-4.

Srikanth, Dr. Geetha. 2021. "Geospatial Technology for Disaster Management." In *ISIM*. https://www.amrita.edu/sites/default/files/isim2021-speaker-presentation-geetha.pdf.

Surjan, Akhilesh Kumar, and Rajib Shaw. 2008. "'Eco-City' to 'Disaster-Resilient Eco-Community': A Concerted Approach in the Coastal City of Puri, India." *Sustainability Science* 3(2): 249–65. doi: 10.1007/s11625-008-0051-3

Tomar, Pallavi. 2020. "Urban Flood Management Using Geo-spatial Techniques –.SGVU J CLIM Change Water." 7: 115–23.

UNCTAD. 2012. "Geospatial Science and Technology for Development: With a Focus on Urban Development, Land Administration and Disaster Risk Management, . New York and Geneva, 1–61.

UNDRR. 2020. "Disaster Risk Reduction in The Republic of India: Status Report 2020." 1–36.

United Nations Development Programme. 2018. "Kerala Post Disaster Needs Assessment: Floods and Landslides-August 2018." no. August: 1–440. https://reliefweb.int/report/india/kerala-post-disaster-needs-assessment-floods-and-landslides-august-2018

Westlund, Scott. 2010. "The Use of Geospatial Technology in Disaster Management." *International Journal of Applied Geospatial Research* 1(3): 17–30. doi:10.4018/jagr.2010070102

Xu, Feng, Xuping Chen, Aizhu Ren, and Xinzheng Lu. 2008. "Earthquake Disaster Simulation for an Urban Area, with GIS, CAD, FEA, and VR Integration." *Tsinghua Science and Technology* 13(Suppl. 1): 311–6. doi:10.1016/S1007-0214(08)70167-6

Zhang, Xiaoling, and Huan Li. 2018. "Urban Resilience and Urban Sustainability: What We Know and What Do Not Know?" *Cities* 72(August 2017): 141–8. 10.1016/j.cities.2017.08.009

24 Analysis of Multi-Environmental/Geo-Hazards Challenges for the City Coimbatore, South India

Dhanya Praveen
Tamil Nadu Agriculture University, Coimbatore, Tamil Nadu, India

Ganapathy Pattukandan Ganapathy
Vellore Institute of Technology (VIT), Vellore, Tamil Nadu, India

CONTENTS

24.1 INTRODUCTION

Geo-hazards vary based on definite spatial settings, whereby enhanced resolution in hazard assessment necessitates detailed assessment at both the local and regional level (Woo, (2017). The most susceptible regions that are prone to the impact of geo-hazards are thickly populated urban areas. These hazards pose severe loss of lives and properties and other natural resources. Climate-induced disasters increase the vulnerability to food insecurity and a reduced ability to alleviate poverty (Alam et al., 2017; Krishna Kumar et al., 2011). Most of the geo-hazards are linked to climate activity and South Asia is particularly vulnerable to geohazards. The critical challenge for disaster management for any nation is the fortification of its population safety and preserving critical infrastructures in a proactive way. Building resilience has become a vital goal forsafeguarding infrastructures (UNISDR, 2015).

With regards to the state of Tamil Nadu, major natural hazards that threaten Tamil Nadu are due to cyclones and associated storm surge (Dhanya and Ramachandran, 2016). However, floods and

DOI: 10.1201/9781003126195-29

flash floods, particularly in urban areas, are not uncommon. The seismicity in general is very low and most of the regions fall under the category of MSK Intensity VI or lower1. Some districts also have some areas liable to cyclonic winds, storm surge, as well as flooding. The sea coast of the state may rarely be subjected to a tsunami generated by a nearby earthquake of magnitude 6.5 or a distant earthquake of magnitude 8.0 or larger. A distance of up to 1.5 km from the sea coast may be damaged if it is on an elevation of less than 5 m about the normal high tide level.

In India, 28% of the Indian population is urban and 60% of our GDP comes from cities. India's urban population is anticipated to rise 50% and going to be the second-largest urban population by 2050. Urban growth needs to be sustainable. Rapid carbon intensive growth may lead to reduced green cover, GHG emissions, rise in heat waves and heat island effects and poor air quality in urban areas (UNHABITAT, 2011). In order to have sustainable urban growth, smart cities play a major part at this juncture. The smart city concept highlights sustainable developments, capacity, and resilience building of human capital and infrastructure (Bakıcı et al., 2013).

Unprecedented growth in an urban population in India imbalances its natural settings. The urban centres become more and more prone to a rise in air, water, and noise pollutions and disasters. In India, urban areas depict the hard reality of economic inequalities that can be seen in the growth of high-rise buildings along with slums. Coimbatore is not an exception. Even during the initial lockdown during the pandemic COVID-19 outbreak in April 2020, it was seen that the city of Coimbatore had an enormous corpus of migrant workers from northern Indian states inhabiting the city. The city has a huge potential to develop its quality of life in terms of water and waste management, sanitation, disaster preparedness, traffic flow, healthcare facilities, etc.

Regional climate models provide the scientific communities with higher-resolution climatic projections for future. It has been used in different parts of the world for climate change detection analysis (Rupa Kumar, 2006; Seneviratne et al., 2012). The mean temperature of India has been enhanced by 0.7°C during 1901–2018 and the average duration of heat wave events is also projected to nearly double by the latter part of the 21st century under the RCP8.5 scenario (Krishnan et al., 2020). Regional disparities in the direction and magnitude of these changes will be the driving force for alterations in hydrological cycle and drought situations in already water-stressed regions. Once in every two and half years, the incidence of droughts and their impacts are visible in the state of Tamil Nadu (Nathan, 1995).

Tropical countries are home to a vast majority of urban slum dwellers, and their health is also threatened by a variety of vector-borne diseases, influenced by social and environmental elements (Campbell-Lendrum and Corvalan, 2007). Apart from this biophysical threats, thickly populated tropics are prone to earthquakes of various magnitude. A probabilistic seismic hazard zonation was carried out for the Tamil Nadu by Menon et al. (2010) and identified 11 areal source zones. The present study area of Coimbatore comes under Tier -II city. The total number of slums in Coimbatore city is 34,343, with a population of 129,181. This represents about 12.29% of Coimbatore's total population. Nevertheless, there are serious environmental, administrative, and socioeconomic trials that Coimbatore city needs to address to fully transform it to a smart city. It is highly imperative to improve our understanding on seismo-tectonic characterization, monitor, and record relevant spatial data (Iyengar et al., 1999, Gupta, 2006, Mohanty et al., 2009). Hence, this chapter is an attempt to improve the existing knowledge in this regard and make the valuable information accessible to the stakeholders.

24.2 MATERIALS AND METHODS

24.2.1 Study Area

Coimbatore is positioned between the latitude 11°1′6″N and longitude 76°58′21″E in south India. It has an average elevation of 411 metres (1,349 ft) above sea level and surrounded by Noyyal River, in northwestern Tamil Nadu (Figure 24.1). It covers an area of 642.12 km^2 (247.92 sq. mi)

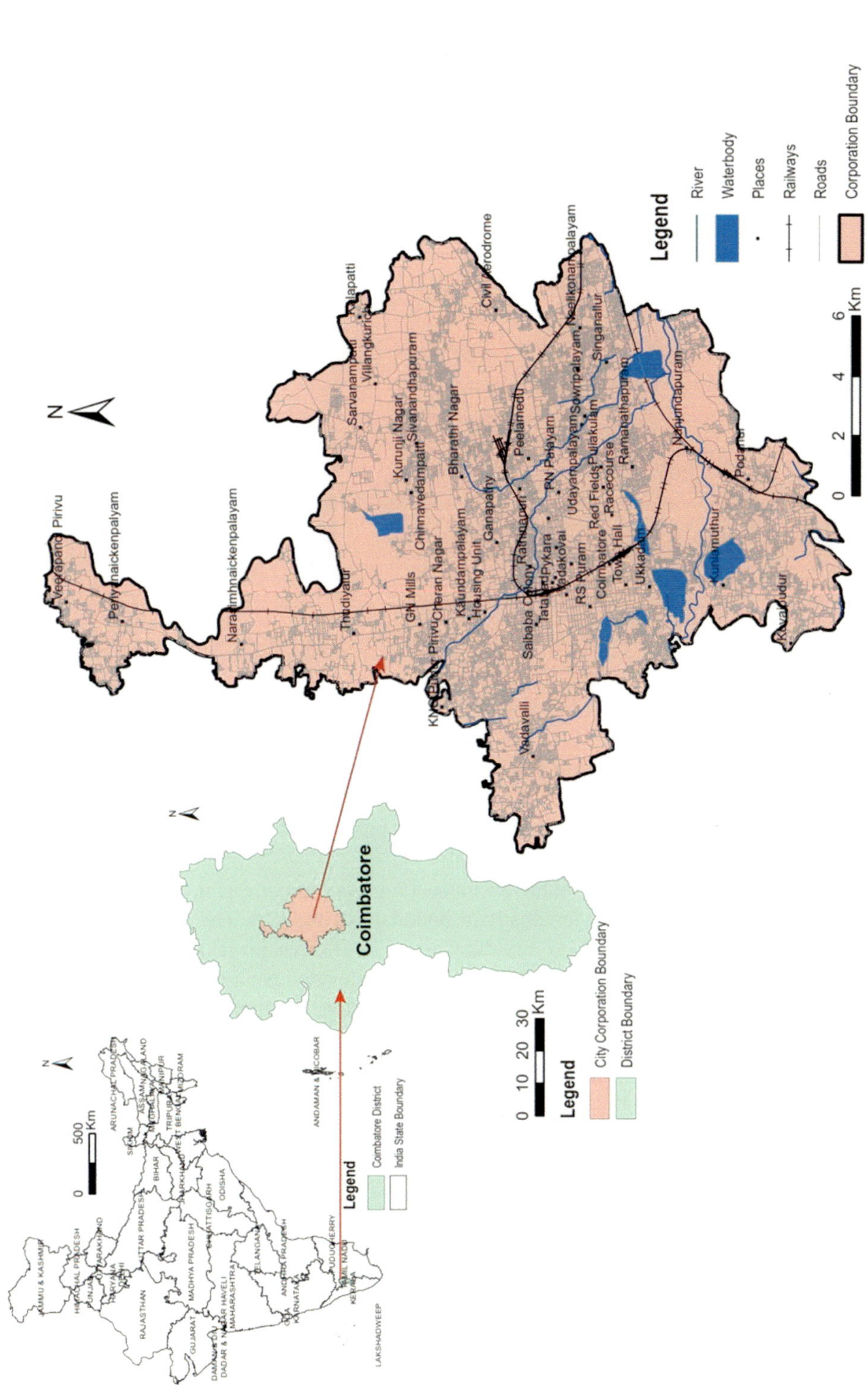

FIGURE 24.1 Location map of the study area.

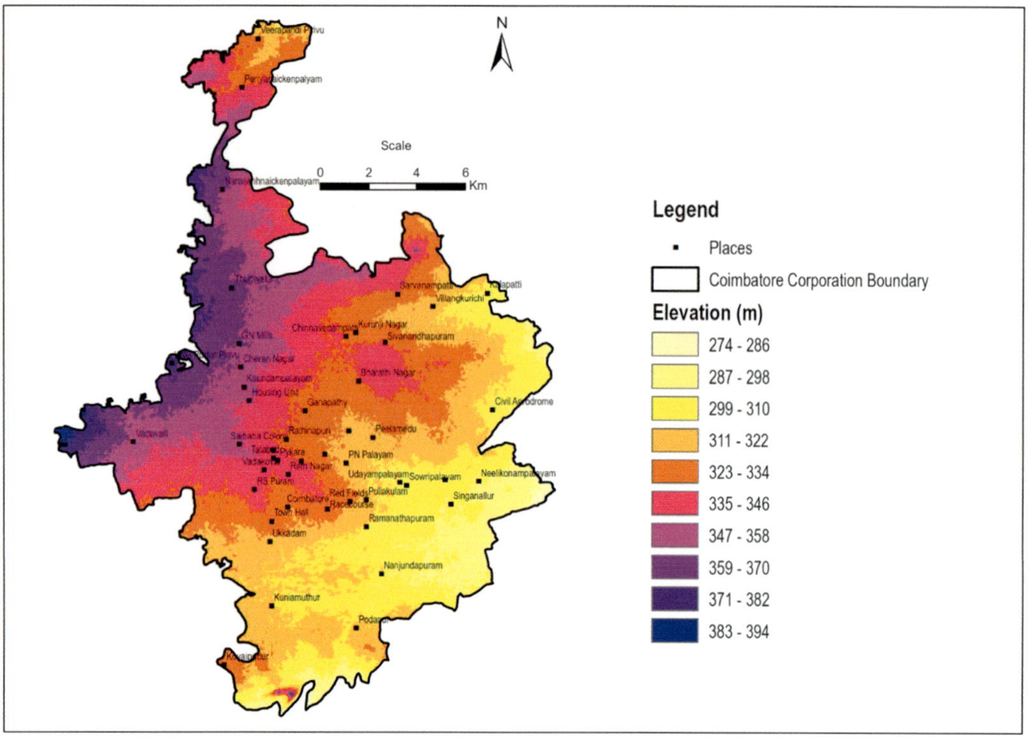

FIGURE 24.2 Digital elevation map of Coimbatore city.

and encircled by the Western Ghats mountain range to the west and the north and with reserve forests of the Nilgiri Biosphere Reserve on the north. Figure 24.2 illustrates that the elevation of the Coimbatore city ranges from 274 mts in the eastern parts to 394 meters in the western parts. The slope is towards the east.

Rainwater during the northeast and southwest monsoon plays a major role in maintaining the river flow in the Noyyal River that shares the southern boundary of the city. The Noyyal River has an extensive system of tanks fed by the river and rainwater. The eight major tanks and wetlands of the city: Singanallur, Valankulam, Ukkadam Periyakulam, Selvampathy, Narasampathi, Krishnampathi, Selvachinthamani, and Kumaraswami. The city has two distinctive topographical regions: majority of the urban area of the city comes under the drier eastern parts and the western part shares boarders with the Nilgiris, Anaimalai, and Munnar ranges.

Coimbatore, a fast-growing Tier-II city, stands as the second-largest city in Tamil Nadu. In the past, robust textile and cotton industry flourished in the city, it was diversified of late into services, IT, jewellery, wet grinders, pumps, poultry, and auto parts.

According to the provisional reports of Census India, the total population of Coimbatore in 2020 is 2,7 86,600. It has grown at 2.85% during past five-year period (Figure 24.3). The density of population of Coimbatore is 731 persons/sq. kms. As there is an increasing demand from a growing population, surface and groundwater resources need to be managed in an effective and integrated way in the future.

24.2.2 Land Use Land Cover Analysis

For evaluating land use land cover, IRS P6AWIFs were utilised in this study. Landsat images were mosaiced together for the assessment, using Erdas Imagine software14. The area of interest was extracted by sub-setting the boundary from the acquired image. The framework of methodology can

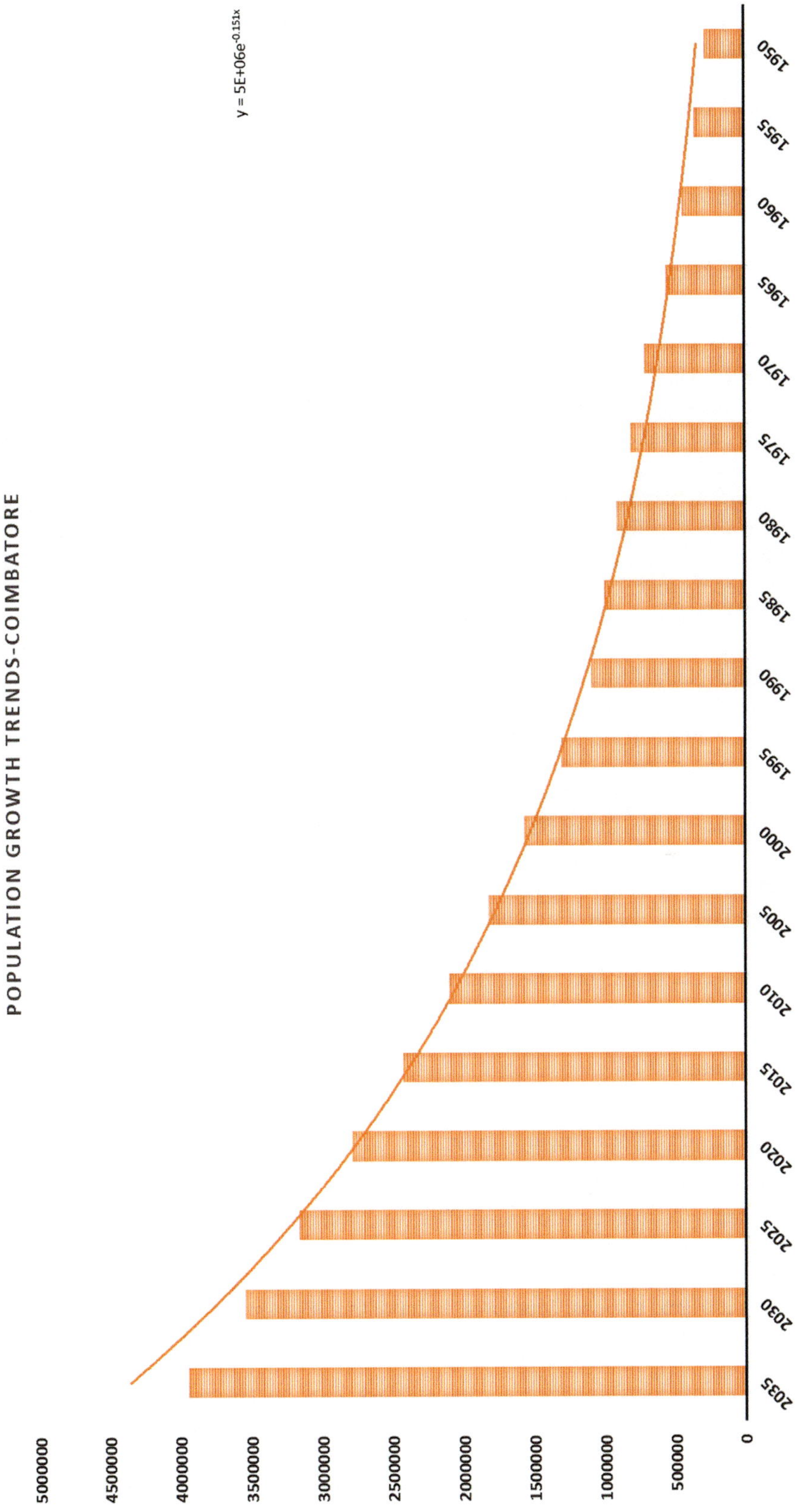

FIGURE 24.3 Projected population for Coimbatore city.

be categorised into five steps: (i) preparation of reference maps for collecting the prevailing and pertinent information in the spatial form, (ii) pre-field grouping of the satellite data, (iii) ground truthing, (iv) post-field correction, and (v) ground truth verification of the final map. Deviations in the unique spectral of reflectance values for each vegetation type was hauled out from digital data by interpreting satellite images. Vegetation looks in shades of red. Hardwood trees display lighter red shades than the coniferous trees. Characteristically, dark red color in the satellite image indicates healthy vegetation including wide leaf and light red color indicates sparse vegetation.

24.2.3 Seismic Hazard Zonation of Coimbatore

Analysing the past records on earthquakes provides an idea of the seismic status of a region. The seismic zonation studies necessitates a selection of varied geological and seismological information. Preserving the details regarding the epicentres, origin time, focus, depth, and magnitude of the fault systems to identify the currently active faults and for future predictions. A collection of past events of Indian earthquakes are available but none of them is up to date and comprehensive. The earliest publication is by Oldham, which gives a list of significant Indian earthquakes up to 1,869. A list of significant earthquakes in peninsular India was published by Gubin. Tandon and Srivastava have also issued a catalogue of earthquakes in India of $M \geq 5.0$ and above, on the basis of historical and instrumental and macro-seismic data available before 1970. Chandra compiled a list of earthquakes up to 1,975 from different sources.

Published literature regarding past earthquakes of $M \geq 2.0$ for a period of around 200 years (1807–2002) was referred from various sources for understanding the present seismicity of Coimbatore, Tamil Nadu. More than 50% of the realized earthquakes are of $M \geq 3$ in the past 200 years of seismic history. Earthquakes of $M \geq 5$ were scattered around Chennai, Villupuram, Ooty, Coimbatore, and Pondicherry off the coast (Ganapathy and Rajarathnam 2011a and 2011b). Apart from above said areas, the M 4 to 4.9 earthquakes are spread around Tiruppattur, Dharmapuri, Salem, Coimbatore, Trichirappalli, and Madurai areas. M 2.0 to 3.9 earthquakes were dispersed in northeastern and southern parts of Tamil Nadu State (Figure 24.4).

Literature reveals that earthquake hazards are not severe but moderate in the state. The maximum probable intensity zone VII does exist in TN with earthquake magnitudes on the Richter scale not exceeding 6.0 in and around the state boundary as shown in Table. As per the Vulnerability Atlas of India (2006), the districts that have a sizable area falling in this zone are Thiruvallur (100%), Chennai (100%), Vellore (100%), Tiruvanamalai (67.1%), Coimbatore (98.2%), Niligiri (97.5%), and Tirunelveli (66.3%), and Kanniyakumari (100%); besides, a few others have smaller percent areas. Earthquakes of $M \geq 4.0$ and $M < 5.0$ (BMTPC 2020, Ganapathy and Rajawat 2014a and 2014b).

24.2.4 Standardized Precipitation Index

Assessing SPI involves analyzing the rainfall anomaly with respect to its mean value for a given time scale, divided by its standard deviation. The precipitation is not a regular distribution, at least for time-scales less than one year. Climatic variables are adjusted so that the SPI makes a Gaussian distribution with zero mean and unit variance. Hence, the amended index permits to compare values related to different regions. Moreover, because the SPI is normalized, wet and dry climates can be monitored in the same way. The categories in the index calculation are provided below (Table 24.1).

McKee et al. (1993) have proposed the standardized precipitation index (SPI). It is applied for the purpose of monitoring and evaluating past drought occurrences in the study area. The SPI consigns a single numeric value to the precipitation, which can be compared across spatio-temporal time scales with distinctly different climates. Long-term precipitation data (1981–2019) has been used to derive the SPI for Coimbatore and is presented in Table 24.1.

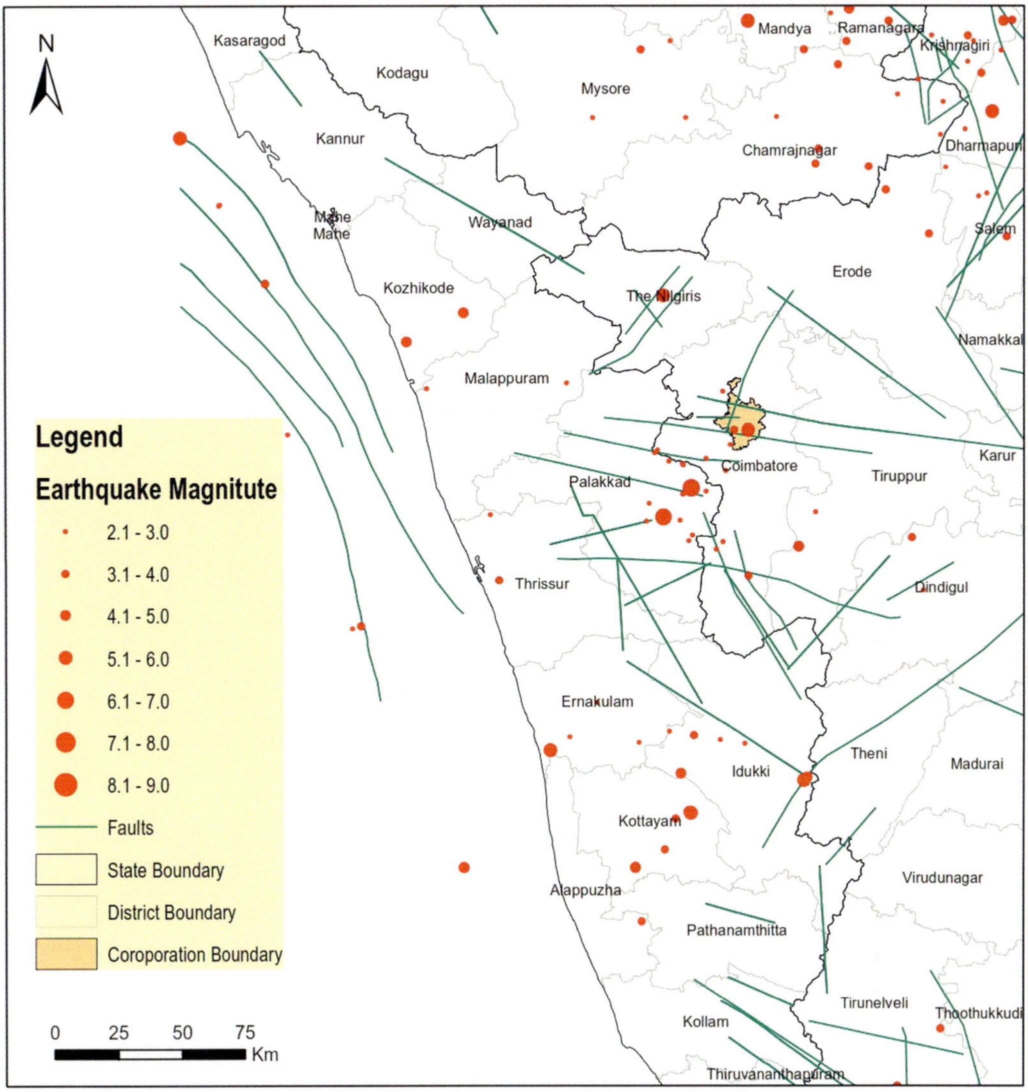

FIGURE 24.4 Seismicity around Coimbatore city.

24.3 RESULTS AND DISCUSSION

24.3.1 Status of Land Use Land Cover

Land use land cover analysis for the study area of Coimbatore is being carried out using IRS P6AWIFs, 2019, with a scale of 1: 250,000. The reference classification is taken from ISRO Bhuvan Methodology. The total area of Coimbatore metropolitan corporation covers 239.6 sq. km area. Out of that 23%, i.e., 55.1 sq. km areas are under built-up areas. About 40.6 sq. km areas cover fallow land and 11.5% of the area covers waste lands; 1.4% of the area is covered by water bodies, which covers 3.2 sq. km (Figure 24.5 and Table 24.2).

Generally, kharif crop can be identified based on field checks to know their phenology and cropping pattern. Generally in the Coimbatore District, the varieties are short-duration varieties sowing from April to May. For the present study, the existing land use pattern is refered from NRSCs, Bhuvan land use map classification. The built-up areas are classified as urban and rural

TABLE 24.1
Catogarization of SPI Values

SPI Values	Classes
>2	Extremely wet
1.5 to 1.99	Very wet
1.0 to 1.49	Moderately wet
–0.99 to 0.99	Near normal
–1 to –1.49	Moderately dry
–1.5 to –1.99	Severely dry
< –2	Extremely dry

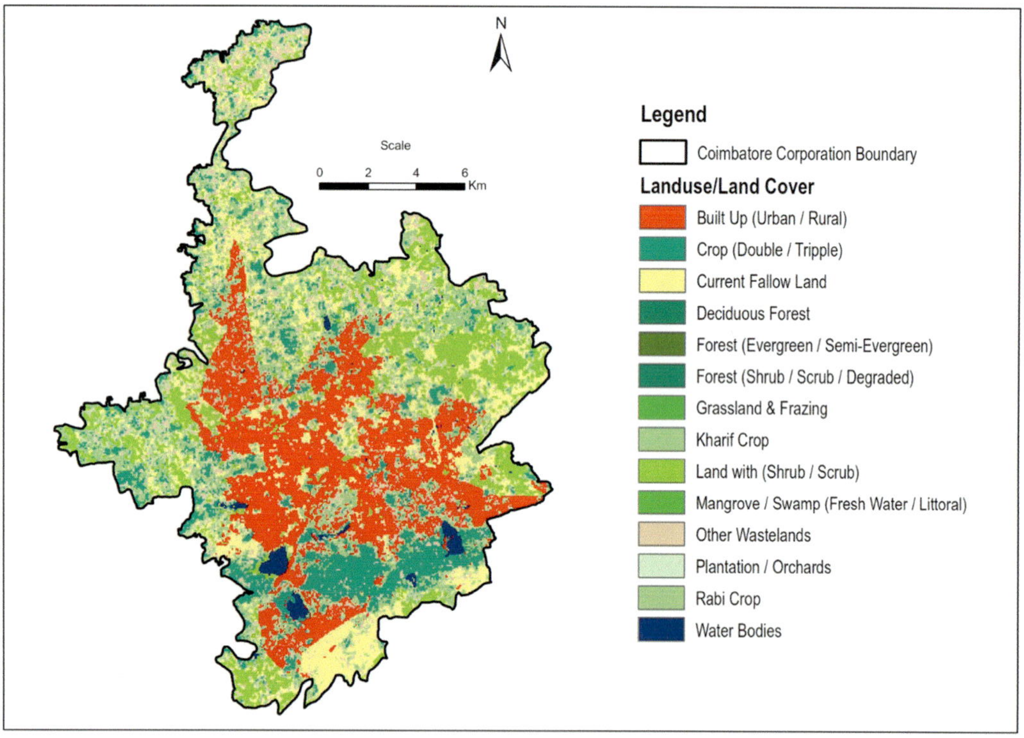

FIGURE 24.5 Land use land cover status of Coimbatore city as per 2019.

areas. Generally, the building types will be helpful to classify the urban and rural areas. However, high-resolution satellite images are required for the same. Since it was difficult to differentiate clearly and demarcate urban and rural areas, it is given as total built-up land. The central business district of the city is confined to the town hall, Ukkadam, and Poo Market. The wholesale market and small-scale industries can be seen in Gandhipuram. Ganapathi is the central business area, saibaba colony. The industrial belt extends to Chinnavedam patti, Avinashi road, Mettupalayam road, and Pollachi axial roads. The slum areas of Coimbatore are located mainly in the ukkadam areas. High-class/posh residential areas can be seen in RS Puram, Race Course road, etc. The city's latest spatial expansions can be found in the northwest directions, mainly to Periyanaicken Palayam, Thondamuthur areas, etc. Military areas comprise Race cource and CRPF camp areas.

TABLE 24.2
Land Use/Land Cover Classification of the Study Area

Sl.No	Land Use/Land Cover Type	Area (Sq. km)	Area (%)
1	Built Up (Urban/Rural)	55.1	23.0
2	Crop (Double/Tripple)	26.8	11.2
3	Current Fallow Land	40.6	16.9
4	Kharif Crop	24.4	10.2
5	Land with (Shrub/Scrub)	32.8	13.7
6	Other Wastelands	27.6	11.5
7	Rabi Crop	29.1	12.1
8	Water Bodies	3.2	1.4
	Total	**239.6**	**100.0**

24.3.2 Earthquake Zonation of Coimbatore

According to the latest issue of IS 1983, Coimbatore city is classified as Zone III, with Zone II corresponding to the least danger and Zone V corresponding to the utmost hazard within the region. Since 1900, there have been no significant earthquakes in Coimbatore. Zone III will be considered an expected magnitude of 6.9 (Figure 24.6). The whole Coimbatore city is under Zone III. Since 23% of the CMA areas are covered by built-up areas, the 1900 Coimbatore earthquake repeats the vulnerability scenario to Coimbatore will be very high and with risk to life of the people. Earthquakes in the recent past have invoked questions about the safety of India's major cities, which are densely populated and have significant infrastructure and economic investment. As a consequence, even moderate incidents can cause major socioeconomic disasters. This is very well applicable to the Coimbatore city as it has to upgrade its urban growth standards. It is critical to evaluate the seismic proneness of the major cities of our country.

Similar works have been published by various researchers. Raghukanth, and Iyengar, (2007) have conducted an appraisal of seismic spectral acceleration in peninsular India. A similar hazard response spectra study for Mumbai city was carried out by his group of researchers. Mahajan et al. (2010) and Sardana et al. (2019) have conducted an assessment on plausible seismic hazards for the northwestern region of the Himalayas. However, Coimbatore city lacks such detailed study to date. The outcomes from this type of research studies form valuable assets as far as preparedness to disasters are concerned.

24.3.3 Standardized Precipitation Index

Water needs of an urban area are hit frequently by unprecedented rainfall variability. Many blocks in Coimbatore are semi-exploited or exploited groundwater status. The long-time scale SPI-12-monthly analysis indicates hydrological droughts situations that have an impact on stream flow and reservoir levels. It puts pressure on drinking, industrial, and irrigation water needs and indirectly impact soil moisture status as well. The six- and three-monthly drought variability analyses are associated with short-term time scales that are 3- and 6-month SPIs. The short-term durations are important to agricultural interest while long terms are important to water supply management interest.

The standardised precipitation index analysis for the Coimbatore district shows a slightly wetting trend, especially for the current decade from 2010 to 2019. During the analysed period from 1981 to 2019, almost 28 periods were neutral, indicating some stability in the annual rainfall. However, there was below-normal rainfall for six years and above-normal rainfall for five years (Figure 24.7). The year 2012 recorded a moderately dry period, followed by dry periods in the

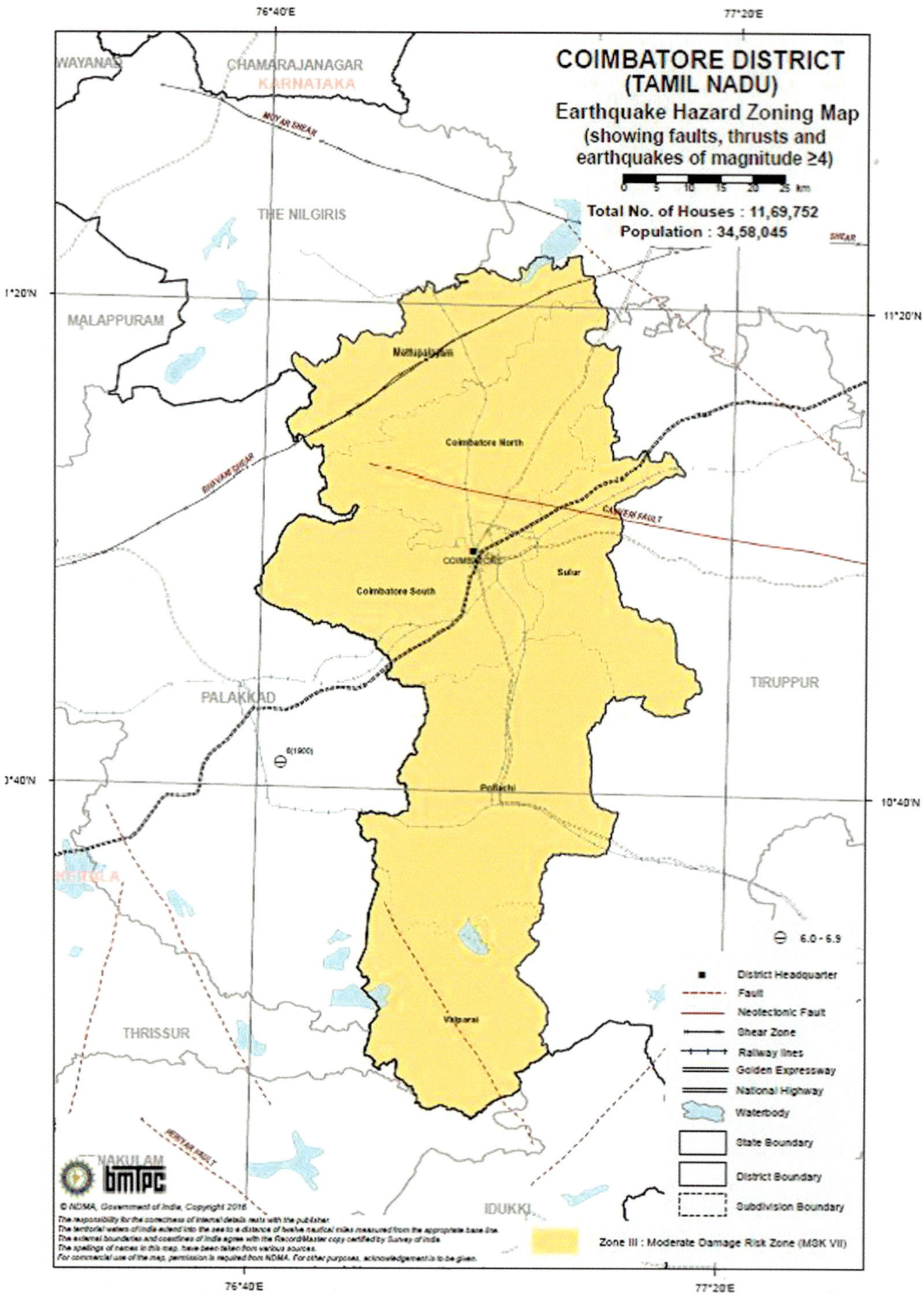

NDMA - BMTPC Earthquake Hazard Zoning Map; Map is Based on digitised data of SOI; Sub-Division Boundary as per Census of India 2011; Seismic Zones of India Map IS: 1893 (Part I) - 2002,BIS; Earthquake Epicentre from IMD; Seismotectonic Atlas of India and its Environs, GSI; Houses/Population as per Census 2011. "(First Edition)"
Disclaimer: The maps are solely for thematic presentation.

FIGURE 24.6 Seismic hazard map of Coimbatore District.

(Source BMTPC, 2020).

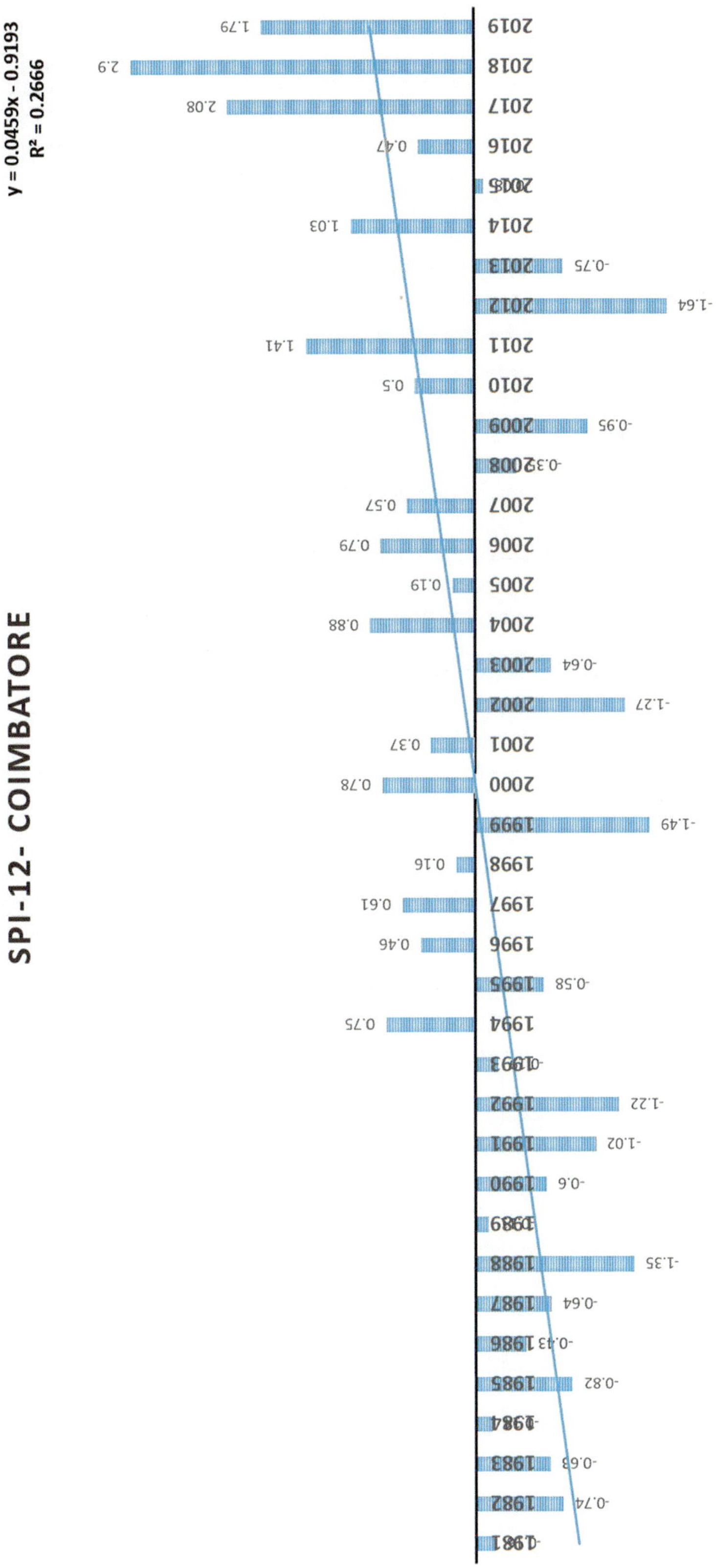

FIGURE 24.7 Rainfall variability analysis during standardized precipitation index.

years 1988, 1991, 1992, 1999, and 2002. Two years, such as 2017 and 2018, were recorded as extremely wet years. In Coimbatore, 2011 and 2014 were wet years and 2019 was a moderately wet year. Coimbatore received above-normal rainfall during 2016 to 2019 continuously in the southwest monsoon period. However, the rainfall during the northeast monsoon season was below normal during the years between 2012 and 2016. In the present decade, the mean annual rainfall received is 667 mm.

It is predicted with medium confidence that droughts will amplify in the already water-stressed areas because of reduced precipitation, combined with enhanced evapotranspiration due to climate change (Seneviratne et al., 2012). It can be expected that the already water scarce areas of Tamil Nadu may reel under water crisis in future(Pandey and Ramasastri 2002) . There may be overdependence of stakeholders on available groundwater resources. Researchers have shown that disproportionate pumping and overextraction of groundwater and may lead to depletion of valuable aquifers in different parts. It may enlarge the likelihood of more earthquakes to occur in the future (Acosta et al., 2018; Roeloffs et al., 2002). Global studies have reported about California that the extensive extraction of groundwater to irrigate cultivable lands could be stressing the San Andreas Fault, which means it could also surge the likelihood of earthquakes occurring in the region (Amos et al., 2014). The scientific reason behind it is wonderfully explained by the researchers that heavy groundwater weighs down the Earth's upper crust; however, as when that groundwater disappears, the crust is lifted, pushing up nearby mountains. Due to this modification, there may be aggravation in the fault line and possibly it is likely to trigger earthquakes in the area. It can also be implicit that extreme rainfall events can also be concomitant with liquefactions and landslide in some areas (Hunt and Menon, 2020). This visibly indicates the cascading anthropogenic effects of water stress on possibility of occurrence of earthquakes in urban areas. As a solution to the critical issue, government needs to have contingency plans for the vulnerable areas focusing on how far and how much continued supply and extraction of groundwater be allowed under its current purview.

Coimbatore will be benefitted hugely from a smart cities mission and ATAL mission for rejuvenation and urban transformation (AMRUT) aims to upgrade the living conditions for urban population. AMRUT works are underway in the city with increasing greeneries, reducing pollution by enhancing smart public transportation facilities, providing more number of non-motorised transport pathways, etc. It is the need of the hour to encourage builders to make more green buildings. Enhancing awareness among the urban dwellers to adopt more energy efficient, water conserving, less air polluting transport systems, conservation of existing lakes, biodiversity, and maintaining road ecology in the city are indispensable at this juncture (Phadtare and Jadhav, 2017). The construction industries should come up with more projects of green building projects in the city. The National Urban Livelihood Mission also aims to improve the livelihood for the urban poor and slum dwellers. Pradhan Mantri Awas Yojana for promoting affordable housing for urban dwellers.

According to Goal 11 of the UN sustainable development goals (SDG), empowering cities and human settlements to be inclusive, safe, resilient, and sustainable has been considered a pressing priority. Enhancing socioeconomic resilience to disasters such as earthquakes, floods, and droughts is highly significant in this context. As reported by the Asian Development Bank (ADB) Report (2016), authorities for urban development and scientific communities must assist city governments in the preparation of seismic and flood-resilient infrastructures and in devising appropriate incentive mechanisms for seismic retrofitting, but in most cases, substantial work and investment is required. Smart models of district level-readiness to disasters can be upgraded and upscaled into state levels and country or regional levels. This study can be considered a pilot step torward understanding the multi-hazard context and preparedness in smart cities such as Coimbatore. Multi-disciplinary and multi-institutional approach can be applied as a way forward for micro-risk zonation and risk assessment (Figure 24.8).

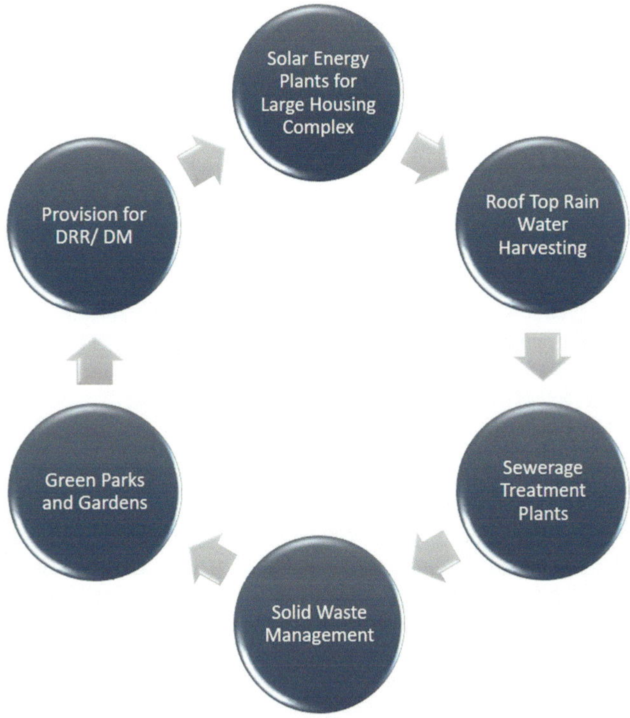

FIGURE 24.8 Way forward for sustainable city development.

24.4 CONCLUSION AND WAY FORWARD

Considering the multi/compound hazard context of Coimbatore city, it is better to adopt sustainable urban growth in these areas. It is advisable that district authorities prepare an action plan considering the hazard vulnerability context of the district in mind at the earliest. Built-up areaa in the city are expanding at a fast pace, along with its population. Effective utilization of the waste lands (11.5%) for afforestation activities and for water harvesting can play a major role in sustainable land utilization. As the whole Coimbatore city is under Zone III, as a consequence, even a moderate level of seismic activity may create more impacts in these areas. Water harvesting and well-developed drainage networks can help in minimizing impacts from drought as a major geohazard faced by the city as there was below-normal rainfall for six years and above-normal rainfall for five years. District and smart city disaster management plans for Coimbatore need to be updated, considering the varying geohazard potential in the purview of climate change. Proactive dissemination of early warnings and drought and flood preparedness strategies are the need of the hour to cope with these geo-hazards. A few of the proactive measures are as follows:

1. Buildings needs to be monitored for ensuring the scope of rooftop rainwater harvesting in the city.
2. Grid-connected solar roof top schemes need to be promoted.
3. There is water scarcity in the city; grey water use has to be promoted, especially for maintaining gardens and green spaces in the city.
4. There is a long way to go as far as solid waste management in the city is concerned, only in large apartments, source segregation of waste is happening, there is accumulation of plastic waste in the city, and less provisioning of dust bins at the present.
5. Green parks and gardens have to be maintained in the city.
6. Surface and groundwater resources need to be managed in an integrated way.

ACKNOWLEDGEMENT

The first author would like to thank the Department of Science and Technology for the financial support.

REFERENCES

Acosta, M., Passelègue, F. X., Schubnel, A., and Violay, M. "Dynamic weakening during earthquakes controlled by fluid thermodynamics." *Nature Communications* 9, no. 1 (2018): 3074. DOI: 10.1038/s41467-018-05603-9

Alam, G. M. M. et al. "Livelihood cycle and vulnerability of rural households to climate change and hazards in Bangladesh." *Environmental Management* 59, no. 5 (2017): 777–791.

Amos, C., Audet, P., Hammond, W. et al. "Uplift and seismicity driven by groundwater depletion in central California." *Nature* 509 (2014): 483–486. DOI: 10.1038/nature13275

Asian Development Bank (ADB) Report. "Reducing Disaster Risk by Managing Urban Land Use, Guidance Note for Planners." *Asian Development Bank* (2016).

Bakıcı, T., Almirall, E., and Wareham, J. A. "Smart city initiative: The case of Barcelona." *Journal of the Knowledge Economy* 4 (2013): 135–148.

Campbell-Lendrum, D., and Corvalan, C. 2007. "Climate change and developing country cities: implications for environmental health and equity." *Journal of Urban Health*. DOI: 10.1007/s11524-007-9170-x

Dhanya, P. and Ramachandran, A. "Farmers' perceptions of climate change and the proposed agriculture adaptation strategies in a semi-arid region of South India." *Journal of Integrative Environmental Sciences* 13, no. 1 (2016). DOI: 10.1080/1943815X.2015.1062031

Ganapathy, G. P., and Rajarathnam, S. "Zonation for seismic geotechnical hazard in urban areas – A case study Chennai City, India." *International Journal of Earth sciences and Engineering* 4, no. 3 (2011a): 436–442.

Ganapathy, G. P., and Rajarathnam, S. "Deterministic Seismic Hazard Assessment for Chennai City." *International Journal of Earth sciences and Engineering* 4, no. 2 (2011b): 233–240.

Ganapathy, G. P., and Rajawat, A. S. "Quantification of Geologic Hazard and Vulnerability for Chennai city, India." *International Journal of Geomatics and Geosciences* 5, no. 1 (2014a): 32–42.

Ganapathy, G. P., and Rajawat, A. S. "Earthquake Damage Scenario Analysis for Chennai City –Using Remote sensing and GIS Techniques." *A Compendium of Research Papers* during the Year 2013, published by Space Application Centre, Ahmedabad (2014b): 193–195.

Gupta, I. D. "Delineation of probable seismic sources in India and neighbourhood by a comprehensive analysis of seismotectonic characteristics of the region." *Soil Dynamics and Earthquake Engineering* 26 (2006): 766–790.

Hunt, K. M. R., and Menon, A. "The 2018 Kerala floods: A climate change perspective." *Climate Dynamics* 54 (2020): 2433–2446. DOI: 10.1007/s00382-020-05123-7

Iyengar, R. N., Sharma, D., and Siddiqui, J. M. "Earthquake history of India in medieval times." *Indian Journal of History Science* 34, no. 3 (1999):181–237.

Krishna Kumar, K., Patwardhan, S. K., Kulkarni, A., Kamala, K., Rao, K. K., and Jones, R. "Simulated Projections for Summer Monsoon Climate over India by a High-Resolution Regional Climate Model (PRECIS)." *Current Science* 101 (2011): 312–326.

Krishnan et al. "Assessment of climate change over the Indian region: A report of the Ministry of Earth Sciences (MoES), Government of India." (2020). Accessed from https://reliefweb.int/report/india/assessment-climate-change-over-indian-region-report-ministry-earth-sciences-moes

Mahajan, A. K., Thakur, V. C., Sharma, M. L., and Chauhan, M. "Probabilistic seismic hazard map of NW Himalaya and its adjoining area, India." *Natural Hazards* 53 (2010): 443–457.

McKee, T. B., Doesken, N. J., and Kleist, J. "Relationship of drought frequency and duration to time scale," In:8th conference on *Applied Climatology*, 17–22, Anaheim, CA (1993). 179–184.

Menon, A., Ornthammarath, T., Corigliano, M., and Lai, C. G. "Probabilistic Seismic Hazard Macrozonation of Tamil Nadu in Southern India." *Bulletin of the Seismological Society of America* 100, no. 3 (2010): 1320–1341.

Mohanty, W. K., Prakash, R., Suresh, G., Shukla, A. K., Walling, M. Y., and Srivastava, J. P. "Estimation of coda wave attenuation for the national capital region, Delhi, India using local earthquakes." *Pure and Applied Geophysics* 166, no. 3 (2009): 429–449.

Nathan, K. K. (1995). "Assessment of droughts in Tamil Nadu". http://digitalcommons.unl.edu/cgi/viewcontent.cgi?article=1057&context=droughtnetnews, accessed on17th July, 2016.

Pandey, R. P., and Ramasastri, K. S. "Incidence of Droughts in Different Climatic Regions." *Hydrological Sciences Journal* 47 (2002): 31–40. DOI: 10.1080/02626660209493020

Phadtare, S. M., and Jadhav, I. "Role of smart cities in sustainable development." *International Journal of Engineering Research and Technology* 10, no. 1 (2017): 45–49.

Raghukanth, S. T. G., and Iyengar, R. N. "Estimation of seismic spectral acceleration in Peninsular India." *Journal of Earth System Science* 116, no. 3 (2007): 199–214. 87.

Roeloffs, E., Sneed, M., Galloway, D. L., Sorey, M. L., Farrar, C. D., Howle, J. F., and Hughes, J. Water Level Changes Induced by Local and Distant Earthquakes at Long Valley Caldera, California. submitted to Bull. Volc. Geotherm. Res. (2002).

Rupa Kumar, K. "High resolution climate change scenarios for India for the 21st century." *Current Science* 90 (2006): 334–345.

Sardana, S., Verma, A. K., Verma, R. et al. "Rock slope stability along road cut of Kulikawn to Saikhamakawn of Aizawl, Mizoram, India." *Natural Hazards* 99 (2019): 753–767. DOI: 10.1007/s11069-019-03772-4

Seneviratne, S. I., Nicholls, N., Easterling, D., Goodess, C. M., Kanae, S., Kossin, J., Luo, Y., Marengo, J., McInnes, K., Rahimi, M., Reichstein, M., Sorteberg, A., Vera, C., and Zhang, X. "Changes in climate extremes and their impacts on the natural physical environment." In *Managing the Risks of Extreme Events and Disasters to Advance Climate Change Adaptation*, Field, C. B., Barros, V., Stocker, T. F., Qin, D., Dokken, D. J., Ebi, K. L., Mastrandrea, M. D., Mach, K. J., Plattner, G.-K., Allen, S. K., Tignor, M., and Midgley, P. M. (eds.). A Special Report of Working Groups I and II of the Intergovernmental Panel on Climate Change (IPCC). Cambridge University Press, Cambridge, UK, and New York, NY, USA (2012): 109–230.

UNHABITAT (2011). Cities Climate change, global report on human settlements, 2011. London, retrieved on March, 27th.

UNISDR (2015). Sendai Framework for Natural Disaster Reduction 2015–2030. http://www.unisdr.org/we/coordinate/sendai-framework

Woo, G. "Grand Challenges in Geohazards and Georisks." *Frontiers in Earth Science* 5 (2017): 19. DOI: 10.3389/feart.2017.00019

25 Monitoring of Urban Climate Using Geospatial Techniques

Archisman Barat, Sunny Kumar, Aakriti Asim, and P. Parth Sarthi
Central University of South Bihar, Bihar, India

CONTENTS

25.1 INTRODUCTION

The study of urban climates is not very new, since the first reporting of urban heat islands (UHIs) by Howard (1818); many research works had been carried out worldwide. To discuss the geospatial studies of an urban climate one has to follow through the evolution of the UHI studies as UHIs are the most widely studied urban climatic phenomenon. Globally, UHI climatology and magnitudes have been studied since the middle of the last century. Studies by Duckworth and Sandberg (1954), Landsberg (1956), and Chandler (1962) presented many new findings before the world at that time; most of these findings are relevant even today. Kratzer (1956) related atmospheric pollution to UHIs, while Myrup (1969) was one of the pioneers to design and suggest the use of numerical models in UHI study. But all of these studies did have a major drawback, they all are dependent on station/observatory data, and because of that these methods, were not applicable to every location on Earth. The advent of remote sensing opens the doors of entirely new possibilities in monitoring urban microclimates and UHI studies. The global identification of UHIs and quantification of UHI intensity (hereafter, UHII) has become possible only after the use of satellite-based temperature data, first scientifically documented by Rao (1972). Thus, we can mark this research as the premier research of remote-sensing applications in urban environments. However, due to limited coverage of early satellite data like in heat capacity mapping mission (HCMM) (Watson, 1982), a major part of the world, including the Indian subcontinent, did remain unexamined. Exemplification of UHI formations and urban climate studies through geospatial

DOI: 10.1201/9781003126195-30

techniques even in small cities and towns around the world had become possible nearly one and a half decades ago, with the use of moderate resolution image spectroradiometer (MODIS)–based data. Another important data source is advance very-high-resolution radiometer (AVHRR); furthermore, the LANDSAT data is also used extensively (Gallo et al., 1993; Singh et al., 2014, Kotharkar et al., 2018; Sultana and Satyanarayana, 2018; Veena et al., 2020).

25.2 URBAN HEAT ISLAND STUDIES USING REMOTE SENSING

The studies related to UHI types can be roughly divided into three groups based on the data and estimation techniques used (Voogt and Oke, 2003; Lokoshchenko and Korneva, 2015; Bahi et al., 2016). To envisage the importance of remote sensing, one needs to understand the drawbacks of other approaches of urban thermal environment and climate monitoring. The most common approaches are as follows.

Atmospheric UHI (AUHI)

The estimation of atmospheric UHI (sometimes also referred to as classic method for UHI estimation) is done mainly by the observed data recorded at different meteorological stations. It is further divided into the following classifications (Voogt and Oke, 2003; Veena et al., 2020).

a. *Urban Canopy Layer (UCL) UHI or canopy layer UHI (CLHI)*

This is defined for the layer of atmosphere from the surface to the average height of buildings. Thus, UCL-UHII can be estimated in situ using standard meteorological sensors at stations and mobile sensors mounted on vehicles (Makido et al., 2016; Voelkel and Shandas, 2017; Shandas et al., 2019).

b. *Urban Boundary Layer (UBL) UHI*

This layer is just above the UCL. The UBL-UHII is estimated using specialised sensor platforms like balloons, aircraft, and tall towers or by radiosonde. The UBL-UHI is strongly influenced by the underlying urban surface (Voogt and Oke, 2003).

The atmospheric UHI approach (especially UCL-UHI) is based on air temperature and estimates the closest UHII that is actually felt by the organisms (Sheng et al., 2017), but it has some severe demerits. It is difficult to generate and get data due to lack of desired station networks (Jiang et al., 2006; Meng and Liu, 2013; Sheng et al., 2017). It is found to be a very costly method also. The researchers need to set and consider more than 30 meteorological stations for UHI assessment over a single city like Delhi (Bhati and Mohan, 2016). Some other difficulties were also found for the estimation of AUHI intensity, such as the rural station is needed to be free from any influence of UHIs; because of this sometimes researchers had to consider a station as a rural reference site sometimes as far as 80 km (Lokoshchenko, 2014). This method is definitely not feasible for a densely populated landscape like the present study area, as in countries like India, where in a random stretch of 100 km several urban agglomerations (e.g., cities, towns, etc.) are commonly found. Thus, selecting the rural reference far away from the area of interest (city that is being studied) may cause the rural reference site to be influenced by some other nearby urban agglomeration. This method also has another major drawback, because from the classical definition of UHIs, the rural reference should be in the immediate vicinity of the studied city (Bhati and Mohan, 2016) only. Moreover, the UHII is dependent on the choice of rural baseline. Hawkins et al. (2004) have found that a variation of as high as 4 °C is observed due to the choice of rural reference. Thus, the selection of a proper rural location that fulfils all the criteria may not be possible for all the urban agglomerations around the globe.

Underground UHI (UUHI)

This is not a very common approach of UHII estimation. However, it has been observed in some recent research (Lokoshchenko and Korneva, 2015). In this approach, the UHI is calculated using soil temperatures recorded by underground sensors, which again requires a dense and widespread network of measuring stations; thus, it is very difficult to get long-term data for any station or in its rural reference.

From the above examples, we can clearly see that remote sensing has a prevalent edge over classic methods, and hence we will look into this in detail.

Surface UHI (SUHI) or Satellite-Derived UHI or Remotely Sensed UHI

This is a widely used and most feasible technique. It is also an effective and uniform method (Meng and Liu, 2013), pioneered by Rao (1972). In this method, the land surface temperature (LST) is considered as the indicator for measuring an urban heat island (UHI) (Voogt and Oke, 2003, Singh et al., 2014). LST is the skin temperature of the ground (Bhattacharya and Dadhwal, 2003) and it is influenced by the temperature of the soil surface, albedo, vegetation canopy, vegetation bodies, and other features (Qin and Karnieli, 1999). Satellite thermal infra-red (TIR) sensors used for LST determination are primarily based on measurement of top of atmosphere (TOA) radiances, from which temperature can be derived using Planck's Law (Dash et al., 2002; Weng, 2009). In other words, the thermal remote sensors/thermal infrared satellite sensors actually see the patterns of upwelling thermal radiance (Voogt and Oke, 2003). There are many methods and algorithms available for retrieval of temperature, like the radiative transfer equation (RTE) for LANDSAT (Sobrino et al., 2004; Sheng et al., 2017) and the split-window algorithm for MODIS (Hu et al., 2014). The UHI measured with the help of remote sensing is also known as surface UHI or SUHI. Zhou et al (2013) has divided the remote sensing of the UHI into two major parts; first is the use of images with medium spatial resolution (e.g., LANDSAT, ASTER) with spatial resolution of about 100 m (LANDSAT TM had a native spatial resolution of 120 m for a thermal infrared [TIR] band; the latest LANDSAT 9 has 100 m spatial resolution, while ASTER has a 90 m spatial resolution for the TIR band); these are useful for study of spatial structures of UHIs. The second class is the high temporal resolution data by AVHRR, Terra/Aqua MODIS, with spatial resolution of 1,000 m and useful for inter-annual trend prediction (Hung et al. 2006; Pongracz et al., 2006; Wang et al., 2007; Zhou et al., 2011). The UHII measured as SUHII, although being an indirect measure (Voogt and Oke, 2003) is one of most valid means to analyse urban thermal environments (Weng, 2009; Bahi et al., 2016; Sheng et al., 2017). If urban climate is studied under varying land use land cover (LULC) or the UHI is measured as an impact of LULC changes (LULCC), the remote sensing becomes the sole tool to assess because the weather stations cannot show the spatial variation of temperature caused due to LULCC and/or the urban or built-up surroundings (Purkis and Klemas, 2013; Li et al., 2012; Bektaş Balçik, 2014; Dihkan et al., 2015; Bahi et al., 2016). Thus, remote sensing has a great advantage over the classical methods of estimation of climatic variables, especially in urban environments. The SUHI with special reference to LULCC is much needed in the Indian context also, since in the last decade evolving SUHI across many cities of India has been reported (Peng et al., 2012), which can be a direct result of LULCC. A study in Pune, India, recorded up to a 4 °C change in surface temperature during 1999–2006 as a result of a 10% decrease in vegetation cover and 32.68% increase in urban and built-up area for the same period (Nesarikar-Patki and Raykar-Alange, 2012). UHIs, especially at nighttime, are a serious matter of concern if the quality of the urban environment is taken into consideration, and thus there is a need to monitor the magnitude and trend of nighttime UHIs. Because of the UHI, urban residents are deprived of cooling relief even at night (Papanastasiou et al., 2010). The urban heat island also causes serious concerns regarding heat-related illness and poor air quality (Qi et al., 2007; Lai and Cheng, 2010; Swamy et al., 2017). Longer and extreme heat wave episodes (Holderness et al., 2013) have also been reported due to UHIs. Though an UHI does not drastically increase global temperatures (Sarkar and de Ridder, 2011;

Houghton et al., 2001), it severely affects local climate and contributes to extreme events and heat-related mortality (Van Weverberg et al., 2008; Tan et al., 2010; Sarkar and De Ridder 2011; Emmanuel and Krüger, 2012; Bhati and Mohan, 2016). Thus, the monitoring of SUHIs may provide multi-sector preparedness in the context of urban planning.

25.2.1 Surface Urban Heat Island Studies in Gangetic Plains

In India, the SUHI studies are very limited if studies covering multiple cities within a single research are concerned. Thus, spatio-temporal SUHI dynamics within and between the cities are less known. Though there is plenty of literature available on metropolitan cities (Kotharkar et al., 2018), yet SUHI dynamics over the majority of the smaller agglomerations are still undiscovered. There is a lack of attention to the microclimate of fast-growing smaller towns across the Indian subcontinent (Kumar et al., 2017; Barat et al., 2021). As far as specific studies over the Gangetic Plains are concerned, one of the notable research, by Ghosh and Mukhopadhyay (2014), quantified the heat island effects over different cities of Bihar, but this study is very concise in nature and refers to six imageries over two years; thus, the long-term temporal aspect was not well elaborated as well as intra-city spatial dimension of SUHIs required further investigation. If we talk about a single major work across multiple cities over the Indian subcontinent, the work by Peng et al. (2012) can be termed as one of the pioneer works that has documented the SUHIs over multiple cities, including the cities of the Gangetic Plains. However, the work is for a very short period due to limited availability of data at the time when this research was conducted. As the work was done for a global scenario, hence special attention to local environmental and climatic factors was beyond the scope of this research. For all of India, a recent work by Shastri et al. (2017) is reported, which used the Aqua-MODIS data where the temporal stretch of the study spans over one decade. The study is very crucial as it has documented the SUHIs on the cities with >0.1 million population across India, for the very first time. Another study by Kumar et al. (2017) focused on the smart cities of India and also documented the SUHIs over 89 cities of India, including cities of the Gangetic Plains. Kumar et al. (2017) used both Terra and Aqua MODIS data, and they followed their own methodology in urban-rural delineation; hence, the study may not be directly comparable with the former two, but has also provided an in-depth account in the field of SUHI studies over India. The heat island formations were reported for almost all of the major towns of the state of Bihar, and were first reported by Ghosh and Mukhopadhyay (2014). Some other studies showed the average LST to have increased by 2.5 °C for the period of 1989–2014 (Ashraf, 2015) for the city of Patna. For other places like Agra and Aligarh, Ahmad et al. (2011) reported the formation of UHIs using MODIS data. The same research also opined for long-term satellite-based monitoring of UHIs over the Ganga-Yamuna doab region. Recently a research (Dutta and Gupta, 2021) found an increase in regional temperature due to pollution in Gangetic West Bengal. While recently a study by Majumdar and Chatterjee (2020) documented an in-depth analysis of fast urban growth of Kolkata, another research by Dutta et al. (2021) also pointed out an expansion of UHIs for Kolkata and its satellite towns. Some more recent works by Barat et al. (2018) over the Gangetic Plains of Bihar and by Sultana and Satyanarayana (2018) over different cities of India, have also added new findings to the scientific community. Barat et al. (2021) studied the influence of the Ganges River on the SUHIs for the cities of the Gangetic Plains, and documented the significant role of wind and LULC on the SUHI intensity. Zhou et al. (2019) have reported a dearth of SUHI research over India if we compare it against the population load. The same research also emphasised the need for long-term SUHI studies for analysis of inter-annual variation in SUHIs.

25.3 URBANISATION AND SATELLITE-BASED AEROSOL STUDIES

The essential climate variables (ECVs) as defined by the World Meteorological Organization (WMO), are the parameters that are essential in the context of climate change and its monitoring

(WMO, 2017). The parameters like temperature, surface pressure, wind speed and direction, water vapour, clouds, and aerosol properties, etc. are defined as ECVs for the atmosphere matrix. In the context of satellite monitoring of climate change, surely the second most important parameter is aerosols after surface temperature. The UHI and urban particulate pollution are also considered as two major problems that are becoming more severe day by day (Li et al., 2018). Not only the aerosol (as aerosol optical depth (AOD)) is an ECV itself, but also aerosols significantly affect other ECVs like radiation budget (Sarthi et al., 2019), precipitation over urban areas (Paul et al., 2018, Sarangi et al., 2018), temperature (Dutta and Gupta, 2021), and cloud properties (Patil et al., 2017). The aerosols are also linked with the formation of UHIs (Chakraborty et al., 2021) and urban climates (Li et al., 2018). The role of aerosols in atmospheric physics, as a result of rapid progress in understanding aerosol-cloud-climate interactions, has become a topic of great importance of late. The potential for significant and long-term effects on Earth's climate from greenhouse gas emissions, moderated by aerosols (Altaratz et al., 2008; Fuzzi et al., 2015; Kremser et al., 2016; Kreidenweis et al., 2019), is quite evident. Particulate aerosols influence the climate by radiation scattering and absorption. The degree to which aerosol particles affect the radiation budget corresponds with their atmospheric amount and their nature to extinguish radiation (Huggett, 2012; Gopal et al., 2016). Radiation extinguishing is the amount of the radiation dispersal and absorption. It is proportional to the mixing ratio of the aerosol mass and is also a function of particle size and wavelength (Pueschel, 1996; Moteki et al., 2010). The impacts of aerosols on climate are regionally heterogeneous and follow greenhouse gases and emission trends. Sulfate aerosols are one of the major drivers of temperature with aerosol-cloud interactions that are a main source of uncertainty (Graf et al., 1997). Black carbon (BC) aerosols also have an important effect on the urban environment and are studied along with SUHI (Shastri et al., 2017). Aerosols have a great impact on regional patterns of precipitation also (Lau et al., 2009; Trenberth, 2011).

25.3.1 Satellite-Based Aerosol Studies in the Gangetic Plains

India and especially the Gangetic Plains (GP) have always been a focus when it comes to atmospheric quality. The presence of a vast number of polluting sources, namely industries (Banerjee et al., 2011), domestic biomass burning (Murari et al., 2016; Sen et al., 2016, 2017), high vehicular density with limited emission control (Murari et al., 2015), open waste and waste burning practices (Banerjee and Srivastava, 2012; Banerjee et al., 2017), and crustal dust resuspension (Banerjee et al., 2015) are some of the associated causes. Then again, the burning of agricultural residue after harvest (Rastogi et al., 2016) and trans-boundary aerosol movements (Sen et al., 2014; Kumar et al., 2015) underpin regional pollution loading. Because of the dearth of ground-based aerosol monitoring networks, remote satellite sensing has long been used and is a key tool to calculate spatio-temporal aerosol variations and climate impacts across the present area. Ramachandran et al. (2012) conducted a long-term, decadal assessment of Terra-MODIS aerosol (AOD) distribution across India, including selected stations over the Gangetic Plains. An increasing trend of AOD at a few stations like New Delhi depicted the rise in anthropogenic pollution sources including fossil-fuel and biomass-burning activities. Prasad and Singh (2007) also reported similar evidence of increasing satellite-derived (MODIS and MISR) aerosol loading during 2000–2005 over major cities of the GP. Dey et al. (2012), using MISR-recovered AOD, estimated the Indian subcontinent surface PM2.5 for both composition and vertical distribution of aerosols. The study revealed exposure of almost 51% of the population of the subcontinent to high concentrations of particulate matter borne by air. Kumar et al. (2007) reported a relation between MODIS-AOD and surface PM2.5 in New Delhi. Information collected from satellites has opened up a new way of characterizing subtypes of aerosols across distinct spatial and vertical resolutions. Application of prevailing air masses for aerosol classification was made at Varanasi by Tiwari et al. (2015) on the basis of cluster air mass analysis. Kumar et al. (2016) used MODIS-AOD and CALIPSO aerosol vertical profiles to identify fireworks-induced particulate pollution over the entire Indian region. Srivastava et al. (2014) reported the presence of dust over Delhi's national capital throughout the year, with the aerosol layer seasonally varying between 2 km during winter/post-monsoon to 6 km in pre-monsoon/monsoon seasons. These works surely indicate that there is a seasonal trend in aerosol concentrations over the urban agglomerations. These case studies related to remote satellite sensing for the study of aerosol characteristics, distribution, transport, and radiative impacts over the GP provide extremely useful information about changes in climate and air quality induced by aerosols across the region. Mhawish et al. (2018) have discussed the aerosol remote-sensing studies over the Indo-Gangetic Plains (IGP); they have indicated that the majority of the studies conducted over IGP used MODIS- and CALIPSO-based data. Sarangi et al. (2018) studied the role of aerosols in modification of rainfall over cities of the Indo-Gangetic basin (IGB); thus, in turn, influencing the urban climate. In a recent study, Chakraborty et al. (2021) analysed the impact of aerosol on the changes in urban heat islands of the IGB during COVID-19 lockdowns. It may be concluded that although some good research has addressed the aerosol-climate relations in urban scales, there is still a need of urbanisation-specific aerosol studies over this part of the world.

25.4 THE SEASONAL TRENDS OF SUHIS AND SATELLITE-DERIVED AOD OVER THE GANGETIC PLAINS

Remote-sensing products provide the scientific community and policy makers a chance to envisage the climate processes at different scales, as the data is spatially resolvable. Seasonal trends for urban climatic variables thus can be easily studied using remotely sensed data. The SUHI is a microscale phenomenon and is governed by local factors like LULC (Bhati and Mohan, 2016) but at the same time is also influenced by large-scale events like heat waves or cold waves (Kumar et al., 2017, Barat et al., 2021). Thus, the seasonal trends are very important in the context of urban climate change.

25.4.1 Study Area, Data, and Methods

25.4.1.1 Study Area

Five important cities from the Gangetic Plains (Figure 25.1) are selected for the study: Prayagraj (formerly Allahabad), Kanpur, Varanasi, Patna, and Gaya. All of these stations fall in the Indian states of Uttar Pradesh (Prayagraj, Kanpur, Varanasi) and Bihar (Patna and Gaya). These two states cover the entire middle Gangetic Plain (MGP), and these areas fall under the Cwa category in Köppen classification (Farrar et al., 2019), the climatological summaries are shown in Table 25.1. These cities are important settlements directly linked with fast urbanisation. The census records for towns (https://censusindia.gov.in/towns/town.aspx accessed:12th July 2021) show the population of the selected cities as Prayagraj: 1,042,229; Varanasi: 1,203,961; Kanpur: 2,715,555; Patna: 1,697,976 and Gaya: 394,945 (and Bodhgaya: 30,857). These figures may change significantly with the publication of new data for census 2021. The Gangetic Plains are one of the most populous regions of the world, and home to 40% of the people in India (Mishra et al., 2017); it is currently facing the worst environmental implications, especially the urban centres. As the urban climate and the air quality are deteriorating, there is a strong need to study the trends of these climatic perturbations in seasonal scales.

25.4.1.2 Data Sources

Here we will discuss two major environmental problems the urban centres are facing currently. One is the modification of thermal environments, or the UHI/SUHI, and the second is the urban air quality. For the purpose, we have selected two different satellite-derived data sets from Terra-MODIS, so that the results could be more easily inter-comparable to envisage the actual trend for inter-linking of these phenomena. For studying SUHI, Terra-MODIS data from the Monsoon Asia

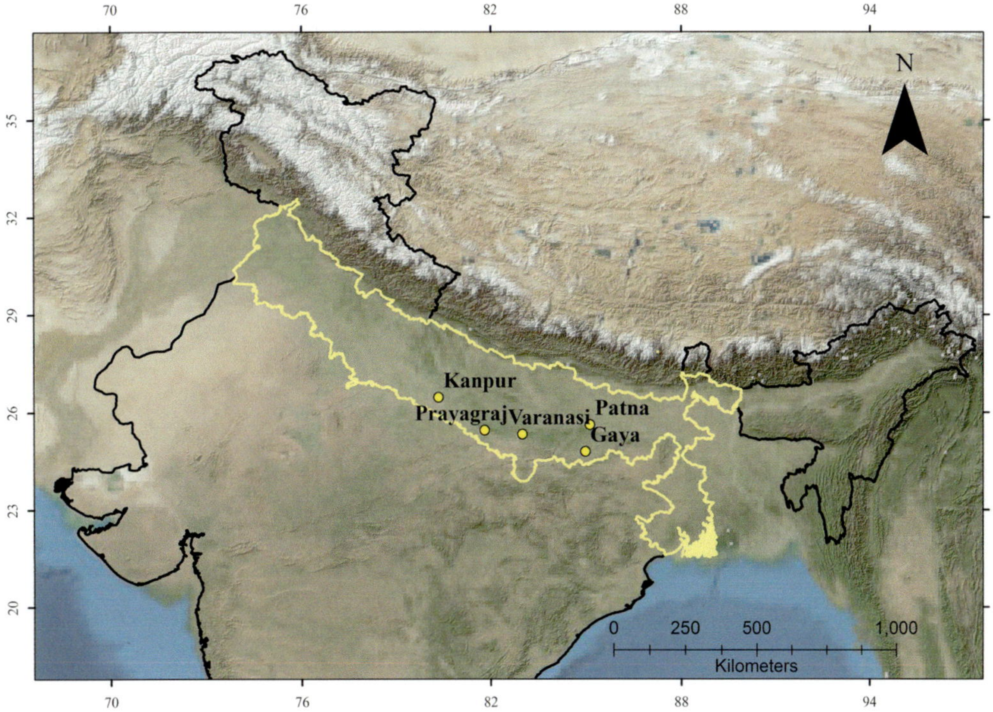

FIGURE 25.1 Map of study area showing selected cities. (Visualisation data source: https://neo.sci.gsfc.nasa.gov/view.php?data setId=BlueMarbleNG-TB).

TABLE 25.1
Climatological Summaries of Selected Cities[a]

S. No.	Name of the Cities	Average Annual Maximum Temperature (in °C)	Average Annual Minimum Temperature (in °C)	Highest Recorded Temperature (in °C)	Lowest Recorded Temperature (in °C)	Average Annual Rainfall (cm)
1.	Kanpur	31.9	18.8	47.3	0.4	79.2
2.	Prayagraj	32.6	20.0	48.8	−0.7	91.8
3.	Varanasi	32.1	19.3	47.2	1.0	101.6
4.	Patna	31.3	19.8	46.6	1.4	115.6
5.	Gaya	31.9	19.2	49.0	1.2	108

Note
[a] (Sources: https://www.imdpune.gov.in/caui/smartcities.html, https://www.imdpune.gov.in/caui/other.html).

Integrated Regional Study (MAIRS) was collected from the Giovanni online data system version 3 (Acker and Leptoukh, 2007). The time frame considered was for 2001–2014 or the MAIRS project data time span. For delineation of urban areas, we have used the IGBP (International Geosphere Biosphere Program) Land Cover (LC) data, and alongside the LST product the LC product was also taken from MAIRS project to ensure better spatial synchronisation between the data sets. We have used topographic base maps from user resources for ArcGIS 10.1 for city identification. The summer monsoon months (June to September) were not considered due to missing data. The representative data product was also selected on the basis of spatial availability of continuous data. For the present study, we have used nighttime LST to envisage how much heat is getting trapped in the urban structures, as from previous studies we know that the nighttime UHI is more impactful than the daytime UHI (Papanastasiou et al., 2010; Barat et al., 2018). We have selected the Terra-MODIS data as its overpass is around 10:30 a.m. and 10:30 pm of local time, and hence the actual contribution of SUHI can be more easily understood, as the trapped heat in the urban structures can be visualised more clearly than Aqua-MODIS (overpass time 1:30 a.m.). The AOD (as AOT) data were collected from NASA -NEO (https://neo.sci.gsfc.nasa.gov). The NEO data sets are cleaned and resampled data and are considered to be suitable for trend analysis studies. The NEO data sets are now being used in various Earth observation studies (Delgado-Baquerizo, 2019; Bagherzadeh et al., 2020; He et al., 2020; Liu et al., 2021; Basu and Salui, 2021). The details of the data sets are given in Table 25.2.

25.4.1.3 Methods

The methods of estimating a surface urban heat island are quite diverse and thus the intensity of the measured SUHI also varies amongst the different research (Shastri et al., 2017, Kumar et al., 2017, Chakraborty and Lee, 2019). Classically, it is the difference between the temperatures of an urban core with its corresponding rural areas. The station-based AUHI determination may be termed much simpler if we compare them with the SUHI studies. The classic estimation of UHI intensity (UHII) is (eq. 25.1)

$$UHII_{u-r} = T_u - T_r \tag{25.1}$$

where T_u is urban temperature and T_r is rural area temperature. It is a widely known fact that for the AUHI studies the air temperature (T_{air}) is considered while for the SUHI studies the land surface temperature (LST) is taken. For the AUHI, the nearest meteorological stations or some platforms with temperature sensors are taken, but in SUHI the pixel-level LST is considered. A major complexity arises when the location of the pixel is chosen, as we know the selection of rural reference sites significantly affects the UHII being calculated (Hawkins et al., 2004). For estimation of SUHI, the tri-zonal method used by Barat et al. (2018) is considered in this study.

This study used a three-layer buffer method adopted and modified from the basic three-layer categorisation by Lowry (1977) and Meng and Liu (2013). The considered method has a classical approach of comparison between the urban zone to a rural buffer, while assigning a suburban buffer in between to eliminate contamination in data. In the present study, the method is applied to some of the cities from a densely populated region of the globe, to ensure better precision (Barat

TABLE 25.2
Details of Data Used

S. No.	Datasets Used	Spatial Resolution	Time Period	Source
1.	IGBP Land Cover Types (MCD12Q1_MAIRS_IGBP.005)	0.5 km × 0.5 km	2001	MODIS
2.	Land Surface Temperature (MOD11A2_MAIRS.005) (8 day product)	1 km × 1 km	01/01/2001-31/12/2014	Terra-MODIS
3.	Aerosol Optical Thickness (AOT) (MODAL2_M_AER_OD) (550 nm Dark_Target_Deep_Blue_Combined)	10 km × 10 km	January 2001-December 2014	Terra-MODIS

et al., 2021). To estimate the SUHI of each of the cities considered in the study, the area of interest is divided into three major categories: urban (U), suburban (SU), and rural (R) based on the LULC data from the MODIS product MCD12Q1_MAIRS_IGBP.005 of the base year (2001). The continuous clustered area under the class urban and built up corresponds to the urban core, which is taken as the urban zone, and this urban zone is buffered with two concentric envelopes of suburban and rural zones. It was also ensured that the data over pixels representing a large water body is not taken into account, and hence such water pixels were removed from the study. The removal of water pixels has been done under a standard protocol across the methods (Shastri et al., 2017, Chakraborty and Lee, 2019, Barat et al., 2021) to ensure the quality of the land surface temperature data being analysed. The difference from urban periphery to suburban periphery and from sub-urban to rural periphery is taken at a distance of 2 km (≈ +0.018°) on each side; precise corrections were made to this value as per the local geodesic requirements. The buffer size is dependent on many factors, including distance between the urban core of interest and next nearest urban core zone (nearby city), comparability of size of the city to the area taken as the rural counterpart, thickness of the suburban buffer required to damp any noise in data, etc. Thus, this optimised distance taken ensures that each of the cities in the study area is free from interferences from neighbouring towns and at the same time each of the segments (U, SU, and R) are spaced enough to show independent trends. Figure 25.2 shows a representation of the scheme used for delineation. The area-weighted LST (as per the buffer shape) is extracted using the built-in functions in a five-dimensional environment of GrADS software (http://cola.gmu.edu/grads/gadoc/gradfuncaave.html), over each zone, and the SUHI intensity (SUHII) is estimated per equation (25.1). For the analysis, the monsoon months of June to September were not taken into account as the data for

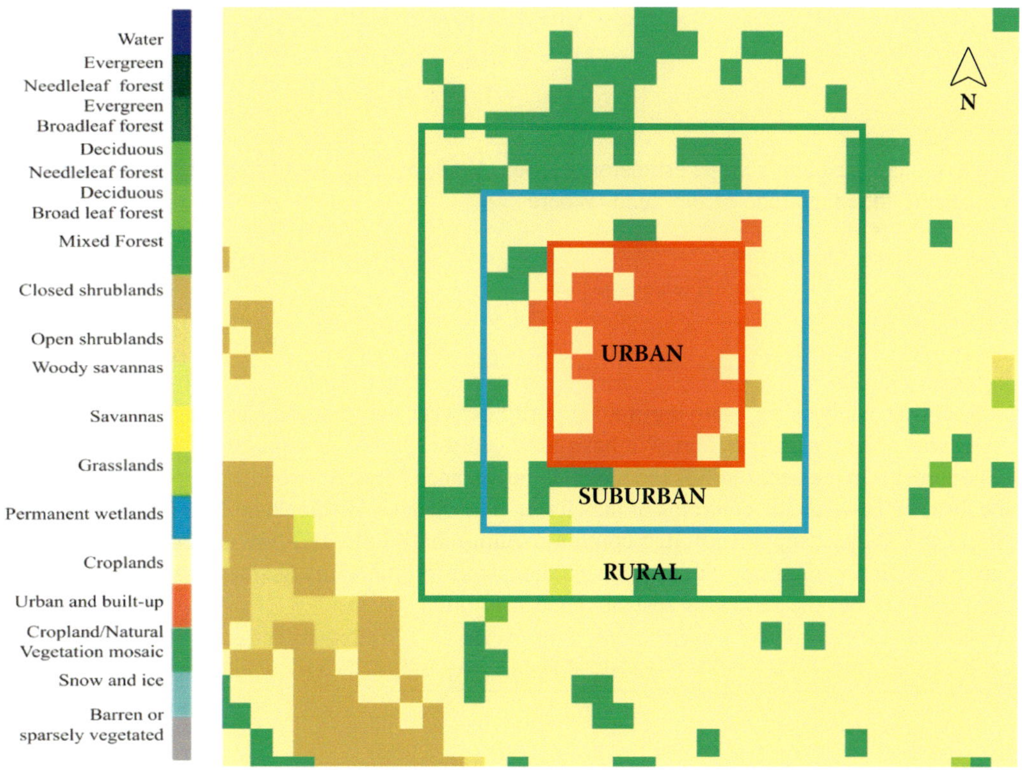

FIGURE 25.2 An overview of the three zone schemes used in the SUHI study (the actual buffers are modified with regard to city morphology, water bodies, etc.).

monsoon months was found to be contaminated with clouds and contained a lot of missing values. The estimated SUHI data for each month is then restructured to seasonal data for the following seasons, pre-monsoon (March to May), post-monsoon (October to November), and winter (December of preceding year to February). The data for AOD was also processed in the same manner. However, the data was extracted over the entire city landscape, including its suburbs and not over the three zones due to the nature of the parameter and data used.

As we were interested in monitoring the urban environment using the remote-sensing tools, hence it was also necessary to envisage the nature of the trend of SUHIIs and the aerosol loadings over the urban areas. This type of analysis not only helps us to understand the changing nature of urban environments but also endorses the fact of multi-dimensional applicability of remotely sensed data in the context of urban environments. The trend analysis was carried out using the Mann-Kendall Test on MiniTab® software. The Mann-Kendall test is a non-parametric test used to determine the existence of a possible significant trend in the data. The test is widely used and is considered to be a good tool for climatic data (Ezber et al., 2007; Kumar et al., 2010). The Mann-Kendall Test evaluates the null hypothesis (H_0) of no significant trend against the alternative hypothesis (H_a) for the significant increasing or decreasing trend. We have calculated the MK test statistic at a 95% significance level. The MK test statistic is defined for N number of data points as follows:

$$MK\ \ Test\ \ Statistic\,(S) = \sum_{i=1}^{N-1} \sum_{j=i+1}^{N} sgn\,(x_i - x_j)\ldots\ldots\ldots \tag{25.2}$$

where

$$\begin{aligned} sgn\,(\mathrm{x_j} - \mathrm{x_i}) &= 1 \ \ \mathrm{if}(\mathrm{x_j} - \mathrm{x_i}) > 0 \\ &= 0 \ \ \mathrm{if}(\mathrm{x_j} - \mathrm{x_i}) = 0 \\ &= -1 \ \ \mathrm{if}(\mathrm{x_j} - \mathrm{x_i}) < 0 \end{aligned}$$

We have also used Sen's Slope estimator (β) (Sen, 1968) over the study area. This value is used for visualising the magnitude of the trend. Where

$$\beta = median\left(\frac{x_i - x_j}{i - j}\right), \forall\, j < i, \ \ldots\ldots\ldots. \tag{25.3}$$

in which 1<j<i<n.

A cluster analysis for studying the similarity between the temporal variations of SUHII and AOD was done for each season. We have used centroid linkage cluster analysis in the Minitab® environment. In the centroid linkage method, the distance between two clusters is considered to be the distance between the centroids of the cluster. The distance is calculated by built-in functions in MiniTab® (https://support.minitab.com/en-us/minitab/18/help-and-how-to/modeling-statistics/multivariate/how-to/cluster-observations/methods-and-formulas/linkage-methods/ accessed on 12 July 2021) as per the following distance matrix formula:

$$d_{mj} = \frac{N_k d_{kj} + N_l d_{lj}}{N_m} - \frac{N_k N_l d_{kl}}{N_m^2} \ \ldots\ldots\ldots. \tag{25.4}$$

where

d_{mj} = distance between the clusters m and j
d_{kl} = distance between the clusters k and l

m = merged cluster consisting clusters k and l, with m = (k,i).
d_{kj} = distance between the clusters k and j
d_{lj} = distance between the clusters l and j
N_k = no. of observations in cluster k
N_l = no. of observations in cluster l
N_m = no. of observations in cluster m

25.4.2 Results and Discussions

The SUHI formation over the selected cities is previously reported by many of the researchers (Peng et al., 2012; Shastri et al., 2017, Barat et al., 2018, Chakraborty and Lee, 2019, Barat et al., 2021). Figure 25.3 is showing land cover along with a well-developed SUHI profile over the selected cities.

From these figures we can clearly see that the urban core is showing a much higher temperature than that of its surrounding regions. As we can see from Figure 25.3, the temperature gradients are very much dependent on LULC and thus cannot be easily studied from station data. Thus, this capability of remote sensing is very useful in the field of urban climate studies, as it helps scientists and policy makers to identify UHI hotspots within the city and the spatial spread of the heat islands. The entire seasonal time series of SUHII was analysed for each city, and the maximum value (amongst all the seasonal averages) for each city was recorded. We then plotted spatial distribution of SUHI for those selected time steps to further study their properties. Thus, Figure 25.3 (a,c,e,g,i) is showing the LULC of the selected cities, whereas Figure 25.3(b,d,f,h,j) is showing the spatial distribution of the SUHI for the same cities for the aforementioned selected times. It was noticed that each city has a different time step for the maximum seasonal mean (hereafter, SM_{Max}) value of SUHII. Not only the years, but also the seasons recording the all-time SM_{Max} of SUHIIs are found to be different for each city. While the post-monsoon of 2009 is found to have the highest value (SM_{Max}) for Prayagraj and Varanasi, similarly the post-monsoon of 2012 recorded the maxima for Patna and Gaya. On the other hand, the peak value was recorded for Kanpur in pre-monsoon of 2012. These differences may be linked with absence of strong synoptic phenomena (Kumar et al., 2017) in post-monsoon, and for Kanpur, the thermal inertia (Wang et al., 2007; Barat et al., 2021) may be the possible cause. The variation discussed surely suggests that the microclimate of each city has its own distinct patterns and drivers for SUHIs and may not be the same for the entire geographical region. From Figure 25.3 (a-j), we can see that the LULC is strongly spatially interconnected with SUHIs over all the selected cities. This finding also endorses the fact that the SUHI monitoring of the cities is better managed by the satellite data in comparison with the station data. While considering the coldest temperature value in rural zones as the base temperature for SUHII plotting, we can see that most of the rural zones (having cropland as LC) has negligible SUHII (≤1 degree Celsius), at the same time urban LC is showing a SUHII of 4 to 8 degrees Celsius. The temporal variation of SUHI can also be linked with LULC change. The seasonal changes in SUHI are influenced by the agricultural cover (Kumar et al., 2017; Shastri et al., 2017), but these effects are out of the scope of current research as the MODIS LC product provides data at annual steps; hence, these aspects are excluded. Outward growth of a city causes changes in LC of non-urban zones from natural covers to urban, and thus in turn it also affects the SUHI values being calculated using static buffers, after a certain period of time. To minimise this temporal effect of LULCC on SUHIIs, we have used the tri-zonal method (Barat et al., 2018; Barat et al., 2021) instead of bi-zonal methods, as mentioned earlier. From the spatial plots (Figure 25.3 (b,d,f,h,j)) we can see the SM_{Max} value of intra-city SUHII can rise up to 8 degrees or greater in cities like Prayagraj (Figure 25.3b) and Varanasi (Figure 25.3f). Patna (Figure 25.3h) and Kanpur (Figure 25.3d) range up to 7 degrees while a smaller town like Gaya (Figure 25.3j) can also possess a SM_{Max} value of 5 degrees. While the most intense SUHI was noticed in the inner locations of the cities, however, the

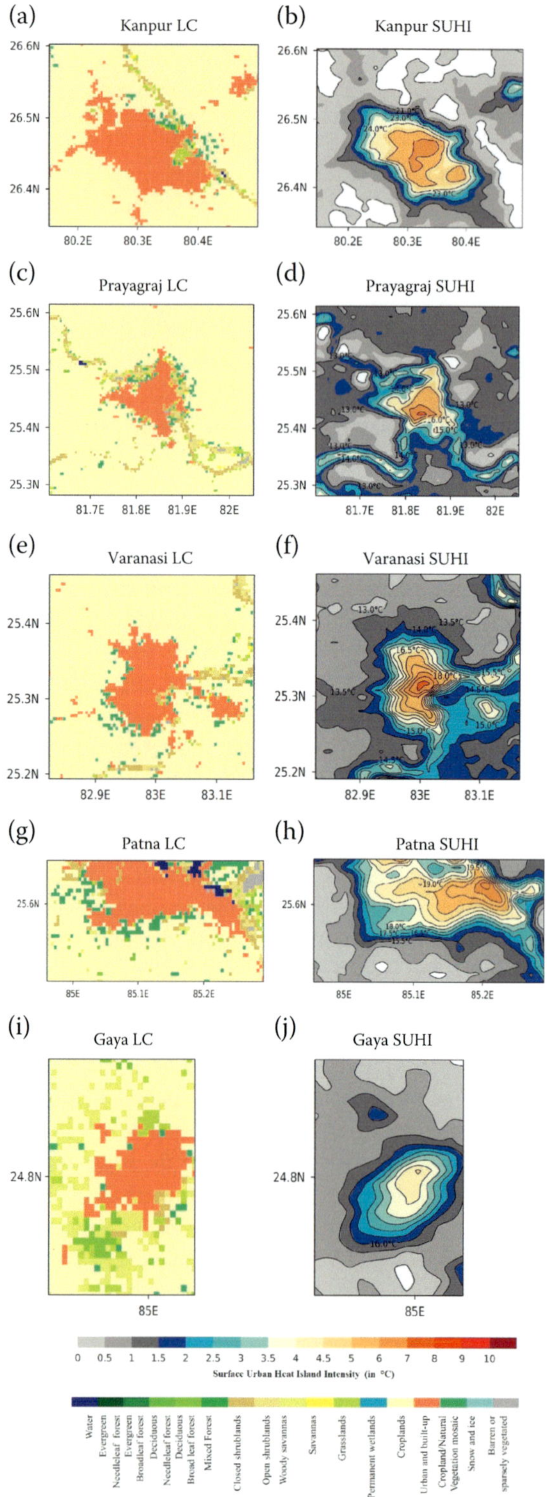

FIGURE 25.3 The land cover (LC) of (a) Kanpur, (c) Prayagraj, (e) Varanasi, (g) Patna, and (i) Gaya and corresponding plots of SUHII for (b) Kanpur, (d) Prayagraj, (f) Varanasi, (h) Patna, and (j) Gaya. The SM_{Max} SUHII (in degrees Celsius) is represented by a color bar with value zero assigned to the coldest pixel in the viewport (from rural zone), while isotherms are showing the LST in °C.

detailed reason of the formation of this core heat zone may be subject to several factors like built-up density, road width, nature of the urban cover (Bhati and Mohan, 2016), etc. and requires the use of urban canopy models (Kusaka and Kimura, 2004) in city-specific studies.

The seasonal time series analysis (Figure 25.4 a-j) shows the temporal variations of the two parameters (SUHII and AOD). It was found that the winter and post-monsoon are the most prominent seasons for strong magnitudes of SUHI and high levels of AOD across all the cities. This may be linked with wind circulation patterns (Nair et al., 2007), vorticity (Sarthi et al., 2019), and is in accordance with previous studies (Kumar et al., 2015). It was also noticed in the present research that for Varanasi, Kanpur, Prayagraj, and Gaya the post-monsoon AOD loadings have increased in a great manner in the recent past. This may be linked with rising anthropogenic pollution in the region (Sen et al., 2017; Kumar et al., 2018). In pre-monsoon season all of the stations are exhibiting lower levels of SUHII if compared with the rest of the seasons; this is maybe because of the prevailing meso-scale circulations as form of heat wave (Wilby, 2003, Kumar et al., 2017, Barat et al., 2021), which has dampened the micro-scale level effects of urbanisation on temperature regime. We can also see a sort of increasing trend in both of the parameters from 2005 onwards in Figure 25.4, which can in turn indicate that the urbanisation may have some effect of aerosol loadings over the urban area too, which may be linked with the findings by Tian et al. (2014). They documented a sharp rise in urbanisation in India from the year 2005 onwards. It should be also noticed that the rate of increment in both of the parameters has been rising in a greater manner in smaller cities; for example, the rise in the SUHI intensity and the AOD for Gaya is found to be greater than that of Prayagraj or Kanpur, while Prayagraj and Kanpur are showing much higher values of SUHIIs and AOD in compared to Gaya. Thus, the monitoring of the smaller towns is also much needed, in which we can say the satellite observations have a greater role to play, as the smaller towns always lack in-situ meteorological stations.

Figure 25.5 (a-f) reveals the inter-linkage of the AOD and SUHII regimes between the cities. For AOD, it is noticed that the regional trends are also reflecting in the similarity dendrograms, for the pre- and post-monsoon the clear demarcation between the cities of western and eastern part of study area. This regional difference has also previously been discussed by Kumar et al. (2018). For the winter season, even a stronger similarity is seen across all the stations, except Patna. This indicates the regional loading is very high and widespread during the winters (Ojha et al., 2020). Patna may have shown a difference because of its high pollution in winter (Jat et al., 2021). While for SUHIs, each of the cities is showing similarities, purely dependent on the local weather conditions of the season. Or, in other words, the geographical distance is not always influencing the level of similarity. This seasonal variability in the similarity leaves a scope of separate analysis, incorporating the station based data of local weather, with these satellite-based results, to know the root causes.

The Mann-Kendall trend (Table 25.3) analysis also points out some interesting results, while the cities like Prayagraj and Kanpur showed no trend in SUHIIs (except an increasing trend in pre-monsoon for Prayagraj), smaller towns like Gaya recorded a significantly increasing trend for all the seasons, while the AOD is showing an increment except for pre-monsoon season across the Gangetic Plains regardless of the station. The probable cause regarding the SUHII trend may be either due to SUHII reaching its saturation level (no more intensification of urbanisation has occurred) or the footprint of SUHI is slowly reaching the rural reference (Kumar et al., 2017) in sub-grid scale; both of these phenomena can be only further analysed using higher spatial resolution data (e.g., LANDSAT) only. On the other hand, the AOD increment can be linked with intensification of regional loadings (Kumar et al., 2018). The AOD magnitude therefore can be related with a regional trend rather than being under urban microscale influence. The Sen's slope (Table 25.4) for the AOD and SUHII also shows a generalised positive value, except for a very tiny negative value in a few instances; that too for pre-monsoon season for AOD only. This trend may be linked to intercontinental transport of

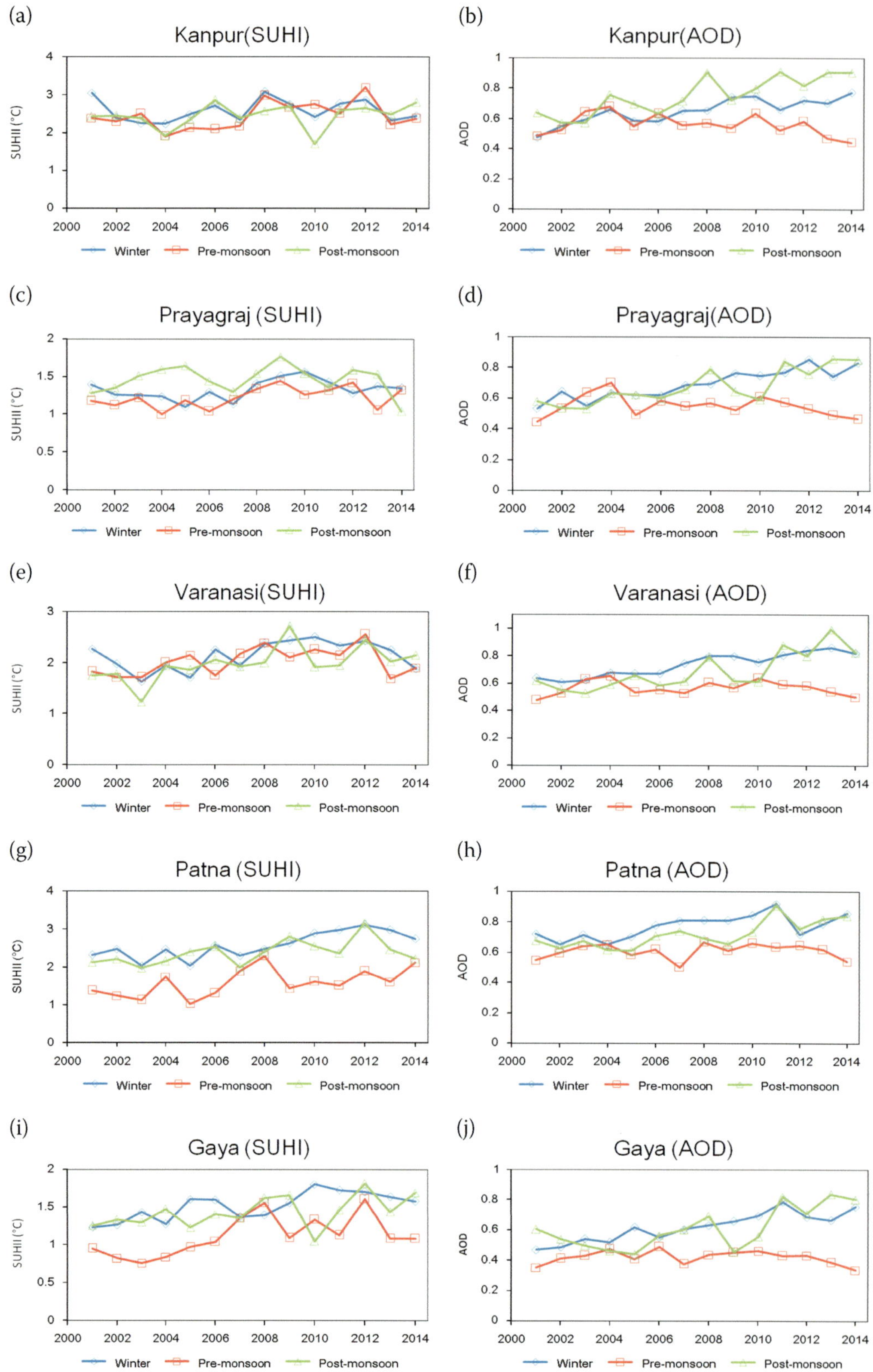

FIGURE 25.4 Time series seasonal analysis of SUHI and AOD over selected cities.

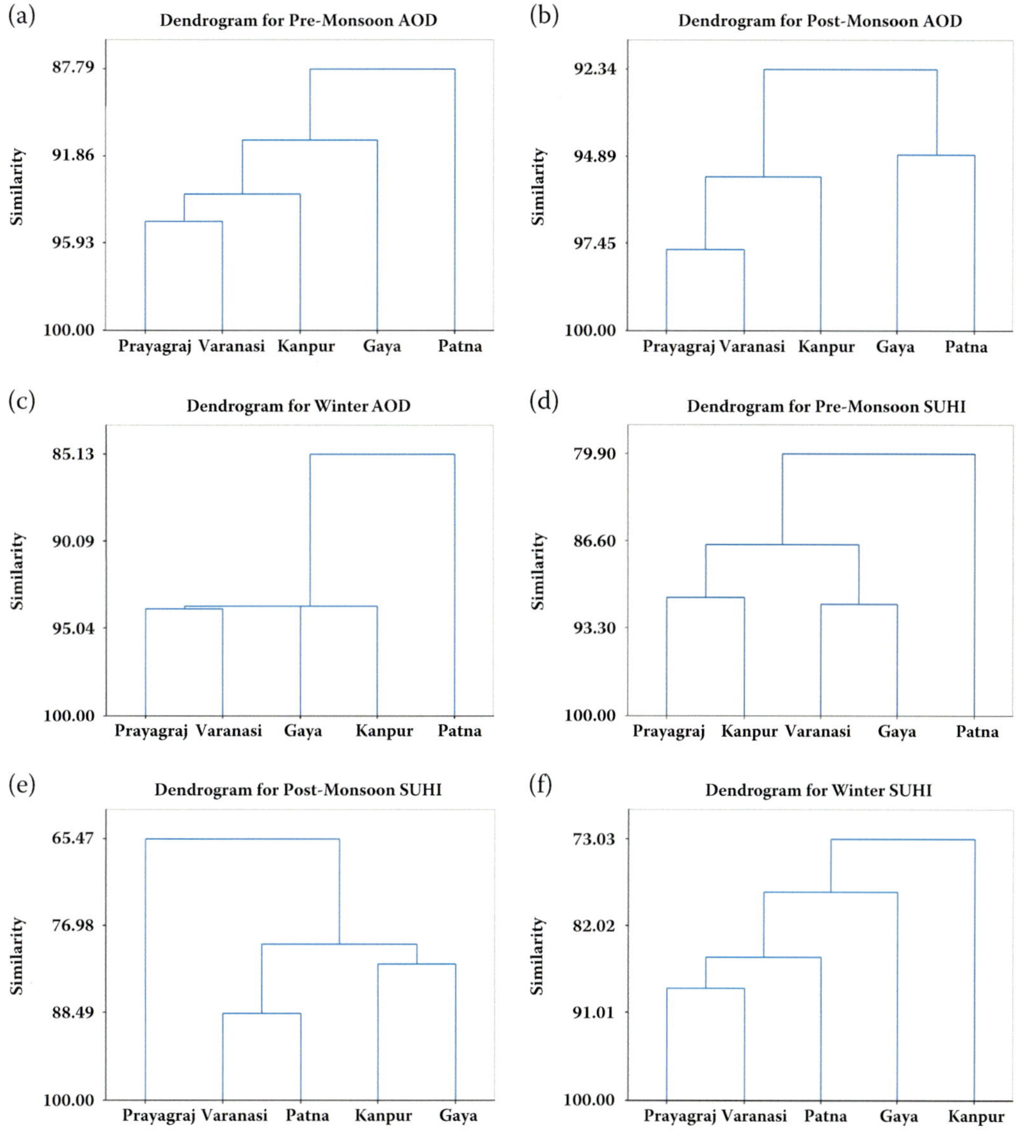

FIGURE 25.5 The centroid linkage dendrograms for showing similarity between cities for (a) pre-monsoon AOD, (b) post-monsoon AOD, (c) winter AOD, (d) pre-monsoon SUHI, (e) post-monsoon SUHI, and (f) winter SUHI.

aerosols, and not to the urban scales, so it requires separate studies to envisage the cause ,because the pre-monsoon season is marked by high levels of AOD of natural (dust) origins (Dey et al., 2004). The urban air quality and UHI have a well-established relationship. UHII is found to cause a rise in tropospheric ozone by 12% (Rosenfeld et al., 1998) besides an increase in other air pollutants. The UHI phenomenon has high implications in the context of air quality and is known to elevate regional atmospheric pollution levels (Sarkar and De Ridder, 2011; Sarrat et al., 2006; Davies et al., 2007). Hence, in the present research, positive values of Sen's slope along with the increasing trends in Man-Kendall test reflect that there is an exigency of monitoring of these parameters to ensure a sustainable urbanisation.

TABLE 25.3
Significant Seasonal Mann-Kendall Trend[a] of SUHII and AOD Variations

		SUHII	AOD
Kanpur	Winter	–	I
	Pre-Monsoon	–	–
	Post-Monsoon	–	I
Prayagraj	Winter	–	I
	Pre-Monsoon	I	–
	Post-Monsoon	–	I
Varanasi	Winter	I	I
	Pre-Monsoon	–	–
	Post-Monsoon	I	I
Patna	Winter	I	I
	Pre-Monsoon	I	–
	Post-Monsoon	I	I
Gaya	Winter	I	I
	Pre-Monsoon	I	–
	Post-Monsoon	I	I

Note:
[a] I = Increasing, D = Decreasing.

TABLE 25.4
Sen's Slope (β) of SUHII and AOD Variations

		SUHII	AOD
Kanpur	Winter	0.009	0.017
	Pre-Monsoon	0.034	–0.007
	Pot-Monsoon	0.02	0.026
Prayagraj	Winter	0.010	0.022
	Pre-Monsoon	0.017	–0.005
	Post-Monsoon	0.002	0.023
Varanasi	Winter	0.026	0.018
	Pre-Monsoon	0.028	0.0009
	Post-Monsoon	0.03	0.024
Patna	Winter	0.065	0.014
	Pre-Monsoon	0.046	0.002
	Post-Monsoon	0.033	0.015
Gaya	Winter	0.03	0.021
	Pre-Monsoon	0.03	–0.001
	Post-Monsoon	0.029	0.023

25.5 CONCLUSIONS

This work is intended to evaluate the potential of satellite-based observations for the purpose of urban climate and atmospheric environment monitoring. We have analysed two parameters most commonly discussed in the context of urban environments. The AOD as an indicator of air quality and SUHII as an indicator of urban thermal environment. The urban heat island phenomenon is found to be quite evident over the entire study area i.e., the Gangetic Plains. All of the cities are found to be affected by the surface urban heat island (SUHI) formations. Our objective to quantify and study the SUHI was based on its seasonal dynamics and temporal characteristics on the basis of data generated for each city it was found that the spatial spread of SUHI is governed by the LULC of the city. The nighttime SUHI is found to be the strongest in the winter months followed by the post-monsoon, which is indicating that the natural cooling is hindered by the urban structures. In these seasons, the temperature falls rapidly after sunset; hence the non-urban zones cool faster than their urban counterparts. This indicates that, when the prevailing mesoscale processes are weak, the SUHI also becomes strongest (Kumar et al., 2017; Barat et al., 2021). Albeit the cities selected also face cold waves too, but the duration of these cold phases is much shorter than the warm months facing heat waves. Hence, the seasonal averaging masks out the effect of cold waves. The intra-station variability of SUHIIs is also very important. Some of the stations like Prayagraj and Varanasi exhibited a strong difference of 7–8 °C in SM_{Max} SUHII between some dense locality and the coolest part of its adjacent rural counterpart. The spatial distribution of SUHIs followed more or less the pattern of urban land cover in most of the stations. However, the spatial spread of the core zone and the symmetry of the SUHI is independent of the city size and morphology. The AOD was found to be following a more regional trend in the seasonal analysis; however, the impact of urbanisation on regional loadings cannot be ruled out. Along with SUHI, the months October–February (post-monsoon and winter) are also more favourable for high AOD values. The Mann-Kendall trend analysis also pointed out increasing trends in the majority of the cities (Prayagraj, Varanasi, Patna, and Gaya for SUHII, and all cities for AOD), along with a positive value of Sen's slope, which gave us a clue of further worsening of these problems. The further development and urbanisation in the future may also increase the problem of SUHI and elevated air pollution reflected through high values of AOD. The SUHI influences numerous sectors like health, energy, pollution, and others; therefore, green town planning and environmentally sound development is much needed in the future. The SUHI can be managed by increasing green spaces and inland water bodies, and by application of engineering and architectural solutions like the use of high albedo building materials, cooler building materials, green roofs, sustainable town planning, etc. The nationwide implementation of strict air pollution control policies and technologies are much needed for control of anthropogenic aerosol loadings, as the regional trends are also found to be very prominent. At the same time, monitoring of the urban climate is also very much needed for risk estimation and evaluation of mitigation measures implemented. Remote sensing is the smartest solution for these monitoring needs and for proper management of the urban climate concerns.

REFERENCES

Acker, James G., and Gregory Leptoukh. "Online Analysis Enhances Use of NASA Earth Science Data." *Eos* 88, no. 2 (2007): 14–7. 10.1029/2007EO020003.

Ahmad, S., H Matloob, H., Warsi, T. R., and Abdullha Khan, M. D. The Evaluation of Heat Island Effect in Various Cities in Ganga-Yamuna Doab Region Using Modis Land Surface Temperature Product. *Asian Journal of Environmental Science* 6, no. 2 (2011): 185–90.

Altaratz, Orit, Ilan Koren, Tamir Reisin, Alex Kostinski, Graham Feingold, Zev Levin, and Yueju Yin. "Aerosols' Influence on the Interplay between Condensation, Evaporation and Rain in Warm Cumulus Cloud." *Atmospheric Chemistry and Physics* 8, no. 1 (2008): 15–24. https://doi.org/10.5194/acp-8-15-2008

Ashraf, M. "A Study Of Temporal Change In Land Surface Temperature And Urban Heat Island Effect In Patna Municipal Corporation Over A Period Of 25 Years (1989–2014) Using Remote Sensing And GIS Technique." *International Journal of Remote Sensing and Geoscience* 4 (2015): 71–7.

Bagherzadeh, Ali, Abdollah Vosugh Hoseini, and Leila Homami Totmaj. "The Effects of Climate Change on Normalized Difference Vegetation Index (NDVI) in the Northeast of Iran." *Modeling Earth Systems and Environment* 6, no. 2 (2020): 671–83.

Bahi, Hicham, Hassan Rhinane, Ahmed Bensalmia, Ute Fehrenbach, and Dieter Scherer. "Effects of Urbanization and Seasonal Cycle on the Surface Urban Heat Island Patterns in the Coastal Growing Cities: A Case Study of Casablanca, Morocco." *Remote Sensing* 8, no. 10 (2016): 829. https://doi.org/10.3390/rs8100829

Banerjee, T., S. C. Barman, and R. K. Srivastava. "Application of Air Pollution Dispersion Modeling for Source-Contribution Assessment and Model Performance Evaluation at Integrated Industrial Estate-Pantnagar." *Environmental Pollution* 159, no. 4 (2011): 865–75. 10.1016/j.envpol.2010.12.026.

Banerjee, T., M. Kumar, R. K. Mall, and R. S. Singh "Airing 'Clean Air' in Clean India Mission." *Environmental Science and Pollution Research* 24, no. 7 (2017): 6399–413. 10.1007/s11356-016-8264-y.

Banerjee, Tirthankar, Vishnu Murari, Manish Kumar, and M. P. Raju. "Source Apportionment of Airborne Particulates through Receptor Modeling: Indian Scenario." *Atmospheric Research 164–165* (2015): 167–87. https://doi.org/10.1016/j.atmosres.2015.04.017

Banerjee, Tirthankar, and Rajeev K. Srivastava "Plastics Waste Management and Resource Recovery in India." *International Journal of Environment and Waste Management* 10, no. 1 (2012): 90–111. https://doi.org/10.1504/IJEWM.2012.048153

Barat, Archisman, Sunny Kumar, Praveen Kumar, and P. Parth Sarthi. "Characteristics of Surface Urban Heat Island (SUHI) over the Gangetic Plain of Bihar, India." *Asia-Pacific Journal of Atmospheric Sciences* 54, no. 2 (2018): 205–14. https://doi.org/10.1007/s13143-018-0004-4

Barat, Archisman, P. Parth Sarthi, Sunny Kumar, Praveen Kumar, and Ashutosh K. Sinha "Surface Urban Heat Island (SUHI) Over Riverside Cities Along the Gangetic Plain of India." *Pure and Applied Geophysics* 178, no. 4 (2021): 1477–97. https://doi.org/10.1007/s00024-021-02701-6

Basu, Eeshan, and Chalantika Laha Salui. "Estimating Particulate Matter Concentrations from MODIS AOD Considering Meteorological Parameters Using Random Forest Algorithm." In *Spatial Modeling and Assessment of Environmental Contaminants*, pp. 591–609. Springer (2021).

Bektaş Balçik, Filiz. "Determining the Impact of Urban Components on Land Surface Temperature of Istanbul by Using Remote Sensing Indices." *Environmental Monitoring and Assessment* 186, no. 2 (2014): 859–72. 10.1007/s10661-013-3427-5.

Bhati, Shweta, and Manju Mohan. "WRF Model Evaluation for the Urban Heat Island Assessment under Varying Land Use/Land Cover and Reference Site Conditions." *Theoretical and Applied Climatology* 126, no. 1–2 (2016): 385–400. 10.1007/s00704-015-1589-5.

Bhattacharya, B. K., and V. K. Dadhwal. "Retrieval and Validation of Land Surface Temperature (LST) from NOAA AVHRR Thermal Images of Gujarat, India." *International Journal of Remote Sensing* 24, no. 6 (2003): 1197–206. https://doi.org/10.1080/01431160210142851

Chakraborty, T., and X. Lee. "A Simplified Urban-Extent Algorithm to Characterize Surface Urban Heat Islands on a Global Scale and Examine Vegetation Control on Their Spatiotemporal Variability." *International Journal of Applied Earth Observation and Geoinformation* 74 (2019): 269–80. https://doi.org/10.1016/j.jag.2018.09.015

Chakraborty, T. C., Chandan Sarangi, and Xuhui Lee. "Reduction in human activity can enhance the urban heat island: insights from the COVID-19 lockdown." *Environmental Research Letters* 16, no. 5 (2021): 054060. http://dx.doi.org/10.1088/1748-9326/abef8e

Chandler, Tony J. "London's Urban Climate." *The Geographical Journal* 128, no. 3 (1962): 279–98.

Dash, P., F. M. Göttsche, F. S. Olesen, and H. Fischer. "Land Surface Temperature and Emissivity Estimation from Passive Sensor Data: Theory and Practice-Current Trends." *International Journal of Remote Sensing* 23, no. 13 (2002): 2563–94. https://doi.org/10.1080/01431160110115041

Davies, F., D. R. Middleton, and K. E. Bozier. "Urban Air Pollution Modelling and Measurements of Boundary Layer Height." *Atmospheric Environment* 41, no. 19 (2007): 4040–9. https://doi.org/10.1016/j.atmosenv.2007.01.015

Delgado-Baquerizo, Manuel. "Obscure Soil Microbes and Where to Find Them." *The ISME Journal* 13, no. 8 (2019): 2120–4.

Dey, Sagnik, Larry Di Girolamo, Aaron van Donkelaar, S. N. Tripathi, Tarun Gupta, and Manju Mohan "Variability of Outdoor Fine Particulate (PM 2.5) Concentration in the Indian Subcontinent: A Remote

Sensing Approach." *Remote Sensing of Environment* 127 (2012): 153–61. https://doi.org/10.1016/j.rse.2012.08.021

Dey, Sagnik, Sachchida Nand Tripathi, Ramesh P. Singh, and Brent N. Holben. "Influence of Dust Storms on the Aerosol Optical Properties over the Indo-Gangetic Basin." *Journal of Geophysical Research D: Atmospheres* 109, no. 20 (2004). https://doi.org/10.1029/2004JD004924

Dihkan, Mustafa, Fevzi Karsli, Abdulaziz Guneroglu, and Nilgun Guneroglu. "Evaluation of Surface Urban Heat Island (SUHI) Effect on Coastal Zone: The Case of Istanbul Megacity." *Ocean and Coastal Management* 118 (2015): 309–16. https://doi.org/10.1016/j.ocecoaman.2015.03.008

Duckworth, Fowler S., and James S. Sandberg. "The Effect of Cities upon Horizontal and Vertical Temperature Gradients." *Bulletin of the American Meteorological Society* 35, no. 5 (1954): 198–207. https://doi.org/10.1175/1520-0477-35.5.198

Dutta, Debjani, and Srimanta Gupta. "Rising Trend of Air Pollution and Its Decadal Consequences on Meteorology and Thermal Comfort Over Gangetic West Bengal, India." In *Spatial Modeling and Assessment of Environmental Contaminants*, pp. 689–720. Springer (2021).

Dutta, Kanaya, Debolina Basu, and Sonam Agrawal. "Synergetic Interaction between Spatial Land Cover Dynamics and Expanding Urban Heat Islands." *Environmental Monitoring and Assessment* 193, no. 4 (2021): 1–22.

Emmanuel, Rohinton, andEduardo Krüger. "Urban Heat Island and Its Impact on Climate Change Resilience in a Shrinking City: The Case of Glasgow, UK." *Building and Environment* 53 (2012): 137–49. https://doi.org/10.1016/j.buildenv.2012.01.020

Ezber, Yasemin, Omer Lutfi Sen, Tayfun Kindap, and Mehmet Karaca. "Climatic Effects of Urbanization in Istanbul: A Statistical and Modeling Analysis." *International Journal of Climatology* 27, no. 5 (2007): 667–79. https://doi.org/10.1002/joc.1420

Farrar, Daniel S., Shally Awasthi, Shaza A. Fadel, Rajesh Kumar, Anju Sinha, Sze Hang Fu, Brian Wahl, Shaun K. Morris, and Prabhat Jha. "Seasonal Variation and Etiologic Inferences of Childhood Pneumonia and Diarrhea Mortality in India." *ELife* 8 (2019): e46202. https://doi.org/10.7554/eLife.46202

Fuzzi, S., U. Baltensperger, K. Carslaw, S. Decesari, H. Denier Van Der Gon, M. C. Facchini, D. Fowler, et al. "Particulate Matter, Air Quality and C*li*mate: Lessons Learned and Future Needs." *Atmospheric Chemistry and Physics* 15, no. 14 (2015): 8217–99. https://doi.org/10.5194/acp-15-8217-2015

Gallo, K. P., A. L. McNab, T. R. Karl, J. F. Brown, J. J. Hood, and J. D. Tarpley. "The Use of NOAA AVHRR Data for Assessment of the Urban Heat Island Effect." *Journal of Applied Meteorology* 32, no. 5 (1993): 899–908. https://doi.org/10.1175/1520-0450(1993)032<0899:TUONAD>2.0.CO;2

Ghosh, Tuhin, and Anirban Mukhopadhyay. *Natural Hazard Zonation of Bihar (India) Using Geoinformatics. Aquaculture*. Vol. 454. Springer Science and Business Media (2014). http://link.springer.com/10.1007/978-3-319-04438-5

Gopal, K. Rama, K. Raja Obul Reddy, G. Balakrishnaiah, S. M. D. Arafath, N. Siva Kumar Reddy, T. Chakradhar Rao, T. Lokeswara Reddy, and R. Ramakrishna Reddy. "Regional Trends of Aerosol Optical Depth and Their Impact on d Properties over Southern India Using MODIS Data." *Journal of Atmospheric and Solar-Terrestrial Physics* 146 (2016): 38–48. https://doi.org/10.1016/j.jastp.2016.05.005

Graf, Hans F., Johann Feichter, and Bärbel Langmann. "Volcanic Sulfur Emissions: Estimates of Source *St*rength and Its Contribution to the Global Sulfate Distribution." *Journal of Geophysical Research Atmospheres* 102, no. 9 (1997): 10727–38. https://doi.org/10.1029/96jd03265

Hawkins, Timothy W., Anthony J. Brazel, William L. Stefanov, Wendy Bigler, and Erinanne M. Saffell. "The Role of Rural Variability in Urban Heat Island Determination for Phoenix, Arizona." *Journal of Applied Meteorology* 43, no. 3 (2004): 476–86. https://doi.org/10.1175/1520-0450(2004)043<0476:TRORVI>2.0.CO;2

He, Yiling, Liangliang Cheng, Junzhe, Bao, Shizhou Deng, Wenmin Liao, Qiong Wang, Benjawan Tawatsupa, Shakoor Hajat, and Cunrui Huang. "Geographical Disparities in the Impacts of Heat on Diabetes Mortality and the Protective Role of Greenness in Thailand: A Nationwide Case-Crossover Analysis." *Science of the Total Environment* 711 (2020): 135098.

Holderness, Tomas, Stuart Barr, Richard Dawson, and Jim Hall. "An Evaluation of Thermal Earth Observation for Characterizing Urban Heatwave Event Dynamics Using the Urban Heat Island Intensity Metric." *International Journal of Remote Sensing* 34, no. 3 (2013): 864–84. https://doi.org/10.1080/01431161.2012.714505

Houghton, John Theodore, Y. D. J. G. Ding, David J. Griggs, Maria Noguer, Paul J. van der Linden, Xiaosu Dai, Kathy Maskell, and C. A. Johnson. *Climate Change 2001*: *The Scientific Basis*. The Press Syndicate of the University of Cambridge (2001).

Howard, Luke. "The Climate of London Deduced from Meteorological Observations, Made at differents Places in the Neighbourghood of the Metropolis. Volume I." J. and A. Arch, Longman, Hatchard, S. Highley [and] R. Hunter (1818), 436.

Hu, Leiqiu, Nathaniel A. Brunsell, Andrew J. Monaghan, Michael Barlage, and Olga V. Wilhelmi. "How Can We Use MODIS Land Surface Temperature to Validate Long-Term Urban Model Simulations?" *Journal of Geophysical Research* 119, no. 6 (2014): 3185–201. https://doi.org/10.1002/2013JD021101

Huggett, Richard J. *Climate, Earth Processes and Earth History*. Springer Science and Business Media (2012).

Hung, Tran, Daisuke Uchihama, Shiro Ochi, and Yoshifumi Yasuoka. "Assessment with Satellite Data of the Urban Heat Island Effects in Asian Mega Cities." *International Journal of Applied Earth Observation and Geoinformation* 8, no. 1 (2006): 34–48. https://doi.org/10.1016/j.jag.2005.05.003

Jat, Rajmal, Bhola Ram Gurjar, and Douglas Lowe. "Regional Pollution Loading in Winter Months over India Using High Resolution WRF-Chem Simulation." *Atmospheric Research* 249 (2021): 105326. https://doi.org/10.1016/j.atmosres.2020.105326

Jiang, X. D., B. C. Xia, and Luo Guo. "Research on Urban Heat Island and Its Environmental Effects of Rapidly Urbanized Regions." *Ecologic Science* 2 (2006): 21.

Kotharkar, Rajashree, Aparna Ramesh, and Anurag Bagade. "Urban Heat Island Studies in South Asia: A Critical Review." *Urban Climate* 24 (2018): 1011–26. https://doi.org/10.1016/j.uclim.2017.12.006

Kratzer, P. A. *Das Stadtklima Die Wissenshaft*, Vol. 90. Braunschweig, Friedr. Vieweg and Sohn (1956), 184 pp.

Kreidenweis, Sonia M., Markus Petters, and Ulrike Lohmann. "100 Years of Progress in Cloud Physics, Aerosols, and Aerosol Chemistry Research." *Meteorological Monographs* 59 (2019): 11.1–11.72. https://doi.org/10.1175/AMSMONOGRAPHS-D-18-0024.1

Kremser, Stefanie, Larry W., Thomason, Marc, von Hobe, Markus, Hermann, Terry Deshler, Claudia Timmreck, Matthew Toohey, et al. "Stratospheric Aerosol—Observations, Processes, and Impact on Climate." *Reviews of Geophysics* 54, no. 2 (2016): 278–335. https://doi.org/10.1002/2015RG000511

Kumar, M., K. S. Parmar, D. B. Kumar, A. Mhawish, D. M. Broday, R. K. Mall, and T. Banerjee. "Long-Term Aerosol Climatology over Indo-Gangetic Plain: Trend, Prediction and Potential Source Fields." *Atmospheric Environment* 180 (2018): 37–50. https://doi.org/10.1016/j.atmosenv.2018.02.027

Kumar, M., R. K. Singh, V. Murari, A. K. Singh, R. S. Singh, and T. Banerjee. "Fireworks Induced Particle Pollution: A Spatio-Temporal Analysis." *Atmospheric Research* 180 (2016): 78–91. https://doi.org/10.1016/j.atmosres.2016.05.014

Kumar, M., S. Tiwari, V. Murari, A. K. Singh, and T. Banerjee. "Wintertime Characteristics of Aerosols at Middle Indo-Gangetic Plain: Impacts of Regional Meteorology and Long Range Transport." *Atmospheric Environment* 104 (2015): 162–75. https://doi.org/10.1016/j.atmosenv.2015.01.014

Kumar, Naresh, Allen Chu, and Andrew Foster. "An Empirical Relationship between PM2.5 and Aerosol Optical Depth in Delhi Metropolitan." *Atmospheric Environment* 41, no. 21 (2007): 4492–503. https://doi.org/10.1016/j.atmosenv.2007.01.046

Kumar, Rahul, Vimal Mishra, Jonathan Buzan, Rohini Kumar, Drew Shindell, and Matthew Huber. "Dominant Control of Agriculture and Irrigation on Urban Heat Island in India." *Scientific Reports* 7, no. 1 (2017): 14054. https://doi.org/10.1038/s41598-017-14213-2

Kumar, Vijay, Sharad K. Jain, and Yatveer Singh. "Analysis of Long-Term Rainfall Trends in India." *Hydrological Sciences Journal* 55, no. 4 (2010): 484–96. https://doi.org/10.1080/02626667.2010.481373

Kusaka, Hiroyuki, and Fujio Kimura. "Coupling a Single-Layer Urban Canopy Model with a Simple Atmospheric Model: Impact on Urban Heat Island Simulation for an Idealized Case." *Journal of the Meteorological Society of Japan* 82, no. 1 (2004): 67–80. https://doi.org/10.2151/jmsj.82.67

Lai, Li-Wei, and Wan-Li Cheng. "Urban Heat Island and Air Pollution—an Emerging Role for Hospital Respiratory Admissions in an Urban Area." *Journal of Environmental Health* 72, no. 6 (2010): 32–6.

Landsberg, Helmut E. *The climate of towns." Man's Role in Changing the Face of the Earth 2,* University of Chicago Press (1956), 584–606 pp.

Lau, William KM, Kyu-Myong, Kim, Christina N, Hsu, and Brent N, Holben. "Possible Influences of Air Pollution, Dust- and Sandstorms on the Indian Monsoon." *World Meteorological Organization Bulletin* 58, no. 1 (2009): 22–30. http://www.csa.com/partners/viewrecord.php?requester=gsandcollection=ENVandrecid=9189011

Li, Huidong, Fred Meier, Xuhui Lee, Tirthankar Chakraborty, Junfeng Liu, Martijn Schaap, and Sahar Sodoudi. "Interaction between Urban Heat Island and Urban Pollution Island during Summer in Berlin." *Science of the Total Environment* 636 (2018): 818–28. https://doi.org/10.1016/j.scitotenv.2018.04.254

Li, Ying Ying, Hao Zhang, and Wolfgang Kainz. "Monitoring Patterns of Urban Heat Islands of the Fast-Growing Shanghai Metropolis, China: Using Time-Series of Landsat TM/ETM+ Data." *International*

Journal of Applied Earth Observation and Geoinformation 19, no. 1 (2012): 127–38. https://doi.org/10.1016/j.jag.2012.05.001

Liu, Guangping, Jingmei Wei, Bala Anand Muthu, and R. Dinesh Jackson Samuel. "Chlorophyll-a Concentration in the Hailing Bay Using Remote Sensing Assisted Sparse Statistical Modelling." *European Journal of Remote Sensing* 54, no. sup2 (2021): 284–95.

Lokoshchenko, M. A. "Urban 'Heat Island'in Moscow." *Urban Climate* 10 (2014): 550–62.

Lokoshchenko, M. A., and I. A., Korneva. "Underground Urban Heat Island below Moscow City." *Urban Climate* 13 (2015): 1–13. https://doi.org/10.1016/j.uclim.2015.04.002

Lowry, William P. "Empirical Estimation of Urban Effects on Climate: A Problem Analysis." *Journal of Applied Meteorology* 16, no. 2 (1977): 129–35. https://doi.org/10.1175/1520-0450(1977)016<0129:EEOUEO>2.0.CO;2

Majumdar, Sushobhan, and Uday Chatterjee. "Modelling Urban Growth Using Urban Growth Deterministic Model in Kolkata Metropolitan Area: A Geo-Statistical Approach." *Modeling Earth Systems and Environment* (2020), 1–9.

Makido, Yasuyo, Vivek Shandas, Salim Ferwati, and David Sailor. "Daytime Variation of Urban Heat Islands: The Case Study of Doha, Qatar." *Climate* 4, no. 2 (2016): 32. https://doi.org/10.3390/cli4020032

Meng, F., and M., Liu. "Remote-Sensing Image-Based Analysis of the Patterns of Urban Heat Islands in Rapidly Urbanizing Jinan, China." *International Journal of Remote Sensing* 34, no. 24 (2013): 8838–53. https://doi.org/10.1080/01431161.2013.853895

Mhawish, Alaa, Manish Kumar, Akhila K. Mishra, Prashant K. Srivastava, and Tirthankar Banerjee. "Remote Sensing of Aerosols From Space: Retrieval of Properties and Applications." In *Remote Sensing of Aerosols, Clouds, and Precipitation*, 45–83. Elsevier (2018). https://doi.org/10.1016/B978-0-12-810437-8.00003-7

Mishra, Anshuman, Sheikh Nizammuddin, Chandana Basu Mallick, Sakshi Singh, Satya Prakash, Niyamat Ali Siddiqui, Niraj Rai, S Justin Carlus, Digumarthi V. S. Sudhakar, and Vishnu P. Tripathi. "Genotype-Phenotype Study of the Middle Gangetic Plain in India Shows Association of Rs2470102 with Skin Pigmentation." *Journal of Investigative Dermatology* 137, no. 3 (2017): 670–7.

Moteki, Nobuhiro, Yutaka Kondo, Tomoki Nakayama, Kazuyuki Kita, Lokesh K. Sahu, Takuya Ishigai, Takeshi Kinase, and Yutaka Matsumi. "Radiative Transfer Modeling of Filter-Based Measurements of Light Absorption by Particles: Importance of Particle Size Dependent Penetration Depth." *Journal of Aerosol Science* 41, no. 4 (2010): 401–12. https://doi.org/10.1016/j.jaerosci.2010.02.002

Murari, Vishnu, Manish Kumar, S. C. Barman, and T. Banerjee. "Temporal Variability of MODIS Aerosol Optical Depth and Chemical Characterization of Airborne Particulates in Varanasi, India." *Environmental Science and Pollution Research* 22, no. 2 (2015): 1329–43. https://doi.org/10.1007/s11356-014-3418-2

Murari, V., M. Kumar, N. Singh, R. S. Singh, and T. Banerjee. "Particulate Morphology and Elemental Characteristics: Variability at Middle Indo-Gangetic Plain." *Journal of Atmospheric Chemistry* 73, no. 2 (2016): 165–79. https://doi.org/10.1007/s10874-015-9321-5

Myrup, Leonard O. "A Numerical Model of the Urban Heat Island." *Journal of Applied Meteorology* 8, no. 6 (1969): 908–18. https://doi.org/10.1175/1520-0450(1969)008<0908:anmotu>2.0.co;2

Nair, Vijayakumar S., K. Krishna Moorthy, Denny P. Alappattu, P. K. Kunhikrishnan, Susan George, Prabha R. Nair, S. Suresh Babu, et al. "Wintertime Aerosol Characteristics over the Indo-Gangetic Plain (IGP): Impacts of Local Boundary Layer Processes and Long-Range Transport." *Journal of Geophysical Research Atmospheres* 112, no. 13 (2007): D13205 1-15.https://doi.org/10.1029/2006JD008099

Nesarikar-Patki, Pradnya, and Pratima Raykar-Alange. "Study of Influence of Land Cover on Urban Heat Islands in Pune Using Remote Sensing." *IOSR Journal of Mechanical and Civil Engineering (IOSR-JMCE)* 3 (2012): 39–43.

Ojha, Narendra, Amit Sharma, Manish Kumar, Imran Girach, Tabish U. Ansari , Som K. Sharma, Narendra Singh, Andrea Pozzer, and Sachin S. Gunthe. "On the Widespread Enhancement in Fine Particulate Matter across the Indo-Gangetic Plain towards Winter." *Scientific Reports* 10, no. 1 (2020): 1–9. https://doi.org/10.1038/s41598-020-62710-8

Papanastasiou, Dimitris K., Dimitris Melas, Thomas Bartzanas, and Constantinos Kittas. "Temperature, Comfort and Pollution Levels during Heat Waves and the Role of Sea Breeze." *International Journal of Biometeorology* 54, no. 3 (2010): 307–17. https://doi.org/10.1007/s00484-009-0281-9

Patil, Nitin, Prashant Dave, and Chandra Venkataraman. "Contrasting Influences of Aerosols on Cloud Properties during Deficient and Abundant Monsoon Years." *Scientific Reports 7*, no. 1 (2017): 1–9. https://doi.org/10.1038/srep44996

Paul, Supantha, Subimal Ghosh, Micky Mathew, Anjana Devanand, Subhankar Karmakar, and Dev Niyogi. "Increased Spatial Variability and Intensification of Extreme Monsoon Rainfall Due to Urbanization." *Scientific Reports* 8, no. 1 (2018): 1–10. https://doi.org/10.1038/s41598-018-22322-9

Peng, Shushi, Shilong Piao, Philippe Ciais, Pierre Friedlingstein, Catherine Ottle, François Marie Bréon, Huijuan Nan, Liming Zhou, and Ranga B. Myneni. "Response to Comment on 'Surface Urban Heat Island across 419 Global Big Cities'." *Environmental Science and Technology* 46, no. 12 (2012): 6889–90. https://doi.org/10.1021/es301811b

Pongracz, Rita, Judit Bartholy, and Zsuzsanna Dezso. "Remotely Sensed Thermal Information Applied to Urban Climate Analysis." *Advances in Space Research* 37, no. 12 (2006): 2191–6. https://doi.org/10.1016/j.asr.2005.06.069

Prasad, Anup K., and Ramesh P. Singh. "Comparison of MISR-MODIS Aerosol Optical Depth over the Indo-Gangetic Basin during the Winter and Summer Seasons (2000-2005)." *Remote Sensing of Environment* 107, no. 1–2 (2007): 109–19. https://doi.org/10.1016/j.rse.2006.09.026

Pueschel, Rudolf F. "Stratospheric Aerosols: Formation, Properties, Effects." *Journal of Aerosol Science* 27, no. 3 (1996): 383–402.

Purkis, Samuel J., and Victor V. Klemas. *Remote Sensing and Global Environmental Change. Remote Sensing and Global Environmental Change*. John Wiley and Sons (2013). https://doi.org/10.1002/9781118687659

Qi, Jun, Linsheng Yang, and Wuyi Wang. "Environmental Degradation and Health Risks in Beijing, China." *Archives of Environmental and Occupational Health* 62, no. 1 (2007): 33–7. https://doi.org/10.3200/AEOH.62.1.33-37

Qin, Zhihao, and A. Karnieli. "Progress in the Remote Sensing of Land Surface Temperature and Ground Emissivity Using NOAA-AVHRR Data." *International Journal of Remote Sensing* 20, no. 12 (1999): 2367–93. https://doi.org/10.1080/014311699212074

Ramachandran, S., Sumita Kedia, and Rohit Srivastava. "Aerosol Optical Depth Trends over Different Regions of India." *Atmospheric Environment* 49 (2012): 338–47. https://doi.org/10.1016/j.atmosenv.2011.11.017

Rao, P. K. "Remote Sensing of Urban 'Heat Islands' from an Environmental Satellite." *Bulletin of the American Meteorological Society* (1972): 647–8.

Rastogi, N., A. Singh, M. M. Sarin, and D. Singh. "Temporal Variability of Primary and Secondary Aerosols over Northern India: Impact of Biomass Burning Emissions." *Atmospheric Environment* 125 (2016): 396–403. https://doi.org/10.1016/j.atmosenv.2015.06.010

Rosenfeld, Arthur H., Hashem Akbari, Joseph J. Romm, and Melvin Pomerantz. "Cool Communities: Strategies for Heat Island Mitigation and Smog Reduction." *Energy and Buildings* 28, no. 1 (1998): 51–62. https://doi.org/10.1016/S0378-7788(97)00063-7

Sarangi, Chandan, S. N. Tripathi, Yun Qian, Shailendra Kumar, and L. Ruby Leung. "Aerosol and Urban Land Use Effect on Rainfall around Cities in Indo-Gangetic Basin from Observations and Cloud Resolving Model Simulations." *Journal of Geophysical Research: Atmospheres* 123, no. 7 (2018): 3645–67.

Sarkar, Abhijit, and Koen De Ridder. "The Urban Heat Island Intensity of Paris: A Case Study Based on a Simple Urban Surface Parametrization." *Boundary-Layer Meteorology* 138, no. 3 (2011): 511–20. https://doi.org/10.1007/s10546-010-9568-y

Sarrat, C., A. Lemonsu, V. Masson, and D. Guedalia. "Impact of Urban Heat Island on Regional Atmospheric Pollution." *Atmospheric Environment* 40, no. 10 (2006): 1743–58. https://doi.org/10.1016/j.atmosenv.2005.11.037

Sarthi, P. Parth, Sunny Kumar, Archisman Barat, Praveen Kumar, Ashutosh K. Sinha, and Varsha Goswami. "Linkage of Aerosol Optical Depth with Rainfall and Circulation Parameters over the Eastern Gangetic Plains of India." *Journal of Earth System Science* 128, no. 7 (2019): 171. https://doi.org/10.1007/s12040-019-1204-8

Sen, A., A. S. Abdelmaksoud, Y., Nazeer Ahammed, Mansour A. Alghamdi, Tirthankar Banerjee, Mudasir Ahmad Bhat, A. Chatterjee, et al.. "Variations in Particulate Matter over Indo-Gangetic Plains and Indo-Himalayan Range during Four Field Campaigns in Winter Monsoon and Summer Monsoon: Role of Pollution Pathways." *Atmospheric Environment* 154 (2017): 200–24. 10.1016/j.atmosenv.2016.12.054.

Sen, A., Y. Nazeer Ahammed, B. C. Arya, T. Banerjee, G. Reshma Begam, B. P. Baruah, A. Chatterjee, et al. "Atmospheric Fine and Coarse Mode Aerosols at Different Environments of India and the Bay of Bengal During Winter-2014: Implications of a Coordinated Campaign." *Mapan – Journal of Metrology Society of India* 29, no. 4 (2014): 273–84. 10.1007/s12647-014-0109-x.

Sen, Avirup, Yadiki Nazeer Ahammed, Tirthankar Banerjee, Abhijit Chatterjee, Anil Kumar Choudhuri, Trupti Das, Narayan Chandara Deb, et al. "Spatial Variability in Ambient Atmospheric Fine and Coarse

Mode Aerosols over Indo-Gangetic Plains, India and Adjoining Oceans during the Onset of Summer Monsoons, 2014." *Atmospheric Pollution Research* 7, no. 3 (2016): 521–32. https://doi.org/10.1016/j.apr.2016.01.001

Sen, Pranab Kumar. "Estimates of the Regression Coefficient Based on Kendall's Tau." *Journal of the American Statistical Association* 63, no. 324 (1968): 1379–89. https://doi.org/10.1080/01621459.1968.10480934

Shandas, Vivek, Jackson Voelkel, Joseph Williams, and Jeremy Hoffman. "Integrating Satellite and Ground Measurements for Predicting Locations of Extreme Urban Heat." *Climate* 7, no. 1 (2019): 5. https://doi.org/10.3390/cli7010005

Shastri, Hiteshri, Beas Barik, Subimal Ghosh, Chandra Venkataraman, and Pankaj Sadavarte. "Flip Flop of Day-Night and Summer-Winter Surface Urban Heat Island Intensity in India." *Scientific Reports* 7 (2017): 40178. https://doi.org/10.1038/srep40178

Sheng, Li, Xiaolu Tang, Heyuan You, Qing Gu, and Hao Hu. "Comparison of the Urban Heat Island Intensity Quantified by Using Air Temperature and Landsat Land Surface Temperature in Hangzhou, China." *Ecological Indicators* 72 (2017): 738–46. https://doi.org/10.1016/j.ecolind.2016.09.009

Singh, Ram Babu, Aakriti Grover, and Jinyan Zhan. "Inter-Seasonal Variations of Surface Temperature in the Urbanized Environment of Delhi Using Landsat Thermal Data." *Energies* 7, no. 3 (2014): 1811–28. https://doi.org/10.3390/en7031811

Sobrino, José A., Juan C. Jiménez-Muñoz, and Leonardo Paolini. "Land Surface Temperature Retrieval from LANDSAT TM 5." *Remote Sensing of Environment* 90, no. 4 (2004): 434–40. https://doi.org/10.1016/j.rse.2004.02.003

Srivastava, Parul, Sagnik Dey, P. Agarwal, and George Basil. "Aerosol Characteristics over Delhi National Capital Region: A Satellite View." *International Journal of Remote Sensing* 35, no. 13 (2014): 5036–52. https://doi.org/10.1080/01431161.2014.934404

Sultana, Sabiha, and A. N. V. Satyanarayana. "Urban Heat Island Intensity during Winter over Metropolitan Cities of India Using Remote-Sensing Techniques: Impact of Urbanization." *International Journal of Remote Sensing* 39, no. 20 (2018): 6692–730.

Swamy, Gsnvksn, S. M. Shiva Nagendra, and Uwe Schlink. "Urban Heat Island (UHI) Influence on Secondary Pollutant Formation in a Tropical Humid Environment." *Journal of the Air and Waste Management Association* 67, no. 10 (2017): 1080–91.

Tan, Jianguo, Youfei Zheng, Xu Tang, Changyi Guo, Liping Li, Guixiang Song, Xinrong Zhen, et al. "The Urban Heat Island and Its Impact on Heat Waves and Human Health in Shanghai." *International Journal of Biometeorology* 54, no. 1 (2010): 75–84. https://doi.org/10.1007/s00484-009-0256-x

Tian, Hanqin, Kamaljit Banger, Tao, Bo, and Vinay K. Dadhwal. "History of Land Use in India during 1880-2010: Large-Scale Land Transformations Reconstructed from Satellite Data and Historical Archives." *Global and Planetary Change* 121 (2014): 78–88. https://doi.org/10.1016/j.gloplacha.2014.07.005

Tiwari, S., A. K. Srivastava, A. K. Singh, and Sachchidanand Singh. "Identification of Aerosol Types over Indo-Gangetic Basin: Implications to Optical Properties and Associated Radiative Forcing." *Environmental Science and Pollution Research* 22, no. 16 (2015): 12246–60. https://doi.org/10.1007/s11356-015-4495-6

Trenberth, Kevin E. "Changes in Precipitation with Climate Change." *Climate Research* 47, no. 1–2 (2011): 123–38. https://doi.org/10.3354/cr00953

Van Weverberg, K., K. De Ridder, and A. Van Rompaey. "Modeling the Contribution of the Brussels Heat Island to a Long Temperature Time Series." *Journal of Applied Meteorology and Climatology* 47, no. 4 (2008): 976–90. https://doi.org/10.1175/2007JAMC1482.1

Veena, K., K. M. Parammasivam, and T. N. Venkatesh. "Urban Heat Island Studies: Current Status in India and a Comparison with the International Studies." *Journal of Earth System Science* 129, no. 1 (2020): 1–15. https://doi.org/10.1007/s12040-020-1351-y

Voelkel, Jackson, and Vivek Shandas. "Towards Systematic Prediction of Urban Heat Islands: Grounding Measurements, Assessing Modeling Techniques." *Climate* 5, no. 2 (2017): 41. https://doi.org/10.3390/cli5020041

Voogt, J. A., and T. R. Oke. "Thermal Remote Sensing of Urban Climates." *Remote Sensing of Environment* 86, no. 3 (2003): 370–84. 10.1016/S0034-4257(03)00079-8.

Wang, Kaicun, Jiankai Wang, Pucai Wang, Michael Sparrow, Juan Yang, and Hongbin Chen. "Influences of Urbanization on Surface Characteristics as Derived from the Moderate-Resolution Imaging Spectroradiometer: A Case Study for the Beijing Metropolitan Area:D22S06 1–12." *Journal of Geophysical Research Atmospheres* 112, no. 22 (2007). https://doi.org/10.1029/2006JD007997

Watson, K. "Regional Thermal-Inertia Mapping from an Experimental Satellite (Powder River Basin, Wyoming)." *Geophysics* 47, no. 12 (1982): 1681–7. https://doi.org/10.1190/1.1441317

Weng, Qihao. "Thermal Infrared Remote Sensing for Urban Climate and Environmental Studies: Methods, Applications, and Trends." *ISPRS Journal of Photogrammetry and Remote Sensing* 64, no. 4 (2009): 335–44. https://doi.org/10.1016/j.isprsjprs.2009.03.007

Wilby, Robert L. "Past and Projected Trends in London's Urban Heat Island." *Weather* 58, no. 7 (2003): 251–60. https://doi.org/10.1256/wea.183.02

WMO. "Essential Climate Variables." (2017, June 27). https://public.wmo.int/en/programmes/global-climate-observing-system/essential-climate-variables

Zhou, Decheng, Jingfeng Xiao, Stefania Bonafoni, Christian, Berger, Kaveh Deilami, Yuyu Zhou, Steve Frolking, Rui Yao, Zhi Qiao, and José A. Sobrino. "Satellite Remote Sensing of Surface Urban Heat Islands: Progress, Challenges, and Perspectives." *Remote Sensing* 11, no. 1 (2019): 48. https://doi.org/10.3390/rs11010048

Zhou, Ji, Ji Zhou, Yunhao Chen, Jinfei Wang, Wenfeng Zhan, and Jinfei Wang. "Maximum Nighttime Urban Heat Island (UHI) Intensity Simulation by Integrating Remotely Sensed Data and Meteorological Observations." *IEEE Journal of Selected Topics in Applied Earth Observations and Remote Sensing* 4, no. 1 (2011): 138–46. https://doi.org/10.1109/JSTARS.2010.2070871

Zhou, Ji, Yunhao Chen, Xu Zhang, and Wenfeng Zhan. "Modelling the Diurnal Variations of Urban Heat Islands with Multi-Source Satellite Data." *International Journal of Remote Sensing* 34, no. 21 (2013): 7568–88. https://doi.org/10.1080/01431161.2013.821576

Index